BURT FRANKLIN: BIBLIOGRAPHY & REFERENCE 40

The Invention of Printing:
A Bibliography

The Invention of Printing: A Bibliography

Edited by Douglas C. McMurtrie

With the assistance of John Adamson

BURT FRANKLIN

New York , N. Y.

Published by LENOX HILL Pub. & Dist. Co. (Burt Franklin)
235 East 44th St., New York, N.Y. 10017
Originally Published: 1936
Reprinted: 1970
Printed in the U.S.A.

S.B.N.: 8337-23421
Library of Congress Card Catalog No.: 71-153487
Burt Franklin: Bibliography and Reference Series 40

FEDERAL WORKS AGENCY

WORK PROJECTS ADMINISTRATION (Illinois)

      Charles P. Casey, State Administrator
      H. M. McCullen, District Manager

DIVISION OF COMMUNITY SERVICE PROGRAMS

      Evelyn S. Byron, State Director
      Amelia H. Baker, District Director

Research and Records Programs Section

      Frank J. Morris, State Chief
      William C. Harder, District Chief

CHICAGO PUBLIC LIBRARY OMNIBUS PROJECT

      Alex Ladenson, Project Supervisor
      Claire B. Benepe, Project Technician
      John Adamson, Unit Supervisor

CHICAGO PUBLIC LIBRARY - SPONSOR

      Carl B. Roden, Librarian
      Nathan R. Levin, Assistant Librarian

CHICAGO CLUB OF PRINTING HOUSE CRAFTSMEN - CO-SPONSOR

      Douglas C. McMurtrie, Chairman
      Committee on the Invention of Printing

TABLE OF CONTENTS

INTRODUCTION

Presented in the following pages is the product of the first
attempt, within the past half century, to compile a comprehensive
bibliography of published materials on the invention of printing
with movable types, which is widely and properly recognized as one
of the great events in the history of civilization. The last published bibliography of the subject appeared in the first volume of
the three-volume Geschichte der Erfindung der Buchdruckkunst by
Antonius van der Linde, published in 1886.

The need for a comprehensive list of source materials on this
important subject occurred to the present writer in 1938, as we
were approaching 1940, the year agreed upon throughout the world
for commemoration of the 500th anniversary of the invention of
printing with movable types. It may here be explained that there
is no evidence establishing the exact month or year of the invention; but the documentary record points to 1440 as a likely date.

Since it was obvious that such a compilation would require the
effort of an extensive clerical and bibliographical force, I proposed to the authorities in Chicago of the Work Projects Administration the setting up of a project with this aim in view. Official approval of the enterprise was readily forthcoming, contingent
only upon provision by some sponsor of a contribution sufficient to
cover the costs of materials, equipment, and professional direction.
The latter being available without expense, I proposed sponsorship

of the project, covering the other costs, to the Chicago Club of
Printing House Craftsmen, the organization in Chicago of the production executives in the printing and allied trades. The board
of governors of this organization took an enlightened view of the
proposal, approving it heartily, and appropriating, under three
successive administrations, the funds required to carry through
the project.

When it is considered that the primary interest of the Chicago Club of Printing House Craftsmen is in problems of printing
production, the significant contribution by this organization to
the scholarship of its industry will, I am confident, merit widespread commendation. The Club set up a Committee on the Invention
of Printing, under the chairmanship of the undersigned, to direct
the project professionally and dispense its sponsorship fund.
Without this practical support the project could never have been
undertaken.

Special credit for support is due to the presidents of the
Club during the four administrations through which the project
has been operating, Messrs. Richard C. Crehore, Jack Hagen,
Gradie Oakes, and Arthur Brooks, and to the members of the
boards of directors functioning during these years.

The Work Projects Administration provided the entire project
payroll, including the practical full-time supervision of the work.
As will be obvious, its appropriation has run into many thousands
of dollars. Actual work on the project began in the school

building at Huron and Wells streets, Chicago, on October 26, 1939.
On January 26, 1940, the separate "Printing Bibliography Project"
was incorporated, as one of its activities, into the "Chicago
Public Library Omnibus Project", and the staff was moved to 1400
West Washington Boulevard. The Chicago Public Library had from
the beginning acted as "official sponsor" of the project, the
Craftsmen's Club being known technically as the "co-sponsor."

Soon after the project got under way, the present writer, as
chairman of the Special Committee on Library Holdings of the Committee on Historical Source Materials of the American Historical
Association, became interested in the possible great increase in
materials for research in American libraries, through intensive
specialization in acquisition policies of reference and research
libraries. It seemed apparent that a prerequisite to intensive
specialization in any subject was a thorough bibliographical
exploration of the available printed materials in that field.
It was suggested [1] that the field of knowledge might be broken
down into a subject classification, and that comprehensive bibliographies on each subject might be compiled with the aid (then
available) of relief labor, with the cooperation of and professional
guidance by the respectively interested learned societies. It was
felt that the resulting bibliographies would provide helpful
guides for library specialization in the respective subjects.

[1] McMurtrie, Douglas Crawford. A suggested program for aug-
menting materials for research in American libraries. [Report
to the Committee on historical source materials of the American
historical association.] Chicago, 1939.

The project on printing bibliography recently undertaken appeared to provide a practical example of subject bibliography projected along these lines. Hence the procedure and methods received specially careful thought.

Since a large number of sources had to be examined systematically for materials bearing on the history of printing, it was thought best, while the search was being made, to record all titles on the broad subject of _printing_. The indexing of periodical articles was restricted, however, to _history of printing_, largely because another WPA project in Chicago, under the sponsorship of the Newberry Library, was engaged in indexing all locally available files of journals on the printing and allied trades. The titles on printing history indexed by this latter project were courteously put at the disposal of our staff.

Procedure

The record of titles was made on paper slips, the size of standard library cards, so that each title could be typed in original, with two carbon copies. This provided three copies of each title, one of which could be placed in a general file arranged alphabetically by author, one arranged by subject classification, and the third kept together with other titles from the same source, so that the adequacy and accuracy of coverage of that source could at any time be checked.

The first and most obvious effort was to record on slips

the titles in all published bibliographies on the subject we were undertaking to cover. Foremost among these was the annual now entitled Bibliographie des Buch- und Bibliothekswesen, the titles in a few sections of which applied to our field of interest. Next were listed the titles in the bibliography in the first volume of van der Linde's work to which reference has already been made.

Titles in the three volumes of Bigmore and Wyman's excellent Bibliography of printing, first published serially in a printing journal, and then republished in book form between the years 1880 and 1886, were transcribed on slips. In this bibliography were many intelligent annotations.

We next transcribed all titles within the scope of our interest in the printed catalogues of four great printing libraries: the Saint Bride Foundation Library, in London; the Börsenverein der deutschen Buchhändler, in Leipzig; the Vereeniging ter Bevordering van de Belangen des Boekhandels, in Amsterdam; and the Cercle de la Librairie, in Paris. It was a handicap that the war cut off correspondence with the librarians of these collections with respect to bibliographical details.

The volume of the printed catalogue of materials on bibliography in the Royal Library at the Hague, published as recently as 1903, provided titles of many important materials, particularly those on the history of Dutch printing, in that institution.

In the fine library of the British Patent Office at London are some collected volumes of Dutch materials on printing history,

apparently originally assembled by Jacobus Koning, the contents
of which we would have liked to record in detail, but this did
not prove feasible. This note as to their existence, however,
may prove helpful to scholars undertaking specialized research
on the traditional Dutch view of the invention controversy.

Of the leading American collections of materials on printing,
only that of the Newberry Library, Chicago, is represented, even
partially, by a catalogue. The best collection on our subject in
this country is undoubtedly that in the Columbia University Library,
recently strengthened to a noteworthy degree by acquisition of the
collection formerly belonging to the American Type Founders Company. Unfortunately no full record of this library's holdings
was available to us, though we trust its most important titles
are represented in our list. It is to be hoped that the authorities of this library will check the present list and contribute
for a supplement any additional titles uncovered.

Other good American collections on printing are to be found
at the Harvard College Library, Cambridge, Mass.; the Providence
Public Library, Providence, R. I.; the New York Public Library,
and the Grolier Club, New York City; and the Library of Congress,
Washington, D. C.

The authorities of the Library of Congress generously made
available to us printed cards for all titles on printing, and the
Chicago Club of Printing House Craftsmen contributed the cost of
microfilming all cards in the printing classification in the

public catalogue of the New York Public Library. So it is to be
presumed that we have a fairly complete record of the holdings of
these two great libraries within our subject field.

From here on, the exploration became more laborious and
relatively less productive with respect to the effort expended.
We examined, for example, the entire file of the Zentralblatt für
Bibliothekswesen, noting titles in lists of books and pamphlets
received for review, and reference in footnotes to or lists of
authorities appended to articles of significance on our subject.
The articles in this journal bearing on our subject were indexed.

This same procedure was followed with respect to other important
bibliographical journals published throughout the world: Transactions of the Bibliographical Society (of London), Papers of the
Bibliographical Society of America, the Zeitschrift für Bücherfreunde, the historic Serapeum, the Bulletin du Bibliophile, the
Bibliographe Moderne, the Bulletin du Bibliophile Belge, La Bibliofilia, the Börsenblatt für den Deutschen Buchhandel, the Neuer
Anzeiger für Bibliographie und Bibliothekswesen, Nordisk Tidskrift
för Bok och Biblioteksväsen, and others.

The several series of publications of the Gutenberg Gesellschaft were fully indexed as to contents. These important publications have never, however, given much attention to bibliographical
record of published materials within their field of interest.

Schweizerisches Gutenbergmuseum, the quarterly official
publication of the Gutenbergmuseum at Bern, Switzerland, proved

exceedingly helpful to us. The editor adopted the commendable practise of printing in each issue a full record of publications received or acquired for the library. This record provided us with many titles of which we would not otherwise have known. My felicitations to Dr. Karl Lüthi, director of this institution.

A number of books provided numerous titles, among them Biblio-theca bibliografica Italica by Ottino and Fumagalli, The invention of printing by T. L. DeVinne, The book; the story of printing and bookbinding by the present writer, and others.

Every title in one book was grist for our mill. I refer to Die Jubelfeste der Buchdruckerkunst by Louis Mohr, published at Vienna in 1886. Mohr's list contributed materially to our list of commemorative publications. In addition, a collected set of publications commemorating the fourth centenary of the invention in 1840, preserved in the library of the Grolier Club of New York, the titles of which were courteously communicated to us by Mr. George L. McKay, helped further in the same direction.

In the private library of the undersigned are many ephemeral as well as standard publications on the invention of printing, all of which were of course available to the project staff for exam-ination and description.

Hundreds of other journals, books, pamphlets, booksellers' catalogues, bibliographies, etc., were examined during the course of the program and the titles duly recorded on slips and added to our bank of references.

- x -

In all, something like 90,000 titles on printing and its history were recorded and filed. This file, covering a far wider subject field than that of the list now published, will remain available for further working and publication, when and if opportunity offers.

———————————

After assembling titles from every source of which we could think, the next procedure was to sort out every title relating in any way to the <u>invention</u> of printing, which was to be the subject of the first list to be compiled and published.

Multiple slips for the same title were first brought together. The standard works were of course represented by slips copied from many different sources. The best title (generally the Library of Congress printed card for such titles) was then selected as the master card, and all recorded locations were transferred to it.

Each title of an independent book or pamphlet was cleared through the Union Catalog of the Library of Congress, through the courtesy of its director, Mr. George A. Schwegmann, Jr. This process gave us more locations for books already located, and provided one or more locations for some books for which we had titles without record of location of any copy. But, of course, many titles came back to us without record of location in any American library.

When some of our titles came back from the Union Catalog

with the indication that no copies had been reported by any
American library, we then tried to find some location overseas.
These titles were searched in the printed catalogues of the
British Museum, the Bibliothèque Nationale, the Prussian Gesammt-
katalog, and other printed institutional catalogues. This search
enabled us to record locations for many such titles.

The titles copied from library catalogues bore, of course,
an automatic indication of location.

The final result of all this research is that some of our
titles are located only in libraries overseas, some only in
libraries in the United States, some in both, and some, of
course, as yet unlocated.

I may digress a moment here to stress the value -- yes,
the necessity -- of location of copies in any bibliography
intended to serve a useful purpose. Up until recent years,
bibliographers acknowledged no obligation to the scholars
consulting their lists to report where one or more copies
might be found. Many are the students who have pursued for
twenty years the book or pamphlet once found listed by a re-
liable bibliographer, but never succeeding in finding a copy.
Yet the man who originally listed the title had undoubtedly
seen a copy and knew the library in which it could be found.
But he had not taken the trouble to note this item of information, so essential when we refer to rare and little-known
material.

The importance of locating titles in bibliographies is today being acknowledged by an ever-increasing number of scholars, but the practise should become universal. We still see published important bibliographies of rare material which include no information as to where the originals may be found. So it behooves all scholars to preach, in season and out of season, that every bibliography should indicate the location of one or more copies of every title for which a location is known.

It is worthy of some interest, I believe, that this is, to the best of our knowledge, the first consequential bibliography ever published to record systematically locations in libraries both domestic and foreign. As such, let us hope it is a pioneer, for such range of locations must certainly increase its usefulness to scholars alike at home and abroad.

Locations are indicated by symbols. For libraries in the United States we use the symbols officially approved by the Union Catalog of the Library of Congress, an exhaustive list of which were published by the American Imprints Inventory in 1939, and a supplement has since been published.

The efficient indication of locations in European libraries presented more of a problem, for there existed no accepted system of symbols for such institutions. Since it seemed inevitable, with the growing trend of scholarship to international scope, that such a code of symbols was needed, the present writer undertook to compile one, to be submitted to bibliographers throughout the world for criticism and revision. Libraries in Europe were first embraced within its scope, but since it was evident that the symbols for European libraries must eventually be fitted into a world scheme, the undertaking was widened to construct a system of symbols for all countries of the world.

The tentative list of world location symbols has been published under the title: Proposed list of location symbols for libraries in all countries of the world except the United States. It was issued in 1941 as no. 3 in the present project's series of "Contributions to the Bibliography of Printing." In the proposed system, each symbol consists of three parts indicating, respectively, the continent, the country, and the city together with the institution. The general scheme of symbols may be illustrated by citing those for a few important depositories:

Eu-Ge-LB.   Europe-Great Britain (England)-London, the British Museum

Eu-Gs-EU.   Europe-Great Britain (Scotland)-Edinburgh, the University Library

Af-U-CP.   Africa-Union of South Africa-Capetown, Public Library

As-Pe-IN.   America (South)-Peru-Lima, National Library (or Biblioteca Nacional)

An-C-TU.   America (North)-Canada-Toronto-University of Toronto Library

To facilitate use internationally, names of geographical

divisions are retained, so far as possible, in the local forms.
Thus Spain is Es (Espana), Holland is Ne (Nederland), and so forth.

More details regarding the system are available in the publication already cited. The list for Canada, as improved by Canadian suggestions, is already in use. Official proposals for certain revisions in symbols for other countries have been received and adopted. Within the last few days there came a suggestion from the Prefect of the Vatican Library proposing a slight change in the symbol representing that library. The symbols are already in use by the Committee of the American Library Association concerned with subscriptions by overseas libraries. That committee has contributed helpfully by sending us the names of institutions not in the list and by suggesting the symbols to be assigned to them.

This is, we believe, the first published bibliography in which this new system of location symbols for overseas libraries is used. The user of this list will have a good opportunity to test its practicability.

Of the total of 3228 titles listed, there are 2026 titles of separate or independent publications, either books or pamphlets.

We have failed to locate in any library 514, or less than 25 per cent, of these separately published titles. For 434, or slightly over 20 per cent of the total, we record locations in European libraries, but not in any library in the United States.

Slightly under half of the total, or 948 titles, are not to be found, so far as we could ascertain, in any American library.

Among the 1078 titles located in one or more institutions in the United States, we found 318 in the Library of Congress, 254 in the New York Public Library, 183 in the Newberry Library, 144 in the Harvard College Library, 126 in the John Crerar Library, 122 in the Columbia University Library, 102 in the Boston Public Library, and 90 in the library of the Grolier Club.

This means that the American library holding the highest percentage of titles owns about one-sixth of the recorded publications on this subject.

It should here be pointed out that we do not have a _full_ record of all holdings of the libraries in question. However, we used the best existing mechanisms to record them. The figures must therefore be regarded as possibly incomplete. I am confident that any one of the libraries, upon checking this list, would find it had titles not here credited to it. In spite of this qualification, the admittedly approximate figures will, I believe, be found both interesting and informative.

We are indebted to many scholars for assistance and cooperation. Our first obligation is to the Librarian of Congress, and to Dr. Luther H. Evans, David Mearns, George A. Schwegmann, Jr., Robert Gooch, John Cronin, Miss Florence Hollman, and others on the staff of the Library of Congress. Next I wish gratefully to acknowledge cooperation by Paul North Rice, Gerald McDonald, and others on the staff of the New York Public Library, as well as to Dr. Harry M. Lydenberg, late director of that distinguished institution. Mr.

Charles M. Adams and Miss Dorothy Eggert of the Columbia University
Library have contributed full descriptions of many titles located
only in its notable collection.

Many European colleagues have contributed to the present list
by material sent me before the outbreak of present hostilities.
Among these I think gratefully of W. Turner Berry, librarian of
the St. Bride Foundation in London, Dr. Henry Thomas of the
British Museum, Dr. Henry Guppy of the John Rylands Library,
Manchester, England, Miss Emma Dronckers, librarian of the
"Vereeniging" at Amsterdam, Dr. Isak Collijn, librarian of the
Royal Library at Stockholm, Dr. Lauritz Nielsen of the Royal
Library at Copenhagen, the Director of the Lenin State Library
at Moscow, and of many friends of earlier days who are now
unhappily on the other side of the present world conflict.

To the supervisor of the printing bibliography project during
the past two years, John Adamson, I express my appreciation for
earnest and untiring effort to make this as fine a list as could
be produced. To Alex Ladenson, supervisor of the Chicago Public
Library Omnibus Project, we are all grateful for enthusiastic
support and understanding cooperation. To Claire B. Benepe,
technician of the Omnibus Project the staff is indebted for
bibliographical counsel and direction on many occasions. And
to the authorities of District 3 of the Illinois Work Projects
Administration, we can only express appreciation for their support
and say that we hope the reception accorded this list by biblio-

graphers and historians will give them cause for satisfaction in devoting to its compilation the resources and personnel allocated to the project.

The list as here offered is far from perfect, as no one understands better than I. It suffers from the lack of skilled bibliographical supervision at all stages of its progress. Inaccuracies have certainly crept in. And all defects have been multiplied by the haste to complete compilation and publication before an arbitrary deadline date, imposed by the change-over of WPA activities to service essential to the war effort.

The full accuracy of sub-division of titles by subject cannot be guaranteed. Nor could they be in such a list, unless the text of every book, pamphlet, and article were read and analyzed by qualified experts -- which is manifestly out of the question. So we were under necessity of classifying by subject, as intelligently as possible, from the wording of the title. Certain errors in classification are bound to result from such procedure. But it seemed more helpful to the user of the list to undertake as effective a subject breakdown as possible, in the belief that the positive advantages would more than offset the disadvantage of an occasional error.

I once more reiterate my belief in the wisdom of publishing bibliography while it can be published, rather than holding it twenty years to perfect it, with the result that it never sees the light. This is a first modern reasonably comprehensive list on the present subject. Beyond doubt it will prove helpful to many. Those who use it will detect some errors which they will, I trust, report to the undersigned. Others will, I hope, report titles which we may have missed. And, when happier days are here again, I am confident that many librarians overseas will check this list and favor us with additions and revisions which will make possible the publication, at some later date, of an enlarged and improved edition.

Meanwhile, these first fruits of our sincere and earnest efforts are offered to scholars everywhere interested in the history of the greatest force in civilization: printing.

Douglas C. McMurtrie

950 Michigan Avenue
    Evanston, Illinois
July 20, 1942

KEY TO LOCATIONS

UNITED STATES

CBPac	Pacific Unitarian school for the ministry library, Berkeley, Calif.
CP	Public library, Pasadena, Calif.
CSmH	Henry E. Huntington library and art gallery, San Marino, Calif.
CU	University of California library, Berkeley, Calif.
CtHT	Trinity college library, Hartford, Conn.
CtMW	Wesleyan university library, Middletown, Conn.
CtY	Yale university library, New Haven, Conn.
DCU-H	Catholic university, Huyvernat collection, Washington, D. C.
DGS	U. S. geological survey library, Washington, D. C.
DLC	Library of Congress, Washington, D. C.
DP	U. S. patent office library, Washington, D. C.
DSG	U. S. surgeon general's library, Washington, D. C.
DSI	Smithsonian institution library, Washington, D. C.
GEU	Emory university library, Emory, Ga.
I	Illinois state library, Springfield, Ill.
IC	Chicago public library, Chicago, Ill.
ICJ	John Crerar library, Chicago, Ill.
ICN	Newberry library, Chicago, Ill.
ICU	University of Chicago library, Chicago, Ill.
IEN·	Northwestern university library, Evanston, Ill.
IU	University of Illinois library, Urbana, Ill.
IaU	State university of Iowa library, Iowa city, Iowa.
In	Indiana state library, Indianapolis, Ind.
KyU	University of Kentucky library, Lexington, Ky.
LNH	Tulane university, Howard Tilton memorial library, New Orleans, La.
MB	Public library of the city of Boston, Boston, Mass.
MBAt	Boston Athenaeum, Boston, Mass.
MBMu	Boston museum of fine arts, Boston, Mass.
MBSi	Simmons college library, Boston, Mass.
MBrZ	Zion research library, Brookline, Mass.
MH	Harvard university library, Cambridge, Mass.
MH-BA	Harvard university, Baker library, Cambridge, Mass.
MHi	Massachusetts historical society, Boston, Mass.
MNBedf	Free public library, New Bedford, Mass.
MSaE	Essex institute library, Salem, Mass.
MWA	American antiquarian society library, Worcester, Mass.
MWiW-C	Williams college, Chapin library, Williamstown, Mass.
MdBJ	Johns Hopkins university library, Baltimore, Md.
MdBP	Peabody institute library, Baltimore, Md.
MeB	Bowdoin college library, Brunswick, Me.

MiD	Detroit public library, Detroit, Mich.
MiU	University of Michigan library, Ann Arbor, Mich.
MiU-C	University of Michigan, William L. Clements library, Ann Arbor, Mich.
MnHi	Minnesota historical society library, St. Paul, Minn.
MnU	University of Minnesota library, Minneapolis, Minn.
NB	Public library, Brooklyn, N. Y.
NBB	Brooklyn museum library, Brooklyn, N. Y.
NBC	Brooklyn college library, Brooklyn, N. Y.
NBuG	Grosvenor library, Buffalo, N. Y.
NIC	Cornell university library, Ithaca, N. Y.
NN	New York public library, New York city, N. Y.
NNC	Columbia university library, New York city, N. Y.
NNGr	Grolier club library, New York city, N. Y.
NNH	Hispanic society of America library, New York city, N. Y.
NNP	Pierpont Morgan library, New York city, N. Y.
NNU-W	New York university, Washington square library, New York city, N. Y.
NNUT	Union theological seminary library, New York city, N. Y.
NPV	Vassar college library, Poughkeepsie, N. Y.
NRU	University of Rochester library, Rochester, N. Y.
NcD	Duke university library, Durham, N. C.
NcU	University of North Carolina library, Chapel Hill, N. C.
NcWfC	Wake Forest college library, Wake Forest, N. C.
NjN	Public library, Newark, N. J.
NjP	Princeton university library, Princeton, N. J.
NjR	Rutgers university library, New Brunswick, N. J.
OC	Public library, Cincinnati, Ohio.
OCU	University of Cincinnati library, Cincinnati, Ohio.
OCl	Cleveland public library, Cleveland, Ohio.
OClW	Western Reserve university library, Cleveland, Ohio.
PBL	Lehigh university library, Bethlehem, Penn.
PHC	Haverford college library, Haverford, Penn.
PHi	Historical society of Pennsylvania library, Philadelphia, Penn.
PP	Free library of Philadelphia, Philadelphia, Penn.
PPDrop	Dropsie college library, Philadelphia, Penn.
PPG	German society of Pennsylvania library, Philadelphia, Penn.
PPL	Library company of Philadelphia, Philadelphia. Penn.
PPTU	Temple university library, Philadelphia, Penn.
PPeSchw	Schwenckfelder historical society, Pennsburg, Penn.
PU	University of Pennsylvania library, Philadelphia, Penn.
RP	Providence public library, Providence, R. I.
RPB	Brown university library, Providence, R. I.
RPD	Rhode Island school of design library, Providence, R. I.
RPJCB	John Carter Brown library, Providence, R. I.
ScU	University of South Carolina library, Columbia, S. C.
TxU	University of Texas library, Austin, Texas.
ViU	University of Virginia library, Charlottesville, Va.
WaU	University of Washington library, Seattle, Wash.

DANMARK

Eu-Da-KKb   Kongelige Bibliotek, København

DEUTSCHES REICH

Eu-De-BP   Preussische Staatsbibliothek, Berlin
Eu-De-BU   Universitätsbibliothek, Berlin
Eu-De-BsSU   Staats- und Universitätsbibliothek, Breslau
Eu-De-GtU   Universitätsbibliothek, Göttingen
Eu-De-HlU   Universitätsbibliothek, Halle
Eu-De-KlU   Universitätsbibliothek, Kiel
Eu-De-LBb   Bibliothek der Börsenverein der deutschen Buchhändler, Leipzig
Eu-De-MrU   Universitätsbibliothek, Marburg
Eu-De-MsU   Universitätsbibliothek, Münster
Eu-De-MzG   Bibliothek der Gutenberg-Gesellschaft, Mainz
Eu-De-WN   Nationalbibliothek, Wien

FRANCE

Eu-Fr-PC   Cercle de la librairie, Paris
Eu-Fr-PN   Bibliothèque nationale, Paris

GREAT BRITAIN - ENGLAND

Eu-Ge-LB   British museum library, London
Eu-Ge-LE   British library of political and economic science, London
                school of political and economic science, London
Eu-Ge-LLl   London library, London
Eu-Ge-LP   Library of the patent office, London
Eu-Ge-LSb   Saint Bride foundation library, London

GREAT BRITAIN - SCOTLAND

Eu-Gs-EU   University of Edinburgh library, Edinburgh

NEDERLAND

Eu-Ne-AVb   Vereeniging ter bevordering van de belangen des boekhandels,
                bibliotheek, Amsterdam
Eu-Ne-GK   Koninklijke bibliotheek, 's-Gravenhage [The Hague]
Eu-Ne-GO   Openbare leeszaal en bibliotheek, 's-Gravenhage [The Hague]

S. S. S. R. [Russia]

Eu-Ru-MLe   Vsesoyuznaya Biblioteka imeni V. I. Lenina [V. I. Lenin
             all-union library] Moskva [Moscow]

SVERIGE [Sweden]

Eu-Sv-SK   Kungl. biblioteket, Stockholm
Eu-Sv-UU   Kungl. universitets bibliotek, Uppsala

SCHWEIZ [Switzerland]

Eu-Sz-BeG   Schweizerisches Gutenbergmuseum, Bern

THE INVENTION OF PRINTING: A BIBLIOGRAPHY

I   ANTECEDENTS

A.   IN THE ORIENT

Alibaux, Henri.
   L'invention de l'imprimerie en Chine et en Occident.   Paris, 1937.
   Title from Douglas C. McMurtrie.   [1]

   Ancienneté de l'imprimerie en Chine.   Bulletin du Bibliophile Belge, vol. 4, 1847, p. 340-341.   [2]

Bullen, Henry Lewis.
   Histories of printing and paper in China and Japan.   Far Eastern Review (Shanghai), vol. 12, 1915, p. 195-197.
   Bibliography: p. 197.   [3]

Burch, R. M.
   Some notes on early printing in the East.   British and Colonial Printer and Stationer, vol. 47, 1900, p. 305; vol. 48, 1901, p. 341; vol. 49, 1902, p. 237.   [4]

Burty, M. P.
   The invention of printing.   Publishers' Weekly, vol. 29, Apr. 1885, p. 499.   [5]

Carter, Thomas Francis, 1882-1925.
   The Chinese background of the European invention of printing. Gutenberg Jahrbuch, vol. 3, 1928, p. 9-14.   [6]

----   The Chinese origins of movable type.   Ars Typographica, vol. 2, 1925, p. 3-36.   [7]

----   The invention of printing in China and its spread westward, by Thomas Francis Carter ... New York, Columbia university press, 1925.   3 prel. leaves, [v]-xviii p., 1 leaf, 282p.   plates, fold. map, facsims., fold. tab.   24 cm.
   Published also as thesis (Ph.D.) Columbia university, 1925.
   Bibliography: p.[261]-273.   [8]
   CSmH   DLC   ICJ   ICN   MB   MSaE   NN

----   The invention of printing in China and its spread westward, by Thomas Francis Carter ... New York, Columbia university press [1931]   xxvi p., 1 leaf, 282p., 1 leaf.   plates, fold, map, facsims., fold. tab.   23 cm.

"Revised edition, October, 1931."
"Thomas Francis Carter.   October 26, 1882-August 6, 1925, signed:
D. C. M.: p. [vii]-xii.
Bibliography: p. [261]-274.   [9]
DLC

Cohn-Antenorid.
    Ein Vorgänger von Gutenberg in China.   Globus, vol. 78, no. 2,
1900, p. 33-35.   [10]

Curzon, R. Baron de la Zouche.
    History of printing in China and Europe.   Philobiblon Society.
Miscellanies, vol. 6, 1860-1861, p. 3-33.   [11]

Daland, Judson, 1860-
    The evolution of modern printing and the discovery of movable
metal type by the Chinese and Koreans in the fourteenth century,
by Judson Daland ... [Lancaster, Pa., Lancaster press, inc., 1931]
209-234p.   illus.   24 cm.
    Cover-title.
    Reprint from Franklin Institute.   Journal, vol. 212, no. 2.
    Also appeared in General Magazine and Historical Chronicle,
    vol. 36, 1933, p. 49-65.   [12]
    NN   Eu-Ge-LB

Duyvendak, J. J. L.
    Coster's Chineesche voorouders.   De Gids, vol. 89, 1925, p.
344-357.   [13]

    The earliest printing in the world.   Book Worm (London), vol.1,
1888, p. 201-202, 291-292.   [14]

    Early printing.   Inland Printer, vol. 1, no. 12, Sept. 1884,
p. 9.   [15]

    Early printing in China.   Chambers' Edinburgh Journal, vol. 11,
1849, p. 174-175.   [16]

Erkes, Eduard.
    Buch und Buchdruck in China.   (In Gutenbergfestschrift, zur
Feier des 25jaehrigen Bestehens des Gutenbergmuseums in Mainz 1925.
Hrsg. von A. Ruppel.   Mainz, Verlag der Gutenberg-Gesellschaft
[1925]   p. 338-341)   [17]
    DLC   ICN   MB   MH   NN   NNC   Eu-De-BP   Eu-Ge-LB
    Eu-Ne-AVb   Eu-Sz-BeG

Fischer von Waldheim, Gotthelf, 1771-1853.
    Les caractères mobiles dans l'antiquité.   Union Syndicale et
Fédération des Syndicats des Maîtres Imprimeurs de France.
Bulletin Officiel, no. 2, Feb. 1928, p. 57-58.   [18]

Fuhrmann, Otto Walter.
    The invention of printing.   Dolphin, vol. 3, 1938, p. 25-27.   [19]

Gallotti, J.
    L'invention de l'imprimerie en Chine.   Arts et Metiers
Graphiques, no. 38, 1933, p. 37-41.   [20]

Horgan, Stephen Henry.
    Is this the oldest printed book?   [Diamond Sutra, May 11, 868]
Inland Printer, vol. 86, no. 2, 1930-1931, p. 57-58.   [21]

Hülle, Hermann, 1870-
    Über den alten chinesischen Typendruck und seine Entwickelung
in den Ländern des Fernen Ostens.   Von Professor Hermann Hülle ...
[Berlin] Gedruckt auf Veranlassung der H. Berthold Messinglinien-
fabrik und Schriftgiesserei A.-G., 1923.   2 prel. leaves, 15p.
facsim.   23.5 cm.
    In portfolio.
    Printed on double leaves in Japanese style.
    "Gedruckt als Privatdruck der Berthold'schen Hausdruckerei in
    500 mit der Hand numerierten Exemplaren auf echt China-Papier."
    Bibliographical foot-notes.   [22]
    DLC   NN

Julien, Aignan Stanislas, 1797-1873.
    Documents sur l'art d'imprimer à l'aide de planches en bois,
de planches en pierre et de types mobiles, inventé en Chine, bien
long-temps avant que l'Europe en fît usage; estraits des livres
chinois, par M. Stanislas Julien ... [Paris, Imprimerie royale,
1847] 16p.   22 cm.
    Caption title.
    Reprint from Journal Général de l'Instruction Publique et des
    Cultes, 1846.
    Also appeared in Comptes Rendus des Séances de l'Académie des
    Sciences, vol. 24, 1847, p. 1002-1009.   Same, Journal Asia-
    tique, 4th ser., vol. 9, 1847, p. 511-519.   [23]
    DLC   MdBP   OCl   Eu-Fr-PN   Eu-Ne-GK

----   L'imprimerie en Chine au sixième siècle de notre ère, par
Stanislas Julien ... Extrait du Journal Général de l'Instruction
Publique et des Cultes.   Paris, Dupont [1847?]   10p.   21 cm.   [24]
    MSaE   Eu-Fr-PN   Eu-Ge-LB

Laufer, Berthold, 1874-1934.
    Descriptive account of the collections of the Chinese, Tibetan,
Mongol, and Japanese books in the Newberry library.   Chicago,
[1913]   ix, 42p.   front., facsims. (1 fold.)   23 cm.   [25]
    DLC   ICJ   ICN   Eu-Fr-PN

----   Paper and printing in ancient China [by] Berthold Laufer.

Chicago, Printed for the Caxton club, 1931.   33, [1]p., 1 leaf.
23.5 cm.
    "Of this book prepared as a lecture for the members of the
Caxton club of Chicago ... two hundred and fifty copies have been
printed from type by the Pynson printers of New York."   [26]
DLC   ICN   MB   MiU   NN   NjN

---- Papier und Druck im alten China.   Imprimatur (Hamburg),
vol. 5, 1934, p. 65-75.   [27]

Löffler, Klemens.
    Der Buchdruck der Ostasiaten und Gutenberg.   Germania, no. 373,
Aug. 12, 1925.   Same, Echo der Gegenwart, no. 201, Aug.27, 1925.
Same, Bayerischer Kurier, Oct. 29, 1925.   [28]

Lofgren, B.
    Boktryckarkonstens kinesiska anor.   Svenska Boktryckareforen-
ingens Meddelanden, vol. 31, 1926, p. 77-83.   [29]

Mullie, P. Jos.
    De uitvinding der drukkunst in China.   Koninklijke Vlaamsche
Academie voor Taal- en Letterkunde.   Verslagen en Mededeelingen
(Gent), 1934, p. 253-280.   [30]

Nachod, O.
    Der älteste erhaltene Blockdruck: Japanische Dharani-Zettel
von 770.   Zeitschrift des Deutschen Vereins für Buchwesen und
Schrifttum, 1918, p. 60-61.   [31]

Peake, Cyrus Henderson, 1900-
    Additional notes and bibliography on the history of printing
in the Far East.   Gutenberg Jahrbuch, vol. 14, 1939, p. 57-61.   [32]

---- The origin and development of printing in China in the
light of recent research.   Gutenberg Jahrbuch, vol. 10, 1935,
p. 9-17   [33]

Pelliot, Paul.
    Ancienneté de l'imprimerie.   Union Syndicale et Fédération
des Syndicats des Maîtres Imprimeurs de France.   Bulletin Officiel,
no. 2, Feb. 1928, p. 49.   [34]

Pil, C. S.
    Early Korean movable type.   Inland Printer, vol. 75, June
1925, p. 410.   [35]

    Printing a thousand years ago.   Printer, vol. 3, no. 6, Nov.
1860, p. 130.
    A tomb discovered in India containing a press with movable type.[36]

Renker, Armin, 1891-
... Papier und Druck im Fernen Osten.   Mainz, Gutenberg-Gesellschaft, 1936.   2 prel. leaves, 7-55, [1]p. incl. plates, facsims.
21 cm.   (Kleiner Druck der Gutenberg-Gesellschaft, nr. 25)   [37]
    DLC   ICN   MB   Eu-De-BP   Eu-De-WN   Eu-Ne-AVb

----   Papier und Druck im Fernen Osten ... Ein Vortragensentwurf
mit Lichtbildern ... Bearbeiter: Amt für Berufserziehung und Be-
triebsführung der Deutschen Arbeitsfront.   Berlin [1937]   31p.
30.5 cm.   [38]
    NN

Satow, Ernest M.
    Further notes on movable types in Korea.   Transactions of the
Asiatic Society of Japan, vol. 10, 1882, p. 252-259.   [39]

----   On the early history of printing in Japan.   Transactions
of the Asiatic Society of Japan, vol. 10, 1882, p. 48-83.   [40]

Schierlitz, Ernst.
    Anfänge der Druckkunst in China und Deutschland.   China-Dienst,
vol. 3, 1934, p. 100-104.   [41]

Schlegel, Gustaaf, 1840-1903.
    Chinesische Bräuche und Spiele in Europa ... Breslau, R. Nisch-
kowsky, 1869.   1 prel. leaf, 32p.   21.5 cm.
    Inaugural-Dissertation, Jena.
    DLC   MH   NjP   [42]

Sotzmann, Johann Daniel Ferdinand.
    Der chinesische Bücherdruck, nach Stanislaus Julien.   Serapeum,
vol. 9, no. 4, 1848, p. 49-59.   [43]

Stübe, R.
    Die Erfindung des Druckes in China und seine Verbreitung in
Ostasien.   Beiträge zur Geschichte der Technik, vol. 8, 1918,
p. 88 et sqq.   [44]

Ting Wen-Yuan.
    Von der alten chinesischen Buchdruckkunst.   Gutenberg-Jahrbuch,
vol. 4, 1929, p. 9-17.   [45]

    Very ancient printing.   National Lithographer, vol. 38, May
1931, p. 43.   [46]

Waley, Arthur.
    Note on the invention of woodcuts.   New China Review (Hong-
Kong), vol. 1, 1919, p. 412-415.   [47]

B.   IN EUROPE

   1 Textile Printing

Depierre, Joseph, 1839-
   L'impression des tissus, spécialement l'impression à la main à
travers les âges et dans les divers pays. L'impression au moyen de
planches en relief. Divers procédés de gravure (bois, clichés
métalliques), planches pour impression à la main, planches pour
perrotine, matières premières, outils, mise en oeuvre, impression
simultanée en plusieurs couleurs, compartiments, fondus, feutrages,
etc., etc.   Par Joseph Depierre ... Mulhouse (Alsace), C. Stukel-
berger [etc., etc.] 1910.   [6], 131, [1]p.   illus., 10 plates,
(part col., part fold.)   29 cm.   [48]
   ICJ

Fleury, Édouard Husson.
   Les manuscrits à miniatures de la Bibliothèque de Laon étudiés
au point de vue de leurs illustrations.   Laon, 1863. 2 pts in 1 vol.
   Textile printing: part 2, p. 4 et sqq.   [49]
   Eu-Fr-PN   Eu-Ge-LB

Forrer, Robert, 1866-
   Les imprimeurs de tissus dans leurs relations historiques et
artistiques avec les corporations; par R. Forrer ... Strasbourg,
C. Muh & cie., 1898.   55p., 2 leaves incl. illus., 10 plates
(1 double) 22 cm.
   DLC   NjP   Eu-De-LBb   Eu-Fr-PN   Eu-Ge-LB   Eu-Ne-AVb

----   Die Kunst des Zeugdrucks vom Mittelalter bis zur Empirezeit.
Nach Urkunden und Originaldrucken bearb. von Dr. R. Forrer ...
Strassburg i. Els., Schlesier und Schweikhardt, 1898.   104p.
81 plates (part col.) incl. front.   32 cm.   [51]
   DLC   MB   Eu-De-LBb   Eu-Fr-PN   Eu-Ge-LB

----   Die Zeugdrucke der byzantinischen, romanischen, gothischen
und spätern Kunstepochen.   Strassburg, 1894.   39, [4]p.   illus.
57 plates (part col.)   29.5 cm.   [52]
   MB   MH   NjP   Eu-De-LBb   Eu-Fr-PN   Eu-Ge-LB

Gremps, P. Max.
   Der Stoffdruck als Vorläufer des Buchdrucks.   Das Schiff
(Beiblatt zu den Typographischen Mitteilungen), 1925, p. 17-19.   [53]

Keller, Ferd.
   Die Tapete von Sitten.   Ein Beitrag zur Geschichte der Xylo-
graphie mit einigen Bemerkungen.   Mittheilungen der antiquarischen
Gesellschaft in Zürich.   Band XI, Heft 6.   Zürich, 1857. 4to.   [54]
   Eu-De-LBb   Eu-Ge-LB

2   Playing cards

Breitkopf, Johann Gottlob Immanuel, 1719-1794.
    Versuch, den Ursprung der Spielkarten, die Einführung des Leinen-
papieres, und den Anfang der Holzschneidekunst in Europa zu er-
forschen.   Von Joh. Gottl. Imman. Breitkopf ... Leipzig, J. G. I.
Breitkopf, 1784-1801. 2 vol. in 1.   plates (part fold.) 26x21 cm.
    Vol. 2 published by Roch und Compagnie.
    Vol. 2 has added t.-p.: Beyträge zu einer Geschichte der
    Schreibekunst ... Von Johann Gottlob Immanuel Breitkopf ...   [55]
    DLC   ICJ   MB   MWA   NN   Eu-De-LBb   Eu-Fr-PN   Eu-Ge-LB

British Museum.   Department of prints and drawings.
    Catalogue of the collection of playing cards bequeathed to the
Trustees of the British Museum by the late Lady Charlotte Schreiber.
Comp. by Freeman O'Donoghue ... Printed by order of the Trustees.
London, Longmans & co. [etc.] 1901.   vii, 228p.   25.5 cm.
    "Books relating to cards and card playing," p. 214-219.   [56]
    DLC   ICJ   ICN   NN   OCl   Eu-Ge-LB

Chatto, William Andrew, 1799-1864.
    Facts and speculations on the origin and history of playing
cards. By William Andrew Chatto ...   London, J. R. Smith, 1848.
vi, [2], 343, [1]p.   illus., plates (part col.)   22.5 cm.   [57]
    DLC   ICJ   MB   MdBJ   NN   NjP   Eu-De-LBb   Eu-Fr-PN   Eu-Ge-LB

Garnier, Jacques Marie.
    Histoire de l'imagerie populaire et des cartes à jouer à Chartres,
suivie de recherches sur le commerce du colportage des complaintes,
canards et chansons des rues.   Chartres, imp. de Garnier, 1869.
viii, 450p.   12mo.   [58]
    Eu-De-LBb   Eu-Fr-PC   Eu-Ge-LB

Hargrave, Catherine Perry.
    A history of playing cards and a bibliography of cards and
gaming; compiled and illustrated from the old cards and books in
the collection of the United States playing card company in
Cincinnati.   Boston and New York, Houghton Mifflin co., 1930.
xxiv p., 1 leaf, 468p.   illus., plates, col. front., col. plates.
31.5 cm.
    Bibliography: p. [369]-449.   [59]
    DLC   ICN

Horr, Norton Townshend.
    A bibliography of card-games and of the history of playing cards.
Cleveland, O., C. Orr, 1892.   79p.   8vo.   [60]
    ICJ   Eu-De-LBb   Eu-Fr-PN   Eu-Ge-LB

[Lacroix, Paul] 1806-1884.
    Curiosités de l'histoire des arts, par P. L. Jacob, bibliophile

[pseud.] ... Paris, A. Delahays, 1858.   2 prel. leaves, 410p.,
1 leaf.   17 cm.
   Each article followed by a bibliography of the subject treated.
   Contents include: Recherches sur les cartes à jouer.   [61]
   DLC   MB   NN   Eu-Fr-PN

Lacroix, Paul, 1806-1884.
   L'origine des cartes à jouer.   Paris, Techener, 1835.   12p.
8vo.   [62]
   Eu-De-LBb   Eu-Fr-PN   Eu-Ge-LB

Lehrs, Max.
   Die ältesten deutschen Spielkarten des königlichen Kupferstich-
kabinets zu Dresden.   Dresden [n.d.]   41p.   4to.   [63]
   Eu-Fr-PN

Lozzi, Carlo, 1829-
   Le antichi carte da giuoco.   Bibliofilia, vol. 1, May-June 1899,
p. 37-46.   [64]

Maignien, Edmond.
   Recherches sur les cartiers et les cartes à jouer à Grenoble.
Grenoble, impr. de J. Allier, 1887.   34p.   8vo.   [65]
   NN'   Eu-De-LBb   Eu-Fr-PN   Eu-Ne-GK

Merlin, Romain.
   Les cartes à jouer.   Bruxelles, 1857.   8vo.
   "Extrait de la Revue universelle des arts, publiée à Paris et
à Bruxelles, sous la direction du Bibliophile Jacob."   [66]
   Eu-De-LBb

----   Origine des cartes à jouer.   Recherches nouvelles sur les
naïbis, les tarots et sur les autres espèces de cartes.   Ouvrage
accompagné d'um album de 74 [73] planches offrant plus de 600
sujots la plupart peu connus ou tout à fait nouveaux.   Paris, 1869.
4to.   [67]
   Eu-De-LBb   Eu-Ge-LB

Peignot, Gabriel i.e. Étienne Gabriel, 1767-1849.
   Recherches historiques et littéraires sur les danses des morts
et sur l'origine des cartes à jouer ... Par Gabriel Peignot.   Dijon,
Paris, V. Lagier, 1826.   lx, 367, [1]p.   front., 5 plates 21 cm. [68]
   DLC   ICJ   MB   MH   MdBP   NN   Eu-De-LBb   Eu-Ne-GK
   Eu-Sz-BeG

Pinchart, Alexandre.
   Recherches sur les cartes à jouer en Belgique.   Bruxelles, 1870.
8vo.
   Reprint from Bulletin du Bibliophile Belge, 3d ser., vol. 4,
   1869, p. 5, 37, 69; vol. 5, 1870, p. 285.   [69]
   Eu-De-LBb   - 8 -

Reiffenberg, Frédéric Auguste Ferdinand Thomas, baron de, 1794-1850.
    Sur l'anciennes cartes à jouer.   Bruxelles, ca. 1850. 8vo.   [70]
    Eu-Ge-LSb

Schreiber, Wilhelm Ludwig, 1855-1932.
    ... Die ältesten Spielkarten und die auf das Kartenspiel bezug
habenden Urkunden des 14. und 15. Jahrhunderts ... Strassburg,
J. H. E. Heitz, 1937.   xii, 176p., 1 leaf, incl. front., illus.
XII plates (part fold.) fold. tab.   25.5 cm.
    At head of title: W. L. Schreiber.
    Preface signed: Paul Heitz.
    "Literatur der Kartenspiele und Spielkarten": p. 165-168.
    "Nachtrag zu Schreibers Literatur über Spielkarten und
    Kartenspiele": p. 168-170.   [71]
    DLC   NN

Singer, Samuel Weller, 1783-1858.
    Researches into the history of playing cards; with illustra-
tions of the origin of printing and engraving on wood ... By
Samuel Weller Singer.   London, R. Triphook, 1816. xvi, [2],
277, [1] p., 3 leaves, [281]-373, [3]p.   front., illus.,
plates (part col.)   28.5 cm.
    Title in red and black.
    Only 250 copies printed.   [72]
    CSmH   DLC   ICJ   MB   MH   NN   Eu-De-LBb   Eu-Ge-LB

Société des bibliophiles françois, Paris.
    Jeux de cartes tarots et de cartes numérales du quatorzième au
dix-huitième siècle, représentés en cent planches d'après les
originaux, avec un précis historique et explicatif; publiés par la
Société des bibliophiles français.   Paris, Crapelet, 1844.
6 prel. leaves, 22p., 1 leaf.   100 plates (part col.; incl. the
added t.-p.)   36x30 cm.
    Half-title: Cartes à jouer.
    "Tiré à trente-deux exemplaires sur grand papier in-folio, et à
    cent exemplaires sur petit papier in-folio."
    "Table bibliographique et raisonnée des ouvrages relatifs aux
    cartes à jouer": p. [19]-22.   [73]
    CSmH   DLC   NN   Eu-Ge-LB

Soulanges, E.
    Inventions et découvertes ou les curieuses origines.   Les
cartes à jouer.   La galvanoplastie.   L'imprimerie.   La lithographie.   Le papier.   La photographie.   11e édition.   Tours,
1879.   8vo.   [74]

Van Rensselaer, May King, 1848-
    The devil's picture-books: a history of playing-cards, by Mrs.
John King Van Rensselaer ... New York, Dodd, Mead & co., [ca. 1890]
viii, [4], 11-207p.   24 plates (part col., incl. front.) 25 cm.   [75]
    ICJ   Eu-De-LBb   - 9 -

Weigel, Theodor Oswald, 1812-1881.
    Die Spielkarten der Weigel'schen Sammlung. Mit 8 Facsimile.
Leipzig, T. O. Weigel, 1865. 45, [1]p. illus., 8 plates
(3 col.)   40.5x30 cm.
    "Nur in 100 Exemplaren gedruckt."   [76]
    DLC   NN   Eu-De-LBb

Willshire, William Hughes, fl. 1839-1879.
    A descriptive catalogue of playing and other cards in the
British museum, accompanied by a concise general history of the
subject and remarks on cards of divination and of a politico-
historical character. By William Hughes Willshire, ... printed by
order of the Trustees.   [London, Chiswick Press], 1876.   x, 360,
viii, 87p. front., xxiii plates (part col., incl. 1 diagr.)
26.5 cm.   [77]
    DLC   DP   ICJ   NN   Eu-De-LBb   Eu-Ge-LB   Eu-Ne-AVb

    3.   Woodcuts and Metal Engravings

Alvin, Louis Joseph.
    Les commencements de la gravure aux Pays-Bas; rapport à l'Académie
de Belgique sur le concours de 1857.   Bruxelles, 1857.   8vo.
    Title from Hind, Arthur. A short history of engraving and
    etching. 1908.   [78]

Arrigoni, Luigi.
    Xilografia italiana inedita.   Milano, 1884.   7p.   plates.
32 cm.   [79]
    ICN   Eu-De-LBb   Eu-Fr-PN   Eu-Ge-LB

Baader, Joseph.
    Beiträge zur Kunstgeschichte Nürnbergs.   Nördlingen, 1860-1862.
2 vols.   8vo.
    Contents.--Formschneider. Briefmaler. Kartenmaler. Illuminis-
    ten. Der Briefmaler Hanns Guldenmund.   [80]
    Eu-De-LBb   Eu-Ge-LB

Baer, Leo, 1880-
... Holzschnitte auf Buchumschlägen aus dem XV. und der ersten
Hälfte des XVI. Jahrhunderts, herausgegeben von Leo Baer; mit 18
Abbildungen. Strassburg, J. H. E. Heitz, 1936. 11, [1]p.
mounted plates (1 double) 37x28.5 cm. (Einblattdrucke des
fünfzehnten Jahrhunderts, hrsg. von P. Heitz. 90. Bd.)
    Illustrated lining-papers (in color)
    Bibliography: p. [12]   [81]
    DLC   MH

- 10 -

Blum, Andre, 1881-
Les origines de la gravure.   Hippocrate, vol. 1, 1933,
p. 895-922.   [82]

----   Xylographiques françaises de la fin du 14e siècle.   Gazette
des Beaux-Arts, 15th ser., vol. 5, 1927, p. 152-158.   [83]

Bouchot, Henri François Xavier Marie, 1849-1906.
... Un ancêtre de la gravure sur bois; étude sur un xylographe
taillé en Bourgogne vers 1370.   Paris, É. Lévy, 1902.   xii, 131p.,
1 leaf.   illus., plates (part fold.)   32x23 cm.
     At head of title: Henri Bouchot.   [84]
     DLC   ICJ   MB   Eu-Ge-LB

----   Les deux cents incunables xylographiques du département des
estampes ... Paris, Librairie Centrale des Beaux-Arts, 1903.
2 vols.   [85]
     NN

Brunet y Bellet, José, 1818-
... L'escriptura, lo gravat, l'imprempta, lo llibre per Josep
Brunet y Bellet ... Barcelona, Tip. "L'Avenç," 1898.   x, 299p.,
2 leaves.   25.5 cm.   (His Erros historics, vol. 5)
     "Tirada de 200 exemplars."   [86]
     DLC   ICJ

Brussels. Bibliothèque royale de Belgique.
     Documents iconographiques et typographiques de la Bibliothèque
royale de Belgique; fac-similé photo-lithographiques avec texte
historique & explicatif par mm. les conservateurs & employés de la
Bibliothèque royale; pub. sous la direction et avec le concours de
m. le conservateur en chef. Avec autorisation de m. le ministre
de l'intérieur.   Bruxelles, Librairie européenne C. Muquardt;
[etc., etc.] 1877.   3 prel. leaves, 73, 3-16p.   illus., 66 plates
(part mounted, 1 col.) on 40 leaves.   54.5x37 cm.
     In 6 divisions, each with special half-title, not included in
     collation.
     Contents.--Alvin, L. Spirituale Pomerium.--Hymans, H. Gravure
     criblée. Sainte Barbe. (XVe siècle). Impressions négatives.
     Sainte Dorothée--Saint Benoît. (XVe siècle).--Ruelens, Ch.
     La Vierge de 1418.--Petit, J. Vue de Louvain.--Fétis, É.
     Les neuf preux.--Ruelens, Ch. Légende de Saint Servais.   [87]
     DLC   Eu-De-LBb   Eu-Ge-LB

     Die Buchdruckerkunst und ihre Vorläufer.   Journal für Buch-
druckerkunst, no. 8, 1859, col. 101.   [88]

Derschau, Hans Albrecht von.
     Holzschnitte alter deutscher Meister in den Originalplatten
gesammelt von Hans Albrecht von Derschau; als ein Beytrag zur

Kunstgeschichte hrsg. und mit einer Abhandlung über die Holzschneidekunst und deren Schicksale begleitet von Rudolph Zacharias Becker ...
Gravures en bois des anciens maîtres allemands ... Gotha en Saxe,
L'éditeur, 1808-16.   3 vols.   351 plates (part mounted, part fold.)
on 123 leaves.   59 cm.
    German and French in parallel columns.   [89]
    DLC   Eu-Ge-LB

Dodgson, Campbell, 1867-
    Catalogue of early German and Flemish woodcuts preserved in the
department of prints and drawings in the British museum. By Campbell
Dodgson.   London, British museum, 1903-1911. 2 vols. 8vo.   [90]
    DLC   ICN   NN   Eu-Fr-PN   Eu-Ge-LB   Eu-Ge-LSb   Eu-Ne-AVb

----   The invention of wood-engraving; a French claim considered.
Burlington Magazine, vol. 3, no. 8, 1903, p. 205-209.   [91]

Dutuit, Eugène, 1807-1886.
    Manuel de l'amateur d'estampes, par M. Eugène Dutuit; ouvrage
contenant: 1º Un aperçu sur les plus anciennes gravures, sur les
estampes en manière criblée, sur les livres xylographiques, sur les
estampes coloriées, sur les cartes à jouer, sur quelques livres à
figures du quinzième siècle, sur les danses des morts, sur les
livres d'heures; un nouveau catalogue de livres de broderie et un
essai sur les nielles ou gravures d'orfevres: 2º Les écoles
italienne, allemande, flamande et holandaise, française et anglaise.
Et enrichi de fac-similes des estampes les plus rares reproduites
par l'héliogravure... Paris, A. Levy; etc., etc., 1881-1888.   4 vols.
in 5.   front. (t. 1, 2. ptie) plates, ports, 29.5 cm., and atlas
of xxxvii plates, 32.5 cm.
    The work was to have been published in 8 volumes and an atlas,
but volumes 2, 3, 7 and 8 never appeared. cf. Lorenz, Catalogue
générale de la librairie française, and Vicaire, Manuel de
l'amateur des livres du XIXº siècle.
    "M. Eugène Dutuit (signed Gustave Pawlowski) vol. 1, part 2,
p. i-xii.
    Bibliography: vol. 1, part 2, p. lxv-lxxii; vol. 4, p. [v]-xi;
vol. 5, p. [vii]-x; vol. 6, p. [iii]-iv.
    Vol. 1, part 2, "Publication continuée sous les auspices de
M. Auguste Dutuit."   [92]
    CU   DLC   ICN   MH   NBB   Eu-De-BP   Eu-De-LBb   Eu-Fr-PN
Eu-Ge-LB

Guillot, Gaëtan.
   ... Les moines précurseurs de Gutenberg. Étude sur l'invention
de la gravure sur bois et de l'illustration du livre.   Par Gaëtan
Guillot ... Paris, Bloud et cie. [1906]   62p.   facsims.   28.5 cm.
(Science et religion. Études pour le temps présent)   [93]
    DLC   ICJ   Eu-Fr-PN

Guillot, Gaëtan.
Les origines de la gravure sur bois dans les monastères français,
d'après un ouvrage récent, Archives de la France monastique.
Revue Mabillon, vol. 1, 1905, p. 73-95.   [94]

[Guppy, Henry] 1861-
Stepping stones to the art of typography. By the editor. John
Rylands library, Manchester. Bulletin, vol. 12, 1928, p. 83-121.
   "An amplification of the lecture delivered in the John Rylands
   library on the 10th February, 1927."
   "Authorities": p. 120-121.   [95]

---- ----   Reprint.   Manchester, The University press; London,
New York [etc.] Longmans, Green & co., 1928.   45p.   facsims.
26 cm.
   "Authorities": p. 44-45.   [96]
   DLC   RPJCB   Eu-Ge-LB

Gusman, Pierre, 1862-
... La gravure sur bois et d'épargne sur métal du XIVe au XXe
siècle.   Paris, R. Roger et F. Chernoviz, 1916.   299, [1]p.
illus.   27.5 cm.
   "Il a été tiré de ce livre ... six cents exemplaires, sur vélin
   de rives au filigrane de l'ouvrage, numérotés de 1 à 600 ... "
   Printer's mark (première marque d'imprimeur parisien.
   (Caillaut) Adaptation) on t.-p.
   "Ouvrage publié avec le concours de l'Académie des inscrip-
   tions et belles-lettres.   Fondation Eugène Piot."
   "Bibliographie": p. [287]-293.   [97]
   DLC   MB   NBB   NN   NjP

----   Gravure sur bois et taille d'épargne.   Historique et
technique.   Paris, 1933.   234p.   [98]
   NN

[Heineken, Karl Heinrich von] 1706-1791.
Idée générale d'une collection complette d'estampes. Avec
une dissertation sur l'origine de la gravure & sur les premiers
livres d'images.   Leipsic et Vienne, J. P. Kraus, 1771.
8 prel. leaves, 520, [32]p.   28 (i.e. 33) plates (part fold.)
21 cm.
   Modeled on the collection in the "Kupferstichkabinett",
   Dresden.   [99]
   DLC   NN   WaU   Eu-Fr-PN   Eu-Ge-LB

Heller, Joseph, d. 1849.
Geschichte der Holzschneidekunst von den ältesten bis auf
die neuesten Zeiten, nebst zwei Beilagen, enthaltend den Ursprung

der Spielkarten und ein Verzeichniss der sämmtlichen xylographischen
Werke, von Joseph Heller. Mit sehr vielen Holzschnitten. Bamberg,
C. F. Kunz, 182?. xii, 457, [1]p., 1 leaf. illus., plates
(part fold.) 20.5 cm.
 Bibliography: p. 390-396.   [100]
 DLC ICJ Eu-Fr-PN Eu-Ge-LB

Hind, Arthur Mayger, 1880-
 An introduction to a history of woodcut, with a detailed survey
of work done in the fifteenth century, by Arthur M. Hind ... with
frontispiece and 483 illustrations in the text ... London, Constable
& co. ltd., 1935. 2 vols. front., illus. 26 cm.
 Paged continuously.
 Bibliographical references at the end of each chapter and in
the foot-notes.
 "Books illustrated with woodcuts", vol. 2, p. 783-814.   [101]
 DLC ICN NN

---- A short history of engraving and etching, for the use of
collectors and students, with full bibliography, classified list
and index of engravers. London, A. Constable, 1908. xviii,
473p. fig., plates. 24 cm.   [102]
 DLC ICJ ICN Eu-Fr-PN

---- History of engraving and etching from the fifteenth century
to 1914. London, 1923. 3d ed. xviii p., 1 leaf, 487p.   [103]
 ICN

Hutchinson, S. A.
 Before movable type. Brooklyn Museum Quarterly, vol. 14, 1927,
p. 127-135.   [104]

[Jansen, Hendrik] 1741-1812.
 Essai sur l'origine de la gravure en bois et en taille-douce,
et sur la connoissance des estampes des XVe. et XVIe. siècles;
où il est parlé aussi de l'origine des cartes à jouer et des
cartes géographiques; suivi de recherches sur l'origine du papier
de coton et de lin; sur la calligraphie, depuis les plus anciens
temps jusqu'à nos jours; sur les miniatures des anciens manuscrits;
sur les filigranes des papiers des XIVe., XVe. et XVIe siècles;
ainsi que sur l'origine et le premier usage des signatures et des
chiffres dans l'art de la typographie ... Avec XX planches. Paris,
F. Schoell, 1808. 2 vols. 19 (i.e. 20) plates (part fold., 1 col.)
21x13.5 cm.
 Dedication signed Jansen.
 Table des auteurs cités dans cet ouvrage: vol. 2, p. [319]-346.[105]
 DLC IaU NN.NjN Eu-Fr-PN Eu-Ge-LB

Kindlinger, Nikolaus, 1749-1819.
 Nachricht von einigen noch unbekannten Holzschnitten, Kupfer-
stichen und Steinabdrücken aus dem fünfzehnten Jahrhundert.

Von Niklas Kindlinger.   Frankfurt am Main, Hermann, 1819.
vi, 56p.   20.5 cm.   [106]
    DLC   Eu-Ge-LB

Koning, Jacobus, 1770-1832.
    Impressions and facsimiles of woodcuts and type of the fif-
teenth century: with a few modern woodcuts illustrative of the
same period. Collected and described by J. Koning.   n.d.
Folio.
    MS descriptions.   [107]
    Eu-Ge-LP

Kristeller, Paul, 1863-1931.
    Kupferstich und Holzschnitt in vier Jahrhunderten, von Paul
Kristeller; mit 259 Abbildungen.   Berlin, B. Cassirer, 1905.
x, 595, [1]p.   illus.   26 cm.
    "Verzeichnis einer Reihe der wichtigsten Schriften über den
    Bilddruck": p. [567]-574.   [108]
    DLC   ICJ   MB   NBB   NN   Eu-Fr-PN
    3d ed. 1921: CSmH   ICU   MH
    4th ed. 1922: CtY   MH   NN

Laborde, Léon Emmanuel Simon Joseph, marquis de, 1807-1869.
    De l'imprimerie dans l'antiquité; des différents genres
d'impressions connus des anciens.   Revue Archéologique, 1st ser.,
vol. 5, 1848, p. 120-125.   [109]

Langer, Bruno.
    Die Druckkunst vor Gutenberg und neue Erfindungen.   Zeit-
schrift für Deutschlands Buchdrucker, vol. 40, no. 1, 1928,
no. 1, 1928, p. 1-2   [110]

Lempertz, Heinrich, 1816-1898.
    Beiträge zur ältern Geschichte der Buchdruck- und Holzschneide-
kunst, von Heinrich Lempertz. 1. Heft. Mit Abbildungen. 2. verm.
Aufl.   Köln, J. E. Renard, 1839.   1 prel. leaf, [25]p.   illus.,
facsims. (part col., part mounted)   25.5x21 cm.
    Title from cover.
    No more published.
    The 1st edition (1838) was published under cover-title: Biblio-
    graphische und xylographische Versuche von H. Lempertz.   [111]
    DLC   Eu-Fr-PN

Lippmann, Friedrich.
    Ueber die Anfänge der Formschneidekunst und des Bilddruckes.
Repertorium für Kunstwissenschaft, (Stuttgart), vol. 1, 1876,
p. 215-248.   [112]

Massmann, Hans Ferdinand, 1797-1874.
    Die Xylographa der Königlichen Hof- und Staatsbibliothek sowie

der Königlichen Universitätsbibliothek in München. Aus dem
"Serapeum" besonders abgedruckt. Leipzig, 1841. 40p. facsims.
8vo.   [113]
    Eu-De-LBb   Eu-Fr-PN   Eu-Ge-LB   Eu-Ne-AVb

McMurtrie, Douglas Crawford, 1888-
    Paving the way for the invention of printing, by Douglas C.
McMurtrie. San Francisco, 1937. [7]p. 23 cm.
    "Reprinted from the Share your knowledge review for February,
1937."   [114]
    DLC   MB   NN   Eu-Ne-AVb

Monnoyer, Charles.
    Recherches sur les origines de l'imprimerie avant Gutenberg.
Conférence Guéranger, séance du 16 novembre 1888. Le Mans,
1888. 16p. 8vo.   [115]
    Eu-Fr-PN   Eu-Ge-LB   Eu-Ge-LSb

Ottley, William Young, 1771-1836.
    An inquiry into the origin and early history of engraving,
upon copper and in wood, with an account of engravers and their
works, from the invention of chalcography by Maso Finiguerra, to
the time of Marc' Antonio Raimondi. By William Young Ottley,
F. S. A. London, Printed for J. and A. Arch by J. M'Creery, 1816.
2 vols. illus., plates (part fold) 29 cm.
    Paged continuously.   [116]
    CSmH   DLC   ICJ   ICN   MdBP   NN   PBL

P-t, H.
    Aus der Geschichte der Holzschneidekunst. <u>Graphische Technik</u>,
vol. 5, 1937, p. 36-39.   [117]

Papillon, Jean Michel, 1698-1776.
    Histoire de la gravure en bois et des graveurs fameux, tant
anciens que modernes, qui l'ont pratiqué. [Paris, 1736].
400p. 12mo..   [118]
    Eu-Fr-PN

---- Traité historique et pratique de la gravure en bois, par
J. M. Papillon ... Ouvrage enrichi des plus jolis morceaux de sa
composition & de sa gravure ... Paris, P. G. Simon, imprimeur,
1766. 2 vols. front. (port.) illus., plates (part col.)
diagrs. 21 cm.   [119]
    DLC   MBMu   MH   NBB   NN   NjN   Eu-De-LBb   Eu-Fr-PN
    Eu-Ge-LB

Pfister, Kurt, 1895-
    Die primitiven Holzschnitte. München, Holbein-Verlag, 1922.
29p., 1 leaf. 44 plates (part col.) 25 cm.

"Von diesem Buch wurden 100 Exemplare in Leder gebunden eun
vom Verfasser handscriftlich gezeichnet."   [120]
    CtY   MH   MiU   Eu-Ne-AVb

Pilinski, Adam, ed.
    Monuments de la xylographie.   [15th cent.]   Reproduits en
facsimilé.   Précédés d'une notice par Gustave Pawlowski.   Paris,
A. Pilinski et fils, 1882-1886.   8 vols.   33.5 cm.   [121]
    CSmH   ICN   MH   Eu-De-LBb

Pitman, Vincent.
    Early printers and late inventions.   British and Colonial
Printer and Stationer, vol. 101, no. 21, Nov. 1927, p. 325-327.   [122]

    Printing before printing presses.   American Bookmaker, vol.
6, no. 3, Mar. 1888, p. 53.   [123]

Reiffenberg, Frédéric Auguste Ferdinand Thomas, baron de, 1794-1850.
    La plus ancienne gravure connue avec une date.   Avec une fac-
simile.   Bruxelles, 1845.   4to.
    "Extrait du tome XIX des Mémoires de l'Académie royale des
    sciences de Bruxelles."   [124]
    Eu-De-LBb   Eu-Ge-LB

Renouvier, Jules, 1804-1860.
    Histoire de l'origine et des progrès de la gravure dans les
Pays-Bas et en Allemagne jusqu'à la fin du quinzième siècle;
par Jules Renouvier ...   Bruxelles, M. Hayez, 1860.   2 prel.
leaves, ii, 317p., 1 leaf.   22.5 cm.
    "Mémoire couronné par l'Académie royale de Belgique, le
    23 septembre 1859."
    "Extrait du t. X des Mémoires couronnés et autres mémoires,
    publiés par l'Académie royale de Belgique."   [125]
    DLC   MB   NN   Eu-Fr-PN

Requeno [y Vives], Vincenzo, 1743-1811.
    Osservazioni sulla chirotipografia, ossia antica arte di
stampare a mano; opera di D. Vincenzo Requeno ... Roma, M. de
Romanis e figli, 1810.   1 prel. leaf, 106p.   19 cm.   [126]
    DLC   NjP   Eu-De-LBb   Eu-Fr-PN   Eu-Ge-LB

Schmidt, M.
    Die frühesten und seltensten Denkmale des Holz- und Metall-
schnittes aus dem 14. und 15. Jahrhundert nach den Originalen
im K. Kupferstich-Cabinet und in der K. Hof- und Staats-Biblio-
thek in München durch Lichtdruck als Facsimiles reproducirt.
Mit erläuterndem Text herausgegeben von M. Schmidt.   Nürnberg,
[1883-1884]   3 vols.   Folio.   [127]
    Eu-De-LBb

Schreiber, Wilhelm Ludwig, 1855-1932.
   Darf der Holzschnitt als Vorläufer der Buchdruckerkunst betrachtet
werden ... Leipzig, O. Harrassowitz, 1895.   1 prel. leaf, 66p.   24 cm.
   Reprint from Zentralblatt für Bibliothekswesen, vol. 12, 1895,
   p. 201-266.   [128]
   DLC   NN   Eu-De-BP   Eu-Ge-LB

----   Handbuch des Holz- und Metallschnittes des XV. Jahrhunderts ...
Leipzig, 1926-1930.   8 vols.
   A second edition, but in German, of the first three volumes and a
   translation of the other volumes of his Manuel de l'amateur.   [129]
   ICN

----   Holschnitt und Inkunabelforschung.   Zentralblatt für Bibliothekswesen, vol. 23, 1906, p. 237-242.   [130]

----   Manuel de l'amateur de la gravure sur bois et sur métal au
XVe siècle, par W. L. Schreiber ... Berlin, A. Cohn; [etc., etc.]
1891-1911.   8 vols. in 9.   illus., CXXI plates (part col.) on
104 leaves.   25 cm.   (vol. 6-8: 42.5 cm.)
   Vols. 4-5: Leipzig, O. Harrassowitz.
   Vols. 1-4, 6-8 "tiré à 300 exemplaires"; vol. 5 "tiré à 400
   exemplaires".
   Bibliography: vol. 1, p. xiii-xvi; vol. 2, p. ix-xiv;
   vol. 3, p. x-xvi; vol. 4, p. xi-xiv; vol. 5^a, p. xxi-xxiv.   [131]
   DLC   MiU   Eu-De-LBb

----   M. Bouchots Ansichten über die Erstlinge der Holzschneidekunst.   Zeitschrift für Christliche Kunst,   vol. 21, no. 2-4,
1908.   [132]

----   Vorstufen der Typographie.   (In Festschrift zum fünfhundertjährigen Geburtstage von Johann Gutenberg, herausgegeben von Otto
Hartwig.   Leipzig, O. Harrassowitz, 1900.   p. 30-72; Mainz ed.,
p. 25-58)   [133]
   CSmH   DLC   ICJ   MH   NjP   Eu-De-BP   Eu-Ne-AVb   Eu-Ne-GK

Schretlen, Martinus Joseph Antonius Maria, 1890-
   Dutch and Flemish woodcuts of the 15th century, with a foreword
by M. K. Friedlaender.   London, E. Benn, ltd., 1925.   viii p.,
1 leaf, 71p., 2 leaves.   plates (facsims.)   32.5 cm.   [134]
   CSmH   DLC   MB   NBB   NN   Eu-Ne-AVb

Servolini, L.
   La techica xilografia antica.   Rassegna Grafica, vol. 5, no. 50,
1930.
   Title from Bibliographie des Bibliotheks und Buchwesens.   [135]

[Sotzmann, Johann Daniel Ferdinand]
... Älteste Geschichte der Xylographie und der Druckkunst überhaupt,
besonders in der Anwendung auf den Bilddruck.   Ein Beitrag zur

Erfindungs- und Kunstgeschichte.   [Leipzig, F. A. Brockhaus, 1837]
[447]-[600]p.   18.5 cm.
     Reprint from Historisches Taschenbuch, vol. 8, 1837.   [136]
     MH   NN   NNC   Eu-De-LBb   Eu-Ge-LSb

----   Die xylographischen Bücher eines in Breslau befindlich
gewesenen Bandes jetzt in dem Königl. Kupferstich-Kabinet in Berlin.
Aus dem "Serapeum" besonders abgedruckt.   Leipzig, 1842. 8vo.   [137]
     Eu-De-LBb   Eu-Ge-LB   Eu-Ne-AVb

Townsend, W. G. P.
     A short historical account of woodcuts and wood engraving.
Penrose's Annual, vol. 30, 1928, p. 81-92.   [138]

Venturi, Lionello.
     Sulle origini della xilografia.   Arte, vol. 6, 1903, p. 265-
270.   [139]

Vienna. Albertina.
     Einzel-Formschnitte des fünfzehnten Jahrhunderts aus der
Erzherzoglichen Kunstsammlung Albertina in Wien, herausgegeben
von Dr. Heinrich Röttinger ... Mit 30 Lichtdrucknachbildungen.
Strassburg, J. H. E. Heitz, 1911.   8, [2]p., 1 leaf., 30 mounted
plates (4 fold.)   36x28 cm. (Einblattdrucke des fünfzehnten
Jahrhunderts, hrsg. von Paul Heitz. [26])   [140]
     DLC

Weigel, Theodor Oswald, 1812-1881.
     Katalog frühester Erzeugnisse der Druckerkunst der T. O.
Weigel'schen Sammlung.   Auszug aus dem Werke: Die Anfänge der
Druckerkunst von T. O. Weigel und Dr. A. Zestermann.   Leipzig,
Weigel, 1872.   274p.   8vo.   [141]
     ICN   NN   NNC   Eu-De-LBb

----   Verzeichniss der xylographischen Bücher des XV. Jahrhunderts. Leipzig, 1856.   8vo.
     Reprint from Serapeum, vol. 18.   [142]
     Eu-De-LBb   Eu-Ge-LB   Eu-Ne-AVb

Willshire, William Hughes, fl. 1839-1879.
     A descriptive catalogue of early prints in the British museum:
German and Flemish schools.   London, Longmans & co. [etc.]
1879-1882.   2 vols.   fronts., plates.   26.5 cm.   [143]
     ICN   Eu-De-LBb   Eu-Ge-LB   Eu-Ge-LSb

     4.   Block Books

     The art of printing before presses.   American Art Printer,
vol. 2, no. 5, 1888, p. 8.   [144]

Berjeau, Jean Philibert, 1809-1891.
   Catalogue illustré des livres xylographiques.   Par. J. Ph.
Berjeau.   Londres, C. J. Stewart, 1865.   viii, 116p.   facsims.
23 cm.
   Only 105 copies printed.   [145]
   DLC   ICN   NN   RPJCB   Eu-De-LBb   Eu-Fr-PN   Eu-Ge-LB
   Eu-Ne-CK

---- Speculum humanae salvationis: le plus ancien monument de la
xylographie et de la typographie réunies.   Reproduit en fac-similé
avec introduction historique et bibliographique, par J. Ph. Berjeau.
Londres, C. J. Stewart, 1861.   lxxii, 33, [1]p., facsim.: 64 numb.
leaves.   31.5 cm.
   CtHT   DLC   MBSi   NN   NjP   Eu-Fr-PN   Eu-Ge-LB   Eu-Ne-AVb [146]
   Eu-Ne-GK

Bernard, Auguste Joseph, 1811-1868.
   Archéologie typographique ... Bruxelles, F. Heussner, 1853.
47p.   22 cm.
   "Extrait du tome 1., 2. série, du Bulletin du Bibliophile Belge.
   Tiré à 100 exemplaires."   [147]
   ICN   Eu-De-LBb   Eu-Ge-LB   Eu-Ge-LSb   Eu-Ne-AVb

Biblia pauperum.
   Biblia pauperum.   Reproduced in facsimile from one of the copies
in British museum; with an historical and bibliographical introduction by J. Ph. Berjeau.   London, J. R. Smith, 1859.   38p.
40 facsim.   39 cm.
   Bibliographers who described the block books and the Biblia
   pauperum, followed by a chronological list of books referring
   to the Biblia pauperum and block books in general: p. 17-21.   [148]
   DLC   MB   NN   Eu-Fr-PN   Eu-Ge-LB   Eu-Ne-GK

Björkbom, Carl, 1898-
   Blockböcker.   Svenska Boktryckareforeningens Meddelanden,
vol. 39, no. 10, 1934, p. 313-317.   [149]

Conway, William Martin, baron, 1856-
   Notes on some of the blockbooks of the Netherlands.   Bibliographer, vol. 3, 1883, p. 124-129, 160-164; vol. 4, 1884, p. 28-
34.   [150]

---- The woodcutters of the Netherlands in the fifteenth century.
In three parts: I. History of the woodcutters.   II. Catalogue of
the woodcuts.   III. List of the books containing woodcuts.   By
William Martin Conway.   Cambridge, University press, 1884.   xvii,
[2], 359, [1]p.   23 cm.   [151]
   CSmH   DLC   ICN   MB   MH   MdBP   NjP

Cust, Lionel Henry, 1859-1929.
The Master E. S. and the 'Ars moriendi'; a chapter in the history
of engraving during the XVth century, with facs. reproductions of
engravings in the university galleries at Oxford and the British
museum; by Lionel Cust ... Oxford, Clarendon press, 1898.   2 prel.
leaves, 61 p. incl. plates, facsims.   33 cm.   (Prints and drawings from Oxford collections, no. 1)
    Ars moriendi block-book reproduced from the copy in the British
    museum: p. 37-61.   [152]
    CSmH   DLC   ICJ   ICN   MB   Eu-De-LBb   Eu-Fr-PN
    Eu-Ge-LB   Eu-Ne-AVb

Geffcken, Johannes, 1803-1864.
Der Bildercatechismus des fünfzehnten Jahrhunderts und die
catechetischen Hauptstücke in dieser Zeit bis auf Luther, mitgetheilt und erläutert von Johannes Geffcken ... I. Die zehn Gebote,
mit 12 Bildtafeln nach Cod. Heidelb. 438 ... Leipzig, T. O. Weigel,
1855.   viii p., 1 leaf, 114p., 1 leaf, 218 col., [1]p.   12 plates.
27 cm.
    The text proper is followed by "Siebenundzwanzig Beilagen,"
    extracts from ms. and early printed editions of the catechism,
    218 columns, and by the 12 plates (facsim. of the "Decalogus")
    from the Palatine cod. 438.
    To this copy is added a facsimile (12 plates) of the 3d ed.
    Of the "Symbolum apostolicum" prepared for Geffcken about 1855,
    but not placed on the market until 1866. cf. Schreiber,
    Manuel, vol. 4, p. xv.   [153]
    DLC   MB   NjP   Eu-Fr-PN   Eu-Ge-LB

Groebe, Dirk.
Beschrijving van een nieuwlings ontdekt exemplaar van de Biblia
Pauperum en de Ars Moriendi, met eenige aanmerkingen, inzonderheid
betreffende het verhaal van Atkyns, wegens den oorsprong der boekdrukkunst in Engeland uit Haarlem, met het facsimile van een der
houtsneêprenten van de Biblia Pauperum.   Amsterdam, 1839.   8vo. [154]
    Eu-Ne-AVb   Eu-Ne-GK   Eu-Ne-GO

Guichard, Joseph Marie, 1810-1852.
Notice sur le Speculum humanae salvationis.   Paris, Techener,
1840.   131p.   23 cm.   [155]
    DLC   ICN   Eu-De-LBb   Eu-Fr-PN   Eu-Ge-LB   Eu-Ne-AVb

---- Recherches sur les livres xylographiques. Bulletin du
Bibliophile (Paris), 4th ser., no. 3-4, 1840-1841, p. 115-134;
no. 6, p. 187-202; no. 7, p. 247-251; no. 8, p. 297-306; no. 16-
17, p. 709-742.   [156]

Haebler, Konrad, 1857-
Xylographische Donate. Gutenberg Jahrbuch, vol. 3, 1928,
p. 15-31.   [157]

Haebler, Konrad, 1857-
  Zum studium der altniederländischen Donate. Zentralblatt
für Bibliothekswesen, vol. 35, 1918, p. 242-254.   [158]

Heidenheimer, Heinrich, 1856-
  Die Donat-Frage und Venedig. Bibliofilia, vol. 4, Oct.-Nov.
1902, p. 249-252.   [159]

Hochegger, Rudolf, 1862-1895.
  Ueber die Entstehung und Bedeutung der Blockbücher mit besonderer Rücksicht auf den Liber regum seu Historia Davidis; eine
bibliographisch-kunstgeschichtliche Studie zugleich ein Beitrag
zur Geschichte des Unterrichtswesens; von privatdocent Dr. Rudolf
Hochegger ... Leipzig, O. Harrassowitz, 1891. viii, 67, [1]p.
front. (facsim.) 23.5 cm.   (On cover: Beihefte zum Centralblatt
für Bibliothekswesen. VII)   [160]
    Nos. V-VIII form Vol. 2 of the series.
    DLC ICJ MB MH Eu-De-LBb Eu-Fr-PN Eu-Ge-LB
    Eu-Ne-AVb

Holtrop, Jan. Willem, 1806-1870.
  Description des éditions connues du Donatus d'origine holland-
aise. Algemeene Konst- en Letterbode, 1840, p. 51.   [161]

----   Monuments typographiques des Pays-Bas au quinzième siècle;
collection de fac-simile d'après les originaux conservés à la
Bibliothèque royale de La Haye et ailleurs, pub. avec l'autorisation de son excellence le ministre de l'intérieur, par J.-W
Holtrop ... La Haye, M. Nijhoff, 1868. xiii, 126p., 1 leaf, [10]p.,
1 leaf. 133 plates on 131 leaves (incl. facsims.) map.
37.5x28.5 cm.   [162]
    CSmH DLC ICJ IaU MB MH NN NcU PBL RPJCB
    Eu-Fr-PN Eu-Ge-LB Eu-Ne-GK

[Masséna, Victor, prince d'Essling, duc de Rivoli] 1836-1910.
  Le premier livre xylographique italien imprimé à Venise vers
1450. Paris, Gazette des beaux-arts, 1903. 44p., 1 leaf.
illus., 15 plates. 28x22 cm.
    At head of title: Prince d'Essling.
    Caption title: Passio D. N. Iesu Christi; livre xylographique
    imprimé à Venise vers 1450.   [163]
    DLC ICJ MB Eu-Fr-PN Eu-Ge-LB Eu-Ge-LSb Eu-Ne-AVb

Massmann, Hans Ferdinand, 1797-1874.
  Literatur der Todtentänze. Beytrag zum Jubeljahre der Buch-
druckerkunst. Leipzig, T. O. Weigel, 1840. 135p. fold tab.
  "Aus dem Serapeum besonders abgedruckt."
    ICN Eu-De-LBb Eu-Fr-PN Eu-Ge-LB   [164]

Reuss, Eduard.
   Die deutsche Historienbibel vor der Erfindung des Bucherdrucks.
(In his Beiträge zu den theologischen Gesellschaft zu Strassburg.
Jena, 1855,   p. 3-136)   [165]
      Eu-De-LBb

Schreiber, Wilhelm Ludwig, 1855-
... Basels Bedeutung für die Geschichte der Blockbücher, von W. L.
Schreiber.   Mit 5 Abbildungen.   Strassburg, J. H. E. Heitz
(Heitz & Mündel) 1909.   ix, 49p., 1 leaf.   v plates (incl. fac-
sim.)   25 cm.   (Studien zur deutschen Kunstgeschichte.   106)   [166]
      DLC   ICJ   ICN   MH   NBB

----   Die Entstehung und Entwicklung der Biblia pauperum unter
besonderer Berücksichtigung der uns erhaltenen Handschriften von
W. L. Schreiber.   29 Textillustrationen und 1 Lichtdrucktafel.
(Sonderabdruck aus: P. Heitz und W. L. Schreiber, Biblia pauperum.
Nach dem einzigen Exemplar in 50 Darstellungen.)   Strassburg,
J. H. E. Heitz (Heitz & Mündel) [1903]   1 prel. leaf, 45p.   fac-
sims.   33 cm.   [167]
      DLC   ICJ   Eu-De-LBb   Eu-Ne-AVo

----   Der Totentanz; Blockbuch von etwa 1465.   27 Darstellungen
in photolithographischer Nachbildung nach dem einzigen Exemplar
im Codex palat. germ. 438 der Heidelberger Universitäts-Biblio-
thek.   Mit einer Einleitung von W. L. Schreiber.   Leipzig, K. W.
Hiersemann, 1900.   4 prel. leaves, facsim. (27 leaves. illus.)
30.5 cm.
      Half-title: Die Blockbücher des Codex palat. germ. 438 der
      Heidelberger Universitätsbibliothek.   Zum ersten Male voll-
      ständig in getreuer Nachbildung herausgegeben.
      "Nur in 100 exemplaren hergestellt."   [168]
      DLC   ICJ   MH   Eu-Ne-GK

Sotheby, Samuel Leigh, 1805-1861.
   Memoranda relating to the block-books preserved in the Bibliothèque impériale, Paris, made October M.DCCC.LVIII., by Samuel
Leigh Sotheby ... London, Printed for the author by T. Richards,
1859.   23p.   illus.   36 cm.
      The illustrations are facsimiles of water-marks.   [169]
      DLC   MB   NN   OCl   Eu-Ge-LB

----   Principia typographica.   The block-books, or xylographic
delineations of scripture history; issued in Holland, Flanders
and Germany, during the fifteenth century, exemplified and considered in connexion with the origin of printing.   To which is
added an attempt to elucidate the character of the paper-marks of
the period.   A work contemplated by the late Samuel Sotheby, and

                              - 23 -

carried out by his son, Samuel Leigh Sotheby ... London, Printed
for the author by W. McDowall, 1858.   3 vols.   facsims.   (part
col.)   37 cm.
    Of the 250 copies printed, 220 were sold at auction May 5,
    1858.   [170]
    DLC   ICJ   MB   MH   MWA   MdBP   MiU-C   NN   NjP   Eu-De-LBb
    Eu-Ge-LB   Eu-Ge-LSb   Eu-Ne-AVb   Eu-Ne-GK

Sotheby, Samuel Leigh, 1805-1861.
    Specimen of Mr. S. Leigh Sotheby's Principia typographica, an
extensively illustrated work, in three volumes, imperial quarto,
on the block-books, or xylographic delineations of Scripture history issued in Holland, Flanders, and Germany, during the fifteenth
century; on their connexion with the origin of printing, and on the
character of the water-marks in the paper of the period.   London,
1858.   4 prel. leaves, xvi, [25]p.   8 plates (1 double) incl.
facsims.   35 cm.
    New t.-p., notice and list of purchasers ([4]p.) distributed
    June 1, 1858.   Original t.-p. reads: Specimen-notice for the
    disposal of Mr. S. Leigh Sotheby's Principia typographica [etc.]
    Contains the introduction, list of plates, indexes and some
    extra plates from the Principia.   [171]
    DLC   MBrZ   NN

Speculum humanae salvationis.
    Speculum humanae salvationis, ein niederländisches Blockbuch,
herausgegeben von Ernst Kloss.   München, R. Piper & Co., 1925.
43, [1]p., 1 leaf.   2 plates and facsim: 63p.   woodcuts.   27 cm.
    Reproduction of the first edition with Latin text (Xyl. 37,
    Staatsbibliothek, München) without name of printer, place or
    date.   Ascribed by the editor to a press in the region of
    Utrecht, ca. 1475-79.
    "Die Faksimile-Ausgabe des Blockbuches Speculum humanae salva-
    tionis ... wurde ... in München im Jahr 1925 von der Kunstanstalt
    Ganymed in Berlin in einer einmaligen numerierten Auflage von
    550 Exemplaren auf handgeschöpft Zanders-Bütten gedruckt ... "   [172]
    DLC   MiU   NN   Eu-De-BP

Stöger, Franz Xaver.
    Zwei der ältesten deutschen Druckdenkmäler beschrieben und in
neuem Abdruck mitgetheilt ... München, G. Jaquet, 1833.   [6],
84p.   4 facsims.   22 cm.
    Contents: Die sieben freuden Maria - Das leiden Christi.   [173]
    NNC   OCl   Eu-De-BP   Eu-De-LBb   Eu-Ge-LB

Zapf, Georg Wilhelm, 1747-1810.
    Von einer höchstseltenen und noch unbekannten Ausgabe der
Ars moriendi.   Augsburg, 1806.   8vo.   [174]
    Eu-De-LBb   Eu-Ge-LB   Eu-Ge-LSb

Zestermann, August Christian Adolf.
  Die Unabhängigkeit der deutschen xylographischen Biblia pau-
perum von der lateinischen xylographischen Biblia pauperum.
Nachgewiesen von Dr..August Christian Adolf Zestermann.   Leipzig,
T. O. Weigel, 1866.   cover-title, 23, [1]p.   facsim.   39.5 cm. [175]
    DLC   ICN   NN   Eu-De-LBb

    5   Binders Stamps

Falk, Franz, 1840-1909.
  Der Stempeldruck vor Gutenberg und die Stempeldrucke in
Deutschland.   (In Festschrift zum fünfhundertjährigen Geburts-
tage von Johann Gutenberg, herausgegeben von Otto Hartwig.
Leipzig, O. Harrassowitz, 1900.   p. 73-79)   [176]
    CSmH   DLC   ICJ   MH   NjP   Eu-De-BP   Eu-No-AVb   Eu-No-GK

Husung, Maximilian Joseph, 1882-
  Neues Material zur Frage des Stempeldrucks vor Gutenberg.
(In Gutenbergfestschrift, zur Feier des 25jaehrigen Bestehens des
Gutenbergmuseums in Mainz 1925.   Hrsg. von A. Ruppel.   Mainz,
Verlag der Gutenberg-Gesellschaft [1925] p. 66-72)   [177]
    DLC   ICN   MB   MH   NN   NNC   Eu-De-BP   Eu-Ge-LB
    Eu-Ne-AVb   Eu-Sz-BeG

Theele, Joseph, 1889-
  Einzeltypenstempel auf Kölner Einbänden.   Ein weiterer Beitrag
zum Stempeldruck vor Gutenberg.   Gutenberg Jahrbuch, vol. 1, 1926,
p. 9-13.   [178]

A   GENERAL WORKS

1   16th Century

Estienne, Henri.
   Artis typographicae querimonia, de illiteratis quibusdam typographis,
propter quos in contemptum venit. Autore Henrico Stephano. Epitaphia
graeca & latina doctorum quorundam typographorum, ab eodem scripta.
[Paris?] H. Stephanus, 1569. 4 prel. leaves, [33]p. 23.5 cm.
   Reissued in Wolf, J. C. Monumenta typographica. Hamburg, 1740.
   vol. 1, p. 41-71.   [179]
   DLC   ICN   Eu-Fr-PN   Eu-Ge-LB

Menapius, Gulielmus Insulanus.
   Statera chalcographiae, qua bona ipsius & mala simul appenduntur
& numerantur. Basil, 1547. 8vo. (In Wolf, J. C. Monumenta
typographica. Hamburg, 1740. vol. 1, p. 1046-1104)   [180]

Richter, Matthias, 1528-1564.
   De typographiae inventione, et de praelorum legitima inspectione,
libellus brevis et utilis, per Matthaeum Iudicem. Coppenhagii,
excudebat Iohannes Zimmerman, Anno 1566.   86p.   8vo.
   Reissued in Wolf, J. C. Monumenta typographica. Hamburg,
   1740.   vol. 1, p. 72-170.   [181]
   Eu-Da-KKb   Eu-Fr-PN   Eu-Ge-LB

Rocca, Angelo, 1545-1620.
   De typographiae artis inventione et praestantia. (In De Bib-
liotheca Vaticana. Romae, 1591)
   Title from Bigmore & Wyman.   [182]

Schroedter, Ernst Christian.
   De typographia, disputabunt publice praeses M. Ernestus Christianus Schroedterius, Wittenberga-Saxo, & respondens Jac. Frideri-
cus Kunad, Dalehn, Misn. die I Septembris, Anno O. R. M DC XCVII
[1597] in Auditorio Minori. Wittenbergae, per Christianum Schroed-
terum, Acad. Typ. (In Wolf, J. C. Monumenta typographica.
Hamburg, 1740.   vol. 2, p. 614-632)   [183]

2   17th Century

Atkyns, Richard, 1615-1677.
   The original and growth of printing: collected out of history,
and the records of this kingdome. Wherein is also demonstrated,
that printing appertaineth to the prerogative royal; and is a
flower of the crown of England. By Richard Atkyns, esq; White-Hall,
April the 25th 1664. By order and appointment of the right Honourable, Mr. Secretary Morice, let this be printed. Tho: Rych aut.

London: Printed by John Streater, for the author, 1664. 5 prel.
leaves, 24p. front. 22x17 cm.
   Dedication and Epistle to the Parliament signed: Richard Atkins.
   First published anonymously as a broadside, without date.
   British museum gives date, 1660?
   Marginal notes partly in ms.   [184]
   DLC   ICJ   MB   NN   PBL   Eu-Ge-LB   Eu-Ge-LSb

Authaeus, Philipp Ludwig.
   Warhafftige historia von Erfindung der Buchdruckerey-Kunst,
ex manuscriptis Philippi Ludovici Authaei. Typis Blasii Ilsneri,
MDCLXXXI [1681]
   Title from van der Linde, Geschichte der Erfindung ...   [185]

---- ----   Reissued in Lersner, Achilles Augustus. Der ...
Stadt Francfurt am Mayn Chronica ... 1706.   [186]
   NN   Eu-Ge-LB

Beichlingen, Zacharias von.
   Fons bibliothecarum inaestimabilis: das ist: Wahrer Unter-
richt vom Uhrsprung, Fortgang, Lobe, Nothwendigkeit, Nutzen,
Freyheit, Rechten und Gerechtigkeit der Buchdruckereyen oder
derselben Officianten und Verwandten ... Eisleben, Andreas Koch,
1669. 24 leaves. 18.5 cm.   [187]
   NIC   NN   Eu-Ge-LB

Besold, Christoph, 1577-1638.
   Pentas dissertationum philologicarum ... [3] De inventione typo-
graphiae. Tubingae, 1620. 1 prel. leaf, 28p., 1 leaf. 18.5 cm.
   Reissued in Wolf, J. C. Monumenta typographica. Hamburg,
1740.   vol. 1.   [188]
   NN   Eu-Ge-LB   Eu-Ge-LSb

Bockenhoffer, Johann Philipp.
   Exempla literarium typographicorum, quae reperiuntur in Regiae
majestatis & Academiae Hafniensis typographia, primo erecta a Petro
Jani Morsingio, deinde aucta a Henrico et Georgio Gödianis, Corni-
ficio Luft, tandem renovata a Johanne Philip. Bockenhoffer, Regiae
majestatis & Academiae Hafniensis. Typographis. Hafniae. Anno
M.DC.XCI [1691]. 28p.   20x31 cm.
   The section on the invention of printing reissued in Wolf, J. C.
   Monumenta typographica. Hamburg 1740. vol. 2, p. 965-978.
   Title-page reproduced by Douglas C. McMurtrie in his Early type-
   founders of Denmark, in Gutenbergfestschrift, Mainz [1925]
   p. 376-384, 1 fold. plate.   [189]
   Eu-Da-KKb

Boeclerus, Joannes Henricus.
   Oratio habita kalend. Octobr. Anno MDCXL. Cum publice magistros
& baccalaureos crearet; in qua de typographiae, Argentorati inventae,
divinitate & fatis, saeculari pietate disseritur. Argentorati, 1654.
(In Wolf, J. C. Monumenta typographica. Hamburg, 1740. vol. 2,
p. 166-188)   [190]

Boxhorn, Marcus Zuerius, 1612-1653.
... De typographicae artis inventione, & inventoribus, dissertatio. Lug-
duni Batavorum, ex officina Hieronymi de Vogel, 1640. 51, [1]p. 19x15 cm.
  Reissued in Wolf, J. C. Monumenta typographica. Hamburg, 1740.
  vol. 1, p. 813-865.   [191]
  DLC   Eu-Ge-LB   Eu-Ge-LSb

----   Ex Marci Zuerii Boxhornii Historia universali sacra & profane,
paginae 946-952. Lugd. Bat., 1652. 4to. (In Wolf, J. C. Monumenta typographica. Hamburg, 1740. vol. 1, p. 866-868)   [192]

----   Ex Marci Zuerii Boxhornii Theatro sive Hollandiae comitatus
& urbium nova descriptione, pag. 134 et sqq. Amstelodia, 1632.
4to. (In Wolf, J. C. Monumenta typographica. Hamburg, 1740.
vol. 1, p. 537-546)   [193]

Cabrera Nuñez de Guzman, Melchor de, 17th cent.
... Discurso legal, historico, y politico, en prueba del origen, pro-
gresses, utilidad, nobleza, y excelencias del arte de la imprenta; y
de que se le deben (y à sus artifices) todas las honras, exempciones,
inmunidades, franquezas, y privilegios de arte liberal, por ser,
como, es arte de las artes. Don Melchor de Cabrera Nuñez de Guzman,
Abogado en los Reales Consejos. En Madrid, en la Oficina de Lucas
Antonio de Bedmar. Año M.DC.LXXV [1675] 2 prel. leaves, 39 numb.
leaves. 29 cm.
  At head of title: Titular, y protector del noble arte de la
  imprinta.   [194]
  ICN   NNH

Catherinot, Nicolas.
  L'art d'imprimer. Par le sieur Catherinot. [At end, p. 12:
A Bourges ce 10. Mars 1685] 12p. 23 cm.
  Reissued in Latin in Wolf, J. C. Monumenta typographica.
  Hamburg, 1740. vol. 2, p. 935-964.
  A facsimile of this pamphlet, reproduced from one of the only
  known copies in the Bibliothèque nationale, Paris, is being
  currently issued by Douglas C. McMurtrie.   [195]
  Eu-Fr-PN

  Der Druckerei zu Chemnitz, erste Blätter von der löblichen und un-
schätzbaren Buchdruckerkunst Erfindung, Nutz und Beforderung.
Chemnitz, 1661. 4to.
  Title from Schult, O. A. Gutenberg, oder Geschichte der
  Buchdruck ... 1840.   [196]

  An essay on writing, and the art and mystery of printing. A
translation out of the anthology ... [From a broadside, printed at
London, in the year 1696] (In The Harleian Miscellany. London,
1808-1813. 30.5 cm. vol. 1, 1808, p. 526-528)
  Verso.   [197]
  ICU   OClW

Fritsch, Ahasverus.
Dissertatio de abusibus typographiae tollendis. Arnstad,
1662, & cum Diss. de Zygenorum origine, vita et moribus. Jena,
1664. (In Wolf, J. C. Monumenta typographica. Hamburg,
1740. vol. 2, p. 428-455) [198]

---- Dissertatio de typographis caput primum de arte typographica in genere. Summaria. De artis typographicae origine
remissive, No. 1. Commendatur ars typographica, No. 2, 3,
et 4. Abusus artis hujus maximus, No. 5 et sqq. (In Wolf,
J. C. Monumenta typographica. Hamburg, 1740. vol. 2, p.
503-549) [199]

Holsten, Andreas.
D. D. Dissertatio academica de renascentis litteraturae
ministra typographia quam ex consensu ampliss. facult. philosoph.
in Regia ad Salam Academ. praeside Laurentio Norrmanno Graec.
litt. prof. ord. publicae bonorum ventilationi modeste sub-
mittit Andreas Holstenius, E. F. vestm. in auditorio Gustaviano
Majori ad diem Junii anno M DC LXXXIX. Holmiae, excudebat
J. G. Eberdt. [10], 43p. 9x15.5 cm.
Reissued in Wolf, J. C. Monumenta typographica. Hamburg,
1740. vol. 2, p. 550-594. [200]
Eu-Sv-UU

Hugo, Hermann, 1588-1629.
De prima scribendi origine et universa rei literariae anti-
quitate cui notas ... scribebat Hermannus Hugo ... Antverpiae,
apud B. & I. Moretus, 1617. 227, [3]p. 17.5 cm. [201]
ICU NN NjP ScU Eu-Fr-PN Eu-Ge-LB

Kramer, D. Daniel.
Grundlicher Bericht, wo, wenn und wer die Buchdruckker-
kunst erfunden? ... Leipzig, 1634. 8vo.
Title from Seitz, J. C. Het derde jubeljaar ... Haerlem, 1740. [202]

La Caille, Jean de, d. 1720.
Histoire de l'imprimerie et de la librairie, où l'on voit son
origine & son progrés, jusqu'en 1689. Divise'e en deux livres. Paris,
Chez J. de la Caille, 1689. 2 prel. leaves, 322, [26]p. 26 cm. [203]
DLC ICN NjP RP Eu-Fr-PN Eu-Ge-LB Eu-Ne-GK

La Salle, de, sieur de Lestang.
Tradition sur l'invention de l'imprimerie. Extraordinaire du
Mercure Galant (Paris), vol. 8, Oct. 1679. [204]

Le Callois, Pierre.
Traitté des plus belles bibliotheques de l'Europe. Des premiers
livres qui ont été faits. De l'invention de l'imprimerie. Des imprimeurs. De plusieurs livres qui ont été perdus & recouvrez par
les soins des sçavans. Avec une methode pour dresser une bibliotheque. Par le Sieur Le Callois. Paris, E. Michallet, 1680.

6 prel. leaves, 210, [3]p.   16 cm.
    Paged irregularly.
    DLC   NN   NjN   Eu-Fr-PN   Eu-Ge-LB

Le Gallois, Pierre.
    ----   [2d ed.]   Paris, E. Michallet, 1685.   6 prel. leaves,
240p.   14 cm.   [206]
    DLC   ICJ   MB   MH   NN   NjN   Eu-Ge-LB

Le Gesne.
    De l'origine de l'imprimerie. Mercure Galant (Paris), vol. 8,
1679, p. 216-228.   [207]

    Loca selecta scriptorum variorum de arte typographica. Ex Achilles
Pirminii Gassari Annalibus Augstburgensibus in I. B. Menckeniis Scrip-
tioribus Rerum. Germ. Tom. I, p. 1660. (In Wolf, J. C. Monumenta
typographica. Hamburg, 1740. vol. 2, p. 1016-1232)   [208]

Maier, Michael, 1568-1622.
    Verum inventum, hoc est, Munera Germaniae, ab ipsa primitus reperta
... et reliquo orbi communicata, etc. Francofurti ad Moenum, 1619. 8vo.
    De typographica: chapter 5.   [209]
    MH   Eu-Ge-LB

---- ----   [German translation] Franckfurt am Main, 1619.   [210]
    Eu-Ge-LB

Mallinckrodt, Bernard von, 1591-1664.
    De ortu ac progressu artis typographicae. Dissertatio historica,
in qua praeter alia pleraque ad calcographices negocium spectantia
de auctoribus et loco inventionis praecipuè inquiritur, proque
Moguntinis contra Harlemenses concluditur: a Bernardo a Mallinkrot ...
Coloniae Agrippinae, apud I. Kinchium, 1640. 11 prel. leaves, 125,
[2]p., 4 leaves. 20.5 cm.
    Added t.-p., engr., dated 1639.
    Enumerates 110 "auctores, qui pro Moguntinis testantur"; 13
    "auctores qui pro Harlemensibus testantur"; 11 "dubii et ambigui
    qui Harlemensium meminerunt."
    Reissued in Wolf, J. C. Monumenta typographica, Hamburg, 1740.
    vol. 1, p. 547-812.   [211]
    DLC   ICJ   MB   NN   Eu-Fr-PN   Eu-Ge-LB   Eu-Ge-LP   Eu-Ne-GK

Moller, Daniel Wilhelm.
    Dissertatio de typographia. Altdorfii, 1692. 4to.
    Title from Horne, T. H. An introduction to the study of typo-
    graphy. 1814.
    Reissued in Wolf, J. C. Monumenta typographica. Hamburg,
    1740. vol. 2, p. 607-614.   [212]

----   Dissertatio de typographia, cura Friderici Roth-Scholtzii.
Norimbergae, 1727. 4to.

Title from Typothetae of the city of New York. Catalogue
of books in the library ... 1896.   [213]

Natolinus, Joannis Baptistus.
   Joannis Baptistae Natolini, typographi nobilissimae civitatis
Utinensis, dissertatio de arte imprimendi, italice edita, Urini,
anno aerae christianae CIƆIƆCVI, [1606]. Folio. (In Wolf,
J. C. Monumenta typographica. Hamburg, 1740. vol. 2,
p. 910-934)   [214]

Naudé, Gabriel, 1600-1653.
   Addition a l'histoire de Louys XI. Contenant plusieurs recherches curieuses sur diverses matieres. Par Gabr. Naudé.
A Paris, chez Francois Targa, au premier pilier de la grand'
Salle du Palais, devant les Consultations, au Soliel d'or.
M.DC.XXX. Avec privilege du Roy. [24], 378, [14]p. 16.5 cm.
   p. 224: Chapitre VII. Que l'impression a esté premierement
   receuë, & establis en France pendant son Regne: avec une curieuse
   digression sur l'invention d'icelle.
   Chapter 7 reissued in Latin in Wolf, J. C. Monumenta typographica. Hamburg, 1740. vol. 1, p. 486-536.
   DLC   MH   NjN   NjP   Eu-Fr-PN   [215]

Panciroli, Guido, 1523-1599.
   Res memorabilis. 1631. (Salmuth, Heinrich. De typographiae
artis impressoriae inventione, verissima historia. vol. 2, p. 311)[216]
   NNC

Rivinus, Andreas, 1600-1656.
   Controversiae de artis typographicae inventione, ab Andr. Rivino,
al. Bachman, sedatae. Germanica latine reddidit Juvenis ornatissi-
mus, Ludovicus Klefekerus. (In Wolf, J. C. Monumenta typographica.
Hamburg, 1740. vol. 1, p. 1031-1039)   [217]

Saubert, Johann.
   Historia bibliothecae reip. Noribergensis, quabus oratiunculis
illustrata; quarum altera de ejus structoribus et curatoribus,
altera de rarioribus quibusdam et scitu dignis agit, authore J.
Sauberto, ecclesiae Noribergensis ad div. Sebaldi pastore, etc.
Accessit ejusdam cura et studio appendix de inventore typographiae
itemque catalogus librorum proximis ab inventione annis usque ad
A. C. 1500 editorum. Noribergae, typis Wolfgangi Enderi, 1643.
xii, 214p. 16mo.
   Typographical appendix: p. 106. "Claims invention of printing
   for Fust, assisted by Gutenberg." (Note in Bigmore & Wyman)   [218]
   Eu-De-LBb   Eu-Ge-LB

Smith, R.
Of the first invention of the art of printing. [Manuscript]
ca. 1670. 4to. [219]
Eu-Ge-LSb

Starck, Sebastian Gottfried.
Brevia historica oratio de arte typographica nobilissima, clarissima, utilissimaque, habita à M. Sebast. Gottfr. Starckio, mittweidensi misnico, SS. Theol. Baccalaureo & Scholae Nicol. Lips. Conrectore. E germanica lingua in latinum translata à Juvene ornatissimo Ludovico Klefekero, Gymnasii Hamburgi cive dignissimo. Lipsia, 1640. 4to. (In Wolf, J. C. Monumenta typographica. Hamburg, 1740. vol. 1, p. 1014-1030) [220]

Starcke, Peter.
Jesu succurente & incluto philosophorum ordine, in illustri tilieto, benevole concedente, de ortu typographiae, sub praesidio clarissimi & perexemii, Dr. M. Johannis Stohrii, ablassensis misnici, SS. Theol. cultoris, & alumn. elector. Fautoris sui ac suorum studiorum promotoris observandi plurimum, solenniter disputabit Petrus Starcke, Taubenheim. Misn. phil. bac. & al. El. ad IX Kal. Nov. Anno a partu Virginis MDCLXVI [1666] H. L. Q. C. (In Wolf, J. C. Monumenta typographica. Hamburg, 1740. vol. 2, p. 456-494) [221]

Tentzel, Wilhelm Ernst.
Discours von Erfindung der löblichen Buch-Drucker-Kunst in Teutschland bey Gelegenheit ihres anscheinenden fünfften Jubel-Jahrs, kurtz und grünlich entworfen. Gotha, 1700. 96p. 12mo.
Reissued in Latin in Wolf, J. C. Monumenta typographica. Hamburg, 1740. vol. 2, p. 644-700. [222]
Eu-De-LBb   Eu-Ge-LB   Eu-Ge-LSb

[Vester, Christian?]
Bono cum Deo omnium artium auctore! Nobilissimam artem typographicam, qua primam ejus originem, egregium adparatum variaque commoda, in usum lectorum arti typographicae faventium, Halae paucis descripsit quidam artis impressoriae cultor. Germanica latine reddidit Ludovicus Klefekerus, Halae Saxonum, typis Chr. Vesterus. (In Wolf, J. C. Monumenta typographica. Hamburg, 1740. vol. 2, p. 495-502) [223]

3   18th Century

[Baer, Friedrich Karl] 1719-1797.
Lettre sur l'origine de l'imprimerie, servant de réponse aux observations publiées par M. Fournier le jeune, sur l'ouvrage de

M. Schoepflin, intitulé Vindiciae typographicae. A Strasbourg,
M.DCC.LXI [1761] 44p.   18.5 cm.
   Reissued in Fournier, Pierre Simon. Traités historiques
et critiques sur l'origine et les progrès de l'imprimerie ...
Paris, J. Barbou [1758-1763?].   [224]
Eu-De-LBb

Bertrand-Quinquet, Mme. Suzanne (Girieux)
   Traité de l'imprimerie. Paris, An VII [1799].   viii, 288p.
10 plates. 4to.
   The work treats of: The origin of printing, types and their
use, impositions, orthography and punctuation, presswork,
management of a printing office, etc.
NNC   NjN   Eu-Fr-PN   Eu-Ge-LB   [225]

   Boktryckerikonstens första upfinnelse.   Nya Svenska Mercurius,
1761, p. 49-55.   [226]

Breitkopf, Johann Gottlob Immanuel, 1719-1794.
   Ueber die Geschichte der Erfindung der Buchdruckerkunst.   Bey
Gelegenheit einiger neuern darüber geäusserten besondern Meynungen.
Nebst der vorläufigen Anzeige des Inhaltes seiner Geschichte der
Erfindung der Buchdruckerkunst.   Von Johann Gottlob Imman. Breit-
kopf. Leipzig, J. G. I. Breitkopf, 1779. 1 prel. leaf, [3]-56p.
22 cm.
   The projected history, of which the author completed part one
in ms. and left material for part two, was never published.   [227]
DLC   NN   Eu-Fr-PC   Eu-Fr-PN   Eu-Ge-LB   Eu-Ge-LP
Eu-Ge-LSb   Eu-Ne-GK

Burges, Francis.
   Some observations on the use and original of the noble art and
mystery of printing. Norwich, 1701. 17p.   8vo. (In The
Harleian Miscellany.   London, 1808-1813.   30.5 cm.   vol. 3,
1809, p. 154-157)   [228]
ICU   OClW

Cogan, Thomas.
   The Rhine; or a journey from Utrecht to Francfort; chiefly by
the borders of the Rhine, and the passage down the river, from
Mentz to Bonn. Described in a series of letters, written from
Holland, to a friend in England, in the years 1791 and 1792.
2 vols. London, 1793. 8vo.
   p. 140-213, letters xxxix, xl, xli, xlii: The invention of
printing.   [229]
Eu-Ge-LB   (Also 1794 ed.)

Des Roches, Jean, 1740-1787.
   Neue Untersuchung über den Ursprung der Buchdruckerkunst;
worinnen gezeigt wird, dass man die ersten Vorbilder davon den

Brabantern zu danken habe.   (In Breitkopf, Johann Gottlob Immanuel. Ueber die Geschichte der Erfindung der Buchdruckerkunst. Leipzig, J. G. I. Breitkopf, 1779.   p. 13-31)   [230]
    DLC   NN   Eu-Fr-PC   Eu-Fr-PN   Eu-Ge-LB   Eu-Ge-LP   Eu-Ge-LSb
Eu-Ne-GK

---- Nieuw onderzoek naar den oorsprong der boekdrukkunst; waarin getoond word, dat men de eerste denkbeelden daar van aan de bra- banders verschuldigd is.   Hedendaagsche Vaderlandsche Letter- Oeffeningen Waar in de Boeken en Schriften ... Mengelwerk.   Zevende deels, tweede stuk ... Amsterdam, 1778.   no. 7, p. 298-308; no. 8, p. 352-374.   [231]

---- Nouvelles recherches sur l'origine de l'imprimerie dans lesquelles on fait voir que la première idée en est due aux Bra- bançons ... lu à la séance du 8 janvier 1777.   Académie Royale des Sciences des Lettres et des Beaux Arts. Mémoires, vol. 1, 1780, p. 523-549.   [232]

    Ehren-Gedichte auf edle freye Kunst-Buchdruckerey und deren Ursprung, Fortgang und Nutzbarkeit.   1739.
    Title from Peddie, R. A.   Subject index of books published up to and including 1880.   vol. 3, 1939.   [233]

Enderes, Johann Friedrich.
    Offentliche Rede von dem Ursprung und Werth der Buchdruckerey; bey Gelegenheit der Deposition eines Kunst-verwandten abgelegt. Speyer, 1766.   4to.   [234]
    Eu-De-LBb

Engel, Samuel.
    Lettre sur l'origine de l'imprimerie et sur diverses éditions anciennes.   Journal Helvetique (Mercure Suisse), Nov. 1742, p. 47- 75.   [235]

---- Remarques sur l'origine de l'art de l'imprimerie, adressées aux éditeurs du "Journal helvetique" [signed: S. Engel. Berne, le 25 juillet 1741]   n.p., n.d.   32p.   8vo.
    Reprint from Journal Helvétique (Mercure Suisse), 1741, p. 352-372.   [236]
    Eu-Fr-PN   Eu-Ne-GK

    An enquiry into the origin of printing in Europe, by a lover of the art.   London, Gibson, 1752.   55p.   8vo.   [237]
    DLC (In Miscellaneous pamphlets: 52, no. 1.)   Eu-Ge-LSb

Ernesti, Johann Heinrich Gottfried, 1664-1723.
    Die Wol-eingerichtete Buchdruckerey, mit hundert und acht- zehn Teutsch-Lateinisch-Griechisch und Hebräischen Schrifften,

vieler fremden Sprachen Alphabeten, musicalischen Noten,
Calender-Zeichen, und Medicinischen Characteren, ingleichen allen
üblichen Formaten bestellet und mit accurater Abbildung der
Erfinder der löblichen Kunst, nebst einer summarischen Nachricht
von den Buchdruckern in Nürnberg, ausgezieret. Am Ende ist das
gebräuchliche Depositions - Büchlein angefüget. Nürnberg,
gedruckt und zu finden bey Johann Andreae Endters seel. Sohn
und Erben. 1721. 140, [24]p. 19.5x25.5 cm.   [238]
    ICN   ICU   Eu-Ge-LSb
    1733 ed.: DLC   Eu-Fr-PN   Eu-Ge-LB

Falckenstein, Karl.
    Geschichte der Buchdruckerkunst. <u>Hamburgische Beyträge</u> <u>zur</u>
<u>Aufnahme</u> <u>der</u> <u>Gelehrten</u> <u>Historie</u> <u>und</u> <u>der</u> <u>Wissenschaften</u>, vol. 2,
1740, p. 301.   [239]

Fournier, Pierre Simon, 1712-1768.
    De l'origine et des productions de l'imprimerie primitive en
taille de bois; avec une réfutation des préjugés plus ou moins
accrédités sur cet art; pour servir de suite à la Dissertation
sur l'origine de l'art de graver en bois. Par M. Fournier le
jeune ... Paris, Impr. de J. Barbou, 1759. 263p. 18.5 cm.
    Reissued in Fournier, Pierre Simon. Traités historiques et
    critiques sur l'origine et les progrès de l'imprimerie ... Paris,
    J. Barbou, [1758-1763?]   [240]
    DLC   ICJ   MH   NN   Eu-De-LBb   Eu-Fr-PN   Eu-Ge-LB
    Eu-Ge-LSb

----   Dissertation sur l'origine et les progrès de l'art de graver
en bois, pour éclaircir quelques traits de l'histoire de l'imprimerie,
& prouver que Guttemberg n'en est pas l'inventeur; par Mr Fournier
le jeune, graveur & fondeur de caractères d'imprimerie.   A Paris,
de l'imprimerie de J. Barbou, M.DCC.LVIII [1758] 92, [4]p.
18.5 cm.
    Reissued in Fournier, Pierre Simon. Traités historiques et
    critiques sur l'origine et les progrès de l'imprimerie ... Paris,
    J. Barbou, [1758-1763?]   [241]
    ICJ   ICN   MB   MH   NN   NNC   Eu-De-LB   Eu-Fr-PN
    Eu-Ge-LB   Eu-Ge-LSb

----   Observations sur un ouvrage intitulé Vindiciae typographicae
[par J. D. Schoepflin] pour servir de suite au traité de l'origine
& des productions de l'imprimerie primitive en taille de bois. Par
M. Fournier le jeune.   A Paris, De l'imprimerie de J. Barbou,
M.DCC.LX [1760] 62p. 18.5 cm.
    Reissued in Fournier, Pierre Simon. Traités historiques et
    critiques sur l'origine et les progrès de l'imprimerie ... Paris,
    J. Barbou, [1758-1763?]   [242]
    ICJ   MH   NN   NNC   Eu-Fr-PN   Eu-Ge-LB

---- Remarques sur un ouvrage intitulé Lettre sur l'origine de
l'imprimerie, &c. pour servir de suite au Traité de l'origine et
des productions de l'imprimerie primitive en taille de bois. Par
M. Fournier le jeune. A Paris, de l'imprimerie de J. Barbou,
M.DCC.LXI [1761] 84p. 18.5 cm.
    Reissued in Fournier, Pierre Simon. Traités historiques et
    critiques sur l'origine et les progrès de l'imprimerie ... Paris,
    J. Barbou, [1758-1763?]   [243]
    ICJ   NN   RP   Eu-De-LBb   Eu-Fr-PN   Eu-Ge-LB

---- Traités historiques et critiques, sur l'origine et les progrès de l'imprimerie. Par M. Fournier le jeune, graveur & fondeur
de caractères d'imprimerie. A Paris, De l'imprimerie de J. Barbou,
rue & vis-à-vis la Grille des Mathurins. [1758-1763?]   2 leaves,
t.-p. with blank verso and table of contents followed by seven
pamphlets. 18.5 cm.   [244]
    NN   Eu-Fr-PN   Eu-Ge-LB   Eu-Ne-GK

Fox, John.
    The benefit and invention of printing; by J. F., that famous
martyrologist. Extracted out of his "Acts and Monuments."
London, 1704. 4to.   [245]
    Eu-Ge-LB

Fugger, Jean George.
    De l'origine et des productions de l'imprimerie primitive.
Paris, 1759. 8vo.   [246]
    Hoe

Fürstenau, Johann Hermann, 1688-1756.
    Dissertatio de initiis typographicae physiologicis.   Rinteln,
1740. 3 Bog. 4to.   [247]
    Eu-De-LBb   Eu-Ge-LSb

Gando, François.
    Lettre de François Gando le jeune, graveur & fondeur de caractères
d'imprimerie. [At end of letter, p. 11: A Paris, ce 12 mai 1758]
11p.
    Reissued in Fournier, Pierre Simon. Traités historiques et
    critiques sur l'origine et les progrès de l'imprimerie ...
    Paris, J. Barbou, [1758-1763?]
    A note on p. 11 says that the letter had already been pub-
    lished with editorial changes in Mercure de France, July
    1758, p. 175.   [248]
    NN   Eu-Fr-PN   Eu-Ge-LB

Gessner, Christian Friedrich, d. 1756.
    Die so nöthig als nützliche Buchdruckerkunst und Schrift-
giesserey, mit ihren Schriften, Formaten und allen dazu gehörigen
Instrumenten abgebildet auch klärlich beschrieben, und nebst einer

kurzgefassten Erzählung vom Ursprung und Fortgang der Buchdruckerkunst, überhaupt, insonderheit von den vornehmsten Buchdruckern
in Leipzig und andern Orten Teutschlandes im 300 Jahre nach
Erfindung derselben and Licht gestellet. Mit einer Vorrede von
Herrn Johann Ergard Kappens ... Leipzig, C. F. Gessner, 1740-1745.
4 vols. 18 cm.
    Title varies slightly.
    By C. F. Gessner and J. G. Hager.   [249]
    DLC   MH   NY   NNGr   Eu-De-LBb   Eu-Ge-LB

Ghesquière, Joseph Hippolyte.
    Lettre sur les nouvelles recherches [de J. Des Roches] sur
l'origine de l'imprimerie. L'Esprit des Journaux Français et
Étrangers, vol. 6, 1779, p. 224.   [250]

----   Reflections de M. l'Abbé J. Ghesquière sur deux pièces
relatives à l'histoire de l'imprimerie, publiées dans l'Esprit
des journaux, p. 236 & suivants du mois de novembre 1779, & page
240 & suivants du mois de janvier 1780. Seconde édition.
Nivelles, Chez E. H. J. Plon, 1780. 32p. 19.5 cm.   [251]
    ICJ   NY   Eu-Fr-PN

Hagenbusch, Johannes Theophius.
    Dissertatio academica de typographiae origine, habita Giessae
sub praesidio Imman. Weberi, Professoris Jurium.   Giessae, 1711.
    Title from Seitz, J. C. Het derde jubeljaar ... Haarlem, 1740. [252]

Hallbauer, George Christian.
    ... De scriptura, eius origine natura et variis modis praecipue
per literas ex aere fusas prodromum ad memoriam secularem inventae
divina providentia anno 1440 artis typographicae. Jenae, I. F.
Schillius, 1739. sm 4to.   [253]
    Eu-Fr-PN   Eu-Ge-LB

[Harris, John]
    A pleasant and compendious history of the first inventors and
instituters of the most famous arts, misteries, laws, customs and
manners in the whole world. Together, with many other rarities and
remarkable things rarely known, and never before made publick. To
which is added, several curious inventions, peculiarly attributed
to England [and] English-men. The whole work alphabetically di-
gested, and very helpful to readers of history. Licensed October
29th 1685. R.L.S.   London, Printed for John Harris, at the
Harrow against the Church in the Poultrey, 1686. [16], 159,
[4]p. 15 cm.
    Notes on printing, p. 100, 155.   [254]
    ICN   MH   Eu-Ge-LB   Eu-Ge-LSb
    1685 ed.: Eu-Ge-LL1   Eu-Gs-EU

Hoier, Andreas, 1690-1739.
    Observationes variae de originibus typographiae.   Schleswig,
1740.   1 1/2 bog.   4to.   [255]
    Eu-De-LBb

Hugo, Herman, 1588-1629.
    ... De prima scribendi origine et universa rei literariae anti-
quitate, cui notas, opusculum de scribis, apologiam pro Waechtlero,
praefationem et indices adjecit C. H. Trotz, jctus. Trajecti ad
Rhenum, apud Hermannum Besseling, 1738.   20 prel. leaves, 40,
611, [66]p. plates (part fold.) 22 cm.   [256]
    DLC   ICU   Eu-Fr-PN   Eu-Ge-LB

Jackson, John Baptist, 1701-1780?
    An enquiry into the origin of printing in Europe.   [Condensed
from his manuscripts by a friend.]   London, 1752.   [257]
    MH

    Kritische Geschichte der Buchdruckerkunst.   Erster Theil.
Geschichte der Erfindung der Buchdruckerkunst.   [By J. G. I.
Breitkopf?]   [Leipzig? 1780?]   4to.   [258]
    Eu-Ge-LB

Lambinet, Pierre, 1742-1813.
    Recherches historiques, littéraires et critiques, sur l'origine
de l'imprimerie; particulièrement sur ses premiers établissemens, au
XVme siècle, dans la Belgique ... Ornées des portraits et des écussons
des premiers imprimeurs belges; par le citoyen P. Lambinet ... Bruxelles,
Impr. de E. Flon, an VII [1799]   1 prel. leaf, xvi, 500p.   illus.,
plates, port.   21.5 cm.   [259]
    CLC   ICJ   NjN   NjP   Eu-Fr-PN   Eu-Ge-LB   Eu-Ge-LP
    Eu-Ge-LSb
    1798 ed.: DLC   IU   NN

Laval.
    Discours sur l'origine, le progrès et les différents âges de la
librairie et l'imprimerie. 1726.
    Title from van der Linde, Geschichte der Erfindung ...   [260]

Lemoine, Henry, 1756-1812.
    Typographical antiquities.   History, origin, and progress, of
the art of printing, from its first invention in Germany to the
end of the seventeenth century; and from its introduction into
England by Caxton, to the present time ... Extracted from the best
authorities, by Henry Lemoine ... London, S. Fisher, 1797.   156p.
18.5 cm.   [261]
    DLC   ICJ   NN   Eu-Ge-LB   Eu-Ge-LP

Loescher, Valentin Ernst, 1673-1749.
    De artis typographicae utilitate, inventione & libris primo

excusis.   Wittemberg, Stromateus, 1724.   4to.
    Title from van der Linde, Geschichte der Erfindung ...   [262]

[Luckombe, Philip] d. 1803.
    A concise history of the origin and progress of printing;
with practical instructions to the trade in general.   Compiled
from those who have wrote on this curious art.   London, W.
Adlard and J. Browne, 1770.   6 prel. leaves, 502, [4]p. front.,
illus.   21 cm.
    Reissued in 1771 under author's name.   [263]
    DLC   ICJ   ICN   MB   NN   NjN   Eu-De-LBb   Eu-Ge-LB
    Eu-Ne-GK

----   The history and art of printing ... By P. Luckombe ... London,
Printed by W. Adlard and J. Browne for J. Johnson, 1771.   6 prel.
leaves, 502, [4]p.   front., illus.   21 cm.
    A reissue with new t.-p. of the work published anonymously in
    1770 under title "A concise history of the origin and pro-
    gress of printing".   [264]
    DLC   I   ICJ   IaU   MNBedf   MWA   NN   ViU   Eu-Fr-PN
    Eu-Ge-LB

Marchand, Prosper, d. 1756.
    Histoire de l'origine et des prémiers progrès de l'imprimerie;
par mr. Prosper Marchand.   La Haye, P. Paupie, 1740.   xii, 152p.
26 cm.
    Added t.-p., engraved.
----   Supplément à l'histoire de l'imprimerie, de Prosper Marchand: ou additions et corrections pour cet ouvrage.   Paris,
Impr. de P. D. Pierres, 1773.   55p.   27 cm.
    By Barthélemy Mercier, abbé de Saint-Léger.
----   Supplément ... ed. rev. & augm.: avec un mémoire sur l'époque
certaine du commencement de l'année à Mayence, durant le XVe siècle.
Paris, Impr. de P. D. Pierres, 1775.   viii, 221p.   25.5 cm.   [265]
    DLC   ICJ   MB   MH   MdBP   NN   Eu-De-BP   Eu-De-LBb
    Eu-Fr-PN   Eu-Ge-LB   Eu-Ge-LP   Eu-Ge-LSb   Eu-Ne-AVb
    Eu-Ne-GK

Mercier, Barthélemy, 1734-1799.
    Lettre de M. Mercier, abbé de St. Léger de Soissons, à MM.
les auteurs du Journal des Savants, contenant diverses remarques
critiques sur son Supplément à l'histoire de l'imprimerie de P.
Marchand: ou additions et corrections pour cet ouvrage [par B. M.]
[Paris, 1776]   16p.   4to.   [266]
    Eu-Ge-LB

Munch, Benedictus Guill.
    Primaria quaedam documenta de origine typographiae.   Altdorfii,
typis Johannis Adami Hesselii, 1740.   36p.   4to.   [267]
    NN   Eu-Ne-GK

Offenbach, Zacharias Conrad von.
De primitii typographicis, quae Harlemi in curia et Francofurti
in bibliotheca Uffenbachiana adservantur. Amoenitates Literariae,
vol. 9, 1728, p. 969-986.   [268]

[Orlandi, Pellegrino Antonio] 1660-1727.
Origine e progressi della stampa, o sia Dell' arte impressoria
e notizie dell' opere stampate dall' anno M. C.CCC.LVII. sino all'
anno M.D. [Colophon: Superiorum permissu opus sic effigiatum suis
formulis effecit finitum Constantinus Pisarius ... Bononiae ...
M.DCCXXII. ...] 4 prel. leaves, 448, [2]p. illus. 24.5x18 cm.
Dedication signed: Fr. Pellegrino Antonio Orlandi ...   [269]
DLC   IU   MB   MH   NN   Eu-De-LBb   Eu-Fr-PC   Eu-Fr-PN
Eu-Ge-LB   Eu-Ne-AVb   Eu-Ne-GK

Origin of printing. Cambridge, 1787.
A broadside containing a paragraph headed thus, surrounded with
very elaborate typographical ornament.   [270]
Eu-Ge-LSb

Oudini, Casimir.
Dissertatio de primis artis typographicae inventoribus, quae
in commentariis ejus de Scriptoribus & Scriptis Ecclesiasticis.
Leipzig, 1722. Folio edition, vol. 3, fol. 2741 et sqq. (In Wolf,
J. C. Monumenta typographica. Hamburg, 1740. vol. 2, p. 872-
904)   [271]

Over den oorsprong der boekdrukkunst. [Signed: S] Groningen,
1781. 8vo.   [272]
Eu-Ge-LSb

Palmer, Samuel, d. 1732.
The general history of printing, from its first invention in
the city of Mentz, to its first progress and propagation thro' the
most celebrated cities in Europe. Particularly, its introduction,
rise and progress here in England. The characters of the most
celebrated printers, from the first inventors of the art to the
years 1520 and 1550. With an account of their works ... By S. Palmer,
printer. London, Printed by the author, 1732. vii, [5], 400p.
26 cm.
Completed after the author's death by George Psalmanazar.
"A catalogue of English printers, from the year 1471 to 1600;
most of them at London" (4p.) tipped in.   [273]
DLC   MBAt   Eu-De-LEb   Eu-Ge-LB

---- A general history of printing; from the first invention
of it in the city of Mentz, to its propagation and progress thro'
most of the kingdoms in Europe: particularly the introduction and
success of it here in England. With the characters of the most
celebrated printers, from the first inventors of this art to the

years 1520 and 1550. With an account of their works ... By S. Palmer,
printer. London, printed for A. Bettesworth, C. Hitch, and
C. Davis, 1733. vii, [5], 400p. 25 cm.
  A reissue of the first edition, 1732, printed in red and black.[274]
  DLC ICJ MdBP MiU NBuG NN NjN PU Eu-Fr-PN
  Eu-Ge-LB Eu-Ge-LP Eu-Ne-AVb

Panciroli, Guido, 1523-1599.
  The history of many memorable things lost, which were in use
among the ancients: and an account of many excellent things
found, now in use among the moderns, both natural and artificial.
Written originally in Latin, by Guido Pancirollus; and now done
into English, and illustrated with a new commentary of choice
remarks ... from Salmuth's large annotations ... To this English
edition is added, first, a supplement to the chapter of printing,
shewing the time of its beginning, and the first book printed in
each city before the year 1500. Secondly, what the moderns
have found, the ancients never knew: extracted from Dr. Sprat's
... History of the Royal-society, the writings of the Honourable
Mr. Boyle, the Royal-academy at Paris, &c. Thirdly, an index
to the whole. London, Printed for J. Nicholson, and sold by
J. Morphew, 1715. 2 vols. in 1. 16.5 cm.
  Paged continuously.   [275]
  CSmH DLC DGS ICJ ICN MNBedf MdBP NN NjR
  Eu-Fr-PN Eu-Ge-LB Eu-Ge-LSb

Parker, T.
  A short account of the first rise and progress of printing, with
a complete list of the first books that were published. London,
1763. 64mo.
  Title from Denis, Ferdinand. Nouveau manuel de bibliographie
  universelle. 1857.   [276]

Pater, Paul, 1656-1724.
  De Germaniae miraculo optimo, maximo, typis literarum,
earumque differentiis, dissertatio, qua simul artis typographicae
universam rationem explicat Paulus Pater; pp. Lipsiae, apud
J. F. Gleditsch et filium, 1710. 2 prel. leaves, 91p. illus.,
2 plates. 21x26 cm.
  Title vignette; head-piece; initials.   [277]
  DLC ICN Eu-Fr-PN Eu-Ge-LB

Pellegrini, Domenico Maria, 1737-1820.
  Origine della stampa in Germania riconosciuta dal Sabellico
ignaro della chimerica invenzione in Feltre. Il medesimo non
favorevole alla stampa in Venezia prima del 1469 ... Senza note
tipografiche. n.d. 30p. 8vo.
  Title from Pasterello, Ester. Bibliografia storico-analitica
  dell' arte della stampa in Venezia. 1933.   [278]

Quirini, Angelo Maria, cardinal, 1680-1755.
Angeli Mariae Card. Quirini ... Liber singularis de optimorum
scriptorum editionibus quae Romae primum prodierunt post divinum
typographiae inventum, a germanis opificibus in eam urbem advectum:
plerisque omnibus earum editonum seu praefationibus, seu epistolis
in medium allatis. Cum brevibus observationibus ad easdem, rei
typographicae origini illustrandae valde opportunis. Recensuit,
annotationes, rerumque notabiliorum indicem adjecit, et diatribam
praeliminarem de variis rebus ad natales artis typographicae
dilucidandos facientibus praemisit Jo. Georgius Schelhornius.
Lindaugiae, impensis J. Ottonis, 1761. 4 prel. leaves, 5-266,
[10]p. vi facsims. 23 cm.   [279]
    DLC   NN   NjP Eu-De-BP   Eu-Ge-LL1   Eu-Ne-GK   Eu-Sz-BeG

Reif, Aemilian.
De originibus typographicis programma academicum. Ingolstadii,
1785. 4to.   [280]
    Eu-De-LBb   Eu-Ge-LB

---- ----   1790. ii, 85p. 4to.   [281]
    Eu-Fr-PN

Schelhorn, Johann Georg, 1694-1773.
Amoenitates literariae quibus ... rariora opuscula exhibentur.
Francofurti & Lipsiae, 1725-1731. 14 vols.
    De primitiis typographicis ... : vol. 9, p. 969 et sqq.   [282]
    CBPac   CtY   DLC   ICU   IU   NBC   NN   Eu-Ge-LB

----   Jo. Georgii Schelhornii ... Amoenitates historiae ecclesiasticae
et literariae, quibus variae observationes, scripta item quaedam
anecdota & rariora opuscula, diversis utriusque historiae capitibus
elucidandis inservientia, exhibentur. Francofurti & Lipsiae,
sumptibus D. Bartholomaei & filii, 1737-1738. 2 vols. 18 cm.
    "Notitia librorum quorundam rariorum": vol. 1, p. 777-941.
    "Notae in vetus carmen de originibus typographiae": vol. 1,
    p. 942-962.
    "Notitia librorum, in quibus acta quaedam Concilii tridentini
    collecta exhibentur": vol. 2, p. 380-477.   [283]
    DLC   ICN   MnU   NIC   Eu-Ge-LB

Schwarz, Christian Gottlieb, 1675-1751, praeses.
Primaria quaedam documenta de origine typographiae ... Altorfii,
typis I. A. Hesselii [1740] 3 parts in 1 vol. fold. plate.
21x27 cm.
    Title chronogram: Ipso anno tertIo saeCVLarI typographIae
    DIVIno a VXILIO a GerManIs Im Ventae.
    Partem primam svbiicit Benedictvs Gvilielmvs Mvnch. Partem
    alteram proponit Io. Gvilielmvs Schavbert. Partem tertiam
    proponit Gvstavvs Philippvs Negelein.   [284]
    DLC   NN   Eu-De-LBb   Eu-Ge-LB   Eu-Ge-LE

Smith, John, printer, fl. 1755.
The printer's grammar: containing a concise history of the origin of printing; also, an examination of the superficies, gradation, and properties of the different sizes of types ... tables of calculations; models of letter cases; schemes for casting off copy, and imposing; ... with directions to authors, compilers, &c. how to prepare copy, and to correct their own proofs. Chiefly collected from Smith's edition. To which are added directions for pressmen, &c. ... London, Printed by L. Wayland and sold by T. Evans, 1787. 2 prel. leaves, 369p. forms. 22 cm. [285]
    DLC

Thiboust, Claude Louis, 1667-1737.
C. Ludovicus Thiboust, Eruditissimis Regiae Scientiarium Academiae Sociis, ut in suam Societatem Artem typorum cooptent carmen latinum. (In Wolf, J. C. Monumenta typographica. Hamburg, 1740. vol. 2, p. 632-643) [286]

[Thorn] printer.
A general history of printing wherein is shown the origin of that nobel art. [1732?] [2], 41, [1, 24]p. 25 cm.
    Manuscript.
    Deals with the invention of printing and the origin of printing in England.
    A description of types: p. [24] [287]
    ICJ

Tiraboschi, Girolamo.
Dell' inventione della stampa. (In Prodromo della nuova enciclopedia. Siena, Pazzini e Bindi, 1779) [288]

Toland, John.
Conjectura verosimilis de prima typographiae inventione ... [London, J. Peele, 1726] 297-303p. 8vo.
    Reissued in Wolf, J. C. Monumenta typographica. Hamburg, 1740. vol. 2, p. 872-904. [289]
    NN

---- ----   Also in A collection of several pieces now first published from his original manuscripts. London, 1726. vol. 1. [290]
    Eu-De-LBb

Villarroya, José.
Disertacion sobre el origen del nobilisimo arte tipografico, y su introduccion y uso en la ciudad de Valencia de los Edetanos. Escribiala d. Joseph Villarroya del consejo de S. M. y su alcalde de casa y corte. En Valencia y oficina de d. Benito Monfort año MDCCXCVI [1796]. 2 prel. leaves, 99p. 20 cm. [291]
    NNH

Villeneuve, J. de.
    Primeira origem da arte de imprimir dada a lus dellos primeiros
characteres.   Lisboa, J. A. da Sylva, Impressor de Academia Real,
1732.   4to.
    Title from Maggs Bros. A catalogue of bibliographies and works
    on book-production. Cat. 703. "The first book printed with the
    first types cast in Portugal."   [292]

Watson, James, d. 1722, pub.
    The history of the art of printing, containing an account of
it's invention and progress in Europe: with the names of the famous
printers, the places of their birth, and the works printed by them.
And a preface by the publisher to the printers in Scotland.
Edinburgh, Printed by J. Watson, sold at his shop [etc.] 1713.
24, xlviii, 64p.   illus., fold. plate.   17 cm.
    Contents.--The publisher's preface to the printers in Scotland
    [signed James Watson]--Specimen of types in the printing-house
    of James Watson.--The history of the invention and progress of
    the mysterious art of printing, &c. [a translation of J. de La
    Caille's Histoire de l'imprimerie et de la librairie, livre 1,
    by J. Spotiswood]--A contemplation upon the mystery of man's
    regeneration, in allusion to the mystery of printing [a poem].   [293]
    DLC   ICJ   ICN   MH   Eu-Ge-LB   Eu-Ge-LP   Eu-Ne-AVb
    Eu-Ne-GK

Watts, Isaac, 1674-1748.
    The improvement of the mind: containing a variety of remarks
and rules for the attainment and communication of useful knowledge in religion, in the sciences, and in common life.   London,
Logographic press, 1785.   xvi, 464p.   8vo.
    Preceded by: An address to the public, on the origin of the
    art of printing, with a description of the logographic in-
    vention, by J. Walter, xxiii p.   [294]
    NN   Eu-Ge-LB

Werther, Johann David, fl. 1700.
    Warhafftige Nachrichten der so alt- als berühmten Büch-
drücker-Künst, in welchen vom Ursprung und Fortgang der Buchdruckereyen, von 1440. an biss ietzo 1721. und denen darinn
eingeführten Gebräuchen auch eingeschlichenen Missbräuchen und
Unordnungen gehandelt wird, alles aus bewährtesten und Unordnungen gehandelt wird, alles aus bewährtesten Urkunden, und selbst-
eigener vieljährigen Erfahrung mit grossem Fleiss und Kosten
zusammengetragen und aus unpartheyischen Gemüthe dem Publico mitgetheilet: von Johann David Werthern. Franckfurth und Leipzig,
J. F. Bielcken, 1721.   14 prel. leaves, 503p.   illus. 20.5 cm.
    Head and tail pieces; printers' marks.   [295]
    DLC   Eu-Ge-LB

Willett, Ralph, 1719-1795.
    Memoir on the origin of printing.   Archaeologia, vol. 11,
1794, p. 267-316.   [296]

----   Observations on the origin of printing.   Archaeologia,
vol. 8, 1787, p. 239-251.   [297]

Wolf, Johann Christian, 1689-1770.
    Monumenta typographica, quae artis hujos praestantissimae
originem laudem et abuseum posteris produnt, instaurata studio
et labore Jo. Christiani Wolfii ... Hamburgi, sumtibus C. Heroldi,
1740.   2 vols.   17 cm.   [298]
    DLC   ICJ   ICN   MB   MH   NN   NjN   Eu-De-BP   Eu-Ge-LB
    Eu-Ge-LL1   Eu-Ne-GK

Würdtwein, Stefan Alexander, 1719-1796.
    Bibliotheca moguntina libris saeculo primo typographico
Moguntiae impressis instructa, hinc inde addita inventae typo-
graphiae historia, a Stephano Alexandro Würdtwein ... Augustae
Vindelicorum, C. F. Bürglen, 1787.   251p.   9 facsim.   25 cm.   [299]
    DLC   MBAt   NN

Zapf, Georg Wilhelm, 1747-1810.
    Aelteste Buchdruckergeschichte von Mainz, von derselben Erfin-
dung bis auf das Jahr 1499; verfasst, herausgegeben und mit Anmerkungen erläutert von Georg Wilhelm Zapf ... Ulm, Zu finden in der
Wohlerschen Buchhandlung, 1790.   8 prel. leaves, 163, [12], 46p.
fold. facsim.   20 cm.   [300]
    DLC   ICN   MB   NN

        4   19th Century

Adams, Thomas F.
    Typographia; or, The printer's instructor: a brief sketch of
the origin, rise and progress of the typographic art, with practical directions for conducting every department in an office, hints
to authors, publishers, &c.   By Thomas F. Adams, typographer.
[New ed.] Philadelphia, L. Johnson & co., 1861.   viii, 7-286p.
incl. illus., plates.   19cm.
    Advertising matter: p. 283-285.   [301]
    DLC   MNBedf   NN   Eu-Ge-LE

Alden, Henry M.
    Origin of printing and why the ancients had no printing press.

Eclectic Review, vol. 40, 1824, p. 366.   Same, Irish Quarterly
Review, vol. 8, 1859, p. 20.   Same, Harper's New Monthly Magazine,
vol. 37, 1868, p. 637-641.   [302]

---- ----   New York [1868]
    [Extracted from Harper's New Monthly Magazine, Aug. and Oct.
    1868].   [303]
    CSmH   DLC   ICJ   MnHi

Amati, Giacinto, 1778-1850.
    Ricerche storico-critico-scientifiche sulle origini, scoperte,
invenzioni e perfezionamenti fatti nelle lettere, nelle arti e nelle
scienze; con alcuni tratti biografici della vita dei piu distinti
autori nelle medesime.   Opera dell' abate Don Giacinto Amati ...
Milano, Coi tipi di G. Pirotta, 1828-30.   5 vols.   fronts., illus.,
plates (1 fold.), ports., fold. map, plans, diagrs.   23.5 cm.
    vol. 5: Tipographia del secolo XV.   [304]
    DLC   ICJ   Eu-Fr-PN   Eu-Ge-LB   Eu-Ge-LSb

Aretin, Johann Christoph Anton Maria Franz Xaver, Freiherr von,
    1772-1824.
    Über die frühesten universalhistorischen Folgen der Erfindung
der Buchdruckerkunst.   Eine Abhandlung, vorgelesen in einer öffentlichen Sitzung der Akademie der Wissenschaften in München, als diese
den Tag ihrer Stiftung zum fünfzigstenmale Feyerte am 28. März 1808,
von J. Christ. Freyherrn von Aretin ... München, 1808.   50p., 1 leaf,
facsims.   25 cm.   [305]
    DLC   MH   PP   Eu-Fr-PN   Eu-Ge-LB   Eu-Ne-GK

Astle, Thomas, 1735-1803.
    The origin and progress of writing, as well hieroglyphic as ele-
mentary, illustrated by engravings taken from marbles, manuscripts
and charters ancient and modern: also some account of the origin and
progress of printing. 2d ed., with additions.   By Thomas Astle ...
London, For J. White, 1803.   4 prel. leaves, xxiv, 240p.   front.
(port.)   plates.   47 cm.   [306]
    DLC   ICJ   MB   MH   MWA   MWiW-C   NN   PBL   PP   PU   Eu-Ge-LB
    1st ed.:   Eu-Ge-LB

---- ---- Reissued, London, Chatto & Windus, 1876.   xxiv, 240p.
xxxi plates.   Folio.   [307]
    Eu-Fr-PN   Eu-Ge-LB

Bakhtiarov, A. A.
    Vozniknovenie knigopechataniia v Evrope.   (In his Istoriia
knigi na Rusi ... St. Petersburg, F. Pavlenkova, 1890.   p. 60-72.   [308]
    NN

Bari, Aristide.
   Brevi notizie storiche intorno alla invenzione e progressi
della stampa.   Como, Tipografia dell' Araldo, 1886.   51p.
8vo.   [309]
   Eu-De-LBb

[Barth, Johann Ambrosius] 1760-1813, ed.
   Geschichte der seit dreihundert Jahren in Breslau befindlichen
Stadtbuchdruckerey als ein Beitrag zur allgemeinen Geschichte der
Buchdruckerkunst.   Mit 4 Bildnissen und 4 erläuternden Kupfer-
platten.   Breslau, Grass und Barth, 1804.   1 prel. leaf, vi,
[24], 86p. ports., facsims., tab.   24.5x20.5 cm.
   Edited by Barth, with the collaboration of J. C. D. Geiser and
C. F. Paritius; preface by J. E. Scheibel.
   Part 1: Kurze Geschichte der Erfindung der Buchdruckerkunst.   [310]
   DLC   Eu-Ge-LB   Eu-Ge-LE

Beckmann, Johann, 1739-1811.
   Beyträge zur Geschichte der Erfindung ... Erster-[fünfter] Band.
Leipzig, P. C. Kummer, 1786-1805.   5 vols.   18 cm.   [311]
   ICJ   Eu-Fr-PN   Eu-Ge-LB

----   A history of inventions and discoveries.   Translated from
the German by Wm. Johnston.   2d ed., carefully corrected, and enlarged by a fourth volume ... London, J. Walker & co., 1814.   4 vols.
23 cm.   [312]
   DSG   ICJ   MiD   NN   PHi   PU   Eu-Fr-Pn   Eu-Ge-LB
   Eu-Ge-LSb

---- ----   3d ed., carefully corrected, and enlarged by the
addition of several new articles ... London, Longman, Hurst, Rees,
Orme and Brown, 1817.   4 vols.   21.5 cm.
   Bibliography of the history of inventions, p. 475-518.   [313]
   ICJ

---- ----   Fourth ed., carefully revised and enlarged by Wm.
Francis, and J. W. Griffith ... London, H. G. Bohn, 1846.   2 vols.
8vo.   [314]
   Eu-Fr-PN

Bergnes de las Casas, Antonio, 1800-1879.
   Historia de la imprenta.   Trata de su invención, historia prim-
itiva é introduccion en Europe.   Por d. A. Bergnes.   Barcelona,
Impr. de A. Bergnes y C.ª, calle de Escudellers, no. 13, con
licencia, octubre, 1831.   3 prel. leaves, [7]-84p.   23 cm.   [315]
   ICN

Bernard, Auguste Joseph, 1811-1868.
De l'origine de l'imprimerie. Serapeum, vol. 12, no. 6, 1851,
p. 89-92. [316]

---- De l'origine et des débuts de l'imprimerie en Europe, par
Aug. Bernard ... Paris, Imprimerie impériale, 1853. 2 vols.
facsims. on XIII plates (3 fold.) 21.5 cm.
    DCU-H   DLC   ICJ   MB   MH   MdBP   NN   NjP   Eu-Fr-PN
    Eu-Ge-LB   Eu-Ge-LP [317]

---- l'origine et les débuts de l'imprimerie. Athenaeum
Français, no. 1361, Nov. 1853, p. 1417. Same, Magazin für die
Literatur des Auslandes, no. 128, 1853, p. 509; no. 129, p. 514. [318]

---- Résumé de l'origine de l'imprimerie. Bulletin du Bibliophile Belge, vol. 15 (2d ser., vol. 6), 1859, p. 90-101.
Also reprint. [319]

---- Voyage typographico-archéologique, en Belgique, en Hollande,
en Allemagne, etc. Bulletin du Bibliophile Belge, vol. 10 (2d ser.,
vol. 1), 1854, p. 98-124, 241-255. [320]

Besso, Beniamino.
Le grandi invenzione antiche e moderne. Milano, 1879.
vol. 1, part 1: La stampa. [321]
MiU

Bignan, Anne.
Épitre à quelques ennemis des lumières, sur la découverte de
l'imprimerie, qui a obtenu l'accessit au jugement de l'Académie
Française, dans la séance publique de 25 août, 1829. Paris, 1829.
16p. 8vo.
Also appeared in Almanach des Musées, 1830 p. 37-46. [322]
Eu-Fr-PN

Blades, William, 1824-1890.
The early schools of typography. Book Worm (Berjeau), vol. 5,
Mar. 1870, p. 35-38. [323]

---- On the present aspect of the question -- who was the inventor
of printing? Being a paper read at the meeting of the Library
association of the United Kingdom, at Birmingham, September 20-23,
1887, by William Blades. London [Priv. print] 1887. cover-title,
8p. 28.5 cm.
Running title: Who invented printing?
"A list of books published upon the subject since 1868."--On
inside of back cover.
Reprint from Library Chronicle (London), vol. 4, 1887, p. 135-143.

Also appeared in Printers' Register, vol. 27, 1887, p. 62-64
80-81, 89.   [324]
DLC   Eu-Fr-IN   Eu-Ge-LB

----   The Pentateuch of printing, with a chapter on Judges. By
William Blades.   With a memoir of the author, and list of his
works, by Talbot B. Reed.   London, E. Stock, 1891.   4 prel.
leaves, [vii]-xxvi p., 1 leaf, 117, [1]p.   illus., 2 fold.
plates, ports., facsims.   26.5 cm.
    Added t.-p., illustrated.
    "A chapter on Judges" [bibliography of the Genesis of
    printing]:   p. [97]-103.   [325]
    DLC   ICJ   MB   MH

---- ----   Chicago, A. C. McClurg and company, 1891.   4 prel.
leaves, [vii]-xxvi p., 1 leaf, 117, [1]p.   Front., illus., 2 fold.
plates, ports, facsims.   26.5 cm.
    DLC   I   MdBP   NjP   [326]

Boehm.
    Who is the inventor?   Inland Printer, vol. 2, 1885, p. 380-381.[327]

    Bogtrykkerkonstens opfindelse og udvikling. Christiania, 1836.
8vo.
    Title from van der Linde, Geschichte der Erfindung ...   [328]

    Bogtrykkerkonstens opfindelse og udvikling. (Reprinted in
Nissen, Mart., ed. Norsk Bok-fortegnelse, 1814-1847.   Christiania,
1848)
    Title from Neuer Anzeiger für Bibliographie und Bibliothek-
    swissenschaft, 1861.   [329]

Bohn, Henry George, 1796-1884.
    The origin and progress of printing. A lecture delivered at
Twickenham, April 18th, and repeated by desire at Richmond, April
21st, 1857.   London, Philobiblon Society, 1857.   2 prel. leaves,
108p.   21 cm.
    Philobiblon Society.   Miscellanies, vol. 4   [330]
    IaU   NN   Eu-Fr-PN   Eu-Ge-LB   Eu-Ge-LSb   Eu-Ne-GK

Börckel, Alfred, 1851-1928.
    Die Ansprüche auf die Erfindung der Buchdruckerkunst. Allge-
meiner Anzeiger für Druckereien, Gutenberg number, June 21, 1900. [331]

----   Die graphischen Künste zur Zeit Gutenbergs.   Klimsch's
Jahrbuch, vol. 1, 1900, p. 1-12.   [332]

Bösch, Hans.
    Zur Geschichte der Erfindung der Buchdruckerkunst. Anzeiger
für Kunde der Deutschen Vorzeit, n.s., vol. 29, 1882, p. 75.   [333]

Bouchot, Henri François Xavier Marie, 1849-1906.
The book: its printers, illustrators, and binders, from Gutenberg to the present time. By Henri Bouchot ... with a treatise on
the art of collecting and describing early printed books, and a
Latin-English and English-Latin topographical index of the earliest
printing places. Ed. by H. Grevel. Containing one hundred and
seventy-two fac-similes of early typography, book-illustrations,
printers' marks, bindings, numerous borders, initials, head and tail
pieces, and a frontispiece. New York, Scribner and Welford, 1890.
xv, 383p. incl. front., illus., ports., facsims. 26.5 cm.
    First English translation by E. C. Bigmore, 1887, has title: The
    printed book; its history, illustration and adornment."
    "The art of describing and cataloguing incunabula" (p. [322]-351)
    is a translation of Die Incunabel-Bibliographie, von A. Einsle,
    Wien, 1888.   [334]
    DLC   ICJ   NjP   Eu-Ge-LB   Eu-Ge-LSb

----   Le livre; l'illustration--la reliure; étude historique som-
maire, par Henri Bouchot ... Paris, Maison Quantin [1889?] 320p.
illus. (incl. facsims.)   21 cm.   (Added t.-p.: Bibliothèque de
l'enseignement des beaux-arts)
    Series title also at head of t.-p.
    "Nouvelle edition."
    Reissue of the first edition (1886)   [335]
    DCU-H   DLC   ICN   MB   MH
    1886 ed.: Eu-Fr-PN   Eu-Ge-LB

----   L'oeuvre de Gutenberg; l'imprimerie; l'illustration.
Paris, H. Lecène et H. Oudin, 1887.   240p.   illus.   8vo.
    MB   Eu-Fr-PN
    1888 ed.:   Eu-Fr-PN   Eu-Ge-LB   [336]

----   The printed book, its history, illustration and adornment,
from the days of Gutenberg to the present time.   By Henri Bouchot ...
Tr. and enl. by Edward C. Gibmore.   With one hundred and eighteen
illustrations and facsimiles of early typography, printers' marks,
copies of book illustrations, and specimens of bindings of all ages.
London, H. Grevel and co., 1887.   viii, 312p.   illus. (incl. facsims.)   20.5 cm.   [337]
    DLC   ICJ   NjP   Eu-Fr-PN   Eu-Ge-LB   Eu-Ge-LSb

Boudet, J. B.
    Les origines de l'imprimerie et son introduction en Angleterre,
de M. A. Quantin. Compte rendu.   Paris, 1879.   15p.   8vo.   [338]
    Eu-Ge-LB   Eu-Ge-LSb

[Bradbury, Henry Riley] 1831-1860.
    Printing: its dawn, day, & destiny ... London, Bradbury & Evans,
1858.   40p.   27.5x21.5 cm.

"An address delivered at the Royal institution of Great Britain ...
May 14, 1858."
DLC   ICJ   MiD   Eu-Ge-LSb

Broadmann, G. A.
   Kurzer Abriss der Geschichte der Buchdruckerkunst und deren welt-
historische Bedeutung ... Zwei Vorträge gehalten in Handwerker-Verein
zu Erfurt am 15. März und 12. April 1864.   3d ed.   Erfurt, 1864.
28p.   8vo.   [340]
   Eu-De-LBb   Eu-Ge-LB

Brunet y Bëllet, José, 1818-
... L'escriptura, lo gravat, l'imprempta, lo llibre per Josep Brunet
y Bellet ... Barcelona, Tip. "L'Avenç," 1898.   x, 299p., 2 leaves.
25.5 cm.   (His Erros historics, vol. 5)
   "Tirada de 200 exemplars."
   Contents include: L'imprempta. Propagació de l'imprempta. Qui
va resoldre l'problema? Gutenberg. Harlem. Strasburg.
Maguncia.   [341]
   DLC   ICJ

Bulgakov, F. I.
   Izobretenie knigopechataniĭa.   (In his Illiustrirovannaĭa
istoriĭa knigopechataniĭa i tipografskogo iskustva.   St. Petersburg, A. S. Suvorin, 1889.   p. 63-76)
   NN   Eu-Ru-MLe   [342]

----   Novoe ob izobretenii knigopechataniia.   Bibliograficheskie
Zapiski, no. 1, 1892, p. 52-55.   [343]

Castellani, Carlo, 1822-1879.
   Da chi e dove la stampa fu inventata?   Ovvero Stato presente
della questione sul vero inventore della tipografia e sulla città
che prima esercito quest' arte, esposto da C. Castellani ...
Firenze, Tip. di G. Carnesecchi e figli, 1888.   42p.   22.5 cm. [344]
   DLC   Eu-Fr-PN   Eu-Ge-LSb

----   L'origine tedesca e l'origine olandese dell' invenzione
della stampa; testimonianze e documenti raccolti e illustrati da
C. Castellani ... Venezia, F. Ongania, 1889.   67p.   23 cm.   [345]
   DLC   Eu-Fr-PN   Eu-Ge-LSb   Eu-Ne-GK

----   Lo stato presente questione sull' inventore della tipografia e sulla città che prima l'esercito.   Revista delle
Bibliotoche, vol. 1, no. 5-7, 1888, p. 67-76.   [346]

Chasles, Philarète, 1798-1873.
   Les origines de la presse.   Revue des Deux Mondes, n.s.,
vol. 1, 1843, p. 308-338.   [347]

Chatelain, Mme. Clara (de Pontigny) de, 1807-1876, ed.
Handbook to the history of printing. Ed. by Madame de Chatelain.
London, A. and S. Joseph, Myers, & co., 1855. 25p. 18 cm. [348]
DLC Eu-Ge-LB

Clephan, J.
On the invention of printing. Popular Lecturer, no. 6, 1856,
p. 161-174. [349]

Cochrane, Charles H.
The earliest printer. Controversial claims for the honor of
first printer. Printer and Book Maker, vol. 26, 1898, p. 234-235. [350]

Coggeshall, William Turner, 1824-1867.
The newspaper record, containing a complete list of newspapers
and periodicals in the United States, Canadas, and Great Britain,
together with a sketch of the origin and progress of printing, with
some facts about newspapers in Europe and America, by W. I. Coggeshall. Philadelphia, Lay & brother, 1856. xiv, 194p. illus.
22.5 cm. [351]
DLC MNBodf NN Eu-Fr-PN Eu-Ge-LB

Colombo, Angelo.
Il combinatore e l'impressore. Cenni storici sopra l'origine
della stampa. Milano, 1857. 8vo. [352]
Eu-De-LBb

Danel, Louis, 1857-
Note sur l'origine de la typographie. Lille, Danel, 1884.
16p. facsims. 25.5 cm. [353]
IaU Eu-De-LBb

Daunou, Pierre Claude François, 1761-1840.
Analyse des opinions diverses sur l'origine de l'imprimerie, par
Daunou ... Lue à la séance de l'Institut national, le 2 floréal an 10.
Paris, Renouard, an XI [1803]. 2 prel. leaves, 138p. 20 cm.
Also printed in Mémoires de l'Institut. (Acad. sci. morales et
politiques) t. 4, 1803; also in Lambinet, Origine de l'imprimerie,
1810, t. 1, p. [311]-424. [354]
DLC ICJ NN Eu-Fr-PN Eu-Ge-LB Eu-Ge-LP Eu-Ne-GK

---- Uebersicht der verschiedenen Meinungen über den Ursprung der
Buchdruckerkunst. Aus dem Französischen übersetzt und berichtigt
von Martin Schrettinger. (In Aretin, J. C. von. Beyträge zur Geschichte und Literatur ... München, 1805. vol. 5, p. 161-224, 273-326) [355]
DLC PU

De Vinne, Theodore Low, 1828-1914.
The invention of printing. Quadrat, vol. 3, June 1875, p. 88. [356]

De Vinne, Theodore Low, 1828-1914.
The invention of printing. A collection of facts and opinions
descriptive of early prints and playing cards, the block books of the
fifteenth century, the legends of Lourens Janszoon Coster, of Haarlem,
and the work of John Gutenberg and his associates. Illustrated with
facsimiles of early types and woodcuts. By Theo. L. De Vinne ...
New York, F. Hart & co., 1876. 4 prel. leaves, [5]-556p. incl.
front., illus., facsim. 24 cm.
    Published in 5 parts; with the last part cancels were issued to
be substituted for p. 43-46, 369-370, 375-576 incorrectly
printed, also the half sheet containing Contents, and Illustrations to be inserted between sig. [1] and [2], before the
Preface.   [357]
    CSmH   DLC   MnU   NN   Eu-Fr-PC   Eu-Ne-AVb
    London, 1876: Eu-Ge-LB   Eu-Ge-LP   Eu-Ge-LSb

---- ----   2d ed.   London, Treubner, 1877.   [358]
    ICN   NjP   Eu-Ge-LL1   Eu-Ge-LP   Eu-Ne-GK

---- ----   2d ed.   New York, F. Hart & co.; [etc., etc.] 1878.
4 prel. leaves, 7-557p. front., illus. (incl. ports., maps, facsims.) 24 cm.
    "Authorities consulted": p. [543]-545.   [359]
    CSmH   DLC   ICJ   ICN   MH   MdBP   MnU   NN   NjP   WaU
    Eu-De-LBb   Eu-Ge-LB   Eu-Ne-GK

---- ----   New York, G. Bruce's son & co., 1878.   168 numb.
leaves. illus. 31x24.5 cm. [With Bruce's New York type-foundry.
Specimens of printing types ... New York, 1882]
    Printed on one side of leaf only, printed pages facing each
other; with 13 sizes of Bruce's standard Roman types, from
great primer down to diamond, a few pages in each type.   [360]
    DLC   ICN

Degeorge, Léon, 1843-
... L'imprimerie en Europe aux XVe et XVIe siècles; les premières
productions typographiques et les premiers imprimeurs. Paris, E.
Paul, L. Huard et Guillemin, 1892. 2 prel. leaves, [vii]-xii,
137p., 1 leaf. 15.5 cm.   [361]
    CSmH   DLC   ICN   MB   MH   Eu-Fr-PN   Eu-Ge-LB   Eu-Ne-GK

Delandine, Antoine François, 1756-1820.
    Histoire abrégée de l'imprimerie, ou Précis sur son origine, son
établissement en France, les divers caractères qu'elle a employés,
les premiers livres qu'elle a produits ... et les ouvrages remarquables
dont elle fut l'objet; par Ant. Fr. Delandine ... Paris et Lyon [1814]
3 prel. leaves, 176p. 22 cm.
    "Cet ouvrage sert de Discours préliminaire au Catalogue raisonné
des livres imprimés de la Bibliothèque de Lyon [t. 1, 1816,
p. 1-176] Il en a été tiré cent exemplaires à part pour les
amis de l'auteur."

Also reprinted in Delandine's Mémoires bibliographiques et littéraires, 1817, p. 309-484.   [362]
DLC   MB   MH   Eu-Fr-PN   Eu-Ge-LB   Eu-Ge-LSb

Dell' invenzione della stampa, ecc. Adria, 1872.   4to.
Title from van der Linde, Geschichte der Erfindung ...   [363]

Delprat, Guillaume Henri Marie, 1791-1871.
    Dissertation sur l'art typographique contenant: un apperçu his-
torique de ses progrès durant le XV et le XVI siècle et des recherches
sur l'influence de cet art sur les lumières de l'espèce humaine.
Par G. H. M. Delprat ... Mémoire, qui a remporté le prix dans le concours proposé en 1816 par la Société provinciale des arts et des
sciences à Utrecht ... Utrecht, J. Altheer, 1820.   2 prel. leaves,
[3]-138p., 1 leaf.   22.5 cm.
    Added t.-p.: Over den voortgangen de verbreiding der boekdrukkunst
    in de vijftiende en zestiende seuw ...   [364]
    DLC   NN   Eu-Ne-GK

Desclosières, Gabriel.
    Biographie des grande inventeurs dans les arts et l'industrie.
Imprimerie: Lithographie: Hélliographie.   6e édition.   Paris, ca.
1885.   8vo.   [365]
    Eu-Fr-PN   Eu-Ge-LSb

Desormes, Émile, 1850-
    Notions de typographie à l'usage des écoles professionelles;
précédées d'un avant-propos sur l'origine de l'imprimerie, par É.
Desormes, directeur technique de l'école Gutenberg.   Paris, École
professionelle Gutenberg, 41, Rue Denfert-Rochereau, 41,
M DCCC LXXXVIII [1888].   513p.   24.5 cm.   [366]
    NN   Eu-Ge-LE

Didot, Ambroise Firmin, 1790-1876.
    Essai sur la typographie, par M. Ambroise Firmin Didot.   Extrait
du tome XXVI de l'Encyclopédie moderne.   Paris, Firmin Didot frères,
1851.   2 prel. leaves, col. 557-922.   4 plates.   24 cm.
    Bound with this are reprints of the author's articles on
    "Gutenberg", and "Estienne", from the Nouvelle biographie
    générale.
    Reissued 1882 under title: Histoire de la typographie.   [367]
    DLC   MB   NjP   Eu-De-BP   Eu-De-LBb   Eu-Fr-PC   Eu-Fr-PN
    Eu-Ge-LB   Eu-Ge-LL1   Eu-Ne-AVb

----   Histoire de la typographie, par Ambroise Firmin-Didot.
(Extrait de l'Encyclopédie moderne.)   Paris, Firmin-Didot et cie,
1882.   2 prel. leaves, [557]-922 col.   23 cm.   [368]
    DLC   MB   Eu-De-LBb

Disraeli.
The invention of printing.   [From his Amenities of literature]
Compositors' Chronicle, no. 13, Sept. 1841, p. 97; no. 14, Oct.,
p. 106.   [369]

Documenti inediti sull' inventione della stampa.   L'Arte della
Stampa, vol. 15, no. 36, 1885, p. 281-282.   [370]

[Doedes, Jacobus Isaac] 1817-1897.
Lourens Janszoon Coster, Johann Guttenberg en Peter Schöffer.
[Amsterdam, 1849]   p. [705]-741. 22.5 cm.
Caption title.
Signed: J. I. Doedes.
Reprint from De Gids, vol. 2, no. 12, 1849.   [371]
NNC   Eu-De-LBb   Eu-Ne-AVb

Donndorff, Johann August, 1754-1837.
Geschichte der Erfindungen in allen Theilen der Wissenschaften
und Künste von der ältesten bis auf die gegenwärtige Zeit.   In
alphabetischer Ordnung.   Von J. A. Donndorff ... Quedlinburg und
Leipzig, 1817-1821, bey Gottfried Basse.   6 vols.   21 cm.
vol. 1, p. 175-180: Buchdruckerkunst.   [372]
MH   Eu-Fr-PN   Eu-Ge-LB

Dosselaere, J. S. v.
De uitvinding der boekdrukkunst, en deszelfs invoer in Belgie.
1849.
Title from Peddie, R. A. Subject index of books published up
to and including 1880.   vol. 3, 1939.   [373]

Duff, Edward Gordon, 1863-1924.
Early printed books, by E. Gordon Duff.   London, K. Paul,
Trench, Trübner & co., ltd., 1893.   xii, 219p.   front., facsims.
21.5 cm. (Added t.p.: Books about books. Ed. by Alfred W.
Pollard.)   [374]
DLC   ICJ   MB   MH   MdBP   MiU-C   NN   NPV   NjP   RPB
Eu-Fr-PN   Eu-Ge-LB   Eu-Ge-LE   Eu-Ge-LSb   Eu-Ne-AVb
Eu-Ne-GK

Dumortier, Barthélemy Charles.
Note sur l'invention de l'imprimerie, lue à l'Académie des
sciences de Bruxelles, le 4 décembre 1841.   Bulletin de l'Académie
Royale de Bruxelles, vol. 8, 1842, p. 479-480.   [375]

Dupont, Paul François, 1796-1879.
Histoire de l'imprimerie, par Paul Dupont ... Paris, 1854.
2 vols.   18.5 cm.
Vol. 2, appendix: Législation, p. 521-536; Bibliographie,
p. 537-556; Tableau chronologique, p. 557-612.   [376]
DLC   ICJ   NN   Eu-Fr-PN   Eu-Ge-LB
1883 ed.: Eu-Fr-PN   Eu-Ge-LB
- 55 -

Dupont, Paul François, 1796-1879.
Notice historique sur l'imprimerie. Paris, Imprimerie Paul
Dupont, M DCCC XLIX [1849]. [vii], 233p. 26 cm.   [377]
DLC (Thacher Collection) NN NNC Eu-De-LBb Eu-Fr-PN
Eu-Ge-LSb Eu-Ne-GK

Dutuit, Eugène, 1807-1886.
Quel est l'inventeur de l'imprimerie? Le Livre, vol. 4, 1883,
p. 320-334.   [378]

[Duverger, Eugène.]
Comment l'imprimerie a été inventée. Paris, n.d. 20p.   [379]
Eu-Ge-LB

----   Histoire de l'invention de l'imprimerie par les monuments.
Paris, Imprimerie rue de Verneuil, n° 4, 1840. 16 numb. leaves,
2 leaves, 15p., 2 leaves incl. illus., 4 plates, 2 port. (1 col.)
3 facsim. 35.5x27 cm.
Title vignette.
Leaf following numbered leaf 16 is numbered 16*; pages [1], 9,
13 are signed 18, 19 and 20 respectively; page 15 is signed 21.
Plates partly printed on both sides.
"Édition in 4_0 sur Jésus velin superfin tirée à 850 exemplaires."
The polychromatic edition was limited to 150 copies. The plates
were broken after the 1000 copies were printed, as shown by im-
pressions on the final leaf.
Also issued at Strassburg by Treuttel & Würtz.
Half-title: Album typographique éxécuté à l'occasion du jubilé
européen de l'invention de l'imprimerie.
"Les autorités": p. [13]-15.   [380]
DLC ICJ MB NN Eu-Fr-PN Eu-Ge-LB Eu-Ge-LE Eu-Ge-LSb
Eu-Ne-AVb Eu-Ne-GK

An early Spanish notice of the invention of printing. Book
Worm (Berjeau), vol. 4, Sept. 1869, p. 129-151.
A colophon found in Alfonso de la Torre: Vision delectabile de
la philosophia y de las artes liberales, etc.   [381]

Ebert, Friedrich Adolph, 1791-1834.
[On the invention of printing.] (In Allgemeine Encyclopädie der
Wissenschaften und Künste von genannten Schriftstellern bearbeitet.
Leipzig, Brockhaus, 1818-1850. vol. 14, p. 224-226)   [382]

----   Zwischenwort über die streitige Erfindungsgeschichte der Buchdruckerkunst. (In Ueberlieferungen zur Geschichte, Literatur und
Kunst der Vor- und Mitwelt. Dresden, Walthersche Buchhandlung,
1826-1827. vol. 1, no. 13, p. 120-139)   [383]
DLC

Egger, Auguste Émile, 1813-1885.
    Histoire du livre depuis ses origines jusqu'à nos jours, par
E. Egger ... Paris, J. Hetzel et c^{ie} [1880]   2 prel. leaves, [vii]-
xi, 323p.   18.5 cm.   ([Collection Hetzel] Bibliothèque d'édu-
cation et de récréation)   [384]
    DLC   Eu-De-BP   Eu-Ge-LE

    Erfindung der Buchdruckerkunst.   Allgemeine Zeitung, no. 359,
Dec. 12, 1825.   [385]

    Die Erfindung der Buchdruckerkunst.   Allgemeiner Anzeiger,
no. 141, 1900, p. 7.   [386]

    Die Erfindung der Buchdruckerkunst.   Hamburgische Lesefrüchte,
Apr.-May 1840.
    Title from Mohr, Jubelfeste.   [387]

    Die Erfindung der Buchdruckerkunst.   Eine Allegorie in freien
Versen.   [Signed: B.] Protest. Kirchen- und Schulblatt, June 1840.
    Title from Mohr, Jubelfeste.   [388]

    Die Erfindung der Buchdruckerkunst.   Gedicht.   Indicateur de
Strasbourg, no. 37, 1840.
    [Signed: F........r]
    Title from Mohr, Jubelfeste.   [389]

Faccio, Domenico.
    Notizie storico-critico-tipografico-bibliografiche di Guten-
berg, Fust e Schoeffer, primi inventori della stampa.   Padova,
Coi tipi del Seminario, 1844.   96p.   23 cm.   [390]
    ICN   IU   NN

Falk, Franz, 1840-1909.
    Zur Erfindungsgechichte der Buchdruckerkunst.   Mainz, 1883.
8vo.   [391]
    Eu-De-LBb

Falkenstein, Constantin Karl, 1801-1855.
    Geschichte der Buchdruckerkunst in ihrer Entstehung und Aus-
bildung, von Dr. Karl Falkenstein ... Ein Denkmal zur vierten
Säcularfeier der Erfindung der Typographie.   Mit einer reichen
Sammlung in Holz und Metall geschnittener Facsimiles der seltensten Holztafeldrucke, Nachbildungen von Typen alter berühmter
Officinen und Proben von Kunstdrucken nach den neuesten Erfindungen unserer Zeit.   Leipzig, B. C. Teubner, 1840.   xiv, 16p.,
1 leaf, 406p., 1 leaf.   illus., plates, facsims. (part col., part
fold.)   27.5 cm.   [392]
    CSmH   DLC   MB   NN   NNGr   NjN   Eu-De-BP   Eu-Fr-PN
    Eu-Ge-LB   Eu-Ge-LP   Eu-Ge-LSb   Eu-Ne-AVb

Falkenstein, Constantin Karl, 1801-1855.
   Geschichte der Buchdruckerkunst in ihrer Enstehung und Ausbildung,
von Dr. Karl Falkenstein ... Ein Denkmal zur vierten Säcular-Feier der
Erfindung der Typographie. Mit einer reichen Sammlung in Holz und
Metall geschnittener Facsimiles der seltensten Holztafeldrucke, Nachbildungen von Typen alter berühmter Officinen und Proben von Kunstdrucken nach den neusten Erfindungen unserer Zeit.   2. unveränderte
Aufl.   Leipzig, B. G. Teubner, 1856.   iv, 406p.   illus., plates
(part col., part fold.)   facsims. (part col., part fold.)
29x22.5 cm   [393]
   DLC   NN   NjP   Eu-Ge-LB   Eu-Ge-LSb

Faulmann, [Johann Christoph] Karl, 1835-1894.
   Die Erfindung der Buchdruckerkunst, nach den neuesten Forschungen.
Dem deutschen Volke dargestellt von Professor Karl Faulmann ... Mit
36 in den Text gedruckten Abbildungen und einer Stammtafel der Familie
Gänsfleisch-Gutenberg.   Wien [etc.] A. Hartleben, 1891.   viii, 156p.
illus., facsims., fold. tab.   23.5 cm.   [394]
   DLC   ICJ   MB   MdBP   NNC   Eu-Fr-PN   Eu-Ge-LB   Eu-Ge-LSb
   Eu-Ne-GK

----   Histoire de l'imprimerie.   Bibliographie de Belgique, 1883,
p. 2-10.   [395]

----   Illustrirte Geschichte der Buchdruckerkunst, mit besonderer
Berücksuchtigung ihrer technischen Entwicklung bis zur Gegenwart.
Von Karl Faulmann ... Mit 14 Tafeln in Farbendruck, 12 Beilagen und
380 in den Text gedruckten Illustrationen.   Wien [etc.] A. Hartleben,
1882.   2 prel. leaves, viii, 806p.   illus., plates (part col.)
fold. geneal. tab., facsims. (part col.)   24 cm.   [396]
   DLC   ICJ   MH   NjP   PPeSchw   Eu-De-BP   Eu-De-LBb
   Eu-Ne-AVb   Eu-Ne-GK   Eu-Sz-BeG

----   Neue Untersuchungen über die Entstehung der Buchstaben-
schrift, und die Person des Erfinders.   Wien, 1876.   8vo.   [397]
   NN   Eu-Ge-LB   Eu-Ge-LSb

   The first printer.   Book Worm (London), vol. 2, Feb. 1889,
p. 79.   [398]

Foggi, C. A.
   Origine dell' arte della stampa.   Discorso letto del circolo
fra i tipografi di Firenze, Civelli, 1877.   16p.   8vo.
   Title from Bibliotheca bibliografica Italica.   vol. 1, 1889. [399]

Fournier, Henri, 1800-1888.
   The introduction of printing; translated from the French by
Jessie E. Ringwalt.   Printers' Circular, vol. 5, no. 8, Oct. 1870,
p. 321-323.   [400]

Fournier, Henri, 1800-1888.
    Traité de la typographie.   Paris, 1826.   8vo.   [401]
    Eu-Ge-LP

---- ----   2d éd.   Corrigée et augmentée.
Tours, Ad. Mame et Cie., 1854.   xii, 408p.   17 cm.   [402]
    ICN   Eu-Ge-LE   Eu-Ge-LP

---- ----   3d éd.   1870.   492p.   22 cm.   [403]
    ICN   Eu-De-BP

---- ----   4th éd., entièrement revue et augmentée par Arthur
Viot. Paris, Garnier frères, 1904.   vi, 515p.   illus.
18.5 cm.   [404]
    DLC   ICJ   Eu-Ge-LP

Frank, Jos.
    Die Erfindung der Buchdruckerkunst.   Gymnasium, vol. 18, 1900,
col. 706.   [405]

Fresenius, J. F. Th.
    Zur Geschichte der Erfindung des Buchdrucks ... Von J. F. Th.
Fresenius ... Frankfurt am Main, 1840.   39, [1]p.   20 cm.
    Programm--Mittelschule, Frankfurt am Main.
    No. 2 of a vol. of pamphlets lettered: Vermischte Schriften.   [406]
    DLC   ICN   Eu-De-LBb   Eu-Ge-LSb

Fritsch, Friedrich.
    Geschichte der Buchdruckerkunst.   Ein kleines Denkmal, den
Koryphäen derselben geweiht von Friedrich Fritsch ... Nordhausen,
E. F. Fürst, 1840.   viii, 128p.   front. (port.), plate.
17.5 cm.   [407]
    NNC   Eu-De-LBb   Eu-Fr-PN

[Galeati, Paolo]
    Lettura ... sulla invenzione della stampa.   [A jeu d'esprit by
Paolo Galeati] Imola, Tipografia di I. Galeati e figlio, 1890.
3p.   8vo.   [408]
    Eu-Ge-LB

---- ----   Imola, Galeati, 1907.   5p.   4to.   [409]
    Eu-De-BP

Geliger, P.
    Die Erfindung der Buchdruckerkunst.   Litterarisches Echo,
1900, p. 1386-1387.   [410]

Giliberti, Francesco.
    Studi storici sulla tipografia intorno l'origine dell'arte
stampa del tipografo Francesco Giliberti. Palermo, Stabilimento

tipografico dell'autore, 1870.   xviii, [19]-145p.   15.5 cm.   [411]
DLC   IU   MiU   Eu-Ge-LB

Graesse, J. G. T.
Geschichte der Entstehung der Buchdruckerkunst.   Allgemeine
Literaturgeschichte, vol. 3, 1852, p. 1 et sqq.   [412]

Grant, George.
Historical account of useful inventions and scientific discoveries:
being a manual of instruction and entertainment.   London, 1852.
12mo.   [413]
    RPB   Eu-Ge-LB   Eu-Ge-LSb

Gutch, John Mathew, 1776-1861.
    Observations, or notes, upon the writings of the ancients, upon
the materials which they used, and upon the introduction of the art
of printing; being four papers read before the Philosophical and
literary society, annexed to the Bristol institution, at their
evening meetings in 1827. By John Mathew Gutch.   Bristol, Printed
by J. M. Gutch, 1827.   170p.   26 cm.
    "Only twenty-five copies printed, for private distribution."   [414]
    DLC   Eu-Ge-LB   Eu-Ge-LSb

    Gutenberg, Fust and Schöffer, oder kurze Geschichte der Erfindung
der Buchdruckerkunst in Mainz.   Mit Peter Schöffers Bildniss.   1821.
Folio.
    Title from van der Linde, Geschichte der Erfindung ...   [415]

Hahn, R.
    Gutenberg's Erfindung.   Die Umschau no. 26, 1900, p. 501-505.   [416]

Hall, Charles Carter.
    The art of printing, historical and practical ... with biograph-
ical sketches of its founders. Sheffield, Trinitarians, 1860.
16mo.
    Title from van der Linde, Geschichte der Erfindung ...   [417]

Hallam, Henry, 1777-1859.
    The invention of printing.   (In his Literary essays and char-
acters ... London, 1852.   p. 76)   [418]
    IU   MB   NN   Eu-Ge-LB

Hansard, Thomas Curson, 1776-1833.
    Typographia: an historical sketch of the origin and progress of
the art of printing; with practical directions for conducting every
department in an office: with a description of stereotype and lithography.   Illustrated by engravings, biographical notices, and portraits. By T. C. Hansard.   London, Printed for Baldwin, Cradock,

and Joy, 1825.   1 prel. leaf, xvi [7], 939, [25]p., 1 leaf.
front., illus., plates, ports.   24 cm.   [419]
    DLC   ICJ   MB   MdBP   NN   NjP   Eu-Fr-PN   Eu-Ge-LB
    Eu-Ge-LP

Hansard, Thomas Curson, 1813-1891.
    The art of printing, its history and practise from the days
of John Gutenberg, By T. C. Hansard, esq.   Edinburgh, A. and C.
Black, 1851.   vii, 235p.   illus., fold. facsims., fold. plates.
21 cm.
    Issued in 1841 under title: Treatise on printing and type-
    founding ... From the 7th edition of the Encyclopaedia
    brittanica.
    Includes a chapter on lithography by W. Nichol.   [420]
    DLC   ICJ   ICN   MB   MdBP   NjP   Eu-Fr-PN   Eu-Ge-LB
    Eu-Ge-LSb

----   The history and art of printing, copperplate printing, and
typefounding, and on lithographic printing.   Edinburgh, 1840.
8vo.   [421]
    ICN

Hartshorne, Charles Henry, 1802-1865.
    The origin of printing: being the substance of a lecture de-
livered to the Northampton Mechanics institute, December 1851.
By the Rev. Charles Henry Hartshorne, ... Northampton, T. Phillips,
printer, [1852]   16p.   21.5 cm.   [422]
    ICJ   Eu-Ge-LB   Eu-Ge-LSb

Hawes, Stephen.
    Bibliography; or the history of the origin and progress of
printing and bookmaking, embracing the various substitutes for
printed literature, the invention of type, paper, and printing.
Newspaper and book publishing in all their varieties; rare old
books and mss., the discovery and progress of engraving,
lithography, photography, photo-engraving, printing in colours,
and a general review of the literature of the day.   New York,
1874.   8vo.
    Title from Bigmore & Wyman.   [423]

Heffner, L.
    Zur Geschichte der Erfinder der Buchdruckerkunst.   Archiv
des Historischen Vereins von Unterfranken und Aschaffenburg
(Würzburg), vol. 14, 1863, p. 168-174.   [424]

Helbig, Henri Antoine, 1813-
    Examen rapide des prétentions que Strasbourg et Harlem ont
à l'honneur d'avoir inventé l'imprimerie, par H. Helbig.
Bruxelles, F. Heussner, 1855.   15p.   24 cm.

Reprint from Bulletin du Bibliophile Belge, vol. 11 (2d ser.,
vol. 2), 1855, p. 443-455.   [425]
ICJ

Helbig, Henri Antoine, 1813-
    Examen rapide des prétentions que Strasbourg et Harlem ont à
l'honneur d'avoir inventé l'imprimerie, par H. Helbig.   Reissued
in mimeographed form, Chicago, Chicago club of printing house craftsmen, 1941.   cover-title, 14 numb. leaves. 28 cm. (Contributions
to materials on the history of printing, no. 4)   [426]
    CSmH   DLC   IC   ICU   MH   NN   NNC

----   Notes et dissertations relatives à l'histoire de l'imprimerie,
par H. Helbig.   Bruxelles, F. Heussner [1863].   67p.   25.5 cm.
    Reprint from Bulletin du Bibliophile Belge, vol. 18 (2d ser.,
    vol. 9), 1862, p. 26, 106, 256, 356.   [427]
    NNC   Eu-De-LBb   Eu-Fr-PC   Eu-Ne-AVb

Hellwald, Ferdinand von.
    Der Mainz-Harlemer Buchdruckerstreit.   Allgemeine Zeitung,
Feb. 12, 1871.   Same, Börsenblatt für den Deutschen Buchhandel,
vol. 38, no. 42, 1871, p. 478-479.   [428]

    Histoire abrégée des inventions et des découvertes importantes
faites en Europe depuis l'ère chrétienne jusqu'au 19e siècle;
ouvrage couronné par la Société pour l'Instruction élémentaire.
6me édition.   A Bruxelles, et dans les principales villes de
l'étranger, chez tous les libraires . 1843. 131p. 12.5 cm.
    L'invention de l'imprimerie: p. 49.   [429]
    MB   Eu-Ge-LSb

    History of printing.   Guide to Knowledge (London), Oct. 1833. [430]

    History of printing.   1.   Its origin and early improvements.
Printer, vol. 1, 1858, p. 1-2.   [431]

    History of printing.   Printer, vol. 6, 1865, p. 82-83, 98-100,
130-131.   [432]

    History of printing.   Woodcock's Printer & Lithographer, no.
16, Nov. 1882, p. 1051.   [433]

    History of printing from 15th to 19th century.   Penny Magazine,
vol. 6, 1837, p. 501.   [434]

    A history of the art of printing.   [Sections on the invention
of printing] Typographic Messenger, vol. 5, no. 1, Jan. 1870,
p. 1-4; no. 2, Apr., p. 17-18; no. 3, July, p. 33-34.   [435]

Höcker, Oskar, 1840-1894.
    Die Erfindung der Buchdruckerkunst. Kulturgeschichtliche
Erzählung aus dem Mainzer Stadtleben im 15. Jahrhundert. Stuttgart, Süddeutsch Verlags-Institut, 1888.   iii, 147p.   8vo.   [436]

Hoffmann, F. R.
    Die Erfindung des Bücherdruckes als Sagenstoff. Journal für
Buchdruckerkunst, no. 38, 1864, col. 302-305.   [437]

----   Materialien zu einer Geschichte der Typographie. Journal
für Buchdruckerkunst, no. 1, 1855, col. 1-7.   [438]

----   Ueber die Anfänge der Kunst des Bücherdruckes. Journal
für Buchdruckerkunst, no. 4, 1862, col. 25-29.   [439]

Humphreys, Henry Noel, 1810-1879.
    A history of the art of printing from its invention to its
widespread development in the middle of the sixteenth century.
Preceded by a short account of the origin of the alphabet and
the successive methods of recording events and multiplying
manuscript books before the invention of printing ... London,
B. Quaritch, 1867.   224p.   100 plates.   35x24 cm.   [440]
    DLC (Thacher Collection) ICJ   ICU   IU   MH   NN   Eu-Ge-LB
    Eu-Ge-LSb   Eu-Ne-AVb   Eu-Ne-GK

---- ---- [2d. ed] Illustrated by 100 fac-similes in photo-
lithography, executed under the direction of the author ...
London, B. Quaritch, 1868.   xii p., 1 leaf, 216p. 100 plates.
35 cm.   [441]
    CSmH   DLC   I   ICJ   MBAt   MWA   MdBP   Eu-De-LBb   Eu-Fr-PN
    Eu-Ge-LB

Hupp, Otto, 1859-
    Zur Geschichte der Erfindung der Buchdruckerkunst. Zentral-
blatt für Bibliothekswesen, vol. 2, 1885, p. 86-90.   [442]

    The invention of printing. American Bookmaker, vol. 10,
No. 4,   April 1890, p. 98.   [443]

    Invention of printing. Foreign Quarterly Review, vol. 19,
1837, p. 118-134.   [444]

    The invention of printing. Inland Printer, vol. 1, no. 5,
Feb. 1884, p. 5-6.   [445]

    Invention of printing. Popular Science Monthly, vol. 53,
July 1898, p. 429.   [446]

    The invention of printing. Printers' Ink, vol. 24, no. 10
Sept. 1898, p. 12.   [447]

The invention of printing; the beginning of bookmaking. <u>American</u>
<u>Bookmaker</u>, vol. 11, no. 3, Sept. 1890, p. 57-58.   [448]

Ivry, C. d'.
    L'invention de l'imprimerie d'après Munster.   <u>Bibliophile Fran-</u>
<u>cais</u>, vol. 6, Aug. 1872, p. 247-248.   [449]

    Izobretenie knigopechataniĩa.   (In Vseobshchaĩa istoriĩa s IV
stoletiĩa do nashego vremeni. Sostavl. pod rukovodstvom Ernesta
Lavissa, Alf. Rambo.   Perevod V. Nevedomskogo, M. K. Soldatenkova.
1897.   vol. 3, p. 665-667)   [450]
    Eu-Ru-MLe

Janson, Henri, 1741-1812.
    De l'invention de l'imprimerie, ou Analyse des deux ouvrages
publiés sur cette matière par M. Meerman.   Suivi d'une notice
chronologique et raisonée des livres avec et sans date, imprimée
avant l'année 1501 dans les dix-sept provinces des Pays-Bas, par M.
Jacques Visser; et augmentée d'environ deux cents articles par
l'éditeur. Avec une planche.   Paris, F. Schoell, 1809.   xxiv,
392p. 1 facsim. 21 cm.
    Dedication signed: Jansen.   [451]
    ICJ   Eu-Fr-PN   Eu-Ge-LB   Eu-Ge-LSb

Jellonschek, Anton.
    Geschichtliche Nachrichten über die Erfindung, Ausbildung und
Verbreitung der Buchdruckerkunst.   Leipzig, 1874.   4to.
    Title from van der Linde, Geschichte der Erfindung ...   [452]

Jenks, O. S.
    The invention of printing.   <u>Inland Printer</u>, vol. 8, 1891,
p. 495-496, 591-592.   [453]

Johnson, John, 1777-1848.
    Typographia, or the Printers' instructor: including an account
of the origin of printing, with biographical notices of the printers
of England, from Caxton to the close of the sixteenth century:
a series of ancient and modern alphabets, and Domesday characters:
together with an elucidation of every subject connected with the art.
By J. Johnson, printer ... London, Longman, Hurst, Rees, Orme, Brown &
Green, 1824.   2 vols.   fronts. (ports.) illus., plates. 28.5 cm.
    Added t.-p., engraved.   [454]
    DLC   I   ICJ   MB   MNBedf   NN   NjP   Eu-Fr-PN   Eu-Ge-LB
    Eu-Ge-LE

Karlstein, O. von.
    Die Buchdruckerkunst, ihre Vorläufer und Entwicklungen. <u>Alte</u>
<u>und Neue Welt</u>, vol. 34, 1900, p. 577-587.   [455]

Keufer, A.
    Notice sur la découverte de l'imprimerie.   Montevrain, 1889.
8vo.   [456]
    Eu-Ge-LSb

Kiesewetter, L.
    Gedrängte Geschichte der Buchdruckerkunst von ihrer Erfindung
bis auf unsere Tage.   Bearbeitet von Dr. L. Kiesewetter.
Glogau, Carl Flemming, 1840.   iv, 85p.   table.   21 cm.   [457]
    NNC   NNGr   Eu-De-LBb   Eu-Fr-PN   Eu-Ge-LB   Eu-Ge-LSb

Koehler, Woldemar, 1871-
    Zur Entwicklungsgeschichte des Buchgewerbes von Erfindung
der Buchdruckerkunst bis zur Gegenwart.   Nationalökonomisch-
statistisch dargestellt von Dr. W. Köhler.   Gera-Untermhaus
F. E. Köler, 1896.   2 prel. leaves, [vi], 183p.   26.5 cm.   [458]
    ICJ   MH   Eu-Ge-LB   Eu-Ge-LSb   Eu-Ne-AVb

    Kogda i gde izobreteno knigopechatanie.   Finskii Vestnik,
part 2, no. 2, 1847, p. 52-53.   [459]

Kuntz, C.
    Die Erfindung der Buchdruckerkunst, ihre ersten Anfänge und
ihre Entwicklungen, nebst einem Berichte über die vierte
Säkularfeier dieser Erfindung in Strassburg; ein Gedenk- und
Lesebüchlein für Volk und Schule ... Strassburg, Levrault, 1840.
180p.   24mo.   [460]
    Eu-De-LBb   Eu-Fr-PN   Eu-Ge-LSb

La Serna Santander, Charles Antoine de, 1752-1813.
    Dictionnaire bibliographique choisi du quinzième siècle ou
Description par ordre alphabétique des éditions les plus rares et
les plus recherchées du quinzième siècle, précédé d'un Essai historique sur l'origine de l'imprimerie, ainsi que sur l'histoire de son
établissement dans les villes, bourgs, monastères et autres en-
droits de l'Europe ... Bruxelles, J. Tarte, 1805-1807.   3 vols.
22 cm.
    The "Essai historique" was also published separately in 1805.   [461]
    DLC   ICJ   ICN   MB   NN   NjN   NjP   Eu-Fr-PN   Eu-Ge-LB.

----   An historical essay on the origin of printing, translated
from the French of M. de la Serna Santander.   Newcastle, S.
Hodgson, 1819.   xiv, 93, [1]p.   19.5 cm.
    "Advertisement" signed: T. H. [i.e. Thomas Hodgson]
    Translation of "Essai historique sur l'origine de l'imprimerie",
preface to the author's Dictionnaire bibliographique choisi du
quinzième siècle, Bruxelles, 1805-07", and also issued separately.   [462]
    DLC   ICN   MB   MH   NN   Eu-Fr-PN   Eu-Ge-LSb

[Lacroix, Paul] 1806-1884.
Curiosités de l'histoire des arts, par P. L. Jacob, bibliophile
[pseud.] ... Paris, A. Delahays, 1858.   2 prel. leaves, 410p., 1 leaf.
17 cm.
Each article followed by a bibliography of the subject treated.
Contents include: Origine de l'imprimerie.   [463]
DLC   MB   NN   Eu-Fr-PN

----   Histoire de l'imprimerie et des arts et professions, qui se
rattachent à la typographie, comprenant l'histoire des anciennes
corporations et confréries d'écrivains, d'imprimeurs, de libraires,
etc. depuis leur fondation jusqu'á leur suppression en 1789.   Paris,
Edouard Fournier et Ferdinand Seré, 1851.   160p.   27 cm.   [464]
NN   Eu-Fr-PN   Eu-Ge-LB

---- ----   2d ed. 1852.   160p.   illus., 15 plates (facsims.)
27 cm.   [465]
DLC   ICJ   MB   MH   NN   NjN   NjP   Eu-Fr-PN

----   Imprimerie.   (In his Le moyen-âge et la renaissance ... Paris,
1848-1851.   vol. 5)   [466]
DLC   ICJ   MH   NN

Lambinet, Pierre, 1742-1813.
Origine de l'imprimerie, d'après les titres authentiques, l'opinion
de M. Daunou, et celle de M. van Praet; suivie des établissemens de
cet art dans la Belgique et de l'Histoire de la stéréotypie; ornée
de calques, de portraits, et d'écussons, par P. Lambinet ... Paris,
H. Nicolle, 1810.   2 vols.   illus., plate, port., facsims. (1 fold.)
20.5 cm.
New edition of the author's Recherches historiques, littéraires
et critiques sur l'origine de l'imprimerie [1799]   [467]
DLC   ICJ   ICN   MB   MdBP   NN   Eu-De-BP   Eu-De-LBb   Eu-Fr-PN
Eu-Ge-LB   Eu-Ge-LE   Eu-Ge-LL1   Eu-Ge-LSb   Eu-Ne-AVb   Eu-Ne-GK

Legouvé, Ernst.
La découverte de l'imprimerie, pièce de vers qui a remporté le
prix de poésie décerné par l'Académie française dans sa séance publique annuelle de la Saint-Louis 1829 ... Paris, Firmin-Didot frères,
1829.   38p.   8vo.   [468]
Eu-Fr-PN   Eu-Ge-LB

[Lemoine, Henry] 1756-1812.
Typographical antiquities.   Origin and history of the art of
printing, foreign and domestic ... from the infancy of printing, to
the end of the eighteenth century, extracted from the best authorities, by a late bibliopolist.   2d ed., cor. and enl. by T. A. of
the Inner Temple, esq. London, Printed for the editor, 1813.
cx, 111-142, [2]p.   19 cm.
First published 1797.

Author's preface signed: H. Lemoine.
Text from the same type as the 1st edition; preface is slightly
enlarged, but no other alterations have been made.   [469]
DLC   MBAt   Eu-Ge-LP

Levol, Florimond.
    L'invention de l'imprimerie, poème.   Paris, J. Pinard, 1829.
20p.   8vo.   [470]
    Eu-Fr-PN   Eu-Ge-LSb

Lichtenberger, Johann Friedrich, 1743-1831.
    Geschichte der Erfindung der Buchdruckerkunst zur Ehrenrettung
Strassburgs und vollständiger Widerlegung der Sagen von Harlem,
dargestellt von Johann Friedrich Lichtenberger, Professor emeritus
am Strassburgischen Gymnasium.   Mit einem Vorberichte von Hrn.
Johann Godfried Schweighäuser, Professor an der Strassburgischen
Akademie und Correspondent des Instituts.   Nebst Gutenbergs Brust-
bild und sechs Abdrucken von original Holztafeln.   Strassburg,
Verlag von J. H. Heitz, Buchdrucker und Buchhändler; Leipzig, in
Commission bei J. F. Gleditsch, Buchhändler, 1825.   vi, 90p.
22 cm.   [471]
    ICN   Eu-De-LBb   Eu-Fr-PN   Eu-Ge-LB   Eu-Ge-LP

----   Histoire de l'invention de l'imprimerie pour servir de
défense à la ville de Strasbourg contre les prétensions de Harlem,
par J. F. Lichtenberger ... Avec une préface de M. J. G. Schweighaeuser
... Accompagnés d'un portrait de Gutenberg et de huit planches origi-
nales gravées sur bois.   Strasbourg, J. H. Heitz, 1825.   2 prel.
leaves, [iii]-viii, 100p. incl. facsims. front. (port.) 21 cm.
    Translated from the German.   [472]
    DLC   ICJ   ICN   IaU   Eu-Fr-PN   Eu-Ge-LB   Eu-Ge-LP
    Eu-Ge-LSb   Eu-No-GK

----   Initia typographica illustravit Io. Frid. Lichtenberger
... Argentorati, Treuttel et Würtz, 1811.   viii, [2], 259, [1]p.
22.5 cm.   [473]
    DLC   ICJ   ICN   MB   MWA   NN   Eu-Fr-PN   Eu-Ge-LB
    Eu-Ge-LP

----   Réfutation des auteurs qui attribuent l'invention de l'imprimerie à L. Coster.   Manuscript in folio.
    Title from Mohr, Jubelfeste: "The author examines the most
important incunabula and disagrees with Meermann and Koning.
The original, which has not yet been published, is in the
possession of my friend Ferd. Reiber, in Strassburg; a copy of
the same is in my possession."   [474]

Loftie, William John.
    The first printers and their art. Cassell's Magazine, n.s.,
vol. 2, 1870, p. 93-95.   [475]

Lorck, Carl Berendt, 1814-1905.
   Handbuch der Geschichte der Buchdruckerkunst von Carl B. Lorck ...
Leipzig, Verlag von J. J. Weber, 1882-1883.   2 vols.   23.5 cm.   [476]
   IU   LH   MdBP   NjP   Eu-De-BP   Eu-De-LBb   Eu-Fr-PN   Eu-Ge-LB
   Eu-Ge-LSb   Eu-Ne-AVb

Lozzi, Carlo, 1829-
   Delle origini della stampa; saggio storico-critico di Carlo Lozzi.
Edizione di 100 esemplari, due dei quali in carta di lusso, uno per
l'Italia e uno per la Germania, anticamente consociate nella invenzione della stampa ed ora in una grande idea nazionale.   Estratto
dal Giornale della Società di Letture e conversazione scientifiche
di Genova.   Genova, Tip. del Movimento de T. P. Ricci, 1881.
cover-title, [3]-24p.   21.5 cm.   [477]
   ICN   Eu-Ge-LB

----   Dell inventore della stampa, secondo i piu recenti studi
storici e critici su antichi e nuovi documenti.   Bibliofilo,
vol. 5, 1884, p. 33-35, 67-72.   [478]

Macintosh, Charles A.
   Popular outlines of the press, ancient and modern: or, A brief
sketch of the origin and progress of printing, and its introduction into this country: with a notice of the newspaper press.
By Charles A. Macintosh.   London, Wertheim, Macintosh, and Hunt,
1859.   xii, 224p.   17.5 cm.   [479]
   DLC   ICJ   NjP   Eu-Ge-LB

[Madden, John Patrick Auguste] 1808-1889.
   Lettres d'un bibliographe ... [1.--6. série]   Versailles [etc.]
1868-86.   6 vols. and 2 atlases in 4 vols.   illus., plates (part
col.) ports., plans, tables, facsims.   25 cm.
   Ser. 4-6 have added t.-p., engraved.
   Imprint varies: ser. 1-3 (1868-74) Versailles, Impr. de ,E. Aubert
   (cover imprint: Paris, Tross).--ser. 4-6 (1875-86) Paris, E.
   Leroux (added t.-p.: Paris, Impr. Lemercier & cie)
   Six series of studies in the early history and technique of
   printing based largely upon contemporary manuscript sources
   and upon minute examination and analysis of specimens of early
   printing, many of them in possession of the author.   ("He
   utilizes the paleography of the pretypographic era to interpret
   and to illustrate the yet hidden subjects connected with the
   incunabula and their immediate successors." --Bigmore & Wyman)
   Many of the letters are devoted to the printing done at the
   monastery of Weidenbach in Cologne by the Brothers of the
   Common life.
   Most of the material in ser. 3-6 appeared first in La Typologie
   Tucker. (Paris, 1874-86)
   Titles vary slightly, the author's name not appearing on t.-p. of
   ser. 1-4.   [480]
   DLC   ICJ   Eu-De-LBb   Eu-Fr-PN   Eu-Ge-LB   Eu-Ne-AVb

Maini, L.
    Intorno la dissertazione sulla invenzione della stampa del Prof.
A. Zanghellini. Osservazioni critiche. Napoli, 1868. 8vo. [481]
    Eu-Ge-LSb

Malyshev, V.
    Pervye shagi pechatnago slova na Zapade. Kolos'íà, no. 4,
1885, p. 33-58.   [482]

Mane, A.
    Invention de l'imprimerie, poëme, suivi de la Fête Dieu. Angers,
1813. 8vo.   [483]
    Eu-Ge-LB   Eu-Ge-LSb

Manceaux, A.
    L'origine de l'imprimerie. Bibliographie de Belgique, 1888,
95; 1889, p. 2-16.   [484]

Marouze, Paul Hecquet de.
    Histoire de l'imprimerie. Paris, 1862. 8vo.
    Title from Bigmore & Wyman.   [485]

Marshall, David.
    Printing; an account of its invention and of William Caxton,
the first English printer. By David Marshall, esq., advocate.
London and Paris, A. Quantin & co., London, 18 Throgmorton
Street, 1877. 4 prel. leaves, 81, [3]p. 29.5 cm.   [486]
    MB   MH   Eu-Ge-LP

Meschina, Carlo E.
    L'invenzione della stampa.   (In Indicatore generale del
commercio. Napoli, E. Pietrocola, 1885)
    Title from Bibliotheca bibliografica Italica, vol. 1, 1889. [487]

Metz, Friedrich.
    Geschichte des Buchhandels und der Buchdruckerkunst, von Fried-
rich Metz. Darmstadt, Jonghaus, 1835. 2 vols. in 1. 21.5 cm. [488]
    DLC   ICJ   NN   NjP   Eu-Fr-PN   Eu-Ge-LSb   Eu-Ne-AVb

Meurling, Magn. G.
    Dissertatio [acad. praes. auct., resp. Petr. Ad. Kjellberg] de
ortu et progressu artis typographicae. Lundae, litteris Berlin-
gianis, 1805. 20p. 4to.   [489]
    Eu-De-LBb   Eu-Sv-SK

Middleton-Wake, Charles H.
    The invention of printing, a series of four lectures delivered
in the Lent term of 1897. By the Rev. Charles H. Middleton-Wake.
London, J. Murray, 1897. xii, 175, [1]p. xiv facsims. (incl.

front.)   23x18 cm.   [490]
    CSmH   ICJ   ICN   IaU   MB   NN   Eu-Ge-LSb

Mira, Giuseppe Maria.
    Origine e propagazione della stampa.   (In his Manuale teorico-
pratico di bibliografia.   Palermo, Piola, 1861-1863.   2 vols.)   [491]
    Eu-De-LBb   Eu-Ge-LB

Mohr, Louis, 1828-1886.
    Über die Erfindung und Einführung der Buchdruckerkunst im
Allgemeinen.   (In Festschrift zur Säcularfeier der ersten Buchdruckerei von St. Polten.   St. Polten, 1882.   Part 1)   [492]

Møller, Peder Ludvig, 1814-1865.
    Kort fremstilling af bogtrykkerkunstens historie ved P. L.
Møller ... Udgivet af Selskabet for trykkefrihedens brug.   Kjøbenhavn, Trykt, med Hurtigpresse, i Bianco Lunos bogtrykkeri, 1841.
2 prel. leaves, 235, 1p.   17 cm.
    p. 226-235: [Report on the jubilee of printing in the three
    Scandinavian countries]   [493]
    CtY   NN   Eu-De-LBb   Eu-Ge-LB

Mueller, H.
    Die Erfindung der Buchdruckerkunst.   Als Fortsetzung der Abhand-
lund über Menschenwürde und Menschenbildung in no. 47 des Sontags-
blattes.   Sonntagsblatt (Hildesheim), no. 49, Dec. 5, 1824.   [494]

Munsell, Joel, 1808-1880.
    Outline of the history of printing, and sketches of the early
printers.   By Joel Munsell.   Albany, J. Munsell, 1839.   32p.
25 cm.   [495]
    DLC   MB   MNBedf   NN

    Neue Studien über die Geschichte der Erfindung der Buchdrucker-
kunst.   Börsenblatt für den Deutschen Buchhandel, vol. 67, no. 181,
1900, p. 5846-5848.   [496]

 - A new light on the invention of printing.   Inland Printer,
vol. 3, 1886, p. 700-701.   Same, Saturday Review, vol. 61, May
1886, p. 741-742.   [497]

    A new theory of the invention of printing.   Printer and
Bookmaker, vol. 29, Nov. 1899, p. 145.   [498]

Noronha, Tito Augusto Duarte de.
    Ensaios sôbre a história de imprensa.   Lisboa, 1857.
    Title from Der Buchdruck des 15. Jahrhunderts.   [499]

    Notable events in the history of printing.   American Biblio-
polist, vol. 8, no. 80, Apr. 1876, p. 34-38.   [500]

Origin and progress of printing. Monthly Review, vol. 155, 1841, p. 328.   [501]

Origin of printing. Printer, vol. 3, Feb. 1864, p. 53.   [502]

The origin of printing. Woodcock's Printers' and Lithographers' Weekly Gazette, vol. 12, Mar. 1878, p. 157.   [503]

L'origine della stampa a tipi mobili. L'Arte délla Stampa, vol. 14, no. 21, 1884, p. 161-162.   [504]

Origines de l'imprimerie. Magasin Pittoresque, vol. 25, no. 26, June 1857, p. 202-203; vol. 26, no. 24, June 1858, p. 186-188; no. 33, Aug., p. 262-264; no. 37, Sept., p. 193-194.   [505]

Ottley, William Young, 1771-1836.
   An inquiry concerning the invention of printing: in which the systems of Meerman, Heinecken, Santander, and Koning are reviewed; including also notices of the early use of wood-engraving in Europe, the block-books, etc.; by the late William Young Ottley ... With an introduction by J. Ph. Berjeau ... Illustrated with thirty-seven plates, and numerous wood-engravings. London, J. Lilly, 1863. xlii, 377p. illus., xxxv (i.e. 37) plates (2 double; incl. facsims.) 30 cm.
   The author died while the book was in press and the publication of the work was made impossible by the loss of the last sheet and the plates. These were discovered in 1863.   [506]
   DLC   ICJ   MB   MH   MdBP   NN   NjP   Eu-Ge-LP   Eu-Ne-GK

Pache, Constant.
   L'imprimerie, son invention, histoire et légende. Lausanne, Imprimerie Constant Pache - Varidel et cie. 5, Escaliers-du-Marché, 5. 1898. 3 prel. leaves, [7]-63p. 17 cm.
   "Cet opuscule, tiré à très petit nombre, n'est pas mis en vente."   [507]
   ICN

Paroy, Jean Philippe Gui le Gentil.
   Précis sur la stéréotypie, précédé d'un coup d'oeil rapide sur l'origine de l'imprimerie et de ses progrès. Paris, Impr. de Cosson, 1822. 32p. plates. 8vo.   [508]
   Eu-Fr-PN   Eu-Ge-LP

Payan-Dumoulin, Charles François Felix Ernest de.
   Recherches sur l'origine de l'imprimerie. Valence, 1841. 24p. 8vo.   [509]
   Eu-Fr-PN

Porthmann, Jules Louis Melchior, 1791-1820.
   Éloge historique de l'imprimerie, augmenté d'une réfutation des
deux ouvrages: Conspectus originum typographicarum (1761), et
Origines typographicae (1766), de M. Meerman.   Par Jules Porthmann.
[3. éd.]   Paris, A. Porthmann, 1836.   4 prel. leaves, 95 (i.e. 59)p.
27.5 cm.
   Page 59 wrongly numbered 95.
   First and second editions published 1810.--cf. preface.   [510]
   NNC   Eu-Fr-PN   Eu-Ge-LB   Eu-Ge-LP

---- Essai historique sur l'imprimerie.   Paris, 1810.   73p.
8vo.   [511]
   Eu-De-LBb   Eu-Fr-PN   Eu-Ge-LB

Prince, Carlos, 1836-1919.
   Los primeros ensayos del arte de la imprenta y los incunables,
por Carlos Prince.   Lima, Impreso en casa del autor, 1897.   x, 285,
[3]p.   front. (port.)   19.5 cm.
   "Edición de trescientos ejemplares."   [512]
   DLC   ICN

   The printing press.   Printer, vol. 1, no. 1, May 1858, p. 5   [513]

Quantin, Albert.
   Les origines de l'imprimerie et son introduction en Angleterre
par A. Quantin, d'après de récentes publications anglaises.   Paris,
A. Quantin et cie., 1877.   2 prel. leaves, 70, [2]p.   29x20 cm.
   In red borders, ruled.
   275 copies printed.
   Contents.--1. Premiers essais d'imprimerie.   Incunable.--2.
Haarlem et Laurent Coster.--3. Mayence et Jean Gutenberg.--4.
Faust et Schoeffer.--5. William Caxton.   [514]
   DLC   ICJ   MB   NN   RP   Eu-De-BP   Eu-Fr-PC   Eu-Fr-PN
   Eu-Ge-LB   Eu-Ge-LSb   Eu-Ne-AVb

R., J. F.
   Geschichte der Erfindung der Buchdruckerkunst.   Eine kurze für
Jedermann verständliche Darstellung.   Leipzig, Cleve, 1840.   16p.
illus.   8vo.   [515]
   Eu-De-LBb

Recchi, Enrico.
   L'arte della stampa.   Origine, lavori, materiali.   Relazione di
Enrico Recchi.   (Proto della Tipografia della Camera dei Deputati.)
Roma, Tip. Carlo Colombo, 1900.   84 leaves.   4to.   [516]
   Eu-Sz-BeG

Reed, Talbot Baines.
   The invention controversy. Bibliographical Society, London.
Transactions, vol. 3, 1895, p. 88-90.   [517]

---- The invention of printing. British Printer, vol. 3,
Nov.-Dec. 1890, p. 20.   [518]

Reiffenberg, Frédéric Auguste Ferdinand Thomas, baron de, 1794-1850.
   Découverte de l'imprimerie. Nouvelles Archives Historiques
des Pays-Bas, vol. 5, 1830, p. 316.   [519]

---- Notices sur l'histoire de l'invention de l'imprimerie et
tableau des noms des premiers imprimeurs dans les principales
villes de la Belgique et de la date de leurs premières impressions.
Annuaire de la Bibliothèque Royale de Belgique, vol. 1, 1840,
p. xxvii-xxxii.   [520]

Reuleaux, F.
   Le invenzione le arti e le industrie. Torino, ca. 1880. 4to.
   Translated from the German by C. Corradino.
   Vol. 1, part 2: Storia e fabricazione della carta, stampa,
   incisione, ecc.   [521]
   Eu-Ge-LSb

Ritschel von Hartenbach, J.
   Der Buchdruckerkunst Erfindung. Nebst einigen Betrachtungen
über den Nutzen und die Nachteile, welche seit ihrem Ursprunge aus
ihrer verschiedenen Anwendung entstanden sind. Sondershausen und
Leipzig, 1820. 8vo.   [522]
   Eu-Ge-LB

Rossi, Giovanni Bernardo de, 1742-1831.
   Dell'origine della stampa in tavole incise e di una antica e
sconosciuta edizione zilografica del dottore G. Bernardo de-Rossi
... Parma, Dalla Stamperia imperiale, 1811. 12p. 23.5 cm.   [523]
   DCU-H   NN   NNC   NjP   Eu-De-LBb   Eu-Ge-LB

Ruelens, Charles Louis, 1820-1890.
   La question de l'origine de l'imprimerie et le grand concile
typographique. Bruxelles, 1855.
   Reprint from Bulletin du Bibliophile Belge, vol. 11 (2d ser.,
   vol. 2), 1855, p. 1-18.   [524]
   Eu-De-LBb   Eu-Ge-LSb

---- ---- Reissued in mimeographed form, Chicago, Chicago club
of printing house craftsmen, 1941. cover-title, 18 numb. leaves.
28 cm. (Contributions to materials on the history of printing,
no. 3)   [525]
   CSmH   DLC   IC   ICU   MH   NN   NNC

Russell, John, printer, Boston.
    An address presented to the members of the Faustus association, in
Boston, at their annual celebration, Oct. 4, 1808.   By John Russell ...
Pub. agreeable to a vote of the Society.   Boston, 1808.   23p.
21 cm.   [526]
    CSmH   DLC   MB   MWA   NN

Schayes, Antoine Guillaume Bernard, 1808-1859.
    Sur l'invention de l'imprimerie.   Messager des Sciences Histori-
ques et Archives des Arts de Belgique, 1841, p. 422-423.   [527]

Schmidt, Johann August Friedrich.
    Handbuch der Bibliothekswissenschaft, der Literatur- und Bücher-
kunde.   Eine Gedrängte ueber der Handschriftenkunde, der Geschichte
der Buchdruckerkunst und des Buchhandels, der Bücherkenntniss, ... der
Bibliothekenkunde und Bibliothekekonomie und der literärhistorischen
und bibliographischen Schriften.   Weimar, Voigt, 1840.   viii, 472p.
8vo.   [528]
    Eu-Ge-LB

Schneegans, L.
    Principales versions sur l'invention de l'imprimerie.   Revue
d'Alsace, 2d ser., vol. 2, 1836, p. 329-340.   [529]

    A short history of the invention of printing and the correct
manner of masking errors in a printer's proofsheet.   Together with
specimens of type from S. Odell's general printing office. ... London
[1840?]   12mo.   [530]
    Eu-Ge-LB

Skeen, George J. A.
    Printing: the invention of typography.   A lecture.   Colombo,
Ceylon, Government press, 1892.   8vo.
    Title from Grafton & co., cat. 90.   [531]

Skeen, William, 1822?-1872.
    Early typography.   By William Skeen.   Colombo: Ceylon [W. Skeen]
1872.   3 prel. leaves, 5-424p.   22.5 cm.
    Based on an earlier publication printed for private distribution:
    Typography, or Letter press printing in the fiteenth century;
    a lecture on the origin and early history of the art, delivered
    before the members of the Colombo athenaeum, Feb. 24, 1853.
    Colombo, 1853.   (48p.)
    Reissued same year (London, Trübner) with addendum of 2 pages.   [532]
    DLC   ICJ   MH   NN   Eu-De-LBb   Eu-Ge-LB   Eu-Ge-LE   Eu-Ne-AVb

----   An essay on the origin of letter-press printing in the
fifteenth century.   By William Skeen ... London, Trübner & co. [Colombo,
Ceylon, W. Skeen, printer] 1872.   2 prel. leaves, 3-8p., 1 leaf,
9-426p.   22.5 cm.

First issued with imprint Colombo, Ceylon, 1872 (424p.)   [533]
DLC   ICJ   NjP   Eu-Ge-LP

Skeen, William, 1822?-1872.
   The invention of printing. Colombo Observer, 1853.
   Title from van der Linde, Geschichte der Erfindung ...   [534]

----   Typography, or letter press printing in the fifteenth
century. A lecture on the origin and early history of the art
by William Skeen. Delivered before the members of the Colombo
Athenaeum on Thursday, February 24, 1853.   Colombo, Ceylon,
Government press, 1853.   iv, 43p.   19 cm.   [535]
   ICN   MB

Society for promoting Christian knowledge, London.   General
   literature committee.
   The history of printing. Published under the direction of the
Committee of general literature and education, appointed by the
Society for promoting Christian knowledge.   London, Society for
promoting Christian knowledge [1862]   2 prel. leaves, 256p.
col. front. (port.)   illus.   17 cm.   [536]

Sotheby, Samuel Leigh, 1805-1861.
   The typography of the fifteenth century: being specimens of
the productions of the early continental printers, exemplified
in a collection of fac-similes from one hundred works, together
with their water marks. Arranged and edited from the bibliographical collections of the late Samuel Sotheby, by his son,
S. Leigh Sotheby.   London, T. Rodd, 1845.   2 prel. leaves,
65p., 1 leaf, vii p.   100 facsims. on 43 plates, 26 plates
(A-Aa)   36.5 cm.   [537]
   DLC   MB   MWA   NN   Eu-De-LBb

Sotzmann, Johann Daniel Ferdinand.
   Ueber Geschichte der Erfindung der Buchdruckerkunst.   Jahrbücher für Wissenschaftliche Kritik, vol. 2, 1836, p. 921-968.   [538]

Soulanges, E.
   Inventions et découvertes ou les curieuses origines. Les
cartes à jouer. La galvanoplastie. L'imprimerie. La lithographie. Le papier. La photographie. 11e édition.   Tours,
1879.   8vo.   [539]
   Eu-Ge-LSb

Southward, J.
   The origin of printing.   British and Colonial Printer, vol.
45, 1899, p. 203-204.   [540]

- 75 -

Staglieno, Marcello, b. 1829-
    Sui primordi dell' arte della stampa, appunti e documenti.
Genoa, R. Instituto sordo-muti, 1877.   38p.   28 cm.   [541]
    ICN

Stänglen, Karl.
    Kurze Geschichte der Buchdruckerkunst seit ihrer Erfindung bis
auf neueste Zeit, nebst den Biographien einiger der berühmtesten
Buchdrucker aus den sichersten Quellen geschöpft.   Stuttgart,
J. B. Metzler'sche Buchhandlung, 1840.   18p.   18 cm.   [542]
    NNGr   Eu-De-LBb   Eu-Ge-LB

Stark, Adam, 1784-1867.
    Printing: its antecendents, origin, history, and results.   By
Adam Stark ... London, Longman, Brown, Green, and Longmans, 1855.
3 prel. leaves, 122p.   17.5 cm.   [543]
    DLC   ICJ   MB   NN   Eu-Gc-LB   Eu-Ge-LP

Steiff, K.
    Beiträge zur ältesten Buchdruckergeschichte.   Zentralblatt für
Bibliothekswesen, vol. 3, 1866, p. 249-264, 345-350; vol. 4, 1867,
p. 49-60.   [544]

Steinhausen, G.
    Zur Erinnerung an die Erfindung der Buchdruckerkunst.   Nation
(Berlin), vol. 17, no. 35, 36, 1900.   [545]

[Stevenson, William] 1772-1829.
    ... Life of William Caxton.   Pub. under the superintendence of the
Society for the diffusion of useful knowledge ... London, Baldwin and
Cradock; New York, G. and C. Carvill; [etc., etc.] 1828.   1 prel.
leaf, 32p.   23 cm.   (Library of useful knowledge. [no.] 31)
    Caption title: Life of William Caxton, with an account of the
    invention of printing, and of the modes and materials used for
    transmitting knowledge before that took place.   [546]
    DLC

---- ----   2d. ed., 1833.   London, 1833.   [547]
    MB

Strobl.
    Die Erfindung der Buchdruckerkunst.   Zeitschrift für des Real-
schulwesen, 1900, p. 679-681.   [548]

Süss.
    Zur Geschichte der Typographie.   Leipzig, 1840.   8vo.
    Title from Mohr, Jubelfeste.   [549]

Taylor, A. K.
   A short sketch of the invention and early history of printing.
Inland Printer, vol. 15, 1895, p. 394; vol. 16, 1895-1896, p. 290. [550]

Timbs, John, 1801-1875.
   A history of wonderful inventions ... Part I.   New York, Harper
& Brothers, 1849.   vii, 125, [1]p.   18 cm.   [551]
   MB

----   Stories of inventors and discoverers in science and the
useful arts.   A book for old and young.   New York, Harper and
Brothers, publishers, 1860.   xiv, [15]-473p.   19.5 cm.   [552]
   MH-BA
   London, Kent & Co.: CSmH   CtY   MB
   London, Lockwood & Co.: NN

----   Wonderful inventions: from the mariner's compass to the
electric telegraph cable.   By John Timbs, editor of "The Year Book
of Facts," and author of "Things Not Generally Known," etc.   With
numerous engravings.   London, George Routledge and Sons, The
Broadway, Ludgate.   New York, 416 Broome Street [1868?]   xvi,
400p.   illus., plate.   [553]
   CSmH   KyU   MH   Eu-Ge-LB
   1882 ed.: Eu-Ge-LSb

Tiraboschi, Girolamo.
   [Notes on the invention of printing.]   (In his Storia della
letteratura italiana. Firenze, 1807.   vol. 6, p. 159)   [554]
   Eu-Ge-LB

Tomlinson, Charles, 1808-1897.
   On the invention of printing; a lecture.   London, privately
printed, 1865.   8vo.   [555]
   Eu-Ge-LB   Eu-Ge-LSb

Tonelli, Tommaso.
   Cenni istorici sull' origine della stampa e sull' artefice che
primo face uso di caratteri sciolti e fusi.   Firenze, 1830.
57p.   8vo.
   Reprint from Antologia.   Giornale di Scienze, Lettere e Arti,
   vol. 41, no. 121, 1831, p. 27-43; no. 122, p. 50-64; no.
   123, p. 14-35.   [556]
   Eu-Ge-LB

   The true invention of printing.   Inland Printer, vol. 2,
Nov. 1884, p. 69-70.   [557]

Umbreit, August Ernst.
   Die Erfindung der Buchdruckerkunst.   Kritische Abhandlungen zur

Orientirung auf dem jetzigen Standpunkte der Forschung; von August
Ernst Umbreit.   Leipzig, W. Engelmann, 1843.   xxxiv, 243, [1]p.
20.5 cm.   [558]
    DLC   MB   NN   Eu-De-LBb   Eu-Ne-AVb   Eu-Ne-GK

Vallet de Viriville, Auguste, 1815-1868.
    Les inventeurs de l'imprimerie en Allemagne.   Par A. Vallet de
Viriville.   Paris, Pillet fils aîné, 1858.   11p.   24 cm.
    "Extrait de la Revue de Paris, du 1er janvier 1858."   [559]
    DLC   Eu-Ge-LSb

Vincard, B.
    Idée sur l'origine de l'imprimerie, ses progrès jusqu'à ce jour
et la perfection dont elle est encore susceptible.   Paris, [n.d.]
11p.   8vo.   [560]
    Hoe

Vitu, Auguste.
    Histoire de la typographie par Auguste Vitu.   Paris, Librairie
Ch. Delagrave, 15 rue Soufflot, 1886.   [iv], 168, [3]p.   21.5 cm. [561]
    NN   Eu-Ge-LP   Eu-Sz-BeG

Vogel, Emil Ferdinand.
    Geschichte der denkwürdigsten Erfindungen von der ältesten bis
auf die neueste Zeit.   4 vols.   Leipzig, 1842-1843.   16mo.
    Invention of printing: vol. 2, p. 1-27.   [562]
    IU

    Vom Erfinder der Buchdruckerkunst.   Blätter für Literarische
Unterhaltung, Oct. 30, 1879.   [563]

Weigel, Theodor Oswald, 1812-1881.
    Die Anfänge der Druckerkunst in Bild und Schrift.   An deren
frühesten Erzeugnissen in der Weigel'schen Sammlung erläutert von
T. O. Weigel und Dr. Ad. Zestermann.   Mit 145 Facsimiles and vielen
in den Text gedruckten Holzschnitten.   Leipzig, T. O. Weigel, 1866.
2 vols.   illus., port., 145 facsim. (partly col.)   39 cm.
    Half title: Collectio Weigeliana.   325 copies printed.
    Contents.- 1. Bd.   Zeugdrucke.   Metallschnitte.   In Metallrahmen
eingesetzte Holzschnitte.   Holzschnitte.   2. Bd. Xylographische
Werke.   Spielkarten.   Schrotblätter.   Zeigdrucke.   Kupferstiche.
Typographische Werke.   Register.   Wasserzeichen des Papiers.   [564]
    DLC   ICJ   ICN   MH   MdBP   MiU   NN   NjP   Eu-De-BP
Eu-De-LBb   Eu-Ge-LB   Eu-Ge-LP   Eu-Ne-GK

---- Lettre de M. T.-O. Weigel. Livres xylographiques. Origine
de l'imprimerie. Historia S. Crucis.   Le Bibliophile, vol. 2, 1863,
p. 49. Réponse à la lettre de M. T.-O. Weigel ... Le Bibliophile, vol.
2, 1863, p. 98.   [565]

Weigel, Theodor Oswald, 1812-1881.
Ein wichtiges Zeugniss zur Geschichte der Erfindung der
Buchdruckerkunst.   Serapeum, vol. 27, no. 15, 1866, p. 225-230.   [566]

Welches ist das älteste mit beweglichen Lettern gedruckte Buch?
Materialen zu den Sächsischen Ausführungsgesetzen zum Bürgerlichen
Gesetzbuche, no. 4-5, 1899.   [567]

Wenzelburger, T.
Erfindung der Buchdruckerkunst.   Unsere Zeit, vol. 1, 1890,
p. 556-561.   [568]

Who invented printing?   Publishers' Weekly, vol. 53, May 1898,
p. 775.   [569]

Who was the first printer?   St. Paul's, vol. 2, Sept. 1868,
p. 706-718.
Authorship attributed to H. N. Humphreys by the St. Bride Foundation.   [570]

Willett, B.
The invention of printing.   (In his Traits of science and invention ... with biographical notices and incidental anecdotes and
sketches.   London, 1834.   chapter 2)   [571]
Eu-Ge-LSb

Willett, Ralph, 1719-1795.
A memoir on the origin of printing.   In a letter addressed to
John Topham ... by Ralph Willett ... Newcastle, S. Hodgson, 1820.
2 prel. leaves, [iii]-iv, 72p.   24.5 cm.
A reprint edited by Thomas Hodgson, of a paper favoring the
claims of Mainz, which first appeared in Archaeologia, vol.
11, 1794, p. 267-316, and was reprinted by J. T. Brockett,
Newcastle, 1818.
Title vignette.
150 copies printed.   Large paper copy.   [572]
DLC   ICN   MB   MdBP   NN   Eu-De-LBb   Eu-Ge-LB

Willett, Ralph, 1719-1795.
Observations on the origin of printing, in a letter to O. S.
Brereton, Esq.   Newcastle, privately printed, 1819.   8vo.   [573]
Eu-Ge-LB

Wyss, Arthur Franz Wilhelm, 1852-1900.
Gutenberg oder Coster.   Leipzig, 1888.   8vo.
Reprint from Zentralblatt für Bibliothekswesen, vol. 5, 1888,
p. 256-272.   [574]
Eu-Ge-LSb

Wyss, Arthur Franz Wilhelm, 1852-1900.
   Zur Geschichte der Erfindung der Buchdruckerkunst. Quartalblätter des Historischen Vereins für das Grossherzogtum Hessen,
1879, p. 9-26.   Same, Norddeutsche Allgemeine Zeitung (Berlin),
May 1, 8, 1881.   [575]

Zanghellini, Antonio.
   Sulla invenzione della stampa.   Feltre, 1865.   4to.   [576]
   Eu-De-LBb

        5   20th Century

   An age-old discussion still unsettled.   Typographical Journal,
July 1939, p. 36.   [577]

Aitchison, R. T.
   A chart of the history of printing in Europe; compiled and illustrated by R. T. Aitchison.   Printed by the McCormick-Armstrong company. Wichita, 1931. Broadside (map) 61x47 cm.
   An outlined map of Europe (in colors) with significant events in
   printing history printed thereon, showing places and dates.   [578]
   MB   NBuG   NN

Allen, Albert Henry.
   The beginnings of printing, by Albert H. Allen. Berkeley, Calif.,
Lederer, Street & Zeus company, 1923.   1 prel. leaf, 5-53p.
18.5 cm.   [579]
   DLC   ICJ   ICN

Anselmo, Antonio.
   A invencao da imprensa.   Anais das Bibliotecas e Arquivos, vol.
4, 1923, p. 6-13.   [580]

Ara, Pedro.
   Invención y propagación de la imprenta.   Por Pedro Ara, Professor de la Universidad de Madrid.   Gutenberg (Buenos Aires),
vol. 40, no. 18, 1940, p. 5-8.
   Reprinted from the Diario Español, with permission.   [581]

Ardashev, P.
   Izobretenie knigopechataniia po svidetel'stvam i otryvkam
sovremennikov.   (In his Khrestomatiia po vseobshchei istorii,
Novaia istoriia v otryvkakh iz istochnikov.   Kiev, Tip. 2-oi
Arteli, 1914.   p. 85-87)   [582]
   Eu-Ru-MLe

Argent, Henry.
   Gutenberg or Coster? British Printer, vol. 48, May 1936,
p. 278-279.   [583]

Audin, Marius, 1872-
... Histoire de l'imprimerie par l'image ... Paris, Henri Jonquières,
éditeur, rue Visconti, 21, 1928-1929.   4 vols in 3.   illus. (part
mounted), ports. (part mounted), facsims. (part col.)   23 cm.   [584]
   CSmH   DLC   PP   PPDrop

----   Une hypothèse sur les origines de la typographie.   Papyrus,
vol. 11, 1930, p. 717-719; 796-800.   [585]

----   Una ipotesi sulle origine della tipografia.   Rassegna
Grafiche, vol. 6, 1931, p. 11-14.   [586]

----   The mystery of the origin of typography.   Library Association Record, 3d ser., vol. 1, 1931, p. 153-162.   [587]

Ballmann, P.
   Ein zweischneidig Schwert oder die schwarze Kunst des Johann
Gutenberg.   Ravensburg, 1901.   48p.   8vo.   [588]
   Hu-Ge-LB

Barge, Hermann.
   ... Geschichte der Buchdruckerkunst von ihren Anfängen bis zur
Gegenwart; mit 134 teils ganzseitigen Abbildungen, 16 ein- und
mehrfarbigen Tafeln und 1 farbigen Beilage.   Leipzig, P. Reclam
jun. [c1940]   viii, 519, [1]p.   illus. (incl. music), ports.
(1 col.), facsims. (part col.; 1 fold.)   23.5 cm.
   Folded facsimile in pocket.   [589]
   DLC

Basel, Switzerland.   Gewerbemuseum.
   Die Erfindung Gutenbergs.   Basel [1941].   82, [2]p., incl.
6 illus. (reprod.)   23 cm.
   Contains: H. Keinzle, "Zur Einführung in die Ausstellung 'Die
   Erfindung Gutenbergs,'" p. 9-14;   Binz, Gustav, "Die Erfindung
   Gutenbergs," p. 15-19;   Pfister, Arnold, "Die Ausbreitung des
   Buchdrucks im fünfzehnten Jahrhundert," p. 30-52 (incl. "Zeit-
   tabellen zur Ausbreitung des Buchdrucks in fünfzehnten Jahr-
   hunderts," p. 45-52), etc.
   McMurtrie.   [590]

Bashirud-Din, S.
   Origin and history of the art of printing.   Modern Librarian
(Lahore, India), vol. 4, July 1934, p. 161-165.   [591]

Bauer, Friedrich.
   Wer hat die Buchdruckerkunst erfunden?   Klimseh's Jahrbuch,
vol. 17, 1923, p. 3-16.   [592]

Bayley, Harold.
    The invention of printing. (In his A new light on the renais-
sance displayed in contemporary emblems. London, J. M. Dent, 1909.
p. 111-120)   [593]
    DLC   ICJ   MB   MnU   NN   PP   PPL   PPTU

Beckman, E. A. B.
    First printed matter. Saturday Review of Literature, vol. 8,
Apr. 1932, p. 653. Discussion of same, vol. 8, Apr. 1932,
p. 706; May, p. 750.   [594]

    The beginning of typography. Athenaeum, vol. 1, no. 3995,
May 1904, p. 656.   [595]

Binz, Gustav.
    Coster oder Gutenberg. Frankfurter Zeitung, no. 300, Apr. 23,
1922.   [596]

Blades, William, 1824-1890.
    De ortu typographiae; Gutenberg versus Coster. Book Worm
(London), vol. 1, no. 3, Feb. 1888, p. 84-86; no. 4, Mar.,
p. 136-138; no. 5, Apr., p. 177-181; no. 6, May, p. 212-215.
Same, Ars Typographica, vol. 1, no. 4, 1918, p. 30-32.
    Also reprint.   [597]

Blaizot, G.
    L'histoire de l'art de l'imprimerie et l'histoire du livre.
Arts et Metiers Graphiques, vol. 1, no. 11, 1929, p. 661-663.   [598]

Blum, André Salomon, 1881-
    The origins of printing and engraving, by André Blum; trans-
lated from the French by Harry Miller Lydenberg. New York,
C. Scribner's sons, 1940. ix, 226p. incl. front., illus.
(incl. facsims.) double plate. 23.5 cm.
    Translation of the second and third parts of Les origines du
papier, de l'imprimerie et de la gravure. cf. Publisher's
note.
    "Notes": p. 193-211.   [599]
    DLC   ICJ   ICN   NBB

----   Les origines de l'imprimerie. Hippocrate, vol. 1, 1933,
p. 660-689.   [600]

----   Les origines du papier, de l'imprimerie et de la gravure;
illustrées de 80 gravures. Paris, Éditions de la tournelle,
1935. 3 prel. leaves, [11]-252p., 1 leaf. front., illus.
(incl. facsims.) 25 cm.   [601]
    CtY   DLC   ICN   MH   NN   Eu-Fr-PN   Eu-Ge-LB

Bogeng, Gustav Adolf Erich, 1881-
Anmerkungen zur Erfindungsgeschichte der Buchdruckkunst.
Gutenberg Jahrbuch, vol. 6, 1931, p. 38-72.   [602]

---- Geschichte der Buchdruckerkunst, von G. A. E. Bogeng.
Hellerau bei Dresden, Demeter-Verlag [1928-] illus., fold.
map, facsims. (part col., part fold.)   34 cm.
   Cover-title.
   Issued in parts.   [603]
   DLC   MH   NBuG   NN   Eu-Ge-LB

---- Geschichte der Buchdruckerkunst ... Hellerau bei Dresden,
Demeter-Verlag [1930-]   illus., plates, ports., fold. map,
facsims. (part col., part fold.)   35 cm.
   At head of title: G. A. E. Bogeng.
   Originally issued in parts, 1928-   [604]
   DLC   ICN   MB   NjN

Bohigas Balaguer, Pedro, 1901-
   Els primers temps de la imprenta.   (In his Resum d'historia
del llibre.   Barcelona, Editorial Barcino, 1933.   p. 42-51) [605]
   DLC

Bömer, Alois, 1868-
   Coster und Gutenberg oder nur Gutenberg?   Zentralblatt für
Bibliothekswesen, vol. 43, 1926, p. 57-73.   [606]

Bornet.
   Histoire de l'imprimerie.   Union Syndicale et Fédération
des Syndicats des Maîtres Imprimeurs de France.   Bulletin
Officiel, no. 2, Feb. 1930, p. 70-71.   [607]

Brage, H.
   Geschichte der Buchdruckerkunst von ihren Anfängen bis zur
Gegenwart.   Leipzig, Reclam, 1940.   viii, 519p.   illus.,
plates.
   Title from Zentralblatt für Bibliothekswesen, 1940.   [608]

Büchler, Eduard.
   Die Erfindung der Buchdruckerkunst.   (In his Die Anfänge
des Buchdrucks in der Schweiz.   Schweizerisches Gutenbergmuseum, vol. 14, no. 1, 1928, p. 16-25)   [609]

Bullen, Henry Lewis.
   Collectanea typographica.   1.   Our first printer's profits.
2. The first history of printing.   Inland Printer,   vol. 62,
no. 2,   Nov. 1918, p. 193-194.   [610]

Burger, C. P.
    Gutenberg en Coster.   Het Boek, vol. 13, 1924, p. 355-356.   [611]

Burgoyne, F. J. P.
    The origin of movable types.   Library Assistant, vol. 4, 1903-
1905, p. 130-134.   [612]

Butler, Pierce, 1886-
    The origin of printing in Europe, by Pierce Butler.   Chicago,
Ill., The University of Chicago press [1940]   xv, 154, [1]p.
front., illus., facsims.   19.5 cm.
    Half-title: The University of Chicago studies in library
    science.
    "Bibliographical notes":   p. 144-150.   [613]
    DLC   ICN   ICU

Champion coated paper company, New York.
    ... Gutenberg or Coster?   [New York] The Champion coated paper
company, ᶜ1917.   14p.   illus. (incl. ports., facsims.)
23 cm.   (Champion monographs.   Dec. 27, 1917)   [614]
    DLC

Cleaver, Wilbur Fisk.
    Five centuries of printing; a compilation of important events
in the history of typography, by Wilbur Fisk Cleaver ... 2d ed.
(rev. and enl.).   Collaborator: Otto W. Fuhrmann ... Johnstown,
Pa., illus.   25.5 cm.
    Bibliography: 1 leaf at end.   [615]
    DLC   NjN

Collijn, Isak Gustaf Alfred, 1875-
    Boktryckerkonstens uppfinning och guldader.   Boktryckeri
Kalender, vol. 14-15, 1910, p. 1-72.
    Also reprint,   Göteborg, W. Zachrisson, 1911.   [616]

----   Samtida utsagor om boktryckarkonstens uppfinning, av Isak
Collijn.   [Göteborg, W. Zachrissons boktryckeri a.-b., 1921]
15, [1]p.   31 cm.
    Colored initial: tail-piece ("familjen Gensfleischs vapen")
    "Detta särtryck ur 'Liber librariorum' är tryckt ... i 50 ex ..."   [617]
    DLC

    Coster, Gutenberg, allebei of een vraagteeken?   Eigen Haard,
1934, p. 458-462.   [618]

Cowan, Arthur J.
    Anent the invention of printing.   London Typographical Journal,
vol. 54, no. 6, June 1919, p. 597-598.   [619]

Currely, C. T.
    Beginnings of printing and the book.   Canadian Printer and
Publisher, Dec. 1931, p. 30-31, 35, 56.   [620]

De Vinne, Theodore Low, 1828-1914.
    Der Schlüssel zur Erfindung der Typographie, ein Abschnitt
aus dem Werke The invention of printing, by Theo. L. De Vinne,
New York, 1876.   Aus dem Englischen übersetzt von Dr. Oscar
Jolles.   Berlin, 1921.   25p.   illus.   30.5 cm.   [621]
    NN   Eu-De-BP   Eu-Ge-LSb

Degering, H.
    Die Erfindung der Buchdruckerkunst.   (In Bömer, K., ed.
Deutsche Saat in fremder Erde.   Berlin, "Zeitgeschichte",
1936.   p. 153-166)   [622]
    Eu-De-BP   Eu-De-WN

Dieterichs, Karl.
    Die Buchdruckpresse von Johannes Gutenberg bis Friedrich
König, von Karl Dieterichs ... Mainz, Gutenberg-Gesellschaft,
1930.   1 prel. leaf, 5-39, [1]p.   43 plates on 22 leaves.
22.5 cm.   (Beilage zum 28. [i.e. 26.-29] Jahresbericht
der Gutenberg-Gesellschaft, Mainz)   [623]
    DLC   ICJ   ICN   MB   MH   NN   NNU-W   Eu-De-BP
    Eu-De-LBb   Eu-Ne-AVb

Dokkum, J. D. C. van.
    Wie vond de boekdrukkunst uit?   Het Grafisch Museum
(Utrecht), vol. 5, no. 4, 1935, p. 63-68.   [624]

Dols, J.
    Wie heeft de boekdrukkunst uitgevonden?   Bibliotheekleven,
vol. 20, 1935, p. 29-33.   [625]

    Druckerstlinge.   Beiträge zur Buchdruckentwicklungsge-
schichte.   Vierteljahrsschrift für Angewandte Bücherkunde,
vol. 1, 1918, p. 69-73.   [626]

Dumont, Jean, 1853-
    Le livre avant et depuis l'invention de l'imprimerie.
Bruxelles, 1903.   8vo.   [627]

    Die Erfindung Gutenbergs.   Eröffnung der Ausstellung im
Gewerbemuseum Basel.   Basler Nachrichten, Dec. 16, 1940.   [628]

Falk, Franz, 1840-1909.
    Jacob Merstetter, Adam Gelthuss und Johann Faust.   Zentral-
blatt für Bibliothekswesen, vol. 18, no. 5, May 1901, p.
209-214.   [629]

Fitzgerald, Edward C.
A short account of the invention of printing. 2d ed. London,
Macmillan & co., 1914. iv, 128p.
Title from Douglas C. McMurtrie.   [630]

Fleischmann, Franz.
Was hat Gutenberg Erfunden? _Alte und Neue Welt_, vol. 46,
1912, p. 596.   [631]

Forkert, Otto Maurice, 1901-
From Gutenberg to the Cuneo press; an historical sketch of the
printing press, by Otto Maurice Forkert ... Chicago, Ill., The Cuneo
press, inc., 1933. 1 prel. leaf, 7-30p. front., illus.
20.5 cm.   [632]
DLC IC NNC

Frauenfelder, Reinhard.
Die Erfindung der Buchdruckerkunst; zum fünfhundert-jährigen
Jubiläum. _Schaffhauser Schreibmappe für das Jahr 1941_
(9th issue), p. [5]-[10].
Also reprint.   [633]

Fuhrmann, Otto Walter.
The invention of printing. _Dolphin_, vol. 3, 1938,
p. 25-57.   [634]

---- The study of printing history. _Gutenberg Jahrbuch_, vol.
6, 1931, p. 336-340.   [635]

Geschichte der Buchdruckerkunst. Leipzig, 1904. 16mo.
(Miniatur-Bibliothek 610-612)   [636]
Eu-Ge-LSb

Ginsburg, Percy
The inventor of printing. _London Typographical Journal_, vol.
54, no. 3, Mar. 1919, p. 241.   [637]

Giovanni Gutenberg e Cristoforo Colombo preceduti nelle loro
scoperte. _Bibliofilia_, vol. 12, 1910, p. 42.   [638]

Gottschalk, Paul.
Die Buchkunst Gutenbergs und Schöffers, mit einem einleitenden
Versuch über die Entwicklung der Buchkunst von ihren frühesten
Anfängen bis auf die heutige Zeit, von Paul Gottschalk.
Berlin, P. Gottschalk, 1918. 1 prel. leaf, 5-15p., 8 leaves.
viii facsims. 46x34 cm.
Each facsimile preceded by leaf with explanatory text.
Facsimiles in original size of fragments of the following:

Die 42 zeilige Bibel; 36 zeilige Bibel; Das Mainzer
Catholicon; Psalterium 1457; Canon missae 1458;
Durandus 1459; Biblia latina 1462; Missale speciale.   [639]
DLC   ICJ   ICN   ICU   IU   MB   NN   NjP   Eu-De-BP
Eu-De-LBb

Goudy, Frederic W.
    The first types.   Monotype, vol. 8, no. 12, Sept. 1921,
p. 12.   [640]

Grover, Edwin Osgood.
    A footnote to the history of printing, by Edwin Osgood Grover.
Rollins Park, Florida, The Angel Alley press, 1929.   13p.
24mo.
    500 copies printed.   [641]

----   The man who taught the world to read.   Rollins College
Bulletin (Winter Park, Fla.), vol. 36, no. 4, (Selected faculty
papers), 1941, p. 15-26.   [642]

Guibertus, Brother.
    Merkweerdige uitvindingen.   Het papier.   De boek- en
steendrukkunst.   Oostacker, Drukkerij der beroepschool
"Glorieux" [1908?]   91p.   8vo.
    Title from Bibliographie de Belgique, 1908.   [643]

Guppy, Henry, 1861-
    Beginning of the art of typography.   John Rylands Library,
Manchester.   Bulletin, vol. 24, Apr. 1940, p. 18-20.   [644]

----   Beginnings of printing.   British and Colonial Printer
and Stationer, vol. 94, no. 6, Feb. 1924, p. 94.   [645]

Gusman, Pierre, 1862-
    Remarques sur les origines de la typographie.   Congrès
International des Bibliothécaires.   Procès Verbaux, 1925,
p. 372-373.   [646]

Haebler, Konrad, 1857-
... Die Erfindung der Druckkunst und ihre erste Ausbreitung in
den Ländern Europas.   Mainz, Gutenberg-Gesellschaft, 1930.
21, [3]p.   24 cm.   (Kleiner Druck der Gutenberg-Gesellschaft.
Nr. 14)
    At head of title: Vortrag von geh. rat. Prof. Dr. Konrad
    Haebler in der Generalversammlung der Gutenberg-Gesellschaft
    am 22. Juni 1930.   [647]
    DLC   ICN   MB   NN   Eu-Ne-AVb

Haebler, Konrad, 1857-
  "Falsche Gulden"--Blätter aus der Frühzeit der Druckerkunst.
Zeitschrift für Bücherfreunde, vol. 11, no. 6, Sept. 1907, p.
219-233.   [648]

----   Handbuch der Inkunabelkunde.   Leipzig, K. W. Hiersemann,
1925.   4 prel. leaves, 187p.   23.5 cm.   [649]
    DLC   ICJ   ICN   NN   NjP   RPB   Eu-De-BP   Eu-Ge-LB
    Eu-Ge-LL1   Eu-Ne-AVb

----   The study of incunabula, by Konrad Haebler; translated
from the German by Lucy Eugenia Osborne; with a foreword by
Alfred W. Pollard.   New York, The Grolier club, 1933.   xvi p.,
1 leaf, 241, [1]p.   24 cm.
    "One of an edition of three hundred and fifty copies on antique
    wove rag paper."
    "Translated from the German edition of 1925, but embodies also
    certain revisions of the text made by the author in 1932."--
    Translator's note, p. xiii.   [650]
    DLC   ICN   MiU   NjP   TxU

----   Typenrepertorium der Wiegendrucke, von Konrad Haebler ...
Leipzig [etc.] 1905-1924.   5 vols.   facsims. (part fold.)
tables.   24 cm.
    Added t.-p.: Sammlung bibliothekswissenschaftlicher Arbeiten
    begründet von Karl Dziatzko, fortgeführt und hrsg. von Prof.
    Dr. Konrad Haebler ... 19./20., 22./23., 27., 29./30., 39., 40.
    Hft. (II. Serie 2./3., 5./6., 10., 12./13., 22., 23. Hft.)
    Imprint varies: Abt. I, Halle a. S., R. Haupt 1903.--Abt.
    II. Leipzig u. New York, R. Haupt, 1908.--Abt. III[1-2],
    Leipzig, R. Haupt, 1909-10.--Abt. IV-V, Leipzig, O. Harrasso-
    witz, 1922-24.   [651]
    DLC   DSG   ICJ   Eu-Fr-PN   Eu-Ge-LSb

Hall, Charles W.
    The history and development of printing.   National Magazine,
vol. 35, Jan. 1912, p. 642-652.   [652]

Hamilton, Frederick William, 1860-1940.
  ... A brief history of printing ... by Frederick W. Hamilton ...
[Chicago] Pub. by the Committee on education, United typothetae
of America, 1918.   2 vols.   20.5 cm.   (Typographic technical
series for apprentices, pt. VIII, no. 51-52)   [653]
    DLC   ICJ   MB

----   The invention of typography, a brief sketch of the invention of printing and how it came about, by Frederick W.
Hamilton ... [Chicago] Pub. by the Committee on education, United
typothetae of America, 1918.   55p.   illus. (incl. facsims.)

20.5 cm.   (Typographic technical series for apprentices, pt.
VIII, no. 50)
   "Supplementary reading": p. 52.   [654]
   DLC   ICJ   MB   NN

Hargreaves, C.
   The genesis of printing.   Penrose's Pictorial Annual,
vol. 16, 1910-1911, p. 175-176.   [655]

Haynes, Merritt Way.
   The student's history of printing, giving the principal dates,
personages, and events in the development of the typographic art
from earliest times to the present, in chronological order by
Merritt Way Haynes, M. A.   1st ed.   New York [etc.] McGraw-
Hill book company, inc., 1930.   xiii, 118p. incl. front.,
illus., ports.   21 cm.   (Half-title: McGraw-Hill vocational
texts)
   Bibliography: p. 107.   [656]
   DLC   In   MB   NN

Heinike, John C.
   A brief story of the art of printing.   Share Your Knowledge
Review, vol. 21, no. 7, May 1940, p. 20-21.   [657]

Henry, E.
   Strasbourg et la naissance de l'imprimerie.   La Vie en
Alsace, 1931, p. 249-257.   Same, Union Syndicale et Fédération
des Syndicats des Maîtres Imprimeurs de France, May 1932, p. 140;
Sept. p. 260.   [658]

Hernandez, Sanz, F.
   Sobre la invención de la imprenta y su introducción en la
isla de Menorca.   Revista de Menorca, vol. 22, 1927, p.
241-256.   [659]

Herscher, Irenaeus.
   History of printing traced from origin.   St. Bona Venture,
vol. 14, no. 20, Mar. 1940, p. 1.   [660]

   History and art of printing.   Dansville, N. Y., Owen Publishing co., 1906.
   Title from Herscher, Irenaeus.   The three-fold printing
centennial.   New York, 1941.   [661]

Hjerta, Per.
   Boktryckerikonstens uppfinning och guldålder.   Sammandrag
effer senaste forskninger.   Boktryckeri Kalender, vol. 9-10,
1902-1903, p. 1-44; vol. 11, 1904, p. 1-54; vol. 12-13, 1905-
1906, p. 1-45.   [662]

Hobart, H. K.
 How printing came. Open Court, vol. 41, no. 11, Nov. 1927,
p. 662-667.   [663]

Hupp, Otto, 1859-
 Die vermutliche Vorstufe des Typendruckers. Osnadrücker
Tageblatt, Oct. 1, 1924.   [664]

 L'invention de l'imprimerie. Patrie Suisse (Genève),
Nov. 2, 1940.   [665]

Irmisch, Linus.
 Zur Geschichte der "beweglichen Lettern". Zeitschrift für
Deutschlands Buchdrucker, vol. 14, no. 8, 1902, p. 86; no. 47,
p. 575-576.   [666]

Jaggard, William, 1868-
 Printing: its birth and growth, by William Jaggard ... With
illuminated facsimile of the Gutenberg Bible and a portrait of
Caxton. Liverpool, The Shakespeare press, 1908. 16p. col.
front. (facsim.) 24 cm.
  "Exhibits" (a chronological list of 146 specimens from the
  author's collection, illustrating the history of printing, on
  exhibition at the Public Library, Stratford-on-Avon):
  p. [9]-16.   [667]
  DLC   ICJ   MB   Eu-Ge-LSb

Kaplan, L. E.
 Nachalo pechataniia podvizhymi bukvami. (In Samokatov, N. V.
Poligraficheskie proizvodstva. Kratkaia entsiklopediia dlia
shkol i samoobrazovaniia. [Kharkov], Gos. Izd. Ukrainy, 1925.
p. 11-18)   [668]
  Eu-Ru-MLe

Kippenberg, Anton.
 Die Geschichte des Buches. Börsenblatt für den Deutschen
Buchhandel, vol. 71, 1904, p. 10082-10087. Same, Archiv für
Buchgewerbe, vol. 42, 1905, p. 6-13.   [669]

[La Caille, Joan de] d. 1720.
 Watson's [i.e. La Caille's] preface to the history of printing,
1713. Edited with introduction and notes by W. J. Couper. Edin-
burgh, The Darien press, 1913.
  See also Watson, James. no. 293.   [670]
  McMurtrie   Eu-Ge-LSb

Lampe, Ferdinand Charles.
 The origin of printing; concise history of its beginning and
development, helpful to printing instructors and students in the

public schools.   Chicago, Barnhart brothers and Spindler, [1928].
35p.   19.5 cm.   [671]
    MiU

Landau, Paul.
    Die ältesten Meister der schwarzen Kunst.   Das Sammlerkabinett,
vol. 3, no. 1, 1924.   [672]

Leclerq, [Léopold?]
    Deux inventeurs pour une invention: Coster, Gutenberg.   Union
Syndicale et Fédération des Syndicats des Maîtres Imprimeurs de
France.   Bulletin Officiel, 1924, p. 270-273.   [673]

Löffler, Klemens.
    Neues zur Geschichte des Buchdrucks.   Börsenblatt für den
Deutschen Buchhandel, vol. 98, no. 16, Jan. 1931, p. 55-56.   [674]

Lone, Emma Miriam, 1872-
    Some noteworthy firsts in Europe during the fifteenth century,
by E. Miriam Lone ... New York, L. C. Harper, 1930.   xiv, 72, [1]p.,
1 leaf.   front., illus., facsims.   22 cm.
    "Of this book 425 copies have been printed by Fred Anthoensen,
    The Southworth press, Portland, Maine, of which nos. 26-425
    are for sale."   [675]
    DLC   ICN

McMurtrie, Douglas Crawford, 1888-
    The birth of typography.   Inland Printer, vol. 98, no. 3, Dec.
1936, p. 23-27; no. 4, Jan. 1937, p. 61-64; no. 5, Feb.,
p. 45-48.   [676]

----   The book; the story of printing and bookmaking, by Douglas
C. McMurtrie.   New York, Covici-Friede, 1937.   xxx p., 1 leaf,
676p., 1 leaf.   front., illus. (incl. ports., music) plates,
facsims.   25 cm.
    Bibliographies: p. 603-646.   [677]
    DLC   In   NN
    1938 ed.:   ViU

----   Dutch scholar renounces Holland's claim to the invention
of printing.   Share Your Knowledge Review, vol. 22, no. 2, Dec.
1940, p. 8-13.   [678]

----   The golden book; the story of fine books and bookmaking--
past & present, by Douglas C. McMurtrie.   Chicago, P. Covici,
1928.   xiv p., 1 leaf, 410p.   illus. (incl. ports.) facsims.
24 cm.
    "Third edition, January, 1928."
    "References to works of which extensive use has been made":
    p. 389-398.   [679]
    DLC   IU   Eu-Ne-AVb

McMurtrie, Douglas Crawford, 1888-
    A historical background of printing, by Douglas C. McMurtrie.
[Washington, D. C., Printed in the apprentice school, Govt. print.
off., 1937] cover-title, iii, 23p. 24 cm.   [680]
    CSmH   DLC   IC   MB   NN

---- The printing press, its history and its service to civilization. Extract from History of printing (75th anniversary, 1866-1941,
New York printing pressman's union no. 51). New York, 1941.
18-37p. 30 cm.
    Much of the text deals with the invention of printing.   [681]
    DLC

[----] Printing; the story of its invention and its service to
mankind. Issued in the interest of a wider appreciation of the
significance of printing to the community, on the occasion of the
500th anniversary of the invention of printing, by the Chicago club
of printing house craftsmen. Chicago, 1940. 16p. 15.5 cm.
    See other editions listed under Commemorative Writings - 20th
    Century.   [682]
    CtY   DLC   ICU   MH   NN

---- Some facts concerning the invention of printing, the five-
hundredth anniversary of which will be celebrated internationally in
1940. By Douglas C. McMurtrie. Chicago, Chicago club of printing
house craftsmen, 1939. 42p. illus. (port., facsims.) 22 cm.
    "This first edition of fifteen hundred copies for distribution to
    registrants at the 1939 convention of the International association
    of printing house craftsmen was produced in September, 1939."   [683]
    DLC   ICU   NN

---- ---- 2d ed. Chicago, 1939.
    "This second edition of twenty-five thousand copies was printed at
the Fifth educational graphic arts exposition in September, 1939." [684]
    DLC   IC   ICJ   MH   NN   PBL   Eu-Ne-AVb

---- War Gutenberg oder Coster der Erfinder des Buchdruckes?
Aurora und Christliche Woche (Buffalo, N. Y.), vol. 90, no. 8,
Sept. 19, 1940, p. 7.   [685]

Maddox, Harry Alfred.
    Printing, its history, practice, and progress, by H. A. Maddox
... London, New York [etc.] Sir I. Pitman & sons, ltd., 1923.
viii, 151p. front., illus. 22 cm.   [686]
    DLC   ICJ   MB   NN   NjP   Eu-Ge-LB

---- ---- 2d ed. London, Sir I. Pitman & sons, ltd., 1932.
x, 171p. front., illus. 22 cm.   [687]
    DLC   MB   NN

Madsen, Victor Christian, 1865-
   Bogtrykkerkunstens historie. **Handbog i Bibliotekskundskab**,
1912, p. 165-213.   [688]

Mitkevich, V. F., ed.
   Izobretenie knigopechataniia. (In Ocherki istorii tekhniki
dokapitalisticheskikh formatsii. Sostavili B. L. Bogaevskii
I. M. Lur'e, E. CH. Skrzhinskaia, E. A. Tseitlin. Pod obshch.
red., V. F. Mitkevicha. Moskva i Leningrad, Izd-vo Akademii
Nauk SSSR, 1936.   p. 334-350)   [689]
   NN   Eu-Ru-MLe

Morison, Stanley, 1889-
   A brief survey of printing: history and practise, by Stanley
Morison & Holbrook Jackson. New York, A. A. Knopf, 1923. 87,
[1]p.   illus.   23 cm.
   "Printed in England."
   "A small portion of the following outline appeared in a more
condensed form in a printing supplement issued with the
Manchester Guardian, May 23, 1922."
   "A short dictionary of printing terms": p. 80-87.   [690]
   DLC   NN
   London, Office of the Fleuron: ICJ   NN

Mornand, Pierre, 1884-
   L'art du livre et histoire de l'imprimerie.   Paris, J. Meynial,
1929.   110p.   facsims.   front. (port.)   4to.
   At head of title: Fondation Jules Meynial Libraire.   [691]
   NN

Mortet, Paul Louis Charles, 1852-1927.
   Les origines et les débuts de l'imprimerie d'après les recherches
les plus récentes, par Charles Mortet ... Ouvrage accompagné de XXI
planches en phototypie. Paris, Pour la Société française de
bibliographie, 1922. viii, 98p., 1 leaf, and atlas of XXI facsims.
(part fold.)   33x25 cm.
   "Tiré à 300 exemplaires."
   Bibliographical footnotes.   [692]
   DLC   ICN   IU   NN   NjP   Eu-Fr-PN   Eu-Ne-AVb

Moscherosch, Hans Michael, 1601-1669.
   Wie das Pulver und die Buchdruckerey erfunden wurde. [Berlin-
Steglitz], Officina Serpentis, 1919.   22p., 1 leaf. 26 cm.   [693]
   NjP   Eu-De-LBb

Nekrasova, I.
   Kak izobreli knigopechatanie. St. Petersburg, Chital'nia
Narodnoi Shkoly [n.d.]   [694]
   Eu-Ru-MLe

- 93 -

New York Times.
   The story of the recorded word ... [New York, ᶜ1939].   cover-title,
31, [1]p.   illus.   23 cm.
   "To tell the story briefly related in this booklet, the New York
Times has been assembling ... more than two hundred objects now on
exhibition ... From the exhibits have been selected the illustra-
tions in this booklet."   [695]
   DLC

Nicolaus.
   Erfindung der Buchdruckerkunst von technischen Standpunkte. Beiträge zur Geschichte der Technik und Industrie, vol. 11, 1921,
p. 89-96.   [696]

Niel, Richard.
   Laurens Janszoon Coster und Johannes Gutenberg. Zeitschrift
für Deutschlands Buchdrucker, vol. 40, no. 46, 1928, p. 387-388;
no. 47, p. 397-398.   [697]

Orcutt, William Dana, 1870-
   Master makers of the book; being a consecutive story of the book
from a century before the invention of printing through the era of
the Doves press, by William Dana Orcutt.   Garden City, N. Y.,
Doubleday, Doran & company, inc., 1928. 271, [1]p. front. (port.)
20.5 cm.
   Frontispiece accompanied by guard sheet with descriptive letter-
press.
   Bibliography: p. 248.   [698]
   DLC ICJ ICN In MB MWA NN

Oswald, John Clyde, 1872-
   A history of printing, its development through five hundred years,
by John Clyde Oswald ... New York and London, D. Appleton and company,
1928. xx, [1], 403, [1]p. col. front., illus., plates, facsims.
(part. col., 1 double)   24 cm.
   Bibliography: p. 389-[391].   [699]
   DLC ICN In MWA NN WaU Eu-De-BP Eu-Ge-LB

Pache, Constant.
   L'art d'imprimer. Son histoire. Bruxelles, A. Leempoel, 1913.
137p.   illus.   4to.
   Reprinted from Annales de l'Imprimerie, Aug. 1910, p. 105-107. [700]
   NN Eu-Fr-PN

Papst, Johann.
   Der Werdegang von Gutenbergs Erfindung.   Archiv für Buchgewerbe,
vol. 43, 1906-p. 262-271.   [701]

Peddie, Robert Alexander, 1869-
   An outline of the history of printing: to which is added the

- 94 -

history of printing in colours. By Robert Alexander Peddie ...
London, Grafton & co., 1917. 3 prel. leaves, [5]-58p. 21.5 cm.
   "Revised and enlarged edition of lectures delivered before the
   Royal society of arts in 1914."   [702]
   DLC ICJ ICN MB NN NjP Eu-Ne-AVb

Peddie, Robert Alexander, 1869-
   Printing, a short history of the art ... edited by R. A. Peddie
... London, Grafton & co., 1927. ix, [1], 389, [1]p., 1 leaf
19.5 cm.
   Bibliographies at end of chapters.   [703]
   DLC ICN IU In MB NN RPJCB ViU Eu-Ge-LE

Pizzetta, J.
   La historia de un pliego de papel. Gutenberg (Buenos Aires),
vol. 40, no. 18, 1940, p. 44-50.
   On writing materials, manuscript books, the introduction of
   paper into Europe, and the invention of printing.   [704]

Pollard, Alfred William, 1859-
   Fine books, by Alfred W. Pollard ... London, Methuen & co., ltd.
[1912] xv, 331, [1]p. xl plates (incl. front., ports., facsims.)
26 cm. (Half-title: The connoisseur's library. General editor:
Cyril Davenport)
   Series title also on t.-p.
   Contents includes: The invention of printing: Holland; the
   invention of printing: Mainz.   [705]
   DLC

---- The origin and development of printing. London Times,
vol. 29, no. 45346, Oct. 1929.   [706]

---- The story of printing. London Times, Sept. 10, 1912.   [707]

Pollin, Fr. W.
   Wie denken Sie über Buchdrucker und Buchdruckerkunst? Zeitschrift für Deutschlands Buchdrucker, vol. 43, no. 54, 1931,
p. 522.   [708]

   Les precurseurs et les inventeurs de l'imprimerie. Union
Syndicale et Fédération des Syndicats des Maîtres Imprimeurs de
France. Bulletin Officiel, no. 12, Dec. 1929, p. 62-64.   [709]

Proskurnin, N. P.
   Izobretenie knigopechataniía i nachalo ego v Rossii. Moskva,
1918. 24p.   [710]
   Eu-Ru-MLe

Ralston, A. L.
   Who invented the art of printing? Coster - Gutenberg - Fust -
Schoeffer. American Printer, vol. 44, Aug. 1907, p. 643-644. [711]

Rath, Erich von.
    Aufgaben der Wiegendruck-Forschung.   Festvortrag bei der Feier
des 25jährigen Jubiläums des Gutenberg-Museums am 27 Juni 1925 in
Mainz.   Beilage zum 22 bis 24 Jahresbericht der Gutenberg-Gesellschaft. Mainz, 1925.   21, [1]p.   22.5 cm.   [712]

Ravry, André, 1886-
    Les origines de la presse et de l'imprimerie par M. André Ravry
... Paris, Union Syndicale des maîtres imprimeurs de France, 1937.
3 prel. leaves, 5-172p.   illus. (incl. ports., plan, facsims.)
plates (part col., part mounted, 1 fold.)   31.5 cm.   (Bulletin
official de l'Union syndicale des maîtres imprimeurs de France,
Noel, 1937)
    Illustrated t.-p.
    "L'ouvrage ... constitutes, cette année, le texte de notre album
    de Noel, 1937".
    "Bibliographie": p. 160-162.   "Index des titres cités: p. 166-
    172.   [713]
    DSI

Renault, Raoul, i.e., Joseph Eugéne Raoul, 1867-
    Débuts de l'imprimerie.   Quebec, imprimé pour l'auteur, 1905.
72, [1]p.   plate, port., facsims.   26 cm.
    "Tiré à trois cents exemplaires."   [714]
    DLC   ICJ   MB   Eu-Ge-LB

Restrepo, Currea Anibal.
    Origines de la impronta.   Revista de las Indias (Bogota), no.
10, Aug. 1938, p. 41-66.   [715]

Rollins, Carl P.
    A short history of printing.   [Part 1: to 1562]   Publishers'
Weekly, vol. 99, no. 24, June 1921, p. 1745-1748.   [716]

Romain, Jean.
    À propos des origines de l'imprimerie.   Annales de l'Imprimerie,
no. 5, 1913, p. 65-66.   [717]

Root, Azariah Smith, 1862-1927.
    The present situation as to the origin of printing.   Biblio-
graphical Society of America. Papers, vol. 5, 1910, p. 9-21.
    "Read at the 12th meeting of the society at Mackinac Island
    (Mich.)   June 30 and July 5, 1910."

Scheibler, August Hermann, 1854-
    Bogtrykkerkunstens og avisernes historie, af H. Scheibler ...
Med 138 illustrationer. Kristiania, A/s W. C. Fabritius & sønners
forlag, 1910.   x, 288p. incl. col. front., illus. (part col.)
ports., facsims. (part col.)   29.5 cm.
    Title vignette, initials, head and tail pieces in colors.   [719]
    DLC   ICJ   Eu-Ge-LSb

Scheuermann, W.
  Geschichte der Erfindung des Buchdrucks. Kunstwanderer, Apr.
1922, p. 347.   [720]

Southward, J.
  Historical printing: from its origin to the close of the 19th
century. British and Colonial Printer, vol. 48, 1901, p. 128-   [721]
285.

Stevens, Thomas Wood.
  The birthplace of the craft. Inland Printer, vol. 40, 1907,
p. 35-37.   [722]

Stevens, W. E.
  The evolution, invention and progress of printing. Inland
Printer, vol. 50, 1913, p. 857-858; vol. 51, 1913, p. 77, 372,
531, 699, 869; vol. 52, 1913-1914, p. 85, 243, 407, 567.   [723]

Tempest, Henry G.
  The full and true account of the invention of printing. British
Printer, vol. 15, no. 87, May-June 1902, p. 133-134.
    A hoax.   [724]

----   The invention of printing. Caxton's Magazine, n. s.,
vol. 4 suppl. no. 6, Dec. 1902, insert p. 220a-220d.
    A hoax.   [725]

Uhlendorf, Bernhard Alexander, 1893-
  The invention of printing and its spread till 1470, by B. A.
Uhlendorf ... [Chicago, 1932] Cover-title, p. 179-231. 24 cm.
    "Reprinted for private circulation from the Library quarterly,
    vol. II, no. 3, July 1932."   [726]
    DLC

Vecchioni, Cesare, 1880-
... Dalla scrittura alla stampa; cenni storici ... Aquila, Officine
Grafiche Vecchioni, 1915.   145p., 1 leaf.   25.5 cm.
    At head of title: Cesare Vecchioni.   [727]
    MH   Eu-Ge-LB

  1447 das Jahr der Erfindung der Buchdruckerkunst. Allgemeine
Buchhändlerzeitung, no. 42, 1901.   [728]

Walker, E.
    A brief history of printing. London, 1911. 4to.   [729]
    Eu-Ge-LSb

Wehrmann, M.
Die Cramer über die Erfindung der Buchdruckerkunst. Monatsblätter der Gesellschaft für Pommersche Geschichte, vol. 14, 1901,
p. 155.   [730]

Who invented movable type, Coster or Gutenberg? British
Printer, vol. 44, no. 259, May-June 1931, p. 17-18.
    Signed: B. E. J. C.   [731]

Who invented printing? British Printer, vol. 39, no. 232,
Nov.-Dec. 1926, p. 173.
    Signed: C. H. L.   [732]

Williams, Henry Smith.
    The history of the art of printing. London, 1901.
    Title from Herscher, Irenaeus. The three-fold printing
    centennial ... 1940.   [733]

Winship, George Parker, 1871-
    Beginning of printing in the fifteenth century. Publishers'
Weekly, vol. 137, Jan. 1940, p. 43-45.   [734]

----   Gutenberg to Plantin; an outline of the early history of
printing, by George Parker Winship ... Cambridge, Harvard university
press, 1926.   xi, [1], 84, [2]p.   illus. (incl. facsims.)
21.5 cm.   [735]
    DLC   ICJ   ICN   MB   MWA   NjP   RPJCD   Eu-Ge-LB   Eu-Ne-AVb

----   Printing in the fifteenth century.   Philadelphia, University of Pennsylvania press, 1940.   158p.   22 cm.   [736]
    DLC   NN

Zülch, Walter Karl, ed.
    Frankfurter Urkundenbuch zur Frühgeschichte des Buchdrucks.
Aus den Akten des Frankfurter Stadtarchivs zusammengestellt und
hrsg. von Walter Karl Zülch und Gustav Mori.   Frankfurt am Main,
J. Baer & Co., 1920.   4 prel. leaves, 75p.   1 illus.   23.5 cm.   [737]
    DLC   NN   Eu-De-BP   Eu-De-LBb   Eu-De-MzG

B.   RIVAL CLAIMS

    1   For and About Gutenberg

Alary, Jacques.
    Gutenberg et l'imprimerie typographique.   Paris, G. Jousset, 1876.
56p.   22.5 cm.   [738]
    NN   Eu-Fr-PN

Bernard, Auguste Joseph, 1811-1868.
    [Letter concerning, among other things, a claim that the recently
published portrait of Gutenberg does not represent the inventor of
printing.]   Bulletin du Bibliophile Belge, vol. 12, (2d ser., vol. 3),
1856, p. 359-360.   [739]

Bigot, Charles.
    Conférence faite au théâtre de Langres le 9 octobre 1879, par Charles
Bigot, ... sur Gutenberg et l'imprimerie.   Langres, impr. de Dessoye,
1879.   73p.   16mo.   [740]
    Eu-De-LBb   Eu-Fr-PN

Binz, Gustav.
    Was hat Gutenberg erfunden?   Schweizerisches Gutenbergmuseum, vol.
8, no. 1, 1922, p. 4-10; no. 2, p. 34-38.   [741]

Bouchot, Henri François Xavier Marie, 1849-1906.
    L'oeuvre de Gutenberg, l'imprimerie, l'illustration.   Paris, H. Lé-
cene et H. Oudin, 1887.   240p.   8vo.   [742]
    Eu-Fr-PN   (Also 1888 and 1889 eds.)
    Eu-Ge-LB   (1888 ed.)

Bullen, George.
    The Gutenberg controversy.   Inland Printer, vol. 3, Aug. 1886, p.
700-701.   [743]

----   On the presumed earliest printed notice of Gutenberg as the inventor of printing.   Library Association of the United Kingdom.   Transactions and Proceedings, vol. 7, 1890, p. 25-31.   [744]

Bullen, Henry Lewis.
    A defense of Johann Gutenberg, inventor of typography.   Inland
Printer, vol. 66, 1920, p. 190-192.   [745]

----   Who was the first printer?   The Gutenberg-Coster controversy re-
stated.   Publishers' Weekly, vol. 104, no. 9, 1923, p. 661-662.   [746]

Dahl, Johann Konrad, 1762-1833.
    Die Buchdruckerkunst, erfunden von Johann Gutenberg, verbessert und
zur Volkommenheit gebracht durch Peter Schöffer von Gernsheim. Histor-
isch-kritische Abhandlung von J. Konrad Dahl ... Mainz, Johann Wirth,
1832. 54p. facsim. 22 cm.   [747]
    ICN   MB   NN   NNC   Eu-De-LBb   Eu-Fr-PN   Eu-Ge-LB   Eu-Ge-LE
    Eu-Ge-LP   Eu-Ge-LSb

Delon, Charles, 1839-1900.
    Gutenberg et l'invention de l'imprimerie.   Paris, Hachette, 1881.
36p.   14 cm.   [748]
    Eu-Fr-PN   Eu-Ge-LB   Eu-Ge-LSb

----   Gutenberg et l'invention de l'imprimerie, par Ch. Delon. Deuxième édition.   Paris, Librairie Hachette et c^{ie}, 79 Boulevard Saint
Germain, 79, 1884. 36p. illus., port. 14 cm.
    At head of title: Bibliothèque des écoles et des familles.   [749]
    INH   Eu-Fr-PN   Eu-Ge-LE   Eu-Ge-LSb

    Did Gutenberg invent printing?   Bibliographer, vol. 2, no. 9, 1882,
p. 57-59, 150.   [750]

Domel, George.
    Gutenberg: die Erfindung des Typengusses und seine Frühdrucke ...
Köln, Als Privatdruck erschienen, 1919.   vii p., 1 leaf, 108p., 1 leaf.
19 facsims. (1 double.)   24 cm.
    "Literatur-Verzeichnis" p. 107.   [751]
    MH   NN   Eu-De-LBb   Eu-Ge-LB   Eu-Ne-AVb
    2d ed., 1921: CSmH   ICN   ICU   IU   MH   NjP   Eu-De-BP
    Eu-De-LBb

----   Gutenbergs Erfindung im Bilde der Forschung.   Deutscher Buch-
und Steindrucker, vol. 20, 1914, p. 797-801.   [752]

Dyckerhoff, Walter.
    Von Gutenberg zur Gegenwart.   Rhein-Mainische Wirtschafts-Zeitung
(Frankfurt am Main), no. 25, June 18, 1940.   [753]

Dziatzko, Karl Franz Otto, 1842-1903.
    Gutenberg und die Erfindung der Buchdruckerkunst.   Velhagen und
Klasings Monatshefte, June 1900, p. 353-366.   [754]

Ed, Christoph Marquand, 1809-
    Geschichte der Buchdruckerkunst und ihres Erfinders Johann Gutenberg,
seit ihrem Ursprung bis auf unsere Zeit.   Von C. M. Ed.   Hamburg, B.
S. Berendsohn, 1840.   128p.   13 cm.   [755]
    ICN   NN   Eu-Ge-LSb

Ed, Christoph Marquand, 1809-
  Kurzgefasste Geschichte des Buchdrucks, von C. M. Ed, Buchdrucker.
Hamburg, bei Johann August Meissner, 1839.   1 prel. leaf, [iii]-viii,
136p.   20 cm.   [756]
   ICN   NN   NNGr   Eu-Fr-PN   Eu-Ge-LB   Eu-Ge-LSb

Ehwald, Rudolf, 1847-
  Der älteste Zeuge für Gutenberg.   Zeitschrift für Bücherfreunde,
vol. 4, 1900, p. 129-140.   [757]

Falk, Franz, 1840-1909.
  Ein neuer Beleg für Gutenberg als Erfinder der Buchdruckerkunst.
Zentralblatt für Bibliothekswesen, vol. 8, 1891, p. 80.   [758]

----   Das Zeugniss des mainzer Erzbischofs Berthold für Mainz als
Erfindungsstätte der Druckkunst.   Zentralblatt für Bibliothekswesen,
vol. 5, 1888, p. 243.   [759]

Fichet, Guillaume, b. 1433.
  Épître adressée à Robert Gaguin le 1er janvier 1472 par Guillaume
Fichet, sur l'introduction de l'imprimerie à Paris.   Reproduction
héliographique de l'exemplaire unique possédé par l'Université de Bâle.
Paris, H. Champion, libraire de la Société de l'histoire de Paris, 1889.
2 prel. leaves, 5p.   facsim. ([10]p.)   25.5 cm.
   In boards.
   Preface signed: L. D. [i.e. Léopold Delisle]
   " 'Un second exemplaire ... a été, depuis, signalé dans la Biblio-
thèque de l'Université de Fribourg en Brisgau' (Note de m. Delisle)"
-P. Lacombe, Bibliographie des travaux de m. Leópold Delisle, 1902,
p. 232, no. 1129.   [760]
   DLC   ICJ   ICN   NjP   WaU   Eu-Fr-PN   Eu-Ge-LB   Eu-Ne-GK

----   The Fichet letter, the earliest document ascribing to Gutenberg
the invention of printing, by Douglas C. McMurtrie. With a reproduc-
tion of the letter in collotype and a translation of the text by W. A.
Montgomery, Ph. D.   New York, Press of Ars typographica, 1927.
4 prel. leaves, 7-58p. incl. facsim.   (p. [27]-[36])   29 cm.
   "Of this volume there have been printed ... two hundred copies only."
   The facsimile reproduction, from the original in the library of the
   University at Basel, is followed by the Latin text and an English
   translation.   [761]
   DLC   ICN   NN

----   Guillermi Ficheti ... quam ad Robertum Gaguinum de Johanne Gutenberg et de artis impressoriae in Gallia primordiis nec non de ortho-
graphiae utilitate conscripsit epistola.   Ad exemplar ut videtur uni-
cum in aedibus Sorbonae anno MCCCCXXII impressum nunc in Bibliotheca
Basiliensi asservantum denuo edidit Ludovicus Sieber ... Basileae,
Typographia Schweighauseriana, 1887.   14p.   1 plate.   24 cm.   [762]
   ICJ   ICN   NN   Eu-Fr-PN

Fischbach, Friedrich, 1839-
    Ursprung der Buchstaben Gutenbergs.   Mentz, 1900.   24p.   16
plates.   4to.   [763]
    NIC   Eu-Ge-LSb

Fischer von Waldheim, Gotthelf, 1771-1853.
    Beschreibung einiger typographischen Seltenheiten, nebst Beyträgen
zur Erfindungsgeschichte der Buchdruckerkunst ... von Gotthelf Fischer
... Mainz, Auf Kosten des Verfassers, und Nürnberg, bey I. L. S.
Lechner, 1800-04.   6 parts in 1 vol.   2 fold. plates.   facsims.
(part fold.)   21 cm.   [764]
    DLC   ICJ   NN   RPB   Eu-Fr-PN   Eu-Ge-LB   Eu-Ge-LP   Eu-Ge-LSb
    Eu-Ne-GK

------   Essai sur les monuments typographiques de Jean Gutenberg, Mayen-
çais, inventeur de l'imprimerie.   Par Gotthelf Fischer ... Mayence, An
X [1802?]   5 prel. leaves, [3]-102p.   front. (port.)   facsims. (part
col.)   26.5 cm.
    Added t.-p., engraved.   [765]
    DLC   ICJ   ICN   IaU   NN   Eu-Fr-PN   Eu-Ge-LB   Eu-Ne-GK

------   Notice du premier monument typographique en caractères mobiles
avec date connu jusqu'à ce jour, découvert dans les archives de Mayence
et déposé à la Bibliothèque nationale de Paris, par G. Fischer.   A Mayence, chez Théodore Zabern, Imprimeur de la Préfecture du département
du Mont-Tonnerre.   [1804]   [8]p.   folding plate.   24 cm.   [766]
    MB   NN   NNC   Eu-De-LBb   Eu-Fr-PN   Eu-Ge-LB   Eu-Ne-GK

Frère, Édouard Benjamin, 1797-1874.
    Considérations sur les origines typographiques.   Rouen, A. Peron,
1850.   roy. 8vo.
    Extrait du précis des travaux de l'Académie de Rouen, etc.
    In favor of Gutenberg.   [767]
    Eu-De-LBb   Eu-Ge-LB

Frydlender, J.
    Quand et comment naquit l'imprimerie.   Papyrus, vol. 18, 1937, p.
198-199.   [768]

Gama, Jean Pierre, ca. 1775-1861.
    Esquisse historique de Gutenberg par J. P. Gama ... Paris, à la
librairie de Germer Baillère, Rue de l'École-de-Médecine, 17, 1857.
xvi, 59p., 1 leaf.   25.5 cm.   [769]
    DSG   ICN   MH   Eu-Fr-PN   Eu-Ge-LB

Gillot, George.
    Guttemberg; précis sur l'origine de l'imprimerie.   Fonderie Typo-
graphique, vol. 3, no. 32, 1901, p. 353-356.   [770]

Gutenberg i ego izobretenie.   Severo-Zapadnoe Slovo, no. 569,
1900.   [771]

Guttenberg izobretatel' knigopechataniia.   Moskva, O-vo Rasprostraneniia poleznykh knig, 1871.   48p.   (Knizhki dlia shkol.   nr. 2) [772]
Eu-Ru-MLe

Hazel, Oscar J.
The inventor of printing.   London Typographical Journal, vol. 54,
no. 2, Feb. 1919, p. 122.   [773]

Heidenheimer, Heinrich, 1856-
Ein indirectes Zeugniss für Johannes Gutenberg als Erfinder der Drukkunst.   Zentralblatt für Bibliothekswesen, vol. 17, 1900.p.278-281.[774]

Holstein, Ad. von.
Gutenberg, Fust und Schöffer.   Die Erfindung des Druckes mit boweg-
lichen Buchstaben.   Darmstadt, 1876-1877.   32p.   4to.
Title from Bigmore & Wyman.   [775]

Hupp, Otto, 1859-
Gutenberg!--wer sonst; eine Erwiederung.   Gutenberg Jahrbuch, vol.
14, 1939, p. 87-101.   [776]

----   Ein Zahlenbeweis für Gutenberg.   Gutenberg Jahrbuch, vol. 6,
1931, p. 9-27.   [777]

Jensen, J. V., and A. Marcus.
Gutenberg.   Til Bogtrykkerkunstens Historie.   København, 1939.
92p.
Title from Bibliographie des Bibliotheks-und Buchwesens, 1939.   [778]

John Rylands Library, Manchester.
Johann Gutenberg and the dawn of typography: a lecture by the librarian.   1903.   15p.
Title from The London bibliography of social sciences.   vol. 3,
1931.   [779]

Josephson, Aksel Gustav Salomon, 1860-
Johann Gutenberg and the invention of printing.   Syllabus to accompany an exhibition.   Public Libraries, vol. 9, 1904, p. 276-279.   [780]

Kharlamova, T.
Gutenberg i izobretenie knigopechataniia.   Moskva, 1893.   35p. [781]
Eu-Ru-MLe

Kraus, Franz Xaver, 1840-1901.
Johann Gutenberg und die Erfindung der Typographie.   Deutsche Rundschau, vol. 44, 1885, p. 410-424.   [782]

Kraus, Franz Xaver, 1840-1901.
    Johann Gutenberg und die Erfindung der Typographie.   1885.
8vo.   [783]
    Eu-De-LBb

Külb, Philipp Hedwig.
    Geschichte der Erfindung der Buchdruckerkunst. Eine für Jedermann
verständliche kurze Darstellung der durch die neuesten Forschungen ge-
wonnenen Resultate, von Dr. Ph. H. Külb, Stadtbibliothekar zu Mainz.
Mit zwei lithographirten Blättern, das Gutenbergsmonument und die beiden Basreliefs darstellend.   [Mainz, 1837]   iv, 96p.   21.5 cm.   [784]
    ICN   NNC   Eu-Ge-LB   Eu-Ge-LSb

Lehne, Johann Friedrich Franz, 1771-1836.
    Beiträge zur Geschichte der Erfindung der Buchdruckerkunst. Mainz,
Johann Wirth, 1837.   ix, 295p.   21 cm.   [785]
    ICJ   Eu-De-LBb   Eu-Fr-PN   Eu-Ge-LB   Eu-Ge-LE

----   Meine Antwort an Herrn Ebert, die Harlemer angebliche Erfindungsgeschichte betreffend.   Allgemeine Literatur Zeitung, no. 142, June
1826, col. 298-304.   [786]

Linde, Antonius van der, 1833-1897.
    Bijdrage tot de geschiedenis der boekdrukkunst.   Gent, Leliaert,
1887.   16p.   8vo.   [787]
    Eu-De-LBb   Eu-Ge-LB

----   Geschichte der Erfindung der Buchdruckkunst; von Antonius von
der Linde ... Berlin, A. Asher & Co., 1886.   3 vols.   illus., plate,
port., facsim.   33.5x25 cm.
    Paged continuously.
    Title in red and black.
    Contents.-1. Bd. Litteratur. Unhistorische Ansprüche in Mainz,
Strassburg und Feltre. Der holländische Koster Mythus.-2. Bd. Der
Koster Mythus [forts.]-3. Bd. Die Erfindung der Typographie zu Mainz.
Beilagen. Register: Register der Illustrationen. Litteraturregister.
Mythologisches Register. Alphabetisches Register.   [788]
    DLC   ICJ   ICN   MB   MH   MdBP   NN   OCl   Eu-Ge-LB   Eu-Ge-LP
    Eu-Ge-LSb   Eu-Ne-AVb   Eu-Ne-GK

----   Gutenberg.   Vaderlandsche Letteroefeningen voor 1870. Honderd
en tiende jaargang. Eerste deel. Wetenschap en belletrie.   p. 365-
405.   [789]

---- ----   Reprinted, Utrecht, 1870.   8vo.   [790]
    Eu-Ne-AVb

----   Gutenberg. Geschichte und Erdichtung. Aus den Quellen nachgewiesen von Dr. A. v. d. Linde.   Stuttgart, W. Spemann, 1878.   viii,

582p., 1 leaf, xcvii, [1]p.   25.5 cm.   [791]
   DLC   ICJ   ICN   MH   NN   Eu-Ge-LB   Eu-Ge-LSb   Eu-Ne-GK

Linde, Antonius van der, 1833-1897.
   The Haarlem legend of the invention of printing by Lourens Jans-
zoon Coster, critically examined by Dr. A. van der Linde. From the
Dutch by J. H. Hessels, with an introduction, and a classified list of
the Costerian incunabula.   London, Blades, East & Blades, 1871.
xxvi p., 1 leaf, 170p.   fold. tab.   24.5 cm.   [792]
   DLC   ICJ   ICN   NN   Eu-De-LBb   Eu-Ge-LB   Eu-Ge-LP   Eu-Ge-LSb
Eu-Ne-GK

----   Haarlemer halletjes uit Praag.   Nederlandsche Spectator, no. 32,
Aug. 12, 1871, p. 249-250.   [793]

----   De Haarlemsche Costerlegende wetenschappelijk onderzocht door
Dr. A. van der Linde.   2., omgewerkte uitgaaf.   's Gravenhage, M.
Nijhoff, 1870.   5 prel. leaves, 352p.   23.5 cm.
   "In his preface the author begins by saying: This book has its origin in the revision and amalgamation of my article on Gutenberg
which appeared in the Vaderlandsche Letteroefeningen of July 1870,
and my study of the famous Coster question, published in the Nederlandsche Spectator of Dec. 1869 to May 1870.   It is not a reprint,
but a new work."   Note supplied by Miss Emma Dronckers, Librarian
to the Vereeniging ter Bevordering van de Belangen des Boekhandels
te Amsterdam.   [794]
   DLC   ICN   MH   NN   Eu-De-LBb   Eu-Ge-LB   Eu-Ge-LE   Eu-Ge-LSb
Eu-Ne-AVb   Eu-Ne-GK

----   L'invention de l'imprimerie.   Bulletin du Bibliophile Belge,
3d ser., vol. 5, 1870, p. 61-66, 93-106, 125-145, 157-180, 189-203,
205-223, 229-243, 245-253, 261-268.   [795]

----   La legende costérienne de Harlem.   Nouvel examen critique, précédé d'une introduction historique par M. Ch. Ruelens.   Bruxelles,
chez F. J. Olivier, Libraire, 1871.   [2], 126p.   1 table.   21 cm. [796]
   ICJ   Eu-Ge-LB   Eu-Ge-LSb

----   Quellenforschungen zur Geschichte der Erfindung der Typographie.
Das Brevarium Moguntinum.   Eine Studie von Antonius von der Linde.
Wiesbaden, Feller & Gecks, 1884.   [6], 82, [2]p.   23.5 cm.   [797]
   ICJ   Eu-Ge-LB   Eu-Ge-LSb

----   [A translation into English of the most important parts of Gutenberg: Geschichte und Erdichtung.   Stuttgart, 1877.]   ms.   2 vols.
1879.   Folio.   [798]
   Eu-Ge-LSb

Löffler, Klemens.
   Der Streit um Gutenbergs Erfindung. Graphische Nachrichten, vol.
12, July 1933, p. 149.
   Extract from Löffler's article in Augsburger Postzeitung.   [799]

Meisner, Heinrich, 1849-1929.
   Die Erfindung der Buchdruckerkunst. Zum fünfhundertsten Geburtstage
Johann Gutenbergs. Von Oberbibliothekar Dr. Heinrich Meisner und Bibliothekar Dr. Johannes Luther. Mit 15 Kunstbeilagen und 100 Abbildung-
en. Bielefeld und Leipzig, Velhagen & Klasing, 1900. 2 prel. leaves,
116p. illus., col. plates, port., facsims. (part col., 2 fold., 1
double) 26 cm. (Added t.-p: Monographien zur Weltgeschichte ... xi)[800]
   DLC   ICJ   ICN   MN   Eu-De-BP   Eu-Fr-PN   Eu-Ge-LE   Eu-Ge-LSb
   Eu-No-AVb

Micheletti, Giovanni Battista, 1763-1833.
   Presagi scientifichi sull' arte della stampa. Aquila, N. Rietelli,
1814. 190p. 8vo.   [801]
   ICN   Eu-Fr-PN

Mori, Gustav.
   Die Erfindung des Buchdrucks und das Wirken Gutenbergs in Mainz,
Strassburg und Frankfurt a.M. Elsass-Lothringisches Jahrbuch, vol.
19, 1940.   [802]

---- The essence of Gutenberg's invention. New York, D. C. Mc-
Murtrie, 1925. Caption title, 101-144p., incl. illus., plate,
facsims. 35 cm.
   Extracted from Ars typographica, vol. 2, no. 2, Oct. 1925.   [803]
   MiU   Eu-No-AVb

---- Mainz, die Gutenberg-Stadt. Deutscher Buch- und Steindrucker,
vol. 35, Aug. 1929, p. 816-820.   [804]

---- Was hat Gutenberg erfunden? ein Rückblick auf die Frühtechnik
des Schriftgusses. Unter Anlehnung an den am 26. Juni 1920 gelegentlich
der Hauptversammlung der Gutenberg-Gesellschaft in Mainz gehaltenen Vortrag in erweiterter Form dargeboten, von Gustav Mori. Mainz, Verlag
der Gutenberg-Gesellschaft, 1921. 4 prel. leaves, 11-37p. plates,
facsims. (1 fold.) 23 cm.
   "Beilage zum 19. Jahresbericht für das Geschäftsjahr 1919/1920, der
   von der Gutenberg-Gesellschaft demnächst mit dem 18. und 20. Jahresbericht vereint herausgegeben wird."   [805]
   DLC   ICN   Eu-No-AVb   Eu-Sz-BeG

Nielsen, L. Chr.
   Boktryckerikonstens uppfinning och des utveckling i Tyskland ...
Ett bidrag till boktryckerikonstens historia i anledning af Gutenberg-
Jubileet. 1400-1900. Malmö, [Förlagsaktiebolagets Tryckeri], 1898;

København, [A. Leisner och Fr. Weiss], 1900.   vii, 309, [2]p.   illus.
(incl. ports., plans) col. facsim., diagrs.   25.5 cm.   [806]
   MnU

Nieritz, Gustav.
   Gutenberg und seine Erfindung.   St. Gallen Tageblatt, no. 288,
1852.
   Title from Neuer Anzeiger für Bibliographie und Bibliothekswissenschaft, 1854.   [807]

Pfaff, Fridrich, 1855-1917.
   Guillaume Fichets Brief über Erfindung der Buchdruckerkunst.
Zentralblatt für Bibliothekswesen, vol. 5, 1888, p. 201-209.   [808]

Pollard, Alfred William, 1859-
   Gutenberg, Fust, Schoeffer, and the invention of printing.
Library, 2d ser., vol. 8, 1907, p. 69-99.   [809]

Poole, W. F.
   John Gutenberg and the early printers.   Library Journal, vol. 18,
1893, p. 474-475.   [810]

[Roche, Johann Wilhelm] 1764-1835.
   Typographia oder die Buchdruckerkunst, eine Erfindung der Deutschen;
bei Gelegenheit der vierten Harlemer Secularfeier zur Ehre dieser Kunst
in Erinnerung gebracht ... Essen, G. D. Bädeker, 1823.   xii, 40p.
19.5 cm.
   Preface signed: R.
   Also issued in Dutch, translated by G. H. M. Delprat.   [811]
   DLC   ICN   IaU   NNC   Eu-Ge-LP   Eu-Ge-LSb   Eu-Ne-GK

[----]   Typographia: of, Betoog, dat de boekdrukkunst eene uitvinding
der Duitschers is. Uitgegeven, bij gelegenheid van de viering van het
vierde eeuwfeest dier kunst, te Haarlem. Uit het Hoogduitsch. Met
een opholderend naschrift van den Nederduitschen vertaler ... Franeker,
G. Ypma, 1823.   viii, 55p.   23.5 cm.
   Preface signed: R.   [812]
   ICN   NNC   Eu-De-LBb   Eu-Ge-LP   Eu-Ne-AVb   Eu-Ne-GK

Ruppel, Aloys Leonhard, 1882-
   Die Erfindung Gutenbergs, technisch und geistig gesehen.   Graphische Nachrichten, vol. 16, 1937, p. 528.   Same, Deutscher Drucker,
vol. 43, 1937, p. 268.   [813]

----   Gutenbergs uppfinning sedd tekniskt och andligen.   Nordisk
Boktryckarekonst, vol. 38, 1937, p. 171-172.   [814]

----   Neuere Fortschritte der Gutenberg-Forschung.   Archiv für Buchgewerbe und Gebrauchsgraphik, vol. 77, no. 7-8, 1940, p. 241-246.   [815]

Ruppel, Aloys Leonhard, 1882-
Wer ist als Erfinder der Buchdruckerkunst anzusehen, Coster oder
Gutenberg? Typographische Mitteilungen, vol. 22, 1925, p. 96-101.[816]

Sander, J.
Johannes Gutenberg; nebst wiedergaben deutscher Frühdrucke. Westermanns Monatshefte, vol. 167, Mar. 1940, p. 352-358. [817]

Schaab, Carl Anton.
Die Geschichte der Erfindung der Buchdruckerkunst durch Johann Gensfleisch genannt Gutenberg, zu Mainz, pragmatisch aus den Quellen bearbeitet, mit mehr als dritthalb hundert noch ungedruckten Urkunden, welche die Genealogie.Gutenberg's, Fust's und Schöffer's in ein neues Licht stellen, von C. A. Schaab ... Mainz, Auf Kosten des Verfassers, 1830-31.
3 vols. front. (ports.) fold. plates. 21 cm. [818]
    DLC ICJ ICN MH MdBP NjP Eu-De-BP Eu-Ge-LB Eu-Ge-LP
    Eu-Ge-LBb Eu-Ne-AVb Eu-Ne-GK

---- ---- 2d ed. Mainz, 1855. 3 vols. [819]
    Eu-Le-LPb

---- Randglossen zu den Phantasien und Träumereien des Pseudogeistes
Johann Gensfleisch, genannt Gutenberg, an Dr. C. A. Schaab und dem Ausschuss zur Errichtung des Denkmals zu seiner Ehre zu Mainz, Utrecht bei
Robert Natan und gedruckt zu Haag 1835. Mit zwei Anhängen: 1. Historischer Beweis, dass die vierte Jubelfeier der Erfindung der Buchdruckerkunst in dem laufenden Jahre 1836 eintrete und nicht im Jahre 1840, oder
einem andern könne gefeiert werden. II. Ueber die Monumentssache und
was seit dreissig Jahren darin geschehen ist. Von Dr. C. A. Schaab.
Mainz, Auf Kosten des Verfassers, 1836. 1 prel. leaf, viii, [3]-138p.
20 cm. [820]
    DLC Eu-Ge-LB Eu-Ge-LE Eu-Ne-AVb Eu-Ne-GK

Schoepflin, Johann Daniel, 1694-1771.
Dissertation sur l'origine de l'imprimerie, 9 mai 1741. (In Mémoires de littérature, tirés des registres de l'Académie royale des inscriptions et belles-lettres, depuis l'année MDCCXLI, jusques et compris l'année MDCCXLIII. Tome dix-septième. A Paris, de l'Imprimerie
royale, MDCCLI. p. 762-786) [821]

---- Jo. Danielis Schoepflini ... Vindiciae typographicae. Argentorati,
J. G. Bauer, 1760. 3 prel. leaves, 120, 42, [10]p. vii fold. facsims.,
24x20 cm.
    "Documenta typographicarum originum ex argentinensibus tabulariis
    et bibliothecis ...": 42p.
    Contents.-Notitia praevia - Gutenbergii Acta & primordia typographica Argentorati. - Typographia a Gutenbergio continuata & a
    Petro Schoeffero perfecta Moguntiae. - Typographia literarum sculptarum a Gutenbergii sociis continuata & perfecta Argentorati. -

Fabulosa Argentinensium de originibus typographicis traditio. -
Fallaces Fausti inscriptiones. - Typographica argentinensis aera
moguntinensi antiquior. - Typographicae Harlemensium origines. -
Reliqua Gutenbergii fata. - Gutenbergii successores Argentinae us-
que ad Sec. XVI. - Typographi Alsatiae extra Argentoratum. - Typo-
graphi alsatae extra Alsatiam.   [822]
DLC   ICJ   ICN   MB   MH   NN   Eu-De-BP   Eu-De-LBb   Eu-De-MzG
Eu-Ge-LB   Eu-Ne-GK

Schoepflin, Johann Daniel, 1694-1771.
    Vindiciae typographicae, translated by Charles Alexander Nelson,
A.M.   New York, Priv. print., 1938.   ix, 200p., 1 leaf.   illus.
(facsims.)   24 cm.
    With reproduction of original t.-p.
    Edited by I. M. Lydenberg.   cf. p. iv.
    "Fifty copies have been printed ..."   [823]
    CtY   DLC   ICN   MH   NN

Scholderer, Victor.
    The invention of printing.   Library, 4th ser., vol. 21, no. 1,
June 1940, p. 1-25.
    "Read before the Bibliographical society on Monday, 18 March
    1940."   [824]

Schwabe, Benno.
    Alteste Zeugniss für Gutenberg als Erfinder der Buchdruckerkunst.
Mitteilungen für den Verein Schweizerischer Buchdruckereibesitzer,
vol. 16, no. 39, 1891.   [825]

[Sotzmann, Johann Daniel Ferdinand]
    Gutenberg und seine Mitbewerber, oder die Briefdrucker und die Buch-
drucker.   Von J. D. F. Sotzmann.   Besonderer Abdruck aus dem Historischen Taschenbuche für 1841.   [Leipzig, F. A. Brockhaus, 1841]   163,
[1]p.   2 facsims.   19 cm.
    Reprint from Historisches Taschenbuch, n.s., vol. 1, 1841,
    p. 516-676.   [826]
    DLC   ICJ   Eu-De-LBb   Eu-Ge-LE

Tetscher, W.
    Gutenberg und die Erfindung der Buchdruckerkunst.   Das Neue Jahr-
hundert, vol. 2, no. 40, 1900.   [827]

Thoma, Albrecht.
    Johannes Gutenberg, der Erfinder der Buchdruckerkunst.   Munchen,
J. F. Lehmann, 1904.   172p.   plates.
    Julius Lohmeyers Vaterländische Jugendbücherei, vol. 16.
    Title from Bibliographie des Bibliotheks und Buchwesen,
    1905.   [828]

Thudichum, F.
Johann Gutenbergs Erfindung in Strassburg 1429-44. <u>Nord</u> <u>und</u> <u>Süd</u>, Sept. 1896, p. 417-423. [829]

Tomlinson, Laurence Elliott.
Gutenberg and the invention of printing; an anniversary review, with special reference to the Gutenberg Bible, by Laurence E. Tomlinson. [Washington, D. C., Judd & Detweiler, inc., 1938] 4 prel. leaves, 13-51p, 2 leaves, incl. facsims. (1 col.) 26 cm.
Metal medallion of portrait of Gutenberg on cover.
Bibliography: leaf at end. [830]
CtY   DLC   NN

Triqueti, H. de.
Gutenberg (Jean Gensfleisch de Sulgeloch). Découverte de l'imprimerie. Discours adressé aux apprentis dans la séance du Comité de patronage de 3 août, 1856. Paris, Meyrueis, 1856. 8vo.
Title from Bigmore & Wyman. [831]

The true story of Gutenberg's invention of printing. <u>Woodcock's</u> <u>Printer</u> <u>and</u> <u>Lithographer</u>, vol. 17, July 9, 1883, p. 551. [832]

Vallet de Viriville, August, 1815-1868.
Sur la découverte, à Mayence, d'une presse attribuée à Gutenberg. <u>Bulletin</u> <u>du</u> <u>Bibliophile</u> <u>Belge</u>, vol. 13 (2d ser., vol. 4), 1857, p. 359-361. [833]

----- Sur un fragment de la presse conservé à Mayence et que l'on croit avoir appartenu à Gutenberg. <u>Société</u> <u>Royale</u> <u>des</u> <u>Antiquaires</u> <u>de</u> <u>France</u>, 1857, p. 162. [834]

Van Loon, Hendrik Willem, 1882-
Observations on the mystery of print and the work of Johann Gutenberg, by Hendrik Willem Van Loon. [New York] Second national book fair, New York Times, Book manufacturers' institute, 1937. 6 prel. leaves, 7-45, [2]p. incl. front., illus. 20.5 cm.
Illustrated t.-p. [835]
DLC   ICN   NN

Volchanetskaia, E.
Iogann Guttenberg i razvitie knigopechataniia. Moskva, I. D. Sytina, 1905. 95p. illus. (Istor. komissiia pri Uchebnom Otd. Obshchestva rasprostraneniia knig.) [836]
Eu-Ru-MLe

Weber, A.
Gutenberg und seine Erfindung. <u>Historische-Politische</u> <u>Blätter</u> <u>für</u> <u>das</u> <u>Katholische</u> <u>Deutschland</u>, vol. 125, 1900, p. 309-331. [837]

Werner, N. J.
    When Gutenberg first printed.   American Printer, vol. 73, part
1, Aug. 1921, p. 27-28.   [838]

Wetter, Johann, 1795-1877.
    Kritische Geschichte der Erfindung der Buchdruckerkunst durch Johann
Gutenberg zu Mainz, begleitet mit einer, vorhin noch nie angestellten,
genauen Prüfung und gänzlichen Beseitigung der von Schöpflin und seinen
Anhängern verfochtenen Ansprüche der Stadt Strassburg, und einer neuen
Untersuchung der Ansprüche der Stadt Harlem und vollständigen Widerlegung ihrer Verfechter Junius, Meerman, Koning, Dibdin, Otley und Ebert.
Von J. Wetter.   Mit dreizehn grossen Tafeln voll sehr genauer Facsimiles. Mainz, J. Wirth, 1836.   xvi, 806, [1]p.   22 cm. And atlas of
xiii facsim.   35.5x30 cm.   [839]
    DLC   ICJ   ICN   NN   Eu-De-LBb   Eu-Ge-LSb   Eu-Ne-GK

Wikström, Bror Anders.
    The true story about Gutenberg's invention of printing, complete in
seven sheets, drawn by B. A. Wikström.   New York, E. H. Hamburger,
[c1882]   8 leaves.   42.5 cm.   [840]
    NN   NNC   Eu-Ge-LB   Eu-Ge-LSb

Winkler, Theodor.
    Die ersten Druckhäuser und Druckwerke von Mainz.   (In Gedenkblätter
zur Gutenbergfeier zu Mainz 14. Aug. 1837 ... Mainz, [1887]   no. 18) [841]
    Eu-Ge-LB   Eu-Ge-LSb   Eu-Sz-BeG

Wyss, Arthur Franz Wilhelm, 1852-1900.
    Die neuesten deutschen Forschungen zur Gutenbergfrage.   Zentral-
blatt für Bibliothekswesen, vol. 7, 1890, p. 407.   [842]

Zarin, A. E.
    Pervyi knigopechatnik I. Gutenberg i istoriia izobretaniia knigo-
pechataniia.   Moskva, D. P. Efimov, 1915.   61p.   ports.   [843]
    Eu-Ru-MLe

        2   For and About Coster

Aa, Cornelis van der, 1749-1816.
    Iets over de uitvinding en voortgang der boekdrukkunst, voorgelezen
... den 29 December 1802 ... Utrecht, C. van der Aa, 1803.   43p.   8vo. [844]
    NN   Eu-De-LBb   Eu-Ne-GK

    Afscheidslied aan alle lengenaars, op het Kosterfeest van 10. Juli
1823.   Haarlem, 1823.
    Title from Mohr, Jubelfeste.   [845]

- 111 -

Albert, A.
Zur Enthüllung des metallenen Standbildes Lourens Jansz. Coster,
zu Haarlem den 16. Juli 1856. Augsburg [1856] Broadside 28x20 cm.
Poem of four stanzas signed A. Albert.
"Gedrukt auf einer Schnellpresse aus der C. Reichenbach'schen
Maschinenfabrik in Augsburg."   [846]
NNC

Album van feestliederen en gezangen, te zingen door de typographische vereenigingen, die deel zullen nemen aan de onthullings-
feesten, op den 16den Julij 1856, te Haarlem. Haarlem, J. J. van
Brederode [1856] 52, [5]p. 18 cm.   [847]
NN Eu-De-LBb Eu-Ne-AVb

Ampzing, Samuel.
Beschryvinge en de lof der stad Haerlem in Holland: in rijm bear-
beyd: ende met veele oude ende nieuwe stucken buyten dicht uyt ver-
scheyde kronijken, handvesten, brieven, memorien ofte gehengenissen,
ende diergelyke schriften verklaerd ende bevestigd. Mitgaders Petri
Scriverii Lavre-Kranz voor Laurens Koster van Haerlem, eerste vinder
van de boekdruckerye ... Haerlem, Adriaen Rooman, 1628.   [88], 520,
[6], 124p.   Portrait of Lourens Koster.   Plates and plans.   18 cm.
"Petri Scriverii Lavre-Kranz voor Laurens Koster" has a special
title-page and separate pagination.
p. 375: Boekdruckerije te Haerlem von Laurens Janszen Koster
gevonden omtrent het jaer 1440.   [848]
ICN IU MH NN Eu-De-LBb Eu-Fr-PN Eu-Ge-LB
Eu-Ne-AVb Eu-Ne-GK

Antzenius, R. H.
Lierzang, bij de ontdekking en inwijding van de eerzuil voor
Lourens Janszoon Koster, in den Harlemmer-Hout, den 10 Julij 1823.
Haarlem, 1823.
Title from Mohr, Jubelfeste.
Reissued in Loosjes, Vincent. Gedenkschriften ... Haarlem, 1824. [849]

Bagford, John, 1650-1716.
An essay on the invention of printing. Philosophical Trans-
actions of the Royal Society, vol. 25, 1706-1707, p. 2397-2407.
Reissued in Latin in Wolf, J. C. Monumenta typographica.
Hamburg, 1740.   vol. 2, p. 995-1015.   [850]

---- An essay on the invention of printing, by John Bagford. A
transcription of the text of this essay as originally published in
the Philosophical transactions for 1706-1707. ... Chicago, Ill., Committee on invention of printing, Chicago club of printing house
craftsmen, 1940.   1 prel. leaf, 11 numb. leaves.   28 cm.   (Contributions to materials on the history of printing, no. 1)

"Published as a report on Work projects administration Official
project no. OP 65-1-54-273 (3)."
Mimeographed.   [851]
CSmH   DLC   IC   ICU   MH   NN   NNC

Bakker, W. A. P. F. L.
    Een woord in het geding "Haarlem-Mainz."   Haarlem, Joh. Enschedés
Zonen, 1889.   40p.   8vo.   [852]
    Eu-Ge-LB   Eu-Ne-AVb   Eu-Ne-GK

Bauer, Friedrich.
    Vorläufer Gutenbergs.   Klimsch's Jahrbuch, vol. 18, 1924-1925, p.
25-31.   [853]

[Bausch, P.]
    Holland's aanspraken op de uitvinding der boekdrukkunst, een ant-
woord op Pater B. Kruitwagen's bijdrage in het Gutenbergs Festschrift,
1926.   Nieuwsblad voor den Boekhandel, vol. 93, no. 15, Feb. 1926, p.
184-185; no. 17, Mar. 2, p. 207-209; no. 19, Mar. 9, p. 231-233; no.
21, Mar. 16, p. 258-260; no. 23, Mar. 23, p. 282-284.   [854]

----   Houten en doorboorde letters in de 15e eeuw.   Amsterdam, 1929.
16 mo.
    Extracts from various works relating to the invention of printing.[855]
    Eu-Ge-LB

[----]   Lourens Jansz. Coster.   Nieuwsblad voor den Boekhandel, vol.
94, no. 25, Mar. 29, 1927, p. 282-283; no. 28, Apr. 8, p. 315-316; no.
34, Apr. 29, p. 376-377.   [856]

[----]   Louwerijsz Jansz. Koster.   Nieuwsblad voor den Boekhandel, vol.
89, no. 46, June 9, 1922, p. 467-469; no. 50, June 23, p. 506-509; no.
56, July 14, p. 569-572; vol. 90, no. 34, Apr. 27, 1923, p. 375-377; no.
35, May 1, p. 386-389; no. 36, May 4, p. 398-401; no. 38, May 11, p.
426-432; no. 39, May 15, p. 443-445; no. 40, May 18, p. 454-458; no.
43, May 29, p. 490-493; no. 44, June 1, p. 502-506; no. 45, June 5, p.
517-523; no. 47, June 13, p. 551-556; no. 48, June 15, p. 565-572; no.
49, June 19, p. 587-591; no. 50, June 22, p. 599-605; no. 51, June 26,
p. 614-619; no. 52, June 29, p. 634-637; no. 54, July 6, p. 666-671;
no. 55, July 10, p. 682-688.   [857]

---- ----   Reprinted, 1923.   8vo.   [858]
    Eu-Ne-AVb

Beeloo, A.
    Eeuwzang bij het vierde eeuwgetijde van de uitvinding der boekdruk-
kunst.   Werken der Hollandsche Maatschappij van Fraije Kunsten en
Wetenschappen, vol. 7, part 1, 1824.   [859]

Beknopt verhaal van de viering van het vierde eeuwgetijde na de
vinding der boekdrukkunst. Gevierd door de gezamenlijke geëmploijeer-
den der Bataviasche land-drukkerij. Batavia, 1825. 8vo.   [860]
    Eu-Ge-LSb   Eu-Ne-GK

Belinfante, Josephus Justus, 1812-1882.
    Lourens Janszoon Coster. Herinnering aan het Costerfeest gehou-
den te Haarlem op 15., 16. en 17. Julij 1856. Amsterdam, P. D. van
Es, 1856. 12p. 8vo.
    Title from Neuer Anzeiger für Bibliographie und Bibliothekswissen-
schaft, 1865.   [861]

[----] Lourens Janszoon Coster, uitvinder der boekdrukkunst, te Haarlem
omstreeks 1423. Oprigting van het standbeeld tot Coster's eere, der stad
Haarlem aangeboden, als hulde van Neerlands volk. [Amsterdam, Gebr.
Diederichs, 1856] 20p. ports. 31 cm.
    Signed in manuscript: J. J. Belinfante.   [862]
    NNC   Eu-De-LBb   Eu-Ge-LP

    Berigt van een zeer merkwaardig overblyfsel van den arbeid van Lau-
rens Jansz. gemeenlyk Laurens Koster genaamd, eersten uitvinder der
drukkunst, het welk, den 29sten van Grasmaand aanstaande, by den boekverkooper Haak, te Leyden, openlyk zal verkocht worden. Algemeene
Konst- en Letterbode, no. 13, 1809, p. 195-196.
    Also reprint.
    Authorship attributed to Jacobus Koning by van der Linde.   [863]

Bernard, Auguste Joseph, 1811-1868.
    Une rectification à propos de l'article de Ruelens: Un nouveau plai-
doyer en faveur de Laurent Coster. Bulletin du Bibliophile Belge,
vol. 15 (2d ser., vol. 6), 1859, p. 395-398.   [864]

Beschrijving van het feest, dat na 400 Jaren den 10. en 11. Julij
1820 en 3, tot Laurens Koster eer gevierd is aan het Sparen 't is
duidlijker en klaarder dan Filosophie. Haarlem, [1820?] Folio.
    1 page poem.   [865]
    Eu-De-LBb

Beverswijk, J. M. van.
    Feestzang bij het vierde eeuwgetijde van de uitvinding der boekdruk-
kunst. 's Hertogenbosch, H. Palier en zoon, 1823. 10p. 8vo.
    Title from Neuer Anzeiger für Bibliographie und Bibliothekswissen-
shaft, 1867.   [866]

    Bewijzen voor de echtheid en gelijkenis der oude afbeeldingen van
Coster. Ter wederlegging van het "Iets" van den Heer van Westreenen.
Haarlem, 1847. 8vo.   [867]
    Eu-Ge-LB   Eu-Ne-GK

Bilderdijk, Willem.
Over de uitvinding der boekdrukkunst. Eene voorlezing in de tweede klasse van het Konigliche Nederlandsche Instituut. ms. 1809.
Title from van der Linde, Geschichte der Erfindung ...   [868]

[Binger, H.]
Costerlied. Mit Music. [Amsterdam, 1856?] 2p. 8vo.
Title from Mohr, Jubelfeste.   [869]

[----] Het oude en het nieuwe Beeld. Poesie. [Amsterdam, 1856] 2p. 8vo.
Title from Mohr, Jubelfeste.   [870]

Een blik op Coster's Standbeeld; dichtmatige letterproeve door de gezellen ter drukkerij van J. G. La Lau, te Leyden, op Koppermaandag van 1857. 8vo.
Title from van der Linde, Geschichte der Erfindung ...   [871]

De boekdrukkunst, als vaderlandsche uitvinding de hoogste belangstelling waardig van elken Nederlander. Amsterdam, 1851. 8vo.
Title from van der Linde, Geschichte der Erfindung ...   [872]

Boeles, Willem Boele Sophius, 1832-1902.
De uitvinder van de boekdrukkunst te Haarlem, door Mr. W. B. S. Boeles. Groningen, J. B. Wolters, 1897. 44p. 25 cm.   [873]
NN   Eu-De-LBb   Eu-Ge-LB   Eu-Ge-LSb   Eu-Ne-AVb   Eu-Ne-GK

[Bolt, Hendrik].
Artis typographicae natalis trecentesimus vigesimus quintus. [Haarlem, 1765.] 8p. 24 cm.   [874]
MH

Bonné, D.
Het boekdrukken, boertende zamenspraak met zang tusschen klass, een zetter en Jan, een drukker. Ter eere van den uitvinder dier kunst Laurens Janszoon Koster. Vervaardigd door D. Bonné, ter gelegenheid van het vierde eeuwfeest, den 10 Julij 1823. Dordrecht, Blussé [1823] 12p. 23 cm.   [875]
NNC   Eu-De-LBb   Eu-Ge-LSb

[Boogaard, W.]
Algemeen lied ter gelegenheid van de onthulling van het standbeeld, van Laurens Janszoon Coster. [(Printed) Johannisberg, Klein, Forst & Bohn, 1856] 1p. 8vo.
Title from Mohr, Jubelfeste.   [876]

Bosscha, Hermann, 1755-1819.
  Carmen de inventae typographiae laude Kostero Harlemensi nunc tandem
potenter asserta.   Dav. Jac. v. Lennep memoria Hieronymi de Bosch.
Amstelodami, 1817.   4to.   [877]
    Eu-De-LBb   Eu-Fr-PN

---- Hermanni Bosscha poëmata. Editionem curavit Petrus Bosscha,
filius.   Prostant Daventriae apud A. J. van den Sigtenhorst, 1820.
2 prel. leaves, xxiv, 188p.   23 cm.   [878]
    MH

Bowyer, William, 1699-1777, ed.
  The origin of printing. In two essays: 1. The substance of Dr.
Middleton's Dissertation on the origin of printing in England.   II.
Mr. Meerman's Account of the invention of the art at Haarleim, and its
progress to Mentz. With occasional remarks; and an appendix.   2d ed.:
with improvements.   London, Printed for W. Bowyer and J. Nichols, 1776.
xxvi, 176p.   21.5 cm.
    Abridgment of Middleton's Dissertations, 1735, and Meerman's Origines
    typographicae, 1765. Reissued with new t.-p. and supplement (177-
    300p.) in 1781.   [879]
    DLC   ICJ   IU   IaU   MB   MH   MHi   NB   NN   TxU   Eu-Fr-PN
    Eu-Ge-LB   Eu-Ge-LP   Eu-Ne-AVb

Boxman, A.
  Feestzang op het vierde eeuwgetijde van de uitvinding der drukkunst.
(In Loosjes, Vincent. Gedenkschriften ... Haarlem, 1824. p. 215-232)[880]

---- Wenk naar Hooger, bij de viering van het vierde eeuwfeest van de
uitvinding der boekdrukkunst.   Haarlem, 1823.
    Title from Mohr, Jubelfeste.
    Reissued in Loosjes, Vincent.   Gedenkschriften ... Haarlem, 1824.
    p. 227-232.   [881]

Broos, Hermanus.
  Recitata oratine de Laurentio Costero, ad academias transiturus
lectiones a. d. XVIII. decembris MDCCXVI. L. M. Q. D. Haarlemi, suis
ipse typis, quos habet animi causa, excudit Hermanus Broos.   1816.
2 leaves.   4to.
    Title from van der Linde, Geschichte der Erfindung ...   [882]

Brugmans, H.
    Toch Haarlem?   Onze Eeuw, vol. 1, 1904.
    Also reprint.   [883]

Brunet, Gustave.
    Laurent Coster.   (In Nouvelle biographie générale. Paris, MM.
Firmin Didot, frères, 1855.   vol. 12, p. 85-87)
    Title from Bulletin du Bibliophile Belge, 1857.   [884]

Bruun, Christian Walther, 1831-1906.
De nyeste undersøgelser om bogtrykkerkunstens opfindelse, af Chr.
Bruun. Med 6 tavler og 15 figurer i texten. Kjøbenhavn, P. G. Philip-
sen, 1889. viii, 92, [3]p. illus., vi facsims. 34 cm.
   Head-pieces.
   "Udgivet af Forening for boghaandvaerk."
   "Oplagets størrelse 688 expl., hvoraf 38 expl. er trykt paa haand-
   gjort papir."
   Contents.- Fortale.- Laurens Janszoon Coster.- Johan Gutenberg.-
   Det tekniske i bogtrykkerkunstens opfindelse.   [885]
   DLC   ICJ   ICN   Eu-Ge-LB   Eu-Ne-GK

Bullen, Henry Lewis.
   The Coster legend verified? Inland Printer, vol. 72, 1923, p.
297-298.   [886]

---- Laurens Janszoon Coster and the introduction of printing in
Europe. Inland Printer, vol. 66, 1920, p. 358-360.   [887]

Burger, C. P.
   Een korte geschiedenis van de drukkunst. Het Boek, vol. 16, 1927,
p. 283-287.   [888]

Buymer, D.
   Merkwaardig gedenkteeken wegen het vieren van ... vierde eeuwfeest.
[Gedicht] Haarlem, 1823. 4to.
   Title from Mohr, Jubelfeste.   [889]

C., A. V.
   Eerekrans gevlogten om het hoofd van L. J. Koster, uitvinder der
boekdrukkunst. 1823. Folio.
   Title from van der Linde, Geschichte der Erfindung ...   [890]

Campbell, Marinus Frederik Andries Gerardus, 1819-1890.
   De uitvinding van de boekdrukkunst. Het Vaderland, Mar 25,1870. [891]

Capelle, Pierre Adolphe.
   Manuel de la typographie française, ou Traité complet de l'impri-
merie. Ouvrage utile aux jeunes typographes, aux libraires et aux
gens de lettre. Paris, Rignoux, 1826. [3], iv, 90p. 27 cm.
   Sur l'invention de l'imprimerie à Harlem: p. 9-42.   [892]
   ICN   MB   NN   Eu-Fr-PN   Eu-Sz-BeG

Carutti, Domenico, barone di Cantogno, 1821-1909.
   Lorenzo Coster; notizia intorno alla sua vita ed alla invenzione
della tipografia in Olanda ... Torino, Stamperia reale, 1868. 24p.
30.5 cm.
   "Estr. dalle Memorie della Reale accademia delle scienze di Torino,
   serie II, tom. XXVI."   [893]
   ICN   Eu-De-LBb   Eu-Ne-GK

[Claromontius, Gothofred]
In statuam laureatam quam collegium medicum sub auspiciis amplissi-
morum consulum civitatis harlemensis Laur. Costero viro consulari typographiae inventori primo in Horto medico Harlemensi, erexit MDCCXXIII.
Amstelodami, 1823.   Folio.   [894]
    Eu-Ge-LB

[Cleef, P. M. van, Jz.]
Handboek ter beofening der boekdrukkunst in Nederland, voorafgegaan
van eene beknopte geschiedenis dezer kunst.   Te 's Gravenhage, ter
boekdrukkerij van P. M. van Cleef, Jz., 1884.   [vi], 259p.   21.5 cm.
    Historical introduction, plus a manual of printing practice.   [895]
    NN
    1850 ed.: ICN

[Collection of materials on the statue of Coster by W. H. J. v.
Westreenen, A. de Vries, and J. Goel of the years 1847 and 1848, with
a manuscript by A. de Vries.]   8vo.   [896]
    Eu-No-GK

[Collection of miscellaneous songs, music, posters, programs, and
medals relating to the Coster jubilee, celebrated at Haarlem in 1856,
with description of the celebration, and list of contents.]   Large
folio.   [897]
    Eu-No-GK

[Collection of 17 publications on the history of printing by Schinkel, van Westreenen, Marnix, A. de Vries, van der Palm, Loots, Scholte-
ma, Koning, Loosjes, van der Linde, and van Meurs.]   8vo.   [898]
    Eu-No-GK

[Collection of 26 publications relating to the fourth centenary of
the invention of printing, celebrated at Haarlem in 1823.]   8vo. [899]
    Eu-No-GK

Conway, William Martin, baron, 1856-
    Dutch printers and wood-cutters.   Magazine of Art, vol. 4, 1881-
1882, p.190-195, 505-509.   [900]

-----   Old world printing and woodcutting.   Magazine of Art, vol. 7,
1884, p. 68-72.   [901]

-----   The origin of printing.   Academy, vol. 37, 1889, p. 165.   [902]

Coornhert, D.
    Officia Ciceronis, leerende wat joghelijck in allen staten behoort
te doen, bescreuen int Latinjn, door den alder welsprekendsten orator
Marcum Tullium Ciceronen, ende nv eerst vertaelt in nederlantscher
spraken.   Tot Haerlem, by Jan van Zuren.   1561.   12mo.

In de voorrede vindt man de getuigenis van Coornhert "dat de nutte eerste van boekprinten alder eerste binnen Haarlem ghevonden is."[903]
NjP Eu-Ge-LB Eu-Ne-AVb

Costerlegende, erste Bearbeitung. Nederlandsche Spectator, 1869, p. 391; 1870, p. 234.
Title from van der Linde, Geschichte der Erfindung ...   [904]

Die Costerlegende und ihre Verfechter. Die Zeugkiste, 1926, p. 52-60.
Title from Bibliographie des Bibliotheks und Buchwesens, 1926. [905]

Coster-Standbeeld. 16. Julij 1856. [Signed: B.] Haarlem, 1856.
4p. roy. 8vo.
Title from Mohr, Jubelfeste.   [906]

De Fraula.
Note sur l'invention des caractères en bois. Bruxelles, 1840.
4to.
Reprinted from Mémoires de l'Académie de Bruxelles.
Title from van der Linde, Geschichte der Erfindung ...   [907]

Delitzsch, Franz Julius.
Das angebliche Zeugniss eines judischen Geschichtschreibers für die Erfindung der Buchdruckerkunst in Haarlem. Leipzig, 1840.
409 col. Folio.
Title from van der Linde, Geschichte der Erfindung ...   [908]

Destanberg, Napoleon.
Laurens Coster. Drama in dry bedrijven. Antwerp, 1855. 56p.
8vo.   [909]
    Eu-Ne-AVb

De drukkunst; eene verhandeling; uitgesprooken in eene aanzienlyke maatschappy. Amsterdam, 1794. 8vo.   [910]
    Eu-De-LBb

Dunkler, F.
Lourens Janszoon Coster. Triomph-marsch gecomponeerd en gearrangeerd voor de piano. Haag, 1856. 4to.
Title from van der Linde, Geschichte der Erfindung ...   [911]

Dusseau, P. J. V.
De boekdrukkunst en derzelven uitvinder Laurens Jansz. Koster. Amsterdam, M. Westerman & zoon [1859] vii, 162p. 12mo.   [912]
    Eu-Ge-LP Eu-Ge-LSb Eu-Ne-AVb

Duyse, Prudens van.
De goed Koster. Aan Dr. A. de Vries. Volkslied. Haarlem, 1856.

1p. 8vo.
Title from Mohr, Jubelfeste. [913]

Duyse, Prudens van.
Den weledelen Geleerden Heer A. D. Schinkel, ouddruckers, etc.
Gedicht. Gent, 1856. 4p. 8vo.
Title from Mohr, Jubelfeste. [914]

Ebert, Friedrich Adolf, 1791-1834.
Die harlemer Erfindungsgeschichte betreffend. Allgemeine Literatur-Zeitung, no. 49, Feb. 1825, col. 405-408. [915]

---- Neue Prüfung der holländischen Ansprüche auf die Erfindung der
Buchdruckerkunst. Hermes, vol. 4, 1823, p. 63-85.
Also reprint. [916]

---- Nieuw onderzoek naar de aanspraak van Holland op de uitvinding
der boekdrukkunst, door Prof. Ebert te Wolfenbuttel; en brief wegens
het geschrift van Prof. Friedrich Lehne. (Getrokken uit den Algemeen-
en Konst- en Letterbode). Met een voorrede en eenige aanmerkingen van
Jacobus Koning. Te Haarlem, bij de Wed. A. Loosjes Pz., MDCCCXXV
[1825]. [ii], v, 46p. 22.5 cm. [917]
NN NNC Eu-De-LBb Eu-Ge-LB Eu-Ge-LSb Eu-Ne-GK

Eeden, J. A. van.
Afscheidsgroet aan het standbeeld van L. J. Coster. Haarlem,
1854. 4to.
Jaarzang van Trouw moet blijken.
Title from van der Linde, Geschichte der Erfindung ... [918]

Eckhoff, Wopke.
Nieuwe bijdrage tot de geschiedenis van de boekdrukkunst in Neder-
land; bevattende een betoog, dat de eerste druk van de Oude Friesche
Wetten, door Hidde Camminghe, bezorgd omstreeks 1484 is gedrukt te
Leeuwarden, medegedeeld bij gelegenheid der Typographische tentoon-
stelling te Haarlem in 1856. Workum, H. Branderburgh en zoon, 1856.
19p. 8vo. [919]
Eu-Fr-PN Eu-Ge-LB Eu-Ge-LSb Eu-Ne-GK

Eerekroon voor Lourens Koster ... op Koppel-Maandag. Amsterdam,
1803. 1 leaf. Folio.
Title from van der Linde, Geschichte der Erfindung ... [920]

De eeuwigduurende lamp, ontstooken voor het beeltenis van Laurens
Koster, mitsgaders de uitbreiding en verklaaringe van de zeer uitmun-
tende Gedenkponningen ter vereeuwiging van de Lof van Haarlem, wegens
de voor drie eeuwen aldaar gevondene boekdrukkunst; gemaakt door den
konstigen medailleur Martinus Holtzhey, te Amsterdam MDCCXL. Te
Haarlem, gedrukt bij Mozes van Hulkenroy, aan de Markt, naast het Ver-
gulde Vlies, in Lourens Koster, eerste uitvinder der boekdrukkunst.

[Haarlem, 1740].   4to.   [921]
   Eu-De-LBb

Ellis, Charles, fl. 1699.
   Letter [claiming the invention of printing for Coster]. Philosophical Transactions of the Royal Society, vol. 23, no. 286, 1703, p.
1416.
   Reissued in Latin in Wolf, J. C. Monumenta typographica. Hamburg,
   1740.   vol. 2, p. 979-995.   [922]

----   A letter written by the Reverend Charles Ellis claiming the invention of printing for Coster and a letter in refutation of that
claim; a transcription of the texts of these letters as originally
published in the Philosophical transactions for 1703 ... Chicago, Ill.,
Committee on invention of printing, Chicago club of printing house
craftsmen, 1940.   11 numb. leaves.   28 cm.   (Contributions to materials on the history of printing, no. 2)
   "Published as a report on Work projects administration Official
   project no. OP 65-1-54-273 (3)."
   Mimeographed.   [923]
   CSmH   DLC   IC   ICU   MH   NN   NNC

Enschedé, Charles, 1855-1919.
   Fonderies de caractères et leur matériel dans les Pays-Bas du XVe
au XIX° siècle. Notice historique principalement d'après les données
de la collection typographique de Joh. Enschedé en zonen à Haarlem;
par Ch. Enschedé ... Haarlem, De erven F. Bohn, 1908.   xxxiv p., 1
leaf, 404p.   illus., facsim.   38.5x28.5 cm.   [924]
   DLC   NN   NjN   Eu-Fr-PN

----   Laurens Janszoon Coster.   Aantwoord aan Fruin.   Nederlandsche
Spectator, no. 22, 1904.   [925]

----   Laurens Jansz. Coster de uitvinder van de boekdrukkunst, door
Mr. Ch. Enschedé. Vervolg op het Technisch onderzoek naar de uitvinding van de boekdrukkunst.   Haarlem, De erven F. Bohn, 1904.   1 prel.
leaf, 56p.   27 cm.   [926]
   DLC   ICJ   ICN   Eu-De-BP   Eu-Ge-LSb   Eu-Ne-AVb

----   Technisch onderzoek naar de uitvinding van de boekdrukkunst,
door Mr. Ch. Enschedé.   Haarlem, F. Bohn, 1901.   2 prel. leaves,
86p.   26.5 cm.   [927]
   DLC   ICJ   ICN   MH   NN   Eu-Ge-LSb   Eu-Ne-GK

Enschedé, Jan Willem, 1865-
   Beknopt overzicht van den tegenwoordigen stand van het onderzoek
naar de uitvinding der boekdrukkunst.   Leiden, 1903.   8vo.
   Reprint from Taal en Letteren, 1903.   [928]
   Eu-Ne-AVb

                                  - 121 -

Feestklanken opgedragen aan de typographische vereenigingen in
Nederland bij den aanvang van 1859 ... Overgedrukt uit het tijdschrift
"Laurens Coster", I^e Jg., Afl. 9.   Utrecht [1859]   16mo.
   A collection of pieces, chiefly in verse.   [929]
   Eu-Ge-LB

Feestlied, ter gelegenheid van de onthulling van het standbeeld van
Lourens Janszoon Coster te Haarlem.   Haarlem, Joh. Enschedé, 1856.
8vo.
   Title from van der Linde, Geschichte der Erfindung ...   [930]

Feestzangen op het vierde eeuwgetijde na de uitvinding der drukkunst
door Lourens Janszoon Koster, gevierd op den geboortedag van Z. M. den
Koning op den 24 Augustus 1823, door de geemploijeerden der Bataviasche
Landsdrukkerij.   Batavia, 1823.   8vo.
   Contains 13 songs, one in Malayan.
   Title from van der Linde, Geschichte der Erfindung ...   [931]

Feestzangen, ter gelegenheid van de herdenking aan de plegtige onthulling aan het standbeeld van L. J. Coster; gevierd te Groningen door
de gesamenlijke beoefenaars der boekdrukkunst, den 19 Julij 1856.
[Groningen, 1856?]
   Title from van der Linde, Geschichte der Erfindung ...   [932]

Festival at Haarlem in honor of Coster.   London Magazine, vol. 8,
1823, p. 272-275.   [933]

Les fêtes de Harlem.   Bulletin du Bibliophile Belge, vol. 12 (2d
ser., vol. 3), 1856, p. 295-296.   [934]

Flanor, C. Vosmaer.
   Proefondervindelik bewijs alsdat Dr. v. d. Linde des Duivels is,
want anders zouwi dat beroerde boek over Gutenberg niet geschreven
hebben, daar toch niks geen nieuws in staat zeit Dek, dat zeit-i.
Opgedragen aan Markus Roost.   Met een prentje.   's Gravenhage, Martinus Nijhoff, 1879.   4to.
   Title from van der Linde, Geschichte der Erfindung ...   [935]

Fruin, Robert.
   Enschedé's jongste bijdrage tot de Costerzaak.   Nederlandsche
Spectator, no. 14, 1904.   [936]

----   De Haarlemsche uitvinder der boekdrukkunst.   Genealogie der
familie Coster betreffend, gegen Rutgers van der Loeff.   Tijdschrift
voor Boek- en Bibliotheekswezen, vol. 3, 1905, p. 75-76.   [937]

----   De huidige stand van het Costervraagstuk, door Mr. R. Fruin.
Uitgegeven door "De Vereeniging Haarlem."   Haarlem, De erven F. Bohn,
1906.   19p.   20 cm.   [938]
   NN   Eu-No-AVb

Fruin, Robert.
    Mainz of Haarlem.   Amsterdam, 1888.   8vo.
    Reprint from De Gids, vol. 1, 1888, p. 49-94.   [939]
    Eu-De-LBb   Eu-Ne-AVb

----   Nieuws aangaande de Costerzaak.   Nederlandsche Spectator, no.
8, 1904.   [940]

----   De uitvinding der boekdrukkunst.   Leidsch Dagblad, June 14-15,
1870.   [941]

G., J. H.
    Onze Schutspatroon.   Gedicht.   [Haarlem, 1856?]   3p.   8vo.
    Title from Mohr, Jubelfeste.   [942]

Gebhard, J. H.
    Ons lied.   [Haarlem, 1856?]   1 leaf, 2p.   8vo.
    Title from Mohr, Jubelfeste.   [943]

    Geloofwaardige bewijzen, dat de boekdrukkunst te Haarlem is uitge-
vonden.   Middelburg, 1806.   12mo.
    Title from van der Linde, Geschichte der Erfindung ...   [944]

Gerlings, Herman.
    Het oordeel van Humphreys over het regt van Koster op de uitvinding
der drukkunst.   (In Gerlings, Herman. Haarlemsche bijdragen, bijeen-
gebragt door Mr. H. Gerlings Oz.   Te Haarlem, bij De Erven F. Bohn,
1869)   [945]
    NN

    Gezangen voor de kinderen der Stads-Armen-Scholen bij gelegenheid
van het vierde eeuwgetijde van de uitvinding der boekdrukkunst door
Laurens Janszoon Koster; gevierd binnen Haarlem, den 11. Julij 1823.
Haarlem, 1823.   sm. 8vo.
    Title from Mohr, Jubelfeste.   [946]

Guicciardini, Lodovico, 1521-1589.
    Descrittione di M. Lodovico Guicciardini patritio fiorentino, di
tutti i Paesi Bassi, altrimenti detti Germania Inferiore. Con piu
carte de geographia del paese, & col ritratto naturale di piu terre
principali. Al gran re Cattolico Filippo d'Austria. Con amplissimo
indice di tutte le cose piu memorabili. Scruta mini.   Anversa, Apresso
Guglielmo Siluic, stampatore regio, 1567.   296, [19]p.   30.5 cm. [947]
    MB   MH   NjP   PU   Eu-Fr-PN

----   Descrittione di M. Lodovico Guicciardini patritio fiorentino,
di tutti i Paesi Bassi, altrimenti detti Germania Interiore. Con tutte
le carte di geographia del paese, & col ritratto naturale di molte terre
principali; riueduta di nuouo, & ampliata per tutto piu che la meta
dal medesimo autore ... Con amplissimo indice di tutte le cose piu

                              - 123 -

memorabili. Anversa, Appresso C. Plantino, stampatore regio, 1581.
12 prel. leaves, 558, [17]p. incl. col. front, col. fold. plates,
port., maps, col. coats of arms. 32.5 cm.
> Title within ornamental border in colors; initial in colors.
> Second edition. For a detailed description of this edition see
> Annales Plantiniennes, 1. ptie., p. 251-253. [948]
> DLC   MH   Eu-Fr-PN   Eu-Ge-LB

Guicciardini, Lodovico, 1521-1589.
> Descrittione di M. Lodovico Guicciardini ... di tutti i Paesi Bassi,
> altrimenti detti Germania Inferiore ... Riueduta di nuouo, & ampliata
> per tutto la terza volta del medesimo autore ... Anversa, Appresso C.
> Plantino, 1588. 16 prel. leaves, 432, [18]p. front., plates,
> port., maps, coats of arms. 33 cm.
> Title within ornamental border. [949]
> DLC   ICN   MB   NN   NjP   PBL   Eu-Fr-PN   Eu-Ge-LB

Haarlem. Commissie tot onderzoek naar het jaar der uitvinding van
de boekdrukkunst.
> [Rapport.] Haarlem. 1822. 51p. 21.5 cm.
> No title-page.
> Reprint in Loosjes, Vincent. Gedenkschriften ... Haarlem, 1824. [950]
> NN

Haarlem. Typographische tentoonstelling, 1856.
> Catalogus van voorwerpen ingezonden ter algemeene typographische
> tentoonstelling gehouden te Haarlem, bij gelegenheid der plegtige
> onthulling van het metalen standbeeld van Lourens Janszoon Coster.
> [Haarlem, Erven F. Bohn, pref. 1856]   viii, 52p.   23.5 cm.   [951]
> MH   NN   NNC   Eu-De-LBb   Eu-Ne-AVb

Haarlems en Kosters regt op de uitvinding der boekdrukkunst, gehandhaafd tegen twee aanvallen in de Arnhemsche Courant en de Bij.
[Haarlem, 1823?]   18p.   23 cm.
> Caption title.
> "Getrokken uit den Algemeenen Konst- en Letterbode 1823, no. 45 en
> 46."
> Authorship attributed to Abraham de Vries by van der Linde. [952]
> NNC   Eu-Ne-AVb

Hazeu, Johann.
> Gedenk-zuil ter eere van Laurens Janszoon Koster, uitvinder der on-
waadlerbare boekdrukkunst, bij de viering van het vierde eeuwfeest te
Haarlem. Amsterdam, 1824. 8vo. [953]
> Eu-De-LBb

[Heineken, Karl Heinrich von] 1706-1791.
> Anmerkungen über die Beweisthümer, welche die holländischen Scri-
benten anführen, dass Laurens Janson Coster die Buchdruckerkunst

erfunden habe. Nachrichten, vol. 2, 1769, p. 241-314.
   Title from van der Linde, Geschichte der Erfindung ...   [954]

Herbert, W.
   Abstract of Bagford's History of typography; also, lists of authors
who have written on the origin and progress of printing. Collected
by R. Smith. 1782. 46, 65 leaves. 4to.
   "This abstract was taken from a copy of Mr. Smith's, in the Publ.
   Lib. Cambr. Dd. 11-91. 254 leaves. per W. H., Sep. 1782."   [955]
   Eu-Ge-LP

   Herinnering aan het Costerfeest te Haarlem. Bij de onthulling van
Coster's metalen standbeeld. Amsterdam, 1856. 8vo.   [956]
   Eu-Ge-LSb

   Herinnering aan het vierhonderd-vijftig-jarig bestaan der boekdrukkunst. Gevierd door de Boekverkoopers-Vereeniging "Ons Doel", te Amsterdam, op Woensdag, 23 Julij, 1872. Amsterdam, 1873. 8vo.   [957]
   Eu-Ge-LSb   Eu-Ne-AVb

Hervet, L. C.
   Ode à Laurens Koster, inventeur de l'art de l'imprimerie, à Haarlem
en 1423. Par L. C. Hervet, artiste du Théatre Français. À Amsterdam,
10 Juillet, 1823. 10p. 20 cm.
   Half-title: Ode à Laurens Koster.
   Printer's ornament: leaf at end.   [958]
   MH

Hessels, Jan Hendrik, 1836-1907.
   A bibliographical tour. Library, 2d ser., vol. 9, 1908, p. 282-
308.   [959]

----   Classified list of the Costeriana....[n.p., 1887] 8 numb.
leaves. 25 cm.   [960]
   ICN   Eu-Ge-LSb

----   Did Gutenberg invent printing? Bibliographer, vol. 2, 1882,
p. 57-59.   [961]

----   The Gutenberg fiction: a critical examination of the documents
relating to Gutenberg, showing that he was not the inventor of printing, by J. H. Hessels. London, A. Moring limited, 1912. xiv, 219,
[1]p., 1 leaf. 25.5 cm.
   "Originally appeared in 'The Library,' 1909 [-1912]"   [962]
   DLC   MWA   NN   Eu-De-BP   Eu-Fr-PN   Eu-Ge-LSb   Eu-Ne-AVb

----   Gutenberg: was he the inventor of printing? Printing Times
and Lithographer, n.s., vol. 6, no. 62, 1880, p. 25-29; no. 63, p.
56-59; no. 64, p. 81-84; no. 65, p. 103-104; no. 67, p. 166.   [963]

Hessels, Jan Hendrik, 1836-1907.
Gutenberg: was he the inventor of printing? An historical
investigation embodying a criticism of Dr. van der Linde's "Guten-
berg." By J. H. Hessels. London, B. Quaritch, 1882. 3 prel.
leaves. [vii]-xxvii, 201p. fold. tab., facsim. 23 cm.
"Only 200 copies printed for sale." [964]
CSmH DLC I ICJ ICN MH NN Eu-De-LBb Eu-Fr-PN
Eu-Ge-LB Eu-Ge-LSb Eu-Ne-AVb Eu-Ne-GK

---- Haarlem de geboorteplaats der boekdrukkunst, niet Mainz, door
J. H. Hessels ... Haarlem, Johannes Enschedé & zonen, 1888. xx,
166p. 26.5 cm. [965]
NN NNC Eu-De-LBb Eu-Fr-PN Eu-Ge-LB Eu-Ne-AVb Eu-Ne-GK

---- Haarlem the birth-place of printing, not Mentz: by J. H. Hessels ...
London, E. Stock & co., 1887. xiv, 85p. 26 cm. [966]
DLC ICJ ICN MB MWA NN Eu-De-LBb Eu-Fr-PN Eu-Ge-LB
Eu-Ge-LSb Eu-Ne-AVb Eu-Ne-GK

---- The history of the invention of printing. Academy, vol. 31,
1887, no. 782, p. 307-308; no. 783, p. 325-326; no. 784, p. 343-344;
no. 785, p. 361-362; no. 786, p. 379; no. 787, p. 395-396; no. 788,
p. 411-413; no. 789, p. 431-432; vol. 32, 1887, no. 791, p. 9-10; no.
792, p. 24-25; no. 793, p. 40-41; no. 794, p. 55-56; no. 795, p. 71;
no. 796, p. 86-88; no. 797; p. 102-105. [967]

---- John Gutenberg and the invention of printing. Saturday Review,
vol. 55, 1882, p. 635. [968]

---- Laurens Janszoon Coster verdraaid en verminkt, naar aanleiding
van G. Zedler, Von Coster zu Gutenberg. Het Book, vol. 11, 1922, p.
97-113, 141-160. [969]

---- The so-called Gutenberg documents. Library, 2d ser., vol. 10,
1909, p. 152-167, 253-287, 386-417; 3d ser., vol. 2, 1911, p. 183-211,
289-313, 396-421; vol. 3, 1912, p. 64-89, 195-220. [970]

---- Some notes on the invention of printing. Bibliographical
Society, London. Transactions, vol. 9, 1908, p. 11-14. [971]

---- Typography. (In Encyclopaedia Britannica, 9th ed., 1888.
vol. 23, p. 681-697) [972]

---- ---- (In Encyclopaedia Britannica, 11th ed., 1911. vol. 27,
p. 519-534) [973]

---- De uitvinding der boekdrukkunst. Overdrukt uit de Nederlandsche
Spectator, 1871. 's Gravenhage, 1871. roy. 8vo. [974]
Eu-De-LBb Eu-Ne-AVb

[Hessen, Willem] 1702-1741.
    Parnas vreuchden, over het derde eeuwjaar van de geboorte der druk-
konst, CIꓛ CCCC XX I IX., door Laurens Koster. Te Haarlem, gedrukt by
Izaak vander Vinne, boekdrukker en verkooper in de Warmoestraat. 1731.
8p. 19 cm. [975]
    NN

---- Parnas vreuchden, ter onsterfelyker gedagtenis over het derde
eeuwjaar van de uitvinding der noit volpreese boek-drukkonst, door
Laurens Jansz. Koster, in zyn leven schepen der stad Haarlem. Waar
by gevoegd is de uitlegging van de gedenkpenning op het derde eeuwjaar,
't geen nu in den jare MDCCXL drie eeuwen heeft geduurd, gemaakt door
den Konstryken Medailleur N. van Swinderen in 's Hage. Te Haarlem, by
Moses van Hulkenroy, aan de Markt &c. 1740. [976]
    Eu-De-LBb   Eu-Ge-LSb

Hinlópen, F. C.
    De uitvinding der boekdrukkunst, eene oorzaak van Godverheerlij-
king. Een woord, na het gevierde feest, uitgesproken den 20sten
Julij 1856 ... te Haarlem. Haarlem, Kruseman, 1856. 20p. 8vo. [977]
    Eu-Ge-LB   Eu-Ge-LSb

    Historisch spel der boekdrukkunst, opgedragen aan de Nederlandsche
jeugd. door D. S. Tweede druk. Te Amsterdam, bij Gebroeders van
Arum, [184-?] Pamphlet of 32p. 8.5x5.5 cm. and plate 23x30.5 cm.
in case 9x7 cm. [978]
    NN

Hooufft, David, and B. C. De Lange.
    Programma wegens de viering van het vierde eeuwfeest der uitvinding
van de boekdrukkunst, door Lourens Janszoon Koster, te Haarlem den 10.
en 11. Julij 1823. Haarlem, 1823. 11p. 8vo.
    Reissued in Loosjes, Vincent. Gedenkschriften ... Haarlem, 1824.
    p. 403-416. [979]
    DLC   LCJ   MH   NN   NNC   Eu-De-LBb   Eu-Fr-PN   Eu-Ge-LB
    Eu-Ge-LSb

Hubbens, Arthur.
    Gutenberg n'est pas l'inventeur de l'imprimerie. Revue de
Hollande, vol. 2, June 1917, p. 1284-1297.
    Also reprint. [980]

Huet, Conrad Busken, 1826-1886.
    Johann Gutenberg. (In Huet, Conrad Busken. Litterarische fan-
tasien en kritieken ... Haarlem, H. D. Tjeeuk Willink [1881-1888]
vol. 4, p. 1-11) [981]
    DLC   MB   MH   Eu-Fr-PN

---- Jonker Johan v. Gutenberg benevens hoffelijk, smaakvol en
welopgevoed bewijs, dat Dr. v. d. L. er een hoop baboes op nahoudt.

Batavia, 1871.   Folio.
   Title from van der Linde, Geschichte der Erfindung ...   [982]

Huffel, N. G. van.
   De uitvinding van de boekdrukkunst.   Drukkers Weekblad, vol. 24,
1934, p. 250-252.   [983]

   Hulde aan Laurens Janszoon Coster uitvinder der boekdrukkunst.
[Standbeeld] Gedrukt op de typographische tentoonstelling, Haarlem,
15-19 Julij 1856, geheel ten voordeele der armen, door O. D. Emrik.
1p.   8vo.
   Title from Neuer Anzeiger für Bibliographie und Bibliothekswissenschaft, 1867.   [984]

   De ijzeren drukpers aan de bezoekers der tentoonstelling te Haar-
lem, by gelegenheid van het feest ter eere van Lourens Janszoon
Coster, op den 15., 16. en 17. Julij 1856.   Haag, 1856.   1p.
Folio.
   Title from Mohr, Jubelfeste.   [985]

Immig, C., Jr.
   De portretten van Laurens Janszoon Coster.   Het Tarief, Coster
number, 1923.   [986]

----   De uitvinding van de boekdrukkunst.   Graphica (Brussels), vol.
4, no. 13, 1923, p. 186-190; no. 15, p. 211-214.
   Also reprint.   [987]

Jones, Albert Y.
   The legend of Haarlem and Coster.   (In Jones, Albert Y. A journey to Holland in the nineteenth century.   Oxford, Clarendon Press,
1810.   p. 372-384)
   Title from Douglas C. McMurtrie.   [988]

Junius, Adrianus, 1511-1575.
   Batavia. In qua praeter gentis et insulae antiquitatem, originem
... aliaque ad eam historiam pertinentia, declaratur quae fuerit vetus
Batavia ... quae item genuina inclytae Francorum nationis fuerit sedes.
Ex officina Plantiniana: [Antwerp] 1588.   4to.   [989]
   ICN   Eu-Do-LBb   Eu-Fr-PN   Eu-Ge-LB

---- ----   Dordrecht, 1652.   12mo.   [990]
   ICN

Junius, Francisc.
   De schilder-konst der oude.   Middelburgh, Zacharias Roman, 1641.
4to.   [991]
   Eu-Do-LBb

- 128 -

Kade, Reinhard.
Eine bibliographische Seltenheit in Freiberg in Sachsen. Speculum humanae salvationis. Zentralblatt für Bibliothekswesen, vol. 4, no. 7, 1887, p. 301-304. [992]

Kampen, Nicolass Godfried van, 1776-1839.
Geschichte der europäischen Staaten. Herausgegeben von A. H. L. Heeren und F. A. Ukert. Geschichte der Niederlande, von N. G. van Kampen ... Hamburg, 1831-1833. Bei Friedrich Perthes. 2 vols. fold. tables. 20 cm.
   Vol. 1, p. 211: "Das Jahr der eigentlichen Erfindung ist von der haarlemer Commission zur vierten Säcularfeier auf 1423, wohl zu fruh, festgesetzt. Die Jahre zwischen 1430 und 1440 kommen uns wahrscheinlicher vor."   [993]
   I   ICN   IaU   MH   NN   Eu-Ge-LB

Klasses, H. J.
The invention of printing.   British and Colonial Printer, vol. 47, Aug. 1900, p. 105-106.   [994]

Koenen, D. P. M.
   Kort verslag van het plaats gehad hebbende in de Algemeene 's Lands Drukkerij te Batavia op den 24sten Augustus 1823 bij de viering van het vierde eeuwfeest van de uitvinding der drukkunst door Lourens Koster Jz. [Batavia, 1823?] Folio.
   Title from van der Linde, Geschichte der Erfindung ...   [995]

Koning, Cornelis de.
   Bij de herstelling van het beeld van Laurens Jansz. Koster, in den gevel van het nieuw geboude huis.   1818.   Algemeene Konst- en Letterbode, no. 37, 1818, p. 102-103.   [996]

---- Lierzang, bij de ontdekking en inwijding van de eerzuil voor Lourens Jansz. Koster, in den Haarlemmer-Hout, den 10 julij 1823. (In Loosjes, Vincent. Gedenkschriften ... Haarlem, 1824. p. 181-195)   [997]

---- Der Nagedachtenis van Lourens Janszoon Koster, toegewijd bij den Gedenksteen in den Achthoek, op het vierde eeuwfeest der boekdrukkunst.   Haarlem, 1823.
   Title from Mohr, Jubelfeste.   [998]

---- Op het instorten der aloude woning van Laurens Jansz. Koster, op den 13 Mei 1818.   Algemeene Konst- en Letterbode, no. 25, 1818, p. 386-387.   [999]

---- Tafereel der Stad Haarlem en derzelver geschiedenis van den vroghste tijden af tot op den tegenwoordigen toe.   Haarlem, bij. A. Loosjes, 1807-1808.   4 vols.   8vo.   [1000]
   Eu-Fr-PN   Eu-Ge-LB

Koning, Gerrit van Enst.
   De vergoding van Gutenberg in onze dagen; of tien vragen, tot
bewijs, etc. Met eene voorrede en aanteekeningen. Groningen, 1842.[1001]
   Eu-Ge-LB

Koning, Jacobus, 1770-1832.
   Aanteekeningen over de geschiedenis der boekdrukkunst, over incuna-
belen, zeldzame drukken, uittreksels uit brieven betrekking hebbende
op de uitvinding der boekdrukkunst, enz.   [ms. of 350 leaves,
with index.]   Folio.   [1002]
   Eu-Ne-AVb

----   Bijdragen tot de geschiedenis der boekdrukkunst, door Jacobus
Koning. Lid van het zeeuwsch genootschap, van de maatschappij der
wetenschappen te Haarlem en die der nederlandsche Letterkunde te
Leyden.   Te Haarlem, bij de. Wed. A. Loosjes, Pz., MDCCCXVIII [1818]
1 prel. leaf, ii, [1]-212, [1]p.   22.5 cm.
   Supplement to his Verhandeling over den oorsprong, de uitvinding,
verbetering en volmaking der boekdrukkunst.   [1003]
   ICN   MH   MiU   NN   NNC   Eu-De-LBb   Eu-Fr-PN   Eu-Ge-LB
   Eu-Ne-AVb   Eu-Ne-GK

----   [Collection of original matter in ms. inscribed "Bijdragen tot
de geschiedenis der boekdrukkunst" arranged in sections, lettered
A-U]   2 vols.   [1816-1850?]   Folio.   [1004]
   Eu-Ge-LP

----   Conspectus og berigt aangaande de verhandeling over de uitvinding, verbetering en volmaking der boekdrukkunst.   Amsterdam,
1817.   8vo.   [1005]
   Eu-Ge-LB

----   Dissertation sur l'origine, l'invention et le perfectionne-
ment de l'imprimerie. Par Jacques Koning ... Couronnée par la
Société hollandoise des sciences à Harlem au mois de mai 1816.   Tr.
du hollandois.   Amsterdam, S. Delachaux, 1819.   viii p., 2 leaves,
180p.   vii fold. plates.   22 cm.   [1006]
   DLC   ICJ   NN   Eu-De-LBb   Eu-Fr-PN   Eu-Ge-LP   Eu-Ge-LSb
   Eu-Ne-GK

----   De drukkunst, eene verhandeling uitgesprooken in eene aanzien-
lijke maatschappij.   Te Amsterdam bezyden het standhuis ... Amsterdam,
1794.   24p.   8vo.   [1007]
   Eu-Ge-LSb   Eu-Ne-AVb

----   In welk jaar dezer eeuw behoort het vierde jubel van de uitvinding der boekdrukkunst te Haarlem, gevierd te worden? In twee
brieven van den Heere J. Koning ... aan den ... Heere A. de Vries ...
Haarlem, A. Loosjes, 1822.   11p.   22 cm.   [1008]
   NNC

Koning, Jacobus, 1770-1832.
Miscellanea typographica. [A collection of excerpta, broad-
sides, circulars and pamphlets relating to the history of printing.]
2 vols. 8vo.
Chief contents:
Vol. 1. 70 pieces, chiefly excerpts from the Algemeene Konst- en
Letterbode.
Vol. 2. 65 pieces, including pamphlets by W. Eckhoff, van Lennep,
J. I. Doedes,etc.   [1009]
Eu-Ge-LP

----   Stukken behoorende tot het vierde eeuwfeest der uitvinding van
de boekdrukkunst door L. J. Coster, 1823. [64 pieces collected and
arranged with notes and table of contents by J. K.] 1822-1825.
2 vols. 8vo.   [1010]
Eu-Ge-LP

----   Thesauriers Rekeningen der stad Haarlem van het jaar 1417 tot
1475. ms. 332p. Folio.
Title from van der Linde, Geschichte der Erfindung ...   [1011]

----   [Tracts and excerpta relating to the invention of printing.]
Haarlem, etc. [1818-1825] 10 pieces.   8vo.
Includes his Bijdragen tot de geschiedenis der boekdrukkunst,
Haarlem, 1818-20; Nieuw onderzoek naar de aanspraak van Holland
op de uitvinding der boekdrukkunst door Prof. Ebert; en brief
wegens het geschrift van F. Lehne ..., Haarlem, 1825; and Vier
brieven, gewisseld tusschen J. Scheltema en J. Koning over de
laatste tegenspraak van het regt van Haarlem op de uitvinding
der drukkunst, Haarlem, 1823.   [1012]
Eu-Ge-LP

----   [Typographia illustrata. Plates and woodcuts illustrative
of the history of the art of printing. Collected by J. K.] ca.
1820.   [1013]
Eu-Ge-LP

----   Verhandeling over den oorsprong, de uitvinding, verbetering
en volmaking der boekdrukkunst. Door Jacobus Koning ... Door de
Hollandsche maatschappij der wetenschappen te Haarlem, in Mei 1816,
met den gouden eerprijs bekroond. Haarlem, A. Loosjes, Pz., 1816.
2 prel. leaves, viii p., 3 leaves, [3]-475, [1], viii, xvi p., 2
fold. leaves incl. 1 tab. VIII (i.e. 9) plates (part fold.)
22 cm. (Added t.-p.: Letter- en oudheidkundige verhandelingen van
de Hollandsche maatschappij der wetenschappen te Haarlem. 2. deel) [1014]
DLC ICJ NN Eu-De-LBb Eu-Fr-PN Eu-Ge-LB Eu-Ge-LP
Eu-Ge-LSb Eu-Ne-AVb Eu-Ne-GK
Eu-Ge-LB: Another copy. Few ms. notes [by F. A. Ebert?]

Korte beschrijving der boeken door Lourens Janszoon Koster, te
Haarlem, tusschen de jaren 1420 en 1440 gedrukt; alsmede van eenige
merkwaardigheden tot de geschiedenis van L. J. Koster betrekkelijk,
bij gelegenheid van het vierde eeuw-feest van de uitvinding der
boekdrukkunst, in de Kerk der doopsgezinde gemeente aldaar ten toon
gesteld, op den 10en en 11en Julij 1823. [Haarlem, 1823]. 20p.
23.5 cm.
   Apparently by Abraham de Vries. cf. Doorninck, J. I. van. Ver-
monde en naamlooze schrijvers, deel 1, no. 486.
   Reissued in Loosjes, Vincent. Gedenkschriften ... Haarlem, 1824.
p. 418-438.   [1015]
NNC   Eu-De-LBb   Eu-Ge-LSb

   Korte en klaare beschrijving, wanner en van wien de loffelijke
konst van boekdrukken eerst gevonden is binnen Haarlem. (In Nieuwe
Haerlemsche Mercurius. Almanach. Haerlem, 1765)   [1016]
   Eu-Ge-LB

Kortebrant, Jakob, 1697-1777.
   Jakob Kortebrant's Lof der drukkunste, te Haerlem uitgevonden door
Laur. Janszoon Koster, omtrent het jaer MCCCCXL; op haer derde eeuw-
getyde. Met nodige aanmerkingen. Delf, P. Vander Kloot, 1740.
2 prel. leaves, 79p. illus. 26x17.5 cm.
   In verse.
   Title-vignette.   [1017]
DLC   Eu-De-LBb   Eu-Fr-PN   Eu-Ge-LB   Eu-Ge-LSb   Eu-Ne-AVb

Kossmann, F.
   Nieuws over den oorsprong der boekdrukkunst. Onze Eeuw, vol.
24, 1924, p. 161-173.
   Also reprint.   [1018]

Kruitwagen, Bonaventura.
   Die Ansprüche Hollands auf die Erfindung der Buchdruckerkunst.
(In Gutenbergfestschrift, zur Feier des 25jaehrigen Bestehens des
Gutenbergmuseum in Mainz 1925. Hrsg von A. Ruppel. Mainz, Verlag
der Gutenberg-Gesellschaft [1925] p. 353-370)   [1019]
   DLC   ICN   MB   MH   NN   NNC   NNGr   Eu-De-BP   Eu-Ge-LB
   Eu-Ne-AVb   Eu-Sz-BeG

----   Hoe staat het met de kwestie over de uitvinding van de boekdrukkunst? Nieuwsblad voor den Boekhandel, vol. 104, 1937, p. 636-
642.   [1020]

----   De uitvinding van de boekdrukkunst en hare eerste voortbren-
gelsen. Handeling van de Maatschappij der Nederlandsche Letterkunde
te Leiden, 1917-1918, p. 17-52.   [1021]

Laborde, Léon Emmanuel Simon Joseph, marquis de, 1807-1869.
   Notice sur Coster. Artiste, vol. 4, 1839, p. 114.   [1022]

Lalanne, Ludovic.
  Curiosités bibliographiques.   Paris, 1845.   16mo.   (Bibliothèque de poche.)
    The invention of printing at Harlem: p. 67, 92-96.   [1023]
    Eu-Fr-PN   Eu-Ge-LB

Langendyk, Pieter.
    Lofdicht op het eerbeeld van Laurens Koster, eerster vinder der
drukkunst, kunstig uitgehouwen door M. G. v. Heerstal, en opgerecht
binnen de stadt Haarlem, in den Artsenyhof, in den jaare 1723.
Haarlem, 1723.   4to.
    Title from van der Linde, Geschichte der Erfindung ...   [1024]

Langenschwarz, Maximiliaan.
    De vergoding van Gutenberg in onze dagen; of, tien vragen, tot
bewijs, dat Johann Gutenberg niet de uitvinder der boekdrukkunst
was ... Met eene voorrede en aanteekeningen van G. van Enst Koning
... Groningen, Oomkens, 1842.   cover title, 4 prel. leaves, [v]-viii,
71p.   22 cm.   [1025]
    ICN   MHi   NNC   Eu-De-LBb   Eu-Ge-LB   Eu-Ge-LP   Eu-Ne-AVb
    Eu-Ne-GK

----   Die Gutenberg-Schwärmerei unsrer Tage; oder zehn Fragen als
Beweis, dass Johann Gutenberg nicht Erfinder der Buchdruckerkunst
war.   Leipzig, 1841.   vi, 84p.   20.5 cm.   [1026]
    NNGr   Eu-De-LBb   Eu-Ge-LB   Eu-Ge-LP

----   Tien vragen van eenen Hoogduitscher, als bewijs dat Johann
Gutenberg niet de uitvinder der boekdrukkunst is.   Eene hulde aan
Laurens Jansz. Koster.   Deventer, 1856.   iv, 42p.   8vo.   [1027]
    Eu-Ge-LSb

    Laurens Coster.   16 July 1856.   n.p. [1856]   4p.   roy. 8vo.
    Signed: D. P.
    At end: "Overgedrukt uit het Weekblad van het regt, no. 1764."
    Title from Neuer Anzeiger für Bibliographie und Bibliothekswissen-
    schaft, 1867.   [1028]

    Laurens Janszoon Koster.   Een liedje bij de onthulling van zijn
standbeeld.   Rotterdam, Altmann & van der Palm, 1856.   6p.
22.5 cm.   [1029]
    NNC   Eu-Ge-LB

    Laurier-Krans, gevlogten om't hoofd van L. Koster, eerste uit-
vinder der boekdrukkunst binnen Haarlem.   Haarlem, 1726.   4to.   [1030]
    Eu-De-LBb   Eu-Ge-LP   Eu-Ge-LSb

    Lauwerkrans opgedragen aan Dr. A. de Vries, door de typographische
vereenigingen in Nederland.   Gedicht.   Haarlem, 1856.   8vo.
    Title from Mohr, Jubelfeste.   [1031]

[Lee, Abraham van] 1805-1869.
  Haarlems regt op de eer van de uitvinding der boekdrukkunst gehand-
haafd; of beknopt overzigt van den stand der zaak, vooral na het on-
derzoek van den heer De Vries, en de toelichtingen van de heeren
Schinkel en Noordziek. Door A. v. L. ... Tweede druk. Amsterdam,
M. H. Binger, 1848.   vi, [7]-34p.   22 cm.   [1032]
  MH   NNC
  1st ed. 1843:   Eu-Ge-LP   Eu-Ne-AVb   Eu-Ne-GK

Lehne, Johann Friedrich Franz, 1771-1836.
  Einige Bemerkungen über das Unternehmen der gelehrten Gesellschaft
zu Harlem, ihre Stadt die Ehre der Erfindung der Buchdruckerkunst zu
ertrotzen. Von Friedrich Lehne ... Mainz, Florian Kupferberg, 1823.
32p.   21.5 cm.
  "Aus der Zeitschrift: Der Spiegel."   [1033]
  ICN   NNC   Eu-De-LBb
  1825 ed.:   Eu-Fr-PN   Eu-Ge-LB   Eu-Ge-LP

---- Historisch-critische Prüfung der Ansprüche welche die Stadt
Haarlem auf den Ruhm der Erfindung der Buchdruckerkunst macht, durch
Beleuchtung der Ansichten ihrer Bertheidiger: des Herrn, Dr. Ebert,
Hofbibliothekars zu Dresden, und des Herrn. Koning, Obergericht-
schreibers zu Amsterdam. Von Dr. Friedrich Lehne, grossherzl.
Hessischen Professor der Universität und Bibliothekar der Stadt
Mainz. Ex-libris J. Visser, Rotterdam.   Mainz, 1827.   Bei Florian
Kupferberg.   viii, 96p.   21.5 cm.   [1034]
  ICN   NNC   Eu-Ge-LB   Eu-Ge-LE   Eu-Ge-LP

Lennep, David Jacob van, 1774-1853.
  Memoria Hieronymi de Bosch, Instituti regii belgici quondam socii,
rite celebrata in publico Classis tertiae consessu a Davide Jacobo
van Lennep. Et, Carmen de inventae typographiae laude Kostero Harlemensi potenter tandem asserta: auctore Hermanno Bosscha ... [Amstelo-
dami] excuderunt Pieper et Ipenbuur, 1817.   3 prel. leaves, 71p.
26x23 cm.
  Edited by K. Nederlandsch institut van wetenschappen, letterkunde
en schoòne kunsten, Amsterdam.   3. klasse.
  Preface signed: M. Stuart.   [1035]
  DLC   ICN   Eu-De-LBb   Eu-Fr-PN

Lennep, Gerard van.
  Aanmerkingen op de gedenkschriften wegens het vierde eeuwgetijde
van de uitvinding der boekdrukkunst, door Lourens Janszoon Koster,
overgenomen uit de 's Gragenhaagsche Couranten van den 12, 14 en 28
Julij 1824, en vermeerderd met eenige aanteekeningen, strekkende om
aan te toonen dat door dit werk aan de zaak van Haarlem nadeel is
toegebragt. 's Gravenhage, Aan het Bureau der 's Gravenhaagsche
Courant, en bij de voornaamste boekhandelaars van het Koningrijk,
1824.   30p.   23 cm.   [1036]
  MH   Eu-Ge-LB   Eu-Ne-GK

Lennep, Gerard van.
Aanmerkingen wegens een' houten drukvorm, waarin de letters eener bladzyde van een Latynsch Horarium verkeerd gesneden staan, en welke den 29sten van Grasmaand l.l., door den boekverkooper Haak, te Leyden, openlyk verkocht is als een overblyfsel van den arbeid van Laurens Janszoon Koster. Algemeene Konst- en Letterbode, no. 24, 1809, p. 371-376.
Also reprint. [1037]

---- Bijdrage tot de geschiedenis van de uitvinding der boekdrukkunst. 1809. 10p. roy. 8vo.
Contains excerpts from the Koninklijke Courant van Dingsdag den
21sten van Lentemaand 1809. [1038]
Eu-De-LBb Eu-Go-LSb Eu-Ne-AVb

---- Wederlegging van het geschrift van den heere Jacobus Koning
over de houten aanmerkingen wegens den houten Druk-worm, den 29sten
Grasmaans 1809, door den boekverkooper Haak, openlyk te Leyden verkocht. n.d. 8vo. [1039]
Eu-De-LBb

Leven van Lourens Janszoon Koster, Haarlemmer, eerste vinder der
drukkunst. (In Levensbeschrijving van beroemde en geleerde mannen.
Amsterdam, 1730. vol. 2, no. 6, p. 9-82)
Also reprint.
Title from Bigmore & Wyman. [1040]

Librovich, S. F.
Gordost' Garlema. Epizod iz istorii knigopechataniia. St. Peters-
burg, M. O. Wolf, 1915. 30p. ports., illus. [1041]
Eu-Ru-MLe

Loeff, J. D. Rutgers van der.
De Haarlemsche uitvinder der boekdrukkunst. Tijdschrift voor
Boek- en Bibliotheekswesen, vol. 2, 1904, p. 187-192. [1042]

Loosjes, Adriaan Pieterszoon, 1761-1818.
Laurens Koster; tooneelstuk met zang. Haarlem, 1809. vi, 53p.
8vó. [1043]
Eu-De-LBb Eu-Fr-PN Eu-Go-LB Eu-Ne-AVb

Loosjes, Vincent.
Gedenkschriften, wegens het vierde eeuwgetijde van de uitvinding
der boekdrukkunst door Lourens Janszoon Koster, van Stadswege gevierde
te Haarlem, den 10 en 11 Julij 1823; bijeenverzameld door V. Loosjes.
Met platen. Haarlem, V. Loosjes, 1824. [2], liv, [2], 462, [2]p.
front. (port.) 2 plates. 22 cm. [1044]
DLC ICJ MH NN NNC NNGr Eu-De-LBb Eu-Fr-PN
Eu-Go-LB Eu-Go-LSb Eu-Ne-AVb Eu-Ne-GK Eu-Sz-BeG

Loots, Cornelis, 1765-1834.
    Feestzang, bij de viering van het vierde eeuwfeest der uitvind-
ing van de boekdrukkunst, te Haarlem, door Cornelis Loots, ridder
der Orde van de Nederlandschen Leeuw en lid van het Koninklijk-
Nederlandsch Instituut.   Te Amsterdam, bij Johannes' van der Hey en
Zoon, 1823. 15p. 21.5 cm.
    Printing, Poetry.
    Re-issued in Loosjes, Vincent. Gedenkschriften ... Haarlem, 1824.
    p. 201-214.   [1045]
    NN   Eu-De-LBb   Eu-Ge-LSb

    Lourens Janszoon Coster, uitvinder der boekdrukkunst, te
Haarlem, omstreeks 1423. Oprigting van het standbeeld tot Coster's
eere, der stad Haarlem aangeboden, als hulde van Neerlands volk.
[Amsterdam, Gedrukt bij C. A. Spin & zoon, 1856?] 20p. 30.5 cm.
[With Nieuwsblad voor den boekhandel. 's Gravenhage, 1856]
    Caption title.   [1046]
    DLC   Eu-De-LBb

    Lourens Janszoon Coster's Fest zu Haarlem am 16. Juli.
Leipziger Illustrierte Zeitung, vol. 27, no. 686, 1856, p. 127-
128.   [1047]

Maatschappij tot nut van 't algemeen: Hoornsche Dept.
    Het vierde eeuwgetijde van de uitvinding der boekdrukkunst,
gevierd den 10 den van Hooimaand 1823. Door het Hoornsche department de Maatschappij: Tot nut van 't Algemeen. Amsterdam, bij
Vink, 1823. 72p. roy. 8vo.
    Louis Mohr assigns authorship to J. S. Swaan.   [1048]
    NNC   Eu-Ge-LB   Eu-Ge-LP

Marnix, C. H. R.
    Mentz of Haarlem? Johann Gensfleisch von Gutenberg of Laurens
Janszoon Koster? Eene bijdrage tot de geschiedenis van de uitvinding der boekdrukkunst. Door C. H. R. Marnix. Ten voordeele
van het op te rigten standbeeld voor Laurens Janszoon Koster.
's Gravenhage, H. C. Susan, C. Hzoon, 1852. vi, [7]-48p.
22 cm.   [1049]
    MH NN NNC Eu-De-LBb Eu-Fr-PN Eu-Ge-LB Eu-Ge-LP
    Eu-Ne-AVb

McMurtrie, Douglas Crawford, 1888-
    The Dutch claims to the invention of printing, by Douglas C.
McMurtrie. Chicago, 1928. 2 prel. leaves, 7-26p., 1 leaf.
23 cm.
    "Of this volume, Ludlow-set in Nicolas Jenson & Nicolas
Jenson open, there have been printed ... on Batchelor hand-made
paper, four hundred copies only."   [1050]
    DLC ICN NN Eu-Fr-PN Eu-Ge-LB Eu-Ne-AVb

McMurtrie, Douglas Crawford, 1888-
    The Dutch claims to the invention of printing, by Douglas C.
McMurtrie. [2d and rev. ed.] Chicago, 1928. 2 prel. leaves,
7-26p., 1 leaf, 23 cm.
    " ... Printed ... September, 1928 ... two hundred copies only."   [1051]
    DLC   MB   MiU   NjN   Eu-Ge-LB

----   A Dutch typefounder on the invention of printing, by Douglas
C. McMurtrie. New York, Press of Ars typographica, 1926. 13p.
23.5 cm.
    A translation, with an introduction, of the first 6 pages of
    "Fonderies de caractères et leur matériel dans les Pays-Bas du
    XVe au XIXe siècle ... par Ch. Enschedé", published at Haarlem,
    1908.   [1052]
    DLC   NBuG   NN

Mariette, Jean Pierre.
    Lettre ... à Gérard Meerman. Communiquée et annotée par Maurice
Tourneux. Société des Bibliophiles François, vol. 2, no. 7, 1903,
p. 1-34.   [1053]

[Meerman, Gerard] 1722-1771.
    Afkomet leeftijdt, en nakomelingschap van Laurens, uitvinder
der boekdrukkunst. [1797] 8vo.
    Title from van der Linde, Geschichte der Erfindung ...   [1054]

----   Conspectus originum typographicarum, a Meermanno proxime in
lucem edendarum. In usum amicorum typis descriptus. [Amstelodami],
1761. 88p. 16 cm.
    Privately printed as the prospectus of the Origines typographicae
    published in 1765.   [1055]
    CtY   ICN   NN   Eu-Fr-PN   Eu-Ge-LB   Eu-Ge-IP   Eu-Ne-AVb
    Eu-Ne-GK

----   De l'invention de l'imprimerie, ou Analyse des deux ouvrages
publiés sur cette matière, par M. Meerman ... avec des notes historiques et critiques. Suivi d'une notice chronologique et raisonnée
des livres avec et sans date, imprimés avant l'année 1501, dans les
dix-sept provinces des Pays-Bas, par M. Jacques Visser; et augm.
d'environ deux-cents articles par l'éditeur ... Paris, F. Schoell,
1809. xxiv, 392p. plates. 21.5 cm.
    Edited by H. Jansen, with notes by H. Gockinga and C. P. Goujet.
    French translation of the Origines typographicae published at the
    Hague in 1765.   [1056]
    DLC   ICN   NN   Eu-Fr-PN   Eu-Ge-LB   Eu-Ne-GK

----   Origines typographicae. Gerardo Meerman auctore ... Hagae
Comitum, apud Nicolaum van Daalen; [etc., etc.] 1765. 2 vols.
in 1. front. (port.) ix plates. 26 cm.
    An abridged translation of this, together with an abridgment of

Middleton's "Dissertation on the origin of printing in England"
was issued by W. Boyer in 1776 under title: The origin of printing.   [1057]
   DLC   ICJ   MBAt   MWA   NN   Eu-De-BP   Eu-De-LBb   Eu-Fr-PN
   Eu-Ge-LB   Eu-Ge-LP   Eu-Ge-LSb   Eu-Ne-AVb   Eu-Ne-GK   Eu-Sz-BeG

Meerman, Gerard, 1722-1771.
   Plan du traité des origines typographiques, par M. Méerman, con-
seiller & pensionnaire de Roterdam [sic]. Traduit du Latin en François.
A Amsterdam et se trouve à Paris, chez Aug. Mart. Lottin,
l'aîne, Libraire & imprimeur de Mgr le Duc de Berry, rue S. Jacques,
près S. Yves, au Coq. MDCCLXII [1762].   viii, 125p.   20 cm.   [1058]
   NN   Eu-Ge-LB

----   Uitvinding der boekdrukkunst, getrokken uit het Latynsch werk
van Gerard Meerman, met ene voorreden en aantekeningen van Henrik
Gockinga; hierachter is gevoegt ene lyst der boeken, in de Nederland-
en gedrukt voor't jaar MD, opgestelt door Jakob Visser.   Amsterdam,
By P. van Damme, 1767.   2 parts in 1 vol.   26x22 cm.   [1059]
   DLC   ICJ   ICN   NIC   NN   Eu-De-LBb   Eu-Fr-PN   Eu-Ge-LB
   Eu-Ge-LP   Eu-Ge-LSb   Eu-Ne-AVb

Meersch, Polydore Charles van der, 1812-1868.
   Un mot sur la question de l'invention de l'imprimerie, a propos
de l'Essai historique et critique sur l'invention de l'imprimerie,
par Mr Ch. Paeile, par P. C. van der Meersch ... Gand, L. Hebbelynck,
1860.   24p.   23 cm.
   "Extrait du Messager des Sciences Historiques de Belgiques."   [1060]
   ICN   NNC   Eu-De-LBb   Eu-Fr-PC   Eu-Ge-LP   Eu-Ge-LSb

----   Recherches sur la vie et les travaux des imprimeurs belges et
néerlandais, établis à l'étranger, et sur la part qu'ils ont prise
à la régéneration littéraire de l'Europe au XVe siècle; précédées
d'une introduction historique sur la découverte de l'imprimerie et
sur la propagation de cet art en Belgique et en Hollande, par P. C.
van der Meersch ... Tome premier.   Gand, L. Hebbelynck, 1856.   2 prel.
leaves, vii, 492, [2]p.   25 cm.
   No more published.   [1061]
   CSmH   DLC   ICJ   ICN   Eu-Fr-PC   Eu-Ge-LB   Eu-Ne-AVb
   Eu-Ne-GK

Meijer, Hendrik Jr.
   Feestzang op het vierde eeuwgetijde van de uitvinding der drukkunst.
Haarlem, 1823.
   Re-issued in Loosjes, Vincent. Gedenkschriften ... Haarlem, 1824.
   p. 215-226.   [1062]

   Mémoire sur les premières impressions faites à Harlem (et y con-
servées dans l'hôtel de ville). (In Sallengre, Albert Henri. Mémoires.   La Haye, 1716.   vol. 1, part 2, p. 392-398)

Title from Hoffman, F. L. Essai d'une liste chronologique des
ouvrages et dissertations concernant l'histoire de l'imprimerie
en Hollande et en Belgique. Bulletin du Bibliophile Belge,
1856.
[1063]

Méry, François Joseph Pierre André.
L'imagier de Harlem; ou la découverte de l'imprimerie; drame
légende en cinq actes et dix tableaux en prose et en vers, de MM.
Méry et Gérard de Nerval. **Nouv. éd.** Paris, À la Librairie théât-
rale, 1851. 126p. 18.5 cm.
Imprint date on cover: 1852. Bernard Lopez was also a collaborator.
[1064]
CtMW NN NRU Eu-Fr-PN Eu-Ge-LB Eu-Ne-AVb

Meurs, Petrus van, 1818-
De Keulsche kroniek en de Costerlegende van Dr. A. van der Linde
te zamen getoetst. Door Dr. P. van Meurs ... Haarlem, A. C. Kruseman,
1870, viii, 65p. illus. (facsims.) 23 cm.
[1065]
CSmH ICN MH NN NNC Eu-De-LBb Eu-Ge-LB Eu-Ne-AVb

Middleton, Conyers, 1683-1750.
The origin of printing in two essays. I. The substance of Dr.
Middleton's dissertation on the origin of printing in England. II.
Mr. Meerman's account of the invention of the art at Harleim, and
its progress to Mentz. With occasional remarks and an appendix.
2d. edition. London, printed for W. Bowyer and J. Nichols, in
Red-Lion Passage, Fleet-Street, 1776. xvi, 300p. 21 cm.
[1066]
CSmH MB NjN Eu-Ge-LB Eu-Ge-LSb Eu-Ne-GK

Molsdorf, Wilhelm, 1866-
Zur Coster-Ikonographie. Zeitschrift für Bücherfreunde, n.s.,
vol. 15, no. 1, 1923, p. 1-3.
[1067]

Mommaas, C.
Het onthaal aan de typographische Vereenigingen in Haarlem op
den 16. Julij 1856. Verslaag aan alle Kunstbroeders in Nederland.
Utrecht, 1856. 24p. 8vo.
Title from Mohr, Jubelfeste.
[1068]

Müller, G. H.
Die Quellen der Costerlegende. Zentralblatt für Bibliothekswesen,
vol. 28, 1911, p. 145-167, 193-207.
[1069]

Musper, Heinrich Theodor.
Die ältesten Haarlemer Blockbücher. Pantheon, 1938, p. 382-384. [1070]

---- Die Datierung und Lokalisierung der ältesten gedruckten Bücher
von Laurens Janszoon Coster. Graphischen Kunste, n.s., vol. 3,
1938, p. 41-52.
[1071]

Musper, Heinrich Theodor.
Die Haarlemer Blockbücher und die Costerfrage; Fest-Vortrag
gehalten am 26. Juni 1938, in der General-Versammlung der Gutenberg-
Gesellschaft im Kurfürstlichen Schloss zu Mainz, von Heinrich Theodor
Musper.   Mainz, Verlag der Gutenberg-Gesellschaft, 1939.   [10]p.,
1 leaf.   port., facsims.   29 cm.   [Kleiner Druck der Gutenberg-
Gesellschaft.   nr. 34]   [1072]
    DLC   ICN   Eu-De-BP   Eu-De-LBb   Eu-De-MzG   Eu-Ne-AVb

N., N.
Onuitgegeven feestzang op het vierde eeuwfeest van de uitvinding
der boekdrukkunst.   1823.   8vo.
Title from van der Linde, Geschichte der Erfindung ...   [1073]

Nierstrasz, J. L., Jr.
Eeuwzang bij het vierde eeuwgetijde van de uitvinding der boekdrukkunst.   Werken der Hollandsche Maatschappij van Fraije Kunsten
en Wetenschappen, vol. 7, part 1, 1824.   [1074]

Nijhoff, P.
Korte geschiedenis van de vestiging der boekdrukkunst in Nederland
in de 15e eeuw.   Amsterdam, 1853.
Reprint from Nieuwsblad voor den Boekhandel.   [1075]
    Eu-Ne-AVb

Noehden, G. H.
On the pretensions of Laurens Koster, of Harlem, to the invention
of printing with movable type.   Classical Journal, vol. 21, no. 41,
Mar. 1820, p. 117-137.   [1076]

Noordziek, Jan Jacobus Frederik, 1811-1886.
Berigt wegens een exemplaar van den Speculum humanae salvationis
op de Groothertogelijke Bibliotheek te Florenz.   (Overgenomen uit
den Algemeenen Konst- en Letterbode, no. 37, van het jaar 1844.)
8vo.   [1077]
    Eu-De-LBb

----   Beschrijving van twee prachtexemplaren der in het Fransch
uitgegeven werken van ... A. de Vries over de uitvinding der boekdrukkunst.   [Privately printed, The Hague, 1846?]   32p.   8vo.   [1078]
    Eu-Ge-LB   Eu-Ge-LP   Eu-Ne-GK

----   Gedenkboek der Costers-Feesten van 15, 16 en 17 Julij 1856.
Door J. J. F. Noordziek.   Uitgegeven door de Boekhandelaars-Vereen-
iging Laurens Janszoon Coster, te Haarlem, 1858.   xxviii, 360p.
plates.   24 cm.   [1079]
    ICN   MH   NN   NNGr   Eu-De-LBb   Eu-Ge-LB   Eu-Ge-LP   Eu-Ge-LSb
    Eu-Ne-AVb   Eu-Ne-GK

Noordziek, Jan Jacobus Frederik, 1811-1886.
    Het geschilstuk betrekkelijk de uitvinding der boekdrukkunst,
geschiedkundig uiteengezet, door J. J. F. Noordziek.   Haarlem, A. C.
Kruseman, 1848.   viii, 112p., errata slip tipped in.   21 cm.   [1080]
    DLC   NN   Eu-De-LBb   Eu-Fr-PN   Eu-Ge-LB   Eu-Ge-LP   Eu-Ne-AVb
    Eu-Ne-GK

[----]   Uitvinding der boekdrukkunst.   Haarlem, J. Enschedé en
zoonen, 1854.   1 prel. leaf, vi, 82p.   front. illus. (incl. ports.)
plates.   17 cm.   [1081]
    DLC   Eu-Ge-LB   Eu-Ne-GK

Ooston de Bruyn, Gerrit Willem.
    De stad Haarlem en haare geschiedenissen ... Eerste deel.   Te Haar-
lem, by Joannis Enschedé, Stads-drukker, en Jan Bosch, 1765.   341p.
Folio.
    Only "eerste deel" published.
    [The invention of printing]: p. 209-280.   [1082]
    Eu-Ge-LB

Pacile, Charles Louis Eusèbe, 1823-1881.
    Essai historique et critique sur l'invention de l'imprimerie
(par C. Pacille].   (In his Catalogue de la Bibliothèque de la ville
de Lille, 1839-1870.   Théologie, 1859, p. [vii]-cclxxxiv).   Also
issued separately the same year.   A Dutch translation appeared at
Amsterdam, 1867.   [1083]
    DLC   NN   Eu-Ge-LB

---- ----   Paris, Téchener; [etc., etc.] 1859.   2 prel. leaves,
[7]-286p.   fold. facsim.   22 cm.
    Reprinted from the author's Catalogue de la Bibliothèque de la
    ville de Lille.   [1084]
    DLC   MH   NN   Eu-De-LBb   Eu-Fr-PN   Eu-Ge-LB   Eu-Ge-LP
    Eu-Ne-AVb   Eu-Ne-GK

---   Kritiesch onderzoek naar de uitvinding der boekdrukkunst.   Geschiedenis der vinding, waardeering van den daarover gevoerden strijd, een
en ander voorgesteld uit minder en meer bekende bronnen en opgemaakt
uit al het daarover heen- en wedergeschrevene, oorspronkelijk in het
Fransch bewerkt door den heer Ch. Pacile ... Nu, ter afdoende inlichting
der landgenooten van Lourens Jansson Coster, in het Nederlandsch overgebracht door J. H. Rutjes ... Amsterdam, C. L. Van Langenhuysen, 1867.
xx, 267p.   23 cm.
    Dutch translation of the preceding work.   [1085]
    MH   NNC   Eu-De-LBb   Eu-Ge-LB   Eu-Ge-LP   Eu-Ge-ISb
    Eu-Ne-AVb   Eu-Ne-GK

Palm, Johannes Henricus van der, 1763-1840.
    Redevoering op het vierde eeuwfeest van de uitvinding der boek-
drukkunst binnen Haarlem, aldaar uitgesproken op den 10 Julij des
                                - 141 -

jaars 1823 door J. H. van der Palm.   Haarlem, Vincent Loosjes, 1823.
viii, 29p.   23 cm.
   Re-issued in Loosjes, Vincent. Gedenkschriften ... Haarlem, 1824.
   p. 131-156.   [1086]
   MH   NN   NNGr   Eu-De-LBb   Eu-Ge-LSb

Pinto, de.
   Laurens Coster 16. Julij 1856.   Haarlem, 1856.   8vo.
   Title from Mohr, Jubelfeste.   [1087]

Pluim de Jaager, J.
   Morgenwandeling van Laurens Janszoon Koster in den hout bij Haarlem, anno 1423. Dichtstukje ... Dordrecht, J. de Vos, 1823.   16p.
22.5 cm.
   Signed: J. Pluim de Jaager.
   "Voorgelezen aan den vriendschappelijken maaltijde gehouden door
de leden van de Vereeniging ter bevordering van de belangen des
boekhandels, den 12 Julij 1823; na den afloop van derzelver Algemeene jaarlijksche vergadering, en der plegtige Feestviering van
het Vierde eeuwgetijde van de uitvinding der boekdrukkunst, te
Haarlem."   [1088]
   NNC

Prato.
   De haarlemsche Costerlegende.   <u>Het Noorden</u> (Amsterdam), Nov.
3-5, 1870.   [1089]

   Programma der feestviering ter gelegenheid van de onthulling van
het oude standbeeld van Laurens Janszoon Coster te Haarlem, den 15,
16, en 17. Julij 1856.   Haarlem, A. C. Kruseman, 1856.   8p.   8vo.
   Title from van der Linde, Geschichte der Erfindung ...   [1090]

   Programma, wegen de Feestviering in de groote Kerk op Donderdag
den 10 Julij 1823.   Haarlem, 1823.   1 leaf.   8vo.
   Title from Mohr, Jubelfeste.   [1091]

Quarles van Ufford, L. J.
   Beknopte beschrijving der stad Haarlem, kunnende dienen tot eenen
gids bij de beschouwing van Lou Koster en Suze Guerre en van derzelver omstreken.   Haarlem, 1828.   sm. 8vo.
   Title from van der Linde, Geschichte der Erfindung ...   [1092]

Quarles van Ufford, Pieter Nicolaas.
   Beknopt verhaal der uitvinding van de boekdrukkunst anno 1423
door Laurens Janszoon, overleden anno 1439, in leven koster der
Groote Kerk, schepen en thesaurier der stad Haarlem.   Haarlem, 1876.
8vo.
   Reprint from Haarlemer Nieuwsblad, May 17, 24, 31, 1876.   [1093]
   Eu-Ne-AVb

Quarles van Ufford, Pieter Nicölaas.
Eenige regelen ter wederlegging van de Costerlegende van Dr.
A. van der Linde.   Haarlem, J. J. van Brederode, 1872.   23p.
23 cm.
    "Overgedrukt uit Haarlems Nieuwsblad van April, 1872."   Title
    taken from the caption.   [1094]
    MH   NN   Eu-Ge-LB   Eu-Ne-AVb

Rathgeber, Georg, b. 1800.
    Beredeneerde geschiedenis der Nederlandsche schilder-, houtsnij-
en graveerkunst, door Dr. George Rathgeber ... Naar het Hoogduitsch; met
aanteekeningen van den vertaler.   Eerste deel:Van de gebroeders Van Eyck
tot op Albrecht Durer's aanwezigheid in de Nederlanden.   Amsterdam,
M. H. Binger, 1844.   xxxii, 452p., 1 leaf.   front.   23 cm.
    No more published.
    In the notes, the invention of printing and Haarlem's alleged
    right of priority are fully discussed.   [1095]
    NNC   Eu-Ge-LB

Reber, Franz von, 1834-1919.
    De primordiis artis imprimendi ac praecipue de inventione typo-
graphiae harlemensi ... Berolini, typis Gustavi Schade [1856]   37,
[1]p., 1 leaf.   21 cm.
    Inaugural dissertation, Berlin.   [1096]
    DLC   Eu-De-LBb   Eu-Ge-LP   Eu-Ne-AVb   Eu-Ne-GK

Regt, Johannes Karel de, 1821-
    Een blick op de uitvinding der boekdrukkunst en op Haarlem bij
de aanstaande feesten in Julij 1856.   Leyden, 1856.   8vo.   [1097]
    Eu-De-LBb   Eu-Ge-LP

---- Lourens Jansz. Coster, of de uitvinding der boekdrukkunst;
historisch drama met zang, in 2 bedrijven en 3 tafereelen.   Met een
naspel ... Leyden, J, J. Somerwil, 1857.   [8], 108, [1]p.   19 cm.   [1098]
    ICN   MH   NN   Eu-De-LBb   Eu-Ge-LB   Eu-Ge-LSb   Eu-Ne-AVb

Reiber, Fr.
    De primordiis artis imprimendi ac praecipue de inventione typo-
graphiae.   Harlemensis, Berlino, 1856.
    Title from Enciclopedia Italiana di scienze, lettere ed arti ...
    [Bibliography of printing] vol. 33.   [1099]

Reinhart, G. H.
    Op het vierde eeuwgetijde van de uitvinding der boekdrukkunst,
door Lourens Janszoon Koster te Haarlem, gevierd den 10 en 11
Julij 1823.   Vaderlandsche Letteroefeningen, no. 10. Aug. 1823,
p. 499-501.   [1100]

[Renouard, Antoine Augustin] 1765-1853.
    Note sur Laurent Coster, à l'occasion d'un ancien livre imprimé

dans les Pays-Bas.   [Paris, de l'imprimerie de Crapelet, rue de
Vaugirard, no. 9, 1818]   7p.   25.5 cm.   [1101]
    NN   Eu-Fr-PC   Eu-Fr-PN

Renouard, Antoine Augustin, 1765-1853.
    Note sur Laurent Coster, à l'occasion d'un ancien livre im-
primé dans les Pay-Bas.   [Paris: Chez P. Renouard, 1838]   16p.
21.5 cm.   (In his Annales de l'imprimerie des Estiennes.   Paris,
1837-1838.   vol. 2)   [1102]
    NN   Eu-De-LBb   Eu-Fr-PC   Eu-Fr-PN   Eu-Ge-LP

Roemer, J.
    Leerrede over het belangrijke en heilzame van de uitvinding der
boekdrukkunst, door Laurens Janszoon Koster, voor het christendom ...
Leyden, Wortier en zoon, 1823.   30p.   8vo.   [1103]
    Eu-De-LBb

Roest, Meijer, 1821-1890.
    De "Wetenschappelijke moraliteit" van Dr. A. van der Linde, een
poosje maar te luchten gehangen, ten gerieve der lezers van diens
spectator-opstellen en boek over "De Haarlemsche Costerlegende",
door M. Roest Mz. ... Amsterdam, Gebr. Levisson firma D. Proops Jz.,
1870.   1 prel. leaf, vi, 50p.   23 cm.   [1104]
    ICN   MB   MH   NNC   Eu-De-LBb   Eu-Ne-AVb

Roos, S. H. de.
    Waar Laurens Jansz. Coster zijn spijkers kocht.   Nieuwsblad voor
den Boekhandel, no. 9, Feb. 1, 1927, p. 91-92.   [1105]

Ruelens, Charles Louis, 1820-1890.
    Un Laurent Coster Italien.   Bulletin du Bibliophile Belge, 3d
ser., vol. 3, 1868, p. 359-364.
    Also reprint.   [1106]

----   L'odyssée de Laurent Coster en Hollande.   Bulletin du Bibliophile Belge, 3d ser., vol. 3, 1868, p. 152-183.
    Also reprint.   [1107]

----   Un plaidoyer nouveau pour Laurent Coster.   Bulletin du Bibliophile Belge, vol. 15 (2d ser., vol. 6), 1859, p. 301-317.
    Also reprint.   [1108]

Schaaff, J. H. van der
    Levensschetsen van eenige van je voornaamste mannen die in vroeg-
eren tijd, binnen de stad Haarlem geboren zijn, of die aldaar sints
de laatste jaren gewoond hebben.   Haarlem, 1844.   sm. 8vo.
    Concerns L. J. Coster and others.
    Title from van der Linde, Geschichte der Erfindung ...   [1109]

Schaaff, J. H. van der.
    Verhandeling over het nut der boekdrukkunst.   Amsterdam,
1833.   36p.   8vo.   [1110]
    Eu-Ge-LP

Scheffer, Jacob Gijabert de Hoop, 1819-1893.   (pseud. Constanter)
    Uitvinding der boekdrukkunst.   De Navorscher, 1866, p. 129.
Same, Nieuwsblad voor den Boekhandel, vol. 33, 1866, p. 121-122.   [1111]

Scheltema, Jacobus, 1767-1835.
    Bericht und Beurtheilung des Werkes von Dr. C. A. Schaab, betitelt:
Die Geschichte der Erfindung der Buchdruckerkunst, durch Johann Gensfleisch, genannt Gutenberg, zu Mainz.   Von Jacobus Scheltema ... Amsterdam, C. G. Sülpke, 1833.   2 prel. leaves, 227, [1]p.   21.5 cm.
    Translated from the Dutch by H. Pfaff.   [1112]
    DLC   ICN   MH   NN   Eu-Ge-LB   Eu-Ge-LE   Eu-Ge-LP   Eu-Ne-AVb
    Eu-Ne-GK

----   Berigt aangaande het stuk van Dr. G. Braun ... over de contrast-
en der eeuwfeesten te Haarlem in 1823 en te Mentz in 1836.   Utrecht,
1836.   8vo.
    Title from Mohr, Jubelfeste.   [1113]

----   Berigt en beoordeeling van de Verhandeling van Jacob Koning,
over de uitvinding, verbetering en volmaking der boekdrukkunst.
Welke door de Maatschappij der wetenschappen te Haarlem is bekroond.
Amsterdam, H. Gartman, 1817.   180-257p.   22.5 cm.   (In his Ge-
schied- en letterkundig mengelwerk, I, 2)   [1114]
    ICN   MiU   Eu-De-LBb

----   Berigt en beoordeeling van het werk van Mr. C. A. Schaab ge-
titeld: De geschiedenis der uitvinding van de boekdrukkunst, door
Johann Gensfleisch, genaamd Gutenberg te Mentz.   Utrecht, J. G.
van Terveen en zoon, 1832.   [2], xiv, 232p.   [1115]
    ICJ   MH   Eu-Ne-AVb

----   Briefwisseling over de beoordeeling van het werk van C. A.
Schaab, Die Geschichte der Erfindung der Buchdruckerkunst 1829-1835.
    Letters by F. A. Ebert, F. Adelung, G. E. Horst, W. Ottley,
    Jacob Grimm, F. A. Brockhaus, Bunsen, Bourcourd, Coopmans, Ch.
    Clossman, E. Munch, H. Pfaff.   33 pieces and a portfolio of letter
    copies by J. Scheltema]   [1116]
    Eu-Ne-AVb

----   Conspectus of berigt aangaande de verhandeling van Jacobus
Koning, over de uitvinding, verbetering en volmaking der boekdrukkunst.
Amsterdam, Hendrik Gartman, 1817.   81p.   21.5 cm.   [1117]
    ICN   NNC   Eu-De-LBb   Eu-Ne-GK

Scheltema, Jacobus, 1767-1835.
Der Geist Johann Gensfleisch's genannt Gutenberg an C. A. Schaab
und die Mitglieder der Commission zur Errichtung des Denkmals seiner
Ehre zu Mainz.   1834.   Folio.
    ms. with remarks by J. Scheltema and four letters by H. Pfaff and
    J. Scheltema.   [1118]
    Eu-Ne-AVb

[----]   Der Geist Johann Gensfleisch's genannt Gutenberg an dr. C. A.
Schaab.   Und den Ausschuss zur Errichtung des Denkmales zu seiner Ehre
zu Mainz.   Utrecht, Robert Natan, 1835.   66p.   22.5 cm.
    Some libraries attribute authorship to C. A. Schaab.   [1119]
    NNC   Eu-Ge-LB   Eu-Ge-LE   Eu-Ge-LP   Eu-Ne-GK

----   De geloofwaardigheid van Adrianus Junius gehandhaafd, ten op-
zigte van zijne berigten aangaande de uitvinding en beoefening der
boekdrukkunst te Haarlem; door Mr Jacobus Scheltema. ... Utrecht, J.
G. v. Terveen en zoon, 1834.   2 prel. leaves, [3]-148p.   21 cm.
    From his Geschied- en Letterkundige Mengelwerk, VI, 1.   [1120]
    DLC   ICN   Eu-De-LBb   Eu-Ge-LB   Eu-Ge-LE

----   Lettre à MM. les rédacteurs de la Galerie des contemporains
sur la nécessité de rectifier et compléter l'article concernant M.
Koning.   La Haye, de l'imprimerie belgique, 1819.   viii, [9]-38p.
22 cm.   [1121]
    NN   Eu-Ne-AVb   Eu-Ne-GK

----   Levens-schets van Laurens Janszoon Koster.   [Utrecht, J. G.
van Terveen en zoon, 1834.]   [179]-240p.   22.5 cm.
    In his Geschied- en Letterkundige Mengelwerk, III.   [1122]
    MiU   Eu-De-LBb   Eu-Ge-LP   Eu-Ne-AVb

----   Nalezingen op de levensschets van Laurens Janszoon Koster ...
[Utrecht, J. G. van Terveen en zoon, 1834.]
    In his Geschied- en Letterkundige Mengelwerk, VI, 1.   [1123]
    MiU   Eu-De-LBb   Eu-Ge-LP   Eu-Ne-AVb

----   Vier brieven, gewisseld tusschen Mr. Jacobus Scheltema en
Jacobus Koning over de laatste tegenspraak van het regt van Haarlem
op de uitvinding der drukkunst.   Te Haarlem, bij de Wed. A. Loosjes,
Pz., MDCCCXXIII [1823].   iv, [5]-37p.   21 cm.   [1124]
    NN   NNC   Eu-De-LBb   Eu-Fr-PN   Eu-Ge-LB   Eu-Ne-GK

Schinkel, Adrianus David, 1784-1864.
    Beschrijving van twee prachtexemplaren der acht in folio formaat
bestaande afdrukken van de in het Fransch uitgegeven werken over de
uitvinding der boekdrukkunst, van Dr. A. de Vries, met teekeningen
van A. H. Bakker Korff ... door den bezitter, A. D. Schinkel, bestemd
tot een gedenkteeken aan den uitvinder der boekdrukkunst, Lourens

- 146 -

Janszoon Coster.   ['s Gravenhage], 1848.   24p.   25 cm.   [1125]
    NN   Eu-Ge-LP

[Schinkel, Adrianus David] 1784-1864.
    Tweetal bijdragen, betrekkelijk de boekdrukkunst ... 's Gravenhage,
Boekdrukkerij van A. D. Schinkel, 1844.   28p. incl. facsims.   23 cm.
    Contents.- 1. Betoog dat met op hout gesneden beweegbare letters
    boekwerken kunnen gedrukt worden.- II. Brief aan den Heer J. W.
    Holtrop ... over de onlangs nieuw gevonden fragmenten van een'
    Donatus.   [1126]
    DLC   NN   Eu-De-LBb   Eu-Ge-LB   Eu-Ne-AVb

Schreiber, D.
    Der Buchbinder Cornelis und die Erfindung der Buchdruckerkunst.
Deutsches Buchbinderhandwerk, vol. 3, 1939, p. 885-886.   [1127]

Schretlen, Martinus Joseph Antonius Maria, 1890-
    De uitvinding der boekdrukkunst en de Costeroverlevering.   Het
Boek, 2d ser., vol. 12, 1923, p. 275-280.   [1128]

Schrevel, Dirk, 1572-1649.
    Harlemias, ofte, om beter te seggeh, De eerste stichinghe der
Stadt Haerlem, etc.   Haarlem, 1648.   4to.   [1129]
    MH   NN

---- ----   Haarlem, 1754.   [1130]
    ICN   MH   NN

----   Theodori Schreveli Harlemum, sive Vrbis Harlemensis incunabula,
incrementa, fortuna varia, in pace, in bello. Hamorum & Asellorum
factio. Obsidiones. Reformationis cruda initia. Consilia politica.
Schismata ecclesiastica. Tempora Lycostriana. Statua antiqua. Comitum privilegia gratiosa. Regimen politicum, ecclesiasticum, oecono-
micum, militaire & scholasticum. Tum studia incolarum in quavis
facultate & arte, et plura id genus. Lvgdvni Batavorvm, excudebat
S. Matthaei, 1647.   10 prel. leaves, 316p.   19.5 cm.
    Added t.-p., engr.
    In double columns.
    Bibliography: p. 249-270. "Typographiae inventum": p. 270-272.   [1131]
    DLC   ICN   MH   Eu-Ge-LB

Schrijver, Pieter, 1576-1660.
    Petri Scriverii Lavre-crans voor Lavrens Coster van Haerlem, eerste
vinder van de boeckdrvckery. Tot Haerlem, by A. Rooman, ordinaris
stads-boekdrukker, 1628.   5, [1]p., 1 leaf, 5-124p.   19x14.5 cm.
    With Ampzing, Samuel. Beschryvinge en de lof der stad Haerlem ...
    Reissued in Latin in Wolf, J. C. Monumenta typographica. Ham-
    burg, 1740.   vol. 1, p. 209-451.   [1132]
    ICN   IU   MH   NN   Eu-De-LBb   Eu-Fr-PN   Eu-Ge-LB   Eu-Ne-AVb
    Eu-Ne-GK

[Schuitemaker, J.]
    Reis van Jonker Johan Henne Gänsfleisch von Sorgenloch zu Gutten-
berg zum Jungen. [Haarlem, 1856?] 2p. 8vo.   [1133]
    NNC

[----] Wat Coster wist, wat hij niet wist, en wat hij weten mogt.
Haarlem, C. A. Spin en zoon, 1856. 4p. 8vo.
    Title from Mohr, Jubelfeste.   [1134]

Schwegman, Hendrik.
    Berigt wegens de uitvinding om een tekening op een koperplaat
overtebrengen, aan den oeconomischen tak van de Hollandsche Maat-
schappye der wetenschappen te Haarlem. Haarlem, 1793. 8p. 8vo.
    Title from Bigmore & Wyman.   [1135]

Seitz, Johann Christian.
    Annus tertius saecularis inventae artis typographicae, sive Brevis
historica enarratio de inventione nobilissimae artis typographicae, in
qua ostenditur, quo tempore, à quo & ubi locorum ea primùm fuerit inventa, post magis magisque exculta & per orbem terrarum sparsa? Et
quot quantaque commoda ex ea in genus humanum redundarint? Auctore
Johanne Christiano Seiz ... Ex idiomate belgico in gratian exterorum
Latine, & hinc inde auctior reddita ... Harlemi, apud Isaacum et
Ioannem Enschede [1742] 13 prel. leaves, 248, [14]p. fold.
plates. 20 cm.
    Added t.-p., engraved, dated: 1741.   [1136]
    DLC

---- Het derde jubeljaar der uitgevondene boekdrukkonst, behelzende
een beknopt historis verhaal van de uitvinding der edele boekdrukkonst;
waar in onpartydig aangewezen word, manneer, door wien en waar ter
plaatse dezelve eerst uitgevonden, vervolgens hoe langer hoe meer
beschaafd, en verder door de waereld verspreid is geworden? en welke
groote nuttigheden daar aan dezelve toegebragt zyn? Door Johann
Christiaan Seiz, Franco-Germanum. Te Haerlem, de voortbrengeresse
der edele boekdrukkonst, gedrukt by Izaak en Johannes Enschede, Ordinaris Stads-drukkers, 1740. [30], 258, [14]p. front., 5 plates,
(1 fold.) 19 cm.
    "Catalogus der autheuren" p. 1-12.   [1137]
    ICJ   ICN   MH   NN   NNC   NNGr   Eu-De-LBb   Eu-Ge-LP
    Eu-Ne-AVb   Eu-Ne-GK

Smits, Jan, 1775-1857.
    Iets over de uitvinding der boekdrukkunst. Door J. Smits, Jz[n]. te
Dordrecht. Dordrecht, Blussé en Van Braam, 1856. 15p. 22 cm. [1138]
    MH   NNC   Eu-Ge-LP   Eu-Ne-AVb

    Some observations concerning the invention and progress of printing,
to the year 1465. Occasioned by the Reverend Mr. Ellis's Letter in
Philosophical Transactions ... Philosophical Transactions of the Royal

Society, vol. 23, no. 288, 1703, p. 1507-1516.
Also reprint, London, 1705. 8vo.   [1139]

Some observations concerning the invention and progress of printing, to the year 1465. ... Reissued in Ellis, Charles. A letter
written by the Reverend Charles Ellis claiming the invention of printing for Coster and a letter in refutation of that claim ... Chicago, Ill.,
Committee on invention of printing, Chicago club of printing house
craftsmen, 1940.   [1140]
CSmH   DLC   IC   ICU   MH   NN   NNC

Someren, Jan Frederick van, 1852-
De "Gutenberg-Legende". Het Boek, vol. 3, 1914, p. 1-10.   [1141]

Souvenir en programma van het Costerfeest te Haarlem gehouden op
Julij 1856. 's Gravenhage, 1856. 8vo.   [1142]
Eu-Ge-LSb

Spreeuwenliedje, gezongen op het Costersmaal (16. Julij 1856) in
het lokaal: Het Congres van Flora te Haarlem. Haarlem, 1856. 3p.
8vo.
Title from Mohr, Jubelfeste.   [1143]

Staring van den Wildenborch, A. C. W.
Lourens Janszoon Koster. Eeuwzang. (In Loosjes, Vincent.
Gedenkschriften ... Harlem, 1824. p. 196-200.)   [1144]

Staveren, Johannes Samuel van, d. 1842.
Redevoering voor de kinderen der stads-armen-scholen, bij gelegenheid van het vierde eeuwgetijde van de uitvinding der boekdrukkunst
door Laurens Jansz. Koster. Gehouden binnen Haarlem, den 11 Julij
1823. Door J. S. van Staveren ... Haarlem, De Erven F. Bohn, 1823.
30p. 16.5 cm.   [1145]
MH   NN   Eu-De-LSb

[Stockum, W. P. van]
Herinnering aan de uitvinding der boekdrukkunst. Overgenomen uit
het Nieuwsblad van den Boekhandel. 1856. 8vo.
Title from Hoffman, F. L. Essai d'une liste ... concernant l'hist-
oire de l'imprimerie en Hollande et en Belgique. Bulletin du
Bibliophile Belge, 1857)   [1146]

Stückrad, Georg.
Das Jubelfest zu Harlem im Jahr 1823. (In his Programm für das
Gutenberg-Jubiläum des 19. Jahrhunderts. Offenbach, C. Washter-
schauser, 1837. p. 33-54)   [1147]
ICN   ICU   NNC   Eu-De-LBb   Eu-Ge-LB

Sulkowski, J. A. M. de.
Vier-hondordjarig jubelfeest van de uitvinding der boekdrukkunst

door Laurens Janszoon Koster, gevierd te Haarlem, den 10den en 11den
Julij 1823.   13p.   8vo.   [1148]
    Eu-Ge-LSb

[Tiele, P. A.]
    De Haarlemsche boekdrukkers en boekverkoopers in de 15e- 18e eeuw.
Nieuwsblad voor den Boekhandel, no. 20, May 18, 1865, p. 95-96.
    Signed: T. Authorship assigned by the Bibliothek des Börsenvereins
    der deutschen Buchhändler.
    Also reprint.   [1149]

---- L'histoire de l'imprimerie en Hollande.   Bulletin du Bibliophile Belge, 3d ser., vol. 8, 1873, p. 16-23.
    Also reprint.   [1150]

Tollens, H. C.
    Feestzang bij het vierde eeuwgetijde van de uitvinding der boek-
drukkunst.   Werken der Hollandsche Maatschappij van Fraije Kunsten
en Wetenschappen, vol. 7, part 1, 1824.
    Reissued in Loosjes, Vincent. Gedenkschriften ... Haarlem, 1824.
    p. 161-180.   [1151]

Toze, Eobald.
    [The invention of printing at Haarlem, based on Meerman's Conspec-
tus of 1761.]   (In Toze, Eobald. Geschichte der vereinigten Niederlande.   1744.   vol. 1, p. 76)   [1152]
    Eu-Ge-LB

Tronnier, Heinrich Ernst Adolph, 1875-
    Ein "Costerfund" in Mainz.   Gutenberg Jahrbuch, vol. 1, 1926,
p. 144-180.   [1153]

[Tydeman, Hendrick Willem]
    Proeve ter beantwoording van de vraag: "Kan het aan Haarlem met
eenigen grond betwist worden, dat de konst, om met enkel verplaats-
bare letters te drukken, aldaar voor het jaar 1440 door Laurens
Koster is uitgedacht? --En is niet deze konst van daar naar Mentz
overgebracht, en aldaar verbeterd door letters van tin gegoten voor
de houten letters in plaats te stellen?" Mnemosyne (Dordrecht),
vol. 1, 1815, p. 121-217.   [1154]

    Typographenzang, gedrukt en verspreid door Haarlems wegen.
Haarlem, 1856.   3p.   8vo.
    Title from Mohr, Jubelfeste.   [1155]

    Uitvinding der boekdrukkunst.   Haarlem, J. Enschede en zonen,
1854.   [4], vi, 82, [2]p.   front. (port.), illus.   18x14 cm.   [1156]
    ICJ   ICN   MH   Eu-De-LBb   Eu-Ge-LP   Eu-Ge-LSb

De uitvinding der boekdrukkunst door Laurens Janszoon Koster.
Op rijm gebragt voor de Jeugd. Amsterdam, 1856. 12mo.
Title from Mohr, Jubelfeste.   [1157]

Uitvinding van de boekdrukkunst en herdenkings feesten daarven.
Verschillende nummers van de Algemeene Konst- en Letterbode, 1801-1832,
bevattende artikelen over dez onderwerpen. 2 parts. 8vo.   [1158]
   Eu-Ne-AVb

Uitvinding der boekdrukkunst met ophelderende houtsneeplaatjes.
[Excerpt. ms. title] Leiden, A. W. Sijthoff, 1857. sm. 4to.
p. 42-69.
   Koning Collection.   [1159]
   Eu-Ge-LP

Valkenburg, Cornelius van.
   Laus Harlemi, ut inventricis artis typographicae. Quam recitavit
in eadem urbe a. d. XX. Sept. A. C. 1696. 4to.
   Title from van der Linde, Geschichte der Erfindung ...   [1160]

[Varelen, J. E. van]
   Aanbieding ter inteekening, op enne uitgave van afbeeldingen der
chassinetten, bijschriften enz., bij het vierde eeuwfeest van de uitvinding der boekdrukkunst, door Lourens Jansz. Koster; te Haarlem
tentoongesteld, den 11den Julij MDCCCXVIII. [Haarlem, 1825]   [1161]

   Verhandeling over de uitvinding der boekdrukkonst door Laurens
Janszoon Koster te Haarlem. [Clipping]   [1162]
   Eu-De-LBb

   Vierde eeuwfeest ter eere van Lourens Janszoon Koster ... donderdag
en vrijdag, 10. en 11. Julij 1823. Zijnde volgens ingebragt rap-
port ... tuschen 1420 en 1425 niet eigentlijk het geboorte-jaar maar
het geboorte-tijdperk. Als ook de programma, of optogt. Benevens
het bedriegelijke van zijn knegt Faust, daarin voorkomende. Amsterdam, 1823. 8vo.
   Title from Mohr, Jubelfeste.   [1163]

   De viering van het vierde eeuwfeest, der boekdrukkunst, te Haarlem,
den 10 en 11 Julij 1823. Haarlem, met en Maylink [1823]. 16p.
plates, port. 24 cm.   [1164]
   NN NNC Eu-De-LBb

Vos, K.
   De Costerlegende ontward? Enkele opmerkingen naar aanleiding van
Gottfried Zedler's Von Coster zu Gutenberg. Door K. Vos. Haarlem,
Joh. Enschedé en zonen, 1922. 40p. 22 cm.   [1165]
   NN Eu-Ge-LB Eu-Ne-AVb

Vreese, Willem de.
    Een fragment van een Costeriaan. Tijdschrift voor Boek- en
Bibliotheekswesen, vol. 5, 1906, p. 49-51.   [1166]

Vries, Abraham de, 1773-1862.
    Arguments des Allemands en faveur de leur prétention à l'invention
de l'imprimerie; ou Examen critique de l'ouvrage de M. A. E. Umbreit:
Die Erfindung der Buchdruckerkunst. Par A. de Vries ͵. Tr. du hollandais par J. J. F. Noordziek ... Faisant suite aux: Éclaircissements sur
l'histoire de l'invention de l'imprimerie. La Haye, Impr. de A. D.
Schinkel, 1845. xxx, 212p. 24.5 cm.   [1167]
    DLC ICJ MH NN Eu-De-LBb Eu-Ge-LP Eu-Ne-GK

---- Beschrijving van twee prachtexemplaren der 8 folio afdruken
van de Fransch vertaling der werken over de uitvinding der boekdrukkunst. 's Gravenhage, 1828. 8vo.
    Title from Bigmore & Wyman.   [1168]

---- Bewijsgronden der Duitschers voor hunne aanspraak op de uitvinding der boekdrukkunst, of beoordeeling van het werk van A. E.
Umbreit: Die Erfindung der Buchdruckerkunst. Door Abraham de Vries.
's Gravenhage, Boekdrukkerij van A. D. Schinkel, 1844. xvi, 208,
[4]p. 23 cm.   [1169]
    DLC ICJ MH NN Eu-De-LBb Eu-Ge-LB Eu-Ge-LP Eu-Ne-GK

---- Bewijzen voor de echtheid en gelijkenis der oude afbeeldingen
van Coster. Ter wederlegging van het Iets van den Heer van Westreenen. Ten voordeele van het fonds voor de oprigting van het standbeeld. Haarlem, A. C. Kruseman, 1847. 48p. 22.5 cm.   [1170]
    DLC Eu-De-LBb Eu-Ge-LSb Eu-Ne-GK

---- Bijdragen tot de geschiedenis der uitvinding van de boekdrukkunst, door Abraham de Vries ... [Haarlem, 1823?] 95p. 21 cm. [1171]
    NNC Eu-Ne-AVb

---- Boekdrukkunst. Algemeene Konst- en Letterbode, no. 52, 1841,
p. 391-399.
    Also reprint.   [1172]

---- Brief van A. de Vries aan A. D. Schinkel, over Guichard's notice sur le speculum humanae salvationis, met drie bijlagen tot stav-
ing der naauwkeurigheid van het verhaal van Junius wegens de uitvinding der boekdrukkunst en ter wederlegging der meening: dat Coster Koster zou geweest zijn. 's Gravenhage, ter Boekdrukkerij van
A. D. Schinkel, 1841. 2 prel. leaves, [iii]-xii, 144p. 22 cm. [1173]
    ICJ MH NN Eu-De-LBb Eu-Ge-LP Eu-Ne-AVb Eu-Ne-GK

---- Catalogue der zeer fraaije godgeleerde, letterkundige en typographische bibliotheek van Dr. Abr. de Vries, te Haarlem. Verkooping
16-26 Maart 1864. Amsterdam, Frederik Muller; Haarlem, A. C. Kruseman,

1864.   263p.   21 cm.
   Cover title.   [1174]
   NN

Vries, Abraham de, 1773-1862.
   Dissertation sur le nom de Coster et sur sa prétendue charge du
sacristain;-- recherches fait à l'occasion de la IVme fête séculaire
à Haarlem en 1823.   Haarlem, 1823.
   Title from Mohr, Jubelfeste.   [1175]

----   Éclaircissemens sur l'histoire de l'invention de l'imprimerie,
contenant: Lettre à M. A. D. Schinkel, ou réponse à la notice de M.
Guichard sur le Speculum humanae salvationis; - Dissertation sur le
nom de Coster et sur sa prétendue charge de sacristain; - Recherches
faites à l'occasion de la quatrième fête séculaire à Haarlem en
1823.   Par A. de Vries ... Tr. du hollandais par J. J. F. Noordziek ...
La Haye, Impr. de A. D. Schinkel, 1843.   xlii p., 1 leaf, 275,
[1]p.   24 cm.   [1176]
   DLC   ICJ   MH   NN   NNGr   Eu-De-LBb   Eu-Ge-LP   Eu-Ne-GK

----   Hedendaagsche voorstelling van Coster en de uitvinding der
boekdrukkunst in Frankrijk.   Door A. de Vries.   's Gravenhage, Ge-
broeders Belinfante, 1853.   iv, 31p.   24 cm.
   Foreword signed: A. D. Schinkel.
   Some libraries attribute authorship to A. D. Schinkel.   [1177]
   MH   NN   NNC   Eu-De-LBb   Eu-Ge-LB   Eu-Ne-AVb   Eu-Ne-GK

----   Lijst der stukken betrekkelijk de geschiedenis van de uitvinding der boekdrukkunst, berustende op het raadhuis te Haarlem.   Opgemaakt door Dr. A. de Vries ... Haarlem, Joh. Enschedé & zonen, 1862.
50p.   23.5 cm.   [1178]
   NNC   Eu-De-LBb   Eu-Ge-LSb   Eu-Ne-AVb

----   Lotgevallen van Costers woning.   Haarlem, A. C. Kruseman, 1851.
2 prel. leaves, [3]-40p.   24 cm.
   Added t.-p. with ornamental borders.   [1179]
   MH   MiU   Eu-De-LBb

----   Nieuwe bijdragen tot de geschiedenis der uitvinding van de
boekdrukkunst, door Lourens Janszoon Koster te Haarlem.   Amsterdam,
1823.
   Reissued in Loosjes, Vincent.   Gedenkschriften ... Haarlem, V.
Loosjes, 1824.   p. 308-402.   [1180]
   NNC

----   Een voorbeeld van onpartijdigheid in het geschil over de uitvinding der boekdrukkunst.   Algemeene Konst- en Letterbode, no. 21,
1834.   [1181]

Vrolijke liederen der Drukkersgezellen te Dordrecht, toegewijd
aan het vierde eeuwfeest van de uitvinding der boekdrukkunst door
Laurens Janszoon Koster. Gesongen ter gelegenheid van hunnen feest-
vierenden optogt, met eene rijdende en tegelijkwerkende drukpers,
des avonds van des 10 Julij 1823, bij fakkelligt. Dordrecht, 1823.
15p. 8vo.
   Bigmore & Wyman attributes authorship to J. Pluim de Jaager.
   Eu-Ne-GK   [1182]

Wal, F. van der.
De beginselen der typografie, door F. van der Wal, redacteur van
Grafisch Weekblad. Tweede druk. Meppel, H. ten Brink, [1910].
vii, 112p., 1 fold. plate. 22 cm.   [1183]
   NN   Eu-Ge-LSb

Walré, J. van.
   Cantate. [Haarlem, 1823] 4p. 8vo.
   Title from Mohr, Jubelfeste.   [1184]

[----] (pseud. Democriet) XII volksliedekens op bekende wijzen, ter
vervrolijking van Lourens Jansz-Koster's vierde eeuwfeest ... Haarlem,
1823. 8vo.   [1185]
   Eu-Ge-LB

Warnsinck, W. H.
   Eeuwzang op de uitvinding der drukkunst. Vaderlandsche Letteroefeningen ... Mengelwerk, no. 1, 1824, p. 1-19.   [1186]

---- De uitvinding der boekdrukkunst, door Lourens Janszoon Koster
te Haarlem. Anno 1423. Zinnespel. Haarlem, 1823. 8vo.
   Reissued in Loosjes, Vincent. Gedenkschriften ... Haarlem, 1824. [1187]
   Eu-Ne-AVb

---- De viering van het vierde eeuwgetijde der uitvinding van de
boekdrukkunst door Lourens Janszoon Koster. Vaderlandsche Letteroefeningen, of Tijdschrift van Kunsten en Wetenschappen, Waarin de Boeken en Schriften ... Mengelwerk. Twwede stuk voor 1823. no. 11, p.
531-536.
   Reissued in Loosjes, Vincent. Gedenkschriften ... Haarlem, 1824. [1188]

   Weeckelycke Courante van Europa N. 1. -- Gedrukt tot Haarlem
[voon Abraham Castelyn, Ten huyse van zyn Vader Vincent Castelyn
(Op de Marckt) in de Druckerey]. Den 8. January 1656. [Reprinted
by Joh. Enschede en Zoonen, 1856]
   Title from Mohr, Jubelfeste.   [1189]

   De weldaad der boekdrukkunst voor het menschelijk geslacht, dank-
baar herdacht bij de onthulling van het metalen standbeeld ter eere
van Laurens Janszoon Coster te Haarlem, 18 Julij 1856. 's Gravenhage, F. Kloots, 1856. 47p. 8vo.   [1190]
   Hoe

Weller, Emil Ottokar, 1823-1886.
Lorenz Coster als Erfinder der Buchdruckerkunst. Serapeum, vol. 30, no. 16, 1869, p. 121.   [1191]

Westreenen van Tiellandt, Willem Hendrik Jacob, baron van, 1783-1848.
Aanmerkingen op de "Gedenkschriften wegens het 4e eeuwgetijde van de uitvinding der boekdrukkunst, door L. J. Koster," overgenomen uit de 's Gravenhaagsche Couranten van den 12, 14 en 28 Julij 1824, en vermeerderd met eenige aanteekeningen, strekkende om aan te toonen, dat door dit werk aan de zaak van Haarlem is toegebracht. 's Graven-hage, 1824.   8vo.   [1192]
   Eu-Ge-LB   Eu-Ne-AVb

----   Iets over de afbeeldingen van Laurens Jansz. Koster, door den Baron van Westreenen van Tiellandt.   Gravenhage en Amsterdam, De Gebroeders van Cleef, 1847.   16p.   23.5 cm.
   Reprinted from the journal "de Tijd".   [1193]
   DLC   Eu-De-LBb   Eu-Ge-LSb

----   De invoering der boekdrukkunst te 's Gravenhage.   Algemeene Konst- en Letterbode, no. 53, 1828, p. 405-409.   [1194]

----   Korte schets van den voortgang der boekdrukkunst in Nederland, in de XV^{de}, en haare verdere volmaaking in de XVI^{de} en XVII^{de} eeuw: door W. H. J. Baron van Westreenen van Tiellandt.   's Gravenhage en Amsterdam, Gebroeders van Cleef, 1829.   37p.   22x13.5 cm.
   Bibliographical foot-notes.   [1195]
   DLC   NN

----   Verhandeling over de uitvinding der boekdrukkunst; in Holland oorspronkelijk uitgedacht, te Straatsburg verbeterd en te Mentz voltooid; door W. H. J. van Westreenen ... 's Hage, P. van Daalen Wetters, 1809.   3 prel. leaves, 181, [3]p.   20 cm.   [1196]
   DLC   ICJ   MH   NN   Eu-De-BP   Eu-De-LBb   Eu-Ge-LB   Eu-Ge-LP
   Eu-Ne-AVb   Eu-Ne-GK

----   De zoogenaamde bewijzen voor de echtheid en gelijkenis der oude afbeeldingen van Koster.   's Gravenhage, 1848.   8vo.   [1197]
   Eu-Ge-LSb   Eu-Ne-AVb   Eu-Ne-GK

Wiaorda, Henricus.
Naauwkeurige verhandelinge van de eerste uytvindigen en uytvinders van veele ... konsten en wetenschappen ... Amsterdam, 1733.   24p.   8vo.[1198]
   Eu-Ge-LB

Wild, Albert.
Ueber die Erfindung der Buchdruckerkunst.   (In his Die Nederlande; ihre Vergangenheit und Gegenwart.   2 vols.   Leipzig, 1862.   vol. 2, p. 455)   [1199]
   Eu-Ge-LB

Wilson, J. S.
   Proeven van zelfdruk. Hulde aan L. Jz. Koster, bij gelegenheid
der onthulling van het metalen standbeeld 15 Juli 1856.   Meppel,
1856.   4to.   [1200]
   Eu-Ne-GK

   Zamenspraak tusschen een' Haarlemmer en een' Antwerpenaar, over
de uitvinding der boekdrukkunst.   De Bij, no. 2, 4, 1823.
   Only 4 numbers of De Bij appeared, hence the article lacks its
conclusion.   [1201]

Zeggelen, Willem Josephus van, 1811-1879.
   Costerliedjes. Souvenir aan Haarlems Julijfeesten in 1856.
Door W. J. Van Zeggelen.   Haarlem, A. C. Kruseman, 1856.   viii,
56p.   15.5 cm.   [1202]
   MH   NNC

Zijll, W. C. van.
   Mijmering van het oude standbeeld van Laurens Janszoon Coster.
Ten voordeele van het feest der onthulling van diens standbeeld.
Hilversum, 1856.   16p.   8vo.   [1203]
   Eu-Ge-LB

   De zwitserse eenvoudigheid, klaagende over de bedorvene zeden
voeler Hollandse doopsgezinden.   Te Haarlem, gedrukt by de Wed.
H. van Hulkenroy, aan de Markt, in Laurens Koster.   1713.
4to.
   Port. of Coster.
   Title from van der Linde, Geschichte der Erfindung ...   [1204]

      3   For and About Waldfoghel

Achard, Paul.
   Simples notes sur l'introduction de l'imprimerie à Avignon et
sur les différentes phases de cette industrie.   Bulletin Historique
et Archéologique de Vaucluse, vol. 1, 1879, p. 181-190, 235-248,
279-290.   [1205]

Aldrich, Stephen J.
   Procope Valdfoghel, goldsmith and printer.   Library, 1st ser.,
vol. 2, 1890, p. 217-219.   [1206]

Axon, William E. A.
    Printing at Avignon in 1444. Academy, vol. 38, 1890, p. 33.   [1207]

Bayle, Gustave.
    La question de l'imprimerie à Avignon en 1444 et 1446; par M.
Gustave Bayle ... (Extrait des Mémoires de l'Académie de Nimes, année
1900) Nimes, A. Chastanier, 1900. 90p. 25.5 cm.   [1208]
    DLC ICN MB MH Eu-Fr-PN Eu-Ge-LB

Biegelaar, A. J.
    De boekdrukkunst te Avignon. Gent, A. Siffer, [1892?] 8p. 8vo.
    Reprint from Dietsche Warande.   [1209]
    Eu-Ge-LB

Blégier-Pierregrosse, le comte de.
    Notice sur l'origine de l'imprimerie à Avignon. Avignon, Impri-
merie Chaillot jeune, n.d. 8p. 8vo.
    Title from Delalain, Paul Adolphe. Essai de Bibliographie de
    l'histoire de l'imprimerie. 1903.   [1210]

Claudin, Anatole, 1833-1906.
    Les origines de l'imprimerie en France. Premiers essais à Avig-
non en 1444. Par A. Claudin ... Paris, A. Claudin, 1898. 2 prel.
leaves, 14p., 1 leaf. 23 cm.
    Reprint from Bulletin du Bibliophile, (Paris), vol. 65, 1898,
    p. 1-14.
    100 copies printed.   [1211]
    CSmH DLC Eu-Fr-PN Eu-Ge-LB Eu-Ge-LSb

Duhamel, Léopold, 1842-1922.
... Les origines de l'imprimerie à Avignon. Note sur les documents
découverts par M. l'abbé Requin. Avignon, Seguin frères, imprimeurs-
éditeurs, 13, rue Bouquerie, 13, 1890. 15p. 22.5 cm.
    At head of title: L. Duhamel, archiviste du département de Vau-
    cluse.   [1212]
    DLC (Thacher Collection) IaU MB MH NN NNC Eu-Fr-PN
    Eu-Ge-LB Eu-Ge-LSb

Fruin, Robert.
    Een nieuwe medelinger van Gutenberg (l'abbé Requin's L'imprimerie
à Avignon en 1444. Paris, 1890). Amsterdam, 1890. 8vo.
    Reprint from De Gids, vol. 54, (4th ser., vol. 8), 1890, p. 342-
    348.   [1213]
    Eu-Ne-AVb

Goebel, Theodor.
    Die Buchdruckerei zu Avignon. Börsenblatt für den Deutschen
Buchhandel, vol. 57, no. 204, Sept. 1890, p. 4598-4600.   [1214]

An incident in the history of typography. Waldfoghel of Avignon
and his artificial writing process. <u>British</u> <u>and</u> <u>Colonial</u> <u>Printer</u>,
vol. 42, June 1898, p. 334.   [1215]

The invention of printing. <u>Inland</u> <u>Printer</u>, vol. 7, Aug. 1890,
p. 1022.
     Claim for Avignon, 1444.   [1216]

Pansier, Pierre, 1864-
... Histoire du livre et de l'imprimerie à Avignon du XIVme au XVIme
siècle ... Avignon, Aubanel frères, 1922.   3 vols. in 1.   fronts.
(vol. 1-2) illus., facsims.   25 cm.
     At head of title: P. Pansier.
     Part of facsimiles in colors.   [1217]
     DLC   ICN   NN   NjP   Eu-De-BP   Eu-Fr-PN   Eu-Ge-LLl
     Eu-Ne-AVb

Philippe, C.
     Note sur Guillaume Fichet. L'imprimerie à Avignon en 1414.
<u>Revue</u> <u>Savoisienne</u>, vol. 32, 1891, p. 272-278.   [1218]

Requin, Pierre Henri, 1851-1917.
     Documents inédits sur les origines de la typographie.   Paris, E.
Leroux, 1890.   24p.   25 cm.   (France. Comité des travaux historiques et scientifiques. Bulletin historique et philologique)   [1219]
     IaU   MiU   Eu-De-LBb   Eu-Fr-PN   Eu-Ne-AVb

----   L'imprimerie à Avignon en 1444.   Paris, A. Picard, 1890.
20p.   23 cm.   [1220]
     DLC   ICJ   ICN   MB   MdBP   Eu-De-LBb   Eu-Fr-PC   Eu-Fr-PN
     Eu-Ge-LB   Eu-Ge-LSb   Eu-Ne-GK

----   Origines de l'imprimerie en France (Avignon, 1444) par l'abbé
Requin ... Paris, Cercle de la librairie, 1891.   15, 21p.   illus.
(facsims.)   23 cm.
     Development of a study published the preceding year, entitled
     "L'imprimerie à Avignon en 1444."
     "Extrait du Journal général de l'imprimerie et de la librairie
     du 28 février, 1891."   [1221]
     DLC   MB   MH   Eu-Fr-PC   Eu-Fr-PN   Eu-Ge-LB   Eu-Ge-LSb
     Eu-Ne-AVb   Eu-Ne-GK

----   La question de l'imprimerie à Avignon en 1444 et en 1446.
Réponse à M. Bayle. Édition de La Revue historique de Provence.
Marseille, 1902.   45p.   8vo.
     On the back of the title-page is the following information:
     Numéros de Décembre 1901 et de Janvier 1902 de la "Revue."   [1222]
     IU   Eu-Fr-PN

Schubert, Anton.
    Zur Geschichte der Familie Waldvogel.   Zentralblatt für Biblio-
thekswesen, vol. 16, 1899, p. 500-501.   [1223]

    4   For and About Castaldi

Bernardi, Jacopo, 1813-1897.
    Intorno a Panfilo Castaldi da Feltre, e alla invenzione dei car-
atteri mobili per la stampa; memoria e dissertazioni dei signori ...
Jacopo cav. Bernardi ... Antonio Zanghellini, e Antonio Valsecchi ...
Milano, Pietro Agnelli, 1866.   56p.   front., port.   30.5 cm.
    Contains bibliographies.   [1224]
    MH   NNC   Eu-De-LBb   Eu-Fr-PC

----   Nuovamente di Panfilo Castaldi da Feltre, inventore de caratteri
mobili e della scoperta di un prezioso documento che lo Riguarda ne
Regii Archivii di Milano.   L'Arte della Stampa, vol. 10, 1880, p.
319.   [1225]

[----]   Panfilo Castaldi da Feltre e l'invenzione dei caratteri
mobili per la stampa.   Milano, Stabilimento Civelli, 1865.   47p.
col'd. coat of arms, illus. (ports.)   31 cm.
    "E dolcissimo invito quello che dalle Associazioni degli operai
    tipografi milanesi mi si fa di scrivere alcuni cenni sul ... Pan-
    filo Castaldi da Feltre ..." p. 7, signed Ab Jacopo dott Bernardi. [1226]
    ICN   MH   MiU   NN   Eu-De-LBb

Carbone, Giunio.
    Par l'inaugurazione del monumento a Panfilo Castaldi in Feltre.
Firenze, Barbéra, 1868.   8vo.
    Title from Bibliotheca bibliografica Italica.   vol. 1, 1889.   [1227]

Carutti, Domenico, barone di Cantogno, 1821-1909.
    Notice sur Pamfilo Castaldi.   Amsterdam, 1867.   8vo.
    Reprint from Verslagen Mededeelingen Kongliche Akademic.   Letter-
    kunde, deel 11.   [1228]
    Eu-Ne-GK

Cechetti, Bartolomeo.
    Autografi di Panfilo Castaldi.   Archivio Veneto, 2d ser., vol.
33, 1887, p. 538.   [1229]

    [Collection of printed documents relating to claims of Castaldi
to the invention of printing.]   Folio.   [1230]
    Eu-Ge-LSb

Fornari, P.
Panfilo Castaldi, maestro dal stampo, o l'invenzione dei caratteri
mobile ... Milano, Agnelli, 1880.   24p.   8vo.   [1231]
Eu-De-LBb   Eu-Ge-LSb

Fumagalli, Giuseppe, 1863-1939.
... La questione di Pamfilo Castaldi.   Milano, U. Hoepli, 1891.   127p.
20.5 cm.
At head of title: Giuseppe Fumagalli.   [1232]
CSmH   ICJ   ICN   MnU   Eu-Fr-PN   Eu-Ge-LB

Ghinzoni, P.
Panfilo Castaldi.   L'Educatore Italiano, Dec. 1880, p. 697-699.[1233]

The legend of Castaldi.   Printing Times and Lithographer, vol.
3, Oct. 1877, p. 205-206.   [1234]

La leggenda di Panfilo Castaldi.   L'Industria della Stampa, vol.
7, no. 3, 1934, p. 7-26.   [1235]

Luciani, Tommaso.
Panfilo Castaldi di Feltre medico in Capo d'Istria.   Giornale
la Provincia dell' Istria (Capo d'Istria), no. 17, Sept. 1, 1884.   [1236]

Minotto, A. S.
Monumenti a Vittorino de Rambaldoni e Panfilo Castaldi in Feltre
1869.   Feltre, Societa Panfilo Castaldi, 1869.   4to.   [1237]
Eu-Ge-LB

Morelli, G.
Panfilo Castaldi inventore dei caratteri mobili.   Rassegna
Grafica, vol. 6, no. 60, 1931, p. 1-2.   [1238]

Motta, Emilio.
Panfilo Castaldi, Antonio Planella, Pietro Ugleimer ed il Vescovo
d'Aleria.   Nuovi documenti per la storia della tipografia in Italia
tratta degli Archivi Milanesi.   Torino, Rocca, 1884.   23p.   8vo.
Reprint from Revista Italiana, vol. 1, 1884, p. 252-272.   [1939]
Eu-De-LBb

Nai, P.
I primi quattro tipografi di Milano: Castaldi, Zarotto, Lavagna,
Valdarfer.   Archivo Storico Lombardo, vol. 61, 1934, p. 569-594.   [1240]

Pamphilo Castaldi, the inventor of movable type?   Book Worm
(Berjeau), vol. 1, 1866, p. 185-187.   [1241]

Panfilo Castaldi.   Communicazioni nel Giornale degli eruditi e
dei curiosi.   Padova, Crescini, n.d.   8vo.
Title from Bibliotheca bibliografica Italica.   vol. 1, 1889.   [1242]

Panfilo Castaldi ed i suoi increduli. L'Arte della Stampa,
vol. 10, 1880, p. 369.   [1243]

Petit, Louis D.
   Iets over Panfilo Castaldi. Naar het Fransch van Ch. Yriarte.
Amsterdam, 1889.
   Reprint from Nieuwsblad voor den Boekhandel.   [1244]
   Eu-Ne-AVb

Praloran, Giovanni.
   Delle origini e del primato della stampa tipografica; di Giovanni
Praloran. Milano, Tip. della Società cooperativa fra tipografi ed
arti affini, 1868.   xvi, 172p.   front. (port.) illus., plates
23 cm.
   Contents.- Preambolo.- Biblioteca della tipografia.- pte. 1.
   Storia della quistione.- pte. 2. Rassegna critica.- pte. 3.
   Panfilo Castaldi.   [1245]
   DLC   IU   NN   Eu-De-IBb   Eu-Fr-PN   Eu-Ge-LB

Rosa, Cesare.
   Panfilo Castaldi da Feltre. La Tipografia Italiana, vol. 1,
1869, p. 42.   [1246]

Rose, Ferdinand.
   Panfilo Castaldi aus Feltre. Journal für Buchdruckerkunst, no.
25, 1865, col. 205-210.   [1247]

Scarabelli, Luciano.
   Di Panfilo Castaldi a Monsignore Jacopo Bernardi Feltrense vicario
vescovile a Pinerola. Il Buonarotti, vol. 3 (n.s., vol. 1), 1866,
p. 196-200.
   Also reprint.   [1248]

Sigillo, Il.
   De Panfilo Castaldi. Il Tomitano (Feltre), vol. 9, no. 14,
July 16, 1880, p. 109.   [1249]

Volpe, Riccardo.
   Panfilo Castaldi in una seduta del consiglio dei nobili della
citta di Belluno ai 12 Luglio 1464.   Belluno, Deliberali, 1888.
10p.   8vo.
   Title from Bibliotheca Italiana, vol. 2, 1895.   [1250]

5   For and About Brito

Bergmans, Paul Jean Etiènne Charles Marie, 1868-1935.
  ... L'imprimeur Jean Brito et les origines de l'imprimerie en Belgique,
d'après le livre récent de M. Gilliodts-Van Severen. Causerie faite
à la Société d'histoire et d'archéologie de Gand, le 15 février 1898.
Gand, Impr. V. van Doosselaere, 1898. 17p. 22 cm.   [1251]
    DLC   Eu-Ne-AVb

Bocarmé, Albert Visart de.
    Recherches sur les imprimeurs brugeois, par Albert Visart de Bo-
carmé, président de la Commission de la Bibliothèque communale de
Bruges. A Bruges, Chez Desclée, De Brouwer et Cie. Editeurs, 10,
Quai au Bois, M. CM. XXVIII [1928]. 74p. 27 cm.   [1252]
    NN   Eu-Ne-AVb

Bockenheimer, Karl Georg, 1836-1914.
    Johann Brito aus Brügge, der angebliche Erfinder der Buchdrucker-
kunst. Von K. G. Bockenheimer. Mainz, [Mainzer] Verlagsanstalt
und Druckerei, A.-G., 1898. iv, 46p. 22.5 cm.   [1253]
    DLC   Eu-Ge-LB   Eu-Ge-LSb

Caullet, Gustave
    La deffense de monseigneur le duc et madame la duchesse d'Aus-
triche et de Bourgongne. Description de cet incunable, précédée d'un
aperçu critique sur la carrière et l'oeuvre de Jean Brito.   Courtrai,
Eug. Bayaert, 1907. 26p. plates.   Bulletin du Cercle Historique
et Archéologique de Courtrai, vol. 4.   [1254]
    Eu-De-LBb

    Documents relatifs aux recherches sur l'invention de l'imprimerie
á Bruges. Chronique Graphique, vol. 12, 1937, p. 3555-3565, 3601,
3603, 3605-3607, 3629-3633.   [1255]

Gilliodts-Van Severn, Louis, 1827-
    L'oeuvre de Jean Brito, prototypographe brugeois; étude critique
pour servir d'introduction à l'histoire de l'ancienne corporation
des librairiers et imprimeurs de Bruges, par L. Gilliodts-Van Severen
... Bruges, Imprimerie de L. de Plancke, 1897. 1 prel. leaf, 514p.
1 leaf. 25 cm.
    "Extrait des Annales de la Société d'émulation pour l'étude de
    l'histoire et des antiquités de la Flandre, 5° sér., t.x, xlvii°
    vol., 1897."   [1256]
    DLC   NN   Eu-Fr-PN   Eu-Ge-LB

----   La question de Jean Brito.   Revue des Bibliothèques, vol.
8, 1898, p. [128]-133.   [1257]

Hölscher, G.
    Belgien und die Erfindung der Buchdruckerkunst.   Börsenblatt für
den Deutschen Buchhandel, vol. 66, no. 13, Jan. 1899, p. 428-429.   [1258]

Maene, A.
    Le cas Brito.   Jean Brito, est-il l'inventeur de la typographie?
Gulden Passer, n.s., vol. 14, 1936, p. 65-76.   [1259]

Nieuwenhuyzen, J.
    Jan Brito en de uitvinding der boekdrukkunst.   Wetenschappelijk
Vlaamsch Congres voor Boek en Bibliotheekwezen.   Handelingen, no.
4, 1937, p. 18-27.
    Summary in English, p. 27.   [1260]

Rommel, H.
    L'oeuvre de Jean Brito, prototypographe brugeois, par H. Louis
Gilliodts-Van Severen ... Etude analytique sur l'invention de l'imprimerie à Bruges, par le chanoine H. Rommel ... [Bruges], Imprimerie
de St. Augustin, Desclée, de Brouwer et Cie, 1898.   51p.   22 cm.
    A review of "L'oeuvre de Jean Brito..." par L. Gilliodts-Van
Severen.   Bruges, 1897.   [1261]
    ICJ   NN   Eu-De-LBb   Eu-Fr-PN   Eu-Ge-LB   Eu-Ne-GK

Seyl, Antoine.
    Les arguments que l'on oppose aux titres de Gutenberg.   Chron-
ique Graphique, vol. 11, 1936, p. 3285-3291.   [1262]

----   Le cas Brito.   Chronique Graphique, vol. 12, 1937, p. 3669-
3671.   [1263]

----   Une gloire nationale reconquise.   Bruges berceau de l'imprimerie.   Chronique Graphique, vol. 10, 1934, p. 2617-2623.   [1264]

----   Jean Brito et l'invention de l'imprimerie.   Chronique Graphique, vol. 10, 1934, p. 2577-2583.   [1265]

----   Le mystère des premiers imprimés brugeois.   Chronique Graphique, vol. 10, 1935, p. 2813-2819.   [1266]

----   Les origines brugeoises de l'imprimerie.   Chronique Graphique, vol. 13, 1938, p. 4043-4047.   [1267]

----   Les Pays-Bas; berceau de la typographie, par Antoine Seyl.
Bruxelles, Éditions des arts et industries graphiques, 1940.   16p.
18 cm.
    At head of title: Le V⁰ centenaire de l'imprimerie.   [1268]
    McMurtrie.

----   Qui inventa l'imprimerie en Europe? La Belgique peut et doit
revendiquer cet honneur en faveur du prototypographe brugeois Jean

Brito.   Chronique Graphique, vol. 10, 1934, p. 2541-2545.   [1269]

---- Le rival belge de Johann Gutenberg: Jean Brito de Bruges.
Chronique Graphique, vol. 10, 1934, p. 2733-2739.   [1270]

Vincent, A.
   Jean Brito, l'imprimeur brugeois, inventa-t-il la typographie?
Bulletin Mensuel du Musée du Livre, vol. 17, Nov. 1934.   [1271]

   Who was the inventor of printing?   A new claimant.   Jean Brito,
vs Gutenberg and Coster.   British and Colonial Printer, vol. 42,
May 1890, p. 294-295.   [1272]

      6   Other Claims

Bailleul, Antoine.
   Petite dissertation sur un monument typographique qui ferait re-
monter la découverte de l'imprimerie à 1414, avec des Observations
qui prouveraient qu'elle est même antérieure à cette date.   1817.
4p.   Folio.   [1273]
   Eu-Fr-PN

Beaulacre, Leonard.
   Lettre sur le Livre de la Sapience imprimé à Bâle, avec le date
de l'an 1444.   Bibliotheque Germanique (Amsterdam), part 21, 1731,
p. 98-119.   [1274]

Berlan, Francesco, 1821-1886.
... La invenzione della stampa a tipo mobile fuso rivendicata all'
Italia.   Con due tavole fotolitografate.   Firenze, A spese dell'
autore, 1882.   viii, 298p.   2 fold. facsim.   20 cm.
   Some chapters of the work were pub. in the Florentine journal
La Nazione, April-May 1882.
   The author contends that movable type was invented at Rome by
Sweynheim and Pannartz, and that all books printed before their
Cicero 1467 were block-books.   [1275]
   DLC   Eu-Fr-PN   Eu-Ge-LB

Broeckx, C.
   Notice sur un livre de médicine prétendument imprimé en 1401.
Académie d'Archéologie de Belgique.   Annales, 1847, p. 326-342.   [1276]

Budik, Peter Alcantara.
   Mentelin, berühmter und geschickter Drucker.   (In Budik, Peter
Alcantara.   Vorschule für bibliothekarisches Geschäftsleben.
München, G. Franz, 1848. p. 34)   [1277]
   DLC   Eu-Fr-PN   Eu-Ge-LB

Comme quoi, Mentel ou Mentelin, et non Guttenberg, serait pour le
quart d'heure, l'inventeur de l'imprimerie. Lettre du 28 Mai
adressée au redacteur des Affiches de la ville de Schlettstadt.
[Signed: V] Affiches de Schlettstadt, no. 22, 1840.
   Answered in Strassburger Wochenblatt, no. 50, 1840.
   Title from Mohr, Jubelfeste.   [1278]

Dorlan, A.
   Quelques mots sur l'origine de l'imprimerie, ou résumé des
opinions qui en attribuent l'invention à Jean Mentel, natif de
Schlestadt.   [Three-line quotation from Epist. ad Clariss. virum
Gab. Naudé, by Jean Schot.] Schlestadt, de l'imprimerie de F.
Helbig, place d'Armes, 289, 1840. 38, [2]p.   7 plates.   21 cm. [1279]
   NN   Eu-De-LBb   Eu-Fr-PN   Eu-Ge-LP   Eu-Ne-AVb

Gachet, Emile.
   L'invention de l'imprimerie n'est due ni à Gutenberg ni à Laurent
Coster.   Bulletin du Bibliophile Belge, vol. 11 (2d ser., vol. 2),
1855, p. 187-190.
   Attributes invention to a Brabançon, Louis van Vaelbecke, ca.1300[1280]

----   Sur l'invention de l'imprimerie.   Académie Royale des Sciences et des Belles Lettres de Bruxelles.   Bulletin, vol. 6, 1839, p.
459-461.   [1281]

Haarhaus, I. R.
   Ein neuer Erfinder der Buchdruckerkunst.   Börsenblatt für den
Deutschen Buchhandel, vol. 2, no. 170, 1895, p. 1362.   [1282]

Leclerc, Émile.
   Essai historique sur l'imprimerie.   La Fonderie Typographique,
vol. 8, no. 92, 1906, p. 247-249; no. 93, p. 279-281; no. 95, p.
353-355; no. 96, p. 392-394; vol. 9, no. 97, 1907, p. 16-18; no. 98,
p. 56-60; no. 99, p. 91-94; no. 101, p. 155-156; no. 107, p. 350-351;
no. 108, p. 385-387.   [1283]

----   Jean Mentel (ou Mentelin) veritable inventeur de la typographie.   La Fonderie Typographique, vol. 3, no. 29, 1903, p. 209-214;
no. 30, p. 257-259.   [1284]

[Mentel, Jacques] 1597-1671.
   Brevis excursus de loco, tempore et authore inventionis typographiae. Ad clarissimum Gabrielem Naudaeum, Parisiensem.   Parisiis,
excudebat typographus, M.DC.XLIV [1644]
   Reissued in Wolf, J. C. Monumenta typographica. Hamburg,
   1740.   vol. 2, p. 189-236.   [1285]
   McMurtrie

----   Iacobi Menteli ... De vera typographiae origine paraenesis ...
Parisiis, ex officina Roberti Ballard, 1650.   4 prel. leaves, 119p.

illus.   23 cm.
   First published anonymously in 1644 under title: Brevis excursus
de loco, tempore et authore inventionis typographiae.
   Claims that Johannes Mentelin of Strassburg (according to some
authorities an ancestor of the author) was the inventor of print-
ing.
   Reissued in Wolf, J. C. Monumenta typographica.   Hamburg,
1740.   vol. 2, p. 237-366.   [1286]
   DLC   MBAt   NN   NNC   Eu-De-LBb   Eu-Fr-PN   Eu-Ge-LB
Eu-Ne-AVb

Mentel, Jacques, 1597-1671.
   Observationes Jac. Mentelii de praecipuis typographis, &
typographiae origine, transcriptae ex Codice baluziano, qui in
Bibliotheca Regia Parisiis Asservantur.   (In Wolf, J. C.   Monumenta
typographica.   Hamburg, 1740.   vol. 2, p. 367-403)   [1287]

Schorbach, Karl, 1851-
   Der Strassburger Frühdrucker Johann Mentelin (1458-1478); Studien
zu seinem Leben und Werke, von Karl Schorbach, mit 19 Tafeln. Mainz,
Verlag der Gutenberg-Gesellschaft, 1932.   3 prel. leaves, ix-xv,
270p., 1 leaf, 25p.   xix plates (facsims., part double)   29.5 cm.
(Added t.-p.; Veröffentlichungen der Gutenberg-Gesellschaft, XXII)
   "Anhang: Bibliographische Beschreibung der Druckwerke Johann
   Mentelins. Gedruckt von der Firma Karras, Kröber & Nietschmann,
   Druckerei u. Verlag, Halle (Saale)": 1 leaf, 25p., following p.
   270.   [1288]
   CSmH   DLC   ICJ   ICN   MB   NN   NNC   Eu-De-BP   Eu-De-BU
Eu-De-BsSU   Eu-De-GtU   Eu-De-HlU   Eu-De-KlU   Eu-De-MrU
Eu-De-MsU   Eu-Ge-LB   Eu-Ne-AVb

----   Strassburgs Anteil an der Erfindung der Buchdruckerkunst.
Freiburg im Breisgau, J. C. Mohr, P. Siebeck, 1892.   [577]-655p.
1 fold. facs.   22.5 cm.
   Caption title: Sonderabdruck aus der Zeits. f. d. Geschichte
des Oberrheins, N. F. VII, 4.   [1289]
   ICJ   NN

Trocsanyi, Z.
   Wer galt im 16. Jahrhundert in Ungarn als Erfinder der Buchdruckerkunst?   Ungarische Rundschau für Historische und Soziale Wissenschaften, 1913, p. 221.   [1290]

Willems, J. F.
   Berigten wegens de bookprinters van Antwerpen, ten jare 1442, enz.,
door J. F. Willems.   Gent, Book- en Steendrukkery van F. en E.
Gyselynck, 1844.   vi, [7]-61p.   1 plate.   20.5 cm.   [1291]
   NN   NNC   Eu-De-LBb

A.   GENERAL

Adam, Carl.
    Die Ergebnisse der Gutenbergforschung.   Typographische Mit-
teilungen, vol. 20, 1923, p. 72-73.   [1292]

Audin, Marius, 1872-
    La métallographie et le problème du livre.   Gutenberg Jahr-
buch, vol. 5, 1930, p. 11-52.   [1293]

    Die Buchdruckerpresse von Gutenberg bis Friedrich König.
[Signed: A. G.]   Deutscher Buch- und Steindrucker, vol. 33, 1926,
p. 53-56, 142-144.   [1294]

    Un curioso ritratto di Gutenberg.   L'Arte della Stampa, vol.
14, no. 17, 1884, p. 133-134.   [1295]

Fry, Francis.
    Gutenberg's first printing press.   Notes and Queries, 2nd ser.,
vol. 11, no. 262, Jan. 1861, p. 23-24.   [1296]

Gage, Harry Lawrence.
    How Gutenberg made his types.   From the researches and recon-
structions of Herr Gustav Mori.   Brooklyn, N. Y., Morgenthaler
Linotype co., 1927.   4to.
    Reprint from Linotype Magazine, vol. 18, no. 11, Sept. 1927.   [1297]

Garnett, Porter.
    The hand-press.   Dolphin, vol. 1, 1933, p. 96-106.   [1298]

Gusman, Pierre, 1862-
    Jean Gutenberg et quelques techniques de son temps.   Byblis,
vol. 2, 1923, p. 52-60.   [1299]

    Gutenberg oder das Rätsel der Buchstaben.   Katechetische
Monatsschrift, 1908, p. 124.   [1300]

    Gutenberg und die ältesten Drucke.   Österreich-Ungarische
Buchdruckerei-Zeitung, 1911, p. 97-98.   [1301]

    Gutenberg's and Schöffer's types.   Results of international
interest in the preservation of the works of Gutenberg.   American
Printer, vol. 82, no. 12, 1926, p. 45.   [1302]

[Haebler, Konrad] 1857-
... Warum tragen Gutenbergs Drucke keine Unterschrift? [Leipzig,
O. Harrassowitz, 1902]   p. [103]-108. 22.5 cm.
    Caption title.
    Signed: K. Häbler, Dresden.
    Reprint from Zentralblatt für Bibliothekswesen, vol. 19, 1902.   [1303]
    NNH   Eu-Ge-LSb

---- Zur Typenkunde des XV Jahrhunderts.   Zeitschrift für Bücherfreunde, n.s., vol. 1, 1909, p. 136-145.   [1304]

Hessel, Alfred.
    Von der Schrift zum Druck.   Zeitschrift des Deutschen Vereins
für Buchwesen und Schrifttum, vol. 6, 1923, p. 89-105.   [1305]

[Hirtz, D.]
    Konrad Sahspach. 1436. Gutenbergs Presse.   Indicateur de
Strasbourg, no. 38, 1840.
    Title from Mohr, Jubelfeste.   [1306]

Hodgkin, John Eliot.
    Rariora; being notes of some of the printed books, manuscripts,
historical documents, medals, engravings, pottery, etc., etc.,
collected (1858-1900) by John Eliot Hodgkin, F. S. A.   Vol. I[-III]
London, S. Low, Marston & company, ltd. [1902] 3 vols. illus.,
port., facsim. (part col., part fold.) 28.5x22.5 cm.
    Title within decorative border; head-pieces, initials, floreated
    endpapers, numerous facsimiles of title-pages, autograph let-
    ters, etc., etc. "Printed by Bemrose and sons, limited, at
    their press in the parish of Saint Peter in the town of Derby
    M.CMII."   [1307]
    DLC   ICJ   MiU   NN   WaU   Eu-Ge-LB

Hoe, Robert, 1839-1909.
    A short history of the printing press and of the improvements
in printing machinery from the time of Gutenberg up to the present
day. New York, 1902. 89p. front., plates. 27.5 cm.   [1308]
    DLC   ICJ   ICN   MB   NN   Eu-Ge-LP

Hoehne, Otto.
    Gutenbergs Technik nach 500 Jahren.   Archiv für Buchgewerbe
und Gebrauchsgraphik, vol. 77, no. 7-8, 1940, p. 269-271.   [1309]

Holland, Rupert S.
    Gutenberg and the printing press. (In Holland, Rupert S.   His-
toric inventions. Philadelphia, 1911.   p. 9-41)   [1310]
    DLC   NN

Hölscher, G.
   Von der angeblichen ersten Buchdruckerpresse Gutenbergs. Allgemeine Buchhändlerzeitung, no. 38, 1900.   [1311]

Rupp, Otto, 1859-
   Gutenberg und die Nacherfinder. Gutenberg Jahrbuch, vol. 4,
1929, p. 31-100.
   Criticism of the hypotheses of Zedler and Enschedé.   [1312]

   Instruktion für den Betrieb der Gutenberg-Presse des Gutenberg-
Museums zu Mainz. Mainz, 1936. 8 leaves.   [1313]
   Eu-De-BP

Klein, Karl, 1806-1870.
   Sur Gutenberg et le fragment de sa presse, trouvé dans la maison où il a établi sa première imprimerie. Traduit d'un manuscrit
de Ch. Klein. Mayence, Imprimerie de J. Gottsleben, 1856.
1 prel. leaf, 69p. illus. 21 cm.   [1314]
   ICJ   ICN   IU   Eu-Ge-LSb

----   [German translation] Mainz, 1857.   [1315]
   Eu-De-LBb

----   Über Gutenberg und das Fragment der ersten Druckerpresse.
Hamburgische Litterarische und Kritische Blätter, no. 1, 1857.   [1316]

----   Über Gutenberg und das im ersten Druckhaus desselben auf-
gefundene Fragment seiner Presse. Von K. Klein. Nach einem
Vortrag am 9. April dieses Jahres im hiesigen Alterthums-Verein.
(Abdruck aus dem Mainzer Wochenblatt 1856 nr. 45 ff.) Mainz,
Seifert, 1856. 8p. 21 cm.   [1317]
   IU   Eu-Ge-LSb

Klemm, Heinrich, 1819-1886.
   Johann Gutenbergs erste Buchdruck-Presse vom Jahre 1441.
Wieder aufgefunden bei einem Neubau im ehemaligen Gutenberg'schen
Druckhause zu Mainz am 22. März 1856. Separat-Abdruck aus dem
Catalogo des Bibliographischen Museums, von Heinrich Klemm ... Dres-
den, H. Klemm, 1884. 15p. plates. 18 cm.   [1318]
   DLC   ICJ   Eu-Fr-PN   Eu-Ge-LSb

König, H.
   Schrift und Schriftverzierung zu Gutenberg's Zeit. Allgemeiner Anzeiger für Druckereien, Gutenberg number, June 21, 1900. [1319]

Madan, Falconer, 1851-1935.
   Early representations of the printing press. Bibliographica,
vol. 1, 1895, p. 223-248, 499-504.   [1320]

Müller, Bruno.
    Wie mag wohl Gutenberg seine ersten brauchbaren Typen herge-
stellt haben?   Berlin, 1931.   [1321]
    •CSmH   MiU   Eu-Ge-LB

Pottinger, David T.
    The history of the printing press.   Dolphin, vol. 3, 1938,
p. 323-344.   [1322]

Riemelk.
    Die älteste Gutenbergtype.   Allgemeine Buchhändlerzeitung,
1902, p. 219-?21.   [1323]

Ruppel, Aloys Leonhard, 1882-
    Die Technik Gutenbergs und ihre Vorstufen.   Berlin, Vidi-
Verlag, 1940.   64p.   illus.   8vo.
    Reprint from Deutsches Museum.   Abhandlungen und Berichte,
    vol. 12, no. 2.   [1324]
    Eu-Sz-BeG

Schmidt, Benno.
    Technisches und Wirtschaftliches an Gutenbergs Erfindung.
Zeitschrift für Deutschlands Buchdrucker, vol. 38, no. 84, 1926.
p. 697.   [1325]

Stempel, D.
    Figuren-Aufstellung zur grossen Psalter-type [Kegel 14, 7 mm].
Nach der ursprunglicher Gussverfahren Gutenbergs in den Jahre
1914-1939 hergestellt.   Frankfurt a.M. Süd, 1939.
    Title from Bibliographie des Bibliotheks und Buchwesens, 1939.   [1326]

Wehrhan, Otto Friedrich, ed.
    Gutenberg's erster Druck, oder Facsimile der ersten Seite des
ersten in der Welt gedruckten Buches.   Bei Gelegenheit der
vierten Säcularfeier des Typendrucks, mit einer kurzen geschichtlichen Erläuterung, herausgegeben von O. F. Wehrhan.   Dresden,
Just. Naumann, 1840.   Folio.
    Title from Mohr, Jubelfeste.   [1327]

Zedler, Gottfried, 1860-
    Auszug aus dem Vortrage über den ältesten Gutenbergischen
Stempel.   Gutenberg-Gesellschaft.   Jahresbericht, 1906,
p. 14-21.   [1328]

----   Der Verbleib der ältesten Gutenbergtype.   Zentralblatt für
Bibliothekswesen, vol. 21, 1904, p. 388-396.   [1329]

B. EARLY PRIMITIVE PRINTS

Astronomischer Kalender für 1448. Zeitschrift für Bücher-
freunde, vol. 6, 1900, p. 342.   [1330]

Bernhart, Mathias.
Meine Ansicht von der Geschichte der Entstehung, Ausbildung und
Verbreitung der Buchdruckerkunst. Bey Veranlassung des neu ent-
deckten Kalenders: "ein Manung der Cristenheit widder die Durken"
für das Jahr 1455. Von Mathias Bernhart, Königl. baier. Hoff-
bibliothek-Secretaire. München, bey E. A. Fleischmann, 1807.
1 prel. leaf, [3]-46p. 16 cm.   [1331]
    ICN   Eu-Fr-PN   Eu-Ge-LB   Eu-Ge-LSb   Eu-Ne-AVb

Garland, H.
An unrecorded specimen of Gutenberg printing 1450. Bookman's
Journal, vol. 2, 1920, p. 252.   [1332]

    Gutenberg's principal production. Early edition credited as
his work. Inland Printer, vol. 48, 1911, p. 237.   [1333]

    Gutenbergs Türkenkalender für das Jahr 1455, rekonstruierter
Typendruck von hölzerner Handpresse mit Handrubrizierung. [Mainz,
Gutenberg-Gesellschaft, 1928] cover-title, facsim. ([9] p.) [1]p.
27 cm. (Kleiner Druck der Gutenberg-Gesellschaft. nr. IX^a)
    Wiedergabe des im Dezember 1454 gedruckten sogenannten Türken-
kalenders auf das Jahr 1455, des ersten vollständig erhaltenen
Druckes in deutscher Sprache nach einer Lichtdruckwiedergabe des
im Besitze der Münchener Staatsbibliothek befindlichen Origi-
nals."   [1334]
    DLC   IU   NN   Eu-Ge-LSb   Eu-Ne-AVb

Haebler, Konrad, 1857-
Le soi-disant Cisianus de 1443, et les Cisianus allemands.
Bibliographe Moderne, vol. 6, 1902, p. 5-40, 188-210.   [1335]

Hölscher, G.
Zwei Drucke Gutenbergs? Börsenblatt für den Deutschen
Buchhandel, vol. 67, 1900, p. 5250-5253.   [1336]

Joachim, Johannes.
[Article on Eyn manung der cristenheit widder die durken]. (In
Dziatzko, Karl Franz Otto, ed. Beiträge zur Theorie und Praxis
des Buch- und Bibliothekswesens. Leipzig, M. Spirgatis, 1894-
1904. vol. 6, 1901, p. 87-102)   [1337]
    ICJ   ICN   IU   MB

McMurtrie, Douglas Crawford, 1888-
    The first typographic printing. Is the Mainz fragment of the
"World judgment" the earliest specimen? By Douglas C. McMurtrie.
Chicago, Priv. print., 1935. 9, [1]p. illus. (incl. facsims.)
22.5 cm.
    "Two hundred copies reprinted from the American printer for
    May 5, 1924."   [1338]
    DLC   MB   NN   RPJCB   Eu-Ne-AVb

... Das Mainzer Fragment vom Weltgericht, der älteste Druck mit der
Donat-Kalender-Type Gutenbergs ...   Der Canon Missae vom Jahre
1458 der Bibliotheca Bodleiana zu Oxford ... Mainz, Gutenberg-Gesellschaft, 1904. 3 prel. leaves., 51p. illus., XI facsim.
(10 fold.) 29x22 cm. (Added t.-p.: Veröffentlichungen der Gutenberg-Gesellschaft III)
    1. Das Mainzer Fragment vom Weltgericht: A. Philologische
    Studien zum Text und zum Druck, von Prof. Dr. Edward Schröder.
    B. Typographische und zeitliche Stellung, von Dr. Gottfried
    Zedler. C. Technische Untersuchung des Weltgerichts-Druckes
    und seiner Typen, von Heinrich Wallau.   Mit 1 Tafeln in Licht-
    druck.   [1339]
    DLC   ICJ   ICN   MH   Eu-Ge-LSb

Mori, Gustav.
    Der Türkenkalender für das Jahr 1455; eine druckhistorische
Studie, von Gustav Mori.   Mainz, Gutenberg-Gesellschaft, 1928.
[18]p.   27 cm. (On cover: Kleiner Druck der Gutenberg-Gesellschaft.   Nr. IX b)   [1340]
    DLC   ICN   IU   MH   NN   Eu-Fr-PN   Eu-Ne-AVb

Neuhaus, Johannes, 1869-1922, ed.
    Das erste gedruckte Buch Gutenbergs in deutscher Sprache;
nach dem einzigen Exemplare in München zum ersten Mal vollständig
herausgegeben und erläutert von Johs. Neuhaus. Kjøbenhavn, S.
Bernsteen, 1902. 3 prel. leaves, facsim. ([9]p.), 37, [1]p.
25.5 cm.
    Cover-title: Die Mahnung, Mainz, 1454; Kjøbenhavn, 1902.   [1341]
    DLC   Eu-Ge-LSb   Eu-Sz-BeG

    Le piu antiche impressione di Gutenberg.   Bibliofilia, vol.
13, 1911, p. 314.   [1342]

Ricci, Seymour de, 1881-
    Catalogue raisonné des premières impressions de Mayence (1445-
1467) par Seymour de Ricci. Avec une planche en phototypie.
Mainz, Gutenberg-Gesellschaft, 1911. 2 prel. leaves, ix, 166p.
facsim. 28.5 cm. (Added t.-p.: Veröffentlichungen der Gutenberg-
Gesellschaft.   VIII, IX)
    Description of 112 incunabula, of which 66 only are to be found
    in Hain and Copinger; each item accompanied by a census of copies

and a bibliography.
This excellent work records not only the imprints of the early
Mainz press above specified, but also all the other issues of
the Gutenberg-Fust-Schoeffer presses. It is an invaluable
document to the student of the history of the invention of
printing. [1343]
DLC   ICJ   ICN   MB   RPJCB   Eu-De-BP   Eu-De-LBb   Eu-De-MzG
Eu-Fr-PN

Scholderer, Victor, 1880-
Das Mainzer Fragment vom Weltgericht.   Library, 2nd ser.,
vol. 6, 1905, p. 221-223. [1344]

Schröder, Edward, 1858-
Das Mainzer Fragment vom Weltgericht; ein Ausschnitt aus dem
deutschen Sibyllenbuche.   Mainz, Gutenberg-Gesellschaft, 1908.
cover-title, 3 prel. leaves, 235p.   illus.   xiv facsims.
(part. col., part. fold.)   29x22 cm.   (Veröffentlichungen der
Gutenberg-Gesellschaft no. 5-7, p. 1-9) [1345]
   DLC   IC   ICN   MB   MH   NN   Eu-De-BP   Eu-De-MzG
   Eu-Ge-LB   Eu-Ge-LSb

Schwenke, Paul, 1853-1921.
Aelteste Gutenbergtype.   Deutsche Literatur Zeitung, vol. 23,
1902, p. 2125-2128. [1346]

----   Gutenberg und die Type des Türkenkalenders.   Zentralblatt
für Bibliothekswesen, vol. 18, 1901, p. 288-296.
   Also reprint. [1347]

----   Die Türkenbulle Papst Calixtus III.   Ein deutscher Druck von
1456 in der ersten Gutenbergtype.   In Nachbildung herausgegeben
und untersucht von Paul Schwenke.   Mit einer geschichtlich-
sprachlichen Abhandlung von Hermann Gegering.   Berlin, M. Bres-
lauer, 1911.   [6], 38, [2]p.   13 facsim.   26.5 cm.   (Seltene
Drucke der Königlichen Bibliothek zu Berlin, I) [1348]
   ICJ   ICN   ICU   MiU   NN   NNC

----   Zum ältesten Buchdruck.   Zentralblatt für Bibliothekswesen,
vol. 21, 1904, p. 283-284. [1349]

Wyss, Arthur Franz Wilhelm, 1852-1900.
Ein deutscher Cisianus für das Jahr 1444 gedruckt von Guten-
berg ...   Strassburg, J. H. E. Heitz, 1900.   19p.   facsim.   4to.
(Drucke und Holzschnitte des XV. und XVI. Jahrhunderts in getreuer
Nachbildung.   V) [1350]
   DLC   MB   NN   Eu-Ge-LB   Eu-Ge-LSb   Eu-Ne-GK

----   Gutenbergs Cisianus zu Deutsche.   Zentralblatt für Bibliothekswesen, vol. 18, 1901, p. 145-150. [1351]

Wyss, Arthur Franz Wilhelm, 1852-1900.
    Die Türkenkalender für 1455. Ein Werk Gutenbergs. (In Fest-
schrift zum fünfhundertjährigen Geburtstage von Johann Gutenberg,
herausgegeben von Otto Hartwig.   Leipzig, O. Harrassowitz, 1900.
p. 380-401)   [1352]
    CSmH   DLC   ICJ   ICN   MH   NjP   Eu-De-BP   Eu-Ne-AVb
    Eu-Ne-GK

----   Der Türkenkalender für 1455.   Ein Werk Gutenbergs, von Arthur
Wyss.   Mainz, P. von Zabern, 1900.   cover-title, 17p.   facsim.
29x23.5 cm.
    At head of title: Aus der Festschrift der Stadt Mainz zum 500
    jährigen Geburtstage von Johann Gutenberg.   [1353]
    ICJ

Zedler, Gottfried, 1860-
    Die älteste Gutenbergtype, von Dr. Gottfried Zedler ... Mit 13
Tafeln in Lichtdruck.   Mainz, Verlag der Gutenberg-Gesellschaft,
1902.   3 prel. leaves, 57p.   12 facsim.   (part fold.) fold.
tab. 20x22 cm. (Added t.-p.: Veröffentlichungen der Gutenberg-Gesellschaft, I)
    Continued and supplemented by Schwenke's Die Donat- und Kalen-
    dertype, Mainz, 1903. (Veröffentlichungen der Gutenberg-
    Gesellschaft, II)
    Contents.--Ein neu entdeckter astronomischer Kalender für das
    Jahr 1448.   Mit einer astronomischen Untersuchung von Prof. Dr.
    Julius Bauschinger zu Berlin und einem sprachlichen Beitrag von
    Prof. Dr. Edward Schröder zu Marburg.--Der Pariser 27 zeilige
    Donat und die Beschaffenheit der ältesten Gutenbergtype.--Die
    übrigen, mit der Gutenbergischen Urtype hergestellten Mainzer
    Drucke und ihr Drucker.   [1354]
    DLC   IC   ICJ   ICN   MB   NN   Eu-De-BP   Eu-Ge-LSb
    Eu-Ne-GK

----   Ein neu ausgefundener Gutenbergdruck.   Zentralblatt für Bibliothekswesen, vol. 18, no. 10, 1901, p. 501-503.   [1355]

Zinner, E.
    Der astronomische Kalender von 1448.   Gesellschaft für Typen-
kunde des XV. Jahrhunderts. Beiträge zur Inkunabelkunde, n.s., vol.
2, 1938, p. 128-130.   [1356]

C‡ EDITIONS OF THE DONATUS

Aubert, M.
    Les anciens Donats de la Bibliothèque Nationale.   Bibliographe
Moderne, vol. 13, 1909, p. 225 et sqq.   [1357]

Collijn, Isak Gustaf Alfred, 1875-
   Fragmente eines 30 zeiligen Donats in der DK-type aus dem Prager
Thomaskloster. Gesellschaft für Typenkunde des XV. Jahrhunderts.
Beitrage zur Inkunabelkunde, n.s., vol. 2, 1938, p. 62-68.   [1358]

---- Nyfunnet fragment af en 26-radig Donat tryckt med Gutenbergs 42-
radiga bibeltyp, af Isak Collijn ... [Uppsala, Almqvist & Wiksells
boktryckeri, 1922] cover-title, [185]-190p. 26 cm.
   Reprint from Nordisk Tidskrift för Bok och Biblioteksvasen,
   vol. 9, 1922, p. 185-190.   [1359]
   DLC

Kattermann, Gerhard.
   Neue Donatfragmente Gutenbergs in der Type der 36-zeiligen Bibel.
Börsenblatt für den Deutschen Buchhandel, vol. 103, no. 185, 1936. [1360]

---- Neue Karlsruher Bruchstücke eines 30 zeiligen Donats in der
DK-type. Gesellschaft für Typenkunde des XV. Jahrhunderts.
Beiträge zur Inkunabelkunde, n.s., vol. 2, 1938, p. 69-78.   [1361]

Keil, Henri.
   Grammatici Latini ex recensione H. Keilii.   Lipsiae, 1857-
1880. 8 vol. 4to.
   The preface to vol. 4 contains study of texts of the Donatus
   and deals with its use in the middle ages, and even after the
   invention of printing.   [1362]
   Eu-Fr-PN   Eu-Ge-LB

Schwenke, Paul, 1853-1921.
   Donatstudien. Zentralblatt für Bibliothekswesen, vol. 22,
no. 11, Nov. 1905, p. 529-535; vol. 23, no. 10, Oct. 1906,
p. 449-456; vol. 24, no. 3, Mar. 1907, p. 112-116.   [1363]

---- Die Donat- und Kalender-Type.   Nachtrag und übersicht von
Dr. Paul Schwenke ... mit einem Abdruck des Donat-Textes nach den
ältesten Ausgaben und mit 7. Tafeln in Lichtdruck. Mainz, Ver-
lag der Gutenberg-Gesellschaft, 1903.   3 prel. leaves, 49p.
7 facsim. (part fold.)   29 cm. (Added t.-p.: Veröffentlichungen
der Gutenberg-Gesellschaft. II)
   Continues and supplements Zedler's Gutenbergtype, Mainz, 1902.
   (Veröffentlichungen der Gutenberg-Gesellschaft. I)   [1364]
   DLC ICJ ICN MB NN Eu-De-BP Eu-De-MzG Eu-Ge-LB
   Eu-Ge-LSb

---- Neue Donatfunde.   Zentralblatt für Bibliothekswesen, vol. 22,
1905, p. 529-535.   [1365]

---- Neue Donatfragmente in Gutenbergtypen.   Zentralblatt für
Bibliothekswesen, vol. 30, 1913, p. 261-263.   [1366]

Schwenke, Paul, 1853-1921.
   Neue Donatstücke in Gutenbergs Urtype.   Zentralblatt für
Bibliothekswesen, vol. 25, 1908, p. 70-75.   [1367]

----   Ein neues Donatfragment der Kalendertype in München.   Zentralblatt für Bibliothekswesen, vol. 23, 1906, p. 452-454.   [1368]

----   Weitere Donatbruchstücke in der ersten Gutenbergtype.   Zentralblatt für Bibliothekswesen, vol. 32, 1915, p. 269-273.   [1369]

Schwetscke, Karl Gustav, 1804-1881.
   De Donati minoris fragmento Halis nuper reberto excursus.
Halis, 1839.   4to.   [1370]
   Eu-De-LBb

Stempel, D.
   Figuren-Aufstellung zur Donat-Kalender B 36-Type [Kegel 8,
28 mm].   Nach der ursprunglicher Gussverfahren Gutenbergs in den
Jahre 1924-1939 hergestellt.   Frankfurt a.M. Süd, 1939.
   Title from Bibliographie des Bibliotheks und Buchwesens, 1939. [1371]

Zedler, Gottfried, 1860-
   Ein neu aufgefundener, mit der 42 zeiligen Bibeltype gedruckter
26 zeiliger Donat.   Gutenberg Jahrbuch, vol. 9, 1934, p. 72.   [1372]

----   Ein neuer, mit der 42 zeiligen Bibeltype in ihrem Urzustande
gedruckter Donat.   Gutenberg Jahrbuch, vol. 8, 1933, p. 26-30.   [1373]

----   Ueber die Donat und Kalendertype.   Zentralblatt für Bibliothekswesen, vol. 20, 1903, p. 513-526.   [1374]

D.   INDULGENCES

Clemen, Otto Constantin, 1871-
   Alte Einblattdrucke.   Bonn, Marcus & Weber, 1911.   77p.
(Kleine Texte für Vorlesungen und Uebungen, vol. 86)   [1375]
   Eu-De-LBb   Eu-Ge-LLl   Eu-Sz-BcG

Dziatzko, Karl, 1842-1903.
   Die gedruckten Ablassbriefe von 1454 und 1455.   (In his
Beiträge zur Gutenbergfrage.   Berlin, A. Asher & Co., 1889.
p. 56-86)   [1376]
   CSmH   DLC   ICJ   ICN   MB   MH   Eu-De-BP   Eu-De-LBb
   Eu-Fr-PN   Eu-Ge-LSb   Eu-Ne-AVb   Eu-Ne-GK

Ein jüngst aufgefundener Exemplar des Ablassbriefes von 1455 und ein bisher unbekannter Druck der Fust-Schöffer'schen Presse vom Jahre 1461. Serapeum, vol. 24, no. 6, 1863, p. 81-82. [1377]

Laborde, Léon Emmanuel Simon Joseph, marquis de, 1807-1869.
Débuts de l'imprimerie à Mayence et à Bamberg, ou Descriptions des lettres d'indulgence du pape Nicholas V ... imprimées en 1454; par Léon de Laborde. Paris, Techener, 1840. 2 prel. leaves, 31p. plates, facsims. 34 cm. [1378]
DLC ICJ MH NN Eu-De-LBb Eu-Fr-PN Eu-Ge-LB
Eu-Ne-GK

Lichtenberger, Johann Friedrich, 1743-1831.
Indulgentiarum literas Nicolai V, P. M. pro regno Cypri impressas anno 1454 matricumque epocham vindicavit, initia typographica supplevit J.-Frid. Lichtenberger. Argentorati, 1816. ii, 16p. 4to. [1379]
Eu-Fr-PN Eu-Ge-LB

Pertz, Georg Heinrich, 1795-1876.
Ueber die gedruckten Ablassbriefe von 1454 und 1455. Aus den Abhandlungen der Königlichen Akademie der Wissenschaften. Berlin, 1857. 4to. [1380]
DLC ICN MBAt MdBP Eu-Ne-GK

Preisendanz, K. and Paul Schwenke.
Zwei neue Exemplare der Ablassbriefe von 1455. Zentralblatt für Bibliothekswesen, vol. 36, 1919, p. 175-178. [1381]

Ruelens, Charles Louis, 1820-1890.
Une nouvelle lettre d'indulgence. Bulletin du Bibliophile Belge, vol. 12 (2d ser., vol. 3), 1856, p. 24-26. [1382]

Schwenke, Paul, 1853-1921.
Ein neues Datum für den 31 zeiligen Ablassbrief von 1454. Zentralblatt für Bibliothekswesen, vol. 26, 1909, p. 30; vol. 27, 1910, p. 219. [1383]

Sotzmann, Johann Daniel Ferdinand.
Ueber die gedruckten Literae indulgentiarum Nicolai V. Pont. Max. pro regno Cypri von 1454 und 1455. Serapeum, vol. 4, no. 18, 1843, p. 273-285; no. 19, p. 289-299. [1384]

Zedler, Gottfried, 1860-
Die Mainzer Ablassbriefe der Jahre 1454 und 1455, von Prof. Dr. Gottfried Zedler ... Mit 16 Tafeln in Lichtdruck, einer Tafel in Zinkätzung und 14 Textabbildungen darunter zwei Typentafeln. Mainz, Gutenberg-Gesellschaft, 1913. 3 prel. leaves, 116p. illus. 29 cm. and portfolio of XVII plates (incl. 15 facsims.) 37.5 cm. (Added t.-p.: Veröffentlichungen der Gutenberg-Gesell-

schaft, XII-XIII)
Initials; tail-pieces.
The facsimiles reproduce 3 manuscripts of the indulgence, and
6 issues each of the 30 line indulgence and the 31 line in-
dulgence.   [1385]
DLC IC ICJ ICN MB NN Eu-De-BP Eu-Ge-LB
Eu-Ge-LLl Eu-Ge-LSb

E.   42-LINE BIBLE

Ashley, Frederick William, 1863-
The greatest book in the world: the Gutenberg Bible.   School
Life, vol. 17, no. 3, Nov. 1931, p. 43-44.   [1386]

----   The Vollbehr incunabula and the Book of books; address by
Frederick W. Ashley, chief assistant librarian of the Library
of Congress, before the Eleventh national conference on printing education at a session held in the Library of Congress audi-
torium, Washington, District of Columbia, on the twenty-seventh
day of June, anno Domini nineteen hundred and thirty-two.   [Wash-
ington, U. S. Govt. print. off., 1932] [19]p. fronts. (incl.
port.) 33.5x26.5 cm.
Colophon: Designed and printed by George Henry Carter ... public
printer of the United States of America ... to the number of four
hundred and twenty copies bound in parchment, impressed on
handmade paper with Cloister types in two columns of forty-two
lines each and illuminated with handmade initial letters similar
to the Gutenberg Bible in the Library of Congress ... MCMXXXII.
Title within ornamental border; vignette; tailpiece.   [1387]
DLC   NjP

Bernhart, Johann Baptist.
Das Druckjahr der Kosmographie des Ptolomaeus 1462.   Namen
der Buchdrucker des Joannis de Turrecremata Explanatio in
Psalterium Cracis impressa.   Schreiberzüge im Theuerdank 1517;
Kennzeichen und Alter von Gutenberg und Faust in Mainz gedruckter
lateinischen Bibel.   München, 1804-1805.   8vo.
Title from Bigmore & Wyman.   [1388]

----   Untersuchung über die von Gutenberg ... gedruckte lateinische
Bibel.   (In Aretin, J. C. von.   Beyträge zur Geschichte und
Literatur ... München, 1804.   no. 11-12)   [1389]
DLC   PU

Bessmertny, Alexander.
Die Kostbare Gutenbergbibel.   Der Tag, no. 168, July 1925.   [1390]

Bible.   Latin (ca. 1450-1455.   Mainz, Gutenberg (42 lines))
    1913.
    [Biblia latina, Moguntiae, Joh. Gutenberg, ca. 1450-55.
Leipzig, Inselverlag, 1913-14]   2 vols.   facsim.   44x31.5 cm.
    Colophon: Diese Faksimile-Ausgabe des ersten [-zweiten] Bandes
    der zweiundvierzigzeiligen Gutenberg-Bibel erschien im Jahre
    1913 [-14] im Insel-Verlag zu Leipzig.   Die Wiedergabe in
    mehrfarbigem Lichtdruck erfolgte durch die Hofkunstanstalt
    Albert Frisch in Berlin nach dem Pergament-Exemplar der König-
    lichen Bibliothek in Berlin und dem der Ständischen Landes-
    bibliothek in Fulda.   Gedruckt wurden 300 Exemplare / davon Nr.
    1-3 auf Pergament / die übrigen auf van Gelder-bütten.   Durch
    Professor Ansgar Schoppmeyer in Berlin wurden die Exemplare Nr.
    1-3 mit der Hand ausgemalt und bei diesen / wie auch bei 10
    Exemplaren auf Büttenpapier Nr. 4-13 / das Gold mit der Hand
    aufgelegt.   Der Einband ist dem Fuldaer Exemplar nachgebildet.
    Published under the direction of Dr. Paul Schwenke.   [1391]
    DLC   ICN   MB   NjP   Eu-De-BP   Eu-De-LBb   Eu-Ge-LSb
    Eu-Ne-AVb   Eu-Sz-BeG

----   Gutenberg Bible page, 1450-1455, a facsimile.   Baltimore,
N. T. A. Munder [1939]   1 leaf.   41 cm.   [1392]
    ICJ

----   Johannes Gutenbergs zweiundvierzigzeilige Bibel.   Er-
gänzungsband zur Faksimile-Ausgabe, herausgegeben von Paul
Schwenke.   Leipzig, Insel-Verlag, 1923.   viii, 95 numb.
leaves, 54p., 1 leaf.   illus.   48x32.5 cm.
    "Vorwort" signed: Anna Schwenke geb. Schomberg.
    Includes facsimiles (95 numb. leaves) of variants found in
    different copies.
    Contents. - Vorwort. - Inhalt. - Inhaltsverzeichnis der
    Gutenbergbibel. - Verzeichnis der Tafeln des Ergänzungs-
    bandes. - Tafeln 1-95. - Die Gutenbergbibel, von Paul Schwenke
    [mit Verzeichnis der bekannten Exemplare]--Anhang: 1. Das
    Helmaspergersche Notariatsinstrument. 2. Übersicht der de
    Ricci- und der Schwenke-Nummer 17.--Alphabetisches Namen-
    und Sachverzeichnis.   [1393]
    DLC   ICN   MB   NjP   Eu-De-BP   Eu-De-LBb   Eu-Ge-LSb
    Eu-Ne-AVb   Eu-Sz-BeG

Bockwitz, Hans H.
    Die Gutenbergbibel (mit mehrfarbigen Beilagen).   Archiv
für Buchgewerbe und Gebrauchsgraphik, vol. 77, no. 7-8, 1940,
p. 239-240.   [1394]

Bullen, Henry Lewis.
    The Gutenberg Bible.   Inland Printer, vol. 71, 1923,
p. 874.   [1395]

Claudy, C.
Gutenberg Bible for $8,000. Publishers' Weekly, vol. 118,
July 1930, p. 279-280.
Reprint from Scientific American, Apr. 23, 1881.   [1396]

Collins, Ross Alexander, 1880-
... The Vollbehr collection of incunabula; speech of Hon. Ross
A. Collins of Mississippi in the House of representatives Friday,
February 7, 1930. [Washington, U. S. Govt. print. off., 1930]
7p.   29x23 cm.
   Caption title.
   Reprint from the Congressional record, Seventy-first Congress,
   second session.   [1397]
   DLC   IU   MB   MH   NNC

[Delisle, Léopold Victor] 1826-1910.
   Les Bibles de Gutenberg, d'après les recherches de Karl
Dziatzko.   [Paris, Imprimerie nationale, 1894]   13, [1]p.
4 fold. facsim.   30x23 cm.
   Caption title.
   "Extrait du Journal des savants, juillet 1894."
   A review of Dziatzko's Sammlung bibliothekswissenschaft-
   licher Arbeiten (with special reference to Heft 4, "Gutenbergs
   früheste Druckerpraxis")   [1398]
   DLC   MH   Eu-Fr-PN   Eu-Ge-LB

Dziatzko, Karl Franz Otto, 1842-1903.
   Gutenbergs früheste Druckerpraxis.   Auf Grund einer mit Hülfe
der Herren Dr. Phil. W. Bahrdt, Dr. Phil. Karl Meyer und Cand. Phil.
J. Schnorrenberg ausgeführten Vergleichung der 42zeiligen und
36zeiligen Bibel, dargestellt von Karl Dziatzko.   Mit 8 Licht-
drucktafeln.   Berlin, A. Asher & Co., 1890.   ix, [1], 136p.
viii plates. (incl. facsims.)   24 cm.   (Added t.-p.: Sammlung bibliothekswissenschaftlicher Arbeiten; hrsg. von Karl Dziatzko.
IV. Hft.)   [1399]
   DLC   ICN   MB   MH   Eu-Fr-PN   Eu-Ge-LB   Eu-Ge-LSb
   Eu-Ne-CK

----   Das Helmasperger'sche Notariatsinstrument vom 6 November, 1455.
[With a facsimile of the document]   (In his Beiträge zur Gutenberg-
frage.   Berlin, A. Asher & Co., 1889.   p. 1-40)   [1400]
   CSmH   DLC   ICJ   ICN   MB   MH   Eu-De-BP   Eu-De-LBb
   Eu-Fr-PN   Eu-Ge-LSb   Eu-Ne-AVb   Eu-Ne-GK

----   Satz und Druck der 42-zeiligen Bibel.   (In his Beiträge zur
Theorie und Praxis des Buch- und Bibliothekswesens ... Leipzig,
M. Spirgatis, 1894-1904.   vol. 7, 1902, p. 90-108)   [1401]
   ICJ   IU   MB   Eu-Fr-PN   Eu-Ge-LB

Emerson, Edwin, 1869-
    Incunabulum incunabulorum.   The Gutenberg Bible on vellum in
the Vollbehr collection.   An authentic story of the choicest book
of Christendom told anew, by Edwin Emerson.   New York, Tudor press
[^c1928]   3 prel. leaves, 9-54, [1]p. incl. front., illus., ports.,
tab.   22.5 cm.
    "Table of all the known Gutenberg Bibles on vellum still extant":
    p. [8]   [1402]
    DLC   ICN   MB   MH   MWA   NN   ViU

Falk, Franz, 1840-1909.
    Bibelstudien, Bibelhandschriften und Bibeldrucke in Mainz, vom
achten Jahrhundert bis zur Gegenwart; von Franz Falk ... Mainz, F.
Kirchheim, 1901.   vi p., 1 leaf, 336p.   illus., facsim.   23.5 cm.
    Contents.- 1. Buch.   Mittelalter.   Von S. Bonifatius bis Guten-
    berg, 750-1450.--2. Buch.   Neuere Zeit.   Von Gutenberg bis zur
    Gegenwart (1450-1900)   [1403]
    DCU-H   DLC   ICJ   ICN   MB   MH   Eu-De-BP   Eu-Fr-PN
    Eu-Ge-LB

----   Une étude bibliographique sur les impressions mayencaises de la
Bible.   Der Katholik, 1899, p. 334-343, 448-455.   [1404]

    The first book printed with separate types.   American Printer,
vol. 52, 1911, p. 330-331.   [1405]

Fitzgerald, Percy.
    The first printed book and its printers.   Complete bibliography
of Gutenberg and the Mazarin library copy of the Bible 1450-1455
A. D.   Gentleman's Magazine, vol. 286, no. 2018, 1899, p. 132-150.
Same, Book-Lovers' Magazine, vol. 1, 1900, p. 292-300.   [1406]

Fuhrmann, Otto Walter.
    A critical review of H. L. Johnson's "Gutenberg and the Book of
Books."   American Book Collector, vol. 2, 1932, p. 36-40.   [1407]

    Getreuer Abdruck von Typen aus der allererston godruckton Bibel.
(Psalm 119 V. 129-136)   [Stuttgart, 1840]
    Printed on an antique press, on St. John's day, in the Market
    place at Stuttgart, as a memorial of the fourth centenary of
    printing.
    Title from Mohr, Jubelfeste   [1408]

    Getreuer Probedruck von der Guttenberg'schen 42zeiligen Bibel.
[Hamburg, 1840]   1 leaf.   4to.
    Title from Mohr, Jubelfeste.   [1409]

    Gutenberg and his Bible.   A reproduction of a page of the
famous Gutenberg Bible.   American Printer, vol. 80, no. 6, 1925,
p. 50.   [1410]

The Gutenberg Bible.   Inland Printer, vol. 8, Apr. 1891,
p. 660.   [1411]

The Gutenberg Bible.   Publishers' Weekly, vol. 52, Aug. 1897,
p. 236-238.   [1412]

Hinck, H.
    Eine Gutenberg-Bibel in der Washingtoner Kongress-Bibliothek.
Die Einkehr, vol. 11, 1930, p. 157-158.   [1413]

Johnson, Henry Lewis, 1867-
    Gutenberg and the Book of books, with bibliographical notes,
reproductions of specimen pages and a listing of known copies, by
Henry Lewis Johnson.   New York, W. E. Rudge, 1932.   [24]p.   col.
plate, col. facsims.   41.5 cm.
    The plate and each of the facsimiles accompanied by guard sheets
    with descriptive letterpress.
    "Seven hundred and fifty copies for sale in the United States
    and in Great Britain."   [1414]
    DLC   MB   MiU   NjP   ViU   Eu-De-BP

Keogh, Andrew.
    The Gutenberg Bible as a typographical monument.   Yale Univer-
sity Gazette, vol. 1, 1926, p. 1-6.   [1415]

Klug, Otto.
    Gutenbergs unsterbliche Kunst, mit prächtiger Wiedergabe einer
Seite der 42zeiligen Bibel.   Schweizer Graphische Mitteilungen
(St. Gallen), Oct. 1940.   Same, Schweizer Reklame (Zürich),
Oct. 1940.   [1416]

Lenhart, J. M.
    The Gutenberg Bibles.   American Catholic Quarterly Review,
vol. 39, no. 156, Oct. 1914, p. 593-617.   [1417]

Liedtke, A.
    Biblja Gutenberga w Pelpinie.   Torun, 1936.   11p.   2 plates.
4to.   (Wydawnictwo Tow.   Bibljufilow im. Lelewela w. Toruniu,
6)   [1418]
    CtY   NN

Lüthi-Tschanz, Karl Jakob.
    Um die 42 zeilige Bibel Gutenbergs.   Schweizerisches Guten-
bergmuseum, vol. 18, no. 3, 1932, p. 145-148.   [1419]

Martineau, Russell, 1831-1898.
    Notes on the Latin Bible of forty-two lines, 1455.   Biblio-
graphica, vol. 2, 1896, p. 333-342.   [1420]

Maugerard, Dom. Jean Baptiste.
   Mémoire lu à la séance du 24 soût 1789, de la Société royale,
sur la découverte d'un exemplaire de la Bible connue sous le nom
de Guttemberg, accompagnée des renseignements qui prouvent que
l'impression de cette Bible est antérieure à celle du Psautier
de 1457. Metz, 1789. 7p. 16mo.   [1421]
   Eu-Fr-PN

Müller, H. G.
   Die ersten Besitzer der Gottinger 42 zeiligen Gutenberg-Bibel.
Zeitschrift des Historischen Vereins für Niedersachsen, 1910,
p. 135-143.   [1422]

Muller, Julius W.
   Gutenberg Bibles. A list of the 45 known copies of the first
book ever printed. Publishers' Weekly, vol. 111, no. 8, 1927,
p. 691-694.   [1423]

Newton, A. Edward.
   The greatest book in the world. (In his The greatest book in
the world and other papers ... Boston, Little & Brown, 1925.
p. 3-53)   [1424]
   DLC   MB   MWA   NN   ViU   Eu-De-BP

---- A noble fragment, being a leaf of the Gutenberg Bible
1450-1455. A bibliographical essay. New York, 1921.   [1425]

   Observations on the Mentz Bible. London, 1811. 8vo.
   Title from Bigmore & Wyman.   [1426]

Price, Iram.
   A Gutenberg Bible dismembered. Library Journal, vol. 49,
1924, p. 142.   [1427]

Proctor, Robert George Collier, 1868-1903.
   The Gutenberg Bible. Library, 2d ser., vol, 2, 1901, p. 60-66. [1428]

---- ---- (In Bibliographical Essays. London, Chiswick press,
1905.   p. 45-53)   [1429]

Raschl, Thiemo.
   Zum Verkaufe der St. Pauler Gutenberg-Bibel, von Fr. Thiemo
Raschl, O. S. B. Gutenberg Jahrbuch, vol. 6, 1931, p. 341-343. [1430]

Reichner, Herbert, 1899-
   Die Gutenberg-Bibel der Sammlung Vollbehr; Schicksale des kost-
barsten Buches, von Herbert Reichner ... Wien [Jahoda & Siegel Buch-
druckerei] 1927. 1 prel. leaf, [5]-27p., 1 leaf. plate, fold.
facsim. 19.5 cm.   [1431]

"Verzeichnis der erhaltenen Exemplare der 42-zeiligen Bibel":
p. [19]-21. "Verzeichnis der wichtigsten Literatur über die
42-zeilige Bibel, im besonderen über des Exemplar der Sammlung Dr. Vollbehr": p. [22]-27.
    DLC ICN MB MWA NN NjP. Eu-De-BP Eu-Ne-AVb   [1432]

Ricci, Seymour de, 1881-
... The Gutenberg Bible; the first printed book, the Melk copy,
described by Seymour de Ricci. To be sold by order of the owner,
Edward Goldston, London, England, Monday evening, February fifteenth.
... New York, The Anderson galleries, 1926. 3 prel. leaves, 3, [1]p.,
incl. facsim. 25.5 cm.
    This copy is known as the Melk Bible because of its possession
    by the Benedictine monastery in Melk, Austria.   [1433]
    DLC ICJ MiU-C RPJCB

Ruppel, Aloys Leonhard, 1882-
    Eine Gutenberg-Bibel wieder in Mainz. Zeitschrift für Deutsch-
lands Buchdrucker, vol. 38, no. 35, 1926, p. 281-282.   [1434]

Schwenke, Paul, 1853-1921.
    Johannes Gutenbergs zweiundvierzigzeilige Bibel; Ergänzungsband
zur Faksimile-Ausgabe. Herausgegeben von Paul Schwenke. Im Insel-
Verlag zu Leipzig, 1923. viii, 95 numb. leaves, 54p., 1 leaf.
48 cm.   [1435]
    NN Eu-Sz-BeG

---- Untersuchungen zur Geschichte des ersten Buchdrucks, von Dr.
Paul Schwenke ... [Burg b. M., Druck von A. Hopfer, 1900] ix, 90p.
illus., double plate, facsims., tables. 28 cm.
    Half-title.
    Cover-title: Festschrift zur Gutenbergfeier, herausgegeben von
    der Koeniglichen Bibliothek zu Berlin. Am 24. Juni 1900.
    Contents: Vorbemerkung.-- Die 42 zeilige Bibel.-- Die 36
    zeilige Bibel.   [1436]
    DLC ICJ MB MH NN Eu-De-BP Eu-Ne-AVb Eu-Ne-GK
    Eu-Sz-BeG

Stevens, Henry, 1819-1886.
    The Bibles in the Caxton exhibition MDCCCLXXVII; or, A biblio-
graphical description of nearly one thousand representative Bibles
in various languages, chronologically arranged from the first Bible
printed by Gutenberg in 1450-1456 to the last Bible printed at the
Oxford university press the 30th June 1877 ... Special ed. rev. and
carefully cor., with additions ... by Henry Stevens ... London, H.
Stevens; New York, Scribner, Welford & Armstrong, 1878. 4 prel.
leaves, 151, [1]p. 24 cm.   [1437]
    DLC ICJ MB MH MWA MdBP MiU-C NN NeWfC NjP
    RPJCB Eu-Ge-LB

Stone, Edward Lee, 1864-1938.
    The great Gutenberg Bible. [Roanoke, Va., Press of the Stone
printing and manufacturing company, 1930]   cover-title, [19]p.
incl. plates, ports., facsims.   22 cm.
    Half-title: The St. Paul copy of the Gutenberg Bible.
    "Twenty-five hundred and twenty-five copies ... printed."
    Contains Foreword by Ross A. Collins, Speech by Pater Dr. Herman
    Peissl on handing over the Bible to Dr. Otto H. F. Vollbehr, and
    Reply by Dr. Vollbehr.
    Accompanied by descriptive leaflet signed: Edward L. Stone.   [1438]
    DLC   ICN

Stöwesand, Rudolf, 1892-
... Der heutige Bestand der Welt an Gutenbergbibeln, mit besonderer
Berücksichtigung derer in den alten Einbänden. Wolfenbüttel,
Heckners Verlag, 1929. 28p. illus. 24.5 cm. (Archiv für
Schreib- und Buchwesen. Sonderheft Nr. 2)   [1439]
    NN   NNC

Stübel, Bruno.
    Über ein neu aufgefundenes Exemplar der 42 zeiligen Gutenberg-
Fust'schen Bibel. Serapeum, vol. 31, no. 16, 1870, p. 241-248.   [1440]

Tinker, C. B.
    The significance to Yale of the gift of the Gutenberg Bible.
Yale University Gazette, vol. 1, 1926, p. 7-13.   [1441]

U. S. Congress. Senate. Committee on the Library.
... Purchase of Vollbehr collection of incunabula ... Report. [To
accompany H. R. 12696] ... [Washington, U. S. Govt. print. off.,
1930]   6p.   23 cm. (71st Cong., 2d sess. Senate. Rept. 965)
    Calendar no. 998.
    Submitted by Mr. Fess. Ordered printed June 18, 1930.   [1442]
    DLC

----   Vollbehr collection of incunabula ... Report. [To accompany
H. R. 12696] ... [Washington, U. S. Govt. print. off., 1930]   3p.
24 cm. (71st Cong., 2d sess. House. Rept. 1769)
    Submitted by Mr. Luce. Committee to the Committee of the
    whole House on the state of the Union and ordered printed,
    June 4, 1930.   [1443]
    DLC

Valentine, U.
    Gutenberg and his Book of books. International Studio, vol.
91, Sept. 1928, p. 53-60.   [1444]

    The Vollbehr proffer and the Gutenberg Bible. Library
Journal, vol. 55, 1930, p. 226.   [1445]

Von den zwei erstgedruckten Bibeln.   Börsenblatt für den
Deutschen Buchhandel, vol. 67, no. 185, 1900, p. 5952-5954.   (1446)

Zedler, Gottfried, 1860-
   Das Helmaspergersche Notariatsinstrument und die 42 zeilige
Bibel.   Zentralblatt für Bibliothekswesen, vol. 24, 1907, p. 193-
207.   [1447]

----   Die sogenannte Gutenbergbibel sowie die mit der 42zeiligen
Bibeltype ausgeführten kleineren Drucke, von Gottfried Zedler.
Mit 9 Abbildungen im Text und 52 Tafeln.   Mainz, 1929.   Verlag
der Gutenberg-Gesellschaft.   3 prel. leaves, xi-xvi, 125p.
illus., plates, facsims.   29 cm.   (Veröffentlichungen der
Gutenberg-Gesellschaft.   XX)   (1448)
      ICN   MB   MH   Eu-De-BP

   Zu Ehren unseres Altmeisters Johannes Gutenberg; Gutenbergs
Bibel zu 42 Zeilen.   Gutenberg-Jugend (Winterthur and Luzern),
no. 617, June-July 1940.   (1449)

F.   36-LINE BIBLE

   Many of the articles on the 42-line Bible discuss this Bible
also. See also under the heading: 42-line Bible.   (1450)

Freys, Ernst.
   Zum Rubrikenverzeichnis der 36 zeiligen Bibel.   Zentralblatt
für Bibliothekswesen, vol. 35, 1918, p. 167-170.   (1451)

Geldner, Ferdinand.
   Ein unbeachteter Einblattdruck der Type der sechsunddreissig-
zeilen Bibel der Universitätsbibliothek München.   Zentralblatt
für Bibliothekswesen, vol. 57, no. 5-6, May-June 1940, p. 278-292.
   A broadside in the 36-line Bible type, known for 25 years but
not recorded in all the Gutenberg literature.   (1452)

Helbig, Henri Antoine, 1813-
   Le Bible de 36 lignes; dissertation bibliographique.   Bulletin
du Bibliophile Belge, 3d ser., vol. 13, 1878, p. 223-233.   (1453)

----   Une découverte pour l'histoire de l'imprimerie. Les plus
anciens caractères de Gutenberg et ce qui en est advenu. - Albert
Pfister imprimeur à Bamberg. - La Bible de 36 lignes. Par Henri
Helbig.   Bruxelles, F. Heussner, libraire ancienne et moderne,
Place Sainte-Gudule, 1855.   16p.   22.5 cm.   (1454)

"Tiré à 50 exemplaires."
Reprint from Bulletin du Bibliophile Belge, vol. 11 (2d ser.,
vol. 2), 1855, p. 18-32.
Bibliography: p. 12-16.   [1455]
ICN   NNC   Eu-Ge-LSb

Schelhorn, Johann Georg, 1694-1773.
   De antiquissima latinor. Bibliorum editione ceu primo artis
typographicae foetu et rariorum librorum phoenice ... Jo. Georgii
Schelhornii diatribe. Ulmae, apud J. F. Gaum, 1760.   36p.
23x18 cm.   [1456]
   CtY   DLC   NN   Eu-De-LBb   Eu-Ge-LB

Zedler, Gottfried, 1860-
   Die Bamberger Pfisterdrucke und die 36 zeilige Bibel, von Prof.
Dr. Gottfried Zedler ... Mit 22 Tafeln in Lichtdruck, einer Tafel in
Autotypiedruck, einer Typentafel in Text und 9 weiteren Abbildungen.
Mainz, Gutenberg-Gesellschaft, 1911.   3 prel. leaves, 113p.   illus.,
xxiii plates (incl. 22 facsims.)   28.5 cm.   (Added t.-p.: Veröffent-
lichungen der Gutenberg-Gesellschaft X, XI)
   Holds that the 36 line Bible could not have been printed by
   Pfister.   [1457]
   DLC   IC   ICJ   ICN   MB   Eu-Ge-LB

G.   MISSALE SPECIALE

Collijn, Isak Gustaf Alfred, 1875-
   Ein neuaufgefundenes Exemplar des L. Rosenthalschen Missale
speciale.   Gutenberg Jahrbuch, vol. 1, 1926, p. 32-46.   [1458]

----   Ett nyfunnet exemplar av det L. Rosenthalska Missale
speciale.   Nordisk Tidskrift för Bok och Biblioteksväsen, vol.
12, 1925, p. 189-204.
   Also reprint.   [1459]

Enschedé, Charles, 1855-1919.
   Gutenbergs eerste drukwerk volgens Otto Hupp en De oudste
Gutenbergtype volgens Gottfried Zedler.   Amsterdam, Roever,
Krober & Bakels, 1902.   8vo.
   Reprint from Nieuwsblad voor den Boekhandel, 1902.   [1460]
   Eu-Ge-LSb   Eu-Ne-AVb   Eu-Ne-GK

----   Le premier ouvrage imprimé de Gutenberg, d'après Otto Hupp,
par Ch. Enschedé ... Besançon, Jacquin, 1903.   27p.   8vo.
   Reprint from Bibliographe Moderne, vol. 7, 1903.   [1461]
   Eu-Fr-PN

Falk, Franz," 1840-1909.
 Wieder ein Missale speciale. Zentralblatt für Bibliothekswesen, vol. 18, 1901, p. 214-217.
 [1462]

Haebler, Konrad, 1857-
 Das Missale speciale Constantiense. Gutenberg Jahrbuch, vol.
5, 1930, p. 67-72.
 [1463]

Hölscher, G.
 Ein Buch Gutenbergs. Börsenblatt für den Deutschen Buchhandel,
vol. 66, no. 1, Jan. 1899, p. 7-9.
 [1464]

Hupp, Otto, 1859-
 Das Gutenbergische Missale. Zentralblatt für Bibliothekswesen,
vol. 20, 1903, p. 182-187.
 [1465]

———— Gutenbergs erste Druck. Ein weiterer Beitrag zur Geschichte
der ältesten Druckwerke; von Otto Hupp. 1902. München-Regensburg,
G. J. Manz [1902] cover-title, 98p. incl. illus., plate, facsim.,
tab. 31.5x23 cm.
 Supplementary to his first study, "Ein Missale speciale; Vorläufer des Psalteriums von 1457. Beitrag z. Geschichte d.
 ältesten Druckwerke, 1898."
 DLC ICJ ICN MB MH NN Eu-Fr-PN Eu-Ge-LB   [1466]
 Eu-Ge-LSb Eu-Ne-GK

———— Ein Missale speciale, Vorläufer des Psalteriums von 1457.
Beitrag zur Geschichte der ältesten Druckwerke, von Otto Hupp.
1898. München-Regensburg, Nationale Verlagsanstalt, Buch- und
Kunstdruckerei [1898] cover-title, 30p. incl. facsim. 31x23 cm. [1467]
 DLC ICJ ICN MB MH Eu-Fr-PN Eu-Ge-LB Eu-Ge-LSb
 Eu-Ne-AVb

———— Le premier ouvrage imprimé de Gutenberg. Bibliographe
Moderne, vol. 7, 1903, p. 118-142.
 Footnote: A paru en hollandais dans la Nieuwsblad v. d.
 Boekhandel, 1902, no. 61, 62, 63.
 [1468]

———— Zum Streit um das Missale speciale Constantiense. Ein
dritter Beitrag zur Geschichte der ältesten Druckwerke von Otto
Hupp. 1917. Verlag von J. E. Ed. Heitz, Heitz & Mündel, Strassburg im Els. Gedruckt von Dr. C. Wolf & Sohn, München. 1 prel.
leaf, 141, [1]p. illus., facsims. 30 cm.
 CSmH MH NN Eu-Do-BP Eu-Ge-LB   [1469]

Kunz, E. F.
 The Missale speciale once more. Literary Collector, vol. 6,
no. 1, May 1903, p. 10-13.
 [1470]

Misset, Eugène, 1850–
  Le premier livre imprimé connu. Un missel spécial de Constance,
oeuvre de Gutenberg avant 1450; étude liturgique et critique par E.
Misset ... Paris, H. Champion, 1899.   41p. incl. 2 facsims.   24 cm.
  "Extrait du Bibliographe moderne, 1899, n° 4."   [1471]
  DLC   ICN   MB   NN   Eu-Ge-LB   Eu-Ge-LSb

Olschki, Leo Samuel, 1861–
  Un messale speciale di Constanza.   Bibliofilia, vol. 1, 1899,
p. 221-223.   [1472]

Paltsits, Victor Hugo.
  Missale speciale: being a further examination of the pretentions
urged in behalf of this early specimen of typography.   New York,
1900.   11p., 1 leaf.   21 cm.
  50 copies reprinted from the Publishers' Weekly, Mar. 31, 1900.   [1473]
  DLC   ICJ   MB   NNUT   Eu-Ge-LB

––––   The newly-found edition of the Missale speciale; an examination
of the pretensions urged in behalf of this new addition to our typographic incunabula.   By Victor H. Paltsits ... [New York, 1899]   7p.
13 cm.
  25 copies reprinted from the Publishers' Weekly, May 20, 1899.   [1474]
  DLC   MB   Eu-Ge-LB

Rivers, John.
  The Gutenberg Missal controversy.   Library World, vol. 6, 1904,
p. 173-175.   [1475]

Rosenthals, L.
  Das Missale speciale.   Börsenblatt für den Deutschen Buchhandel,
vol. 66, no. 194, 1899, p. 5978-5981.   [1476]

Schmidt, Adolf, 1857–
  Das Missale speciale L. Rosenthals.   Zentralblatt für Bibliothekswesen, vol. 16, 1899, p. 368-372.   [1477]

Stein, [Frederic Alexandre] Henri, 1862–
  Une production inconnue de l'atelier de Gutenberg, Missale
speciale.   Paris, 1899.   8vo.
  Reprint from Bibliographe Moderne, vol. 2, no. 11, 1898,
  p. 297-306.   [1478]
  Eu-De-LBb

––––   Ein unbekanntes Erzeugnis aus Meister Gutenberg's Offizin.
Börsenblatt für den Deutschen Buchhandel, vol. 66, Jan. 1899,
p. 498-501.   [1479]

Weale, William Henry James, 1832-1917.
The newly discovered Missale speciale. Library, 2d ser., vol.
1, 1900, p. 62-67. [1480]

Zedler, Gottfried, 1860-
Das Rosenthalsche Missale speciale. Zentralblatt für Bibliothekswesen, vol. 20, 1903, p. 187-191. [1481]

---- Das vermeintlich Gutenbergsche Missale. Zentralblatt für
Bibliothekswesen, vol. 20, 1903, p. 32-55. [1482]

H. PSALTER OF 1457

Borovsky, F. A.
Die dritte Ausgegeben des Psalteriums vom Jahre 1457. Zeitschrift für Bücherfreunde, vol. 3, no. 9, 1899, p. 343-344. [1483]

Boze, C. G. de.
Notice du premier livre imprimé portant une date certaine:
Psalmorum Codex. Moguntiae: 1457. (In Histoire de l'Académie
royale des inscriptions et belles lettres ... depuis l'année
MDCCXXXVIII jusques et compris l'année MDCCXL. Tome quatorzième.
A Paris, de l'Imprimerie royale, 1743. p. 254-266) [1484]

Dibdin, Thomas Frognall.
Account of the first printed psalters at Mentz in the years
1457, 1459 and 1490. London, 1807. 8vo.
Title from Bullen, George, ed. Caxton celebration catalogue ...
1877. [1485]

Eichler, Ferdinand.
Kleine Beiträge zur Geschichte der Buchdruckerkunst. Gutenberg
Jahrbuch, vol. 10, 1935, p. 65-69. [1486]

Falk, Franz, 1840-1909.
Die Mainzer Psalterien von 1457, 1459, 1490, 1502, 1515 und 1516
nach ihrer historisch-liturgischen Seite. (In Festschrift zum
fünfhundertjährigen Geburtstage von Johann Gutenberg, herausgegeben
von Otto Hartwig. Leipzig, O. Harrassowitz, 1900. p. 320-324) [1487]
    CSmH   DLC   ICJ   MH   NjP   Eu-De-BP   Eu-Ne-AVb   Eu-Ne-GK

McMurtrie, Douglas Crawford, 1888-
The Mainz Psalter of 1457 ... by Douglas C. McMurtrie. Chicago,
Priv. print., 1931. 6p. 23 cm.
"Two hundred copies reprinted from the Rotarian for February,
1931." [1488]
    DLC   MBrZ   Eu-Sz-BeG

Martineau, Russell, 1831-1898.
The Mainz Psalter of 1457. Bibliographica, vol. 1, 1895,
p. 308-323.
Detailed collations of nine known copies for variant readings,
press corrections, etc. With a double plate of the first page
of the Psalter, in colors. [1489]

Moser.
Das Fust-Schöffersche Psalterium latinum von 1457, erworben im
Jahre 1843 für die Königliche Öffentliche Bibliothek in Stuttgart.
Serapeum, vol. 5, no. 9, 1844, p. 129-137; no. 10, p. 145-156;
no. 11, p. 161-171; no. 12, p. 177-182. [1490]

Theele, Joseph, 1889-
Die Fuldaer Psalterfragmente von 1457. Fundbericht. Gutenberg Jahrbuch, vol. 11, 1936, p. 57-58. [1491]

Tronnier, Adolph, 1875-
... Von Gutenberg, dem Mainzer Psalter und einem Schelmenstreich.
Mainz, Gutenberg-Gesellschaft, 1936. 2 prel. leaves, 7-22p.,
1 leaf. illus. (incl. port., facsims.) 24.5 cm. (Kleiner
Druck der Gutenberg-Gesellschaft. 24) [1492]
DLC ICN MB Eu-De-MzG Eu-Ne-AVb

Zedler, Gottfried, 1860-
Die Technik und Urheberschaft der Psalterinitialen. Gutenberg
Jahrbuch, vol. 12, 1937, p. 30-34. [1493]

---- Die Typen des Fust-Schöfferschen Psalteriums. Gutenberg
Jahrbuch, vol. 13, 1938, p. 69-77. [1494]

Zobeltitz, Fedor von.
Ein Vorläufer des Psalteriums von 1457. Zeitschrift für Bucher-
freunde, vol. 2, 1898-1899, p. 417-419. [1495]

I. CANON MISSAE OF 1458

Collijn, Isak Gustaf Alfred, 1875-
Ein neugefundenes Blatt des Canon Missae 1458. Gutenberg Jahrbuch, vol. 10, 1935, p. 70-73. [1496]

---- Ett nyfunnet blad av Canon Missae 1458. Nordisk Tidskrift
för Bok och Biblioteksväsen, vol. 21, 1934, p. 3-8.
Also reprint. [1497]

Falk, Franz, 1840-1909.
    Der Canon Missae vom Jahre 1458 in liturgischer Beziehung.
(In Der Canon Missae vom Jahre 1458 der Bibliotheca bodleiana zu
Oxford ... Mainz, Gutenberg-Gesellschaft, 1904. Veröffentlichungen
der Gutenberg-Gesellschaft III)   [1498]
    DLC   ICJ   ICN   Eu-Fr-PN   Eu-Ge-LSb

Fitzgerald, Edward C.
    A note on the Canon Missae of 1458.   English Historical Review,
vol. 44, 1921, p. 21-94.   [1499]

Holter, Kurt.
    Ein Reindruck des Canon Missae von 1458 in der Nationalbibliothek
in Wien.   Gutenberg Jahrbuch, vol. 13, 1938, p. 78-82.   [1500]

J.   LATER PSALTERS AND MISSALES

Baer, Joseph.
    Das Psalterium von 1459 (gedruckt zu Mainz von Johann Fust und
Peter Schoeffer).   Frankfurt am Main, Joseph Baer [1905]   4to.
    Title from Bibliographie des Bibliotheks und Buchwesens, 1905. [1501]

Becker, C.
    Neu aufgefundene Bruckstücke eines Exemplars des Psalteriums
von 1467.   Serapeum, vol. 7, 1846, p. 61-62.   [1502]

Beyer, Fritz.
    Die sogenannten nicht datierten und die 1502 datierten Schöffer-
Psalterien und ihre Druckeigentümlichkeiten.   Gutenberg Jahrbuch,
vol. 13, 1938, p. 124-134.   [1503]

Falk, Franz, 1840-1909.
    Die Drucke des Missale Moguntinum.   Zentralblatt für Biblio-
thekswesen, vol. 2, 1885, p. 309; vol. 3, 1886, p. 305-319.
    Also reprint.   [1504]

----   Die Mainzer Psalterien von 1457, 1459, 1490, 1502, 1515 und
1516 nach ihrer historisch-liturgischen Seite.   (In Festschrift
zum fünfhundertjährigen Geburtstage von Johann Gutenberg, herausgegeben von Otto Hartwig.   Leipzig, O. Harrassowitz, 1900.
p. 320-324)   [1505]
    CSmH   DLC   ICJ   MH   NjP   Eu-De-BP   Eu-Ne-AVb   Eu-Ne-GK

----   Missale Moguntinum, sine loco, 1482.   Zentralblatt für
Bibliothekswesen, vol. 1, 1884, p. 56-60.   [1506]

Falk, Franz, 1840-1909.
Der Tractatus de sacrificio Missae, Moguntiae. Zentralblatt
für Bibliothekswesen, vol. 2, 1885, p. 21-23.
Also reprint. [1507]

Haebler, Konrad, 1857-
Ein Psalterium aus der Offizin des Peter Schöffer. Zentralblatt für Bibliothekswesen, vol. 24, 1907, p. 155-163. [1508]

Pollard, Alfred William, 1859-
The great Latin psalter of Fust and Schoeffer, 1459. Book-
Lovers' Magazine, vol. 6, part 1, 1905-1907, p. 24-26. [1509]

Roberts, W.
The Latin psalter of 1459. Athenaeum, vol. 2, 1904, p. 732-
733. [1510]

Schwenke, Paul, 1853-1923.
Ein nationales Denkmal in Gefahr. Psalterium von 1459.
Berlin, 1906.
Title from Bibliographie des Bibliotheks und Buchwesens, 1906. [1511]

Starkenstein, Emil.
Ein neuentdecktes Blatt des Psalters von 1459. Gutenberg Jahrbuch, vol. 14, 1939, p. 119-120. [1512]

Stollreither, Eugen.
Ein unbekanntes Blatt des Psalters von 1459 gefunden in der
Universitätsbibliothek Erlangen. Gutenberg Jahrbuch, vol. 11,
1936, p. 59-60. [1513]

Tronnier, Adolph, 1875-
Die Missaldrucke Peter Schöffers und seines Sohnes Johann.
Mainz, Gutenberg-Gesellschaft, 1908. cover-title, 3 prel. leaves,
235p. illus., xiv facsims. (part col., part fold.) 29x22 cm.
(Veröffentlichungen der Gutenberg-Gesellschaft, no. 5-7, p. 28-
220) [1514]
    DLC   IC   ICN   MB   MH   NN   Eu-De-BP   Eu-De-MzG   Eu-Ge-LB
    Eu-Ge-LSb

Wallau, Heinrich Wilhelm.
Die zweifarbigen Initialen der Psalterdrucke von Johann Fust
und Peter Schöffer. (In Festschrift zum fünfhundertjährigen
Geburtstage von Johann Gutenberg, herausgegeben von Otto Hartwig.
Leipzig, O. Harrassowitz, 1900. p. 325-378. Mainz ed., p. 261-
304) [1515]
    CSmH   DLC   ICJ   MH   NjP   Eu-De-BP   Eu-Ne-AVb   Eu-Ne-GK

Wallensis, Tho.
   Expositiones super Psalterium.   1481.   Folio.
   Title from Bullen, George, ed.   Caxton celebration catalogue.
   1877.   [1516]

Zedler, Gottfried, 1860-
   Die 42zeilige Bibeltype in Schöfferschen Missale Moguntinum
von 1493.   Mainz, Gutenberg-Gesellschaft, 1908.   cover-title,
3 prel. leaves, 275p.   illus., xiv facsims. (part col., part fold.)
29x22 cm.   (Veröffentlichungen der Gutenberg-Gesellschaft no. 6,
p. 10-27)   [1517]
      DLC   IC   ICN   MB   MH   NN   Eu-De-BP   Eu-De-MzG   Eu-Ge-LB
      Eu-Ge-LSb

K.   THE CATHOLICON

Bömer, Alois, 1868-
   Die Schlussschrift des Mainzer Catholicon-Drucks von 1460.
(In Abb, Gustav, ed.   Von Büchern und Bibliotheken.   Berlin,
Struppe & Winckler, 1928.   p. 51-55)   [1518]
      DLC   ICJ   NjP   OCU   Eu-De-BP   Eu-Ge-LB

Falk, Franz, 1840-1909.
   Der muthmassliche Verfasser der Schlussschrift des Catholicon
von 1460.   Zentralblatt für Bibliothekswesen, vol. 5, 1888, p. 306-
312.   [1519]

   Hat Gutenberg in der Unterschrift seines Catholicons von 1460
Mainz als Erfindungsort der Buchdruckerkunst bezeichnet?   Neue
Mitthcilungen aus dem Gebiet Historisch-Antiquarischer Forschungen,
vol. 4, no. 1, 1838, p. 169.
   Signed: W.   [1520]

Hiersemann, Karl W.
   Catholicon 1460.   Der zweite monumentale Drucke aus Johann
Gutenbergs Presse.   Leipzig [1927?]   Folio.
   Text in English and German.   [1521]
      MH   MnU

Hopkins, Frederick M.
   The Mainz Catholicon of 1460.   Publishers' Weekly, vol. 130,
Nov. 1936, p. 2106-2108.   [1522]

Längin, Theodor.
   Der Catholiconhymnus Gutenbergs.   Zentralblatt für Bibliothekswesen, vol. 55, 1938, p. 205-211.   [1523]

Moon, George Washington, 1823-1909.
   The oldest type-printed book in existence: a disquisition on
the relative antiquity of the Pfister and Mazarin Bibles and the
"65-line A" Catholicon: prefaced by a brief history of the in-
vention of printing: by George Washington Moon.   London, Priv.
print. [Chiswick press] 1901.   2 prel. leaves, 47p.   5 facsims.
on ii plates (1 fold.)   27.5x22 cm.
   Half-title: The "65-line A" Catholicon.
   "Only 241 copies were printed."
   "Works referred to": p. 45-47.   [1524]
   DLC   ICJ   IaU   MB   MH   MiU   NN   Eu-Fr-PN   Eu-Ge-LB
   Eu-Ge-LSb   Eu-Ne-GK

Ruppel, Aloys Leonhard, 1882-
   Probleme um das Mainzer Catholicon von 1460.   Gutenberg Jahrbuch, vol. 13, 1938, p. 83-96.   [1525]

Stillwell, Margaret Bingham, 1887-
   Gutenberg and the Catholicon of 1460; a bibliographical essay
by Margaret Bingham Stillwell, together with an original leaf of
the Catholicon.   New York, E. B. Hackett, The Brick row book shop,
inc., 1936.   5 prel. leaves, 27, [1]p.   43.5 cm.   [1526]
   CtY   DLC   MB   MH

Zedler, Gottfried, 1860-
   Das Mainzer Catholicon, von Dr. Gottfried Zedler ... Mit 11 Tafeln
in Lichtdruck, einer Typentafel im Text und 22 weiteren Textabbildungen.   Mainz, Gutenberg-Gesellschaft, 1905.   3 prel. leaves,
75p.   illus., xi plates (facsim.)   29x22 cm.   (Added t.-p.:
Veröffentlichungen der Gutenberg-Gesellschaft.   IV)   [1527]
   DLC   ICJ   ICN   MB   NN   Eu-Ge-LSb

----   Die Schlussschrift des Catholicon.   Zeitschrift für Bücherfreunde, vol. 40, 1936, p. 47-50.
   Additional notes by K. F. Bauer: p. 49-50.   [1528]

L.   OTHER EARLY PRINTING

Bechstein, L.
   Fust und Schöffer.   Sechs noch unbekannte Producte der Presse
Fusts und Schöffers von 1461.   Serapeum, vol. 1, 1840, p. 305-
309, 367-368; vol. 2, 1841, p. 46-47.
   Also reprint.   [1529]

Beyssac, Gabriel M.
   Notes sur la Bible de Mayence de 1462.   [Chartres, Durand, 1923]
19p.   21 cm.

Reprint from Bulletin du Bibliophile, n.s., vol. 2, 1923,
p. 447-465.   [1530]
NN   Eu-Ce-LB

Bohatta, Hanns, 1864-
  Die Schöffer'schen Canones für Mainz, Breslau und Krakau.
Wien, Gilhofer & Ranschburg, 1933.   8p.   8vo.   [1531]
  Eu-De-BP   Eu-De-WN   Eu-Ge-LB   Eu-Ge-LSb

Falk, Franz, 1840-1909.
  Die Ausgaben des directorium missae der Mainzer Kirche.
Zentralblatt für Bibliothekswesen, vol. 5, 1888, p. 206-210.
  Also reprint.   [1532]

----   Ein kaum bekannter Mainzer Druck der Summa de articulis
fedei des Aquinaten.   Zentralblatt für Bibliothekswesen, vol.
2, 1885, p. 328-330.   [1533]

----   Die Mainzer Brevier ausgaben.   Leipzig, 1887.   8vo.
  Eu-Ge-LSb   [1534]

----   Ein neu aufgetauchter Fust-Schöfferschen Druck.   Germania,
Nov. 5, 1896, literary supplement.   [1535]

----   Der P. Schöfferdruck "Ingang der Himmel."   Zentralblatt
für Bibliothekswesen, vol. 19, 1902, p. 581-583.   [1536]

----   Die Schuler Gutenberg's, Fust's und Schoeffer's.   Zentralblatt
für Bibliothekswesen, vol. 4, 1887, p. 216.   [1537]

Haapanen, Toivo.
  Missale Hafniense vetus.   Ett hittills okändt danskt missale
tryckt i Mainz af Peter Schöffer omkring är 1484.   Nordisk
Tidskrift för Bok och Bibliotheksväsen, vol. 9, 1922, p. 29-37.   [1538]

Heidenheimer, Heinrich, 1856-
  Das Begleitgedicht zum Justiniani Institutiones Druck von
1468.   (In Gutenberg Festschrift, zur Feier des 25jaehrigen
Bestehens des Gutenberg-Museums in Mainz 1925.   Hrsg. von A.
Ruppel.   Mainz, Verlag der Gutenberg-Gesellschaft [1925]   p. 108-
117)   [1539]
    DLC   ICN   MB   MH   NN   NNC   Eu-De-BP   Eu-Ne-AVb   Eu-Sz-BeG

----   Johannes Gutenberg in den Schöfferschen Drucken des deutschen
Livius.   Zeitschrift für Bücherfreunde, vol. 2, no. 8-9, 1898-
1899, p. 368-371.   [1540]

Helbig, Henri Antoine, 1813-
  Additions et corrections aux listes chronologiques des anciennes
impressions de Mayence avec date, qui ont été publiées jusqu'à ce

jour. Gand, L. Hebbelynck, 1840. 10, [2]p. 21.5 cm.
    Reprint from Messager des Sciences Historiques et Archives des
    Arts de Belgique, 1842, p. 124-166, 343-347; 1843, p. 415-418.   [1541]
    ICJ   NNC   Eu-Ge-LB

Helbig, Henri Antoine, 1813-
    Les dernières impressions de Pierre Schoeffer de Gernsheim.
    Bulletin du Bibliophile Belge, 3d ser., vol. 11, 1876, p. 288-300.   [1542]

----   Liste des ouvrages imprimé à Mayence par Frederic Heuman,
avec les anciens caractères de Gutenberg.   Bulletin du Biblio-
philé Belge, vol. 11 (2d ser., vol. 2), 1855, p. 21-32.   [1543]

Hiersemann, Karl W.
    Biblia latina; die 48-zeilige Bibel Exemplar auf Pergament.
Mainz, J. Fust & P. Schoeffer, 1462. With a description in English. Offered for sale by Karl W. Hiersemann, Leipzig.   [Leipzig,
1929]   1 leaf, 7p.   32 cm.
    Contains description, in German and English, of a copy of the
    1462 Bible on parchment, but lacking 16 pages.
    McMurtrie   [1544]

Jacobs, Friedrich.
    Mainzer Drucke von Erfindung der Buchdruckerkunst bis zum Er-
löschen der Schöfferischen Offizin.   Beiträge zur Älteren Literatur
oder Merkwürdigkeiten der Herzoglichen Öffentlichen Bibliothek zu
Gotha, vol. 1, 1835, p. 327-368.   [1545]

Knaus, Hermann.
    Über Verlagereinbände bei Schöffer ... Gutenberg Jahrbuch, vol.
13, 1938, p. 97-108.   [1546]

Meyer, Wilhelm.
    Bücheranzeigen des 15. Jahrhunderts.   Zentralblatt für Biblio-
thekswesen, vol. 2, no. 11, Nov. 1885, p. 437-463.
    With reproduction of Schoeffer's list of 1469-1470.   [1547]

Müller, Joseph, 1839-1880.
    Ein Autographon Peter Schöffer's in einer Incunabel der Koenig-
lichen und Universitaets-Bibliothek zu Koenigsberg i. Pr. mit litho-
graphirtem Facsimile, hrsg. von Joseph Mueller.   Koenigsberg i. Pr.,
Huebner & Matz, 1869.   2 prel. leaves, [5]-8p.   2 facsims.
29 cm.   [1548]
    DLC

Naumann, Robert.
    Bemerkungen zu dem Artikel: Absetzungsbulle Pius II gegen
Diether von Isenburg vom Jahre 1461.   Serapeum, vol. 12, no. 15,
1861, p. 236-240.   [1549]

Naumann, Robert.
  La Bulle du Pape Pie II, imprimée en 1461 par Jean Gutenberg.
Bulletin du Bibliophile Belge, vol. 9, 1852, p. 144-145.   [1550]

Prinet, Max.
  Un exemplaire de la Bible de 1462 conservé à la Bibliothèque
de l'Arsenal. Bibliographe Moderne, vol. 25, 1930-1931, p. 12-17. [1551]

Riedner, W.
  Peter Schöffers Anzeige des Decretum Gratiani und der Dekretalen
Gregor IX von 1472. Zeitschrift für Bücherfreunde, vol. 12, 1908-
1909, p. 153-154.   [1552]

Rosen.
  Ein unbekannter Holzschnitt der Schöfferschen Offizin. Gutenberg Jahrbuch, vol. 8, 1933, p. 133-135.   [1553]

Roth, F. Wilhelm Emil, 1853-
  Zur Geschichte des Mainzer Verlags und Buchdrucks im 15. bis 16.
Jahrhundert. Hessische Chronik, vol. 5, 1916, p. 93-95.   [1554]

Suchier, W.
  Ein Exemplar der Fust-Schöfferschen Bibel von 1462 in Braun-
schweig. Braunschweigische Landeszeitung und Braunschweiger
Tageblatt, no. 279, June 18, 1909.   [1555]

Weale, William Henry James, 1832-1917.
  Bemerkungen zu dem Mainzer und Trierer Missalia. Zentralblatt
für Bibliothekswesen, vol. 4, 1887, p. 550-552.
  Also reprint.   [1556]

M. PRINTING AT BAMBERG

Camus, Armand Gaston, 1740-1804.
  Notice d'un livre imprimé à Bamberg en CIƆCCCCLXII, lue à
l'Institut national, par Camus.   Paris, Baudouin, an VII [1799].
1 prel. leaf, 24p. 5 plates. 36x27 cm.
    Caption title: Notice d'un livre imprimé 4 par Albert Pfister,
  et contenu dans un volume nouvellement arrivé à la Bibliothèque
  nationale.   [1557]
    DLC   MB   MdBP   NN   Eu-Fr-PN   Eu-Ge-LB   Eu-Ge-LSb
    Eu-Ne-GK

Gusman, Pierre, 1862-
  Le premier livre de typographie illustré imprimé par Pfister
à Bamberg 1460. Byblis, vol. 7, 1928, p. 81-85.   [1558]

Hulthem, Charles Joseph Emmanuel van.
... Discours prononcé par C. van H. en presentant au conseil la notice d'un livre imprimé à Bamberg en 1462, par le cit. Camus. [Paris] An VII [1799].   8vo.
    At head of title: Corps législatif. Conseil des Cinq-cents.   [1559]
    Eu-Ge-LB

Jaeck, Joachim Heinrich, 1777-1847.
    Ein kleiner Beitrag zur Geschichte der Buchdruckerkunst in Bambergs Umgebung.   Serapeum, vol. 7, no. 3, 1846, p. 33-38.   [1560]

Murr, Christoph Gottlieb von, 1733-1811.
    Aelteste Buchdruckerey-Geschichte Bambergs. (In his Merk-würdigkeiten der fürstbischöflichen Residanzstadt Bamberg. Nürnberg, Grattenauerische Buchhandlung, 1799)   [1561]
    DLC   Eu-Fr-PN   Eu-Ge-LB

Scholderer, Victor, 1880-
    Albrecht Pfister of Bamberg.   Library, 3d ser., vol. 3, 1912, p. 230-236.   [1562]

Schramm, Albert, 1880-
    Die Drucke von Albert Pfister in Bamberg.   Leipzig, Verlag vor. K. W. Hiersemann, 1922.   iv, 7p.   38 plates.   Folio. (Der Bilderschmuck der Frühdrucke, I)   [1563]
    NN   Eu-De-LBb

Schwenke, Paul, 1853-1921.
    Zum Pfisterschen Donat.   Zentralblatt für Bibliothekswesen, vol. 21, 1904, p. 566-567.   [1564]

Sprenger, Placidus Johann Philipp, 1735-1806.
    Aelteste Buchdruckergeschichte von Bamberg, wo diese Kunst, neben Mainz, vor allen übrigen Städten Deutschlands zuerst ge-trieben worden; aus der Dunkelkeit hervorgezogen und bis 1534 fortgeführt, auch mit ein paar Abhandlungen versehen von P. Placidus Sprenger ... Nürnberg, In der Grattenauerischen Buchhand-lung, 1800.   vi p., 1 leaf, 86p.   facsim.   25.5x21.5 cm.   [1565]
    DLC   MWA   Eu-Ge-LB

Zedler, Gottfried, 1860-
    Quellen zur Geschichte des Bamberger Buchdrucks im fünfzehnten Jahrhundert.   Gutenberg Jahrbuch, vol. 5, 1930, p. 149-157.   [1566]

N. PRINTING AT ELTVILLE

Gutenberg a Eltville. *L'Arte della Stampa*, vol. 14, no. 21, 1884, p. 162. [1567]

Kutsch, F.
Die Beziehungen Gutenbergs zu Eltville. *Nassauische Annalen*, vol. 56, 1936, p. 185-188. [1568]

Roth, F. Wilhelm Emil, 1853-
Die Druckerei zu Eltville a. Rh. 1467-1476. *Allgemeiner Anzeiger für Druckereien*, vol. 29, 1902, p. 1630. [1569]

---- Die Druckerei zu Eltville im Rheingau und ihre Erzeugnisse. Ein Beitrag zur Bibliografie des 15. Jahrhunderts, von F. W. E. Roth. Mit einem Facsimile des Vocabularius ex quo de 1477. Augsburg, Verlag des Literarischen Instituts von M. Huttler, 1886. 30p., 1 leaf, incl. geneal. tab. facsim. 24.5 cm.
Contents.--Johann Gutenbergs zweite Druckerei und ihr verhältnis zur Eltviller Presse.--Die Eltviller Druckerei.--Die Eltviller Druckwerke.--Die Bechtermuntze.--Die Stätte der Eltviller Druckerei.--Anlagen. [1570]
DLC ICJ ICN MH Eu-De-LBb Eu-Ge-LB Eu-Ge-LSb

---- Gutenberg und die Buchdruckerei zu Eltville 1467-1476. *Zeitschrift für die Osterreichische Gymnasium*, vol. 62, 1913, p. 961-965. [1571]

---- Gutenberg und die Eltviller Druckerei. *Hessische Chronik*, vol. 5, 1916, p. 230. [1572]

---- Die Mainzer Patrizierfamilie Bechtermünze zu Eltville und die Eltviller Druckerei. *Nassovia*, vol. 12, 1911, p. 285-287. [1573]

---- Zur Geschichte der Eltviller Buchdruckerei 1467-1476. *Zentralblatt für Bibliothekswesen*, vol. 18, 1901, p. 114-121. [1574]

Ruppel, Aloys Leonhard, 1882-
Eltville als Frühdruckstadt, von Dr. Aloys Ruppel ... Mainz, Verlag der Gutenberg-Gesellschaft, 1938. 93p.,. 1 leaf. illus. (incl. facsims., geneal. tables) 21.5 cm. (Kleiner Druck der Gutenberg-Gesellschaft, Nr. 31) [1575]
CSmH DLC ICN MB Eu-Ne-AVb Eu-Sz-BeG

---- Gutenberg und Eltville. *Zeitschrift für Deutschlands Buchdrucker*, vol. 43, 1931, p. 472-473. [1576]

Schaefer, Hans.
Johannes Gutenberg in Eltville am Rhein (1465-1467). *Graphische Nachrichten*, vol. 19, no. 6, June 1940, p. 232. [1577]

Zedler, Gottfried, 1860-
  Die Zeugnisse für Gutenbergs Aufenthalt in Eltville, von G.
Zedler. Separat-Abdruck aus: Annalen des Vereins für Nassauische
Altertumskunde und Geschichtsforschung, Band XXXI, Heft 2, 1900.
n.p. ₍1900₎   cover-title, ₍215₎-222p.   26 cm.   ₍1578₎
    ICN

O.   THE ZEDLER HYPOTHESIS

Zedler, Gottfried, 1860-
  Die Erfindung Gutenbergs und der chinesische und frühholländische
Bücherdruck.   Gutenberg Jahrbuch, vol. 3, 1928, p. 50-57.   ₍1579₎

──── Gutenberg-Forschungen von Dr. Gottfried Zedler ... Mit vier
Tafeln.   Leipzig, O. Harrassowitz, 1901.   4 prel. leaves, 165 ₍1₎p.
iv plates, (1 fold.)   23 cm.   ₍1580₎
    DLC   ICJ   ICN   MB   MH   Eu-De-BP   Eu-Ge-LB   Eu-Ge-LSb
    Eu-Ne-AVb

──── Der holländische Frühdruck in Lichte der heutigen Gutenberg-
forschung.   Bibliofilia, vol. 24, 1923, p. 293-301.   ₍1581₎

──── Der holländische Frühdruck und die ersten Versuche Gutenbergs
in Strassburg.   Gutenberg Jahrbuch, vol. 5, 1930, p. 53-66.   ₍1582₎

──── Ein letztes Wort zu Coster-Gutenberg Frage.   Zentralblatt
für Bibliothekswesen, vol. 46, 1929, p. 329-333.   ₍1583₎

──── Mein Kampf um das Buch "Von Coster zu Gutenberg."   Zentralblatt für Bibliothekswesen, vol. 54, 1937, p. 223-226.   ₍1584₎

──── Die neuere Gutenbergforschung und die Lösung der Costerfrage.   Frankfurt am Main, J. Baer & Co., 1923.   63, ₍1₎p.
2 illus.   22.5 cm.   ₍1585₎
    DLC   NN   NjP   Eu-Ge-LB   Eu-Ne-AVb

──── Probleme und methode der heutigen Gutenbergforschung.
Zentralblatt für Bibliothekswesen, vol. 30, 1913, p. 404-417.   ₍1586₎

₍Zedler, Gottfried₎ 1860-
  Van Coster tot Gutenberg.   Nieuwsblad voor den Boekhandel,
no. 10, Feb. 3, 1922, p. 95-96; no. 14, Feb. 17, p. 134-136; no.
15, Feb. 24, p. 157-159; no. 18, Mar. 3, p. 183-185; no. 22, Mar.
17, p. 223-225; no. 24, Mar. 24, p. 242-245; no. 28, Apr. 7, p.
281-284; no. 30, Apr. 14, p. 303-305.   ₍1587₎

Zedler, Gottfried, 1860-
    Von Coster zu Gutenberg.   Der holländische Frühdruck
und die Erfindung des Buchdrucks.   Mit 26 Doppeltafeln und 49
Abbildungen, darunter 8 Typentafeln.   Leipzig, K. W. Hiersemann,
1921.   3 prel. leaves, [v]-viii, [2], 194p., 1 leaf.   illus.,
xxvi double facsim. (part col.)   diagrs.   29 cm.   On verso of t.-p.:
Mit Unterstützung der Holländischen Gesellschaft der Wissenschaften
zu Haarlem.   [1588]
    DLC   ICJ   ICN   MB   NN   NjP   Eu-De-BP   Eu-De-LBb
    Eu-Ge-LLl   Eu-Ne-AVb   Eu-Sz-BeG

----   Zur Coster-Gutenbergfrage.   Zentralblatt für Bibliothekswesen, vol. 43, 1926, p. 357-380.   [1589]

----   Zur Halbtausendjahrfeier der Erfindung der Buchdruckerkunst ...
von Gottfried Zedler.   Limburg an der Lahn, Limburger Vereins-
druckerei, G.M.B.H., 1936.   32p.   24 cm.
    Contents.-1. In welchem Jahr sollte die Feier stattfinden?--
    2. Was hat Coster in Haarlem erfunden und wodurch ist Gutenberg
    zum Erfinder der Buchdruckerkunst geworden?--3. Was hat Gutenberg
    gedruckt?   [1590]
    DLC   NN

IV   FUST and SCHOEFFER

Ackersdijck, W. C.
   Iets over het nageslacht van den vermaarden mentzischen boek-
drukker Petrus Schöffer naar 's Hertogenbosch verhuisd, en aldaar
uitgestorven.   Vaderlandsche Letteroefeningen, no. 6, May 1817,
Mengelwerk, p. 279-283.
   Also reprint.   [1591]

Bernard, Auguste Joseph, 1811-1868.
   Lettre [concerning a point of dispute with J. Wetter relating
to the relationship between Schoffer and Fust.]   Bulletin du
Bibliophile (Paris), no. 1, Jan. 1851, p. 30-32.   Same, Serapeum,
vol. 12, 1851, p. 97-99.   [1592]

[Boisserand, M.]
   Une quittance de Pierre Schoeffer.   Bibliothèque de l'École
des Chartes, 3d ser., vol. 1, 1849, p. 68-69.   [1593]

Börckel, Alfred, 1851-1928.
   Mainzer Drucker und Druckereien seit Gutenberg.   Allgemeiner
Anzeiger für Druckereien, 1902, p. 2 et sqq.   [1594]

Bullen, Henry Lewis.
   More about Fust and Schoeffer's device.   American Printer,
vol. 49, 1910, p. 724-725.   [1595]

Burger, Konrad, 1856-1912.
   Buchhändleranzeigen des 15. Jahrhunderts.   In getreuer Nach-
bildung herausgegeben von Konrad Burger ...   Leipzig, K. W.
Hiersemann, 1907.   4 prel. leaves, 15, [1]p.   32 facsims.
(mounted)   44.5 cm.   [1596]
   CSmH   DLC   ICJ   ICN   NN   Eu-Ge-LB

Campbell, Marinus Frederik Andries Gerardus, 1819-1890.
   Pierre Schoeffer de Gernsheim.   Bulletin du Bibliophile Belge,
3d ser., vol. 12, 1877, p. 46-47.   [1597]

Dahl, Johann Konrad, 1762-1833.
   Historisch-topographisch-statistiche Beschreibung der Stadt
und des Amtes Gernsheim in Grossherzoglich-Hessischen Fürsten-
thume Starkenburg.   Mit Urkunden.   Darmstadt, 1807.   8vo.
   Geschichte des Peter Schöffer von Gernsheim: p. 82-92.   [1598]
   Eu-Ge-LB

----   Peter Schöffer von Gernsheim, Miterfinder der Buchdruckerkunst.   Eine historische Skizze; mit einer kurzen Geschichte
der Erfindung jener schönen Kunst überhaupt.   Von Konrad Dahl.

Wiesbaden, Ludwig Schellenberg, 1814.   23p.   fold. geneal.
table.   18.5 cm.
    Also appeared in Vogt und Weitzels Rheinischen Archiv, 1814,
p. 260-283.   [1599]
    NNC   Eu-Ne-GK

Falk, Franz, 1840-1909.
    Der gelehrte Korrektor Adrian O. S. B. der Peter Schöfferschen
Druckerei zu Mainz.   Zentralblatt für Bibliothekswesen, vol. 16,
1899, p. 233-237.   [1600]

---- Hat sich Johann Fust zu Mainz eines Nachdrucks Johann
Mentelin zu Strassburg gegenüber schuldig gemacht?   Zentral-
blatt für Bibliothekswesen, vol. 1, no. 6, 1884, p. 246-247.   [1601]

---- Peter Schöffer als Clericus.   Zentralblatt für Bibliothekswesen, vol. 19, 1902, p. 547.   [1602]

    Festlied bei der Enthullung des Denkmales für Peter Schöffer
in Gernsheim, des Vollenders der Buchdruckerkunst.   Gesungen von
sämmtlichen anwesenden Buchdruckern.   Gernsheim, 1836.   2p.
8vo.
    Title from Mohr, Jubelfeste.   [1603]

Franchini, Ettere.
    Giovanni Fust.   Rassegna Grafica, vol. 6, no. 58, 1931.   [1604]

---- Pietro Schoeffer.   Rassegna Grafica, vol. 6, no. 59,
Feb. 1931, p. 5-6.   [1605]

    Fust, der Erfinder der Buchdruckerei.   [Drama]   Mainz, 1792.
56p.   12mo.   [1606]
    Eu-Ge-LSb

Hagelstange, Alfred.
    Festvortrag ... am 23. Juni 1907 in der Gutenberg-Gesellschaft
zu Mainz über Gutenbergs Erbe und die Pflichten der Gegenwart
im Gegenüber.   Gutenberg-Gesellschaft.   Jahresberichte, 1907,
p. 25-45.   [1607]

Hartenbach, J. Ritschel von.
    Der Buchdruckerkunst Erfindung.   Nebst einigen Betrachtungen
über den Nutzen und die Nachtheile ... Sondershausen, 1820.   8vo.
    " ... and Schoeffer was the father of typefounding": p. 25.
    Title from van der Linde, Geschichte der Erfindung ...   [1608]

Heidenheimer, Heinrich, 1856-
    Aus der Geschichte der Familie Fust-Schöffer.   Eine Erinnerung
zum Johannistage.   Zeitschrift für Deutschlands Buchdrucker, vol.
14, no. 25, 1902, p. 305-306.   [1609]

Heidenheimer, Heinrich, 1856–
Peter Schöffer, der Kleriker.   Zentralblatt für Bibliothekswesen, vol. 19, 1902, p. 451-455.   [1610]

Helbig, Henri Antoine, 1813–
Les concurrents de Pierre Schoeffer à Mayence pendant le XVe
siècle.   Bulletin du Bibliophile Belge, 3d ser., vol. 11, 1876,
p. 22-25.   [1611]

Jacobs, Emil, 1868–
Nachkommen Peter Schoeffers?   Zeitschrift für Bücherfreunde,
vol. 8, 1904-1905, p. 405-406.   [1612]

Kentenich, Gottfried, 1873–
Die Buchdruckerfamilie Schöfer und Franz von Sickingen.
Zentralblatt für Bibliothekswesen, vol. 27, no. 2, 1910, p. 70-71. [1613]

Klee, Otto.
Noch einmal die Kleriker.   Zentralblatt für Bibliothekswesen,
vol. 20, no. 7, July 1903, p. 325-333.   [1614]

Külb, Philipp Hedwig.
Peter Schöffer der Vollender der Buchdruckerkunst.   Gernsheim,
1836.   15p.   8vo.   [1615]
Eu-Fr-PN   Eu-Ge-LSb

Künzel, Heinrich.
Peter Schöffer von Gernsheim, der Miterfinder der Buchdruckerkunst.   Zur Erinnerung an seine Verdienste bei der am 9. Juni
1836 stattfindenden feierlichen Enthüllung des von der Stadt Gernsheim ihrem Mitbürger errichteten Standbildes dargebracht.
Darmstadt, C. W. Leske, 1856.   15p.   8vo.   [1616]
Eu-De-LBb

Lange, Adolph.
Peter Schöffer von Gernsheim, der Buchdrucker und Buchhandler ...
Leipzig, Hermann, 1864, 20p.   (Beiträge zur Geschichte des Buch-
handels, der Buchdruckerkunst und der verwandten Künste und Ge-
werbe. 1)   [1617]
ICN   MB   NNC   Eu-Ge-LB

Linde, Antonius van der, 1833-1897.
Johann Fust.   (In Allgemeine deutsche Biographie.   Leipzig,
1878.   vol. 8, p. 267-271)   [1618]

Maaslieb, W.
Peter Schoeffer und die Erfindung der Buchdruckerkunst.   Ein
Kulturbild für die reifere Jugend ... Neu-Ruppin [1868]   188p.
plates.   4to.   [1619]
Eu-Ge-LB

Mone, Franz Joseph.
Schirmbrief für den Buchdrucker Peter Schöffer. Zeitschrift
für die Geschichte des Oberrheins, 1850, p. 309-314.
[1620]

Peter Schoeffer. Printers' Circular, vol. 8, no. 2, 1873,
p. 43.
Reprint from American Encyclopaedia of Printing.
[1621]

Peterson, Eugen.
Peter Schöffer, der Miterfinder der Buchdruckerkunst.
Zeitschrift für Deutschlands Buchdrucker, vol. 37, no. 14, 1925,
p. 91-92.
[1622]

Pollard, Alfred William, 1859-
An essay on colophons, with specimens and translations, by
Alfred W. Pollard, and an introduction by Richard Garnett.
Chicago, The Caxton Club, 1905. xx, 198p., 1 leaf, incl. facsims. 28.5 cm.
Title in red and black; initials in red.
"The publication committee of the Caxton club certifies that
this copy of 'An essay on colophons' is one of an edition
consisting of two hundred and fifty-two copies on French
hand-paper and three copies on imperial Japanese paper,
printed from type, and completed in the month of August,
nineteen hundred and five."
DLC   ICJ   MB   MiU-C   NN   TxU
[1623]

---- Peter Schoeffer at work. Book-Lovers' Magazine, vol. 6,
part 2, 1905-1907, p. 50-55.
[1624]

Programm der Festlichkeiten bei der Enthüllung des Denkmales
für Peter Schöffer von Gernsheim, des Vollenders der Buchdruckerkunst. Am. 9. Juni 1836. Gernsheim, 1836. 4p. 8vo.
Title from Mohr, Jubelfeste.
[1625]

Programm des musikalischen Dankfestes in der Kirche zu Gernsheim und Erklärung der damit verbundenen Aufstellung der allegorischen Transparent-Gemälde am Tage der Enthüllung des Denkmales von Peter Schöffer, welches die Gemeinde in einer kolos-
salen Statue aus Sandstein, erfunden und ausgeführt von dem
Hofbildhauer Scholl in Darmstadt, aus dankbarer Verehrung ihrem
Mitbürger aus eigenen Mitteln gesetzt hat. Gedruckt bei Stahl &
Bekker in Darmstadt [1836] 4p. 4to.
Title from Mohr, Jubelfeste.
[1626]

Roth, F. Wilhelm Emil, 1853-
Die Mainzer Buchdruckerfamilie Schöffer. Zentralblatt für
Bibliothekswesen, vol. 18, 1901, p. 61-65.
[1627]

Roth, F. Wilhelm Emil, 1853-
    Zur vierhundertjährigen Gedenkfeier des Todes von Peter
Schoeffer dem Aelteren, Buchdrucker der Stadt Mainz 1454 bis 1502.
Allgemeiner Anzeiger für Druckereien, vol. 29, 1902, p. 1792 et
sqq.   [1628]

Ruppel, Aloys Leonhard, 1882-
    Peter Schöffer aus Gernsheim; Festvortrag zur Hundertjahr-
feier der Errichtung des Schöfferdenkmals gehalten im Rathause zu
Gernsheim am 27. September 1936, von Dr. Aloys Ruppel ... Mainz,
Gutenberg-Gesellschaft, 1937.   62p., 1 leaf.   front., illus.
(facsims.)   21 cm.   (Kleiner Druck der Gutenberg-Gesellschaft.
Nr. 26)
    "Literatur": p. 59-62.   [1629]
    DLC   IC   ICN   MB   Eu-Ne-AVb   Eu-Sz-BeG

----   Peter Schöffer der ältere.   (In Altmeister der Druckschrift,
in Gutenberg-Jahr 1940 gedruckt und herausgegeben von der Schriftgiesserei D. Stempel AG, Frankfurt a.M.   p. 22-24)
    McMurtrie   [1630]

----   Zur Nachkommenschaft Peter Schöffers aus Gernsheim.   Gutenberg Jahrbuch, vol. 12, 1937, p. 269-271.   [1631]

Sayers, G. A.
    The fathers of our craft: Peter Schoeffer.   Caxton's Magazine,
vol. 31, 1929, p. 616-618.   [1632]

Schaab, Carl Anton, 1767-1835.
    Kritische Bemerkungen über Dahls neueste Schrift: Peter Schöffer,
Miterfinder der Buchdruckerkunst, Mainz.   Mainz, 1833.   8vo.   [1633]
    Eu-Ge-LB

Schenk zu Schweinsberg, Gustav Ferdinand Karl Johann Ernst
    Ludwig, freiherr, 1842-
    Mainzer Buchdruckerrechnung.   Quartalblätter des Historischen
Vereins für das Grossherzogtum Hessen, no. 3-4, 1882, p. 15.   [1634]

Schmidt, Adolf, 1857-
    Eine Mainzer Buchdruckerrechnung von 1480.   Zentralblatt für
Bibliothekswesen, vol. 29, 1912, p. 25-26.   [1635]

    Das Schöffer-Fest zu Gernsheim am 9ten Juni, 1836.   Journal
für Buchdruckerkunst, 1836, p. 98-103.   [1636]

    Some new facts concerning Fust and Schoeffer.   American Book-
maker, vol. 3, no. 5, Nov. 1886, p. 147.   Same, Book Lore, vol.
5, Jan. 1887, p. 45.   [1637]

Stricker, Thomas Perry, 1898-
... Herr Faust and his goose flesh. Los Angeles [Priv. print.]
1940. [8]p. 18 cm.
   "Edition: 50 copies."   [1638]
   DLC

Strieder, Jacob, 1877-
   Fünf neu-aufgefundene Briefe des Mainzer Buchdruckers Peter
Schöffer. _Gutenberg Jahrbuch_, vol. 8, 1933, p. 69-74.   [1639]

Velke, Wilhelm, 1854-
   Zu den Bücheranzeigen Peter Schöffers. Mainz, Gutenberg-
Gesellschaft, 1908. cover-title, 3 prel. leaves, 235p. illus.
xiv facsims. (part col., part fold.) 29x22 cm. (Veröffent-
lichungen der Gutenberg-Gesellschaft no. 5-7, p. 221-235)   [1640]
   DLC   IC   ICN   IB   MH   NN   Eu-De-BP   Eu-De-MzG
   Eu-Ge-LB   Eu-Ge-LSb

Verreyt, Charles C. V.
   Het geslacht Schoeffer later Scheffer en Scheffers te
's-Hertogenbosch van 1541-1796, in betrekking tot de boekdrukkunst door Ch. C. V. Verreyt. 's-Gravenhage, Genealogisch-
heraldisch archief, 1888. 2 prel. leaves, 142p. illus.,
plate. 21.5 cm.   [1641]
   NNC   Eu-Ne-CK

Wehmer, Carl.
   Ein frühes Korrekturblatt aus der Schöfferschen Offizin.
Gutenberg Jahrbuch, vol. 7, 1932, p. 118-122.   [1642]

Wetter, Johann, 1795-1877.
   C. Henlif oder Henekis, Buchhändler zu Mainz, der Geschäfts-
genosse P. Schöffers ... (Abgedruckt aus der Zeitschrift des
Vereins zur Erforschung der rheinischen Geschichte und Alter-
thümer.) Mainz, 1851. 8vo.   [1643]
   Eu-Ge-LB

Willax, W.
   Peter Schöffer der Verbesserer und Vollender der Typographie.
Schulmitteilungen der Buchdrucker-Fachschule (München), vol. 7,
1921, p. 26-27, 37-39.   [1644]

Zedler, Gottfried, 1860-
   Peter Schöffer und seine Söhne. Konflikt mit dem Könige von
Schöffernamen des 15. und 16. Jahrhunderts aus dem Gernsheimer
Gerichtsbuch. _Zentralblatt für Bibliothekswesen_, vol. 20, 1903,
p. 378-385.   [1645]

Berjeau, Jean Philibert, 1809-1891.
    Essai bibliographique sur le Speculum humanae salvationis;
indiquant la passage de la xylographie à la typographie, par
J. Ph. Berjeau.   (Introduction de l'édition fac-simile de ce
monument xylographique.)   Londres, C. J. Stewart, 1862.   lxxii p.
facsim.: 24 leaves.   illus.   32.5 cm.   [1646]
    1U   NBuG   Eu-De-LBb   Eu-Fr-PN   Eu-Ge-LL1   Eu-Ne-AVb

Breitenbach, Edgar.
    ... Speculum humanae salvationis, eine typengeschichtliche Unter-
suchung, von Edgar Breitenbach; mit 12 Tafeln.   Strassburg, J. H. E.
Heitz, 1930.   4 prel. leaves, 277, [1]p., 1 leaf.   xii plates.
25.5 cm.   (Studien zur deutschen Kunstgeschichte.   Hft. 272)
    "Katalog der Handschriften": p. 5-[43]   [1647]
    CSmH   DLC   MB   MH   NN   Eu-Ge-LB

Buhler, Curt Ferdinand.
    New Coster fragments of the Doctrinale.   Gutenberg Jahrbuch,
vol. 13, 1938, p. 59-68.   [1648]

Campbell, Marinus Frederik Andries Gerardus, 1819-1890.
    Annales de la typographie néerlandaise au XVe siècle, par
M.-F.-A.-G. Campbell ... La Haye, M. Nijhoff; [etc., etc.] 1874.
xii, [6], 629, [1]p.   24 cm.   [1649]
    CSmH   DLC   ICJ   MB   MH   MdBP   NN   Eu-Ne-GK

---- ---- 1. [-4] supplément.   La Haye, M. Nijhoff, 1878-1890.
4 vols.   24 cm.   [1650]
    CSmH   DLC   ICJ   MdBP   Eu-Ne-GK

Doudelet, Charles.
    ... Le "Speculum humanae salvationis" à la Bibliothèque nationale
de Florence.   Gand, Librairie néerlandaise, 1903.   3 prel. leaves,
42p., 1 leaf.   illus., facsims.   26.5 cm.
    "Il a été tiré de cet ouvrage: douze exemplaires sur papier Japon
impérial, numérotés de 1 à 12 et cent cinquante exemplaires sur
papier velin, numérotés de 13 à 162 ..."
    On verso of t.-p.: Ouvrages illustrés du même auteur.
    "Travaux des auteurs les plus autorisés qui ... se sont occupés de
cette matière" [i.e. de savoir si la priorité de l'invention des
caractères mobiles devait s'attribuer à telle nation ou à telle
autre] -- Avant-propos.   [1651]
    DLC   ICJ

Enschedé, Jan Wilhelm, 1865-
   Een drukkerij buiten Mechelen voor 1466.   Het Boek, vol. 7,
1918, p. 286-292.   [1652]

Falk, Franz, 1840-1909.
   Das Speculum humanae vitae, sein Verfasser und sein Uebersetzer.
Neuer Anzeiger für Bibliographie und Bibliothekswissenschaft, no.
487, 1878, p. 194-197.   [1653]

Guichard, Joseph Marie, 1810-1852.
   Notice sur le Speculum humanae salvationis, par J. Marie Guichard.
Paris, Techener, 1840.   131p.   23 cm.   [1654]
      DLC   Eu-De-LBb   Eu-Fr-PN   Eu-Ge-LB   Eu-Ne-AVb

Harzen, Ernst.
   Ueber Alter und Ursprung der frühesten Ausgaben des Heilspiegels
oder des Speculum humanae salvationis.   Archiv für die Zeichnenden
Künste, 1855-1856, p. 3-15; suppl., p. 1-12.   [1655]

Hesse, Friedrich Ludwig.
   Ueber das Speculum humanae salvationis.   Serapeum, vol. 16, no.
13, 1855, p. 193-203; no. 14, p. 209-221; no. 15, p. 225-232; no.
16, p. 241-255; no. 17, p. 257-267.   [1656]

Kattermann, Gerhard.
   Neue Karlsruher Bruchstücke eines 30 zeiligen Donatus in der
niederländischen Speculumtype.   Gutenberg Jahrbuch, vol. 14, 1939,
p. 102-108.   [1657]

Nemeitz, Joachim Christoph.
   Von den zu Harlem aufbehaltenen raren Buch.   [Speculum humanae
salvationis.]   (In his Vernüfftige Gedanken über allerhand historische, critische und moralische Materien ... Franckfurt a.M., 1739.
p. 34-44)
   Title from Bulletin du Bibliophile Belge, 1856.   [1658]

Perdrizet, Paul Frédéric, 1870-
   Étude sur le Speculum humanae salvationis, par Paul Perdrizet ...
Paris, H. Champion, 1908.   x, 178p., 1 leaf.   25.5 cm.
   Results of the author's personal researches, which have also been
   incorporated in "Speculum humanae salvationis" written in collabor-
   ation with Jules Lutz (vol. 1, part 1 and vol. 2, part 1 issued
   Mülhausen 1907)   [1659]
      DLC   MB

Podesta, B.
   L'esemplare fiorentino della prima edizione latina dello speculum
humanae salvationis. (Lettura al Prof. Carlo Castellani.)   Rivista
delle Biblioteche, vol. 1, no. 8-10, 1888, p. 126-132.   [1660]

Proctor, Robert George Collier, 1868-1903.
 Additions to Campbell's Annales de la typographie néerlandaise au
15e siècle.   London, Priv. print., 1897.   79p.   23.5 cm.   (Tracts
on early printing, III)
    Fifty copies printed.   [1661]
    DLC   IU   Eu-Fr-PN   Eu-Ge-LB   Eu-Ge-LSb   Eu-Ne-GK

----   List of the founts of type and woodcut devices used by the
printers of the Southern Netherlands in the fifteenth century.
London, Priv. print., 1895.   48p.   3 plates.   23.5 cm.   (Tracts
on early printing.   I)
    Fifty copies printed.   [1662]
    DLC   Eu-Fr-PN   Eu-Ge-LB   Eu-Ge-LSb   Eu-Ne-GK

Ruelens, Charles Louis, 1820-1890.
 Sur le Speculum humanae salvationis, par Ch. Ruelens.   Bruxelles,
F. Heussner, Librairie ancienne et moderne, Place Saint-Gudule, 1855.
24p.   22.5 cm.
    Reprint from Bulletin du Bibliophile Belge, vol. 11 (2d ser., vol.
    2), 1855, p. 165-177.
    Fifty copies printed.   [1663]
    CSmH   Eu-De-LBb   Eu-Ne-AVb

Weigel, Theodor Oswald, 1812-1881.
 Widerlegung der Angabe: ein Exemplar des Speculum humanae salvationis in holländischer Sprache befinde sich in der akademischen
Bibliothek zu St. Petersburg.   Serapeum, vol. 10, no. 14, 1849,
p. 209-218; no. 15, p. 225-237.   [1664]

Zedler, Gottfried, 1860-
 Der älteste Buchdruck und das frühholländische Doktrinale des
Alexander de Villa Dei, von Gottfried Zedler; mit 24 Tafeln.   Leiden,
A. W. Sijthoff, 1936.   6 prel. leaves, 71p.   24 plates (incl. fac-
sims.) on 12 leaves.   28.5 cm.
    Supplementary to the author's Von Coster zu Gutenberg.   cf. Vor-
    wort.   [1665]
    CSmH   DLC   ICJ   ICN   NN   Eu-Ne-AVb   Eu-Ne-GK

VI   GUTENBERG

A.   GENEALOGY

Abstammung und Verwandtschaft Gutenbergs.   Archiv für Hessische
Geschichte und Alterthumskunde, vol. 14, 1875, p. 132.   [1666]

Holbig, Henri Antoine, 1813-
   La généalogie de Jean Gutenberg, inventeur de l'imprimerie recti-
fiée d'après les documents.   Bulletin du Bibliophile Belge, 3d ser.,
vol. 9, 1874, p. 141-148.   [1667]

Howorth, Henry H.
   The parentage of Gutenberg the printer.   Academy, vol. 48, no.
1230, Nov. 30, 1895, p. 461.   [1668]

Hupp, Otto, 1859-
   Das Wappen Gutenbergs.   (In Gutenbergfestschrift, zur Feier des
25jaehrigen Bestehens des Gutenbergmuseums in Mainz 1925.   Hrsg. von
A. Ruppel.   Mainz, Verlag der Gutenberg-Gesellschaft [1925] p.1-3)[1669]
   DLC   ICN   MB   MH   NN   NNC   NNGr   Eu-De-BP   Eu-Ge-LB
   Eu-Ne-AVb   Eu-Sz-BeG

Roth, F. Wilhelm Emil, 1853-
   Friele und Henne Gensfleisch zur Laden und deren Erben.   Ein
Beitrag zur Mainzer Patriziergeschichte.   Hessische Chronik, vol.
1, no. 4, Apr. 1912, p. 127-131.   [1670]

Saum, Auguste.
   La famille Gensfleisch à Strassbourg.   [Strassbourg, Berger-
Sevrault, 1866]
   Reprint from Bibliophile Alsacien, vol. 4, 1866, p. 201-204.   [1671]
   MB   Eu-De-LBb   Eu-Ge-LSb

----   The Gutenberg family at Strassbourg.   Book Worm (Berjeau),
vol. 3, 1868, p. 7-8.   [1672]

Schenk zu Schweinsberg, Gustav Ferdinand Karl Johann Ernst Ludwig,
   freiherr, 1842-
   Genealogie des Mainzer Geschlechtes Gänsfleisch.   (In Festschrift
zum fünfhundertjährigen Geburtstage von Johann Gutenberg, herausgegeben von Otto Hartwig.   Leipzig, O. Harrassowitz, 1900.   p. 80-
162)   [1673]
   CSmH   DLC   ICJ   ICN   MH   NjP   Eu-De-BP   Eu-Ne-AVb
   Eu-Ne-GK

Schenk zu Schweinsberg, Gustav Ferdinand Karl Johann Ernst Ludwig,
   freiherr, 1842-
   Konrad Henkis von Gutenberg, der Geschaftsgenosse des Peter
Schöffer.   Quartalblätter des Historischen Vereins für das Grossherzogtum Hessen, n.s., vol. 11, 1900, p. 635.   (1674)

Seidenberger, Johann Baptist, 1860-1923.
   Die Zünftkampfe in Mainz und der Anteil der Familie Gensfleisch.
(In Gutenberg-Feier in Mainz.   1900 ... [Mainz] Mainzer Verlags-
Anstalt und Druckerei [1900])   (1675)
      DLC   ICJ   ICN   MH   Eu-Fr-PN   Eu-Ge-LB   Eu-Ge-LSb
      Eu-Ne-AVb

Tronnier, Adolph, 1875-
   Von Einbandspiegeln, Mainzer Rechnungsbuchern und Gulten der
Gensfleisch-Familie.   Gutenberg Jahrbuch, vol. 11, 1936, p. 30-
47.   (1676)

B.   DOCUMENTS

Berlan, Francesco, 1821-1886.
   Un nuovo documento au Guttemberg.   Archivio Veneto, 2d ser., vol.
27, 1884, p. 234-266.   (1677)

Bernays, Heinrich.
   Der Process zwishen Gutenberg und der Erben von Georg Dritzehn.
Quartalblätter des Vereines für Literatur und Kunst zu Mainz, vol.
4, no. 1, 1833, p. 3-21.   (1678)

Bogeng, Gustav Adolf Erich, 1881-
   Die grossen Gutenberg-Prozesse.   Börsenblatt für den Deutschen
Buchhandel, vol. 95, no. 248, 1928, p. 1173-1175.   (1679)

Castellani, Carlo, 1822-1879.
   L'originale dello strumento Helmasperger 6 November 1455, recente-
mente scoperto dal D'Carlo Dziatzko e i fatti risultanti datale
scoperta.   Rivista delle Biblioteche, vol. 2, 1889, p. 74-76.   (1680)

[Claudin, Anatole] 1833-1906.
   Un nouveau document sur Gutenberg.   Témoignage d'Ulric Gering,
le premier imprimeur parisien, et de ses compagnons en faveur de
l'inventeur de l'imprimerie.   [Paris, Typ. A. Quantin, 1884]
4p.   30 cm.
   Caption title.
   Reprint from Le Livre, bibliographie retrospective, Nov. 1884,   (1681)
      DLC   ICJ   Eu-Fr-PN   Eu-Ge-LSb

De Villiers, Peter.
The signature of Gutenberg, by P. DeVilliers, M. D.   London,
Published by Kerby and Endean, 190 Oxford Street, MDCCCLXXVIII [1878]
28p.   25.5 cm.
"This edition consists of three hundred copies only."
Contents:-Facsimile of a Letter of Indulgence and of two
signatures of Gutenberg.- The signature of Gutenberg.   Biblia
Sacra Gutenbergiana.- The Catholicon.- The Letter of Indulgence.-
The two signatures of Gutenberg.- The pretended handwriting of
Gutenberg.   [1682]
ICN   NN

Dziatzko, Karl Franz Otto, 1842-1903.
Beiträge zur Gutenbergfrage, von Karl Dziatzko.   Mit einem
Lichtdruck-Facsimile des Helmasperger'schen Notariats-Instrumentes
vom 6. November 1455 nach dem Original der K. Universitäts-Biblio-
thek zu Göttingen.   Berlin, A. Asher & Co., 1889.   4 prel. leaves,
89p.   fold. facsim.   24 cm.   (His Sammlung bibliothekswissenschaftlicher Arbeiten ... Berlin, 1889.   2. Hft.)   [1683]
   CSmH   DLC   ICJ   ICN   MB   MH   Eu-De-BP   Eu-De-LBb
   Eu-Fr-PN   Eu-Go-LSb   Eu-Ne-AVb   Eu-Ne-GK

Fuhrmann, Otto Walter.
Gutenberg and the Strasbourg documents of 1439;   an interpreta-
tion by Otto W. Fuhrmann.   To which has been appended the text of
the documents in the original Alsatian, the French of Laborde, and
modern German and English translations; sketches by Fritz Kredel.
New York, Press of the Woolly whale, 1940.   x p., 1 leaf, 260p.,
1 leaf incl. illus., facsims.   26 cm.
   Illustrated lining-papers.
   Gutenberg's seal on t.-p.
   Initials.
   "The facsimiles 1 to 13 [p. 147-151] and the watermarks [p. 153]
have been reproduced ... from the lithographic tracings in Count
Léon de Laborde's book Débuts de l'imprimerie à Strasbourg, Paris,
1840.   Facsimile 14 [p. 152] has been taken from a pamphlet en-
titled Gutenberg, lithographed by students of the Strasbourg
Industrial School, 1840, (from the copy in the library of the
Grolier club, New York).   All are shown in the exact size of the
originals, preserved by the tracings."- Author's note, p. [146].
"Published in celebration of the 500th anniversary of the
invention of printing from movable types.   The body matter
is hand set in Bruce Rogers' 14-point centaur ... Only 660
copies have been printed."
   Bibliography: p. [237]-253.   [1684]
   DLC   NN   NjF   ViU

Laborde, Léon Emmanuel Simon Joseph, marquis de, 1807-1869.
Débuts de l'imprimerie à Strasbourg, ou recherches sur les
travaux mystérieux de Gutenberg dans cette ville, et sur le procès

qui lui fut intenté en 1439 à cette occasion; par Léon de Laborde.
Paris, Techener, 1840.   83p.   iii fold. plates.   27.5 cm.   [1685]
   DLC   ICJ   ICN   MB   MH   MdBP   NNGr   NjP   Eu-De-LBb
   Eu-Fr-PN   Eu-Ge-LB   Eu-Ge-LP

Lacroix, Paul, 1806-1884.
   Procès de Gutenberg; XIIe dissertion du bibliophile Jacob.   Paris,
1847.
   Title from Dupont, Paul.   Histoire de l'imprimerie. 1854.   [1686]

Lobstein, Jean-Martin-François-Théodore.
   Manuel du notariat en Alsace, ou Notices sur la composition de
toutes les études de cette ancienne province ... et sur les actes
déposés dans lesdites études et dans les dépôts publics, avec la
nomenclature des fonctionnaires qui les ont reçus ... précédées
d'une histoire du notariat, générale, et particulière aux
diverses localités de cette province ... par J.-F. Lobstein,...
Strasbourg, Treutel et Wurtz, 1844.   xvi, 369p.   8vo.   [1687]
   Eu-Fr-PN

McMurtrie, Douglas Crawford, 1888-
   Gutenberg's life recorded in documents.   New and interesting
information on the activities of Johann Gutenberg, his invention
of printing, and his financial tribulations derived from twenty-
eight contemporary documents.   Inland Printer, vol. 105, no. 4,
July 1940, p. 50-52.   [1688]

----   The life and work of Johann Gutenberg as recorded in con-
temporary documents.   Invention of printing anniversary committee,
International association of printing house craftsmen.   Chicago,
1940.   10p.   23 cm.
   Reprint from Share Your Knowledge Review, vol. 21, no. 8,
   June 1940, p. 6-13.   [1689]
   DLC   ICU   NN

Mayr, Ludwig Wilhelm.
   Der Prozess Fust's gegen Gutenberg im Jahre 1455.   Theile vom
Abschnitt einer von der Königlichen Ludwig-Maximilians-Universität
München im Jahre 1856 gekrönten Preisschrift über die Erfindungs-
geschichte der Buchdruckerkunst als Inaugural-Abhandlung.   München,
J. G. Weiss, 1858.   23p.   21.5 cm.   [1690]
   ICJ

Ruppel, Aloys Leonhard, 1882-
   Ein angeblicher Originalbrief Gutenbergs aus dem Jahre 1438.
Gutenberg Jahrbuch, vol. 5, 1930, p. 73-76.   [1691]

Schorbach, Karl, 1851-
   Neue Strassburger Gutenbergfunde.   (In Gutenbergfestschrift, zur
Feier des 25 jährigen Bestehens des Gutenbergmuseums in Mainz 1925.

Hrsg. von A. Ruppel.   Mainz, Verlag der Gutenberg-Gesellschaft
(1925)   p. 130-143)
   Also appeared in Gutenberg Jahrbuch, vol. 1, 1926, p. 14-31.   (1692)
   DLC ICN MB MH NN NNC NNGr Eu-De-BP Eu-Ge-LB
   Eu-Ne-AVb Eu-Sz-BeG

Schorbach, Karl, 1851-
   Des Rechtsstreit der Ennelin zu der Iserin Thür gegen Johann
Gutenberg im Jahre 1437, und Ennel Gutenberg.   Zentralblatt für
Bibliothekswesen, vol. 19, 1902, p. 217-228.   (1693)

---- Die urkundlichen Nachrichten über Johann Gutenberg.   (In
Festschrift zum fünfhundertjährigen Geburtstage von Johann Gutenberg,
herausgegeben von Otto Hartwig.   Leipzig, O. Harrassowitz, 1900.
p. 163-319.   Mainz ed., p. 183-256)   (1694)
   CSmH DLC ICJ ICN MH NjP Eu-De-BP Eu-Ne-AVb
   Eu-Ne-GK

Stammler, Rudolf, 1856-
   Die Rechtshandel des Johann Gutenbergs.   (In Festschrift ... für
Wilhelm von Brünneck.   Halle, 1912.   p. 1-25)   (1695)
   McMurtrie

---- ---- (In Stammler, Rudolf.   Deutsches Rechtsleben ... Charlotten-
burg, Pan-Verlag, 1928.   p. 1-22)   (1696)
   DLC MH Eu-De-BP

C.   BIOGRAPHY

Altaev, A. A.
   Svetochi pravdy.   Ocherki i kartinki iz zhizni velikikh liudei.
Izd. 5-e.   Moskva, I. D. Sytin, (1918)   367p.   illus., port.   (1697)
   Eu-Ru-MLe

Bakhtiarov, A. A.
   Iogan Gutenberg, ego zhizn' i deiatel'nost' v sviazi s istoriei
knigopechataniia.   Biograficheskii ocherk.   St. Petersburg, F.
Pavlenkova, 1893.   94p.   94p.   front., port.
   Zhizn' zamechatel'nykh liudei.   Biograficheskaia biblioteka F.
Pavlenkova.   (1698)
   Eu-Ru-MLe

Benner, R. C.
   Les derniers temps de la vie de Gutenberg.   L'Alsace Française,
vol. 7, no. 41, 1927.   (1699)

Bernard, Auguste Joseph, 1811-1868.
  Gutenberg--his troubles and achievements. Translated from
the French by F. S. Burrell. Inland Printer, vol. 5, Nov. 1887,
p. 90-92; Dec., p. 152-153; Jan. 1888. p. 224-225; Feb., p. 323-
324.   [1700]

Birkenfeld, Günther, 1901-
  Johann Gutenberg, sein Leben und seine Erfindung.   München und
Berlin, 1939.   56p.   [1701]
    Eu-Ne-AVb

Bockenheimer, Karl Georg, 1836-1914.
  Gutenberg. (In Gutenberg-feier in Mainz, 1900 ... [Mainz],
Mainzer Verlags-Anstalt und Druckerei A.-G. [1900]   [1702]
    DLC   ICJ   ICN   MH   Eu-De-BP   Eu-Fr-PN   Eu-Ge-LB
    Eu-Ge-LSb   Eu-Ne-AVb

----   Gutenberg's Grabstätte.   Von Dr. K. G. Bockenheimer ...
Mainz, 1876.   Verlag von J. Diemer, Ludwigsstrasse 10.   2 prel.
leaves, 21p.   plan (fold.)   23 cm.   [1703]
    MH   Eu-De-LBb   Eu-Fr-PN   Eu-Ge-LB   Eu-Ge-LSb

Bockwitz, Hans H.
  Urkunden zu Gutenbergs Lebenslauf. Archiv für Buchgewerbe und
Gebrauchsgraphik, vol. 77, no. 7-8, 1940, p. 247-250.   [1704]

Bömer, Alois, 1868-
  Das Bild Gutenbergs. Zentralblatt für Bibliothekswesen, vol. 53,
1936, p. 284-297.   [1705]

Börckel, Alfred, 1851-1928.
  Gutenberg. Sein Leben, sein Werk, sein Ruhm.   Zur Erinnerung an
die 500jährige Geburt des Erfinders der Buchdruckerkunst für weitere
Kreise dargestellt von Alfred Börckel ... Giessen, E. Roth, 1897.
5 prel. leaves, 122p.   front., illus., ports., facsims.   28.5 cm. [1706]
    DLC   ICJ   ICN   MB   Eu-Fr-PN   Eu-Ge-LB   Eu-Ge-LSb

----   Gutenberg und die Anfänge seiner Kunst in Frankreich. Frankfurter Zeitung, no. 73, 1900.   [1707]

----   Gutenberg und seine berühmtesten Nachfolger im ersten Jahr-
hundert der Typographie nach ihrem Leben und Wirken dargestellt von
Alfred Börckel. Mit einundfünfzig Abbildungen.   Frankfurt a. M.,
Klimsch & Co., 1900.   xii, 211p.   front. (port.) illus.   21.5 cm.
(On cover: Klimsch's graphische Bibliothek, Bd. V)   [1708]
    DLC   ICJ   ICN   MB   Eu-Fr-PN   Eu-Ge-LB   Eu-Ge-LSb

Börckel, Alfred, 1851-1928.
    Mainz als Gutenbergstadt vor 70 Jahren. (In Studien aus
Kunst und Geschichte Friedrich Schneider zum 70en Geburtstage ...
Freiburg im Br., Herder, 1906.   p. 19-27)   [1709]
    Eu-De-BP

Carlson, Axel A.
    Gutenberg; hans liv, hans werk och sättningarna därför, av Axel
A. Carlson.   Oskarshamm, Oskarshamms-Bladets boktryckeri, 1924.
96p.   illus. (incl. facsims., ports.)   8vo.   [1710]
    NN

Carro, Jean de.
    Jean Gutenberg né en Bohême.   Bulletin du Bibliophile Belge,
vol. 3, 1846, p. 484-486.   [1711]

Cherskii, L. F.
    Ioann Guttenberg i Ivan Fedorov.   St. Petersburg, Energiĩa,
1905.   iv, 32p.   illus.   [1712]

---- ----   Moskva, M. V. Kliukin, 1913.   40p.   port., illus.   [1713]
    Eu-Ru-MLe

Conrad, Gustav.
    Die Adam Gelthuss'sche Inschrift zu Ehren Johann Gutenbergs.
(In Dziatzko, Karl Franz Otto, ed.   Beiträge zur Theorie und
Praxis des Buch- und Bibliothekswesens ... Leipzig, M. Spirgatis,
1894-1904.   vol. 5, 1900, p. 13-25)   [1714]
    ICJ   ICN   IU   MB   Eu-Fr-PN   Eu-Ge-LB

Crous, E.
    Gutenberg.   (In Peddie, R. A., ed.   Printing, a short history
of the art.   London, Grafton & Co., 1927.   p. 1-5)   [1715]
    DLC   ICN   IU   In   MB   NN   RPJCB   ViU   Eu-Ge-LE

Danzer, Beda.
    Die Cistercienser und die Erfindung Gutenbergs.   Cistercienser
Chronik, no. 535, 1933, p. 259-261.   [1716]

Daunou, Pierre Claude François, 1761-1840.
    Guttemberg.   n.p., n.d.   8vo.   [1717]
    NN   Eu-Ge-LSb

De Vinne, Theodore Low, 1828-1914.
    The art of Gutenberg.   The early opposition to printing.
American Printer, vol. 30, 1900, p. 341.   [1718]

---- The Gutenberg anniversary.   A biography of the inventor and
some of his works.   American Printer, vol. 30, 1900, p. 218-221.
Same, Outlook, vol. 65, no. 1, May 1900, p. 31-37.   [1719]

Delecluze, Etienne Jean, 1781-1863.
    Jean Gutenberg, 1450; l'imprimerie.   Paris, Bourdier & Cie.,
1862. 43p. 8vo.   [1720]
    Eu-Fr-PN   Eu-Ge-LSb

Dertsch, Richard, 1894-
    Mainz zur Zeit Gutenbergs, Festvortrag gehalten bei der Eröffnungs-
feier der Gutenberg-Festwoche der Stadt Mainz am 20. Juni 1937 von
Dr. Richard Dertsch ... Mainz am Rhein, Gutenberg-Gesellschaft; [etc.,
etc.] 1937. 2 prel. leaves, 7-26p., 1 leaf. illus. 21 cm.
(Kleiner Druck der Gutenberg-Gesellschaft. Nr. 30)   [1721]
    DLC   ICN   Eu-De-BP   Eu-De-LBb   Eu-De-MzG

Didot, Ambroise Firmin, 1790-1876.
    Gutenberg (Jean ou Hans Gensfleisch) par M. Ambroise Firmin-Didot.
Extrait de la Nouvelle biographie générale ... [Paris, Firmin Didot
frères, fils et cie., 1859] [891]-916 col. 24 cm. [With his
Essai sur la typographie. Paris, 1851]
    Caption title.   [1722]
    DLC   ICN   Eu-De-LBb   Eu-Ge-LB   Eu-Ge-LSb

Dingelstedt, Franz, freiherr von, 1814-1881.
    Gutenbergs letzte Flucht. Fragment. <u>Morgenblatt</u> (Stuttgart),
no. 37-47, 1840.
    Title from Mohr, Jubelfeste.   [1723]

----   Iean Gutenberg, premier maître imprimeur, ses faits &
discours les plus dignes d'admiration, & sa mort. Ce récit fidèle,
écrit par Fr. Dingelstedt, est ici traduit de l'allemand en françois
par Gustave Revilliod. Genève, J. G. Fick, imprimeur, 1858.
1 prel. leaf, 69, [1]p. plates. 30.5 cm.
    Title vignette: Grande marque de Iosse Badius.   [1724]
    CSmH   DLC   ICN   MB   MdBP   MnU   NN   Eu-De-LBb   Eu-Fr-PC
    Eu-Fr-PN   Eu-Ge-LB   Eu-Ge-LP   Eu-Sz-BeG

----   Jean Gutenberg. Traduction par G. Revilliod. <u>Papyrus</u>,
vol. 14, 1933, p. 151-155, 225-228, 293-296, 425-428, 555-558,
621-626.   [1725]

----   John Gutenberg, first master printer, his acts and most remarkable discourses, and his death. From the German by Caroline
Wintour. London, Truebner & co., 1860. 4, 141p. 21.5 cm.
    Large paper. "Only one hundred copies printed."   [1726]
    CSmH   DLC   ICJ   ICN   IaU   MB   MdBP   NN   PBL
    Eu-De-LBb   Eu-Ge-LB   Eu-Ge-LP

----   Sechs Jahrhundert aus Gutenbergs Leben. Kleine Gabe zum
frossen Feste. Text von Dr. Franz Dingelstedt in Fulda; mit Rand-
zeichnungen von Prof. Friedr. Müller in Cassel. Holzschnitte von
Andrew, Best und Leloir in Paris und Prof. F. W. Gubitz in Berlin.

Druck von Jerome Hotop in Cassel. Cassel, J. Hotop, 1840.
3 prel. leaves, [3]-47p. illus. 35x26 cm.
    Poem in six cantos, entitled respectively: 1440, 1540, 1640,
1740, 1840, ??40.   [1727]
    DLC MBAt Eu-Fr-PN   Eu-Ge-LB

Domínguez, José de Jesús.
    Juan Guttemberg. Conferencia por el Dr. José de Jesús Domínguez.
Imprenta de M. Fernández. Mayagüez, 1882.   34p.   15.5 cm.   [1728]
    ICN

Dziatzko, Karl Franz Otto, 1842-1903.
    Gutenberg-Forschungen. Göttingische Gelehrten Anzeigen, vol.
164, 1902, p. 980-1000.   [1729]

———— Johann Gutenberg and the invention of printing. Literary
Collector, vol. 6, 1903, p. 69-81.   [1730]

———— Was wissen wir von dem Leben und der Person Joh. Gutenbergs?
[Leipzig, 1895] [34]-55p. 23.5 cm.
    "Der Text dieses Aufsatzes—ohne die Anmerkungen—gibt im wesent-
lichen einen Vortrag wieder, den ich im Winter 1892/93 in Göttin-
gen gehalten habe."—p. 36.
    Reprinted from his Beiträge zur Theorie und Praxis des Buch- und
Bibliotheks-Wesens, II. (Sammlung bibliothekswissenschaftlicher
Arbeiten. Hft. 8)   [1731]
    DLC ICN Eu-Fr-PN Eu-Ge-LB Eu-Ge-LSb

Eichenberg, Julius.
    Gutenberg und die Rechtswissenschaft. Börsenblatt für den
Deutschen Buchhandel, vol. 67, no. 136, June 1900, p. 4551-4552. [1732]

Falk, Franz, 1840-1909.
    Gutenberg, seine Person und seine Erfindung. Nach einem Vortrag,
gehalten in der Versammlung der Lehrer-Bezirks-Vereine Mainz und
Nieder-Olm am 22. November 1899; von Franz Falk ... Mainz, J. Falk III,
Söhne, 1900. 32p. illus. (incl. facsims.) 20 cm.   [1733]
    DLC ICJ Eu-De-BP Eu-Fr-PN Eu-Ge-LSb

———— Jvo Wittig von Hammelburg in Mainz. [Leipzig, O. Harrassowitz, 1889] 256-261p. 21.5 cm.
    Caption title.
    "Separatabdruck aus dem Centralblatt für Bibliothekswesen ... " [1734]
    DLC Eu-De-LBb

———— Der "Pilger" im Wappen der Gansefleisch zu Mainz in rechter
Deutung. Zentralblatt für Bibliothekswesen, vol. 20, 1903, p.
526-528.   [1735]

Filippov, N.
   Ioann Gutenberg, pervyi izobretatel' knigopechataniia. 2-e.
St. Petersburg, 1900. 32p. illus.   [1736]
   Eu-Ru-MLe
   3d ed., 1911: Eu-Ru-MLe

Fleischmann, Franz.
   Gutenberg im Licht der Schulbücher. Archiv für Buchgewerbe,
vol. 11, 1910, p. 143-146.   [1737]

France, Anatole, 1844-1924.
... Jean Gutenberg; suivi du Traitté des phantosmes de Nicole Lange-
lier; compositions de G. Bellenger, Bellery-Desfontaines, F. Florian
et Steinlen, gravées par Deloche, Ernest et Frédéric Florian, Froment,
Mathieu ... Paris, E. Pelletan, 1900. 6 prel. leaves, viii, 28p.
front., illus., port. 26.5 cm.
   Illustrated cover. Title and text in red and black.
   Tirée à 113 exemplaires, plus un pour chacune des bibliothèques
d'état.   [1738]
   DLC   ICJ   Eu-Fr-PN

Goudy, Frederic W.
   Gutenberg, father of printing. Modern Lithographer, vol. 8,
no. 2, Feb. 1940, p. 26-30, 69.   [1739]

Graf, P. W.
   Johannes Gutenberg. Graphische Nachrichten, vol. 19, no. 6,
June 1940, p. 203-232.   [1740]

Guillaume, B.
   Notice biographique et éloge de Jean Gutenberg, inventeur de
l'imprimerie. Chauny, 1861. 24p. 8vo.   [1741]
   Eu-De-LBb

   Gutenberg. A nyomdászat sa vele rokon szakmák Közlönye.
Erlau, 1866-1867. 4to.
   Title from van der Linde, Geschichte der Erfindung ...   [1742]

   Gutenberg et ses emules les premiers ateliers. Union Syndicale
et Fédération des Syndicats des Maîtres Imprimeurs de France.
Bulletin Officiel, no. 11, Nov. 1927, p. 62-85.   [1743]

   Die Gutenbergstadt Mainz. Zeitschrift für Deutschlands Buchdrucker, vol. 41, no. 62, 1929, p. 497-498.   [1744]

Heidenheimer, Heinrich, 1856-
   Die Heimatstadt der Druckkunst. Archiv für Buchgewerbe, vol.
42, 1905, p. 106-109.   [1745]

- 221 -

Helquerra y Garcia, A. de la.
  Gutenberg. Barcelona, Araluce, 1930. 144p.
  Title from Bibliographie des Bibliotheks und Buchwesens, 1930. [1746]

Hensler, Erwin.
  Gutenberghäuser in Mainz. Zeitschrift für Deutschlands Buchdrucker, vol. 20, no. 64, 1908, p. 803. [1747]

Hetzer, Theodor.
  Gutenberg und seine Kunst. Leipzig, Johann Ambrosius Barth
Verlag, 1940. 28p. 8vo. (Leipziger Universitätsreden, no. 3) [1748]
  Eu-Sz-BeG

Hohler, Emmerich Th.
  Zur Frage welcher Nation Johann von Gutenberg, der Erfinder der
Buchdruckerkunst angehöre. Wiener Zeitung, Mar. 22, 1840.
  Title from van der Linde, Geschichte der Erfindung ... [1749]

Howorth, Henry H.
  Gutenberg and Strassburg--some grave doubts. Academy, vol. 49,
no. 1233, 1896, p. 12-13. [1750]

---- Gutenberg-Corrigenda. Academy, vol. 49, no. 1238, 1896,
p. 78. [1751]

Hupp, Otto, 1859-
  Das Bild Gutenbergs. Gutenberg Jahrbuch, vol. 10, 1935, p. 18-
64. [1752]

Ihme, F. A.
  Gutenberg und die Buchdruckerkunst im Elsass. Von F. A. Ihme.
Strassburg, C. F. Schmidt, 1891. 52p. 23 cm. [1753]
  DLC   ICJ   MB   Eu-Fr-PN   Eu-Ge-LB   Eu-Ge-LSb

Juchhoff, Rudolf, 1894-
  Wandlungen des Gutenbergbildes. Zentralblatt für Bibliothekswesen, vol. 57, no. 5-6, May-June 1940, p. 202-214. [1754]

Kessler, P. T.
  Die Wappen im Hause Molsberg zu Mainz, darunter einnoch nicht
veröffentliches Wappen der Gensfleisch. (In Gutenbergfestschrift,
zur Feier des 25jaehrigen Bestehens des Gutenbergmuseum in Mainz
1925. Hrsg. von A. Ruppel. Mainz, Verlag der Gutenberg-Gesellschaft [1925] p. 342-344) [1755]
  DLC   ICN   MB   MH   NN   NNC   NNGr   Eu-De-BP   Eu-Ge-LB
  Eu-Ne-AVb   Eu-Sz-BeG

Ketring, Ruth Anna.
  Johann Neumeister: an assistant of Johann Gutenberg? Library
Quarterly, vol. 1, no. 4, Oct. 1931, p. 465-475. [1756]

Khaynach, Friedrich von.
　　Gutenberg, sein Leben und Wirken, in erzählender Form.　Köln,
1876.　12mo.
　　Title from Bigmore & Wyman.　　　　　　　　　　　　　　　　　[1757]

Koch, Matthias, 1797-
　　Kurzgefasste kritische Geschichte der Erfindung der Buchdrucker-
kunst, mit der ältesten Wiener und Österreichischen Buchdrucker-
geschichte, nebst Widerlegung der Ansprüche der Städte Strassburg
und Haarlem auf die Erfindung und Abfertigung der neuesten Behauptung:
Gutenberg sei ein Böhme und geborner Kuttenberger.　Wien, Singer &
Göring, 1841.　viii, 167p.　8vo.　　　　　　　　　　　　　　　　[1758]
　　Eu-Fr-PN　Eu-Ge-LB　Eu-Ge-LSb

　　Kurzer Abriss der Lebenschreibung Gutenbergs.　Nebst Nachrichten
über die Errichtung und Einweihung seines Denkmals von Thorwaldsen
zu Mainz.　Mainz, 1840.　viii, 207p.　8vo.　　　　　　　　　　[1759]
　　Eu-Ge-LB　Eu-Ge-LSb

Lamartine, Alphonse Marie Louis de, 1790-1869.
　　Gutenberg, inventeur de l'imprimerie.　Par A. de Lamartine ...
Paris, Librairie de L. Hachette et cie., 1853.　iv, 49p.　16.5 cm.
　　Note on p. 49: Cette biographie de Gutenberg est extraite du
　　Civilisateur.　　　　　　　　　　　　　　　　　　　　　　　　[1760]
　　ICN　IaU　MBAt　NN　Eu-Fr-PN　Eu-Ge-LP　Eu-Ge-LSb

---- ----　Deuxième édition.　Paris, L. Hachette et cie., 1866.
[4], 49p.　19.5 cm.　(On cover: Bibliothèque des chemins de fer)　[1761]
　　ICJ　IaU　NN　NNC　Eu-De-LBb　Eu-Fr-PN　Eu-Ge-LSb
　　Eu-Ne-AVb

---- ----　Troisième édition.　Paris, L. Hachette et cie., 1867.
49p.　18 cm.　　　　　　　　　　　　　　　　　　　　　　　　　[1762]
　　PBL　Eu-Fr-PN　Eu-Ge-LE

----　Guttemberg, inventor de la imprenta.　Boletin Bibliografico
Español, vol. 8, no. 5, 1867, p. 59-60; no. 7, p. 81-84; no, 8,
p. 92-96; no. 9, p. 104-108; no. 10, p. 118-120; no. 11, p. 127-129.[1763]

----　Memoirs of celebrated characters.　By Alphonse de Lamartine.
London, R. Bentley, 1854-1856.　3 vols.
　　Includes biography of Gutenberg.
　　A translation of articles from the "Civilisateur"; a literary
　　review by Lamartine, published in parts from 1852-1854.
　　Published also in Paris, 1855-1856, in a collection under
　　title: La vie des grands hommes.　　　　　　　　　　　　　　[1764]
　　DLC　IC　MB　MH　NN　Eu-Ge-LB

---- ----　New York, Harper, 1856.　2 vols.　　　　　　　　　[1765]
　　MdBP　NN

Lamartine, Alphonse Marie Louis de, 1790-1869.
   Memoirs of celebrated characters.   2d. ed., with additions.
London, R. Bentley, 1854-1858.   3 vols.   [1766]
   DLC   Eu-Ge-LB

———— ———— New ed.   London, Winchester (printed),R.Bentley,1860. [1767]
   Eu-Ge-LB

Lehne, Johann Friedrich Franz, 1771-1836.
   Aufschrift an das Haus Gutenbergs, des Erfinders der Buchdrucker-
kunst, zu Mainz 1803.   (In Kulb, P. H., ed.   Gesammelte Schriften.
Mainz, 1837-1839.   vol. 5, p. 377)   [1768]
   Eu-Fr-PN   Eu-Ge-LB

———— Das Haus zum Gensfleisch in Mainz, Stammhaus des Johann
Gensfleisch, genannt Gutenberg, Erfinders der Buchdruckerkunst.
(In Kulb, P. H., ed. Gesammelte Schriften.   Mainz, 1837-1839.
vol. 4, p. 245)   [1769]
   Eu-Fr-PN   Eu-Ge-LB

Lindblom, G. A.
   Johann Gutenberg och Tycho Brahe.   Svenska Boktryckareforeningens
Meddelanden, vol. 29, 1924, p. 181-183.   [1770]

Linde, Antonius van der, 1833-1897.
   Johann Gutenberg.   (In Allgemeine deutsche Biographie.   Leipzig,
1879.   vol. 10, p. 218-220)   [1771]

List, Hermann.
   Thomas und der Meister.   Eine Geschichte un Johannes Gutenberg,
den Erfinder der Buchdruckerkunst.   Stuttgart, B. Gundert Verlag,
1937.   124p.   8vo.   [1772]
   Eu-Sz-BeG

[Lüthi-Tschanz, Karl Jakob] 1876-
   Berühmte Buchdrucker [Teilabdruck von "Berühmte Buchdrucker von
Gutenberg bis Morris."]   Korrespondenz der Neuerscheinungen (Berlin),
Mar. 7, 1935.   Same, Darmstädter Zeitung, no. 57, Mar. 8, 1935.   [1773]

———— Berühmte Buchdrucker von Gutenberg bis Morris, Vortrag von
Karl J. Lüthi ... Mit xxii Tafeln und 8 Text-Illustrationen.   [Bern,
Buchdruckerei Büchler & Co.] 1935.   30p., 1 leaf.   front., illus.,
xxi facsims.   23.5 cm.   (Bibliothek des Schweizer.   Gutenberg-
museums.   Nr. 4, 1935)
   "Benützte Literatur": p. 25-27.   [1774]
   DLC   Eu-Sz-BeG

———— Gutenberg, Bodoni, Morris.   Een vergelijking hunner kunst.
Grafische Revue, no. 3, 4, 6, 1925.   [1775]

Lüthi-Tschanz, Karl Jakob, 1876–
   Gutenberg, Bodoni, Morris, eine Vergleichung ihrer Kunst;
Vortrag gehalten an der Delegierten-Versammlung des Bildungsver-
bandes Schweiz. Buchdrucker, Samstag den 13. September 1924, im
"Grütlibund", im Chur, von Karl J. Lüthi. Bern, Buchdruckerei
Büchler & Co., 1925. 4 prel. leaves, 38p., 1 leaf, iv facsims.
14.5 cm.
   "Gedruckt in 250 Exemplaren ... "
   "Benützte Literatur": p. 37–38.   [1776]
   DLC   ICJ   Eu-Sz-BeG

Lüthi-Tschanz, Karl Jakob and H. Tribolet.
   De Guetebärgmuseum u sy alti Handpräss. Schweizerisches
Gutenbergmuseum, vol. 21, no. 3, 1935, p. 146–152.
   Transcript of a radio interview over Radio-Bern, conducted
   in Bern-German.
   Also reprint.   [1777]

McMurtrie, Douglas Crawford, 1888–
   Wings for words; the story of Johann Gutenberg and his in-
vention of printing, by Douglas C. McMurtrie, with the collabora-
tion of Don Farran, illustrated by Edward A. Wilson. New York,
Chicago [etc.], Rand McNally & company, 1940. 175, [1]p. incl.
illus., 2 facsims. on 1 leaf. 24 cm.
   Illustrated t.-p. and lining papers.   [1778]
   DLC   NN

Malten, H.
   Ist der Erfinder der Buchdruckerkunst ein Mainzer oder ein
Böhme? (In Bibliothek der neuesten Weltkunde. Aarau, 1841.
no. 1, p. 131)
   Title from van der Linde, Geschichte der Erfindung ...   [1779]

Martens, Wilhelm, 1858–
   Johann Gutenberg und die Erfindung der Buchdruckerkunst. Ein
kulturgeschichtliches Bild zur fünfhundertjährigen Gedenkfeier
von Gutenbergs Geburtstag, von Prof. Dr. W. Martens. Karlsruhe,
J. Lang, 1900. 46p. incl. front. illus. (port., facsim.)
21 cm.   [1780]
   DLC   ICJ   MB   MH   Eu-Fr-PN   Eu-Ge-LSb   Eu-Ne-AVb

Marzi, Demetrio.
   Giovanni Gutenberg e l'Italia. Bibliofilia, vol. 2, 1900–
1901, p. 81–135.   [1781]

——— Giovanni Gutenberg preceduto nelle sua scoperta. Bibliofilia, vol. 12, May 1910, p. 71–72.   [1782]

——— Gutenberg und Italien. Antiquitäten-Zeitung, no. 41,
1900.   [1783]

Mazzucotelli, Antonio.
L'arte del Guttemberg ossia la stampa; opera del sacerdote
Antonio Mazzucotelli, parroco di Gorle diocesi di Bergamo, utile ad
ogni ceto e precipuamente alla gioventu' studiosa. Torino, Tip.
dell' oratorio di S. Franc. di Sales, 1863. viii, 295p. 20.5cm.[1784]
ICN IU NN NNC Eu-Ge-LSb

Neeb, Ernst.
Gutenberghauser zu Mainz; Auszug aus dem Festvortrag ... gehalten
in der Mitglieder-Versammlung der Gutenberg-Gesellschaft zu Mainz
am 28. Juni 1908. Gutenberg-Gesellschaft. Jahresberichte, 1908,
p. 27-37. [1785]

----- El origen de Gutenberg. Gutenberg (Buenos Aires), vol. 40,
no. 18, 1940, p. 1-4.
Summary of a lecture delivered at Mainz by Prof. Ernst Neeb;
translated from the French by J. Moras. [1786]

Oberlin, Jérémie Jacques, 1735-1806.
... Essai d'annales de la vie de Jean Gutenberg, inventeur de la
typographie, par professeur Jér. Jacques Oberlin ... A Strasbourg,
dans la salle d'actes de l'Ecole centrale du départment du Bas-
Rhin, le 18 fructidor ... an IX [1801]. [Strasbourg, Impr. de
Levrault, 1801] 1 prel. leaf, 45p. 20 cm. [1787]
DLC ICJ ICN IaU Eu-De-LBb Eu-Fr-PN Eu-Ge-LB
Eu-Ge-LE Eu-Ge-LP Eu-Ne-AVb

----- ----- New edition. Strasbourg, Levrault, 1840. 51p. 20cm.[1788]
NNGr

Oertel, Hugo.
Johann Gutenberg, der Erfinder der Buchdruckerkunst. Zur dank-
baren Erinnerung der deutschen Jugend und dem deutschen Volke
geschildert. Mit vier Abbildungen. Wiesbaden, Julius Niedner,
Verlagshandlung, 1880. 144p. ports. 11.5x15.5 cm. [1789]
PPG Eu-De-LBb

Pamiatnik Guttenbergu, Fausti i Shefferu. Russkii Vestnik, vol.
10, no. 14, 1857, p. 110. [1790]

Peters, Adolf.
Johann Gutenberg; sein Werk, sein Schicksal. [Mainz, 1837]
Title from Mohr, Jubelfeste. [1791]

Potocki, A.
O Jani Gutenbergu i o tem, jak sie ludzie nauczyli pisac i druckowac.
Warszawa, Ksiegarna polska, 1927. 39p.
Title from Bibliographie des Bibliotheks und Buchwesens, 1927. [1792]

Proskuriakov, V. M.
   Ioann Gutenberg.   Moskva, Zhurnal'nogazetnoe ob'-edinenie, 1933.
139p.   illus. (Seriia biografischeskaia.   Zhizn' zamechatel'-
nykh liudei, 19.)   [1793]
   NN   Eu-Ru-MLe

Rodenberg, Julius.
   Die Heimatstadt der Druckkunst.   Zeitschrift für Deutschlands
Buchdrucker, vol. 38, no. 98, 1926, p. 810-811.   [1794]

Roth, F. Wilhelm Emil, 1853-
   Gutenbergstudien.   Nassovia, vol. 14, 1913, p. 105-107, 117-119. [1795]

----   Johannes Gensfleisch zum Gutenberg, Erfinder der Typographie.
Hessische Chronik, vol. 5, 1916, p. 202-210.   [1796]

Ruppel, Aloys Leonhard, 1882-
   Auf der Suche nach dem Grabe Gutenbergs.   Börsenblatt für den
Deutschen Buchhandel, vol. 98, no. 88, 1931, p. 388.   Same,
Graphische Jahrbücher, vol. 52, 1931, p. 153-155.   Same, Gutenberg
Jahrbuch, vol. 6, 1931, p. 345-349.   Same, Schweizerisches Guten-
bergmuseum, vol. 17, no. 2, 1931, p. 91-96.   Same, Zeitschrift für
Deutschlands Buchdrucker, vol. 43, 1931, p. 292-293.   [1797]

----   Das Grab Gutenbergs, von Dr. A. Ruppel ... Mainz, Verlag der
Gutenberg-Gesellschaft, 1930.   2 prel. leaves, 7-37, iv p., 2
leaves.   illus. (plans)   20 cm.   (Kleiner Druck der Gutenberg-
Gesellschaft.   Nr. 13)
   "Anmerkungen": p. i-iv.   [1798]
   CSmH   DLC   ICN   MB   Eu-De-BP   Eu-Ge-LB   Eu-Ne-AVb
   Eu-Sz-BeG

----   Gutenberg in Strassburg. Seine Strassburger Druckversuche.
Frankfurt am Main, Moritz Diesterweg, 1939.   8vo.
   Reprint from Elsass-Lothringisches Jahrbuch, vol. 18, 1939 .   [1799]
   Eu-Sz-BeG

----   Die Heimatstadt der Druckkunst, von Dr. A. Ruppel ... Mainz
[etc.] Verlag der Gutenberg-Gesellschaft, 1926.   36p., 1 leaf.
22 cm.   (Kleiner Druck der Gutenberg-Gesellschaft.   Nr. 2)   [1800]
   DLC   IC   ICN   IU   NN   NjP   Eu-De-BP   Eu-De-LBb
   Eu-Ge-LB   Eu-Ne-AVb   Eu-Sz-BeG

----   Johannes Gensfleisch zum Gutenberg.   (In Altmeister der
Druckschrift, in Gutenberg-Jahr 1940 gedruckt und herausgegeben
von der Schriftgiesserei D. Stempel AG, Frankfurt a.M.   p. 9-
21)   [1801]
   McMurtrie

Ruppel, Aloys Leonhard, 1882-
    Johannes Gutenberg der Erfinder der Buchdruckerkunst. [2d
revised ed.] Leipzig, Friedrich Brandstetter, 1940. 20p.
1 plate. 8vo. [1802]
    Eu-Sz-BeG

---- Johannes Gutenberg, der Sohn des Rhein- Main- Gebietes.
Rhein-Mainische-Wirtschafts-Zeitung (Frankfurt am Main), no. 25,
June 18, 1940. [1803]

---- Johannes Gutenberg; sein Leben und sein Werk, von Aloys
Ruppel ... Berlin, Gebr. Mann, 1939. 3 prel. leaves, 9-224p.
illus. (incl. geneal. tab.) facsims. (3 fold. in pocket) 27.5 cm.[1804]
    DLC   NN   Eu-Ne-AVb

---- Mainz als Gutenbergstadt, von Dr. A. Ruppel ... Mainz, Gutenberg-Gesellschaft, 1928. 2 prel. leaves, 3-21, [1]p. 22.5 cm.
(Kleiner Druck der Gutenberg-Gesellschaft. Nr. 8)
    "Benutzte Literatur": p. 21. [1805]
    DLC   IC   ICN   IU   NN   NjP   Eu-De-BP   Eu-De-LBb
    Eu-Ge-LB   Eu-Ne-AVb   Eu-Sz-BeG

---- När dog Gutenberg? Var ligger han begraven? Grafiskt Forum,
vol. 43, 1938, p. 116-119. Same, Nordisk Boktryckarekonst, vol. 39,
1938, p. 169-171. [1806]

---- Quando mori Gutenberg? Dove è sepolto? Bibliofilia, vol.
40, 1938, p. 328-330. Same, Giornale della Libreria, vol. 51,
1938, p. 113-114. [1807]

---- Die Stadt Mainz und ihr grosser Sohn Gutenberg. Berlin und
Mainz, Kupferberg, 1940. 47p. plates.
    Title from Zentralblatt für Bibliothekswesen, 1940. [1808]

---- Starb Gutenberg eines gewaltsamen Todes? Zeitschrift für
Deutschlands Buchdrucker, vol. 43, 1931, p. 102-103, 112-113. [1809]

---- Tätigkeitsbericht der Gutenberg-Gesellschaft für 1930-1931
mit einem Bericht über die Suche nach dem Grabe Gutenbergs.
Gutenberg Jahrbuch, vol. 6, 1931, p. 344. [1810]

---- Der Totenschild am Grabe Gutenbergs. Gutenberg Jahrbuch,
vol. 12, 1937, p. 35-42. [1811]

---- Über den Wohnort Gutenbergs in seinem letzten Lebensjahren.
Gutenberg Jahrbuch, vol. 3, 1928, p. 58-68. [1812]

---- Wann starb Gutenberg? Wo liegt er begraben? Börsenblatt
für den Deutschen Buchhandel, vol. 105, 1938, no. 56, p. 195-196.

Same, Graphische Jahrbücher, vol. 59, 1938, p. 77-79. Same, Graphische Nachrichten, vol. 17, 1938, p. 357-359. Same, Wochenblatt für Papierfabrikation, Sondernummer, 1938, p. 15-16.   [1813]

Ruppel, Aloys Leonhard, 1882-
   Wo starb Gutenberg? Graphische Jahrbucher, vol. 58, 1937,
p. 173-177.   [1814]

Schaab, Carl Anton, 1761-1855.
   Geschichte der Stadt Mainz von K. A. Schaab ... Mainz, 1841-51.
Auf Kosten des Verfassers. In Kommission bei F. Kupferberg.
4 vols. 20.5 cm.
   Title and imprints vary slightly.   [1815]
   MH   Eu-Ge-LB

Schenk zu Schweinsberg, Gustav Ferdinand Karl Johann Ernst Ludwig,
     freiherr, 1842-
   Ueber Johann Gutenberg's Grabstätte und Namen.   Von Gustav
frhrn. Schenk zu Schweinsberg.   Darmstadt [1881]   21p.   20.5 cm.
   Caption title.
   No. [3] in a vol. lettered Schenk z. S. kl. Aufsätze ...
   "Separatabdruck aus 'Archiv des Histor. Vereins für das
   Grossh. Hessen.' 15 Bd. 2. Hft. S. 337-357."   [1816]
   DLC

Schmidt, Charles Guillaume Adolphe, 1812-1895.
   Nouveaux détails sur la vie de Gutenberg, tirés des archives de
l'ancien chapitre de Saint-Thomas à Strasbourg, par C. Schmidt ...
Strasbourg, Impr. de G. Silbermann, 1841.   cover-title, 8p.
21.5 cm.
   Tail-piece: printer's mark.   [1817]
   DLC   NN   Eu-De-LBb   Eu-Ge-LB

[Schnitzler, J. H.]
   Notice sur Jean Gutenberg, l'inventeur de la typographie.
Extrait de l'Encyclopédie des Gens du Monde, T. XIII, p. 328 et
suiv.   Paris, Duverger, ca. 1840.   3p.   8vo.   [1818]
   Eu-Ge-LSb

Scholderer, Victor, 1880-
   Gutenberg: the man and his invention. Chequered fortunes of
the father of printing. London Times, Jan. 15, 1940. Special
section on commemoration of the five hundredth anniversary of
the invention of printing by movable type, p. i-ii.   [1819]

Schrohe, Heinrich, 1864-
   Mainzer Leben in fünfzehnten Jahrhundert.   (In Gutenberg-
Feier in Mainz.   1900 ... [Mainz] Mainzer Verlags-Anstalt und
Druckerei A.-G. [1900]   [1820]
   DLC   ICJ   ICN   MH   Eu-Fr-PN   Eu-Ge-JB   Eu-Ge-LSb   Eu-Ne-AVb

Sleptsov, N.
  Guttenberg, izobretatel' knigopechataniia. Moskva, Panafidin,
1900. 55p.   [1821]
  Eu-Ru-MLe

Thevet, André, 1502-1590.
  Jean Guttemberg, inventeur de l'imprimerie. (In Thevet, André.
Pourtraits et vies des hommes illustres. Paris, 1584. vol. 2, folios
514-516)   [1822]
  McMurtrie

----   Jean Guttemberg, inventor of printing. A translation by
Douglas C. McMurtrie of the essay in André Thevet's "Vies des hommes
illustres", Paris, 1589. [New York] 1926. 2 prel. leaves, 3-8p.,
1 leaf, incl. front. (port.) 29x23 cm.
    Colophon: Printed in the year MCMXXVI by Douglas C. McMurtrie, New
    York. Typography and calligraphy by Frank E. Powers. The edition
    limited to one hundred & ninety copies ... "   [1823]
  CSmH   DLC   ICN

Theele, Joseph, 1889-
  Das literarische Denkmal für Futenberg, Festvortrag gehalten in der
Generalversammlung der Gutenberg-Gesellschaft in Mainz am 27. Juni 1937
von dem Direktor der Landesbibliothek Fulda, Dr. Joseph Theele. Mainz,
Verlag der Gutenberg-Gesellschaft, 1938. 2 prel. leaves, 7-44p., 1
leaf. 21 cm. (Kleiner Druck der Gutenberg-Gesellschaft. Nr. 32)[1824]
  DLC

Thiel, Rudolf, 1899-
  Kritische Gutenbergstudien. Gutenberg Jahrbuch, vol. 14, 1939,
p. 62-86.   [1825]

Tronnier, Adolph, 1875-
  ... Über Gutenberg-Bildnisse. Mainz, G. A. Walter's Druckerei, G.m.b.H.,
1913. 31p. illus. (11 port.) 24 cm. (Beilage zum 12. Jahresbericht der Gutenberg-Gesellschaft)   [1826]
  DLC   ICJ   ICN   MB   NN   Eu-De-BP   Eu-Go-LB   Eu-Ne-AVb

----   Vier neue Gutenberg-Bildnisse des Gutenberg-Museums, Mainz.
[Mainz, Gutenberg-Gesellschaft, 1930] 1 prel. leaf, 5-31, [1]p., 1
leaf. 4 illus. (ports.) 22.5 cm. (Kleiner Druck der Gutenberg-
Gesellschaft. Nr. 11)   [1827]
  DLC   ICN   ICU   MB   MH   NN   Eu-De-BP   Eu-Go-LB   Eu-Ne-AVb

Vinařický, Karel Alois, 1803-1869.
  Jean Gutenberg, né en 1412 à Kuttenberg en Bohême, bachelier ès
arts à l'Université de Prague, promu le 18 Novembre 1445, inventeur
de l'imprimerie à Mayence en 1450. Essai historique et critique, par
le révérend Charles Winaricky ... Tr. du manuscrit allemand par le

chevalier Jean de Carro ... Bruxelles, A. Vandale, 1847.   104p.
18.5 cm.   [1828]
    DLC   ICJ   ICN   NN   NNUT   Eu-Ge-LP   Eu-Ge-LSb   Eu-Ne-GK

Vinařický, Karel Alois, 1803-1869.
    Johann Gutenberg geboren zu Kuttenberg in Böhmen 1442 ... <u>Oester-
reichische Blätter</u>, no. 90, 1846.   [1829]

---- Johannes Gutenberg. <u>Serapeum</u>, vol. 11, no. 14, 1850, p. 209-
224; no. 15, p. 225-240; no. 16, p. 241-254.   [1830]

Wallau, Heinrich Wilhelm.
    Gutenberg, Techniker und Kunstler; Vortrag gehalten ... am 25. Juni
1905.   Gutenberg-Gesellschaft. <u>Jahresberichte</u>, 1905, p. 10-28.   [1831]

---- Johann Gutenberg.   (In The Catholic encyclopedia.   New York,
1913.   vol. 7, p. 90-91)   [1832]

Wallmark, Peter Adam, 1777-1858.
    Johan Gutenberg; hans uppfinning, dess utbredande och framsteg.
Historiskt utkast i anledning af boktryckeri-konstens fjerde jubel-
ar; uppläst vid den i Frimurar-ordens lokal af Boktryckeri-societeten
föranstaltade fest, den 5 Juli 1840, af dess ordförande P. A. Wallmark
... Stockholm, P. A. Norstedt & söner, 1840.   1 prel. leaf, 114p.
front.   26.5 cm.
    On cover: Tal i anledning af boktryckeri-konstens fjerde jubelar.
    "Berättelse om den, af Boktryckeri-societeten, i anledning af
    boktryckeri-konstens fjerde jubel-ar, den 5 Juli 1840 föranstal-
    tade fest": p. 106-114.   [1833]
    DLC   NN   Eu-Ge-LSb

Wentzke, Paul.
    Strassburg zur Zeit Gutenbergs.   <u>Elsass-Lothringisches Jahrbuch</u>,
vol. 19, 1940.   [1834]

Werdet, Edmond, 1795-1869.
    Gutenberg, Faust, Schoeffer.   (In Werdet, Edmond. Histoire du
livre en France ... Paris, E. Dentu, 1861-1864.   vol. 1, p. 214-292) [1835]
    DLC   ICJ   MB   MH   NN   Eu-Ge-LB

Westfehling, J.
    Gutenberg.   Eine Biographie, zusammengestellt und nach verschiedenen
Quellen bearbeitet.   Winterthur, 1878.   8p.   4to.
    Title from Bigmore and Wyman.   [1836]

Wiesenthal, Heinrich.
    Graphische Techniker: Johannes Gutenberg, Aloys Senefelder, Louis
Jacques Daguerre, Nicephore Niepce. Leipzig, Weigel, 1925.   64p.
8vo.   (Führende Männer, 6)   [1837]
    Eu-De-LBb

Winship, George Parker, 1871–
    John Gutenberg; a lecture at the University of Pennsylvania
delivered on February 14, 1940, by the Rosenbach fellow in bibliography, George Parker Winship ... Chicago, The Lakeside press, 1940.
3 prel. leaves, 38p., 1 leaf.   19.5 cm.
        "There were printed 650 copies as Keepsake no. 65 for the American
    institute of graphic arts; for the Philobiblon club of Philadelphia
    150 copies; and 100 copies for the author and printer."   [1838]
    DLC   NjN

Woski, Zbigniew.
    Jan Gutenberg, szkic biograficzny ... Warszawa, 1894.   32p.
8vo.   [1839]
    Eu-Ge-LB

Wyss, Arthur Franz Wilhelm, 1852–1900.
    War Gutenberg verheiratet?   Zeitschrift für Bücherfreunde,
vol. 4, 1900, p. 335–336.   [1840]

Zedler, Gottfried, 1860–
... Gutenberg und Schöffer im Lichte des Mainzer Frühdrucks ... von Gottfried Zedler.   Mainz, Verlag der Gutenberg-Gesellschaft, 1929–
illus., facsims. (part double)   29 cm.   (Veröffentlichungen der
Gutenberg-Gesellschaft, XX, XXIII)
    Each volume has also special t.-p.   [1841]
    CtY   DLC   ICJ   ICN   NN   Eu-De-BP   Eu-De-LBb   Eu-De-MzG
    Eu-Ge-LB   Eu-Ge-LSb   Eu-Ne-AVb   Eu-Sz-BeG

Zöller, Edmund.
    Johannes Gutenberg von Winaricky.   Serapeum, vol. 11, 1850.
p. 209–223, 225–241.   [1842]

D.   POPULAR WRITINGS

    Alcuni fatti interessanti.   Risorgimento Grafico, vol. 30, no. 7,
July 1935, p. 416–417.   [1843]

    Altmeister Gutenberg, der Erfinder der Buchdruckerkunst.   Zur
Buchdrucker-Jubiläumsfeier in Wien.   Welt-Neuigkeitsblatt (Wien),
no. 99, 1882.   [1844]

Arkad'ev, E. I.
    Guttenberg.   (In Arkad'ev, E. I.   Slovar' bibliofila t. e.
slov, kasaiushchikhsia knizhnago dela ... Moskva, 1890.   p. 33–34)   [1845]
    NN

Bahnsen, Broder.
Gutenberg's Sendung. Ein Spiel in drei Bildern. Berlin, Verlag des Bildungsverbandes der Deutschen Buchdrucker, 1926. 38p. 8vo. [1846]
Eu-De-BP   Eu-De-LBb

Bateman, George W.
Gutenberg - a sketch. Inland Printer, vol. 4, 1887, p. 717-718. [1847]

Berlin, ÎA. A.
Gutenberg. (In Berlin, ÎA. A. Istoriiã knigi. Kul'turno-istor-icheskii ocherk. St. Petersburg, O. N. Popova, 1906. p. 74-81) [1848]
Eu-Ru-MLe

Birch-Pfeiffer, Charlotte, 1800-1868.
Johannes Gutenberg. Original-Schauspiel in drei Abtheilungen. 2. Auflage. Mit einer Ansicht der Statue Gutenbergs in Mainz. Nebst einer kurzgefassten Geschichte der Buchdruckerkunst von ihrem Ursprunge bis zur Gegenwart, und einem Programm der Festlichkeiten am 24., 25. und 26. Juni, in verschiedenen deutschen Städten. Berlin, L. W. Krause, 1840. 87p. 8vo. [1849]
Eu-De-LBb
1863 ed.: NjP   1865 ed.: GEU

Birkenfeld, Günther, 1901-
Die schwarze Kunst. Ein Gutenberg-Roman. Leipzig, Oswald Schmidt, G.m.b.H.: Berlin, Paul Neff Verlag, 1936. 388p. 8vo. [1850]
NN   Eu-Sz-BeG

Björkbom, Carl, 1898-
Gutenberg. Svenska Boktryckareforeningens Meddelanden, vol. 36, p. 316-320, 392-397. [1851]

Bleyer, Hans, 1880-
Gutenbergs Schöpfertraum, Erzählung von Hans Bleyer-Härtl. Verlag der Gutenberg-Gesellschaft, 1930. 19p., 1 leaf. 23 cm. (Kleiner Druck der Gutenberg-Gesellschaft. Nr. 15) [1852]
CSmH   DLC   ICN   MB   MH   NNU-W   Eu-De-MzG   Eu-Ne-AVb

Börckel, Alfred, 1851-1928.
Gutenberg. Illustrierte Zeitung, no. 2973, 1900. [1853]

---- Gutenberg. Historisches Drama in drei Akten ... Mainz, Verlag von Victor von Zabern, 1883. iv, 81, [1]p. 22 cm. [1854]
MB   Eu-Ge-LB   Eu-Ge-LSb

---- Gutenberg, historisches Drama in vier Akten, nach der ersten Fassung neu bearbeitet. Mainz, K. Theyer [1900] 67p. 8vo. [1855]
Eu-Fr-PN   Eu-Ge-LB

Börckel, Alfred, 1851-1928.
   Gutenberg, historisches Drama in vier Akten ... (In Gutenbergfeier
in Mainz. 1900 ... [Mainz] Mainzer Verlags-Anstalt und Druckerei
[1900]   [1856]
   DLC   ICJ   ICN   MH   Eu-Fr-PN   Eu-Ge-LB   Eu-Ge-LSb
   Eu-Ne-AVb

Buchler, G.
   Gutenberg. A portrait composed in brass rule by G. B.   Bern,
1883. Folio.   [1857]
   Eu-Ge-LSb

Bulgakov, F. I.
   Guttenberg. Literaturnye zamentki, radzel 2.   Novoe Vremia, no.
8686, May 4-17, 1900.   [1858]

Camici, Dino A.
   Gutenberg. L'Arte della Stampa, 6th ser., vol. 33, no. 25, 1903,
p. 202-204; no. 30, p. 251; no. 31, p. 259-260; no. 32, p. 266-
267.   [1859]

[Cary, Melbert Brinckerhoff] 1892-
   The missing Gutenberg wood blocks. New York, Press of the Woolly
whale, 1940.   [13]p., 1 leaf, 20 plates, 1 leaf.   22 cm.
   Purports to be reproductions of 20 prints from wood blocks
   possibly contemporary with Gutenberg; a hoax.   [1860]
   DLC   NjN

Cathiau, T.
   Johannes Gutenberg, geb. 1398, gest. 1468. Dramatische Szene.
(In Wedkind, H. Zur 50 jährigen Jubel Feier ... 1879)   [1861]
   Eu-Ge-LSb

Chistiakov, M. B.
   Guttenberg. (In Chistiakov, M. B. Biograficheskie rasskazy.
Sobrany is Zhurnala dlia detei.   St. Petersburg, V. A. Nevel'skii,
1896.   p. 255-271)   [1862]

Clostre, Eugène.
   Gutenberg.   Paris [1850?]   Folio.   [1863]
   Eu-Ge-LSb

Collas, H.
   L'atelier de Gutenberg.   Courrier Graphique, vol. 2, no. 7, 1937,
p. 1-7.   [1864]

Cornwall, Raymond L.
   Gutenberg and what we know of him.   Typographical Journal, vol.
79, no. 4, Oct. 1931, p. 383-386. Same, London Typographical
Journal, June 1932, p. 9; July, p. 13.   [1865]

Daniel', M. N.
Isobretatel' i komediant. (Iogann Gutenberg.) P'esa v 4 aktakh,
8 kart. Russkii tekst L. Ostrovera. Moskva, Iskusstvo, 1938. 92p. [1866]
Eu-Ru-MLe

Danko, E. I.
Ioann Gutenberg. Poema. Ris B. Tronova. Moskva, Raduga, 1925.
23p. [1867]
Eu-Ru-MLe

Delepierre, Octove.
John Gutenberg, first master printer. Philobiblon Society: Miscellanies, vol. 5, 1858-1859, p. 3-141. [1868]

Denisov, L. I.
Pervopechatnik Ioann Gutenberg i Ivan Fedorov. Moskva, Stupin,
1908. 42p. illus. [1869]
Eu-Ru-MLe

Dessoff, Albert.
Der Weg zu Gutenberg. Frankfurter Zeitung, no. 492, July 5,
1929. [1870]

Dürrbach.
Gutenberg's Gattin. Poesie. Druck von F. C. Heitz, im Jahre
des IV. Jubelfestes ... am Vorabend des grossen Festes. Strassburg,
1840. 4p. 8vo. [1871]
Eu-Ge-LSb

Eberle, Johann Georg.
Johannes Gutenberg; Volks-Schauspiel in fünf Aufzügen, von Johann
Georg Eberle. Zweite Auflage. Wien, 1902, Selbstverlag des Ver-
fassers; 11. Bezirk, Leopoldsgasse Nr. 28. Auch in Buchhandlungen
zu haben. 72p. 20.5 cm. [1872]
NN Eu-Ge-LSb

Eenige bijzonderheden uit het leven van Johann Gutenberg. Drukkers Weekblad, vol. 24, 1934, p. 541-542. [1873]

Ehrhardt, Robert.
Johannes Gutenberg, Festspiel in drei Abtheilungen. Halle
an der Saale, P. Goldschmidt, 1902. 24p. 8vo. [1874]
Eu-De-BP Eu-Ge-LSb

Fedorov, Ivan.
Gutenberg-pervopechatnik. (In Modestov, A. P. Zamechatel'nye
rabotniki nauki i tekhniki. Moskva, Assnat, 1927. vol. 1, p. 69-
73) [1875]
Eu-Ru-MLe

- 235 -

Figuier, Louis Guillaume.
    Gutenberg. (In Figuier, L. Svetila nauki. Zhizneopisaniia
zamechatel'nykh uchenykh ot drevnosti i do nashikh dnei i kratkaia
otsenka trudov. Perevod s frants. pod. red. N. Strakhova, 3 vols.
1869-1873. vol. 2, p. 152-207) [1876]
    Eu-Ru-MLe

---- Gutenberg, pièce historique en cinq actes, huit tableaux.
Paris, Tresse et Stock, 1886. 123p. 8vo. [1877]
    Eu-Fr-PN

---- Jean Gutenberg. (In Figuier, Louis. Vies des savants illustres du moyen age ... Paris, 1867. p. 309-370) [1878]
    MBAt   MdBP   NN   Eu-Ne-GK

---- Jean Gutenberg d'après les derniers documents. Revue Contem-
poraine, vol. 6, 1866, p. 48-87. [1879]

Figuier, Mme. Louis, née Juliette Bouscaren.
    ... Gutenberg; drame historique en cinq actes et en prose, par Mme.
Louis Figuier. Paris, Librairie Internationale, 15 Boulevard Mont-
martre; A. Lacroix, Verboeckhoven & C⁰, Éditeurs, à Bruxelles, à
Leipzig et à Livourne, 1869. Tous droits de représentation, de traduction et de reproduction réservés. 106p. 17 cm.
    At head of title: Nouvelle bibliothèque dramatique. [1880]
    NN   Eu-Fr-PN   Eu-Ge-LB   Eu-Ge-LSb

Filippov, A.
    Kogda rodilsia Ioann Gutenberg? Novoe Vremia, no. 8378, July 8,
1899. [1881]

    The first impression; Gutenberg at Mainz. American Printer, vol.
51, 1911, facing p. 569.
    Reproduction by 4-color halftone plates of a painting in the Plantin
museum at Antwerp. [1882]

Foa, Eugénie.
    Gutenberg. (In her Les enfants illustres, contes historiques ...
Paris, A. Bédelet, 1858. p. 33-58) [1883]
    MB   Eu-Fr-PN   Eu-Ge-LB   Eu-Ge-LSb

Fogg, Samuel C.
    A sketch of Gutenberg. Printer, vol. 2, no. 2, 1859, p. 30-31. [1884]

Fournier, Edouard, 1819-1880.
    Gutenberg, drame en cinq actes et en vers. Représenté, pour la
première fois à Paris, sur le Theatre imperial de l'Odéon, le 8 avril
1869. Paris, E. Dentu, Libraire-éditeur, Palais-royale, 17 et 19,
Galerie d'Orleans, 1869. 6 prel. leaves, [3]-137p. 22.5 cm. [1885]
    ICN   Eu-Ge-LB   Eu-Ge-LSb

Franchini, Ettore.
  Giovanni Gutenberg.   Rassegna Grafica, vol. 5, no. 56-57, 1930. [1886]

Frobenius, L.
  Gutenberg.   Sozialistische Monatshefte, 1900, p. 403-407.   [1887]

Fuchs, J. C.
  Gutenberg. Opera. Wien, 1870. Folio.
  Title from van der Linde, Geschichte der Erfindung ...   [1888]

Gotthold, Friedrich August.
  Johann Gutenberg. Akrostichon.   Preussische Provinz-Blätter, vol.
24, [ca. 1840] p. 513-520.   [1889]

Gottner, G.
  Gutenberg. Ein Festspiel. München, 1878. 12mo.   [1890]
  Eu-Ge-ISb

Grieshaber.
  Der grosse Wurf Gutenbergs.   Graphische Jahrbücher, vol. 57, 1936,
p. 155-158.   [1891]

  Gutenberg.   Deutscher Hausschatz in Wort und Bild, vol. 26, no.
35, 1900.   [1892]

  Gutenberg.   Monatsschrift für Deutsche Beamte, 1900, p. 191.   [1893]

  Gutenberg.   Pravitel'stvennyi Vestnik, no. 275, Dec. 10, 1881. [1894]

  Gutenberg and the "yellow" editor. Imaginary conversation of Gutenberg with an American editor.   Blackwood's Edinburgh Magazine, vol.
168, Sept. 19, 1900, p. 399-402.   Same, Living Age, vol. 227, Nov.
1900, p. 451-453.   Same, Eclectic Magazine, vol. 136, 1901, p. 126. [1895]

  Gutenberg burial place.   Publishers' Weekly, vol. 134, no. 3,
July 1938, p. 159.   [1896]

  Gutenberg und Frauenlob. Mainz, 1881. 4to.
  Title from van der Linde, Geschichte der Erfindung ...   [1897]

  Gutenberg und seine Kunst.   Archiv für Post und Telegraphie,
vol. 28, 1900, p. 605.   [1898]

  Gutenberg und seine Zeit.   [Bericht über einem Vortrag von F.
Hönig.]   Deutscher Drucker, vol. 45, no. 533, 1938-1939, p. 209-
212.   [1899]

  Gutenberghiana.   L'Arte della Stampa, vol. 16, no. 37, 1886, p.
291-292; no. 38, p. 299-300; no. 44, p. 347-348; no. 48, p. 380-381;
vol. 18, no. 64, 1888, p. 509-510; no. 65, p. 516-518, 549-550.   [1900]

Gutenberg's burial place.   Inland Printer, vol. 2, Nov. 1884,
p. 58.
Reprinted from London Printers' Register.   [1901]

Gutenberg's Grab.   Gutenbergstube (Bern), vol. 2, no. 3, 1916,
p. 68-69.   [1902]

Gutenbergs letzte Nachkomm.   Frankfurter Zeitung, no. 157, 1900.[1903]

Guttemberg et Fauste; ou le premier imprimeur.   Comedie anecdotique
en cinq actes et en prose.   n.p., n.d.   Folio boards.
ms. of early nineteenth century.
Title from The Library of the late Theodore Low DeVinne ... New York,
1920.   [1904]

Guttemberg.   Illiustrirovannyi Listok, vol. 8, no. 51, 1863,
p. 11-14.   [1905]

Guttenberg, Faust i Sheffer.   Illiustrirovannaia Gazeta, no. 6,
1867, p. 91.   [1906]

Gutzkow, Karl.
   Gutenberg-Reminiszenz.   Deutsche Buchhändelsblätter, vol. 7, no.
3, 1906, p. 77-78.   [1907]

Hanstein, Wolfram von.
   Der vom Gutenberg. Die grosse Liebe im 15. Jahrhundert.   Ein
Roman.   Berlin, Voco-Verlag, 1939.   385p.
   Title from Bibliographie des Bibliotheks und Buchwesens, 1939. [1908]

Helmolt, H. F.
   Gutenberg.   Ehrenbuch des Deutschen Volkes, 1923, p. 73-78.   [1909]

Herrero, B.
   Patria y vicisitudes de Juan Gutenberg.   Gaceta de las Artes
Graficas, vol. 6, no. 5, 1928.   [1910]

Heyck, Ed.
   Gutenberg.   Daheim (Leipzig), vol. 36, no. 38, 1900.   [1911]

Hoffmann, Alfred.
   Gutenberg.   Wissenschaftliche Beilage zur Leipziger Zeitung, no.
57, 1900.   [1912]

Horn, Alban.
   Gutenberg. Ein Volkskalender für die Jünger der schwarzen Kunst.
Zittau, 1876.   12mo.
   Title from Bigmore & Wyman: "An almanack intended for printers, but
   hardly more than a worthless collection of anecdotes, etc."   [1913]

Ioann Gutenberg. Biograficheskii ocherk. Kaleidoskop, no. 20, 1861, p. 157-159. [1914]

Jeger, O.
Gutenberg. (In Jeger, O. Vseobschaia istoriia v 4 tomakh. T. II, Istoriia srednikh vekov. St. Petersburg, A. F. Marks [1904] p. 567) [1915]
Eu-Ru-MLe

Johann Gutenberg. Ueber Land und Meer, vol. 84, no. 38, 1900, p. 608.
Signed: L. H. [1916]

Karintsev, N.
Gutenberg. (In Karintsev, N. Taina knigi. Rasskaz o tom, kak delaiut bumagu i pechataiut knigu. Leningrad, Kniga,1926. p.68-72)[1917]
Eu-Ru-MLe

Kempfert, V.
Gutenberg. (In Kempfert, V. Istoriia velikikh izobretenii. Perevod N. Mirkina pod redakts. i s primechaniiami inzh. F. Davydova. Leningrad, Priboi, 1928. p. 192-198) [1918]
Eu-Ru-MLe

Kimball, Alice Mary.
The story of books and how they came to be. Dallas, Texas, A. T. Walraven Book cover co., 1928. 32p. 19 cm. [1919]
McMurtrie

Kingery, R. E.
A certain John Gutenberg. Hobbies, vol. 45, May 1940, p.86-87.[1920]

———— New light on Gutenberg. Hobbies, vol. 46, Mar. 1941, p. 99-100. [1921]

Kliuch k svetu. Gutenberg. n.p., n.d. 27p. (Knizhka za knizhkoi, 167) [1922]
Eu-Ru-MLe

Klokova, M. P.
Iogann Guttenberg, izobretatel' knigopechataniia. Moskva, Shkol'naia Biblioteka, 1908. 48p. illus. [1923]
Eu-Ru-MLe

Körber, Philipp.
Gutenberg der Erfinder der Buchdruckerkunst. Ein Vorbild für die deutsche Jugend. (In Pantheon der Weltgeschichte. Nürnberg, Lotzbeck, 1848. p. 172 et sqq.)
Title from Neuer Anzeiger für Bibliographie und Bibliothekswissenschaft, 1848-1849. [1924]

Kraus, Franz Xaver, 1840-1901.
   Gutenberg. Allgemeine Zeitung, Dec. 18, 19, 1878.   [1925]

Kurz, Hermann.
   ... Die Guten von Gutenberg, Roman. München, Süddeutsche Monatshefte,
G.m.b.H., 1911. 380, [1]p. 19.5 cm.   [1926]
   DLC   Eu-De-LBb

Lacour-Gayet.
   ¨ Reconnaisance à Gutenberg. Union Syndicale et Fédération des
Syndicats des Maîtres Imprimeurs de France. Bulletin Officiel, no.
11, Nov. 1929, p. 413.   [1927]

Law, Frederick Houk, 1871-
   Gutenberg, Manutius and Caxton, the first great printers. (In
Civilization builders. p. 116-122)   [1928]

Lechmann, P.
   Gutenberg und die Buchdruckerkunst. Die Wahrheit, 1900, p. 303-
312.   [1929]

Ledroit, Johann.
   Johannes Gutenberg und seine Kunst. Mainz, 1900. 34p. 8vo.[1930]
   Eu-De-BP   Eu-Ge-LSb

Leeman van Elck, P.
   Johannes Gutenberg. Neue Zürcher Zeitung, no. 1460, Aug. 12,
1939.   [1931]

Lehmann-Haupt, Hellmut, 1903-
   Gutenberg's first job, and more about price cutting. American
Printer, vol. 89, 1929, p. 35-37.   [1932]

——— Talking of Gutenberg. Publishers' Weekly, vol. 137, Jan.
1940, p. 46-49. Same, Scholastic, vol. 36, Apr. 1940, p. 17-19. [1933]

Levray, Alphonse.
   Gutenberg; scènes historiques. Paris, Meyrueis, 1856. 24p.
12mo.
   Also appeared in Ami de la Jeunesse, no. 3-5, 1856.   [1934]
   Eu-Fr-PN   Eu-Ge-LB   Eu-Ge-LP

   The life of Herr Gutenberg, dedicated to members of the craft.
[Buffalo, 1940] 6 numb. leaves, 2 leaves. 20.5 cm.
   Caption title.
   Cover-title: Anniversary, five hundred years of printing, 1440-
1940.
   Colophon: Of this keepsake ... 110 copies have been privately
printed, for distribution among my friends and members of the

Buffalo club of printing house craftsmen. The type set by myself
in my spare time, printed on a hand press on imported Zerkall
mould made deckle edged paper. Done for the love of the craft
by Emil Georg Sahlin, at Axel Edw. Sahlin typographic service,
Buffalo, New York, March, 1940.
Printed on one side of leaf on opposite pages.   [1935]
DLC

Linkenbach, Hans Ludwig, 1876-
   Johanniswunder, ein Festspiel zur Gutenbergfeier in Mainz; von
Hans Ludwig Linkenbach. Mainz, Verlag der Gutenberg-Gesellschaft,
1932, 4 prel. leaves, [11]-24p., 1 leaf. 21.5 cm. (Kleiner
Druck der Gutenberg-Gesellschaft. Nr. XVIII)   [1936]
   CSmH   DLC   ICN   MB   NN   NNC   NjP   Eu-De-BP

----   The miracle of John Gutenberg, by Hans Ludwig Linkenbach; a
festival play for the Gutenberg celebration in Mainz. Translated
from the German by John Charles Tarr.   [Chiswick] Chiswick poly-
technical school of art [1932]   3 prel. leaves, 9-18p., 1 leaf.
28 cm.   [1937]
   Composed in Monotype Baskerville.
   NNC

Loviagin, A. M.
   Gutenberg. (In Loviagin, A. M.   Osnovy knigovedeniia.   Lenin-
grad, Nachatki Znaniia [n.d.]   p. 39-43)   [1938]
   NN   Eu-Ru-MLe

Lukas, J.
   Johannes Gutenberg, der Erfinder des Buchdrucks. Genossenschaft-
liches Volksblatt (Basel), no. 40, Nov. 2, 1940.   [1939]

Lunkevich, V.
   Gutenberg. (In Lunkevich, V. Chudesa nauki i tekhniki. Vyp.
Btoroi. New York, M. N. Maizel', 1918.   p. 7-12)   [1940]
   NN

MacMahon, Robert C.
   A portrait of Gutenberg and a poem of 1676. American Printer,
vol. 83, 1926, p. 83.   [1941]

Mahncke, Georg Heinrich.
   Johannes von Guttenberg, Erfinder der Buchdruckerkunst, und Dr.
Johann Faust, oder die Zeichen der Zeit dramatisch erzählt [in five
acts]. Als 1er Theil des Handbuchs für Anfänger der Buchdruckerkunst.
Hamburg, 1809. 8vo.   [1942]
   Eu-Ge-LB   Eu-Ge-LSb

Maksimov, A. N.
   Gutenberg i knigopechatanie. Novii Viek, no. 9, 1900, p. 458. [1943]

Marlow, F. (i.e. Wolfram) Ludwig Hermann.
Gutenberg. Drama in fünf Aufzügen. Leipzig, L. H. Bösenberg,
1840. iii, 282p. 8vo.   [1944]
    Eu-De-LBb   Eu-Fr-PN   Eu-Ge-LB

Meller, Clara.
    Johann Gutenberg. Schauspiel. Nach dem gleichnamigen Filmstück
von C. Th. Ohler. Valentine Höfling. 1928.   [1945]
    NN   Eu-De-LBb

Merbach, P. A.
    Gutenberg im Roman und Drama. Ein stoffgeschichtlicher Versuch.
Gutenberg Jahrbuch, vol. 5, 1930, p. 77-103.   [1946]

Metz, J. J.
    Johann Gutenberg, inventor and printer. Industrial Arts and Vo-
cational Education, vol. 25, Dec. 1936, p. 381.   [1947]

Modestov, A. P.
    Ioann Gutenberg. (In Modestov, A. P. Zamechatel'nye rabotniki
nauki i tekhniki. Moskva, Assnat, 1927. vol. 1, p. 50-68)   [1948]
    Eu-Ru-MLe

Morin, E.
    Gutenberg. Revue Suisse, Jan. 1932, p. 16.   [1949]

Mueller, K.
    Guttenberg. (In Mueller, K. Promyhlennost' i tekhnika. St.
Petersburg, Prosveshchenie [n.d.] p. 158-172)   [1950]
    Eu-Ru-MLe

Muller, Julius W.
    Gutenberg's last days; a biography. American Printer, vol. 88,
1928, p. 61.   [1951]

N-v, D.
    Guttenberg. Bibliograficheskie Zapiski, vol. 1, no. 15, 1858,
p. 436-443.   [1952]

Nikolaev, A.
    Gutenberg i ego velikoe izobretenie. Mirskoe Delo, no. 4, 1918,
p. 18-22.   [1953]

    Notes sur Gutenberg. Livre Moderne, vol. 6, May 1885, p. 268.   [1954]

Nover, Jakob, 1845-
    Gutenberg und die Bedeutung der Buchdruckerkunst. Mainz, J.
Wirth'sche Hofbuchdruckerei, 1900. 3 prel. leaves, 9-188p. incl.
illus., plates. 22 cm.
    Half title: Zur Erinnerung an das Mainzer Gutenbergsfest 1900

ihren auswärtigen Freunden gewidmet von Chr. Adt. Kupferberg
& Co. in Mainz.   "Das erste Werk, das in der Geburtsstadt
Gutenbergs auf der Setzmaschine hergestellt ist."
Letterpress in blue within red line border.   [1955]
DLC   ICJ

Novikov, M.
   Iogann Guttenberg. K 500-lettīu so dnīa ego rozhdeniīa.
Izvestiia Knizhnykh Magazinov, no. 8-9, 1900, p. 105-109.   [1956]

Nypels, C.
   Gutenbergs laatste levensjaren.   Drukkers Weekblad, vol. 28,
1938, p. 437.   [1957]

Ohlcr, Conrad P.
   Gutenberg. Fünf Abschnitte aus seinem Leben.   Leipzig, Härtel,
1927.   109p.   [1958]
   Eu-De-LBb

Olivier, George.
   Jean Gutenberg.   Feuilleton de l'Indicateur de la Ville de Strasbourg, no. 1, 2, 3, 1856.   [1959]

Ol'khin, P. M.
   Iogann Guttenberg, izobretatel' knigopechataniīa.   Mainz 1400-
Petersburg 1900.   Sostavleno po porucheniīu Russkogo o-va Deīatelei
Pechatnogo Dela.   St. Petersburg, 1900.   24p.   [1960]
   Eu-Ru-MLe

Passerini, Giuseppe Lando.
   In memoria di Giovanni Gutenberg.   Rivista delle Biblioteche,
vol. 12, no. 6-7, 1901, p. 90-97.   [1961]

Patterson, Emma L.
   More Gutenberg Bibles?   Wilson Library Bulletin, vol. 14, no. 6,
Feb. 1940, p. 445-447.
   A hoax.   [1962]

Pearson, Mrs. Emily Clemens.
   From cottage to castle; the boyhood, youth, manhood, private and
public career of Gutenberg and the story of his invention, the art
of printing, by Emily C. Pearson ... New York, Hurst & co. [c1887]   [1963]
   IU   IaU

---- Gutenberg, and the art of printing. By Emily C. Pearson ...
Boston, Noyes, Holmes and company, 1871.   2 prel. leaves, [iii]-vi,
292p. front., illus., plates.   19 cm.   [1964]
   DLC   ICJ   MB   MH   MWA   MdBP   NN   Eu-Ge-LB   Eu-Ge-LP
   2d ed., [1876]: ICJ

- 243 -

Pearson, Mrs. Emily Clemens.
Gutenberg and the art of printing ... 3d ed.   Boston, D. Lothrop
and company [1880]   2 prel. leaves, [iii]-v, [1], 304p.   front.,
illus., plates.   19 cm.
    DLC   NN   Eu-Ge-LB   Eu-Ge-LSb   [1965]

----   Gutenberg; or, the world's benefactor; a book for boys on
the art of printing.   London, Ward, Lock & co., 1881.   8vo.   [1966]
    Eu-Ge-LB   Eu-Ge-LSb

Petzhold, Artur.
Gutenberg. Festspiel in zwei Bildern.   Berlin, Verlag des
Bildungsverbandes des deutschen Buchdrucker, 1926.   15p.   8vo.   [1967]
    Eu-De-BP   Eu-De-LBb

Pilant, R.
Goodbye Gutenberg.   Wilson Library Bulletin, vol. 15, 1940-1941,
p. 32-33, 275, 375, 786-787.   [1968]

Pimenova, E. K.
Ioann Gutenberg i ego velikoe izobretenie.   Biograficheskii ocherk.
St. Petersburg, O. N. Popova, 1906.   16p.   illus.   [1969]
    Eu-Ru-MLc

Prechtler, Otto.
Johannes Gutenberg. In vier Akten.   Wien, 1843.   8vo.
Title from Bigmore & Wyman.   [1970]

The printer of Mentz.   Compositors' Chronicle, no. 14, Oct. 1841,
p. 111.   [1971]

Redgrave, Gilbert R.
Johann Gutenberg, the first printer.   British Printer, vol. 4,
no. 45, Mar. 1891, p. 5-9.   [1972]

Ritchie, Ward, 1905-
1440, John Gutenberg, 1940; a fanciful story of the 15th century,
by Ward Ritchie.   [Los Angeles, The Ward Ritchie press, 1940]   49p.,
1 leaf.   1 illus.   21 cm.
    Illustrated t.-p.
    "300 copies printed in February, 1940; decorations by Fletcher
    Martin."   [1973]
    DLC   MH   NN   NNC

Riumin, V. V.
Guttenberg.   (In Riumin, V. V., ed. Chudesa tekhniki.   Illiustrirovannaia istoriia uspekhov tekhniki i kartina eia sovremennogo
sostoianiia.   St. Petersburg, P. P. Soikina, 1911.   p. 689-692)   [1974]
    Eu-Ru-MLc

Roderich, M.
    Johann Gutenberg, seine Zeit und seine Erfindung. Dresden, T.
Meinhold [1876] 53p. 4 plates. 8vo. (Illustrierte Gallerie
berühmter Männer und Frauen aller Völker und Zeiten, no. 4)   [1975]
    Eu-De-LBb   Eu-Ge-LB

Rothmund, Frau Toni (Lüdemann) 1877-
... Der unsichtbare Dom; ein Gutenberg-Roman. Leipzig, P. Reclam jun.
[C1937] 305, [1]p., 1 leaf. 19.5 cm.   [1976]
    DLC   NN

Rotondi, Pietro, 1814-
    Guttenberg; o, l'invenzione della stampa. Dramma storico. Milano,
1846. 143p. 22 cm.   [1977]
    ICN   IU   Eu-De-LBb

Ruland, F. W.
    Gutenberg-Album. Photographies par B. Erdmann. Mayence, 1868.
4to.
    Title from Bigmore & Wyman.   [1978]

Rushmore, Arthur W.
    The Mainz diary: 1437-1440, in which new light is shed upon the
cradle days of the art and mystery of printing. Translated from the
German by Albert Bachaus. Edited and with a note by Arthur W. Rushmore. With a critical foreword by Hermann Püterschein ... Madison, N.J.,
The Golden hind press, 1940. xiv, [1]p., 1 leaf, 11, [1]p., 1 leaf.
front., plates, facsim. 26 cm.
    Issued on the occasion of the 500th anniversary of the invention
    of printing from moveable type.
    "Of the first edition ... 250 copies have been bound in boards for
    the friends of the editor, and the balance of the sheets bound in
    with the text of the Christmas issue of Print."
    A hoax.   [1979]
    DLC

Sayers, G. A.
    The fathers of our craft: John Gutenberg. Caxton's Magazine,
vol. 31, 1929, p. 154-156.   [1980]

Schildbach, B.
    Gutenberg. Der Türner, vol. 39, 1937, p. 261-264.   [1981]

Schwemer, R.
    Gutenberg. Allgemeiner Anzeiger für Druckereien, Gutenberg
number, June 21, 1900.   [1982]

Scripps, James Edmund, 1835-1906.
    Gutenberg. Public Libraries, vol. 6, 1901, p. 3-5.   [1983]

Seatelli.
Gutenberg. Revue Suisse Catholique, vol. 16, 1884, p. 17-33. [1984]

Seidel, Robert.
Gutenberg. Freie Innerschweiz (Luzern), July 6, 1940. [1985]

Seyl, Antoine.
The face of Gutenberg. Printing Review, summer, 1931, p. 82.
Condensed from an article in Chronique Graphique. [1986]

----- Le visage de Gutenberg. Chronique Graphique, vol. 6, 1930,
p. 667-672. [1987]

Shchelkunov, M. I.
Gutenberg i ego izobretenie. (In Shchelkunov, M. I. Iskusstvo
knigopechataniia v ego istoricheskom rasvitii. Moskva, Moskov.
Institut Zhurnalistiki, 1923. p. 39-50) [1988]
Eu-Ru-MLe

----- ----- (In Shchelkunov, M. I. Istoriia tekhniki, iskusstvo
knigopechataniia. Moskva i Leningrad, Gos. Izd., 1925. p. 59-77) [1989]
Eu-Ru-MLe

----- Gutenberg, Iogann. (In Bol'shaia Sovietskaia Entsiklopediia.
Moskva, 1930. vol. 20, p. 50-52) [1990]
MH   NN   Eu-Ru-MLe

Shreknik, E. F.
Pervyi izobretatel' knigopechataniia Ioann Gutenberg. Istoriches-
kaia povest'. St. Petersburg, Mishakova, 1895. vii, 64p. port. [1991]
Eu-Ru-MLe

Smirnova, A.
Ioann Guttenberg. Vestnik Vsemirnoi Istorii, no. 7, 1900, p. 144-
152. [1992]

Society for promoting Christian knowledge.
Gutenberg's dream. London [1868] 8p. 8vo. (Tract no.
1,462 of the Society for promoting Christian knowledge)
Title from Bigmore & Wyman. [1993]

Solov'ev-Nesmelov, N.
Mirnyi zavoevatel'. Istoricheskaia povest' iz zhizni Ioanna
Guttenberga, izobretateliia knigopechataniia 1420-1468 g. g. Moskva,
Detzkoie Chtenie, 1900. 158p. illus. [1994]
Eu-Ru-MLe

Sopikov, V. A.
Gutenberg. (In Rogozhin, V. N., ed. Opyt Rossiiskoi bibliografii.

St. Petersburg, 1904.   plate 1, p. 20-22)   [1995]
    MH   NN   Eu-Ru-MLe

Ständer, Bartholomäus.
    Gutenberg; ein Dramen-Fragment, von Bartholomäus Ständer.   Mainz,
Gutenberg-Gesellschaft; [etc., etc.] 1937.   2 prel. leaves, 3-24p.,
1 leaf.   21.5 cm.   (Kleiner Druck der Gutenberg-Gesellschaft. 27)[1996]
    DLC   ICN

Stein, A.
    Gutenberg, 1934.   Deutsches Bucherverzeichniss, vol. 19, 1931-
1935, p. 616.   [1997]

Stein, Paul.
    Johannes Gutenberg.   Kultur-historischer Roman.   Leipzig, Grunow,
1861.   3 vols.   8vo.   [1998]
    Eu-Ge-LB
    2d ed., 1864: Eu-Sz-BeG

Stern, Adolf, 1835-
    Johannes Gutenberg; epische Dichtung von Adolf Stern.   Leipzig,
J. J. Weber, 1873.   4 prel. leaves, 385, [1]p.   20 cm.   [1999]
    DLC   Eu-Ge-LB   Eu-Sz-BeG
    2d ed., 1889: MB

Sternau, C. O.
    Johannes Gutenberg, Episches Gedicht in fünf Gesängen.   Dresden,
Heinrich, 1840.   15p.   8vo.   [2000]
    Eu-Ge-LB

Tissandier, Gaston.
    Guttenberg.   (In Tissandier, Gaston.   Mucheniki nauki.   Perevod s
frants. pod red. F. Pavlenkova.   St. Petersburg [n.d.] p. 140-144) [2001]
    Eu-Ru-MLe

Tränckner, Christian.
    Vom Lesen.   Ein Epilog zum Gutenberg-Gedenkjahr.   Die Literatur
(Stuttgart), Dec. 1940.   [2002]

Trebusch.
    Johannes Gutenberg.   Jungbuchdrucker, vol. 3, 1936, p. 46-50.   [2003]

    Typographikus.   Eine bemerkenswerte Würdigung Gutenberga und
seiner Kunst.   Graphische Nachrichten, vol. 16, 1937, p. 597-600. [2004]

Udal'tsov, A. D.
    Gutenberg.   (In Istoriía srednikh vekov.   T. I. Pod redaktsiei
professorov A. D. Udal'tsova, E. A. Kosminskogo i O. L. Vainsteina.
Moskva, Gos. sots.-ekonom. Izd-vo, 1938.   p. 572-573)   [2005]
    Eu-Ru-MLe

Unser Gutenberg. Mainzer Anzeiger, Feb. 18, 1871.   [2006]

Vil'chinskii, O.
    Ivan Gutenberg. Nauchnoie Obozrenie, no. 8, 1900, p.1421-1427.[2007]

Vinaritskii, K.
    Ian-Gutenberg. S pol'sk. iaz. perevel P. Duborovskii. Moskvit-
ianin, no. 8, 1846, p. 137-151.   [2008]

Wehmer, Carl.
    Gutenberg. Zwei Ausstellungen zur Geschichte des Buchdrucks.
Das Reich (Berlin), July 14, 1940, p. 19.   [2009]

    Wie die Buchdruckerkunst erfunden ward. Briefe des Erfinders
der Buchdruckerkunst an den Franziskaner Andreas, geschrieven vom
Ufer des Rheines um die Mitte des 15. Jahrhunderts. Journal für
Buchdruckerkunst, no. 1, 1845, col. 5-14; no. 2, col. 17-24; no. 4,
col. 41-47.   [2010]

Wood, A. A.
    Popular lectures for the magic lantern. History of printing.
London, 1874.   8vo.   [2011]
    Eu-Ge-ISb

Wratko, Jaroslaw.
    Vier Scenen aus dem Leben Johannes Gutenberg ... Wlastimil (Praha),
vol. 1, no. 1, 1840.   [2012]

Wray, George E.
    400 years of printing ... Gutenberg to Franklin, 1390-1790. Salt
Lake City, Utah, Porte publishing co., 1930.   32p.   17 cm.   [2013]
    IC   IU

Wright, J. H.
    The romance of printing. Caxton's Magazine, vol. 27, Sept. 1925,
p. 592-593.   [2014]

Zatzmann, V.
    Gutenberg. Ein Lebensbild fürs Volk.   Mainz, Zabern, 1900.
48p.   [2015]
    Eu-Ge-LB   Eu-Ge-ISb

Ziegler, Theobald, 1846-1918.
    Gutenberg und sein Werk. Frankfurter Zeitung, no. 165, 1900.   [2016]

------ Menschen und Probleme.   Reden, Vortrage, und Aufsatze von
Theobald Ziegler.   Berlin, G. Reimer, 1914.   vii, [4], 424p.
24.5 cm.
    Gutenberg und sein Werk: p. 1-6.   [2017]
    ICJ

A.   16TH CENTURY

Arnold, Johannes.
De chalcographiae inventione, poëma encomiasticum, Johanne
Arnoldo Bergellano auctore.   [Moguntiae ad diuum Victorem excudebat Franciscus Behem] M.D.XLI [1541]   12 numb. leaves.
19 cm.
    Reissued in Wolf, J. C. Monumenta typographica.   Hamburg,
    1740.   vol. 1, p. 1-40.   [2018]
    NNC   Eu-De-LBb   Eu-Fr-PN   Eu-Ge-LB

B.   17TH CENTURY

    Bericht von Erfindung der Buch Truckerey in Strasburg
[together with two poems in praise of the invention of printing
by J. Frunssheimer and J. Rumpler].   Strassburg, 1640.   4to.   [2019]
    Eu-Ge-LB

Brehm, C.
    Gründlicher Bericht von Erfindung der edlen und hochnütz-
lichen Kunst Buchdruckerey. Auff das nunmehr zwey hundert
jährig eingetretene Jubel-Fest, welches feyerlich zu halten
angesonnen worden von denen Leiptziger belobten Kunstverwandten ... Dresden, 1640.   8 leaves.   4to.
    Reissued in Latin in Wolf, J. C. Monumenta typographica.
    Hamburg, 1740.   vol. 1, p. 930-969.   [2020]
    Eu-De-LBb

    Carmina secularia de typographia, ante annos ipsos CC â
Germanis inventâ. Curabat pariter atque imprimebat Georg.
Baumann typographus Vratislaviensis.   Breslau, 1640.   4to.
    Reissued in Wolf, J. C. Monumenta typographica.   Hamburg,
    1740.   vol. 1, p. 969-1005.   [2021]
    Eu-De-LBb

Closius, Henr.
    In laudem artis typographicae.   Breslau, 1640.   4to.
    Title from Mohr, Jubelfeste.   [2022]

Cramer, Daniel.
  Des heiligen Iobs bleyerne Schreib Täfflein, sampt darin enthal-
tener seiner Bekentniss von Christo ... zum Lob der edlen Drücker
Kunst, wie auch zum letzten Ehren des Erbarn und Wolgeachten Joachim
Rheten, Buchtruckern zu Alten Stettin: welcher den 10. Febr. dieses
1611. Jahrs seliglich entschlaffen ... verhandelt und erkleret.   Alten
Stettin [1611]   4to.
    Reprinted as a Festschrift in 1640.   Also in Hornschuch, Hierony-
    mus.   Ortotypographia.   1634.   [2023]
    Eu-De-LBb

Fürstenau, Philipp C. von.
  Gebundene Lobrede von der hochnütz- und löblichen zweyhundert-
jährigen Buchdruckerey-Kunst, wenn, wo, wie und durch wen sie erfunden worden, bey Volchreycher Versamlung und Einführung eines neuen
Drucker-Gesellens Michael Pfeiffers in Hamburg den 20. Tag des
Hornungs im 1642.   Hamburg, Jacob Rebenlein, Drucker und Verleger
[1642?]   4to.
    Title from Wolf, J. C.   Monumenta typographica ... Hamburg, 1740. [2024]

Gueintz, Christian.
  Lob der edlen und nützlichen Druckerey-Kunst auff das ander hun-
dertjährige Jubel-Fest, so gehalten am Johannes-Tage 1640, auffge-
setzt.   Halle in Sachsen, 1640.   4to.
    Reissued in Latin in Wolf, J. C.   Monumenta typographica.   Ham-
    burg, 1740.   vol. 1, p. 1040-1045.   [2025]
    Eu-De-LBb

Gutner, Johann Gabriel.
  Typographei chemnitiensis primae plagulae, de laudibilis & inaestimabilis artis typographicae inventione, utilitate & incremento,
Chemnitii cum nonnullis accessionibus iterum excusa per Jo. Gabrielem
Gutnerum, typographeon suum primum aperientem, volente magno paritur
Deo ac fortuna, postquam A. C. 1440. atque adeo ante 221 annos haec
nobilis ars primum erat excogitata; & è lingua germanica latine
redditae à Joanne Oswalto, Altonaviensi, Hamb. Gymasii Cive dignissimo.   (In Wolf, J. C.   Monumenta typographica.   Hamburg, 1740.
vol. 2, p. 404-427)   [2026]

  Jubilaeum typographorum lipsiensium: Oder zweyhundertjähriges
Buchdrucker Jubelfest / wie solches deroselben Kunstverwandte zu
Leipzig / am Tage Johannis des Täuffers / anno Christi 1640. und
also gleich 200. Jahr nach Erfindung dieser edlen Kunst / mit
Christlichen Ceremonien celebriret und begangen ... [Leipzig] in
öffentlichen Druck gegeben / und bey den gesampten Buchdruckern
daselbsten zu finden / im Jahr Christi M.DC.XL.   1 prel. leaf,
[137]p.   19 cm.   [2027]
    DLC   NN   NNGr   Eu-De-LBb   Eu-Ge-LE

Kleinwechter, Valentin.
Actus secularis I et II exotericus in laudem typographiae...
Breslau, G. Baumann, 1640.
Title from Mohr, Jubelfeste.
Reissued in Wolf, J. C. Monumenta typographica. Hamburg, 1740.
vol. 1, p. 1005-1014. [2028]

Licimandrus.
Panegyricus in laudem artis typographicae, vernaculo sermone an.
1690 dictus. (In Wolf, J. C. Monumenta typographica. Hamburg,
1740. vol. 2, p. 597-607) [2029]

Olearius.
Löbliche Buchdruckerkunst. Halle, 1640.
Title from Mohr, Jubelfeste. [2030]

Peck, David.
Jubel-jähriges Gedenck- und Dancklied von der edlen Kunst der Buch-
druckerey, so vor zweyhundert Jahren, Anno 1440. durch sonderbare
Schickung Gottes erfunden worden. Leipzig, 1640. 4p. 4to. [2031]
Eu-De-LBb

Rinckhart, Martin.
Trucker-Gedenck-Rinck: Darinnen der hoch-edlen Schreib- und Trucker-
Feder und Teutsch-Landes höchster und letzter Ehren-Preiss. Auff das
andere und verhoffentlich auch letzte ... Jetzo 1640, zu Leipzig gehal-
tene Buch-Trucker Jubel-Fest: bestellet, angestellet und getruckt ...
durch Gregorien Ritzschen und seine Kunstverwandten deselbst zu
Leipzig. [Leipzig, 1640] 4to. [2032]
Eu-De-LBb

Ritzsch, Timotheus.
Emblematisches Jubel-Gedichte, oder Sinnen-Bild auff das zwey
hunderte Jahr nach Erfindung der Hochlöblichen ... Buchdrucker Kunst,
welche im Jahr ... 1440 durch Göttlichen Beystand zum ersten in Teutschland ans Tageliecht bracht worden. Tableau mit einem allegorischen
Bild. Leipzig, am 24. Juni 1640.
Title from Mohr, Jubelfeste. [2033]

Rivinus, Andreas, 1600-1656.
L. Andreae Rivini ... Hecatomba laudum et gratiarum in ludis iterum-
secularibus ob inventam in Germania abhinc annis CC chalcographiam ...
cùm in carminibus quibusdam et epigrammatis, tum vero praecipue in
declamatiuncula solenni, artis typographicae commendationem ... ò variis
scriptoribus celebrante. Lipsiae, Apud typographos, 1640. 32p.
18.5 cm.
Reissued in Wolf, J. C. Monumenta typographica. Hamburg, 1740.
vol. 1, p. 869-880. 2034]
NNC Eu-De-LBb Eu-Ge-LB

Rivinus, Andreas, 1600-1656.
   Panegyrica declamatio, qua artis typographicae initia, progressus,
nobilitas et utilitas summa celebrantur ... Lipsiae, 1640.   4to.
   Reissued in Wolf, J. C.   Monumenta typographica.   Hamburg, 1740.
   vol. 1, p. 881-926.   [2035]
   Eu-De-LBb

Rumpler, J.
   Gedicht von Erfindung und Lob der Buch-Truckerey.   Strassburg,
1640.   4to.
   Title from Mohr, Jubelfeste.   [2036]

Schmidt, Johann, 1594-1658.
   Eine Christliche Danck-Predigt, wegen der im Jahr 1440 neu-erfun-
denen sehr nützlichen Buchdrucker-Kunst, gehalten in Strassburg, An.
1640.   1678.   39p.   64mo.   [2037]
   Eu-Ge-LSb

----   Gott zu Lob, Drey Christliche Danck Predigten: wegen dero im
Jahr 1440 und also vor zweyhundert Jahren, durch Göttliche Eingebung,
in Strassburg erfundenen hochwerthen thewren Buchdrucker-Kunst: 1640.
den 18. 25. Augusti und 1. Septembr. gehalten.   Strassburg, 1641.
4to.
   Reissued in Latin in Wolf, J. C.   Monumenta typographica.   Hamburg,
   1740.   vol. 2, p. 58-165.
   Reissued, Gotha, J. A. Reyher, 1740.   127p.   19 cm.   [2038]
   Eu-Ge-LB

[Schrag, Johann Adam] 1616-1687.
   Bericht von Erfindung der Buch Truckerey in Strassburg.   Getruckt
in Strassburg / bey Moritz Carlen / im Jahr Christi / M.DC.XXXX.
[64]p.   20.5x16 cm.
   Unpaged; 4 prel. leaves, signature A-G^4.
   Interleaved.
   Advocates the theory that printing was invented at Strassburg by
Johannes Mentelin.
   Reissued in Latin in Wolf, J. C.   Monumenta typographica.   Hamburg,
   1740.   vol. 2, p. 1-57.   [2039]
   DLC   NN   Eu-De-LBb   Eu-Ge-LB   Eu-Ne-GK

Tscherning, Andreas.
   Lob der Buchdruckerey.   Breslaw, Georg Baumann, 1640.   4to.   [2040]
   Eu-De-LBb   Eu-Ge-LB

Zeren, P. von.
   Lobrede von der Buchdruckerkunst mit Anmerkungen, darinnen dersel-
ben Erfindung und Alterthum erötert word.   Hamburg, 1642.   4to.
   Title from Bigmore & Wyman.   [2041]

Zweyhundert-jähriger Zeit denckwürdiges Ehren-Lob von der ... Buchdruckerey, wenn, wo, wie und durch wen sie erfunden worden ... Leipzig, Greg. Ritsch, 1640. 1 Bog. 8vo.
     Title from Mohr, Jubelfeste.
     Reissued in Latin in Wolf, J. C. Monumenta typographica. Hamburg, 1740. vol. 2, p. 1075-1081.   [2042]

C.   18TH CENTURY

     Abhandlung von der Buchdrucker-Kunst, und einigen dahin gehörigen Stücken des Alterthums; bey Gelegenheit des dritten Jubel-Jahrs, so in diesem Jahr, wie in den meisten berühmten Städten Deutschlandes, also auch in der Kayserlichen und des Reiche freyen Stadt Bremen, von dasigen beyden Gesellschaften der Brauer- und Janischen ... mit Vergnügen gefeyret worden, eilfertig entworffen.   Bremen, 1740.   106p. 8vo.   [2043]
     Eu-De-LBb   Eu-Ge-LB

Albini, Eliae Engelb.
     Ruhm- und ehrenvolles Andenken der 130 Jahre zu Brieg blühenden Buchdruckerkunst. Brieg, 1740. 2 Bog. Folio.
     Poem.
     Title from Mohr, Jubelfeste.   [2044]

Alex, Siegm. Gabr.
     Als das dritte Jubeljahr der Buchdruckerkunst gekommen, hat auch Franckfurt seine Pflicht an der Oder wargenommen.   Frankfurt a/O., 1740. 4 Bog. 4to.
     Title from Mohr, Jubelfeste.   [2045]

     Als auf die allergnädigst verliehene Erlaubniss Ihro Königlichen Majestät in Preussen einige Buchdruckereyen in Halle das ... dritte Jubiläum der Buchdruckerkunst den 25. Jul. 1740 feyerlich begiengen ... Halle a. S., 1740. Folio.   [2046]
     Eu-De-LBb

     Als das / in Das Ein Tausend, Siebenhundert und / Vierzigste Jahr nach der Heylwerthen / Geburth unseres Erlösers / Jesu Christi / einfallende Dritte Jubel-Fest / Der Buchdrucker-Kunst, / welche in hiesiger Löblicher / Stadt Strassburg / Eben vor Drey-Hundert Jahren / erfunden worden ... [Strassburg, Heitz, 1740] 4p. Folio.
     Title from Mohr, Jubelfeste.   [2047]

     Als der ... J. H. Reussner ... nicht nur das allgemeine Jubiläum der edlen Buchdruckerkunst ... gefeyert, wollten gratuliren die Kunstgenossen der Dorn'schen Buchdruckerey.   Königsberg, 1740.   Folio.
     Title from Mohr, Jubelfeste.   [2048]

Als die edle Buchdrucker-Kunst ihr drittes Jubilaeum begienge,
wollten derselben zu ehren, aus schuldiger Obliegenheit gegenwärtige
Zeilen aufsetzen, die, derselben zugethane Kunst-Verwandte der Lent-
zischen Officin ... den 27 Sept. A. 1740.   Regensburg, 1740.   Folio.[2049]
    Eu-De-LBb

Altare gloriae et honoris arti typographicae saeculum ab inventione
sua tertium Monachii solemnissime celebranti erectum, et singulis
eiusdem cultoribus devotissime consecratum.   [Monachii] Typis Mariae
Magdalenae Riedlin, 1740.   Folio.   [2050]
    Eu-De-LBb

Baumgarten, Siegmund Jacob.
    Betrachtung über Sirach 33, 17. 18. zur feierlichen Begehung des
300 järigen Gedächtnisses der Buchdruckerkunst.   Oeffentliche Jubelzeugnisse welche, bey dem von einigen Buchdruckern zu Halle ... erneuerten Andenken der vor dreyhundert Jahren erfundenen Buchdruckerkunst, von der Hochlöbl. Friedrichsuniversität ... abgelegt worden.
Halle, 1741.   4to.   [2051]
    Eu-Ge-LB

Becker, Petr.
    Plausus honestae societatis typographorum Rostochiensium saecu-
lares publice significat, commendatque et ad audiendam tertia abhinc
die orationem panegyricam decenter invitat.   Rostock, 1740.   Folio.
    Title from Mohr, Jubelfeste.   ⸗   [2052]

Beifreude über die Erfindung und den Wachstum der edelen Kunst der
Buchdruckerei, bei Gelegenheit ihres zum dritten Mal gefeierten Jubelfestes, bezeuget von einem Liebhaber schöner Künsten.   Idstein, 1740.
1 Bog.   Folio.   [2053]
    Eu-De-LBb

Bellermann, Constantin.
    Doron Basilikon. ˙Oder, das mehr als Königliche ... Geschenke der ...
Buch-Druckerye ... Erfurt, J. M. Funcken, 1740.   208p.   fold. front.,
plates.   18 cm.   [2054]
    NNGr

Bequignolle, Joan. Car.
    De statu typographiae superiorum temporum ad hodiernum comparato.
Dissertatio.   Halae Salicae, 1740.   2 Bog.   4to.   [2055]
    Eu-De-LBb

Bey dem Jubelfeste der erfundenen Buchdruckerkunst sowohl, als
auch insonderheit der Hof- und Academischen Reussnerischen Buchdruckerey bezeugten ihre Mitfreude einige auf der Königsberger Universität Studirende.˙ Königsberg, Dorn, 1740.   1 Bog.   Folio.
    Title from Mohr, Jubelfeste.   [2056]

[Boltz, Theodor]
    Bey der a. 1740 einfallenden allgemeinen und auch Preussisch-
Reussnerischen Jubelfeyer der Buchdruckerkunst beobachtete in Be-
zeugung der Danck- und Wunschpflicht seine Mitfreude.   Gedicht.
Königsberg, Hartung, 1740.   1 Bog.   Folio.
    Title from Mohr, Jubelfeste.   [2057]

Brechenmacher, Georg Friedrich.
    Natalen artis typographicae, trecentis abhinc annis feliciter
natae saeculari celebratione agendum ab Seminario ... Oettingae,
a.d. 10. Octr. 1740.   Oettingen, 1740.   Folio.
    Title from Mohr, Jubelfeste.   [2058]

Breitfeld, Christoph Ernst.
    Den Vorzug und Nutzen für allen andern Künste suchte bei dem
sich ereigneten dritten Jubilaeo der edlen Kunst der Buchdruckerey
den 24. Jun. 1740. zu beweisen, und hierüber ebenmässig seine
Freude zu bezeugen ... C. E. B.   Regenspurg, 1740.   Folio.   [2059]
    Eu-De-LBb

    Bresslauiches Jubelgedächtniss der vor dreyhundert Jahren
erfundenen Buchdruckerkunst, in einer vollständigen Sammlung
alles desjenigen, wodurch im Jahre 1740 ... bey der öffentlich
darüber angestellten Freudenbezeugung der in Bresslau über 200
Jahre schon blühenden Baumannischen Buchdruckerey das danckbare
Andencken dieser edlen Erfindung ... erneuert worden.   [Herausgeg.
von Joh. Friedr. Burg] Bresslau, 1740.   33 1/2 Bog.   4to.   [2060]
    Eu-De-LBb

Bünemann, Johann Ludolph.
    Notitiam scriptorum editorum atque ineditorum artem typo-
graphicam illustrantium, intermixtis passim observationibus
litterariis in memoriam saeculi tertii ab inventa typographia
decursi occasione actus oratorii a sedecim juvenibus lectissimis
anno 1740, de Maii decima ... Hanoverae, sub prelo H. G. Hannigii,
1740.   44p.   4to.   [2061]
    Eu-De-LBb   Eu-Fr-PC   Eu-Fr-PN

Buxtorff, August Johann.
    Christliche Danck-Predigt, auf das durch Gottes Gnad erschienene
dritte Jubel-Jahr, der Anno CIↃCCCXL vermittelst Göttlichen Bey-
standes erfundenen höchst-schätzbarsten Buchdruckerkunst, gehalten
den 26. Tag Brachmonat 1740 ... Basel, bei Joh. Christ. [1740] 33,
12p.   4to.   [2062]
    Eu-De-LBb

    Cantata, das Lob des Höchsten, wegen vor 300. Jahren erfundenen
Buchdrucker-Kunst, bey dem am 18. Juli 1740 zu Jena ... feyerlich begangenen Jubel-Feste.   Jena [1740]   Folio .   [2063]
    Eu-De-LBb
                              - 255 -

[Cappelier, Chr. Friedrich]
    Erneuertes Andencken der vor 300 Jahren erfundenen Buchdrucker-
kunst. Ode. Guben, 1740. 2 1/2 Bogen.
    Title from Mohr, Jubelfeste.   [2064]

    Carmen seculare. Leipzig, 1740.
    Title from Mohr, Jubelfeste.   [2065]

Carpov, Jac.
    Vergleichung der Kunst in Erfindung des Schreibens und der Buch-
druckerey. Weimar und Jena, 1740. 18p. 4to.
    Reissued in Weimarischer Beytrag zu feyerlicher Begehung des
    dritten 100 jährigen Jubel-Festes einer wohllöblichen Buchdrucker-
    kunst. Weimar, 1740.   [2066]
    Eu-De-LBb   Eu-Ge-LB

Cless, Wilhelm Jeremias Jacob.
    Drittes Jubel-Fest der Buchdrucker-Kunst, oder Christliches Denck-
und Danckmahl dem allerhöchsten Gott zu Ehren, wegen der vor dreyhundert Jahren erfundenen und bisher erhaltenen edlen Buchdrucker-
Kunst, worinnen vor Erfindung, Ausbreitung und Verbesserung, vom
Nutzen, Lob und Fürtrefflichkeit, vom rechten Gebrauch und Mis-
brauch derselben gehandelt wird, sammt einer Vorrede M. Georg Cunrad
Riegers. Gotha, J. A. Reyher, 1740. 52, 197, [11]p. 19 cm. [2067]
    DLC   Eu-De-LBb   Eu-Ge-LB   Eu-Ge-LSb

    Curiöses Traum-Gesicht, oder Gedicht von Anfang und Erfindung der
edlen höchst-nutzbaren Buchdruckerkunst, so einem, der vil von wohl-
ermeldter Kunst gelesen, gehöret, und geredet, ist vorkommen, und
von ihme bey herrlicher Begehung des dritten Jahr-Hunderts von gedachter Erfindung, samentlichen solcher edlen Kunst-Verwandten zu
Ehren in Reimen verfasset worden, zu München in Bayrn. München,
1740. Folio.   [2068]
    Eu-De-LBb

Deichsel, Johann Gottlieb.
    Germanum typographicae decus in actu publico ob distribuenda mag-
nifici senatus praemia solemni die XVI. Junii A. C. 1740 horis lo-
coque consuetis a juventute Gymnasii Elisabethani selecta consider-
andum significat. Vratislaviae [Breslau] 1740. 112p. Folio.
    Reissued in Bresslauisches Jubelgedächtnis ... 1740.   [2069]
    Eu-De-LBb   Eu-Fr-PN   Eu-Ge-LB

    Den Vorzug der edlen Drucker-Kunst unter denen sieben freyen Kün-
sten wolten ... am Tage ihrer Jubel-Freude, war der 6ste Julii des
1740. Heyl-Jahres zu Erfurt feyerlich celebrieret wurde ... erwegen.
Erfurt [1740] Folio.   [2070]
    Eu-De-LBb

Dienner, Reginald.
    Das grosse Sonnen-Liecht am Firmament des Teutschen Himmels die
edle Buchdrucker-Kunst, ein hell-glantzende Zierde der Katholischen
Welt. In dem Löbl. Gotts-Hauss und Closter-Kirchen der PP. Augus-
tinern in München bey höchst-feyerlichen Angedencken des dritten
Jahr-Hunderts der edlen Drucker-Kunst Anno 1740 durch ein Lob-
und Ehren-Red ... ans Liecht gestellet. München, 1740. Folio.   [2071]
    Eu-De-LBb

Döderlein, Ad.
    Orationem solemnen iamque saecularem, quam in laudem typograph-
iae publice recitaturus est adolescens politissimus ... [Weisenburg
im Nordgau, 1740]
    Title from Mohr, Jubelfeste.   [2072]

    Eine doppelte Denk-Säule bey zweyfacher Jubelfeyer ... aufge-
richtet von sämmtlichen in der Reussnerischen Officin befindlichen
Kunstverwandten. Königsberg, 1740. 1 Bog. Folio.
    Title from Mohr, Jubelfeste.   [2073]

Döring, Christian Gottlob.
    Ode zum dritten Jubelgedächtniss der erfundenen Buchdrucker·
kunst in Jena, den 18. Jul. 1740. Jena, 1740. Folio.   [2074]
    Eu-De-LBb

Dorn, Mart. Eberh.
    Lobgedicht auf das Jubelfest der Buchdruckerkunst. Königsberg,
1740. 1 Bog. Folio.
    Title from Mohr, Jubelfeste.   [2075]

Dresden. Buchdrucker-Gesellschaft.
    Der löblichen Buchdrucker-Gesellschaft zu Dressden Jubel-Ge-
schichte A. 1740, den 24. und 25. Junii. Mit einer Vorrede Herrn
Christian Schöttgens ... Dressden, Gedruckt auf Kosten der Buchdrucker-Societät [1740] 94p. 23.5x19 cm.
    "Historische Beschreibung des dressdnischen Buchdrucker-
Jubilaei, welches am Johannis-Feste den 24. und 25. Junii
1740, gefeyert worden. Nebst darzu gehörigen Beylagen.
Dresden, Gedruckt auf Kosten der Buchdrucker-Societät."
p. [17]-94.   [2076]
    NN   NNC   NNGr   Eu-De-LBb   Eu-Ge-LB   Eu-Ge-LSb

    Dreyfaches Kleeblättlein an die drey Ehrwürdigen Erfinder der
löblichen Kunst-Buchdruckerey, Gutenberg, Faust, Schöffer. Leipzig, 1740.
    Title from Mohr, Jubelfeste.   [2077]

Die dritte Jubel-Freude der ... Buchdrucker-Kunst, solennisirten ...
die sämmtlichen Patronen und Officianten in Erfurt den sechsten
Julii 1740 ... Erfurt [1740]   Folio.   [2078]
   Eu-De-LBb

Das dritte Jubiläum einer löbichen Buchdrucker-Kunst 1740 den 30.
Novemb. in der Königl. Haubt-Stadt Prag gefeiert.--Die Denckmahle
der Gütte Gottes etc.--- Lingua trium saeculorum.-- Apollo olim
Admeti regis tutela. -- F. Kauschke, das gutthätige und danckbare
Adela. -- Jos. Franc. Ant. Kraus, expressa librorum impressio.
Prag, 1740.   Folio.   [2079]
   Eu-De-LBb

Eccard, Carl Christoph.
   Jubelrede bey öffentlicher Versammlung der sämmtlichen Universität,
den 13. Oktober.   Strassburg, 1740.   4to.
   Title from van der Linde, Geschichte der Erfindung ...   [2080]

Egendter.
   Der edlen theuren Kunst, als der Buchdruckerey, so hier in Regenspurg ein Jubel-Fest aufs neu Hochfeyerlich begeht, sey dieses Blatt
geschrieben, und dem Herrn Sättler, auch, der diese Kunst zu üben
niemahlen unterläst, bey solcher Jubel-Freud ... geweyht.   Regenspurg,
1740.   Folio.   [2081]
   Eu-De-LBb

Ehren-Gedichte auf die edle freye Kunst-Buchdruckerey, und deren
Ursprung, Fortgang, und Nutzbarkeit, wessen sich deren Anverwandten,
für andern Künsten, mit Grund der Wahrheit zu rühmen haben; mit
poetischer Feder entworffen.   Frankfurt und Leipzig, 1739.   8vo. [2082]
   Eu-De-LBb

Ehrhardt, Johann Friedrich.
   Aria bey dem ... 3 Jubel-Feste.   Torgau, 1740.   2p.   4to.
   Title from Mohr, Jubelfeste.   [2083]

Eichsfeld, Ephraim Gottlob, 1697-
   Relation, vom wittenbergischen Buchdrucker-Jubiläo 1740, nebst
einer Historischen Nachricht, von allen wittenbergischen Buchdruckern,
welche, seit Erfindung der Buchdrucker-Kunst, sonderlich zur Zeit der
Reformation Lutheri, allhier Druckereyen gehabt haben, ausgefertiget
von Ephraim Gottlob Eichsfelden ... Wittenberg, Gedruckt in eigener
Officin, 1740.   8 prel. leaves, 200p.   21.5x17 cm.   [2084]
   DLC   Eu-De-LBb   Eu-Ge-LE

Epigraphe syncharistica seu carmen leoninosapphicum in solis elo-
gium, nobilissimae typographicae ter jubilanti ore praeconis facun-
dissimi typice consecratum, eiusdem honoribus operâ inclytae socie-

tatis Vötterinanae debitae observantiae ergo adornatum a F. E. C. J.
Monachii, 1740.   Folio.   [2085]
     Eu-De-LBb

Erichson, Johann.
   Die heilsahmen Absichten, welche Gott bey Erfindung und zeitiger
Einführung der edlen Buchdrucker-Kunst in hiesige Reiche, besonders
zu dieser Ihrem Besten, gehabt. Rede, welche den 1. Novbr. des
1740. Jahrs als des dritten Jubel-Jahrs dieser herrlichen Kunst,
in der Teutschen Schule öffentlich gehalten worden.   Stockholm,
gedruckt bey Johann Laurens Horrn, 1740.   36p.   4to.   [2086]
     Eu-De-LBb   Eu-Ge-LB

Ernesti, Johann August, 1707-1781.
   Prolusio qua ad audiendas oratiunculas contrarias IV contra
chalcographiam ... habendas patronos et fautores invitat et quibus
literarum disciplinis et quatenus chalcographia prosit quaerit Io.
Aug. Ernesti ... [Lipsiae, Ex officina Langenhemiana, 1740] xvi p.
21.5 cm.   [2087]
     NNC   Eu-Fr-PN   Eu-Ge-LB

   Die ersten Rudolstädtischen Jubel-Opffer wurden ... Friedrich
Anthon Fürsten zu Schwartzburg ... an dem den 24 Juni 1740,
eingefallenen und mit hoher Concession gefeyerten Jubilaeo der
vor 300 Jahren erfundenen Buchdrucker-Kunst ... überbracht von
dem Factor und sämtlichen Kunst-Verwandten der Löwischen Officin
allhier zu Rudolstadt. Daselbst gedruckt mit Löwischer Wittwen
Schrifften 1740.   Folio.   [2088]
     Eu-De-LBb

Fekno, Peter Paul.
   Deo & magistrati in honorem, aeque ac juventuti patriae masculae
in emolumentum, Actus scholastico-valedictorio-oratorius, de
duplici Germaniae invento, scilicet de typographia et pulvere
pyrio, Lyceo Torgensi anno aerae christianae MDCCXIII die X
Octobr. praesentabitur, ad quem audiendum honorandos patronos,
fautores & amicos humillime invitat Petrus Paulus Fekno, Lyc.
Torgensis Rector.   Torgae, typis Johannis Zachariae Hempii.
(In Wolf, J. C. Monumenta typographica. Hamburg, 1740.
vol. 2, p. 867-872)   [2089]

Feller, Frid. Theoph.
   Als ... die ... edlen ... Buchdrucker-Herrn und sämmtlichen Kunst-
Verwandten ... das dritte Jubel-Fest Anno 1740 feyerten ... Jena,
1740.   Folio.   [2090]
     Eu-De-LBb

Finck, R. Dan.
   Programma de coeli in haec inferiora dominia.   Brandenburg,
1740.   4to.
   Title from Mohr, Jubelfeste.   [2091]

Fleischhauer, Christ. Val.
   Quadruplirter zehnfach verwandelnder Bilder-Reim, in jambisch-
heroischen Versen, als die sehr gelobte Buchdruckerkunst ihr drittes
Jubiläum den 27. Junii 1740 ... feyerlich begieng.   Erfurth [1740]
1 Bog.   Folio.
   Title from Mohr, Jubilfeste.
   Reprinted in Gessner, C. F.   Die so nöthig als nützliche Buch-
   druckerkunst ... Leipzig, 1740-1745.   [2092]

   Franckfurtische Jubelandacht an dem dritten Jubelfest, wegen der
vor 300 Jahren erfundenen Buchdruckerkunst, welches den 24. Juni
1740 in der Reichs-, Wahl- und Handels-Stadt Franckfurt a/M. feyerlich soll gehalten werden.   Franckfurt a/M., 1740.   2 Bog.   8vo.
   Title from Mohr, Jubelfeste.   [2093]

   Freud- und Leyd-Begehung oder Jubel- und Trauer-Fest, da nemlich
in diesem 1740 Jahr ... Carl der Sechste. allerhöchster ... Gönner der
Buchdruckerey Kunst und allerhöchstdessen Kayserl. Thron in eine
Todten-Baar verkehret wird, in welchem diese nemliche Buchdruckerey-
Kunst, ... das dritte ... Jubel-Jahr, ... begehen, und zugleich wegen aller-
höchst gedachten Todes-Fall kläglich ... traurrn, und insonderheit an-
heunt als den 26. Dec. anni ejusdem hochfeuerlich celebriren thut
die devote Buchdruckerey deren Swobodischen Erben, in der Königlichen
Stadt Znymb.   Znaym, 1740.   [2094]
   Eu-De-LBb

   Die Freude derer Frommen zu Zion, bey dem dritten Jubel-Feste der
edlen Buchdrucker-Kunst, und der desswegen angestellten solennen
Jubel- und Danck-Predigt in der evangelischen Kirche zu denen Kauff-
männern den 6ten Julii Anno 1740 in einem kurtzen musikalischen
Dramate vorerwehnten Gottesdienstes erwogen von Joh. Mich. Funcken,
Joh. Dav. Jungnicol, Joh. Heinr. Nonnen und sämmtlichen in derer
Officinen befindlichen Kunst-Gliedern.   Erfurt, 1740.   Folio.   [2095]
   Eu-De-LBb

Freyburg, Christian August, 1684-1743.
   Reliquien von der Dressdnischen und übrigen Ober-Sächsischen
Buchdrucker-Historie.   Dressden [1741]   4to.   [2096]
   Eu-De-LBb

----   Von den allerersten und ältesten Buchdruckern zu Dressden
handelt in diesen Blättern, und kündiget zugleich einen Schulactum
an, der bey dem dreyhundertjährigen Andencken der 1440. erfundenen
Kunst auf den XVII. Jun. zu St. Annen gehalten werden sol, M. Chris-

tian August Freyberg, rector. Dressden, Gedruckt bey der verwitt.
Hof-Buchdr. Stösselin, 1740.   16p.   19.5x17 cm.
    Stamp on t.-p.: Grafl. Stolbergische Bibliothek z. Wernigerode.
    With this are bound: (1) Schöttgen, Christian. Historie derer
    dressdnischen Buchdrucker. Dressden [1740]   (2) [Röllig,
    J. C.] Cantata, auf das dritte Jubel-Fest. [Dressden, 1740]
    (3) Freyberg, C. A. Reliquien von der dressdnischen und übrigen
    obersächsischen Buchdrucker-Historie. Dressden [1741]   (4)
    Müller, D. T. Indicem pleniorem scriptorum typis excusorum ...
    perficit ... D. T. Müller ... Dresdae [1768]   [2097]
    DLC   Eu-De-LBb

Freytag, Frid. Gotthilf.
    Sibillae Erythraeae oraculum de typographia expendit et lectiones
publicas in provinciali schola portensi indicat.   Numburgi [Naum-
berg a. S.] 1740.   2 Bog.   Folio.   [2098]
    Eu-De-LBb

Fuchs, Johann Nicolas Heinrich.
    Als das dritte 100jährige Jubelfest wegen Erfindung der hochlöb-
lichen Buchdruckerkunst fast von allen und jeden Mitgliedern theils
vor, theils an und nach dem Tage Johannis des Täufers 1740 feyerlichst
begangen worden ... wünschte denen Buchdruckerherren und Gesellen zu
Leipzig, Halle, Jena und Erfurt wie auch zu Franckfurt a/M ferneres
Wachsthum und Aufnahme. [Leipzig] 1740.   1 Bog.   4to.
    Title from Mohr, Jubelfeste.   [2099]

Funck, Johann Daniel.
    Als anno 1740 die edle Buchdruckerkunst ihr 300jähriges; die
Reussnerische Buchdruckerey aber ihr 100jähriges Jubelfest beging.
Königsberg, Hartnung, 1740.   1 Bog.   Folio.
    Title from Mohr, Jubelfeste.   [2100]

Funcke, Johann Michael.
    Wollte Gott, der druckenden, das ist, bewegenden und belebenden
Ursache aller Dinge, und sonderlich der ... Buchdrucker-Kunst, bey
erfreulich angebrochener dritten Jubel-Feier, den 6. Julii 1740,
allhier in Erfurt ... demüthigsten Dank abstatten. Erfurt [1740]
Folio.   [2101]
    Eu-De-LBb

Gasser, Johann Michael.
    Vertente saeculo ab inventa typographia tertio ad audiendas ora-
tiones saeculares, quae a.d. III idus Maias 1740 habebuntur ... rogat,
de inventae artis natalibus nonnulla disserens. Hallae Salicae
[1740]   Folio.   [2102]
    Eu-De-LBb

Gedicht zur Feier des Jubelfestes von 1740 von einem Gehülfen der Heitz'schen Buchdruckerei. [Reprinted in] Indicateur du Bas Rhin, no. 51, 1840. [2103]

Gemeinhardt, Johann Casper.
Gedicht über das 300jährige Gedächtniss der 1440 zu Mayntz erfundenen Buchdruckerkunst. Lauban, 1740. 2 Bog.
Title from Mohr, Jubelfeste. [2104]

Gerlach, Benjamin Gottl.
Von der Erfindung der Buchdruckerkunst. Zittau, 1740. 8vo.
Title from Chevalier, C. U. J. Repertoire des sources historiques du moyen age. Paris, 1877-1903. vol. 2)
Louis Mohr lists only the name of Gerlach with the following note, translated from the German: Latin invitation to a declamation [Rede-Uebung] May 3, 1740; the title is missing. [2105]

Gertner, Georg Michael.
Jubilaeum typographicum bambergense, das ist: Feyerliche Begängnuss des dritten Jubel-Festes der vor dreyhundert Jahren in ... Maynz ... glücklich erfundenen edlen Buchdrucker-Kunst, bey welcher Feyerlichkeit ... der Buchdruckerey vorzüglich- und höchst-erspriesliche Verdienste ... in einer Lob- und Dank- Predigt verabfasset ... von Georgio Michaële Gertner ... Bamberg, Gedruckt bey G. A. Gertner, 1740. 28p. 30 cm. [2106]
    DLC

Gertner, Johann Georg Christ.
Das in seiner Hof- und Academischen Buchdruckerey jubilirende Bamberg, als die dritte Jubelfeier der Erfindung der Buchdruckerkunst celebrirt worden. 12. December 1740. Bamberg, 1740. 4 Bog. Folio. [2107]
    Eu-Ge-LSb

Gessner, Christian Friedrich, d. 1756.
Nachricht wie man das Jubelfest ... Ausführliche Nachricht wie das dritte Buchdruckerjubiläum 1740 ... (In his Die so nöthig als nützliche Buchdruckerkunst und Schriftgiesserey ... Leipzig, 1740-1745. vol. 3, p. 114-225) [2108]
    DLC   MH   NN   NNGr   Eu-De-LBb   Eu-Ge-LB

Goetse, Christian Friedrich.
Kalavdoloria, quibus virum praecellentissimum, plurimum venerabilem, clarissimum doctissimumque ... sit acclamabat de tertio artis typographicae jubilaeo feliciter. Sorau, 1740. 2 Bog. 4to.
Title from Mohr, Jubelfeste. [2109]

---- Strena votiva. Sorau, 1740.
Title from Mohr, Jubelfeste. [2110]

[Gollners, Johann]
Typographia Jenensium iubilans seculari et aenigmatico carmine
expressa vel celebrata. Oder die zu Jena jubilirende wohllöbliche
Buchdrucker-Kunst in einem feyerlichen und verdeckten Gedichte ...
entworffen von Johann Gollners A. 1719 verstorbenen ältesten Buchdrucker-Herrn zu Jena sämtliche hinterlassene Kinder den 18. Julii
1740. Jena, 1740. Folio. [2111]
  Eu-De-LBb

[Gottsched, Johann Christoph] 1700-1766.
Cantata welche bey der öffentlichen Gedächtnissrede auf die vor
dreyhundert Jahren erfundene Buchdruckerkunst ... zu Leipzig ... den 27.
Juni 1740 vor und nach der Rede abgesungen worden. Aufgeführt von
Joh. Gottlieb Görnern. Leipzig, 1740. 1 Bog. 4to. [2112]
  Eu-De-LBb

---- Lob- und Gedächtnissrede auf die Erfindung der Buchdruckerkunst ...
(In his Gesammelte Reden. Leipzig, 1749. p. [125]-172) [2113]
  NNGr

---- Ode auf das dritte Jahrhundert der Buchdruckerkunst, welches
im Jahre 1740 den 28. December zu Königsberg gefeyert wurde.
Konigsberg [1740] [2114]
  Eu-De-LBb

Graf, Andr. Christ.
Augspurgische Kinderreden von der edlen Buchdruckerkunst, welche ...
am Thomas- und Johannistage ... einige Schüler des evangel. Gymnasii
allhier öffentlich abgeleget. Augsburg, 1740. 8vo.
Title from Mohr, Jubelfeste. [2115]

Grosch, Gottfried.
Programma de officio deo, artis typographicae causa praestantis
in memor. jubil. tertii. Goslar, 1740. 4to.
Title from Mohr, Jubelfeste. [2116]

---- Sex orationes de multiplici varioque artis typographicae usu
in memoriam hujus artis a tribus inde saecularis inventae renovatum
... Goslar, 1740. 7 Bog. 4to.
Title from Mohr, Jubelfeste. [2117]

Grosse Wunder-Werck welche die Göttliche Vorsichtigkeit in Erfin-
dung der edlen Buchdruckerkunst gewürcket, bey höchst-feyerlicher
Begehung des dritten Jahr-Hundert gedachter Kunst, in ... München ver-
kündet von einem grossen Verehrer dieser höchst nützlich- und edlen
Kunst. München, 1740. Folio. [2118]
  Eu-De-LBb

Grunert, Johann Friederich and others.
An den Allerdurchlauchtigsten ... Herrn Friedrich den Andern, König
in Preussen etc. bey Gelegenheit derjenigen Feyer, die zum Andenken
der vor dreyhundert Jahren erfundenen Buchdruckerkunst auf der Hochlöbl. Friedrichsuniversität zu Halle den 25. Juli 1740 angestellet
worden, allerunterthänigst abgelassen.   [Halle a.S., 1740] Folio.[2119]
    Eu-De-LBb

Halle. Universität.
Oeffentliche Jubelzeugnisse, welche, bey dem von einigen Buchdruckern zu Halle den 25. Jul. 1740 erneuerten Andenken der vor dreyhundert Jahren erfundenen Buchdruckerkunst, von der Hochlöbl. Friedrichsuniversität und andern gelehrten Gönnern feyerlichst abgelegt worden.
Halle, Grunert Gebrüder und Joh. Just. Gebauer, 1741.   312, 36p.
front.   21 cm.   [2120]
    NNC   NNGr   Eu-De-LBb   Eu-Ge-LSb

Hänicker, Samuel.
Immergrünes Ehren-Gedächtniss, und ewigwährendes Lob der hochedlen
und unvergleichlichen Kunst der Buchdruckerey, sonderlich der Frey-
bergischen.   Mit Beutherischer Schrifft daselbst.   [1740]
Folio.   [2121]
    Eu-De-LBb

Hanov, Michael Christoph.
Denkmahl der Danziger Buchdruckereyen und Buchdrucker.   1539-1740.
Danzig, 1740.   4to.   [2122]
    Eu-Ge-LB

Hartung, Johann Heinrich.
Den Satz, dass der Buchdrucker, von welchem das Vaterland einen
gewissen Vortheil erwarten soll, ein rechtschaffener Patriote seyn
müsse. Königsberg, 1740.   2 Bog.   Folio.
Title from Mohr, Jubelfeste.   [2123]

Hecatombe.   Der Tübingischen / Buchdrucker-Gesellschaft / Das ist:
/ Demüthiges und freudiges / Lob- und Dank-Opfer / Vor die / Gnädige
Vorsorge der ewigen Weissheit, / mächtigen Schutz des Hochfürstlichen
Hauses / Würtemberg, / und ununterbrochene Grossgunst des Hochlöblichen / SENATUS ACADEMICI, / Worunter / Die im Jahre 1440 glücklich
erfundene gemeinnützliche / Buchdrucker-Kunst / Besonders allhier in
Tübingen bishero geblühet hat, und zu grösserer Vollkommenheit ge-
diehen, / an ihrem am Tage Jacobi des Grössern / im Jahre 1740 feyer-
lichst begangenen / Dritten Jubel-Fest / dem grossen GOTT, als
Urhebern aller heilsamen Künste, zu / höchsten Ehren, wie auch zu
der sämmtlichen dieser Edlen / Kunst-Verwandten / unterthänigtgehor-
samster / Empfehlung / zu fernerer Gnade, Schutz und Wohlwollen /
Auf der uralten UNIVERSITAET Tübingen / unter vielen Freuden-
Bezeugungen dargebracht, und der dankbaren Nach- / Welt zu einem

Reitzenden Beyspiel der Nachfolge überlassen / Von denen sich
daselbst aufhaltenden Buchdruckern und Kunstverwandten.   Tübingen,
1740.   8p.   Folio.
    Title from Mohr, Jubelfeste.   [2124]

Heller, Johann Bernhard.
    Bey Feyrung des dritten Jubel-Festes der vortrefflichen Buch-
drucker-Kunst den 18ten Julii dieses 1740ten Jahres in Jena.
Jena [1740]   Folio.   [2125]
    Eu-De-LBb

----   Wohlgemeynte Gedancken über Führung einer Buchdruckerey, bey
Feyerung des dritten Jubel-Festes der Buchdrucker-Kunst kürtzlich
eröffnet.   Erfurt, 1740.   10 leaves, 112p.   8vo.   [2126]
    NNGr   Eu-De-LBb

Hendel, Johann Christian.
    Wolte das dritte Jubel-Fest der edlen Buchdrucker-Kunst im Jahr
1740 zu Halle durch nachfolgende Lob- und Freuden-Ode ... an seinem
auswärtig begangenen Hochzeit-Tage (als am Tage des Apostels St.
Jacobi) jauchzend besingen.   Halle, 1740.   4to.   [2127]
    Eu-De-LBb

Hertl, M. Christian Friedrich.
    De librorum in scholis delectu et usu.   Halberstadt [1740]   3
Bog. with music.   4to.
    Title from Mohr, Jubelfeste.   [2128]

Heumann, Christoph August.
    Dissertatio, in qua Fabulam de Juliani Imp. voce extrema: Vicisti
Galileae, certis argumentis confutat ejusque originem in apricum pro-
fert Christophorus Augustus Heumannus ... Gottingae, 1740.   30p.
4to.   [2129]
    Eu-Fr-PN

Heyne, Johann.
    Ioan Heynius, ad memoriam saecularem artis typographicae ante CCC.
annos inventae diebus X. et XI. Febr. 1740 ... Brandeburgi, 1740.
4to.   [2130]
    Eu-De-LBb

    Hilaria typographica Erfordiensia, das ist, historischer Bericht
von der Jubel-Feyer, welche zum Andencken der vor dreyhundert Jahren
erfundenen Buchdruckerkunst am 27. Junij MDCCXL auf der uralten
Universität Erfurth begangen worden nebst der bey solcher Gelegenheit gehaltenen Academischen Rede und noch andern dahin gehörigen
Schriften.   Erfurth, 1740.   7 1/2 Bog.   4to.   [2131]
    NNGr   Eu-De-LBb

Hoeglein, Valent.
   ... Jubilaeum artis typographicae inter festos literati orbis nostri
apparatus tertio redux ... die XII. decembris celebrat Universitas Bam-
bergensis ... Bamberg, 1740.   Folio.
      At head of title: Valent. Hoeglein, Collegii S. J. et Universi-
      tatis Ottoniano Friedr. Rectoris.   [2132]
      Eu-De-LBb

Hoffmann, Christian Ludwig.
   Pêle-Mêle; bestehend in einem historisch-philologischen Discours
von Erfindung der edlen Buchdrucker-Kunst ... nebst einem kurtzen Bericht, wie in Mengeringhausen und Lippstadt endlich eine Buchdrucker-
Officin aufgerichtet ... Bey Gelegenheit des Jubilaei Typographici herausgegeben. Mengeringhausen und Lippstadt, 1740.   4 leaves and 7
Bog. 8vo.   [2133]
      Eu-De-LBb   Eu-Ne-GK

Hoffmann, Johann Daniel.
   Tractatus de typographiis earumque initiis et incrementis in regno
Poloniae et magno ducatu Lithuaniae cum veriis observationibus rem et
litterarium et typographicam ... ex parte illustrantibus.   Dantisci,
1740. 4 leaves, 71p. 4to.   [2134]
      Eu-De-LBb

   Einer / Hohen Obrigkeit / Der hiesigen Königlichen Freyen / Stadt-
Strassburg / Unsern / Gnädigen Gebietenden Herren / Haben bei Gelegenheit / der, in dem Eintausend, Vierhundert und Viertzigsten Jahr nach
der / Heil-Geburt Christi, und also eben vor Dreyhundert Jahren, /
durch die Göttliche Gnade / Hier zuerst erfunden / Buchdrucker-
Kunst, / Und des dabey auf den sechsten Brachmonat dieses jetzt lauffenden / 1740sten Jahrs angeordneten Derselben / Dritten Jubel-Festes, /
Theils ihre geziemende Pflicht an der Tag zu legen, theils auch die
Grösse ihrer Freude / in etwas auszudrucken / folgendes Jubel-Gedicht-
verfertigen lassen und in tiefster Ehrfurcht überreichen sollen, /
Unserer / Gnädig-Gebietender Herren, / Unterthänigste Bürger und Die-
ner / die sämmtliche sich hier aufhaltende / Buchdrucker und Buch-
druckerey-Verwandten. / [Strassburg, 1740] 8p.   Folio.
      Title from Mohr, Jubelfeste.   [2135]

Hueth, Christoph Joseph.
   Der von dem Guten-Berg das Drittenmal gegebene Echo, oder freuden-
voller Ehren-Schall, der von Johann Guttenberg, Anno 1740 erfundenen
... Buchdruckerey-Kunst, zum drittenmal erschallendes Jubel-Jahr, welches
C. J. Hueth, einer ... Wiennerischer Universität Buchdrucker, und Burger
in ... Rötz ... den 6. Dec. 1740.   Hoch-Feyerlich begienge mit ... Gottfried
Zipper und Andreas Hoffer.   [Rötz, 1740]   Folio.   [2136]
      Eu-De-LBb

Hupffer, Hieronymus.
    Lob-Rede auf das bey Gelegenheit der Anno 1440 durch die Gött-
liche Gnade allhier zu Strassburg erfundenen höchst-schätzbarsten
Buchdrucker-Kunst den 6. Brachmonat dieses jetzt lauffenden 1740.
Jahrs feyerlichst begangene Dritte Jubelfest ... Strassburg, Simon
Kürssner, 1740. 16p. 4to.
    Title from Mohr, Jubelfeste   [2137]

    Kurzer Vorbericht von einer umständlichen Nachricht, den Anfang
und Fortgang der Buchdruckerkunst betreffend. Amsterdam, 1740.
Folio.
    Title from Bigmore & Wyman.   [2137a]

Jena. Buchdruckergesellschaft.
    Kurtze Nachricht wie die Buchdruckergesellschaft zu Jena, den 17,
18, 19 und 20ten Juli 1740, ihr drittes Jubelfest nach Erfindung
der edlen Buchdruckerkunst behörig gefeyret. [Jena] Johann Volckmar
Marggraf [1740]   [8]p. 19,5 cm.   [2138]
    NNC

    Jubel-Carmen, dem Hochedlen Rath von den beyden Buchdruckern (Chr.
Ulr. Wagner und Elias Dan. Süss) und sämmtlichen Buchdruckerey-Ver-
wandten unterthänigst dedicirt. Ulm, 22. August 1740. 2 Bog.
    Title from Mohr, Jubelfeste.   [2139]

    Jubilaeum, tam commune inventae ante ccc annos artis typographicae,
quam speciale, fundati ante c annos regii et academici typographaei
Reusneriani, diebus xxvii et xxviii Decembr. a. 1740 solenniter celebratum etc. Königsberg, 1740. 1 Bog. Folio.
    Title from Mohr, Jubelfeste.   [2140]

Jungendres, Sebastian Jac.
    Disquisitio in notas characteristicas librorum a typographiae in-
cunabulo ad a. MD impressorum ... in jubilaei typographici tertii
mnemosynon conscripta. Noribergae, 1740. 3 leaves and 6 Bog.
4to.   [2141]
    Eu-De-LBb

Jungmann, Johann Christian.
    An dem höchst freudevollen Nahmensfest des hochgeboren H. H. Joh.
Ant. Schafgotsch ... welches den 24. Juni 1740 hochgräflich celebrirt
worde, wollte durch nachgesetztes Denckmahl, bey der allgemeynen
dritten Jubel-Freude derer Kunstgenossen der Druckerey ... seinen
Glückwunsch abstatten. Jauer, 1740. 2 Bog. Folio.
    Title from Mohr, Jubelfeste.   [2142]

Jungnicol, Johann David.
    Als die hochlöbliche und hochnützlichste Buchdrucker-Kunst ihr
drittes Jubiläum mit Gott erlebete ... Erfurt, 1740. Folio.   [2143]
    Eu-De-LBb

Kleinknecht, Conrad Daniel, 1691-1753.
Gottheiligte Evangelisch-Lutherische Buchdrucker-Jubel-Freude,
über die besondere göttliche Wohlthat wegen der Anno 1440 ... erfun-
denen, verbessert und bishero gnädig erhaltenen höchstnützlichen
Buchdrucker-Kunst, an ihrem dritten Jubel-Fest ... zu Ulm den 24.
Augusti des 1740. Jahrhunderts gehalten in einem Gespräche von
Conrad Daniel Kleinknecht. Ulm, C. U. Wagner, 1742. 101p. 8vo. [2144]
NNGr   Eu-De-LBb   Eu-Fr-PN   Eu-Ge-LSb

Klemm, Johann Christian, 1688-1754.
Das Angedencken des dritten Jubel-Fests der edlen Buchdrucker-
Kunst auf der Universität Tübingen [1740] welches ... einen histori-
schen Entwurff des Anfangs und Fortgangs dieser edlen Kunst in
Schwaben, und besonders der Academie Tübingen in denen meisten von
A. 1440. biss 1540. als dem ersten Jahrhundert gedruckten Büchern
enthält ... durch Johann Christian Klemm ... Tübingen, Joseph Siegmund
[1740]   111p.   front.   21 cm.   [2145]
NNC   Eu-De-LBb   Eu-Ge-LB   Eu-Ge-LSb

Klettenberg, Johann Erasmus Georg von.
Kurzgefasster historischer Bericht von denen ersten Erfindern der
löblichen Buchdrucker-Kunst. Frankfurt am Mayn, 1741. 16mo.   [2146]
Eu-Fr-PN   Eu-Ge-LB

Knauth, Christian.
Annales typographici Lusatiae superioris, oder Geschichte der Ober-
Lausitzischen Buchdruckereyen ... als ein Beytrag zur Buchdrucker-His-
torie mitgetheilet. Lauban, 1740. 96p. 4to.
Reprinted in: Bresslauisches Jubelgedächtniss ... 1740.   [2147]
Eu-Ge-LB

----   Historischer Abriss von den Anfang und Wachstum der Gelehrsam-
keit in Ober-Lausitz und wie die Ober-Lausitzschen Buchdruckereyen derselben gedienet, bey Gelegenheit des 3ten. Buchdrucker-Jubel-Festes
1740 entworfen von Christian Knauthen ... Leipzig und Görlitz, S. E.
Richter [n.d.]   27p.   4to.   [2148]
Eu-De-LBb   Eu-Fr-PN

Koch, Christ. Bened.
De palingenesia litterarum oratio anniversaria memoriae Zangianae
cumprimis sacra et hac occasione viaentibus impraesentiarum typographiae jubilis dicata. Arnstadt, 1740. 4 Bog. 4to.   [2149]
Eu-De-LBb

Köcher, Johann Christoph.
Ad renovandem in Gymnasio Osnabrugensi artis typographicae memoriam
viros cujuscumque ordinis doctissimos honoratissimosque convocat de
nonnullis ejusdem memorabilibus pauca praefatus J. C. K.   Osnabrugi
[1740]   4to.   [2150]
NN   Eu-Ge-LB

[Köhler, Johann David] 1684-1755.
  ... Eine Gedächtnuss-Müntze auf Johann Guttenberg von Sorgenloch, gennant Gänsfleisch wahrhafftigen Erfinder der Buchdruckerey, von A. 1740.   (In Köhler, Johann David. Historischer Münz-Belustigung vierzehender Theil ... Nürnberg, 1742.   p. 353-360)
    At head of caption title: Der wöchentlichen historischen Münz-Belustigung. 45. Stuck, den 7. November 1742.   [2151]
    MBMu   MH   MdBP

----   Hochverdiente und aus bewährten Urkunden wohlbeglaubte Ehren-Rettung Johann Guttenbergs, eingebornen Bürgers in Mayntz, aus dem alten Rheinländischen Adelichen Geschlechte derer von Sorgenloch, genannt Gänsefleisch, wegen der ersten Erfindung der nie genug gepriesenen Buchdrucker-Kunst in der Stadt Mayntz, zu unvergänglichen Ehren der Teutschen Nation, und insonderheit der löblichen uralten Stadt Mayntz, mit gänzlicher und unwiedersprechlicher Entscheidung des darüber entstandenen dreyhundertjährigen Streits, getreulich und mit allein Fleiss ausgefertigt von Johann David Köhler, Hist. P. P. O. zu Göttingen.   Leipzig, bey Caspar Fritschen, 1741.
8 prel. leaves, 108p.   21.5 cm.   [2152]
    CSmH   ICN   NN   Eu-De-LBb   Eu-Fr-PN   Eu-Ge-LB   Eu-Ge-LP
    Eu-Ne-AVb   Eu-Ne-GK

Kratzenstein, M. Christian Heinrich.
    Der in der duncklen Nacht hellstrahlende Stern der edlen Buchdruckerkunst ... in einer Rede vorgestellet.   Erfurth, 1740.
1 1/2 Bog.   4to.
    Title from Mohr, Jubelfeste.   [2153]

Kraus, Johann Christoph.
    Joannes Christoph. Krausius. Laudes meritissimas nobilissimae artis typographicae, cum Io. Conradus Stoesselius, praestantissimae hujus artis cultor strenuus, ex laudabili typographorum more, in aedibus patris sui, viri honestissimi, solertissimi & peritissimi, Conradi Stoesselii, typographi ac bibliopolae in urbe Chemnitiensi florentissimi, tyrocinium poneret, & documentum artis daret, paucis exponere annisus est amicus, qui nomen suum in fine epistolae profitetur. De lingua vernacula ad verbum expressit Jo. Gerh. Sucksdorfius, Gymnasii Hamburg. Civic egregius. Chemnitii 1729. 26. Nov.   (In Wolf, J. C. Monumenta typographica. Hamburg, 1740. vol. 2, p. 700-704)   [2154]

Kretzschmar, Christ.
    Saecularia typographica nonnulli scholae novae ad Dresdam urbis discipuli d. xiii. Maji ... celebrabunt ... Dresdae, 1740.
2 Bog.   4to.
    Title from Mohr, Jubelfeste.   [2155]

Kreyssig, M. G. C.
Nachlese zum Buchdrucker-Jubiläo in Ober-Sachsen, oder Historie
derer ehemaligen Buchdrucker zu Altenburg, Annaberg, Freyberg, Pirna
und Zwickau, nebst einem Verzeichniss aller dabey gehörigen Schriften.
Dressden, 1741. 1 1/2 Bog. 4to. [2156]
Eu-Ge-LB

Kropffgans, Johann Georg.
Beim den nach Erfindung der edlen Buchdruckerkunst A. R. S. 1740
d. 24 Junii zum Drittenmahl begangenen solennen Jubilaeo sollte auf
Verlangen und im Nahmen Paul Conrad Helds ... den Antheil seiner ge-
hörigen Bey-Freude erklären ... Regenspurg, 1740. Folio. [2157]
Eu-De-LBb

Kühn, Johann Michael.
Das dritte Jubeljahr der edlen Druckerey bemerket diese Zahl
CIƆIƆCCXL. Ich wünsche dies dabey: dass der Patronen Huld ihr
ferner günstig sey! Cottbus, 1740. 2 Bog. Folio.
Title from Mohr, Jubelfeste. [2158]

Kurtze Fragen von der Buchdruckerkunst, zum Nutzen der Jugend in
der Stadt-Schule zu Grimma aufgesetzt von P. S. K. Leipzig, 1740.
1 Bog. 8vo. [2159]
Eu-De-LBb

Kurtze Nachricht wie das Jubilaeum wegen der vor drey hundert
Jahren erfundenen Buchdruckerkunst in der Residenzstadt Gotha den 11.
Julii 1740 celebriret worden. Nebst einem Vorbericht von Joh. Benj.
Huhn. Gotha, gedruckt mit Reyherischen Schrifften [1740] [16]
leaves, xl, 253p. 17 cm. [2160]
NNGr   Eu-De-LBb

Küster, Georg Godofr.
Typographiae ante hos trecentos annos feliciter inventae memoria,
orationibus quibusdam die XXVIII. Mart. in Gymnasio renovabitur ...
Berlin, 1740. 1/2 Bog. 4to.
Title from Mohr, Jubelfeste. [2161]

Lackmann, Adam Heinrich.
Annalium typographicorum selecta quaedam capita. Hamburgi, apud
viduam B. Felgineri et J. C. Bohnium, 1740. iv, 168p. 4to. [2162]
ICN   Eu-De-LBb   Eu-Fr-PN   Eu-Ge-LB   Eu-Ne-AVb

Lange, Johann Christoph.
Die Buchdrucker-Kunst als das letzte und edelste Kleinod der
Kirche am dritten Buchdrucker-Jubelfeste 1740, den 19. Julii in
Budissin gepriesen. Budissin, 1740. 4to. [2163]
Eu-De-LBb

Leich, Johann Heinrich, 1720-1750.
De origine et incrementis typographicae lipsiensis liber 'singularis, ubi varia de litterariis urbis studiis et viris doctis, qui
in ea claruerunt, inserunter. Accedit librorum sec. XV. excusorum
ad Maittairii Annales supplementum. Lipsiae, B. C. Breitkopf,
anno typographiae seculari III [1740] 5 prel. leaves, [3]-147,
[1]p. 24 cm. [2164]
DLC Eu-De-LBb Eu-Fr-PN Eu-Ge-LB

[----] Gepriesenes Andencken von Erfindung der Buchdruckerey, wie
solches in Leipzig beym Schluss des dritten Jahrhunderts von den
gesammten Buchdruckern daselbst gefeyret worden. Leipzig, In
den Buchdruckereyen, 1740. lvi, 176p. illus. 24 cm.
Contents.-- I. Auszüge aus den Predigten, die am Johannistage,
vor der Jubelfeyer alhier und in Grimma gehalten worden.--
II. Einladungsschrift des Dechanten ... Herrn Prof. Menzens, zu
der Jubelrede.-- III. Lob und Gedächtnissrede auf die Erfindung der Buchdruckerkunst, gehalten von Herrn. Prof. Gott-
scheden; wobey der von dem Herrn Prof. Wachter erfundene und
in Genf geprägte Schaupfennig, als ein Zierrath angebracht
worden.-- IV. Cantata ... -- V. Ode auf die Gedächtnissfeyer
der vor dreyhundert Jahren erfundenen Buchdruckerkunst, von
Luis Adolg. Vict. Gottschedinn.-- VI. Das Programma, womit
Herr M. Ernesti zu einer Redeübung auf der Thomasschule, als
Rector derselben eingeladen.-- VII. Carmina in typographiae
solenne seculare tertium celebratum Lipsiae.-- VIII. Lobge-
dichte ... [2165]
DLC NN Eu-De-LBb Eu-Ge-LB Eu-Ge-LSb Eu-Ne-AVb
Eu-Ne-GK

Lengren, Carl.
Kort berättelse om bok-tryckeriets begynnelse och fortgang i
gemen och äfwen uti Sverige. Stockholm, 1740. 4to. [2166]
Eu-De-LBb

---- Kort berättelse om boktryckeriets begynnelse och fortgang i
gemen och äfwen uti Sverige da ahr efter Christi börd, MDCCXL, des
tredje jubilaeum uti Europa firades, framgifwen af Carl Lengren.
Stockholm, Trykt uti thet Kongl. boktryckeriet, 1740. [Stockholm,
1917] 5 prel. leaves, 15-34p., 1 leaf incl. front., port. 26.5 cm.
Colophon: Denna skrift är ett nytryck i 76 numrerade exemplar,
varav nummer 1 tryckt a pergament är till direktören Erik Oldenburg pa 50-arsdagen av boktryckare-vänner i Stockholm överlämnat.
Dekorationerna äro efter teckningar av konstnären Arthur Sjögren
och trycket är utfört hos bröderna Lagerström boktryckare,
Stockholm 1917. [2167]
DLC ICN NN Eu-Ge-LB Eu-Sv-SK

- 271 -

Lentz, Hieronymus.
Die Ausbreitung des göttlichen Lobes sollte bey der dritten Jubel-Feyer, welche zum erfreulichen Andencken der vor Drey-Hundert Jahren erfundenen edlen Kunst Buchdruckerey, vermittelst eines actus oratorii, in ... Regenspurg den 27. Sept. im Jahr 1740 angestellet wurde, zu seinem Haupt-Endzweck setzen.   Regensburg, 1740.   Folio.   [2168]
   Eu-De-LBb

Lentz, Hieronymus and **Seiffert**, Christian Gottlieb.
Pflicht-schuldigstes **Danck**- und **Denck-mahl**, welches bey feyerlicher Begehung des dritten Jubel-Fests der ... Buchdrucker-Kunst, denen ... Herren Stadt-Cummerer und Rath ... Freyer Stadt Regenspurg ... vor die biherige hohe Förderung ... ihrer Officinen unterthänig-gehorsamst aufgerichtet zwey Regenspurgische Bürger und Buchdrucker ... den 27. Sept. A. 1740.   Regenspurg, 1740.   Folio.   [2169]
   Eu-De-LBb

Lerche, Johann Christian.
Jubilaeam typographorum solennitatem ad doctrinam de lege Dei in Decalogi tabulis divinis typis expressam accommodat ... Norimberga, typis J. H. G. Bielingii, 1740.   4to.   [2170]
   Eu-Fr-PN

Lessel, Johann Casper.
Die edle Buchdrucker-Kunst ... Im Jahr Christi 1740 den 24 Juni ... bey dem dritten Jubel-Feste, welches, nach Erfindung dieser Kunst, derselben Verwandten fast in gantz Deutschland und also auch in Brieg veranstaltet ... in einer besonderer Denck- und Danck-Predigt ... betrachtet.   Brieg, [1740]   4to.   [2171]
   Eu-Go-LB

Lesser, Friedrich Christian, 1692-1754.
Typographia iubilans, das ist: Kurtzgefasste Historie der Buchdruckerey, worinnen von dieser edlen Kunst Ursprunge und Anfange, Ausbreitung, Verbesserung, Zierrathan, Nutzen, wie nicht weniger von der Buchdrucker Eigenschaften und Pflichten, und dann von anderer Verhalten gegen dieselbe und deren Kunstverwandten kurtzlich gehandelt wird; bey dem dritten Jubel-Fest derselben, welches dieses Jahr auf Johannis-Tag gefeyert wird, entworffen von Friedrich Christian Lessern ... Leipzig, M. Blochberger, 1740.   8 prel. leaves, 412, [27]p. 27.5 cm.
   There is another edition of the same year with slightly different t.-p.
   "Einleitung" [Literatur]; p. 1-15.   [2172]
   DLC   ICJ   NNGr   Eu-De-LBb

Lestocq, Ludwig.
Bei dem dreihundertjährigen allgemeinen, und besonders auf dem 100jährigen Reussnerischen Freudenfeste der erfundenen und von den

Reussners fortgesetzten Buchdruckerkunst ... Königsberg, 1740. 1
Bog. Folio.
Title from Mohr, Jubelfeste. [2173]

Löchner, Johann Hieronymus.
Drittes Jubelfest in Ansprach 1740. (In Sammlung merkwürdiger
Medaillen. Nürnberg, P. C. Monath, [1740] vol. 4, p. 253) [2174]
Eu-Fr-PN

Lyce, Erdmann Andreas.
Frolockender Widenschall der allgemeinen dritten Jubel-Freude,
über die vor nun dreyhundert Jahren an den gesegneten Ufern des
Rheinstrohms glücklich erfundene ... Buch-Trucker-Kunst. Idstein,
1740. 1 Bog. Folio. [2175]
Eu-De-LBb

Magdeburgischer Beytrag zum Lobe Gottes wegen der vor 300 Jahren
erfundenen Buchdrucker-Kunst ... Magdeburg, 1740. 16 1/2 Bog.
4to. [2176]
Eu-De-LBb

Magerlinus, D. F.
Annus Bibliorum, 1450, primo impressorum Moguntiae, tertium jubi-
laris, hoc anno 1750. Francofurti, 1750. 4to.
Title from Hoe, Richard M. The literature of printing ... London,
1877. [2177]

Memmel, Johann Casp.
Regenspurgisches Denckmahl, der edlen Buchdrucker-Kunst zu schul-
digsten Ehren in ihrem dritten Jubel-Jahre den 24. Jun. A.C. 1740 ...
aufgerichtet. [Regensburg, 1740] Folio. [2178]
Eu-De-LBb

Menz, Friedrich.
Ludos seculares artis typographicae tribus ante seculis ... inventae
nunc seculo redeunte die XXVII. Junii 1740. hora IX, oratione ... in-
dicit ... F. Menzius. 1740.
Reprinted in [Leich, Johann Heinrich] Gepriesenes Andencken ...
Leipzig 1740. [2179]
Eu-De-LBb Eu-Ge-LB

Merckenberger, Johann Wilhelm.
Sein Jubel-Postulat unterfieng sich bey dem dritten Jubel-Feste
der edlen Buchdrucker-Kunst den 24. Jun. A. C. 1740. durch dieses
Blatt aus schuldigster Obliegenheit bekandt zu machen. Regenspurg,
1740. Folio. [2180]
Eu-De-LBb

Merkwürdiges Gespräch im Reiche der Todten zwischen den ersten
Erfindern der Buchdruckerkunst, worinne von den Ursprung, Fortgang
und übrigen Schicksälenderselben gehandelt, und insbesondere der
Stadt Mayntz der Ruhn von der Erfindung solcher Kunst vindiciret
wird: in dem dritten Buchdrucker-Jubiläo der curiösen Welt nebst
einigen remarquablen Neuigkeiten aus dem Reiche der Lebendigen
mitgetheilt. Erfurt, 1740. 8 Bog. ports.   [2181]
    Eu-De-LBb

Metzner, Michael and Appolt, Johann Martin.
    Als das durch göttliche Gnade den 24 Junii Anno 1740 beglückt er-
lebte dritte Jubel-Fest der edlen Kunst Buchdruckerey allhier in
Regenspurg vergnügt celebriret wurde, wollten ihre Bey-Freude damit
gleichfalls an den Tag legen. Regenspurg, 1740. Folio.   [2182]
    Eu-De-LBb

Meuschen, J. G.
    Der dem falschen entgegen gesetzte Rechte Abdruck der Person
Christi, am Festtage Petri und Pauli 1740, als der Jubel-Feyer der
Buchdruckerey, vorgestellt. Coburg, 1740. 8vo.
    Title from Mohr, Jubelfeste.   [2183]

Möller, M. Johann Melchior.
    Die Pflicht und Schuldigkeit gläubiger Seelen an dem durch die
Gnade Gottes erlebten III. Jubiläo der edlen Buchdruckerkunst ...
welches die Buchdrucker zu Erfurth ... den 6. July feyerlichst be-
giengen. Erfurt, 1740. 10 Bog. 4to.   [2184]
    Eu-De-LBb   Eu-Ge-LB

Münden, Christian, 1684-1741.
    D. Christian Mündens ... Danck-Predigt welche am dritten Jubel-Fest
wegen Erfindung der löbl. Buchdrucker-Kunst aus Ps. CII 14-19. zu
Franckfurt gehalten worden. Nebst einem historischen Bericht von
denen ersten Erfindern dieser Kunst denen franckfurtischen Buchdruckern und dem dritten Buchdrucker Jubel-Fest; nach des sel. Herrn
senioris tod vollendet und ausgefertiget durch Joh. Erasm. Georg von
Klettenberg ... Franckfurt, Buchdrucker-Societät, 1741. [18], 267,
[9], 47p. 17 cm.   [2185]
    ICN NN NNC NNGr Eu-De-LBb Eu-Fr-PN Eu-Ge-LB

    Musikalische Texte bey dem sich ereigniten dritten Jubilaeo der
edlen Kunst Buchdruckerey den 24. Jun. 1740 so in der Memmlischen
Officin celebriret wurde. Regensburg, 1740. Folio.   [2186]
    Eu-De-LBb

    Musophili löbliche Vorzüge einer edlen Buchdrucker-Kunst dargethan
in einem Lob- und Ehren-Gedichte ... bey Gelegenheit ihres dritten Jubelfestes so auf der berühmten Universität, Jena 1740, den 18 Juli ...

zum Druck befördert worden durch die sämtlichen Kunst-Verwandten in der Schillischen Buchdruckerey daselbst.   [Jena, 1740]   Folio.   [2187]
  Eu-De-LBb

  Nach dem vor dreyhundert Jahren, etc.   [Description of a token coined on occasion of the third centenary of the invention of printing, celebrated at Breslau, 24 June 1740.]   Breslau [1740] 8vo. [2188]
  Eu-Ge-LB

  Nachricht von einigen, occasione des dritten Jubiläi typographici in der Nieder-Lausitz herausgekommenen Schrifften.   (In Destinata literaria et fragmenta Lusatica.   Lübben, 1738.   p. 409-415)   [2189]
  Eu-De-LBb

Neubauer, Johann.
  Continuirter Schreibkalender auf das Jahr 1740.   Breslau, 1740.   4to.
  Title from Mohr, Jubelfeste.
  Contains a history of printing.   [2190]

Niederle, Georg Elias and Hieronymus Michael Pockwitz.
  Bey der den 6. Julii des 1740sten Jahres ... begangenen Feyer des dritten Jubelfestes der Buchdruckerkunst, wollten ... ihre Jubelfreude bezeugen.   Erfurt, 1740.   Folio.   [2191]
  Eu-De-LBb

Nonne, Johann Heinrich.
  Denck- und Danckmahl an dem den 6ten des Heumonats 1740 in all- hiesiger Evangelischen Kirche zu den Kaufmännern vermittelst einer Gedächtnisspredigt feyerlich begangenen dritten Jubelfeste der ehren Buchdrucker-Kunst.   Erfurt [1740]   Folio.   [2192]
  Eu-De-LBb

Ohlius, Jac. Heinrich.
  Ode auf das Andencken der vor dreyhundert Jahren erfundenen Buchdruckerkunst.   [Gedicht.]   Königsberg, Hartnung, 1740.
  1 Bog.   Folio.
  Title from Mohr, Jubelfeste.   [2193]

Opitz, Johann Carl.
  Incunabula atque incrementa typographiae saec. XV. in usum studio- sae juventutis breviter delineat, Typographos Mindenses strictim re- censet et ad actum oratorium in memoriam saecularem artis, grata erga Deum mente d. XI. Maii habendum invitat.   Mindae, 1740.   4to.   [2194]
  Eu-Ge-LB

----   Singularia artis typographicae a saeculo XVI. carptum exponit et ad actem oratorium in V. iduum April. invitat.   Minden, 1740.
  6 Bog.   4to.
  Title from Mohr, Jubelfeste.   [2195]

Osiander.
Programma rectoris academiae Tübingensis.   24. Juli 1740.
[Tübingen, 1740]   4p.   Folio.
   Title from Mohr, Jubelfeste.   [2196]

Pater, Paulus.
Der Germaniae miraculo optimo, maximo, typis literarum, earumque
differentiis, dissertatio, qua simul artis typographicae universam
rationem explicat Paulus Pater, P. P.   Prostat Lipsiae, apud Jo.
Frider. Gleditsch & filium, Anno M.DCC.X [1710]   91p.
   Reissued in Wolf, J. C.   Monumenta typographica.   Hamburg, 1740.
   vol. 2, p. 705-824; notes in German, p. 825-866.   [2197]
   McMurtrie

Peucer, M. Daniel.
Doctor Martin Lutheri merckwürdiger Sendbrief vom Dollmetschen,
nebst eben desselben erläuternten Ausprüchen von der Buchdruckerey
und den Buchdruckern, als einem Beytrage zu der dritten Jubelfeyer
ausgefertigt.   Leipzig, 1740.   10 bog.   8vo.
   Reprinted in Gessner, C. F.   Die so nöthig als nützliche Buchdruckerkunst ... 1740-45.   vol. 4.   [2198]
   Eu-Ge-LB

Pretin, Maximilian.
Liber Generationis Jesu Christi ... zur Vollkommenheit der Freuden
nach verflossenen dritten Jahrhundert von Erfindung der Buchdruckerkunst in Teutschland an gegenwärtigen Jubeltag von der Joseph-Caro-
linischen Buchdruckerey der Gesellschaft Jesu in Breslau zu einem
Neujahrsgeschenk denen catholischen Herren Kunstverwandten angetra-
gen, in einer Danckpredigt im Jahre 1740 den 4. Janr.   Breslau,
1740.   3 Bog.   Folio.   [2199]
   Eu-De-LBb

Preuss, Sam. Gottl.
Lob der Buchdruckerkunst.   Königsberg, Dorn, 1740.   2 Bog.
Folio.
   Title from Mohr, Jubelfeste.   [2200]

Programma oder Einladungsschrift, einem gesammten Hochedlen und
Hochweisen Rath dieser ... freyen Stadt Ulm ... Antonius Beck ... und die
beiden Buchdruckern Chr. Ulr. Wagner und Elias Dan. Süss.   Ulm,
22. August 1740.   1 Bog.
   Title from Mohr, Jubelfeste.   [2201]

Reinhard, M. Mich. Henr.
De typographia Torgaviensi illustri.   Torgau, 1740.   2 1/2 Bog.
4to.
   Title from Mohr, Jubelfeste.   [2202]

Relatio de origine typographiae, à quo, quo tempore et quo loco illa primum inventa sit, è documentis ad Faustorum de Aschaffenburg familiam pertinentibus, hausta, & e Germanica in latinam linguam translata à Ludovico Klefekero, Hamburgi Gymnasii patrii cive nobilissime. (In Wolf, J. C.   Monumenta typographica.   Hamburg, 1740.   vol. 1, p. 452-485)   [2203]

Rilsch, Theodorus Heinrich.
    Der Finger Gottes bey der Druckerey, womit der ... Buchdrucker-Gesellschaft in Jena zu Ihrem Jubilaeo, welches den 18. Jul. 1740. solenn allda begangen wurde, glückwünschet.   Jena [1740]   Folio.[2204]
        Eu-De-LBb

[Röder, Johann Paul] 1704-1766.
    Acta des zum feyerlichen Andenken der im Teutschland glücklich erfundenen Büchdrücker-Künst zu Nürnberg erbaulich und erfreulich gehaltnen und vollzognen dritten Jübel-Festes ans Licht gestellet von dem sämtlichen Buchdrucker-Collegio.   Nürnberg, gedruckt auf eigene Kosten, 1740.   80p.   1 plate.   34.5 cm.   [2205]
        DLC   NNC   Eu-De-LBb   Eu-Ne-AVb

[Röllig, Joh. Christ.]
    Cantata auf das dritte Jubel-Fest der löblichen Buchdruckerkunst. Dressden, den 24. Junii 1740.   [Dressden, Gedruckt bey J. W. Harpetern, 1740]   4p.   19.5x17 cm.   [With Freyberg, C. A. Von den allerersten und ältesten Buchdruckern zu Dressden.   Dressden, 1740]
    Included also at the end of Christian Schöttgen's Historie derer dressdnischen Buchdrucker, Dressden, 1740, with caption title:
    Cantata.   [2206]
        DLC

Rungo, Christian.
    Incunabula typographiae, actu publico solemni in Gymnasio Mar. Magdeleno exhibita.   [Breslau, 1740]   Folio.
    Reprinted in Bresslauisches Jubelgedächtniss ... 1740.   [2207]
        Eu-Go-LB

    Sammlung derjenigen Schriften und Carminum, welche bey Gelegenheit des dritten Buchdruckerjubiläi, so den 7. Juli 1740 ... vergnügt celebrirt wurde, von vershiedenen Gelehrten hiesigen Ortes mitgetheilt sind ... Eisenach, 1740.   10 Bog.   4to.
    Title from Mohr, Jubelfeste.   [2208]

Scharff, Gottfried Balth.
    Die Hand Gottes bey der vor 300 Jahren erfundenen Buchdruckerkunst, sowohl bey dem Anfang, als bey dem Fortgang derselben.   Schweidnitz, 1740.
    Title from Mohr, Jubelfeste.   [2209]

Schilter, Johann.
Beweis, dass Strassburg sich gewiss und allein rühmen könne
wegen der Erfindung der Buchdruckerey, bey jetzigem dritten Buch-
drucker-Jubilaeo eröffnet ... Arnstadt, 1740. 32p. sm. 8vo.
Extract from Königshoven's Chronik, p. 411 et sqq. [2210]
Eu-De-LBb

Schmidt. Johann.
Die edle Buchdruckerkunst als ein grosse Werk des Herrn in drey
Predigten am anderen Jubilaeo derselben betrachtet von Johann Schmidt;
nun aber zum dritten Jubelfeste herausgegeben mit einer Vorrede von
Erdmann Neumeister. Hamburg, 1740. 4to.
Title from Mohr, Jubelfeste. [2211]

Schmidt, Johann, 1594-1658.
Gott zu lob, Drey christliche Danck Predigten: wegen dero im Jahr
1440. und also vor zweyhundert Jahren, durch göttliche Eingebung, in
Strassburg erfundenen hochwerthen thewren Buchtrucker-Kunst: Nach An-
leitung dessandern Versiculs des 111. Psalms, Gross sindt die Wercke
des Herrn, wer jhr achtet der hat eitel Lust daran. In volckreicher
Versammlung. zu Strassburg anno 1640. den 18. 25. Augusti und 1. Sep-
tembr. gehalten, und, auff Begehren, in Truck gegeben, durch Johannem
Schmidt ... Anno M.DC.XLI. Gotha, J. A. Reyher, 1740. 127p. 19 cm.
With Closs, Wilhelm J. J. Drittes Jubel-Fest der Buchdrucker-
Kunst ... Gotha, 1740.
"Joannis Henrici Boecleri Oratio ... in qua de typographiae ...
divinitate & fatis ... disseritur": p. 109-127. [2212]
DLC Eu-De-LBb Eu-Ge-LSb

Schoepflin, Johann Daniel, 1694-1771.
Programma quo typographia annum 1440 inventae festum seculare
indictum. Lectoribus salutem. X Octobris 1740. (In his Commen-
tationes historicae et criticae ... Basileae, 1741)
Also published separately, Argentorati, 1740. [2213]
ICU NN

Scholze, Heinrich.
Specimen bibliothecae arabicae de typographis arabicis. Ham-
burg, 1740. 2 Bog. 4to.
Title from Mohr, Jubelfeste. [2214]

Schöttgen, Christian, 1687-1751.
Historie derer dressdnischen Buchdrucker. Wobey zugleich alle
hohe Gönner und Freunde der edlen Buchdrucker-Kunst das dritte
Jubel-Fest derselben, am Tage Johannis des Täuffers 1740. Nach-
mittage um 3. Uhr, bey Anhörung einiger teutschen Reden und Music
feyerlich zu begehen gehorsamst ersucht Christian Schöttgen, Rector. Dressden, F. Hekels [Gedruckt bey J. H. Harpetern, 1740]
29, [3]p. 1 illus. 19,5x17 cm.

With Freyberg, C. A.   Von den allerersten und ältesten Buch-
druckern zu Dressden.   Dressden, 1740.
Engraved vignette.
"Cantata [verfasst von Joh. Christ. Röllig]": p. [30]-[32]
(Issued also separately with half-title: Cantata auf das
dritte Jubel-Fest der löblichen Buchdrucker-Kunst)   [2215]
DLC   NNGr   Eu-De-LBb

Schreiber, Thomas Johann.
    Erstlinge der Jubelfeyer in Danzig ergen der vor dreyhundert
Jahren erfundenen Buchdruckerey, ... theils dargebracht, theils
veranlasset und verlegt durch Thom. Joh. Schreiber.   Danzig,
1740.   4to.
    "Mit einem Denkmahl von M. Ch. Hanow, einer Predigt von H.
Bordewisch, Es ist die edle Buchdruckerkunst von Johann
Guttenberg sinnreich erfunden!, einer Ode von Joh. G. Sievert,
Mainz ist der Ort da sie erfunden und Guttenbergh hat sie
erdacht!, und Gedichten von J. G. Fabricus, B. Stabenau,
etc."   (Note from Mohr, Jubelfeste)   [2216]
Eu-De-LBb

Schultz, Christian.
    Bey dem 100jährigen Erinnerungsfeste der belobten Buchdruckerey,
welches das Reussnerische Geschlecht feyerlich begehet ... Königsberg, 1740.   1 Bog.   Folio.
    Title from Mohr, Jubelfeste.   [2217]

Schumacher, Carl Ludwig and Christian Ludwig Horn.
    Freudiges Jubel-Vivat ... an dem beglückten Postulats-Tage (den
27. Junii 1740) derer ... Herrn Johann Heinrich Andreä, ... Heinrich
Remigius Brönner, ... Johann Häffner, ... zugleich auch ein Andencken
dieser dreyhundertjährigen Jubel-Freude, (welche zu Franckfurt am
Mayn in diesem Jahr zum erstenmahl begangen wurde,) ... Gedruckt im
Jubel-Jahr.   Franckfurt a.M., 1740.   Folio.   [2218]
Eu-De-LBb

Schwarz, Christian Gottlieb, 1675-1751, praeses.
    II Odae seculares.   14. Julii 1740.   Norimbergae, 1740.
Folio.   [2219]

Schweisinger, Johann Heinrich.
    Der Memmelischen Officin in Regenspurg wiedmete bey der
dritten Jubel-Feyer der edlen Buchdrucker-Kunst den 24. Jun.
1740. dieses glückwünschende Blatt.   [Regenspurg, 1740]
Folio.   [2220]
Eu-De-LBb

Seelen, Johann H.
    Nachricht von dem Ursprung und Fortgang der Buchdruckerey in der
Reichs-Stadt Lübeck, worinn die Lübeckischen Buchdrucker und aller-
ley von Ihnen gedruckte merkwürdige Bücher und Schriften angeführet
und beschrieben werden. Bey Gelegenheit des in diesem 1740sten Jahre
einfallenden Buchdrucker-Jubilaei ertheilet und mit verschiedenen
zur Gelehrten-Historie gehörigen Anmerkungen. Lübeck, J. Schmidt,
1740. 186p. 8vo.   [2221]
    Eu-De-LBb   Eu-Ge-LB

Sempiterno, Christian Leonhard.
    Vertrauliche Unterredung zwischen Fortunatus und Florianus von
dem zu Franckfurt zu Feyrenden 300jährigen Buchdrucker-Jubiläo,
welches den 24. Juni 1740 am Tage Johannes des Täufers wird begangen
werden. Franckfurt a/M, 1740. 1 Bog. 8vo.
    Title from Mohr, Jubelfeste.   [2222]

Seyler, Georg Daniel.
    Musa Elbingensis jubilans sive actus eucharisticus in mem. secul.
tertii ab inventa feliciter typographia jubilei in athenaeo Druscio
d. xxiv. Nov. 1740. Elbing, 1740. 56p. 4to.
    Title from Mohr, Jubelfeste.   [2223]

Sibilander.
    Das durch die preiswürdige Buchdrucker-Kunst eweiterte Reich der
Musen ... als das dritte Jubel-Fest ... am 18. Juni 1740. in Jena feyerlich begangen wurde ... zum Druck befördert von den sämmtlichen Kunst-
verwandten in der Schillischen Buchdruckerey. Jena [1740] Fol.[2224]
    Eu-De-LBb

Sommer, Johann Jac.
    Der vor 300 Jahren erfundenen und von der Reussnerischen Familie
vor 100 Jahren in Königsberg errichteten Druckerey zu ehren, widmet
dieses frohe Jubellied. Königsberg, 1740. 1 Bog. Folio.
    Title from Mohr, Jubelfeste.   [2225]

Spreng, Johann Jakob.
    Schuldiges Ehren-Gedächtniss der nutzlich als preisswürdigen Buch-
druckerkunst, welche bey Celebrirung des III. Jubilaei nach deren
glücklichen Erfindung Anno 1740 den 27. Juni in ... Basel gestifftet ...
von einer gantzen societät der Buchdruckeren allda. Basel, 1740.
    Title from Mohr, Jubelfeste.   [2226]

Stadler, Erhard.
    Bey abermahliger angestellten Jubel-Freude, zu Ehren der edlen
Buchdruckerkunst und Erinnerung dessen Erfindung, Fortgang und vor-
trefflichen Nutzen, entwurff folgende Zeilen. Regensburg, 1740.
Folio.   [2227]
    Eu-De-LBb

Stargardisches Buchdrucker-Jubilaeum wie es im hiesigen illus-
tren Gröningischen Collegio wegen der vor dreyhundert Jahren erfundenen edlen Buchdrucker-Kunst den 13. Julii 1740, mit Verlangen
Joh. Chn. Falcken, Königliche privilegirten Buchdruckers hieselbst
feyerlich begangen worden.   Stargard [1740]   4to.   [2228]
    Eu-De-LBb

Stieff, Christian.
    Ueber das durch göttliche Gnade den 24. Junii Anno 1740 glück-
lich eingetretene dritte Jubel-Fest der ... Buchdrucker-Kunst, wolte ...
sein ... Vergnügen bezeugen, und ... Herrn Samuel Grass ... als dermaligen
Erben, Besitzer und Forsetzer der ... Baumannischen Buchdruckerey
alles gesegnete ... Wachstrum ... an erwünschen.   Breslau, 1740.
Folio.   [2229]
    Eu-De-LBb

Stoltzenberg, Christoph.
    Erfreuliches Lob- und Danck-Opffer dem grossen Gott zu ehren
bey dem erneuerten Denckmahl der vor 300 Jahren erfundenen edlen
Buchdruckerkunst auf dem Regenspurgischen Gymnasio poëtico den 27.
Sept. des 1740. Jahrs im Nahmen Johann Baptiste Lang.   Bischöff-
lichen Stadt-Buchdruckern abgestattet von dem Choro musico.
Regensburg, 1740.   Folio.   [2230]
    Eu-De-LBb

[Stolle, Gottlieb]
    Memoriam saecularem inventae ante hos trecentos annos artis
typographicae publica celebratione a. d. XVI. Calend. sextilis
anno ... 1740 consecrabit Acad. Jenensis. .Jena, 1740.   Folio
    Title from Mohr, Jubelfeste.   [2231]

----   Universitäts-Programm zur Jubelfeier der Erfindung der
Buchdruckerkunst.   Jena, 1740.   Folio.   [2232]
    Eu-De-LBb

Struck, Michael Anton.
    Einladungs-Schrift, wodurch vornehme Gönner und Freunde der
Buchdruckerey, einer Danck- und Jubel-Rede, wegen dieser vor 300
Jahren erfundenen Kunst, am instehendem [sic] Johannis-Tage, als
den 24. Junii 1740 in dessen Behausung beyzuwohnen, ersuchet
werden.   Wernigeroda [1740]   Folio.   [2233]
    Eu-De-LBb

---- comp.   Wernigerödisches Danck- und Jubel-Fest, welches wegen
der vor 300 Jahren 1440 erfundenen Buchdrucker-Kunst, durch eine
3-tägige Illumination und andern feyerlichen Anstalten in Beyseyn
hoher Gönner und Freunde, wie auch einiger Buchdrucker von Halber-
stadt, Wolffenbüttel und Blanckenburg, zum Preise Gottes, und der

Kunst Andencken, 1740. den 24-26 Junii drey Tage nach einander
celebriret worden.   [Wernigerode? 1740].   8 prel. leaves, 72p.
21x17 cm.   [2234]
   NN

Suchland, Theod. Jac.
   Als anno 1740 die edle Buchdruckerkunst ihr 300jähriges, die
Reussnerische Buchdruckerey aber ihr 100jähriges Jubelfest den 27.
December höchst feyerlich celebriret ... Königsberg, 1740.   1 Bog.
Folio.
   Title from Mohr, Jubelfeste.   [2235]

Taute, Johann Gabriel.
   Wollte die Vortrefflichkeit und den Nutzen der edlen Buchdrucker-
Kunst bey Gelegenheit des Jubilaei, welches den 6 Julii des 1740sten
Jahres zu Erfurt feyerlich celebriret wurde ... erwegen.   Erfurt
[1740]   Folio.   [2236]
   Eu-De-LBb

Theune, C. H.
   De typographiae in rem Christianam meritis et peccatis, programma.
Soraviae, 1740.   4to.
   Title from Bigmore & Wyman.   [2237]

Thiboust, Claude Louis, 1667-1737.
   Typographiae excellentia, carmen notis gallicis illustratum ...
L'excellence de l'imprimerie, poème latin, dédié au roi, par Thiboust,
Claude Louis, traduit par son fils ... Paris, Thiboust, 1754.   28p.
front., port.   18 cm.
   French and latin text.   [2238]
   ICN   NN   Eu-Fr-PN   Eu-Ne-GK

Trautmann, Joan. Christoph.
   De typographia ab scholis ornamenta capiente, iisdemque gratiam
referente, disserit ed ad colloquium familiare d. 25 Aprilis 1740
instituendum invitat.   Lauban, 1740.   1 1/2 Bog.   Folio.
   Title from Mohr, Jubelfeste.   [2239]

   Typographia Luneburgense jubilans.   Als ... das Jubel-Fest der erfundenen Buchdruckerey-Kunst zum dritten Mahl den 24. Junii des 1740-
sten Jahrs in Teutschland feierlich begangen wurde, wollte dasselbe
auch hiedurch an bemeldtem Tage erneuren und zugleich Ihrem Hoch-
geschätzen Buchdrucker-Herrn, ... Herrn. Cornel. Joh. von Stern etc.
dazu schuldigst und gehorsamst Glück und alles fernere Walergehen
anwünschen die sämmtliche Gesellschaft der Stermischen Buchdruckerey ...
Luneberg, [1740]   Folio.   [2240]
   Eu-De-LBb

Über das Merckmahl göttlicher Güte welches sich bey der den 27
Sept. 1740 allhier in Regensburg angestellten Feyrung des ... dritten
Jubel-Festes der edlen Buchdrucker-kunst deutlich entdeckte, wolten
nicht nur ihre herzliche Freude ... an den Tag legen, sondern auch ...
ihr ... Lob-Opffer demüthigst darbringen die in der Seiffartischen
Officin sämmtlich sich befindende Kunst-Verwandte.   Regensburg,
1740.   Folio.   [2241]
    Eu-De-LBb

    Vollständige Beschreibung und Sammlung alles dessen, was bey
dem den 29 Juni 1740 zu Coberg ... wegen der vor 300 Jahren erfundenen edlen Buchdrucker Kunst gefeierten Jubiläo vorgefallen und
abgehandelt worden.   Coberg, 1740.   14 prel. leaves, 176p.
8vo.   [2242]
    NNC   Eu-De-LBb

[Wagner, Christian Ulrich]
    Ulmische Jubel-Reden, welche in dieser des H. R. Reichs freuen
Stadt Ulm am dritten Jubel-Feste, wegen der vor 300 Jahren erfundenen höchstnützlichen Buchdrucker-Kunst ... gehalten worden.   Ulm,
1740.   8 leaves, 109p.   8vo.   [2243]
    NNGr   Eu-De-LBb   Eu-Ge-LB

[Wagner, Mag. Ph.]
    Als ... Fr. von Gollen der Jüngere, das am Tage Thomä den 21.
December in Augsburg celebrirte 3. Jubiläum ... durch eine wohl-
gerathene Oration in gebundener Rede gezieret, wollte hierüber
seine innigste Freude bezeugen ein Wohlbekannter.   Stuttgart,
1740.   4to.   [2244]
    Title from Mohr, Jubelfeste.

Walther, Samuel.
    Die Ehre der vor dreyhundert Jahren erfundenen Buchdruckerkunst,
und was die Stadt Magdeburg von derselben vor Dienst und Vortheile
gehabt, sollte auf obrigkeitliche Veranstaltung, den 29. November:
des jetzlauffenden 1740 Jahres mit einem geringer Beytrag in dem
Gymnasio der alten Stadt Magdeburg sowol durch diesen Vorbericht,
als auch öffentliche Reden zum Preise Gottes.   Magdeburg, 1740.
48p.   4to.   [2245]
    Eu-Ge-LB

    Weimarischer Beytrag zu feyerlicher Begehung des dritten 100järi-
gen Jubel-Festes einer wohllöblichen Buchdrucker-Kunst.   Nebst einer
Vorrede Joh. Gg. Webers.   Weimar, 1740.   48p.   4to.   [2246]
    Eu-De-LBb   Eu-Ge-LB

Werner, Daniel Gottfried.
    Jubel-Rede wegen der im Jahr 1440 erfundenen Buchdrucker-Kunst.
[1740]   4to.   [2247]
    Eu-Ge-LB

Werner, Daniel Gottfried.
    Sub auspiciis ... Regis Borussiae ... Jubilaeum tertium artis typo-
graphicae ... inventae, in collegio Groeningiano ... indicit D. G. W.
Stargardiae [1740] 4to.   [2248]
    Eu-Ge-LB

Wierigi'sche Buchdruckerey, Hamburg.
    Die unsägliche Nutzbarkeit der Buchdruckerkunst an dem dritten
Jubelfeste derselben, so auf Johannis im Jahre 1740 einfiel, in
einigen poetischen Zeilen betrachtet von den sämmtlichen Kunstverwandten. Hamburg, 1740. 2 Bog. Folio.
    Title from Mohr, Jubelfeste.   [2249]

Witter, Johann Jac.
    Jubelgedicht. Strassburg, 1740. 4to.
    Title from van der Linde, Geschichte der Erfindung ...   [2250]

Zäncker, Johann David.
    Bey der doppelten Jubelfreude der edlen Buchdruckerkunst in Preus-
sen, da selbige das dritte Jahrhundert der Erfindung, das Reussnerische Haus aber das erste seines Ruhms feyerte ... Königsberg, 1740.
1 Bog. Folio.
    Title from Mohr, Jubelfeste.   [2251]

Zeiske, Johann Gottfried.
    Wolte bey der Richter und Fritschischen Hochzeit so ... den 19. Juli
in dem dritten Jubelfeste der löblichen Buchdruckerkunst ... gefeyert
ward ... erwägen. Budissin, 1740. 1 Bog. 4to.   [2252]
    Eu-De-LBb

    Zu dem abermaligen 100jährigen Jubelfeste, der erfundenen und ins-
besondere auch allhier seit 100 Jahren unter dem Reussnerischen Namen
glücklich fortgepflanzten Buchdruckerey, welches die hiesige Academie
begehen und am 28. December feyern wird, ladet ... ein Prorector und
Senatus der Königsbergischen Academie. Königsberg, 1740. 1 Bog.
Folio.
    Title from Mohr, Jubelfeste.   [2253]

    Zu dem glücklich erlebten dritten Jubelfeste der vortrefflichen
Buchdruckerkunst, wünschte den Jenaischen Buchdrucker-Herren und
sämtlichen Kunstverwandten ... Jena, 1740. Folio.   [2254]
    Eu-De-LBb

Zunckel, Heinrich Gottfried.
    Da Gottes Gütigkeit ... das dritte Jubel-Fest der Kunst Buchdruck-
erey vergnügt uns feyren läst, so wiel von solcher Kunst ein Mitglied
hier nicht schweigen, vielmehr durch dieses Blatt sich gleichfalls
froh erzeigen. Regensburg, 1740. Folio.   [2255]
    Eu-De-LBb

Zunckel, Heinrich Gottfried.
In LaVDeM Ioannis GVttenbergII InVentorIs artIs typographiCae
et eIVs tertII IVbILaeI.   Regensburg, 1740.   4to.
Title from Mohr, Jubelfeste.   [2256]

Zwey Uebersetzungen ein paar lateinischer Gedichte von dem
Lob der edlen Buchdruckerkunst von P. v. D. F.   Hirschberg, 1740.
2 Bog.   Folio.
Title from Mohr, Jubelfeste.   [2257]

Zwiefaches Jubelopfer, welches dem feyerlichen Andencken der
vor 300 Jahren erfundenen Buchdruckerkunst ... widmeten, die sämmtlichen Glieder der Hartung'schen Kunststätte.   Königsberg, 1740.
2 Bog.   Folio.
Title from Mohr, Jubelfeste.   [2258]

Zwo Cantaten sollten bey dem feyerlichen Jubel-Feste der vor dreyhundert Jahr erfundenen Buchdruckerey zum Andenken einer so Herrlichen Wohlthat vor und nach der zu haltenden Jubel-Rede verfertigt
und abgesungen in [sic] Nahmen der sämtlichen allhiesigen Buchdrucker
Nürnberg, dem [sic] 14 Julii 1740.   Nürnberg, 1740.   Folio.   [2259]
   Eu-De-LBb

D.   19TH CENTURY

Abbildung des grossen Festsalons, welcher zur Jubelfeier ... auf
dem Augustusplatz zu Leipzig errichtet.   Leipzig, Baumgärtner,
1840.   roy. 4to.
Title from Mohr, Jubelfeste.   [2260]

An die Herren Buchhändler und Buchdrucker von C. F. Appun.   18.
Mai 1840.   Bunzlau, 1840.   1 leaf.   4to.
Title from Mohr, Jubelfeste.   [2261]

An die Söhne und Töchter der Waldeckischen Gauen und an die
Freunde und Pfleger der Wissenschaften, um das Gutenberg-Fest
würdig zu feiern.   Einladung.   Arolsen, 1840.   4to.
Title from Mohr, Jubelfeste.   [2262]

An Gutenberg, Akrostichon.   [Mainz, 1837]   8vo.
Title from Mohr, Jubelfeste.   [2263]

An unsere Committenten.   Leipzig 5. Juni 1840.   Das Comité zur
Feier der Erfindung der Buchdruckerkunst.   Leipzig, 1840.   10p.
4to.
Title from Mohr, Jubelfeste.   [2264]

Andenken an das Fest vom 24. Juni als Gedächtnissfeier Gutenberg's und der Erfindung der Buchdruckerkunst.   Lübeck, Aschenfeld, 1840. iv, 40p.   20 cm.   [2265]
    NNGr   Eu-De-LBb

Andenken an die vierten Säcularfeier der Erfindung der Buchdruckerkunst.   26. Juni 1840.   Gedicht.   Hannover, 1840.   4to.
    Title from Mohr, Jubelfeste.   [2266]

Anniversaire séculaire de l'invention de l'imprimerie.   Où en est la souscription pour le Monument Gutenberg?   Mit Antwort hierauf von G. Silbermann und einer neuen Aufforderung des Comités zur Subscription.   Courrier du Bas-Rhin, no. 107, 109, 113, 1836.   [2267]

Anordnung der Festlichkeiten zur Feier des vierten Jubiläums der Erfindung der Buchdruckerkunst am 24., 25. und 26. Juni 1840 zu Leipzig.   Nebst einer Abbildung des zu dieser Feier erbauten Festsalons und dessen Grundriss.   Leipzig, Lorenz, 1840.   4p.   4to.
    Title from Mohr, Jubelfeste.   [2268]

Appel à tous les coeurs droits à l'occasion de la fête de Gutenberg.   Strasbourg, Silbermann, 1840.   4p.   8vo.
    Title from Mohr, Jubelfeste.   [2269]

Appel au monde civilisé pour célébrer dignement la fête séculaire de l'art de l'imprimerie par l'érection d'un monument en l'honneur de son inventeur Jean Gensfleisch de Gutenberg.   Mayence, De l'Imprimerie de F. Kupferberg, 1832.   7p.   22 cm.   [2270]
    NNC

Aufforderung zur Feier des vierten Säcularfestes der Buchdruckerkunst am 24. Juni 1840.   Programm und Beschreibung der Feier. Braunschweig, 1840.
    Title from Mohr, Jubelfeste.
    Reprinted in Journal für Buchdruckerkunst, no. 8, 11, 1840.   [2271]

Augsburg's älteste Druckdenkmale.   Augsburg, 1840.   4 prel. leaves, 80p.   plates (1 fold.)   26 cm.   [2272]
    NNGr

Autobiographie von Friedr. Andrae, Buchdrucker in Leipzig. Niedergelegt zum Feste, etc. etc. Leipzig, 1840.   2p.   roy. 4to.
    Title from Mohr, Jubelfeste.   [2273]

Baier, Johann.
    Zur 500jährigen Gutenberg-Feier in Würzberg.   Gemeinnützige Monatsschrift, 1900, p. 88-92.   [2274]

Baumgarten-Crusius, Ludwig Friedrich Otto.
Festrede bei der akademischen Secularfeier von der Erfindung der
Buchdruckerkunst zu Jena an 23. Juni 1840 gehalten.   Jena, Bran,
1840.   24p.   8vo.   [2275]
Eu-De-LBb   Eu-Ge-LSb

[Baur, N.]
Einladung zur Inaugurations-Feier des Denkmals.   Mainz, 1837.
1p.   4to.
Title from Mohr, Jubelfeste.   [2276]

Bechstein, Ludwig.
Johannes Gutenberg.   1840.   [Prolog zur Fest-Vorstellung im
Theater.]   Erfurt, Fr. Knick, 1840.   8p.   8vo.
Title from Mohr, Jubelfeste.   [2277]

Beck, August.
Das 400jährige Erinnerungsfest der Erfindung der Buchdruckerkunst
durch Johann Gutenberg, feiert am 24. Juni 1840 das Real-Gymnasium
in Gotha.   Gotha, Engelhard-Reyher'sche Druckerei, 1840.   8p.
4to.
Title from Mohr, Jubelfeste.   [2278]

Beissel, Stephan.
Zur Feier des Erfindung des Buchdrucks.   <u>Stimmens aus Maria-
Laach</u>, vol. 39, 1890, p. 343-352.   [2279]

Bekanntmachung, die vierten Säcularfeier der Buchdruckerkunst in
Leipzig betreffend 1. Julius 1839.   Die Buchdrucker-Innung.   Leipzig
[1839]   3p.   4to.
Title from Mohr, Jubelfeste.   [2280]

Bekker, Ernst.
Das Buchdrucker-Wappen.   Ein Versuch demselben seine ursprüng-
liche Gestalt und Bedeutung wieder zu geben.   Als bescheidener Beitrag zur Verherrlichung Gutenberg's.   Entworfen bei Gelegenheit der
Inauguration seines Monuments am 14. August 1837 von Ernst Bekker,
grossherzoglicher Hof- und Cabinets-Buchdrucker in Darmstadt.
Darmstadt, Druck von Stall und Bekker, Hof- und Cabinets-Buchdruck-
erei [1837]   1 prel leaf, [3]-10p.   21.5 cm.   [2281]
ICN   Eu-De-LBb

Bemerkungen eines Elsässers über die Gutenbergs-Feier mit beson-
derer Rücksichtnahme auf die dadurch veranlassten Aeusserungen des
Zeitgeistes.   Strassburg, Le Roux, 1840.   24p.   8vo.
Reprint from <u>Katholisches Kirchen- und Schulblatt für Elsass</u>.   [2282]
Eu-De-LBb

Bemühungen Fr. Lehne's bei der Gesellschaft der Wissenschaften
und Künste zu Mainz im Jahre 1804 zur Errichtung eines Monuments
für den Erfinder der Buchdruckerkunst. (In Kulb, P. H., ed.
Gesammelte Schriften. Mainz, 1837-1839. vol. 4, p. 254-266)   [2283]
    Eu-Fr-PN   Eu-Ge-LB

    Beretning om Sekularfesten i Christiania. Christiania [1840]
40p. 21 cm.   [2284]
    NNGr

Berger, Karl, ed.
    Vierte Säkularfeier der Erfindung der Buchdruckerkunst. Ein
Festdenkmal für Jedermann, gesammelt und herausgegeben von Karl
Berger ... Zum Besten der Carlsruher Gutenbergsstiftung ... Carlsruhe,
1840. Druck und Verlag des Artistischen Instituts (F. Gutsch &
Rupp). iv, 159p. 20.5 cm.   [2285]
    MH   NNGr   Eu-De-LBb   Eu-Ge-LSb

Berlin. Königliche Bibliothek.
    Festschrift zur Gutenbergfeier. Herausgegeben von der Koenig-
lichen Bibliothek zu Berlin am 24. Juni 1900. Berlin, 1900.
3 prel. leaves, [v]-ix, 90p. illus., facsims. 28 cm.   [2286]
    ICJ   ICN   MB   Eu-De-BP   Eu-Ne-AVb   Eu-Ne-GK   Eu-Sz-BeG

[Berliner, A.]
    Souvenir des fêtes des 4, 5 et 6 Avril 1836 en l'honneur de Guten-
berg. Tableau historique et allegorique orné du portrait de Gutenberg et contenant la Cantate de M. M. Hoerter et Redslob, composé
et executé à la plume. Strassbourg, Simon fils, 1836.
    Title from Mohr, Jubelfeste.   [2287]

Berstett, August, freiherr von.
    Versuch einer Münzgeschichte des Elsasses. Mit 14 Kupfertafeln
der vorzügl. Münzen. Freiburg, Ad. Emmerling, 1840. 100p. 4to.
    Title from Mohr, Jubelfeste.   [2288]

    Beschreibung aller bei der vierten Säcularfeier der Erfindung der
Buchdruckerkunst am 24., 25. und 26. Juni in Leipzig stattgefundenen
Festlichkeiten. Ein Denkmal für Mit- und Nachwelt ... Leipzig, Glück,
1840. viii, 87, [1]p. front. 20 cm.   [2289]
    NNGr   Eu-De-LBb

    Beschreibung der vierten Secularfeier der Erfindung der Buchdrucker-
kunst wie dieselbe den 24., 25., 26. Juni in Leipzig gefeiert wurde.
Leipzig, Edouard Meissner, 1840. iv, 24p. front. 21 cm.   [2290]
    NNGr   Eu-De-LBb

Betrachtungen eines Setzers, am Morgen des Einweihungsfestes
der Bildsäule Gutenbergs. 1640. (Gedicht) -- 1740. (Gedicht)
-- 1840. (Bei Gutenberg's Denkmal, am 24. Juni 1840.)   Strassburger Wochenblatt, no. 51, 1840.   [2291]

Bettzeiche, Heinrich.
    Das Jubeljahr 1840 und seine Ahnen. Vergangenheit als Gegen-
wart.   Berlin, Vereinsbuchhandlung, 1840.   8vo.   [2292]
    Eu-Ge-LB

    Der Betzinger beim Buchdrucker-Jubiläum.   [Reutlingen, 1840]
    In Schwäbischen dialect.
    Reprinted in Naze's Schwabenspätzle, Stuttgart.   p. 64-68.
    Title from Mohr, Jubelfeste.   [2293]

Biedermann, Fl. Fr. von.
    Die Kunst Gutenbergs auf der Weltausstellung in Paris.   Allge-
meiner Anzeiger für Druckereien, Gutenberg number, June 21, 1900. [2294]

----   Zum Gutenberg Feier.   Universum, vol. 16, 1900, p. 2277-
2296.   [2295]

Billig, J. C. G.
    Guttenberg-Lieder. Weihgabe zur vierten Säcularfeier der Er-
findung der Buchdruckerkunst am 24.-26. Juni 1840.   Warburg,
Billig, 1840.   15p.   8vo.   [2296]
    Eu-De-LBb

Björklund, F. G.
    Bref ifran Gutenberg, innehallande underrattelser om boktryckar-
konstens uppfinning samt skildringar tutr hans lefnad öfversättning
af F. G. Björklund.   Strengnäs, Carl Erik Ekmarck, 1841.   31,
[1]p.   8vo.
    Title from Almquist, Johan Axel. Sveriges bibliografiska
    litteratur … Stockholm, 1909-1910.   [2297]

Blaser, Fritz.
    Schweizerische Gutenbergfeiern im Jahre 1840.   Schweizer
Graphischer Central-Anzeiger, 1937, no. 1-3.   [2298]

----   Die schweizerischen Festgaben der Gutenbergfeiern 1840.
Gutenberg Jahrbuch, vol. 14, 1939, p. 310-313.   [2299]

    Ein Blick auf die Geschichte der Buchdruckerkunst.   [Berlin,
1840?]   8p.   8vo.   [2300]
    Eu-De-LBb

[Block, August]
    Das Königswort. [Gedicht]   Berlin 25. September 1840.   1p.   4to.
    Title from Mohr, Jubelfeste.   [2301]

Blumenfeld, J. C.
   Die drei Tage Gutenbergs in Strassburg, oder eine Darstellung
dessen, was man gesehen und gehört an diesen drei grossen Tagen,
nebst einer Nachfeier von J. C. Blumenfeld.   Strassburg, G. L.
Schuler, 1840.   iv, 84p.   12mo.   [2302]
   MB   Eu-De-LBb   Eu-Fr-PN   Eu-Ge-LSb

Böck, Joseph.
   An Gutenberg und seine Kunst.   Zum 24. Juni 1882, dem Tage der
vierten Säcular-Jubelfeier der Einführung der Buchdruckerkunst in
Wien.   Wien, 1882.
   Title from Mohr, Jubelfeste.
   Reprinted in Die Heimat, no. 39, 1882.   [2303]

----   Gutenbergbuch.   Eine Verherrlichung der Buchdruckerkunst in
Gedanken und Gedichten aus der Gegenwart.   Wien, 1885.   8vo.   [2304]
   Eu-Ge-LSb

----   Wiens Buchdrucker-Jubiläum am 24. Juni 1882.   Mit Gutenbergs
Porträt.   Wien, 1882.
   Title from Mohr, Jubelfeste.
   Reprinted in Die Heimat, no. 39, 1882.   [2305]

Böckel, Ernst Gottfried Adolf, 1783-1854.
   Die Buchdruckerkunst und die Kirchenverbesserung.   Predigt am
Reformationsfeste 1840 gehalten.   Oldenburg, 1840.   16p.   8vo.   [2306]
   Eu-De-LBb

Bödeker, Hermann Wilhelm.
   Die Geschichte und hohe Bedeutsamkeit der Buchdruckerkunst.   Auf
Anlass der vierten Säcularfeier ihrer Erfindung für die Hannoverschen
Volksschulen dargestellt.   Hannover, Hahn, 1840.   32p.   8vo.   [2307]
   Eu-De-LBb   Eu-Fr-PN   Eu-Ge-LSb

Boysen, Karl.
   Johann Gutenberg-feier.   Fest-rede.   Polytechnischer und Gewerbe-
Verein, vol. 56, 1900, p. 71-88.   [2308]

Brandes, Georg Morris Cohen.
   Bogtrykkerkunstens opfindelse.   Foredrag ved de kjøbenhavnske typo-
grafers 500 aars mindefest for Johan Gutenberg den 18 November 1900.
Kjøbenhavn, udgivet af typografiske foreninger, Bianco Lunos bogtrykkeri,
MCM; Kjøbenhavn, der Nordiske Forlag, bogforlaget Ernst Bojesen, MCM
[1900]   1 prel. leaf., 3-[16]p.   20.5 cm.   [2309]
   ICN   Eu-Ge-LB

   A brief history of early printing.   In commemoration of the semi-
millennial anniversary of the birth of Johannes Gutenberg.   Scientific American Supplement, vol. 50, no. 1279, July 1900, p. 20501-
20502.   [2310]

Briefe über das Gutenberg-Fest in Strassburg. Morgenblatt
(Stuttgart), no. 201-218, 1840.   [2311]

Brückner, G.
     Geschichte der Erfindung der Buchdruckerkunst. Zur 400 jährigen
Gutenbergsfeier oder zum Culturfest der Menschheit im Jahr 1840,
für Volk und Jugend. Schleusingen, 1840. 56p. 18 cm.   [2312]
     NNGr   Eu-De-LBb   Eu-Fr-PN   Eu-Ge-LSb

     Die Buchdrucker der Stadt Mainz an Albert Thorwaldsen, bei seiner
Anwesenheit, dahier den 30. Juni und 1. Juli 1841. Gedicht. Mainz,
Seifertsche Buchdruckerei, 1841. 4p. 8vo.
     Title from Mohr, Jubelfeste.   [2313]

     Das Buchdruckerfest in Stuttgart. Gefeiert den 24. Juni 1840.
In schwäbischen Dialekte vom Verfasser der Schrift "Der Bauer beim
Schillerfest". Stuttgart, Etzel, 1840. 15p. 8vo.   [2314]
     Eu-De-LBb

     Die Buchdruckerkunst. Verfasst und herausgegeben vom Artist.
Institut [F. Gutsch und Rupp] in Carlsruhe. Carlsruhe, 1840.
Roy. Folio.
     Title from Mohr, Jubelfeste.   [2315]

     Buchdrucker-Lied am 4. October 1824. Mainz, Th. v. Zabern,
1824. 4p. 8vo.
     Title from Mohr, Jubelfeste.   [2316]

Buffet, J.
     Hommage à Gutenberg à l'occasion de la Saint-Jean-Porte-Latin
fête de l'imprimerie. [Le Mans] Monnoyer [1857] 2p. 8vo.   [2317]
     Eu-Fr-PN

Burckhardt, Antistes and Carl Rudolph Hagenbach.
     Festreden bei der vierten Säcularfeier der Erfindung der Buch-
druckerkunst in Basel, gehalten im Münster daselbst von Ant. Burckhardt und Prof. Hagenbach den 24. Juni 1840. Nebst einer Beschreibung des Festes. Mit einer Abbildung von Gutenberg's Standbild
nach David d'Angers in Paris. Basel, Schneider, 1840. 50p.
4to.   [2318]
     Eu-Fr-PN   Eu-Sz-BeG

Camerer, J. W.
     Johannes Brenz, der Württembergische Reformator. Mit Porträt.
(Fest-Ausgabe zum 24. Juni 1840.) Stuttgart, 1840. 7 leaves,
113p., 1 leaf. 8vo.   [2319]
     Eu-De-LBb

Catalogue de l'exposition des produits de l'industrie alsacienne, ouverte au Château, du 26 juin au 24 juillet 1840. Strasbourg, Silbermann, 1840. 20p. 8vo.
  Title from Mohr, Jubelfeste.   [2320]

Catalogue des livres destinés à la loterie typographique. Strasbourg, Levrault, 1840. 19p. 12mo.
  Title from Mohr, Jubelfeste.   [2321]

Catalogue des objets compris dans la salle des imprimés et faisant partie de l'exposition aux fêtes de Gutenberg célébrées à Strasbourg les 24, 25 et 26 juin 1840. Strasbourg, Silbermann, 1840. 20p. 8vo.
  Title from Mohr, Jubelfeste.   [2322]

Cenni sulla invenzione della stampa e inaugurazione delle statue di Guttemberg in Magonza e Strasburgo, con note aggiunte. Forli, Dalla stamperia Casali, 1841. 21 cm.
  Contents: - Invenzione della stampa. Statua innalzata a Guttemberg in Magonza [article from Teatro universale; raccolta enciclopedica e scenografica, 1838, vol. 5, no. 205] -- Descrizione del monumento eretto in onore di Guttemberg a Strasborgo [two articles from the Gazzetta privilegiata di Milano, 1840, no. 190, p. 799 and no. 206, p. 854] -- Note aggiunte da Scipione Casali.   [2323]
  NN   Eu-Ge-LB   Eu-Ge-LSb

Chmelarz, Eduard.
  Gutenberg und die Erfindung der Buchdruckerkunst. Vortrag gehalten im Oesterreichischem Museum für Kunst und Industrie am 12. Jänner 1882. Mittheilungen des Kaiserlich Königlichen Oesterreichischen Museums, no. 201, 1882, p. 126; no. 202, p. 158.   [2324]

Collet, Franz.
  Gutenberg. Fest-Cantate für Soli, Chor, Orchester und Declamation. Dichtung von F. Collet. Musik von Stierlin, Adolph. Münster, Regensburg, 1900. 8vo.   [2325]
  Eu-De-BP

Le comité de la Réunion musicale alsacienne à MM. les amateurs et artistes qui ont concouru aux fêtes en l'honneur de Gutenberg. Lettre du 29 avril 1836. [Strasbourg, 1836]
  Title from Mohr, Jubelfeste.   [2326]

Comité du Monument Gutenberg. [Circular] 22 mai 1840. Strasbourg, Heitz, 1840. 1p. 4to.
  The same in German.
  Title from Mohr, Jubelfeste.   [2327]

Comité du Monument Gutenberg. Circular vom 30. März 1840. Strassburg, Heitz, 1840. 1p. 4to.
  Title from Mohr, Jubelfeste.   [2328]

Comité du Monument Gutenberg. Circular vom 30. März 1840.
Strassburg, Schuler, 1840. 1p. 4to.
Title from Mohr, Jubelfeste.   [2329]

Comité du Monument Gutenberg. Circular vom 31 März 1840.
Strassburg, Le Roux, 1840. 2p. 4to.
The same in French.
Title from Mohr, Jubelfeste.   [2330]

Comité du Monument Gutenberg aux habitants de la ville de
Strasbourg. Strasbourg, Berger-Levrault, 1840. 2p. 4to.
The same in German.
Title from Mohr, Jubelfeste.   [2331]

Comité zur vierten Säcularfeier der Erfindung der Buchdruckerkunst. [Frankfurt a.M., 1840?] 4p. 8vo.
Title from Mohr, Jubelfeste.   [2332]

Commission du monument Gutenberg. Invitation d'assister au
Cortège du 26 juin. Strasbourg, Heitz, 1840. 1p. 4to.
Title from Mohr, Jubelfeste.
Reprinted in Niederrheinischer Curier, 1840.   [2333]

Commission du monument Gutenberg. Invitation d'assister au ser-
vice divin, au Temple neuf. Strasbourg, Heitz, 1840. 1p. 4to.
Title from Mohr, Jubelfeste.
Reprinted in Niederrheinischer Curier, 1840.   [2334]

Commission du monument Gutenberg. Mittheilung des Programms an
den Maire vom 30. März 1840. Strassburg, Dannbach, 1840. 1p. 4to.
Title from Mohr, Jubelfeste.
Reprinted in Niederrheinischer Curier, 1840.   [2335]

Cracow. Stowarzyszenie drukarzy Krakowskich.
   Na Cześć Jana Gutenberga. Drukarze stowarzyszenie, Krakowie,
1900.   [2336]
   Eu-Ge-LB

[Creteur, Otto Jonas]
   Johann Guttenberg oder die Erfindung der Buchdruckerkunst.
[Köln, 1837]
   Title from Mohr, Jubelfeste.
   Reprinted in Journal für Buchdruckerkunst, no. 12, 1837.   [2337]

Curtmann, Wilhelm.
   Geschichtchen für Kinder, welche noch nicht lesen, zu erzahlen
von Muttern, Geschwistern und Lehrern. Ein Gedenkbuchlein des
Gutenbergfestes 1840. Offenbach, Ernst Heinemann, 1840. 72p.
17 cm.   [2338]
   NNGr

[Cuvier]
Souvenir religieux de la fête de Gutenberg.   Strasbourg, Berger-
Levrault, 1840.   24p.   18mo.
Title from Mohr, Jubelfeste.   [2339]

Darstellung der Feier des Gutenberg-Festes zu Erfurt am 26. und
27. Julius 1840. Auf Wunsch der Theilnehmer von Comité zusammengestellt.   Erfurt, J. G. Cramer, 1840.   31p.   8vo.
Title from Mohr, Jubelfeste.   [2340]

Decker, Friedrich.
Nacht und Nebel der Vorzeit! und Tageshelle der Gegenwart. Ein
Festlied zur IV. Secularfeier der Erfindung der Buchdruckerkunst.
Stuttgart, 1840.   14p.   8vo.   [2341]
Eu-Ge-LSb

Decker'sche Geh. Ober-Hofbuchdruckerei. Kunstvolle typographische
Composition, einen Tempel mit zwei Seitenthürmen darstellend, in der
offenen Halle Gutenberg's Denkmal. Grosses Tableau.   [Berlin, 1840]
Title from Mohr, Jubelfeste.   [2342]

Delcasso, L.
La puissance et les bienfaits de l'imprimerie. Chant dithyram-
bique. Strasbourg, Derivaux, 1840. 8p. 8vo.   [2343]
Eu-Fr-PN

Delitzsch, Franz Julius.
Der Flügel des Engels. Eine Stimme aus der Wüste im vierten Jubel-
Fest-Jahre der Buchdruckerkunst. Dresden, J. Naumann, 1840.   x,
91p. 8vo.   [2344]
Eu-Do-LBb   Eu-Fr-PN   Eu-Ge-LSb

Delprat, Guillaume Henri Marie, 1791-1871.
Die Brüderschaft des gemeinsamen Lebens. Ein Beitrag zur Geschichte der Kirche, Litteratur und Pädagogik des 14., 15. und 16.
Jahrhunderts. Deutsch von Glieb. Mohnike. Auch eine Gabe zur
vierten Jubelfeier der Typographie. Leipzig, Cnobloch, 1840.
xv, 185, [2]p. 20.5 cm.   [2345]
NNGr   Eu-Ge-LB

Dem Andenken Gutenbergs gelegentlich des Buchdruckerfestes in
Wien am 24. und 25. Juni 1882 zu ehren. Bezugsquellen für Buch-
und Steindruckereien (Wien), June 22, 1882.   [2346]

Dem Andenken Guttenbergs beim Festmahle der vierten Säcularfeier
der Buchdruckerkunst geweiht. Den 5. December 1840. Gedicht.
Königsberg, Hartung'sche Hofbuchdruckerei, 1840. 4p. 8vo.
Title from Mohr, Jubelfeste.   [2347]

Den Manen Gutenberg's am Tage der Enthüllung seines Monumentes
dargebracht von den Mitgliedern der Buchdruckerkunst in Stuttgart.
Journal für Buchdruckerkunst, no. 6, 1837.
    Also reprint.   [2348]

Den Manen Gutenbergs an dem Gedächtnissfeste der Erfindung seiner
Kunst ... Elberfeld, Druck von Chr. Farre, Barmen, 1840. 4p. roy. 8vo.
    Title from Mohr, Jubelfeste.   [2349]

Denkblatt. Künstlerisch componirtes Tableau. Lithograph.   Leipzig, 1840.
    Title from Mohr, Jubelfeste.   [2350]

Denkmal zur vierten Säcularfeier des Typendruckes 1840. Historisch entworfen von O. A. Schulz, artistisch ausgeführt von C. L.
Hirschfeld. Leipzig, Schulz & Thomas, 1840. Folio.
    Title from Mohr, Jubelfeste.   [2351]

Dennhardt, G. W.
... Festrede des Professors Dennhardt am 27. Juli 1840. [Erfurt,
J. G. Cramer, 1840] 12p. 22.5 cm.
    Caption title.
    At head of title: Anhang zur Beschreibung des Gutenbergsfestes
    in Erfurt.   [2352]
    NNC

Der Deutsche Bienenkorb, oder Germaniens alphabetische geordneter
Sprachschatz. Begonnen im Jahre 1840, dem säcular-Jahre der Erfindung der beweglichen Lettern oder der typographischen Buchdruckerkunst durch Gutenberg. Erlangen, Fr. Enke, 1840. 48mo.
    Title from Mohr, Jubelfeste.   [2353]

Dietrich, Ewald Christian Victorin.
    Album deutscher Typographen. Festgabe zur vierten Säcularfeier
der Erfindung der Buchdruckerkunst am 24., 25. und 26. Juni 1840.
Herausgegeben von Dr. E. V. Dietrich, mit Abbildung der Festhalle,
auf Zink gravirt. Leipzig, C. B. Polet, 1840. xxvi, 164p. 16mo. [2354]
    Eu-De-LBb

——— Beschreibung der Feier des Gutenberg-Festes zu Leipzig am 24.,
25. und 26. Juni 1840. Eine Erinnerung an die vierte Säcularfeier
der Erfindung der Buchdruckerkunst. Mit Abbildung der Festhalle,
auf Zink gravirt. Leipzig, C. B. Polet, 1840. 1 prel. leaf,
[123]-164p. front. 17 cm.
    Reprint from his Album deutscher Typographen.   [2355]
    NNGr   Eu-De-LBb   Eu-Fr-PN

Dietz, Benjamin.
    Auf das Fest von Johannes Gutenberg, Erfinder der Buchdrucker-
kunst in Strassburg. Indicateur de Strasbourg, no. 53, 1840.   [2356]

Dölling, Johann Gottl.
    Zu dem feierlichen Schulactus, welcher am 24. Juni als dem 400-
jährigen Jubiläum der Erfindung der Buchdruckerkunst im grossen Hörsaale des hiesigen Gymnasiums gehalten wird, ladet ein der Rector
der Anstalt.   Plauen, A. Wieprecht, 1840.   8p.   8vo.
    Title from Mohr, Jubelfeste.   [2357]

Drehorgel, Tambourin.
    Das Gutenberg-Fest in Leipzig 1840.   Durch farbiges Glas auf-
genommen und in Reimen geschildert.   Leipzig, F. H. Elbert, 1840.
16p.   8vo.
    Title from Mohr, Jubelfeste.   [2358]

    Die drei Tage der Inaugurations-Feier des Monumentes für Johann
Gutenberg in Mainz den 14., 15. und 16. August 1837.   Neuwied, 1837.
16p.   illus.   sm. 8vo.
    Title from Mohr, Jubelfeste.   [2359]

Drobisch, Maur, Guil.
    De Joannis Widmanni Egerani Lipsiensis quondam à A.A.L.L. Magis-
tri compendio arithmeticae mercatorum scientiae mathematicae saeculi
XV. simul atque artis typographiae Lipsiensis insigni monumento.
Solemnia inventae typographiae saecularia rite peragenda concele-
braturus scripsit.   Leipzig, 1840.   33p.   4to.   [2360]
    Eu-Ge-LB

[Duverger, Eugène]
    Zur Erinnerung an die 450jährige Gedenkfeier der Erfindung der
Buchdruckerkunst.   Königsberg i Br., 1891.   31p.   8vo.
    Title from Chevillier, C. U. J.   Repertoire des sources histor-
iques du moyen age ... Paris, 1877-1903.   [2361]

Ebner-Heilbronn, Theodor.
    Stuttgarts Buchhandel und das Gutenberg Fest am 24. Juni 1840 in
Stuttgart.   Börsenblatt für den Deutschen Buchhandel, vol. 67, 1900,
p. 3315-3318.   [2362]

Eckstein, Friedrich August.
    Schriften zur Secularfeier der Erfindung der Buchdruckerkunst.
Allgemeine Literatur-Zeitung (Halle), vol. 2, no. 111-114, 225-228,
suppl. no. 105-107, 1840.   [2363]

Ed, Christoph Marquand, 1809-
    Die Hamburger Säcularfeier der Erfindung des Buchdrucks am 24.
und 27. Juni 1840.   Hamburg, Meissner, 1840.   1 prel. leaf, iv,
68p.   20 cm.   [2364]
    NNGr   Eu-De-LBb   Eu-Ge-LSb

Ed, Christoph Marquand, 1809-
　　Die Mützen von Papier, geweiht den Buchdruckergehilfen bei
Gelegenheit der Enthüllung der Gutenberg-Statue, den 24. Juni 1840.
Indicateur de Strasbourg, no. 51, 1840.
　　Title from Mohr, Jubelfeste.　　　　　　　　　　　　　　　　　[2365]

Edel, Friedrich Wilhelm.
　　Denkschrift für die im Jahr 1840 zu begehende vierte Säcular-
feier der Erfindung der Buchdruckerkunst.　Von Friedrich Wilhelm
Edel ... Strassburg, F. C. Heitz, 1840.　31p.　18 cm.　　　　　　[2366]
　　NNC　Eu-De-LBb　Eu-Fr-PN　Eu-Ge-LSb

　　Einladung zu den Festlichkeiten, welche bei der Inauguration
des Monumentes für Johann Gutenberg in Mainz an 14, 15. und 16.
August 1837 stattfinden werden; mit Programm.　Der Vorstand der
Stadt Mainz.　Juni 1837.　8p.　4to.
　　Title from Mohr, Jubelfeste.
　　Reprinted in Journal Für Buchdruckerkunst, no. 6, 1837, col.
81-87.　　　　　　　　　　　　　　　　　　　　　　　　　　　[2367]

　　Einladung zur Theilnahme an den Berathungen und zur gefälligen
Mitwirkung beim Comité zur Begehung einer würdigen Feier des vierten
Säcularfestes der Erfindung der Buchdruckerkunst. (Vom 8. October
1839)　Frankfurt a.M.　2p.　4to.
　　Title from Mohr, Jubelfeste.　　　　　　　　　　　　　　　　　[2368]

　　Einladung zur vierten Jubelfeier der Erfindung der Buchdrucker-
kunst im grossen Saale der Engelhard-Reyher'schen Buchdruckerei.
Gotha, 1840.　4to.
　　Title from Mohr, Jubelfeste.　　　　　　　　　　　　　　　　　[2369]

　　Einladung zur vierten Säcularfeier der Erfindung der Buchdrucker-
kunst am 23., 24. und 25. Juni 1840 zu Mainz.　(November 1839.　Der
Stadt-Vorstand.)　Mit Programm.　Mainz, Zabern, 1840.　8p.　4to.
　　Title from Mohr, Jubelfeste.　　　　　　　　　　　　　　　　　[2370]

[Ellissen, Ad.]
　　Am Tage Johannes des Täufers den 24. Juni 1840.　Cassel, Th.
Fischer, 1840.　4p.　4to.
　　Title from Mohr, Jubelfeste.　　　　　　　　　　　　　　　　　[2371]

[Enslin]
　　Erster Trinkspruch am Gutenberg-Feste.　Berlin, 1840.　1p.
8vo.
　　Title from Mohr, Jubelfeste.　　　　　　　　　　　　　　　　　[2372]

　　Entwurf zu einem Programm der vierten Säcularfeier der Erfindung
der Buchdruckerkunst.　Leipzig [Dec. 1839]　3p.　Folio.
　　Title from Mohr, Jubelfeste.　　　　　　　　　　　　　　　　　[2373]

Epigramme zur Jubelfeier der Erfindung der Buchdruckerkunst.
Morgenblatt (Stuttgart), no. 154, 1840.
    Title from Mohr, Jubelfeste.   [2374]

    Die Erfindung der Buchdruckerkunst zu Strassburg durch Joh. Guten-
berg. Kurze Notiz, herausgegeben bei Gelegenheit der vierten Säcularfeier dieser Erfindung, welche zu Strassburg den 24sten, 25sten
und 26sten Juni 1840 statt hat ... Strassburg, L. F. LeRoux [1840]
cover-title, 15p. plate. 22.5 cm.   [2375]
    ICJ   MB   NNC   Eu-De-LBb   Eu-Ge-LSb

Erfurt Jubilee.
    [Facsimile illustrating the history of printing in Germany on the]
vierten Säcular-Jubelfeier der Erfindung der Buchdruckerkunst, Erfurt, im Juli 1840. [Erfurt, 1840?] 8vo.
    Title from Catalogue ... of the Typothetae of the city of New York.
1896.   [2376]

    Erinnerung an das vierte Säcularfest der Erfindung der Buchdrucker-
kunst, wie solches in der Weidle'schen Buchdruckerei am 24. Juni 1840
gefeiert wurde.   Berlin, [Weidle], 1840. 14p. 8vo.   [2377]
    Eu-De-LBb

    Eine Erinnerung an das vor 25 Jahren am 24. Juni 1840 in Danzig
im Jäschkenthale gefeierte vierten Säcularfest der Erfindung der
Buchdruckerkunst.   Rückblick auf den in Danzig innerhalb des letzten
Vierteljahrhunderts genommenen Aufschwung der Typographie und der mit
ihr verwandten Gewerbe, sowie der periodischen Presse.   West-
preussische Zeitung, no. 166, 1865.   [2378]

    Erinnerung an den 24. Juni 1840.   Breslau, Grass, Barth & Co.,
1840. 15p. 8vo.
    Title from Mohr, Jubelfeste.   +2379]

    Erinnerung an die Gutenbergs-Feier zu Leipzig im Jahre 1840.
Nach der Natur gezeichnet von C. Liebner, lith. von Böhme.   (Grosses
Tableau mit Ansichten von Leipzig.)   [Leipzig, 1840]
    Title from Mohr, Jubelfeste.   [2380]

    Erinnerung an die vierten Säcularfeier der Erfindung der Buchdrucker-
kunst: der Gutenbergsplatz in Manz.--Der Schöfferplatz in Gernsheim.
Mannheim, Hoff, 1840.   2 copper-engravings in 4to.
    Title from Kayser's Bücher-Lexikon.   [2381]

    Erinnerungs-Denkmal an die 400jährige Jubelfeier der Erfindung
der Buchdruckerkunst. Den 5. December 1840.   Akrostichon: Gutenberg. Königsberg, Dalkowskische Officin, 1840.   1 leaf.   Folio.
    Title from Mohr, Jubelfeste.   [2382]

Erinnerungsfeier in Rückblick auf die Gutenberg-Feste. 1840.
Indicateur de Strasbourg, no. 64, 1840.   [2383]

Erinnerungsschrift an die 500-jährige Geburtstagsfeier Johannes
Gutenbergs zu Nürnberg. Veranstaltet von den Buchdruckern Nürnbergs
am 16. und 17. Juni 1900. Nürnberg, 1900. 51p. 4to.   [2384]
     Eu-De-BP   Eu-Ge-LSb

Die Errichtung des Standbildes Gutenberg's im Garten des Guten-
bergischen Hauses. Vereinsblatt (Mainz), suppl. to no. 11, 1824.[2385]

Erster Bericht des in Leipzig erwählten Comité zur Feier der Erfindung der Buchdruckerkunst. Leipzig, am Neujahrstage 1840.
3p. 4to.
     Title from Mohr, Jubelfeste.
     Reprinted in Hitzig's Pressezeitung, no. 2, 1840, p. 14-16.   [2386]

Erstes Gutenbergfest (1837), und zweiter Gutenbergfeste (1840).
(In Reiss, E. Mainzer Silhouetten und Genrebilder. Mainz, 1841.
p. 1-27)
     Title from Bigmore & Wyman.   [2387]

[Falk]
     Zur denkwürdigen 400jährigen Jubelfeier der Erfindung der Buch-
druckerkunst, den 24. Junius 1840 gesungen in der Concordia-Gesell-
schaft. Arnstadt, Ohlenroth'sche Hofbuchdruckerei, 1840. 4p.
8vo.
     Title from Mohr, Jubelfeste.   [2388]

Falk, Franz, 1840-1909.
     Gutenbergbüchlein für die liebe Jugend. Zum Gutenbergfeste in
Mainz 1900. Von Diöcesan-Archivar Dr. Franz Falk. Mainz, J. Falk
III. Söhne, 1900. 23p. illus. 14.5 cm.   [2389]
     DLC   Eu-Fr-PN

Die Feier des 400 jährigen Jubiläums der Erfindung der Buchdruckerkunst. Königsberger Preussische Staats-, Kriegs- und
Friedens-Zeitung, no. 286, 289, 1840.   [2390]

Die Feier des vierten Jubelfestes der Buchdruckerkunst. Reutlingen, 1840. 8vo.
     Title from Bigmore & Wyman.   [2391]

Die Feier des vierten Säcularfestes der Erfindung der Buchdruckerkunst, in Berlin, 29. August 1840. [Berlin, 1840] 4p. 4to.
     Title from Mohr, Jubelfeste.   [2392]

[Felix, Hilarius]
     Das Gutenberg-Fest, eine poetisch-humoristische Beschreibung zur
Erinnerung an die Feierlichkeiten des 14., 15. und 16. August 1837.

Mainz, 1837.   42p.   12mo.
   Title from Mohr, Jubelfeste.   [2393]

   Festgedicht allen Verehren Gutenbergs und seiner Kunst zur Feier
des vierten Jubelfestes gewidmet.   Dresden, 1840.   Folio.
   Cover-title: Zur vierten Säcular-Feier der Erfindung der Buchdruckerkunst.   Dresden 1840.   [2394]
   Eu-De-LBb

   Festgedicht, dargebracht den Manen Gutenberg's.   Stuttgart, 1837.
   Title from Mohr, Jubelfeste.   [2395]

   Festgedicht zur vierten Säcularfeier der Erfindung des Buchdruckes.
Dargebracht den Manen Gutenberg's.   Zum 24., 25. und 26. Juni 1840.
Bernburg, Gröning, 1840.   12p.   4to.
   Title from Mohr, Jubelfeste.   [2396]

   Festgesang zur 400jährigen Feier der Erfindung der Buchdruckerkunst.   25. Juli 1840.   Elberfeld, Elberf. Zeitungsdruckerei, 1840.
4p.   4to.
   Title from Mohr, Jubelfeste.   [2397]

   Festgesang zur vierten Jubelfeier der Buchdruckerkunst am 5.
December 1840.   Königsberg, Thewing'sche Buchdruckerei, 1840.   8p.
8vo.
   Title from Mohr, Jubelfeste.   [2398]

   Festgesänge zur vierten Säcularfeier der Erfindung der Buchdruckerkunst zu Frankfurt a.M.   1840.   4p.   8vo.
   Title from Mohr, Jubelfeste.   [2399]

   Festlied: "Ein Morgenstrahl aus finsterer Nacht."   Leipzig, 1840.
8vo.
   Title from Mohr, Jubelfeste.   [2400]

   Festlied zur vierten Säcularfeier der Erfindung der Buchdruckerkunst am 5. December 1840.   Von Robert K--g.   Königsberg, Schultz'-
sche Buchdruckerei, 1840.   4p.   8vo.
   Title from Mohr, Jubelfeste.   [2401]

   Festlieder zur vierten Secularfeier der Erfindung der Buchdrucker-
kunst, gesungen auf dem Weissen Hirsch bei Dresden den 22. Juni 1840.
Dresden, 1840.   4p.   8vo.
   Title from Mohr, Jubelfeste.   [2402]

   Fest-Ordnung und Festlieder der am 21. und 22. Junius 1840 in
Neukirchen zu begehenden 400jährigen Gedächtnissfeier der Erfindung
der Buchdruckerkunst.   Eisenach, Druck von F. v. Göckel, 1840.
16p.   sm. 8vo.
   Title from Mohr, Jubelfeste.   [2403]

Fest-Programm des Vereins Hallischer Buchdrucker und Buchhändler
zur Begehung der vierten typographischen Säcularfeier am 18. Juni
1840. Halle, 1840. 3p. 4to.
Title from Mohr, Jubelfeste.   [2404]

Fest-Programm zur Erfurt-Thüringischen Jubelfeier der Erfindung
der Buchdruckerkunst am Johannistage 1840.
Title from Mohr, Jubelfeste.
Reprinted in Erfurter Zeitung, no. 55, May 7, 1840.   [2405]

Festschrift zum drei jährigen Gründungs-Feste des Vereins der
Buchdrucker Kärntens und zur Gedenkfeier an die vor 500 Jahren er-
folgte Geburt Johannes Gutenbergs des Erfinders der Buchdruckerkunst. Klagenfurt, 1898. 8vo.   [2406]
   Eu-De-LBb

Festschrift zum fünfhundertjährigen Geburtstage von Johann Gutenberg, herausgegeben von Otto Hartwig; mit einem Atlas von 35 Tafeln ...
Leipzig, O. Harrasowitz, 1900. 4 prel. leaves, 548p. 5 fold. tab.
and atlas of 35 plates (part fold., incl. col. plates, facsims.)
24 cm. (Added t.-p.: Beihefte zum Centralblatt für Bibliothekswesen ... 8. Bd., Hft. 23)
   Also issued separately.   [2407]
   CSmH   DLC   ICJ   ICN   MH   NjP   Eu-De-BP   Eu-Ne-AVb
   Eu-Ne-GK

Festschrift zum fünfhundertjährigen Geburtstage von Johann Gutenberg, im Auftrage der Stadt Mainz, hrsg. von Otto Hartwig. Mainz
[Kunstdr. von P. von Zabern]; Leipzig, Kommissionverlag von O.
Harrasowitz, 1900. 2 prel. leaves, 455p. illus., 35 plates
(part fold., part double, 1 col., incl. facsims.) 5 fold. geneal.
tab. 30 cm.   [2408]
   DLC   ICJ   ICN   IU   MH   NNGr

Festschrift zur Feier des vierten Säculums der Einführung der
Buchdruckerkunst in Wien am 24. und 25. Juni 1882. [Ludwig
Gerstberger, ed.] Wien, A. Eurich, 1882. 16p. ports.
Folio.
   Portrait of Gutenberg.
   Title from Mohr, Jubelfeste.   [2409]

Die Fest-Tage des Buchdruckers. Eine Sammlung von Prologen,
Festgrüßen, Tafelliedern, Gedichten zu Jubiläen, Toasten, etc.
Leipzig, A. Waldow, 1868. 146p. 13.5 cm.   [2410]
   NNC   Eu-Ge-LB

Fest-Zeitung zum 500jährigen Geburtstags-Jubiläum Gutenbergs und
zur 42. Generalversammlung des Schweizerischen Typographenbundes,
3. und 4. Juni 1900 in Luzern. Luzerner Tages-Anzeiger, suppl.
to no. 126, 1900.   [2411]

Fête séculaire de l'invention de l'imprimerie.--Concerts alsaciens. -- Bal. -- Banquet. Courrier du Bas-Rhin, no. 75, 82, 1836, feuilletons.
 Title from Mohr, Jubelfeste. [2412]

Fête séculaire de l'invention de l'imprimerie par Gutenberg, qui sera célébré à Strasbourg en 1836. Strasbourg, F. G. Levrault, 1836. 4p. 4to.
 Title from Mohr, Jubelfeste. [2413]

Fêtes de Gutenberg. Concert donné à la Salle de spectacle le 24 juin 1840. Cantate allemande avec traduction française par M. Aug. Lamey. Musique de M. Gambs. Strasbourg, Silbermann, 1840. 4p. 4to.
 Title from Mohr, Jubelfeste. [2414]

Fêtes de Gutenberg. [Cortège] Brasseurs, tonneliers et marchands de vin. Compte définitif des Recettes et des Dépenses à l'occasion des fêtes, etc. Strasbourg, Silbermann, 1840. 4p. 4to.
 Title from Mohr, Jubelfeste. [2415]

Fêtes de Gutenberg. Cortège industriel de Strasbourg 25 juin 1840. Strasbourg, Lith. Simon, 1840. Folio. [2416]
 Eu-De-LBb

Fêtes de Gutenberg. Exposition des produits de l'industrie alsacienne, ouverté au château, du 26 juin au 24 juillet 1840. Strasbourg, 1840. 4to.
 Title from Serapeum, vol. 1, 1840. [2417]

Fêtes de Gutenberg. Programme officiel publié par le Maire de la ville. Strasbourg, Dannbach, 1840. 2p. 4to.
 Title from Mohr, Jubelfeste. [2418]

Fêtes de Gutenberg. Relation ... Banquet offert à David d'Angers. Courrier du Bas-Rhin, no. 152-155, 1840.
 Title from Mohr, Jubelfeste. [2419]

Die Foyer des Gutenberg-Festes in Dresden am 24. Junius 1840. [Dresden, 1840] 4p. 4to.
 Title from Mohr, Jubelfeste. [2420]

Filiette, H.
 Ode à Gutenberg. Indicateur du Bas-Rhin, no. 42, 1840.
 Title from Mohr, Jubelfeste. [2421]

Finney, Byron A.
 Gutenberg and the invention of printing. A paper on the celebration of the birth of printing. Inland Printer, vol. 25, 1900, p. 210-216. [2422]

Fischbach, H.
  Gutenberg-Fest. 1840. Gedicht.   Indicateur du Bas-Rhin,
no. 54, 1840.
  Title from Mohr, Jubelfeste.   [2423]

Fischer, Karl Ed.
  Die Buchdruckerei von J. F. Fischer.   Leipzig, 1840.   4to.   [2424]
  Eu-De-LBb

Fischer von Waldheim, Gotthelf, 1771-1853.
  Einige Worte an die Mainzer bei der Feierlichkeit des dem Erfinder der Buchdruckerkunst Johann Gutenberg zu errichtenden Denkmals.   Moskwa, 1836.   16p.   plates.   4to.   [2425]
  NN   Eu-De-LBb   Eu-Ge-LSb

Flathe, Johann Ludwig Ferdinand.
  Die vierte Säcular-Feier der Erfindung Gutenbergs in Dresden
und Leipzig. Ein Gedenkbuch für Gegenwart und Zukunft. Mit einer
getreuen Abbildung des Gutenbergs-Monuments in Mainz und einigen
werthvollen xylographischen Beilagen.   Leipzig, B. G. Teubner,
1840.   130p.   front., facsim.   21 cm.   [2426]
  NNGr   Eu-De-LBb   Eu-Fr-PN   Eu-Ge-LB   Eu-Ge-LSb

Fleischmann, Franz.
  Die Huldigung der Völker. Ein Festspiel, zur 500sten Gedenk-
feier Johann Gutenbergs.   München, Bruckmann, 1900.   42p.   8vo.[2427]
  Eu-De-BP

  Flüchtige Blicke auf die letzten vierzig Jahre des vierten Jahrhunderts der Buchdruckerkunst.   Berlin, Duncker & Humblot, 1840.
36p.   20 cm.
  Preface signed: H. Unger.   [2428]
  NNGr

Frege, Ludwig.
  Deutschlands und Preussens Jubelfreude. Erinnerungen an die
Jahre 1440, 1540, 1640 und 1740.   Berlin, G. Gropius, 1840.
iv, [2], 105p.   18 cm.   [2429]
  NNGr   Eu-De-LBb

Freiligrath, Ferdinand.
  Denkschrift zur F.-Feier in Leipzig am 6. Juli 1867, etc.
Leipzig [1867]   8vo.   [2430]
  Eu-Ge-LB

----   Zur Feier von Gutenberg's 400jährigen Todestage 24. Februar
1868. Dem Fortbildungs-Verein für Buchdrucker und Schriftgiesser
in Leipzig mit herzlichen Grussen gewidmet.   Leipzig, 1868.   2p.
8vo.
  Title from Bigmore & Wyman.   [2431]

[Friederich, G.]
   Rede am vierten Säcularfeste der Erfindung der Buchdruckerkunst,
den 24. Juni 1840.   [Frankfort a.M.?] 1840.   8p.   8vo.
   Title from Mohr, Jubelfeste.   [2432]

Froebel, Gunther.
   ... Album zur vierten Säcularfeier der Erfindung der Buchdruckerkunst,
und zur Jubelfeier fünfzigjähriger Wirksamkeit der Herren Buchdrucker:
Johann Ludwig Knote, Johann Christoph Wilhelm Esefelder, Friedrich
Rudolf Gehring, Johann Ernst Henneberg ... Mit höchster Genehmigung
und mit Unterstützung wohlwollender Freunde veranstaltet, von G.
Froebel ... Rudolstadt, Froebel [1840]   48p.   22 cm.
      At head of title: Anno 1840, am 18. Aug. in Rudolstadt.   [2433]
      NNC   NNGr   Eu-De-LBb

Frölich, K.
   Liederbuch für die im Gutenbergbunde vereinigten Buchdrucker.
Berlin, 1850.   8vo.   [2434]
   Eu-Ge-LSb

Fromman, F. J.
   Rede am Gutenbergs-Feste zu Leipzig, den 25. Junius 1840.   Jena,
Fromman, 1840.   4p.   8vo.
   Title from Mohr, Jubelfeste.   [2435]

Fuelleborn, Georg Gustav.
   Lof der Buchdruckerkunst.   Zur vierten Säcularfeier ... neu aufge-
legt von J. F. W. Weilshäuser.   [Oppeln, 1840]   Folio.
   Title from Mohr, Jubelfeste.   [2436]

Gailer.
   Rede in der Hauptkirche, gehalten am 4. Säcular-Gedächtnissfeste
der Erfindung der Buchdruckerkunst den 24. Juni 1840.   Reutlingen,
J. Raach, 1840.   12p.   8vo.   [2437]
   Eu-Ge-LSb

   Gedächtniss-Tafel zur 400jährigen Jubelfeier der Erfindung der
Buchdruckerkunst am Johannisfeste 1840 allen Bewohnern dieser
Froien und Hansestadt Lübeck gewidmet.   Lübeck, G. C. Schmidt
& Sohn, 1840.
   Title from Mohr, Jubelfeste.   [2438]

   Gedanken über Censur und Pressfreiheit in Beziehung auf Prof.
Gottfr. Herman's gehaltene Festrede und deren durch die Leipziger
Allgemeine Zeitung vom 25. Juli 1840 gegebene Beurtheilung.   Leip-
zig, E. Fleischer, 1840.   28p.   20.5 cm.   [2439]
   NNGr

Gedenkblatt zur vierten Säcularfeier der Erfindung der Buchdruckerkunst. Grosses Tableau in Farben.   Hanover, Gebr. Jänecke, 1840.
   Title from Mohr, Jubelfeste.   [2440]

Gedenkblätter zur Gutenbergfeier am 50. Jahrestage der Errichtung
des Gutenbergdenkmals zu Mainz 14. Aug. 1837. Herausgegeben von den
voreinigten Mainzer Buchdruckern und Buchhändlern m.d.ccc.lxxxvii
[1887]   4to.   [2441]
   Eu-Ge-LB   Eu-Ge-LSb   Eu-Sz-BeG

Gedenkbuch an die festlichen Tage der Inauguration des Gutenberg-
Donkmals zu Mainz am 13., 14., 15. und 16. August 1837. Nebst den
Acten, die Entstehung desselben betreffend und einer kurzen Lebens-
beschreibung Gutenbergs. Mit vier lithographischen Abbildungen.
Mainz, 1837, auf Kosten sämmtlicher Buchhandlungen. In Commission
bei: F. Kupferberg. viii, 207p.   2 plates, 2 fold. plates.
21 cm.   [2442]
   NN   NNC   Eu-Ge-LB   Eu-Ge-LSb

Gedenk-Buch der vierten Jubelfeier der Erfindung der Buchdruckerkunst in Mainz. 1840.   Mainz, Seifert'sche Buchdruckerei [1841]
xxii, 362p.   front., plates.   25 cm.   [2443]
   MiU   Eu-De-LBb

Gedenkbuch der 4ten Säcularfeier der Erfindung der Buchdruckerkunst zu Braunschweig, am Johannisfeste des Jahres 1840.   Braunschweig, 1840.   [6], 100p.   22 cm.   [2444]
   ICJ   NN   NNGr   Eu-De-LBb   Eu-Ge-LSb

Gedenk-Buch zur vierten Jubelfeier der Erfindung der Buchdruckerkunst begangen zu Frankfurt am Main am 24ten und 25ten Junius 1840.
Eine Festgabe herausgegeben von den Buchdruckern, Schriftgiessern
und Buchhändlern.   [Frankfurt a.M., J. D. Sauerländer, 1841]
xiv p., 1 leaf, 320p.   26 cm.   [2445]
   DLC   NN   NNGr   Eu-De-LBb   Eu-Ge-LB   Eu-Ge-LP

Gedenkschrift zur Erinnerung an die 450jährige Jubiläumsfeier
der Erfindung der Buchdruckerkunst in Frankfurt a.M. am 21. und
22. Juni 1890.   Frankfurt a.M., 1890.   8vo.   [2446]
   Eu-Ne-AVb   Eu-Ne-GK

Gedichte zur Feier des Johannistages 1840.   Basel, Schneider,
1840.   80p.   8vo.
   Title from Mohr, Jubelfeste.   [2447]

Geissler, P. C.
 Festtableau zur vierten Säcularfeier der Buchdruckerkunst. Lith-
ogr. von B. Dondorf. Leipzig, Leo, 1840. 26.5x43 cm.
 Title from Mohr, Jubelfeste. [2448]

 Gesang zum Gutenberg-Feste in Dresden am 21. Juni 1840. Dresden,
E. Blochmann, 1840. 4p. 8vo.
 Title from Mohr, Jubelfeste. [2449]

 Gesänge bei der vierten Säcularfeier der Erfindung der Buchdruckerkunst in der Neuen-Kirche. zu Strassburg am 24. Juni 1840. Strassburg, 1840. [2450]
 MB Eu-Ge-LSb

 Gesänge der Lieder-Tafel des Erfurter Musikvereins zur Vorfeier
des Gutenberg-Festes den 26. Juli 1840. Erfurt, Fr. Stickel, 1840.
15p. 8vo.
 Title from Mohr, Jubelfeste. [2451]

 Geschichte der Buchdruckereien in Königsberg. Ausgegeben am Tage
des in Königsberg stattfindenden Buchdrucker-Jubiläums am 5. December 1840. Königsberg, Hartung'sche Hofbuchdruckerei, 1840. 62p.
8vo. [2452]
 NNGr

 Geschichte der Buchdruckerkunst in Basel von den ältesten bis auf
die neuesten Zeiten. Herausgegeben von der historischen Gesellschaft
in Basel. Basel, Schweighauser, 1840. illus. 4to.
 Title from Mohr, Jubelfeste. [2453]

 Geschichte der Buchdruckerkunst und ihres Erfinders Johann Gutenberg. Nebst einem Programme der Festlichkeiten in Leipzig und Berlin zur 400jahrigen Gutenbergs-Feier im Jahre 1840. Eine Festgabe.
Berlin, Koch, 1840. 16p. 20 cm. [2454]
 NNGr Eu-De-LBb

Gothmann, E.
 Gutenberg-Fest. Mit Abbildung der Statue. Strassburg, Dannbach,
1840. 4p. 8vo. [2455]
 Eu-Ge-LSb

Giesebrecht, Ludwig.
 Gutenberg. Oratorium in 3 Abtheilungen, componirt von Karl Löwe.
Berlin, F. W. Gubitz, 1840. 16p. 8vo.
 Title from Mohr, Jubelfeste. [2456]

---- Gutenberg's Bild. Componirt für gemischten Chor mit Orches-
terbegleitung von Karl Czerny. Partitur und Clavier-Auszug.
[Mainz, 1837] 4to.
 Title from Mohr, Jubelfeste. [2457]

Gleditzsch, Hermann.
    Jubiläumsbild.   Leipzig, Hirschfeld, 1840.   Large folio.
82x63x3.5 cm.   [2458]
    Eu-Sz-BeG

Gleich, Ferdinand.
    Guttenbergs-Walzer für das Pianoforte. Componirt zur Feier des
vierhundertjährigen Jubilaeums der Erfindung der Buchdruckerkunst.
14. Werk.   Leipzig, Sturm & Koppe [1840]   1 prel. leaf, 10p.   4to.[2459]
    Eu-De-LBb

Goebel, Theodor.
    Die Gutenberg-Ausstellung in Mainz. Zeitschrift für Deutschlands
Buchdrucker, vol. 12, no. 29, 1900, p. 333-335; no. 30, p. 347-349;
no. 31, p. 359-361.   [2460]

Goetz, Walter.
    Die Bedeutung der Buchdruckerkunst für die Kultur. Zeitschrift
für Deutschlands Buchdrucker, vol. 12, no. 25, 1900, p. 273-275.   [2461]

Goldschmidt, Paul.
    Gutenbergbuch. Festgabe für das deutsche Volk zur 500 jährigen
Geburtstagfeier des Erfinders der Buchdruckerkunst am 24. Juni 1900.
Halle an der Saale, 1900. 64p.   8vo.   [2462]
    Eu-De-BP   Eu-Ge-LB   Eu-Ge-LSb

    Gott grüss die Kunst. Zur Erinnerung an die vierten Säcularfeier
der Erfindung der Buchdruckerkunst durch J. Gutenberg aus Mainz.
Entworfen und ausgeführt durch H. M. Poppen.   Grosses Tableau.
Freiburg i. Br., Univ.-Buchdruckerei der Gebr. Groos, 1840.
    Title from Mohr, Jubelfeste.   [2463]

Gotthold, Friedrich August.
    Zur Feier des vierten Jubiläums der Erfindung der Buchdrucker-
kunst. Ein in der Physic.-ökonom. Gesellschaft geh. Vortrag.
Preussische Provinz-Blätter, vol. 24, [ca. 1840], p. 481-513; vol.
25, p. 33-65.   [2464]

Göttingen. Universität. Bibliothek.
    Katalog der im historischen Saale der K. Universitäts-Bibliothek
zu Göttingen, zur 500jährigen Geburtstagsfeier Johann Gutenberg's am
24. Juni 1900 eröffneten Ausstellung. Göttingen, Univ.-Buchdruck-
erei von Fr. Kaestner, 1900.   v, 37p.   18 cm.
    "Vorwort" signed: Dr. Dziatzko, Direktor.   [2465]
    MH   NNC   Eu-De-BP   Eu-Ge-LSb

Gottwald, Eduard.
    Betrachtungen eines Buchdruckers an Guttenberg's Denkmale, und
des Meisters Traum ... Dresden, Arnold, 1840. 16p.   8vo.   [2466]
    Eu-De-LBb   Eu-Fr-PN

Gottwald, Eduard.
Erinnerungsblätter an die vierte Säcularfeier der Erfindung der
Buchdruckerkunst zu Dresden, 1840. Dresden, 1840. 2, 116p.
ports. 21 cm. [2467]
NNGr Eu-Ge-LB Eu-Ge-LSb

———— Worte der Weihe zur vierten Secularfeier der Erfindung der
Buchdruckerkunst. Gedicht. Dresden, C. C. Meinhold & Söhne,
1840. 4p. 4to.
Title from Mohr, Jubelfeste. [2468]

[Graberg, Fr.]
Proben der Schriftschneiderei, Schrift- und Stereotypengiesserei.
Zürich, 1840. 4to.
Title from Mohr, Jubelfeste. [2469]

[————] Vignetten und Verzierungen für die Buchdruckerpresse.
Zurich, 1840. 4to.
Title from Mohr, Jubelfeste. [2470]

[Graubel]
Jubellied, den Manen Gutenberg's geweiht. Am 21. Juni 1840.
Dresden, 1840. 1 leaf. 8vo.
Title from Mohr, Jubelfeste. [2471]

Grey, Johanna.
Ioannea Graiae, litterae ad H. Bullingerum. Johanna Grey's Briefe
an Heinrich Bullinger. Diplomatischer Abdruck des Originals, nebst
deutscher und englischer Uebersetzung. Denkschrift zum Jubilaeum
der Erfindung der Buchdruckerkunst. Zürich, Orell, Füssli & Co.,
1840. 42p. 4to. [2472]
Eu-De-LBb Eu-Fr-PN

Grieben, Henry.
Fust und Gutenberg. (In Simrock. Rheinsagen, no. 128, p. 271-
273.
Title from Bigmore & Wyman. "A poem in 8 strophes, each of 8
verses, having for its subject the invention of printing. Fust,
or Faust, plays the part of the villian." [2473]

Grosse, Ed.
Johannistag 1900, betreffend Gutenbergfeier. Zur Guten Stunde,
1900, p. 431-436. [2474]

Grossman, Christian Gottlob Leberecht, 1783-1857.
Predigt zur vierten Säcularfeier der Erfindung der Buchdrucker-
kunst am Johannistage 1840, in der Thomaskirche zu Leipzig, gehalten
von Dr. Christian Gottlob Leberecht Grossmann ... Leipzig, Friedrich
Fleischer [1840] 34p. 21.5 cm. [2475]
NNC

Grotefend, Carl Ludwig, 1807-1874.
Geschichte der Buchdruckereien in den hannoverschen und braun-
schweigischen Landen, von Dr. C. L. Grotefend. Hrsg. von F. G. H.
Culemann. Mit 9 Steintafeln. Hannover, Hahn'sche Buchhandlung,
1840. 7 prel. leaves, [118]p. viii facsims. 22.5x18.5 cm.
Title vignette (portrait of Gutenberg) illustrated half-title. [2476]
DLC   Eu-Fr-PN   Eu-Ge-LB

Grotefend, Georg Friedrich, 1775-1853.
Neue Beiträge zur Erläuterung bey babylonischen Keilschrift nebst
einem Anhange über die Beschaffenheit des ältesten Schriftdruckes,
bei der vierten Säcularfeier der Erfindung des Buchdruckes von Gutenberg. Herausgegeben von Dr. Georg Friedrich Grotefend ... Hannover,
Hahn, 1840. 72p. plates. 4to. [2477]
ICU   MH   NN   OCl   Eu-Fr-PN   Eu-Ge-LB

Grucker, M. T. G.
Abschiedsruf an die Handwerker und die Kunstausstellung in Strass-
burg den 24. Juni 1840. Strassburg, Berger-Levrault, 1840. Folio.
Title from Mohr, Jubelfeste. [2478]

---- An Hoerter. Gedicht. Strasbourg, Silberman, 1840. 1 leaf.
8vo.
Title from Mohr, Jubelfeste. [2479]

---- Worte der Liebe bei Austheilung der Gutenbergs-Medaillen an
die Kinder, den 19. Juli 1840. Strassburg, Müller, 1840. 4p.
8vo.
Title from Mohr, Jubelfeste. [2480]

Grün, Karl.
Gutenberg-Lieder. Der Stadt Strassburg gewidmet. Strassburg,
1840. 16p. 8vo. [2481]
Eu-De-LBb   Eu-Fr-PN   Eu-Ge-LSb

Grüneisen, Carl and Eduard Mauch.
Ulm's Kunstleben im Mittelalter. Ein Beitrag zur Culturgeschichte
Schwabens. Ulm, Stettin, 1840. iv, 79p. plates. 8vo. [2482]
Eu-Fr-PN
1854 ed.: Eu-Ge-LB

[Gubitz, F. W.]
Bildnisse mir der Reliefmaschine zum Druck auf der Buchdrucker-
presse. Festgabe zur vierten Säcularfeier der Buchdruckerkunst.
Berlin, 1840. 6 leaves. sm. 4to.
Title from Mohr, Jubelfeste. [2483]

[Gubitz, F. W.]
   Mittheilung an Buchhändler, Buchdrucker und Schriftgiesserei-
Besitzer, betreffend die Feier am 28. und 29. August.   Berlin,
1840.   4to.
   Title from Mohr, Jubelfeste.   [2484]

Guldberg, C. A.
   Historisk udsigt over bogtrykkerkonsten fra dens begyndelse tit
naewaerende Tid. Et Indbydelsesskrift til Sekularfester i Christiania, Trykt i Guldberg & Dzwonkowskys Off., 1840. 24p.   4to.
   Title from Mohr, Jubelfeste.   [2485]

   Gutenberg à Strasbourg; ou, l'invention de l'imprimerie. Diver-
tissement en un acte, mêlé de chant et de danses, pour l'inauguration
de la statue de Gutenberg ... Strasbourg, Chez les principaux libraires,
1840.   35p.   front.   23 cm.
   MB   NNC   NNGr   Eu-De-LBb   Eu-Ge-LSb   [2486]

   The Gutenberg anniversary. Spectator, vol. 84, 1900, p. 917-
918.   [2487]

   Gutenberg.   Bemerkungen eines Elsassers über die Gutenberg-Feier
mit besonderer Rücksichtnahme auf die dadurch veraulassten Aesser-
ungen des Zeitgeistes.   Strassburg [1840?] 8vo.
   Title from Hoe, Richard M. The literature of printing ... London,
1877.   [2488]

   The Gutenberg celebration in Cologne.   Athenaeum, vol. 96, no.
3272, July 12, 1890, p. 62-63.
   Signed: G. S.   [2489]

   The Gutenberg celebrations.   British Printer, vol. 3, no. 16,
1890, p. 2-3.
   Describes celebrations at Mainz, Cologne and Leipzig.   [2490]

   Gutenberg.   Der bestehenden Commission zur Errichtung des Denkmals
gewidmet.   Mainz, 1837.
   Signed: M.
   Title from Mohr, Jubelfeste.
   Reprinted in Journal für Buchdruckerkunst, no. 6, 1837.   [2491]

   Gutenberg Festival in Mainz. A collection of programmes, local
newspapers, leaflets, etc.   Mainz, 1900.   [2492]
   Eu-Ge-LSb

   Gutenberg. Five-hundredth anniversary of his birth.   Nation,
vol. 71, Oct. 4, 1900, p. 272.   [2493]

   Gutenberg, 1400-1468.   [Portrait by Landseer]   Eclectic Magazine, vol. 73, no. 1, 1869, p. 114.   [2494]

The Gutenberg jubilee in Germany in commemoration of the discovery of printing. Foreign Quarterly Review (London), vol. 25, no. 50, 1840, p. 446-457. [2495]

Gutenberg, König, Keppler, Copernicus, Berthold Schwerz. Die fünf Weltumgestalter. Mit Portraiten. Neuer Einsiedler Kalender, 1876.
Title from Bigmore & Wyman. [2496]

Gutenberg ou l'invention de l'imprimerie. Poésie. Strasbourg, 1840. 9p. 8vo.
Signed: M.
Title from Mohr, Jubelfeste. [2497]

Gutenberg, ou l'invention de l'imprimerie. Poésie. [Strasbourg? 1840?] 35p. 8vo.
Title from Mohr, Jubelfeste. [2498]

Gutenberg und die unsterbliche Erfindung der Buchdruckerkunst, sowie deren Vervollkommnung, seit dem Beginn derselben bis auf unsere Zeit; zugleich mit einer kurzen Schilderung derjenigen Männer, welche sich um dieselbe am meisten verdient gemacht haben, mit besonderer Rücksicht auf Deutschland. Eine Festgabe zur vierten Säcularfeier der Erfindung der Buchdruckerkunst den 24., 25. und 26. Juni 1840 allen Jungern und Verehrern derselben gewidmet. Leipzig, Glück, 1840. iv, 44p. 18.5 cm. [2499]
DLC NNGr Eu-De-LBb

Gutenberg und Kleber; Gutenberg und Erwin. [Von K. C.] [Strassburg, 1840]
Title from Mohr, Jubelfeste. [2500]

Gutenberg und Luther. Indicateur de Strasbourg, no. 64, 1840.
Title from Mohr, Jubelfeste. [2501]

Gutenberg-Buchlein. Zur fünfhundertjährigen Gedächtnissfeier des Geburtstages Johann Gutenberg am 24. Juni 1900 herausgegeben von einem Mainzer Schulmann. Zweite verbesserte Auflage. Hannover, C. Meyer, 1900. 32p. illus. 1 plate paged in, 1 port. 8vo. [2502]
ICJ Eu-Ge-LB Eu-Ne-AVb

Die Gutenbergfeier der Königlichen Hofbuchdruckerei Trowitzsch & Sohn in Frankfurt a.d.Oder am 17. Juni 1900. Frankfurt a.d.Oder, 1900. 8vo. [2503]
Eu-Ne-AVb

Die Gutenberg-Feier in Leipzig. Börsenblatt für den Deutschen Buchhandel, vol. 67, no. 141, June 1900, p. 4703-4707.
Signed: V. M. [2504]

Gutenbergfeier in Mainz.   Illustrierte Zeitung, no. 2974, 1900. [2505]

Gutenberg-Feier in Mainz.   Mainzer Journal, vol. 40, no. 189,
1887.   [2506]

Gutenberg-Feier in Mainz.   1900. Festschrift im Auftrage der
Festleitung, herausgegeben von K. G. Bockenheimer.   [Mainz] Verlags-
Anstalt und Druckerei A.-G. [1900] [432]p.   illus., facsims.
25.5 cm.
   Various pagings.
   Each article, except the first, has special t.-p.   [2507]
DLC   ICJ   ICN   MH   Eu-De-BP   Eu-Fr-PN   Eu-Ge-LB
Eu-Ge-LSb   Eu-Ne-AVb

Gutenberg-Fest im Jahre 1840.   Strassburger Bilderbogen, no. 30,
1875.   [2508]

Das Gutenberg-Fest in Gorlitz.   Gorlitz, 1840.   25p.   18 cm. [2509]
NNGr   Eu-De-LBb

Das Gutenberg-Fest in Strassburg.   Morgenblatt (Stuttgart), no.
163-165, 1840.   [2510]

Gutenberg-Fest.   Versammlung der Gelehrten, Buchdrucker und Buchhändler, welche in Folge des Festprogrammes am 16. August 1837 statt-
fand.   Mainz, 1837.   8p.   Folio.
   Title from Mohr, Jubelfeste.
   Reprinted in Journal für Buchdruckerkunst, no. 6, 1837.   [2511]

Die Gutenberg Festtage in Mainz.   Fünf auf die Gutenbergfeier
in Mainz 1900 bezügliche Nummern des Heidelberger Fremdenblattes.
[Heidelberg, Universitäts-Buchdruckerei und Verlag] 1900.   [2512]
Eu-Ge-LSb

Gutenberg-Stiftung für Freunde des goettlichen Wortes, gegründet
bei dem Jubelfeste.   Strassburg, 1840.   4 parts.   8vo.   [2513]
Eu-Ge-LSb

Gutenbergs-Album.   Zur Erinnerung an des vierte Säkularfest der
Erfindung der Buchdruckerkunst, gefeiert zu Ulm, am 24. Juni 1840.
Ulm, Ernst Nübling, 1840.   [188]p.   26 cm.   [2514]
NNC   Eu-De-LBb

Gutenbergs-Archiv.   Sammlung für Kunde deutscher Vorzeit in allen
Beziehungen. Herausgegeben von Ottm. F. H. Schönhuth.   Stuttgart,
Cannstatt, 1840.   8vo.
   Title from Mohr, Jubelfeste.   [2515]

―――   2d ed.   Schwäbische Hall, F. F. Hesgid, 1848.   [2516]
MH   Eu-Ge-LB

Das Gutenbergs-Fest in Erfurt. Leipziger Allgemeine Zeitung,
no. 215, Aug. 2, 1840.   [2517]

Das Gutenbergs-Fest in Mainz am 13-16 August 1837. Journal für
Buchdruckerkunst, no. 8, 1837, col. 113-127; no. 9, col. 129-143;
no. 10, col. 153-166; no. 11, col. 169-183; no. 12, col. 185-199. [2518]

Das Gutenbergs-Fest zu Leipzig am 24., 25., 26. Juni 1840.
Hitzig's Presszeitung, no. 50-52, 1840, p. 434-467.
      Also reprint.
      Title from Mohr, Jubelfeste.   [2519]

Die Gutenbergs-Feste in Strassburg. 24. 25. 26. Juni 1840.
Gedicht. Indicateur de Strassbourg, no. 61, 1840.   [2520]

Haberland, L.
      Lied am Gutenbergs-Feste geweiht. Den 5. December 1840.   König-
berg, Haberland'sche Buchdruckerei, 1840.   4p.   8vo.
      Title from Mohr, Jubelfeste.   [2521]

Habermann, Carl Friedrich.
      Beschreibung der bei der vierten Säcularfeier der Buchdruckerkunst
am 23. und 24. Juni 1840, in Hildburghausen stattgehabten Feierlichkeiten.   Hildburghausen, 1840.   8vo.
      Title from Mohr, Jubelfeste.   [2522]

Hagen, Friedrich Heinrich von der.
      Rede zur vierten Jahrhundertfeier der Buchdruckerkunst in Berlin.
Berlin, 1841.   12p.   8vo.   [2523]
      Eu-Ge-LB

Hagenbach, Carl Rudolph.
      Toast auf die Regierung.   Basel, 1840.   1p.   4to.
      Title from Mohr, Jubelfeste.   [2524]

Half a millenium of printing.   The 500th anniversary of John
Gutenberg.   American Printer, vol. 30, 1900, p. 345.   [2525]

Haltaus, Karl Ferdinand, 1811-1848.
      Album deutscher Schriftsteller zur vierten Säcularfeier der Buch-
druckerkunst, durch Dr. Karl Haltaus.   Leipzig, Fest'sche Verlags-
Buchhandlung, 1840.   xxx, 312p.   front. (port.)   23.5 cm.   [2526]
      MiU   NN   NNC   NNGr   Eu-De-BP   Eu-De-LBb   Eu-Fr-PN
      Eu-Ge-LB   Eu-Ge-LSb   Eu-Ne-AVb   Eu-Ne-GK

Harless, Chr. Fr.
      Die Litteratur der ersten hundert Jahre nach der Erfindung der Ty-
pographie, in den meisten Hauptfächern der Wissenschaften, mit besonderer Rücksicht auf klassische Philologie, Geschichte und Chronik,

Erd- und Länderkunde, Reisen, Naturgeschichte, Medicin und ihre
Zweige, Dichtkunst und Romantik. Ein Beitrag zur Geschichte dieser
Wissenschaften im Mittelalter und seinem Uebergange zur neuern Zeit ...
Leipzig, Fest'sche Verlags-Buchhandlung, 1840. 288p. 21.5 cm. [2527]
    DLC   NNGr   NjP   Eu-Fr-PN   Eu-Ge-LB

Hartman, C. F.
    An Alsa, nach Strassburgs Jubelfeier der Erfindung Gutenbergs
1840. Strassburger Wochenblatt, no. 55, 1840. [2528]

——— An Hörter (Componist der Cantate). Gedicht. Strassburg,
Silbermann, 1840. 8vo.
    Title from Mohr, Jubelfeste. [2529]

——— Gutenberg. Juni 1841. Strassburger Wochenblatt, no. 52,
1841. [2530]

——— Gutenbergs Erfindung. 1436-1440. Strassburger Wochenblatt,
no. 38, 1840. [2531]

——— Die Strassburger Handwerker an Gutenbergs Ehrenfeste. Strassburger Wochenblatt, no. 59, 1840. [2532]

Hase, Oscar von, 1846-1916.
    Der Gutenbergpfennug; eine Dankesschuld des deutschen Buchgewerbes.
Rede zur 450jährigen Gedenkfeier der Erfindung der Buchdruckerkunst
gehalten am 5. Juli 1890 im Deutschen Buchhändlerhause zu Leipsig,
von Dr. Oscar von Hase, Vorsitzendem des Centralvereins für das ge-
samte Buchgewerbe. Leipzig, Druck und verlag von Breitkopf & Härtel,
1890. 17p. 23.5 cm.
    Also appeared in Zeitschrift für Deutschlands Buchdrucker, vol. 2,
no. 28, 1890, p. 287-291. [2533]
    NN   Eu-De-LBb

Hasse, Friedrich Christian August, 1773-1848.
    Kurze Geschichte der Leipziger Buchdruckerkunst im Verlaufe ihres
vierten Jahrhunderts. Einladungsschrift der Universität Leipzig zu
der bei der vierten Säcularfeier der Buchdruckerkunst von ihr veran-
stalteten Feierlichkeit durch ... Prof. Friedr. Chr. Aug. Hasse. Aus
dem lateinischen übersetzt. Nebst einigen xylographischen Beilagen.
Leipzig, B. G. Teubner, 1840. iv, 73p. 3 facsims. on 2 leaves
(1 fold.) 21 cm. [2534]
    DLC   Eu-De-LBb   Eu-Ge-LB

——— Rector academiae orationem in solemnibus typographiae saecular-
ibus quartis. Lipsiae D. XXV. M. Junii H. X. MDCCCXL. In aula academica habendam indicit interprete Frid. Christ. Aug. Hasse, ord.
philos. H. T. Decano. Typographiae Lipsiensis, imprimis saeculi

quarti, historiae brevis adumbratio ... Colophon [p. 56]: Lipsiae, Typis
Guil. Staritzii, Typogr. Acad. [1840] 1 prel. leaf, 56p. fold.
plate. 27 cm.
    "Corrigenda" slip mounted on p. 56.   [2535]
    MH   NN   NNGr   Eu-De-LBb

Hassler, Konrad Dieterich, 1803-1873.
    Die Buchdrucker-Geschichte Ulm's zur vierten Säcularfeier der
Erfindung der Buchdruckerkunst geschrieben von Dr. Konrad Dieterich
Hassler ... Mit neuen Beiträgen zur Culturgeschichte, dem Faksimile
eines der ältesten Drucke und artistischen Beilagen, besonders zur
Geschichte der Holzschneidekunst.   Ulm, Stettin'sche Buchhandlung,
1840.   6 prel. leaves, 156 col., [1]p.   facsims.   32 cm.
    Added t.-p., engr., in colors: Ulm's Buchdruckerkunst ...   [2536]
    DLC   ICJ   MH   Eu-De-BP   Eu-De-LBb   Eu-Fr-PN   Eu-Ge-LB

----   Explicatio monumenti typographici antiquissimi nuper reperti.
Accedunt supplementa nonnulla ad auctoris historiam typographiae
Ulmae.   Stettin, 1840.   16p.   4to.   [2537]
    Eu-Fr-PN

Haton, Martial.
    A Guttemberg et à la fraternité composé à Lagny, à l'occasion de
la Saint-Jean-Porte-latine (1876).   Lagny, impr. de F. Aureau
[1873?]   1p.   4to.   [2538]
    Eu-Fr-PN

Hauschild, J. G.
    Gutenbergs Festtänze: Gutenberg, Schottischer Walzer; Fust,
Gallopp für Pianoforte.   Leipzig, G. Schubert, 1840.
    Title from Mohr, Jubelfeste.   [2539]

[Hausrath, A.]
    Rede am vierten Säcularfeste der Erfindung der Buchdruckerkunst am
24. Juni 1840, vor einem grossen Festzuge in der grösseren Stadkirche
gehalten.   Carlsruhe, 1840.   16p.   20 cm.   [2540]
    NNGr

[Hauthal, Ferdinand]
    Festgedicht zur Jubelfeier der Buchdruckerkunst im Jahre 1840.
Dresden, E. Blochmann, 1840.   6p.   4to.
    Title from Mohr, Jubelfeste.   [2541]

[----]   Lied zum Gutenbergs-Feste in Dresden am 21. Juni 1840.
Dresden, E. Blochmann, 1840.   4p.   8vo.
    Title from Mohr, Jubelfeste.   [2542]

[Hedenus, A. G.]
Pro typographia cum quintum seculum auspicantur. Dresden, C. C. Meinhold & Söhne, 1840. 3p. 4to.
Title from Mohr, Jubelfeste. [2543]

Heidenheimer, Heinrich, 1856–
Johannes Gutenberg zum Gedächtnisse. Zeitschrift für Deutschlands Buchdrucker, vol. 12, no. 25, 1900, p. 272. [2544]

———— Vom Lobe der Druckkunst. Zeitschrift für Deutschlands Buchdrucker, vol. 12, no. 51, 1900, p. 585-587. [2545]

———— Von Ruhme Johannes Gutenbergs. Eine litterar-geschichtliche Studie ... (In Gutenberg-Feier in Mainz. 1900 ... [Mainz] Mainzer Verlags-Anstalt und Druckerei [1900]) [2546]
DLC ICJ ICN NH Eu-Fr-PN Eu-Ge-LB Eu-Ge-LSb
Eu-Ne-AVb Eu-Sz-BeG

Hein, Gustav.
Das Mährlein des Sängers von Mainz. Zur vierten Säcularfeier der Buchdruckerkunst am 24. Juni 1840 von den Kunstgenossen. Troppau, Ad. Trasler, 1840. 4to.
Title from Mohr, Jubelfeste. [2547]

Heinlein, Heinrich.
Festgabe zur vierten Säcularfeier der Erfindung der Buchdruckerkunst. Eine Darstellung der Entstehung, Ausbreitung und Vervollkommnung der Typographie bis zur gegenwärtigen Zeit. Von Heinrich Heinlein ... Mit einer Abbildung des Festsalons. Leipzig, C. Drobisch, 1840. viii, 99p. col. front. 20.5 cm. [2548]
DLC NNGr Eu-De-LBb Eu-Fr-PN

Heinritz.
Versuch einer Geschichte der Buchdruckerkunst im vormaligen Fürstenthum Bayreuth bis zur vierten Säcularfeier der Erfindung derselben. Archiv für Geschichte und Alterthumskunde des Ober-Main-Kreises, vol. 1, 1841. [2549]

Hell, Th.
Festgabe zur vierten Säcularfeier der Erfindung der Buchdruckerkunst. Gedicht. Dresden, C. H. Gärtner, 1840. 1 Bog. Folio.
Title from Mohr, Jubelfeste. [2550]

Heller and Rohm.
Die drei Tage der Enthüllungsfeier des Gutenberg-Monuments am 14., 15. und 16. August 1837. Aufgefasst von einem Frankfurter Typographen. Mit Vorwort, vollständigen Festreden und Anhang. Zum Besten des Gutenberg-Monuments. Frankfurt am Main, 1837.
Title from Hoe, Richard M. The literature of printing ... London, 1877. [2551]

Henné.
   Andenken an das Buchdruckerfest am Johannistage 1840. Gedicht.
[Saint-Gallen, 1840]
   Title from Mohr, Jubelfeste.   [2552]

Hermann, Gottfried, 1772-1848.
   Godofredi Hermanni Oratio in quartis festis secularibus artis
typographicae habita d. XXV. m. Iunii a. MDCCCXL.   Lipsiae, sumptibus Ernesti Fleischeri [1840]   10p.   26 cm.   [2553]
   DLC

[Hervegh, G.]
   Festweihe der Buchdruckerei-Inhaber, ihrer Gehilfen und der Buchhändler von Constanz, zur Jubelfeier der Erfindung der Buchdruckerkunst in St. Gallen, den 24. Juni 1840.   [St. Gallen, 1840]
   Title from Mohr, Jubelfeste.   [2554]

Hesse, Max.
   Zur Erinnerung an die 450jährige Jubelfeier der Erfindung der
Buchdruckerkunst, Leipzig, vom 24. Juni bis 5. Juli 1890.   Leipzig,
1890.   68p.   8vo.   [2555]
   Eu-Ge-LB   Eu-Ge-LSb

Heubner, Gustav.
   Das vereinigte Gutenbergs- und Turnfest der Stadt Plauen am 24.
Juni beschreiben, nebst den dabei gehaltenen Reden und gesungenen
Liedern.   Plauen, 1840.   28p.   20 cm.   [2556]
   MH   NNGr   Eu-De-LBb

Heymann.
   Predigt, bei der Säcularfeier der Erfindung der Buchdruckerkunst,
am 21. Juni in der Kreuzkirche zu Dresden gehalten.   Dresden, 1840.
16p.   8vo.   [2557]
   Eu-De-LBb

Hinze, H. P. F.
   Ein Steinchen zu der Gutenberg-Säule, niedergelegt am 24. Juni
1840.   Lübeck, Rathgens, 1840.   4p.   8vo.
   Title from Mohr, Jubelfeste.   [2558]

   Historische Notiz über den Typendruck in der Stadt Minden.   Als
Festgabe zur vierten Säcularfeier der Erfindung der Buchdruckerkunst
am 24. Juni 1840.   Minden, 1840.
   Title from Mohr, Jubelfeste.   [2559]

Hitzig, Ferdinand, 1807-1875.
   Die Erfindung des Alphabetes.   Eine Denkschrift zur Jubelfeier des
von Gutenberg im Jahre erfundenen Bücherdruckes.   Verfasst von Dr. Ferdinand Hitzig.   Zürich, Orell, Füssli & Co., 1840.   43p.   31.5 cm[2560]
   NN   NjP   Eu-De-LBb   Eu-Fr-PN   Eu-Ge-LB   Eu-Ge-LSb

[Höchel, Carl Hermann]
   Die Heroen der Kunst. Ein charakteristisches Gemälde der ausge-
zeichnesten Typographen früherer Zeit. Ein Denkmal zur Feier des
vierten Jubelfestes geweiht den Manen Gutenberg's. Ulm, 1836.
viii, 95p. front. (port.) 19 cm.   [2561]
   NNGr   Eu-De-LBb

Hölscher, G.
   Allerlei ketzerische Glossen zum Mainzer Gutenbergfest. Allgemeine Buchhändlerzeitung, no. 24, 26, 1900.   [2562]

———   Zum Gedachtnis Gutenbergs. Aus Anlass der Feier seines 500en
Geburtstages am 24. Juni 1900. Börsenblatt für den Deutschen Buchhandel, vol. 67, no. 129, June 1900, p. 4347-4350, 4406-4409.   [2563]

   Hommage des élèves de l'école industrielle de Strasbourg à la
mémoire de Gutenberg. Courrier du Bas-Rhin, no. 143, 1840.   [2564]

Hornig.
   Gutenberg. Indicateur de Strasbourg, no. 31, 1840.
   Poem.   [2565]

Hörter, Ph.
   Cantate en l'honneur de Gutenberg. Composé pour la fête de 1836.
Texte par H. Redslob. Strasbourg, 1836.
   Title from Mohr, Jubelfeste.   [2566]

Höttinger.
   Zur 450jährigen Feier der Erfindung der Buchdruckerkunst, Festrede
gehalten zu Strassburg am 29. Juni 1890. Zeitschrift für Deutschlands Buchdrucker, vol. 2, no. 27, 1890, p. 272-275.   [2567]

Humbourg, A. de.
   Affaire des basreliefs de Gutenberg. Strasbourg, Leroux, 1840.
4p. Folio.
   Title from Mohr, Jubelfeste.   [2568]

———   Monument Gutenberg. Strasbourg, Leroux, 1840. 4p. 8vo.
   Extrait de l'Abeille no. 12.   [2569]
   Eu-Ge-LSb

Immergrün.
   Eine Festgabe zur vierten Jubelfeier der Erfindung der Buchdrucker-
kunst. Wien, Haas, 1840. 11 leaves, 336p. 16mo.   [2570]
   Eu-De-LBb   Eu-Ge-LSb

   Inauguration de la statue Gutenberg à Strasbourg, les 24, 25 et
26 juin 1840. [Annales de la typographie française et étrangère,
Paris, 1840] 11p. 8vo.
   Title from Mohr, Jubelfeste.   [2571]

Inauguration du monument de Gutenberg à Strasbourg. Programme ...
24, 25 et 26 juin 1840. Strasbourg, G. Silbermann, 1840. 2p.
4to. [2572]
  NNGr   Eu-Sz-BeG

Inaugurations-Feier des Monumentes für Johannes Gutenberg. Ein
Blatt der Erinnerung. [Mainz, 1837] Broadside.
  Title from Mohr, Jubelfeste. [2573]

Instituto catalán de las artes del libro, Barcelona.
  A Gutenberg. Barcelona, 1900. 2 prel. leaves, 84p. illus.,
plates, ports., facsims. 27.5 cm. (Revista gráfica, 1900) [2574]
  NNC   Eu-Ge-LSb

L'invention de l'imprimerie à Strasbourg par J. Gutenberg. Courte
notice publiée à l'occasion du quatrième anniversaire séculaire ...
célèbré à Strasbourg le 24, 25 et 26 juin 1840. Strasbourg, Leroux
[1840] cover-title, 15p. 22.5 cm. [2575]
  NNC   NNGr   Eu-De-LBb   Eu-Ge-LSb

Jaeck, Joachim Heinrich, 1777-1847.
  Denkschrift für das Jubelfest der Buchdruckerkunst zu Bamberg am
24. Juni 1840, als Spiegel der allseitigen Bildungs-Verhältnisse seit
unserer geschichtlichen Periode, verfasst von Heinrich Joachim Jäck ...
(Mit XIX Schriftmustern, der Abbildung des Bibliothek-Gebäudes, der
Jubel-Medaille, und dem Portrait des Authors.) Erlangen, im Ver-
lage von Ferdinand Enko, 1840. viii, 192p. front. (port.), fold.
facsim. 21 cm. [2576]
  ICN   MH   Eu-De-LBb   Eu-Ge-LB   Eu-Ge-LSb

Johannes Gutenberg. Porträt lith. von C. Brandt. Leipzig, 1840.
Large folio.
  Title from Mohr, Jubelfeste. [2577]

Jubelblatt, den Manen der Erfinder der Buchdruckerkunst, Gutenberg, Fust und Schöffer, bei Anlass der vierten Säcularfeier ihrer
Erfindung am St. Johannistage 1840, aus Liebe zur Kunst und in Verehrung der Erfinder von dem Buchdrucker Ernst Friedrich Hammerich
und seinen Gehilfen. Altona, 1840. Imper. folio.
  Title from Mohr, Jubelfeste. [2578]

Jubelblatt zur vierten Säcularfeier der Buchdruckerkunst. Berlin,
Hänel, 1840.
  Title from Mohr, Jubelfeste. [2579]

Jubelbrief zur vierten Säcularfeier der Buchdruckerkunst an alle
Völker der Erde. Leipzig, Dederich, 1840. 1p. 4to.
  Signed: Christianus.
  Title from Mohr, Jubelfeste. [2580]

Die Jubelfeier der Buchdruckerkunst.   Leipziger Allgemeine Zeitung, no. 179, 180, 182, 1840.   [2581]

Die Jubelfeier der Buchdruckerkunst in Leipzig.   Börsenblatt für den Deutschen Buchhandel, vol. 7, 1840, col. 1412-1421, 1445-1452, 1477-1482, 1509-1515, 1549-1552, 1589-1592.   [2582]

Jubel-Feier des 450sten Geburtsjahres der Erfindung der Buchdruckerkunst, begangen von Magdeburgs Buchdruckern am Sonntag, den 22. Juni 1890, im Garten und in den Sälen der Gesellschaft zur Freundschaft. [Magdeburg, Gedruckt in der Buchdruckerei A. Wohlfeld, 1890]   cover-title, [8]p.   28 cm.   [2583]
    NNC

Das Jubelfest der Buchdruckerkunst in Erfurt.   Börsenblatt für den Deutschen Buchhandel, vol. 7, 1840, col. 1791-1794, 1813-1815.   [2584]

Jubelfestzug.   Tableau betreffend die Aufstellung und Anordnung des Zuges. Leipzig, 1840. Folio.
    Title from Mohr, Jubelfeste.   [2585]

Jubelklänge bei der vierten Säcularfeier der Erfindung der Buchdruckerkunst am 21. Juni 1840. Dresden, C. C. Meinhold & Söhne, 1840. 4p. 4to.
    Title from Mohr, Jubelfeste.   [2586]

Jubelklänge zum Feste der vierten Säcular-Feier der Erfindung der Buchdrucker-Kunst, den 24. Juni 1840 in St. Gallen. Denkblatt gewidmet von den Besitzern und Gehülfen der Buchdruckereien, der Schriftgiessereien und den Buchhandlungen St. Gallens. St. Gallen, Wartmann'sche Offizin, 1840. Broadside. 55x72 cm.
    Printed in six colors.   [2587]
    Eu-Sz-BeG

Jubelschrift zu Johann Gutenberg's 400jähriger Feier im Jahre 1840. Berlin, 1840.
    Title from Mohr, Jubelfeste.   [2588]

Jubeltableau zur Erinnerung an die Gutenberg-Feier. Leipzig, Polet, 1840.
    Lithograph.
    Title from Mohr, Jubelfeste.   [2589]

Jubiläums-Büchlein; oder, Geschichte, wie die Buchdruckerkunst in Deutschland erfunden worden ist, nebst ander'm, was dazu gehört. Erzählt für's Volk und für Freunde des Volkes. Mannheim, Heinrich Hoff, 1840. 48p. front. 17.5 cm.   [2590]
    NNC   Eu-De-LBb

Kade, Emil.
Die vierte Säcularfeier der Buchdruckerkunst zu Leipzig am 24. 25. 26. Juni 1840. Eine Denkschrift im Auftrage des Comité zur Feier der Erfindung der Buchdruckerkunst, verfasst von Dr. Emil Kade. Leipzig, Druck von Breitkopf und Härtel, 1841. 2 prel. leaves, 82p. 23 cm. [2591]
    DLC   NN   Eu-De-LBb   Eu-Ge-LSb

[Kastner]
1840! Essai de solutions d'un probleme transcendant de linguistique proposé le 1 janvier 1840 ou lettre à M. Pillet ainé avec dedicace aux manes de Gutenberg. Strasbourg, Dérivaux, 1840. 200p. 8vo.
    Title from Mohr, Jubelfeste. [2592]

[----] Prospectus d'un essai de meditations philosophiques, politiques et religieuses, à publier par souscription et dont le programme est dedié aux manes de Gutenberg. Strasbourg, Silbermann, 1840. 4p. 8vo.
    Title from Mohr, Jubelfeste. [2593]

Keysser, Adolf, 1850-
Stadtbibliothek in Koeln. Katalog einer Ausstellung von Druckerwerken bei Gelegenheit der Gutenberg-Feier 1900. Koeln, M. DuMont Schauberg, 1900. vi, 10p. 8vo. [2594]
    Eu-De-BP

Klein, Theodore.
Strassburgs Jubelfeier der Erfindung der Buchdruckerkunst am 24., 25. und 26. Juni 1840. Strassburg, 1840. 4to. [2595]
    Eu-Ge-LSb

---- Strophen gesungen von allen Anwesenden bei der Enthüllungsfeier der Gutenberg-Statue, den 24. Juni. Strassburg, 1840. 8vo.
    Title from Mohr, Jubelfeste. [2596]

Koehler, Gustav
Zur Geschichte der Buchdruckerei in Görlitz. Eine Festschrift. Görlitz, Heyn'sche Buchdruckerei, 1840. illus. 3 leaves, 23p. 8vo. [2597]
    Eu-Fr-PN   Eu-Ge-LB

Köning, H.
Festbilder aus Mainz. Zeitung für die Elegante Welt, no. 172-176, 1837. [2598]

Körner, Friedrich.
Johannes Gutenberg; mit farbigem Kunstblatt, nach einem Oelgemälde
von G. Bartsch. (In Das neue Buch der Welt. Stuttgart, 1878.
no. 1, p. 1-4)
Title from Bigmore & Wyman. [2599]

Köster, Albert, 1862-1924.
Festrede zur fünfhundert jährigen Geburtsfeier Johannes Gutenberg,
gesprochen in Mainz am 24. Juni 1900 von Albert Köster. Leipzig,
B. G. Teubner [1900] 30p. 24,5x20 cm. [2600]
ICJ MH NNGr Eu-Fr-PN Eu-Ge-LSb Eu-Ne-AVb

Krause, L'. W., firm, printers.
Beschreibung der Feier des vierten Säcularfestes der Erfindung der
Buchdruckerkunst in der Officin von L. W. Krause am 24. Juli 1840.
Eine Denkschrift für die Theilnehmer des Festes. Berlin, 1840.
32p. fold. plate. 15 cm. [2601]
NNGr Eu-De-LBb

Krebs, C.
Gutenbergs-Festlied. Hamburg, Schubert & Co., 1840. 4to.
Title from Mohr, Jubelfeste. [2602]

Kreyssig, Johann Gottlieb.
Memoriam Joannis Gutenbergii, artis typographicae inventoris,
inter solemnia saecularia ex a. D. 9 usque 7 calendas quintiles a.
1840. Lipsiae quartum instaurata recoluerunt J. T. Kreyssig et
Eduardus Augustus Diller. Misenae, typis C. E. Klinkichtii et
fil [1840] 12p. 4to. [2603]
Eu-Fr-PN

Krüger, Gustav.
Predigt zur Belehrung seiner Gemeinde über die nahe Feier des
vierhundertjährigen Jubelfestes der Buchdruckerkunst am zweiten
Pfingstfeiertage gehalten und mit erläuternden geschichtlichen Anmerkungen auf Verlangen in Druck gegeben. Delitzsch, 1840. 23p.
8vo. [2604]
Eu-De-LBb

Kuntz, C.
Gesänge und Cantate bei der vierten Säcularfeier der Erfindung
der Buchdruckerkunst in der neuen Kirche, den 24. Juni. Strassburg,
Fr. C. Heitz, 1840. 8p. 8vo. [2605]
Eu-Ge-LSb

Kunze, Gustav.
Gutenberg-Festklänge oder musikalische Erinnerungen an drei grosse
Tage des Jahres 1840. Potpourri für Pianoforte op. 40. Leipzig,
1840. 2p. 4to. [2606]
Eu-De-LBb

Laboulaye, E.
   Izobretenie Gutenberga i ego znachenie dlĩa istorii t͡sivilizat͡sii.
(In Laboulaye, E. Gosudarstvo i ego predely v svĩazi s sovremennymi
voprosami administratsii, zakonodatel'stva i politiki.   St. Peters-
burg, N. I. Lamanskii, 1868.   p. 150-155)   [2607]
   Eu-Ru-MLe

Lachmann, Karl.
   Zwanzig alte Lieder von den Nibelungen.   Zur 400jährigen Jubelfeier der Buchdruckerkunst gedruckt bei Rud. Lud. Decker.   Berlin,
1840.   3 leaves, 155p.   Folio.   [2608]
   Eu-Ge-LB

[Lakje-Chiarini]
   Couplets dédiés aux membres des Concerts alsaciens.   Strasbourg,
1836.   4to.
   Title from Mohr, Jubelfeste.   [2609]

Lamey, August.
   Gutenberg oder das Fest der Buchdruckerkunst.   Cantate.   Strass-
burg, 1840.
   Title from Mohr, Jubelfeste.   [2610]

Lappenberg, Johann Martin, 1794-1865.
   Zur Geschichte der Buchdruckerkunst in Hamburg am 24. Juni 1840
... Hamburg, J. A. Meissner, 1840.   lxxxvi, 123, [1]p.   27.5 cm. [2611]
   DLC   ICJ   ICN   MH   Eu-De-LBb   Eu-Fr-PN   Eu-Ge-LB
   Eu-Ne-GK

Lasker, J.
   Die 400jährige Jubelfeier der Erfindung der Buchdruckerkunst am
25. Juli 1840.   Eine Erinnerungsschrift.   Danzig, Gerhard, 1840.
48p.   20 cm.   [2612]
   NNGr

Laun, Friedrich, pseud. [i.e. Friedrich August Schutze]
   Ludwig Philipp und Napoleon.   Zum Andenken an das Jahr 1840 und
dessen Jubelfeier der Buchdruckerkunst.   Gedicht.   Dresden, Arnold,
1840.   31p.   8vo.   [2613]

Le Roux.
   Auf Gutenberg.   Bei Errichtung seiner Bildsäule in Mainz.
Gedicht.   Mainz, 1837.   8vo.
   Title from Mohr, Jubelfeste.
   Reprinted in Journal für Buchdruckerkunst, no. 6, 1837.   [2614]

Lehmann, C. D.
   Gutenberg und der neue Geisterbund, besungen zum Andenken an die
vor vierhundert Jahren ans Licht getretene Erfindung der Buchdrucker-

kunst. Kamenz, C. J. Krausche, 1840. ii, 132p. 8vo. [2615]
    Eu-De-LBb   Eu-Fr-PC   Eu-Ge-LB

Lehmann, J.
    Guttenberg's Statue in Strassburg.   Berlin, 1840.   1 leaf.
    Im Universitätsgebäude gedruckt.
    Title from Mohr, Jubelfeste.
    Reprinted in Magazin für Literatur des Auslandes, vol. 23, no.
    116, Sept. 1840.   [2616]

Lehr, Paul.
    À la mémoire de Gutenberg.   Strasbourg aux 24, 25 et 26 juin
    1840.   Strasbourg, 1840.   2p.   4to.
    German translation, by Th. Klein, on back page.
    Title from Mohr, Jubelfeste.   [2617]

Leipzig.   Deutsche Buchhändlerbörse.
    Verzeichniss der Gegenstände, welche zur vierten Säcularfeier ...
    in der deutschen Buchhändler-Börse in Leipzig ausgestellt sind.
    Leipzig, Ph. Reclam, 1840.   30p.   17 cm.   [2618]
    NNGr

Leipzig.   Universitätsbibliothek.
    Verzeichniss einiger in der akademischen Aula am 25. und 26. Juni
    1840 zur Ansicht aufgestellter, in der hiesigen Universitäts-Biblio-
    thek aufbewahrter alter Druckwerke.   Nebst einem Verzeichniss der
    Leipziger Buchdrucker von 1480-1580.   Leipzig, F. A. Brockhaus,
    1840.   14p.   21 cm.   [2619]
    NNGr

Lekisch, Hermann.
    Die Gutenbergfeier in Mainz.   Das Neue Jahrhundert, vol. 2, no.
    40, 1900.   [2620]

Lenz, Max.
    Zum Gedächtnisstage Johann Gutenberg's.   Hamburg, 1900.   8vo.
    (Zeitfragen: Aufsätze a. d. Hamburger Correspondenten)   [2621]
    Eu-Ne-GK

Leser, J.
    Gutenberg.   24. Juni 1840.   Strassburg, Dannbach, 1840.   2p.
    8vo.
    Title from Mohr, Jubelfeste.
    Reprinted in Indicateur de Strasbourg, no. 51, 1840.   [2622]

Lesné, Mathurin Marie.
    À la gloire immortelle des inventeurs de l'imprimerie.   Paris,
    chez l'auteur, 1840.   11p.   8vo.   [2623]
    Eu-Fr-PN

- 324 -

Levrault, Louis.
   À la presse.   Strasbourg, Berger-Levrault, 1840.   3p.   8vo.
   Title from Mohr, Jubelfeste.   [2624]

[----]   Couplets chantes par tous les assistants à la fête de la
cérémonie de l'inauguration de la statue de Gutenberg, 12-24 juin
1840.   Strasbourg, 1840.   8vo.
   Title from Mohr, Jubelfeste.   [2625]

Liebenau, Theodor von.
   Ueberblick über die Geschichte der Buchdruckerei der Stadt Luzern.
Gedenkblatt zur 500jährigen Gutenbergfeier.   Luzern, Buchdruckerei
H. Keller, 1900.   62p.   23 cm.   [2626]
   DLC   ICJ   MH   Eu-Sz-BeG

   Lied zur Erinnerung an die Erfindung der Buchdruckerkunst durch
Gutenberg.   [Dresden, 1840]   2p.   8vo.
   Title from Mohr, Jubelfeste.   [2627]

   Lieder am Feste zu Ehren von Johann Gutenberg zu Mainz am Oct.
1824 ... Mainz, 1824-1827.
   9 pieces folded to 8vo.
   ms. t.-p.
   Collected by Jac. Koning.   [2628]
   Eu-Ge-LP

   Lieder bei der Gutenbergs-Feier in Königsberg.   Den 5. December
1840.   [Königsberg] Dalkowski [1840]   cover-title, [8]p.   20.5 cm. [2629]
   NNC

   Lieder bei der vierten Säcularfeier der Erfindung der Buchdruckerkunst am 24. Juni 1840.   Bremen, Druck von C. Schünemann, 1840.
6 leaves.   8vo.
   Title from Mohr, Jubelfeste.   [2630]

   Lieder bei Gelegenheit der vierten Säcularfeier der Erfindung
der Buchdruckerkunst dargeboten.   Den 24. Juni 1840.   Bremen, J. G.
Heyse, 1840.   14p.   8vo.
   Title from Mohr, Jubelfeste.   [2631]

   Lieder zur 400jährigen Jubelfeier der Erfindung der Buchdruckerkunst.   Den 25. Juni 1840.   Chemnitz, Pickenhahn, 1840.   8 leaves.
8vo,
   Title from Mohr, Jubelfeste.   [2632]

   Lieder zur vierten typographischen Säcularfeier.   Gesungen auf
der Rabeninsel bei Halle am 29. August 1840.   Halle, Buchdruckerei
Gebauer-Schwetschke, 1840.   30p.   8vo.
   Title from Mohr, Jubelfeste.   [2633]

[Liesegang, Ed.]
Zur Feier der 400jährigen Jubiläums der Erfindung der Buchdruckerkunst am 25. Juli 1840.   Elberfeld, Schlottmann'sche Officin, 1840.
4p.   4to.
Title from Mohr, Jubelfeste.   [2634]

Lindow, O.
Johannes Gutenberg.   Lied.   Componirt von W. Schwarz.   Berlin,
Wolff & Co., 1840.   4to.
Title from Mohr, Jubelfeste.   [2635]

Lippmann, J.
Die Gutenbergfeier in Mainz.   Illustrierte Zeitung, no. 2975,
1900.   [2636]

Lisch, George Christian Friedrich, 1801-1883.
Geschichte der Buchdruckerkunst in Meklenburg bis zum Jahre 1540,
von G. C. F. Lisch ... Mit einem Anhange über die niederdeutsche Bearbeitung des Reineke Voss.   Aus den Jahrbüchern des Vereins für Mek-
lenburgische Geschichte und Alterthumskunde [Jahrg. IV, 1839] besonders abgedruckt.   Mit einer Steindrucktafel.   Schwerin, In Commission in der Stiller'schen Hofbuchhandlung, 1839.   viii p., 1 leaf,
281p.   fold. facsim.   21.5 cm.   [2637]
DLC   ICJ   ICN   Eu-De-BP   Eu-De-LBb   Eu-Fr-PN   Eu-Ge-LB
Eu-Ge-LL1

Lommatzsch, C. A. W.
Festpredigt zum Gedächtniss Johannes des Täufers und Johannes
Gutenbergs, gehalten zu Keilhau und Eichfeld bei Rudolstadt den
28. Junius 1840.   Jena, 1840.   30p.   8vo.   [2638]
Eu-De-LBb

Lorenz, Baron von.
Gedächtnissfeier erschienener Buchdruckerkunst.   Strassburger
Wochenblatt, no. 65, 1840.
Reprinted from Dresdner Zeitung.
Title from Mohr, Jubelfeste.   [2639]

Loterie typographique de Strasbourg.   Circulaire des ouvriers
du 23 août 1840.   Strasbourg, Silbermann, 1840.   1p.   4to.
Title from Mohr, Jubelfeste.   [2640]

Löwe, Karl, 1796-1869.
Gutenberg.   Oratorium von Ludwig Giesebrecht, componirt zur Feier
der Inauguration der Bildsäule Johann Gutenbergs in Mainz.   Opus 55.
Clavier-Auszug.   [Mainz, 184?]   Folio.   [2641]
MB   Eu-De-LBb

Lübecker Festlied, gesungen beim Gutenberg-Mahle am 24. Juni
1840. Lübeck, Rathgens, 1840. 4p. 8vo.
Title from Mohr, Jubelfeste.   [2642]

Luchet, Auguste, 1806-1872.
Récit de l'inauguration de la statue de Gutenberg et des fêtes
données par la ville de Strasbourg les 24, 25 et 26 juin 1840. Par
Auguste Luchet ... Paris, Pagnerre, éditeur, Rue de Seine, 1840.
152p. front. (port.) 13 cm.   [2643]
    MH   Eu-De-LBb

Lücke, Gottfried Christian Friedrich.
Festrede zur vierhundertjährigen Jubelfeyer der Erfindung der
Buchdruckerkunst den 24sten Juni 1840 zu Göttingen in dem grossen
akademischen Hörsaale gehalten. Göttingen, Vandenhoek & Ruprecht,
1840. 16p. 8vo.   [2644]
    Eu-De-LBb   Eu-Ge-LB   Eu-Ge-LSb

Ludewig, Hermann.
Zur Bibliothekonomie. Festgabe zur vierten Säcularfeier der
Erfindung der Buchdruckerkunst von G. H. Gärtner, Buchdruckerei-
Besitzer. Dresden, 1840. xxx, 41p. 8vo.   [2645]
    Eu-Fr-PN   Eu-Ge-LB

Lyser, J. B.
Das Wort. Guttenbergs-Lieder. Leipzig, Sturm & Koppe, 1840.
16p. 8vo.
Title from Mohr, Jubelfeste.   [2646]

Mäder.
Der Segen der Buchdruckerkunst. Strassburg, Berger-Levrault,
1840. 14p. 8vo.
Sermon in the Reformed church, June 21, 1840.   [2647]
    Eu-De-LBb

Mainz. Commission zur Errichtung eines Monuments für Johann
    Gutenberg.
Aufruf um das herannahende Säcularfest der Buchdruckerkunst
durch Errichtung eines Monuments zu ehren ihres Erfinders Joh.
Gensfleisch zum Gutenberg, würdig zu feiern. Mainz, Kupferberg,
1832. 7p. 22 cm.   [2648]
    DLC   ICN   NNC   Eu-Ge-LB

Mainz. Festleitung der Gutenberg-Feier 1900.
Gutenberg-Feier in Mainz 1900. Katalog der typographischen Aus-
stellung. 23. Juni bis 22. Juli. Mainz, Buchdruckerei von H.
Prickarts, 1900. 87p. 20 cm.   [2649]
    ICJ

Mann, Ed.
    Gutenberg. Ein poetisches Gedicht der bestehenden Commission
zur Errichtung des Denkmals gewidmet. Strassburg, Dannbach [1840]
Folio.   [2650]
    Eu-Fr-PN

Marnix, C. H. R.
    Beschrijving van het Gutenberg-Feest te Mentz. Haag, Athenäum,
1837. 8vo.
    Title from van der Linde, Geschichte der Erfindung ...   [2651]

Meisner, Heinrich and Johannes Luther.
    Die Anfänge der Buchdruckerkunst. Fünfhundertjahrfeier des
Geburtstages Gutenbergs. Zeitschrift für Bücherfreunde, vol. 3,
no. 11-12, 1900, p. 409-456.   [2652]

Mel'gunov, N. A.
    Mainzkoe torzhestvo v chest' Gutenberga 15 avgusta 1837. Pere-
vod iz Journal des debats. [n.p., n.d.] 8p. 25 cm.   [2653]
    Eu-Ru-MLe

Melzer, C. Ph.
    Buchdruckerei-Besitzer und Buchhändler in Leipzig. Leipzig,
1840. 4to.
    Title from Mohr, Jubelfeste.   [2654]

Mendelssohn-Bartholdy, Felix.
    Festgesang zur Eröffnung der ersten Tage der vierten Säcularfeier
... auf dem Markte zu Leipzig stattfindenden Feierlichkeiten. Für
Männerchor und Orchester. Klavierauszug. Leipzig, Breitkopf &
Härtel [1840?] 22p. 34 cm.   [2655]
    ICN   Eu-De-LBb

Mercier, M. T.
    Chant séculaire à l'occasion de l'inauguration du monument érigé
le 24 juin 1840, dans la ville de Strasbourg, à la mémoire de Gutenberg, inventeur de l'imprimerie. Paris, Desrez, 1840. 8vo.
    Title from Mohr, Jubelfeste.   [2656]

Meyer, Heinrich, 1812-1863.
    1840. Gutenbergs-Album. Hrsg. von Dr. Heinrich Meyer. Braun-
schweig, J. H. Meyer; Philadelphia, J. G. Wesselhöft; [etc., etc.,
1840] 3 prel. leaves, xxi p., 1 leaf, 348, [4]p. front., 5
plates, 8 port., 4 facsim. 32 cm.
    Also issued the same year in cheaper edition (on small paper,
    and without plates and facsimiles)   [2657]
    DLC   ICJ   MnHi   NNGr   Eu-De-BP   Eu-De-LBb   Eu-Ge-LB
    Eu-Ge-LSb

Meyer, L. E.
Die Buchdruckerkunst in Augsburg bei ihrem Entstehen. Eine
Denkschrift zur Feier des vierten Säkular-Festes der Erfindung
Guttenberg's. Mit breiter Einfassung und Holzschnitten. Augs-
burg, Kollmann, 1840. 88p. plates (1 fold.) 26 cm. [2658]
    NNGr   Eu-De-LBb

Meyer-Köchlin, Val.
Les casques de papier. Couplets dédiés aux ouvriers typographiques. Mulhouse, Bareta, 1840. 2p. 8vo.
    Reprint from Indicateur de Strasbourg, no. 51, 1840.
    Title from Mohr, Jubelfeste. [2659]

Mezger, G. C.
Augsburgs älteste Druckdenkmale und Formschneiderarbeiten ...
nebst einer kurzen Geschichte des Bücherdruckes und Buchhandels
in Augsburg. Von G. C. Mezger ... Augsburg, J. P. Himmer, 1840.
80p. plates (1 fold.) 26 cm. [2660]
    NNGr   Eu-Ge-LB

Milchsack, Gustav, 1850-1919.
    Gutenberg, sein Leben und seine Erfindung. Rede bei der Guten-
bergfeier des Braunschweigischen Buchdrucker-Vereins gehalten von
Gustav Milchsack. Wolfenbuettel, J. Zwissler, 1900. vii, 32p.
24 cm. [2661]
    DLC   ICJ   MH   Eu-Ge-LB

Mohnike, G.
Geschichte der Buchdruckerkunst in Pommern. Stettin, A. F.
Bülow, 1840. vi, 138p. roy. 8vo. [2662]
    Eu-Ge-LB

Mokelott, Alex.
Gutenberg-Salon-Galopp. opus 11. Leipzig, J. Wunder, 1840.
    Title from Mohr, Jubelfeste. [2663]

---- Gutenberg-Salon-Walzer, aufgeführt bei Gelegenheit der
vierten Säcularfeier ... Mit Abbildung des Festsalon. opus 10.
Leipzig, J. Wunder, 1840.
    Title from Mohr, Jubelfeste. [2664]

Monument du Gutenberg, dessiné & gravé sur acier par Ch. A.
Schuler. Strasbourg, 1840. Folio.
    Title from Mohr, Jubelfeste. [2665]

Monument en l'honneur de Gutenberg à Strasbourg. Album
Alsacien, no. 6, 1839, p. 87-92. [2666]

Morrison, Michael A.
   Johann Gutenberg, 1400-1900. Independent, vol. 52, no. 2687,
May 1900, p. 1315-1316.   Same, Scientific American Supplement, vol.
50, July 7, 1900.   [2667]

[Mosche, C.]
   Festhymne zur 400jährigen Gedächtnissfeier Gutenberg's an der
Erfindung der Buchdruckerkunst.   In Musik gesetzt.   Text.   Lübeck,
1840.   4p.   8vo.
   Title from Mohr, Jubelfeste.   [2668]

Moser, K.
   Pinselstriche zum Gesammtbilde des industriellen Umzuges.   25.
Juni 1840.   Indicateur de Strasbourg, no. 53, 1840.   [2669]

Michler, Karl.
   Gutenberg.   Zur vierten Säcularfeier der Buchdruckerkunst.
Berlin, Crantz, 1840.   16p.   8vo.
   Title from Mohr, Jubelfeste.   [2670]

[Müller, A.]
   Gutenberg oder das Fest der Buchdruckerkunst.   Cantate.   Strass-
burg, 1840.   5p.   roy. 8vo.
   Title from Mohr, Jubelfeste.   [2671]

Müller, H.
   Zum Gutenbergsfeste.   Journal für Buchdruckerkunst, no. 1, 1838.
col. 13-14.   [2672]

Müller, J. H.
   Ueber den syrischen Nomenclator des Thomas à Novaria.   Eine Ab-
handlung, der Engelhard-Reyher'schen Buchdruckerei zugeeignet am
Buchdrucker-Jubiläum 1840.   16p.   8vo.
   Title from Mohr, Jubelfeste.   [2673]

Müller, Nikolaus, 1770-1851.
   Beschreibung des Festes dem Andenken der Erfinders der Buchdrucker-
kunst, Johann Gensfleisch zum Gutenberg, gefeiert im Mainz am 4. Okt-
ober 1824, von sämmtlichen Herren, Schriftsetzern, Buchdruckern und
Schriftgiessern daselbst, bei Gelegenheit der Einweihung des dem
grossen Erfinder von der Casino-Gesellschaft im Hofe zum Gutenberg
gesetzten Denksteins.   Aus den Akten zusammengestellt von N. Müller
... Mainz, Florian Kupferberg, 1824.   64p.   fold. plate.   22.5 cm. [2674]
   NN   NNC   Eu-De-LBb   Eu-Fr-PN   Eu-Ge-LB   Eu-Ge-LSb
   Eu-Ge-LP

----   Lied, gesungen am Weihungsfeste: "Dort strahlt uns entgegen
sein hehres Bild."   Mainz, J. Wirth, 1824.   6p.   4to.
   Title from Mohr, Jubelfeste.   [2675]

Müller, Nikolaus, 1770-1851.
   Lied: "Im schönsten Vereine der Freude."   Mainz, Kupferberg,
1824.   4p.   4to.
   Title from Mohr, Jubelfeste.   [2676]

----   Lied: "Mit Gutenberg's Bildniss vertraulich vereint."
Mainz, Druck in Reuling's Officin von Wilh. Seifert, 1824.   4p.
4to.
   Title from Mohr, Jubelfeste.   [2677]

----   Lied zum Geburtsfeste der Buchdruckerkunst.   Stuttgart,
1840.   8vo.
   Title from Mohr, Jubelfeste.   [2678]

----   Liedern an Wiehungsfeste des zu Ehren Gutenberg's errichteten
Denksteins im Hofe zum Gutenberg in Mainz 1824, mit Abbildung des
Denksteins, und eine extra Beilage des Vereinblattes, die Beschreibung der Errichtung des Standbildes Gutenbergs im Garten des Guten-
berg-Hauses 4. October 1827 enthaltend, mit die Reden und Poesien
der Herren Lehne, Schaab, Huguier und Le Roux.   Mainz, 1827.   8vo.
   Title from Bigmore & Wyman.   [2679]

----   "Der Menschheit Genius schuldete den Stempel."   Mainz, Th.
v. Zabern, 1824.   4p.   4to.
   Title from Mohr, Jubelfeste.   [2680]

   Nachrichten über die Gutenberg-Feier in Leipzig.   Hitzig's
Presszeitung, no. 49, 1840, p. 428-432.   [2681]

   Nachruf eines Blinden auf die Feste Gutenbergs in Strassburg.
Indicateur de Strasbourg, no. 53, 1840.
   Signed: F.....z.   [2682]

Naumann, C. J.
   Beschreibung seiner Buchdruckerei.   Leipzig, 1840.   4to.
   Title from Mohr, Jubelfeste.   [2683]

Née de la Rochelle, Jean François, 1751-1838.
   Éloge historique de Jean Gensfleisch dit Guttenberg, premier
inventeur de l'art typographique à Mayence.   Par M. J. F. Née de
la Rochelle ... Paris, D. Colas, 1811.   2 prel. leaves, vi, 158p.
front. (port.)   21.5 cm.   [2684]
   DLC   ICJ   ICN   Eu-Fr-PN   Eu-Ge-LB   Eu-Ge-LP

Neff, P.
   Denkblatt über Johann Gutenberg.   Stuttgart, 1840.
   Title from Mohr, Jubelfeste.   [2685]

Neudecker, Chr. Gottl.
   Ad memoriam artis typographicae ante 400 annos feliciter inventae
pia mente gratoque animo recolendam verba numeris nexae hebraica
scripsit.   Gotha, Engelhard-Reyher'sche Buchdruckerei, 1840.   4p.
4to.
   Title from Mohr, Jubelfeste.   [2686]

   Das Neue Testament.   Deutsch durch Dr. Martin Luther.   Nach der
letzten Ausgabe von 1545.   Leipzig, im Verlag der Buchdrucker-Innung,
1840.   8vo.   [2687]
   Eu-De-LBb

   Das Neue Testament unseres Herrn und Heilandes Jesu Christi, nach
der Uebersetzung Dr. Martin Luthers.   Festausgabe zur Säcularfeier ...
Aus Nonpareilleschrift stereotypirt.   Stuttgart, J. B. Metzler, 1840.
3 leaves, 555p.   16mo.   [2688]
   Eu-De-LBb

   Das Neue Testament unseres Herrn und Heilandes Jesu Christi (und
der Psalter).   Verdeutscht von Dr. Martin Luther.   Buchdrucker-Jubi-
läums-Ausgabe.   Mit Titelstahlstich, Titelvignette, Widmungsblatt,
2 Facsimiles und farbigen Initialen.   Stuttgart, S. G. Liesching,
1840.   7 leaves, 113p., 1 leaf.   4to.   [2689]
   Eu-De-LBb

Neukomm, Sigism.
   Te Deum laudamus.   Composé pour la fête d'inauguration du monu-
ment de Jean Gutenberg à Mayence.   Mayence [1837?]   [2690]
   Eu-De-LBb

   Der Nibelunge Lied, Abdruck der Handschrift des Freiherrn Joseph
von Lassberg.   Mit Holzschn. nach Originalzeichnungen von Ed. Bende-
mann und Jul. Hübner.   Leipzig, Otto und Georg Wigand, 1840.
[404]p.   illus.   31 cm.   [2691]
   ICN   Eu-Ge-LB

[Niemann, H.]
   Gutenberg in seiner Werkstatt.   Lithogr. von L. Zöllner & Schlick.
Erinnerungsblätt an die vierten Säcularfeier ... Leipzig, J. J. Weber,
1840.   44x52 cm.
   Title from Mohr, Jubelfeste.   [2692]

Nies, Friedrich.
   Denkschrift seiner Druckerei und Hieroglyphen und ägyptische
Schriftproben.   Leipzig, 1840.   3 leaves.   4to.
   Title from Mohr, Jubelfeste.   [2693]

Die öffentliche Feier des vierten Säcular-Festes der Erfindung
der Buchdruckerkunst in Berlin, am 25. und 26. September 1840.
Zum Besten der Gutenberg Stiftung.   Berlin, A. W. Hayn, 1841.
136p.   22.5 cm.   [2694]
    NNC   Eu-De-LBb

[Opitz, G.]
    Erinnerungsblatt an die 400jährige Jubelfeier der Erfindung
und Einführung der Buchdruckerkunst. Lithograph.   Leipzig,
Pönicke, 1840.
    Title from Mohr, Jubelfeste.   [2695]

    Ordnung der Liturgie für den Gottesdienst in der Thomaskirche
zur vierten Säcularfeier ... am 24. Juni 1840.   Leipzig, Breitkopf
& Härtel, 1840.   4p.   8vo.
    Title from Mohr, Jubelfeste.   [2696]

    Ordnung der Trinksprüche und Lieder beim Festmahle der Guten-
bergs-Feier zu Erfurt am 27. Juli 1840.   Erfurt, Ohlenroth'sche
Buchdruckerei, 1840.   15p.   8vo.
    Title from Mohr, Jubelfeste.   [2697]

Ortlepp. Ernst.
    Gedicht zum Gutenberg-Fest.   Leipzig, Zirges, 1840.   16p.
8vo.   [2698]
    Eu-De-LBb   Eu-Ge-LSb

Ortlepp, Johann Carl.
    Festgabe für den deutschen Landmann.   Eine Predigt, auf Veran-
lassung der vierhundertjährigen Jubelfeier der Erfindung der Buchdruckerkunst am 2. Sonnt. nach Trin. 1840, in der Kirche zu Blum-
berg bei Trogau gehalten und zum Drucke befördert von J. C. Ortlepp ... Halle, C. A. Kümmel [1840]   16p.   22 cm.   [2699]
    NNC   Eu-De-LBb

Ott-Usteri.
    Eröffnungsrede der Jahresversammlung der Museums-Gesellschaft,
am Jubelfeste der Erfindung der Buchdruckerkunst den 24. Juni 1840.
Nebst dem Verzeichnisse der am Festtage ausgestellten typographischen Merkwürdigkeiten mit erläuternden Bemerkungen von J. Casp.
Orelli.   Zürich, Orell, Füssli & Co., 1840.   40p.   12mo.   [2700]
    Eu-De-LBb   Eu-Ge-LSb

Pall von Pallhausen, Vincenz, 1759-1817.
    Denkmal in Stereotypen den Manen Gutenberg's ... [München,
1805]   [2701]
    Eu-De-BP   Eu-Ge-LB

Pall von Pallhausen, Vincenz, 1759-1817.
Denkmal in Stereotypen den Manen Gutenberg's geweiht von Vincenz
von Pallhausen im Jahre 1805, und zur vierten Säcularfeier der Buchdruckerkunst mit lithographirten Federzeichnungen zu Johannis 1836
hrsg. von Progel. ⌜München, 1836⌝ viii, 16p. 28 cm.   ⌜2702⌝
    ICN

    Pamiatnik Guttenbergu v Frankfurte na Maine.   Illiustratsiia,
vol. 9, no. 208, 1862.   ⌜2703⌝

Pangkoffer, Joseph Anselm and Joseph Rudolph Schuegraf.
Geschichte der Buchdruckerkunst in Regensburg. Mit zwey lith.
Tafeln.   Regensburg, G. J. Mantz, 1840.   vi, ⌜2⌝, 56p.   2 plates.
22 cm.   ⌜2704⌝
    DLC   ICN   Eu-Ge-LB

Paris. Bibliothèque nationale.
A la mémoire de Jean Gutenberg. Hommage de l'Imprimerie nationale
et de la Bibliothèque nationale.   Paris, Imprimerie nationale, 1900.
77p., 16 leaves, ⌜2⌝p. incl. port. 17 plates (facsims.)   42.5 cm.
    Each plate accompanied by leaf with explanatory letterpress.
    Four plates have facsimiles on verso also.
    Preface signed: Leopold Delisle.   ⌜2705⌝
    DLC   ICJ   ICN   NN   Eu-Fr-PN   Eu-Ge-LB   Eu-Ge-LSb   Eu-Ne-GK

Pierer, Heinrich August.
Festgruss zur IV. Säcularfeier der Erfindung der Buchdruckerkunst
am 24. Juni 1840 in gastlichen Leipzig. Dargebracht von der Hofbuchdruckerei in Altenberg.   Altenberg, 1840. 4 leaves. 4to.   ⌜2706⌝
    Eu-De-LBb   Eu-Ge-LSb

Pischon, Friedrich August.
Kurze Geschichte der Erfindung der Buchdruckerkunst und ihres
segensreichen Einflusses, Einladung zur bevorstehenden vierhundertjährigen Gedächtnisfeier Gutenbergs und der Buchdruckerkunst am 24.
Juni 1840 zunächst für die Schulen.   Berlin, C. A. Wolff, 1840.
16p. plates. 19 cm.   ⌜2707⌝
    NNGr   Eu-De-LBb   Eu-Fr-PN   Eu-Ge-LB

————   Von dem Einflusse der Erfindung der Buchdruckerkunst auf die
Verbreitung des göttlichen Wortes.   Berlin, 1840. 19p. 4to.
    Program of the Preussische Haupt-Bibelgesellschaft for 1840.   ⌜2708⌝
    Eu-De-LBb   Eu-Ge-LB

Preusker, Karl, 1786-1871.
Gutenberg und Franklin. Eine Festgabe zum vierten Jubiläum der
Erfindung der Buchdruckerkunst; zugleich mit Antrag zur Gründung von
Stadt- und Dorf-Bibliotheken. Allen Buchdruckern, Buchhändlern, Ge-
lehrten, überhaupt allen deutschen Männern welche an Fortschreitender

Menschheits-Bildung regen Antheil nehmen gewidmet von Karl Preusker,
Konigl. Sächs. Rentamtmann zu Grossenhayn. Ritter des K. S. Civil-
Verdienstordens.   Leipzig, 1840.   Verlag von Heinrich Weinedel.
1 prel. leaf, 64p.   20 cm.   [2709]
   ICN   MB   NNGr   Eu-De-LBb   Eu-Fr-PN   Eu-Ge-LSb

Priem, Johann Paul.
   Zum Gutenbergfeste.   (In his Festliche und heitere Stunden.
Dramatische Spiele und Gedichte.   Nürnberg, 1865)   [2710]
   Eu-Ge-LB

   Programm am 24., 25., 26. Juni.   Hannover, Druck von Gebr.
Jänecke, 27. Mai 1840.
   Title from Mohr, Jubelfeste.   [2711]

   Programm, betreffend die Festfeier am Johannis-Feiertage.   24.
Juni 1840.   Reutlingen, 1840.   1p.   Folio.   [2712]
   Eu-Ge-LSb

   Programm der Gutenberg-Feier.   Frankfurt a. M., 1840.
   Title from Mohr, Jubelfeste.
   Reprinted in Börsenblatt für den Deutschen Buchhandel, no. 221,
1840.   [2713]

   Programm der vierten Säcularfeier der Erfindung der Buchdruckerkunst.   Erfurt [Hennings u. Hopf] 1840.   11p.   22 cm.   [2714]
   NNC

   Programm der vierten Säcularfeier der Erfindung der Buchdruckerkunst.   Leipzig [Breitkopf] 1840.   11p.   27.5 cm.   [2715]
   NNC   Eu-Ge-LSb

   Programm der vierten Säcularfeier der Erfindung der Buchdruckerkunst.   Leipzig, Glück, 1840.   16p.   17 cm.   [2716]
   NNGr

   Programm des Zuges der Darmstädter Buchdruckerei-Genossen zur
Einweihung des Denkmals.   [n.p., n.d.]   2p.   4to.
   Title from Mohr, Jubelfeste.   [2717]

   Programm.   Grosses Tableau in Farbendruck.   Hannover, Druck von
Gebr. Jänecke, 1840.
   Title from Mohr, Jubelfeste.   [2718]

   Programm.   Inauguration des Monuments für Johann Gutenberg in
Mainz, 14., 15. und 16. Juni 1837.   Journal für Buchdruckerkunst,
no. 6, 1837, col. 87-90.   [2719]
   Also reprint.

Programm, mittelst dessen zur Begehung der Säcularfeier der Buchdruckerkunst durch die Oberlausitzische Gesellschaft der Wissenschaft
eingeladen wird. Gorlitz, 1840. 15p. 4to.
Title from Mohr, Jubelfeste.   [2720]

Programm vom Könige genehmigtes, zur vierten Säcularfeier der
Erfindung der Buchdruckerkunst am 28. und 29. August 1840. Berlin,
Hayn, 1840. 7p. 8vo.
Title from Mohr, Jubelfeste.   [2721]

Programm zu der Feier des 400jährigen Jubiläums der Erfindung der
Buchdruckerkunst am 24. Juni 1840. Plauen, 1840. 2p. 4to.
Title from Mohr, Jubelfeste.   [2722]

Programm zum 24. und 25. Juni 1840. Veröffentlicht von F. W.
Gubitz, J. Petsch, Lehmann, F. H. v. d. Hagen und C. F. Rundenhagen.
Berlin, 1840. 4to.
Title from Mohr, Jubelfeste.   [2723]

Programm zur Begehung der vierten Säcularfeier der Erfindung der
Buchdruckerkunst am 24. und 25. Juni. Mit farbiger Einfassung.
Hannover, Druck von Gebr. Jänecke, 4. April 1840.
Title from Mohr, Jubelfeste.   [2724]

Programm zur Begehung der vierten Säcularfeier der Erfindung der
Buchdruckerkunst, 23., 24. Juni 1840. Bremen, Druck von C. Schüne-
mann, 1840. 1 leaf. Folio.
Title from Mohr, Jubelfeste.   [2725]

Programm zur vierten Säcularfeier ... am 24. und 25. Juni 1840.
Stuttgart, Das Comité, 13. März 1840. 4p. roy. 4to.
Title from Mohr, Jubelfeste.   [2726]

Programm zur vierten Säcularfeier der Erfindung der Buchdruckerkunst in Berlin am 28. und 29. September 1840. [Berlin, 1840]
6p. 8vo.
Title from Mohr, Jubelfeste.   [2727]

Programme des fêtes, qui auront lieu à Strasbourg pour l'inauguration de la statue de Gutenberg et de la célébration du IV. anniversaire seculaire de l'invention de l'imprimerie. Strasbourg,
Silbermann, 1840. 4p. 4to.   [2728]
    Eu-Ge-LSb

Puhlmann.
Beschreibung des Jubelfestes ... in der Deckerschen Officin in
Potsdam, am 25. und 26. September 1840. Potsdam, 1840.
Title from Mohr, Jubelfeste.   [2729]

Quatrième fête séculaire de l'invention de l'imprimerie.
Revue d'Alsace, 2d ser., vol. 2, Feb. 1836.   [2730]

Rede gehalten auf dem grünen Berg, an die vereinigten Buchdruckergehilfen, von einem Mitgliede der Gesellschaft, am 24.
Juli 1840.   Wochentl. Mittheilungen, vol. 1, July 1840.   [2731]

Reden am Gutenbergsfest zu Arolsen, 24. Juni 1840.   Arolsen,
Speyer, 1840.   35p.   20.5 cm.   [2732]
    NNC   Eu-De-LBb

Redslob, H.
    Cantate en l'honneur de Gutenberg.   Musique de Ph. Hoerter de
Strasbourg.   (In Réunion musicale Alsacienne.   Souvenir des fêtes
de 1836.   Strasbourg, 1836.   p. 45-47)
    Title from Bigmore & Wyman.   [2733]

Rée, Paul Johannes.
    Festrede zur Feier der 450jährigen Erfindung der Buchdrucker-
kunst. Nürnberg, Johannisfest 1890.   Nürnberg, G. P. J. Bieling-
Dietz, 1890.   [2734]
    Eu-Ge-LB

Reiss, Eduard.
    Erstes Gutenbergfest 1837.   (In his Mainzer Silhouetten und
Genrebilder. Ein Panorama des heutigen Mainz.   Mainz, 1841.
p. 1-12)
    Title from Mohr, Jubelfeste.   [2735]

----   Zweites Gutenbergfest 1840.   (In his Mainzer Silhouetten
und Genrebilder ... Mainz, 1841.   p. 13-27)   [2736]

Reissinger, C. G.
    Deutsches Lied zur vierten Säcularfeier des Gutenberg-Festes in
Musik gesetzt, gedichtet von Richard Teubner.   Leipzig, 1840. 4to.
    Title from Mohr, Jubelfeste.   [2737]

Réunion musicale alsacienne.   Concerts alsaciens par L. Jolly.
Bal par Ed. Barrois.   Revue d'Alsace, 2d ser., vol. 1, 1836,
p. 318-337.   [2738]

Réunion musicale alsacienne.   Fêtes en l'honneur de Gutenberg
des 4, 5 et 6 avril 1836.   Courrier du Bas-Rhin, no. 85-88, 1836. [2739]

Réunion musicale alsacienne.   Souvenir des fêtes de l'année
1836.   Strasbourg, 1836.
    p. 45-47: Cantate en l'honneur de Gutenberg.   Libretto by
    H. Redslob, music by Ph. Hoerter.
    Title from Mohr, Jubelfeste.   [2740]

Reuss.
Würzburgs erste Drucke.   (1497-1500)   Serapeum, vol. 1, 1840.
p. 97-104.   [2741]

Rhenus. Sonntagsblatt für Literatur, Kunst und Bürgerleben.
The numbers from Oct. 2 to Oct. 24, 1824, contain all articles
concerning the celebration of the unveiling of the monument in
the Gutenberg-Hof and a picture of the monument.
Title from Mohr, Jubelfeste.   [2742]

Richter, E. F.
"Heilig und hehr ist der Name des Herrn." Hymne für Chor und
Orchester, aufgeführt am 24. Juni 1840 bei der kirchlichen Feier
der Erfindung der Buchdruckerkunst.   Klavier-Auszug.   Leipzig,
Breitkopf & Härtel, 1840.   roy. 4to.   [2743]
    Eu-De-LBb

Richter, Johann Andreas Leberecht, b. 1772-
Festgabe.   Warum sollte die Feier der Erfindung der Buchdruckerkunst eine allgemeine für die gänze Welt sein?   Quedlinburg, Basse,
1840.   iv, 48p.   20.5 cm.   [2744]
    NNGr   Eu-De-LBb   Eu-Fr-PN

Ritschel von Hartenbach, J.
Neues System geograph. Charten zugleich mit ihrem Colorit auf der
Buchdruckerpresse herzustellen.   Bei Gelegenheit der vierten Säcularfeier ... herausgegeben.   Leipzig, Wunder, 1840.   xvi, 80p.
20.5 cm.   [2745]
    NNGr   Eu-Ge-LB

Rödiger, Christian Friedrich.
Fünf Gesänge betreffend die vierten Secularfeier zu Leipzig.   Im
October 1839.   Leipzig, Breitkopf & Härtel [1839]   25p.   roy.
8vo.   [2746]
    Eu-De-LBb

----   Gesang beim Zusammenlegen der Facklein auf dem Marktplatze
als Beschluss der vierten Säcularfeier ... den 26. Juni 1840. Leipzig,
Breitkopf & Härtel, 1840.   4p.   8vo.
Title from Mohr, Jubelfeste.   [2747]

Röhr, Johann Friedrich.
Predigt am Johannis-Feste 1840 als am vierten hundertjährigen
Jubelfests der Buchdruckerkunst in der Haupt- und Stadt-Kirche zu
Weimar.   (In Weimar's Album zur vierten Säcularfeier ... Weimar,
Albrecht, 1840.   p. 325-342)   [2748]
    ICN   IEN   NNC   NjP   Eu-De-LBb   Eu-Ge-LB   Eu-Ge-LSb
    Eu-Ne-AVb

Rollé, Ad.
    Gutenberg. Gedicht. Strassburg, Dannbach, 1840. 1p. 8vo.
    Title from Mohr, Jubelfeste.   [2749]

Rückmann, Fr.
    Vierte Säcularfeier ... Leipzig, 1840. 2 leaves. roy. 4to.
    Title from Mohr, Jubelfeste.   [2750]

Rudolph, Hermann.
    Kurze Geschichte der Erfindung der Buchdruckerkunst im Jahre 1440.
Eine Vorbereitungsschrift auf die vierte Säcularfeier dieser Erfindung im Jahre 1840, für Schule und Haus ... Meissen, Klinkicht [1840]
cover-title, 2 prel. leaves, iv, 66p. 17 cm.   [2751]
    ICJ   ICN   Eu-De-LBb   Eu-Ge-LSb

    Rundgesang beim Banket als alsatischen Singvereins bei der vierten
Gedächtnissfeier Gutenberg's zu Strassburg den 3. April 1836. "Wir
sehen am Rhein nach langer Zeit uns wieder." [Strassburg, 1836]
    Title from Mohr, Jubelfeste.   [2752]

    Rundgesang zur Jubelfeier der 400jährigen Erfindung der Buch-
druckerkunst am 21. Juni 1840.   Dresden, C. H. Gärtner, 1840.
4p. 8vo.
    Title from Mohr, Jubelfeste.   [2753]

Rungenhagen, C. F.
    Die beiden Sterne von August Zeune, zur vierten Säcularfeier der
Erfindung der Buchdruckerkunst am 25. September 1840 in Musik gesetzt. Partitur. Berlin, 1840. 5p. 4to.
    Title from Mohr, Jubelfeste.   [2754]

Sabel, J. Ch.
    Predigt bei der Feier des Buchdrucker-Jubiläums in Heidelberg,
gehalten in der Kirche zu St. Peter am 24. Juni 1840. Heidelberg,
Winter, 1840. 8vo.
    Title from Mohr, Jubelfeste.   [2755]

Saphir, Moritz Gottlieb, 1795-1858.
    Nachfeier der Nachdrucker zum Guttenbergfeste. Eine dramatisch-
episch-drastisch-komisch-literarisch-typographische Jubel- und Tri-
umphscene in abgerissenen Bildern ... Aus Saphir's fliegendem Album ...
Leipzig, 1846. 8vo.   [2756]
    Eu-De-LBb   Eu-Ge-LB

---- Nachfest der Nachdrucker zum Gutenbergfeste. (In Funck, E.
Buch deutscher Parodieen und Travestieen. Erlangen, 1840-1841.
vol. 2, p. 275, 313-316)   [2757]
    RPB

Sarnow, Emil.
Die typographische Ausstellung zur Gutenbergfeier in Mainz.
Zentralblatt für Bibliothekswesen, vol. 27, 1900, p. 425-429.   [2758]

Schaab, Carl Anton, 1767-1835.
Das Jahr 1436. Erfindungsjahr der Buchdruckerkunst und die Bildung
einer Jury über das Säcularjahr. Mainz, 1837. 16p. 8vo.
Title from Mohr, Jubelfeste.   [2759]

Schäfer, Johann Wilhelm, 1809-1880.
Historischer Bericht von der Erfindung, Verbreitung und Vervollkommnung der Buchdruckerkunst. Eine Festgabe zur diesjährigen vierten Säcularfeier, von Dr. Johann Wilhelm Schaefer. Bremen, Carl Schünemann,
1840. 2 prel. leaves, [vii]-viii, 96p. front. 19.5 cm.   [2760]
NNC NNGr Eu-De-LBb Eu-Ge-LB Eu-Ge-LE

Schäffer, H.
Johann Gensfleisch von Gutenberg. Zur vierten Säcularfeier am
24. Juni 1840. Berlin, Gropius, 1840.
Title from Mohr, Jubelfeste.   [2761]

Scheffer, H.
Festcantate, gedichtet von Freudentheil. Hamburg, 1840. 4to.
Title from Mohr, Jubelfeste.   [2762]

Scherzer, Karl von, 1821-1903.
Die Buchdruckerkunst und der Kulturfortschritt der Menschheit.
Berlin, 1882. (Vorträge und Abhandlungen herausgegeben von der
Volkswirtschaftlichen Gesellschaft, no. 31)   [2763]
DLC Eu-De-BP

Schlegel.
Geschichte Gutenberg's und seiner grossen Erfindung, für das
deutsche Volk bearbeitet. Leipzig, R. Friese, 1840. 40p. 16mo.   [2764]
Eu-De-LBb Eu-Ge-LB

Schlinck, Philipp Franz.
Hymne, gedichtet zum Gutenberg-Feste in Mainz. Mainz, 1837.
Title from Mohr, Jubelfeste.
Reprinted in Journal für Buchdruckerkunst, no. 6, 1837.   [2765]

Schlussgesang bei der Erinnerungsfeier des Gutenberg-Festes.
Veranstaltet am 26. Juni 1841 in den Räumen des Leipziger Schützen-
hauses. Leipzig [1841] 1p. 8vo.
Title from Mohr, Jubelfeste.   [2766]

Schlussgesang zum Buchdrucker-Jubelfestmahle in Leipzig. Am 24.
Junius 1840. Von einem Fest- und Kunstgenossen aus Thüringen.
Leipzig, 1840. 1p. roy. 8vo.
Title from Mohr, Jubelfeste.   [2767]

Schmaltz, Johann Carl Stephan, 1810-1843.
   Aufforderung zur Gründung und Vermehrung von öffentlichen Bücher-
Sammlungen für Volksschulen ... Als Denkmal der 400jährigen Denkfeier
der Erfindung der Buchdruckerkunst.   Leipzig [1840]   10p.
20.5 cm.   [2768]
   NNGr

---- Das Jubiläum der Buchdruckerkunst im Jahre 1840!   Nebst
geschichtlichen Nachrichten über die Jubelfeiern in den Jahren
1540, 1640 und 1740, und Ankündigung eines Lexikon's sammtlicher
Buchhändler und Buchdrucker, von Erfindung der Buchdruckerkunst
an.   Von J. C. St. Schmaltz.   Quedlinburg und Leipzig, G. Basse,
1836.   iv, 35p.   22.5 cm.
   Argument in favor of the celebration of the fourth centenary
   of the invention of printing in 1840 as opposed to 1836.   [2769]
   DLC   MH   Eu-De-LBb   Eu-Ge-LB   Eu-Ne-AVb

Schmidt, Charles Guillaume Adolphe, 1812-1895.
   Plaintes d'un laïque allemand du XIV siècle sur la décadence de
la chrétienté.   Opuscule publié pour la première fois à l'occasion
du IV. anniversaire de l'invention de l'imprimerie, d'après un manuscrit de la Bibliothèque de Strasbourg.   Strasbourg, Schmidt &
Grucker, 1840.   15p.   8vo.   [2770]
   Eu-De-LBb

Schmidt, G.
   Nachhall des vierten Gutenberg-Jubels in Sachsen.   Gedicht.
(In his Musenstunden.   Leipzig, 1839)   [2771]
   Eu-De-LBb

Schmitz, J. P.
   Sonetten-Alphabet.   Huldigung dem Johann Gutenberg bei der feier-
lichen Inauguration seines Denkmals zu Mainz am 14. August 1837.
Bingen, 1837.   24p.   8vo.   [2772]
   Eu-De-LBb   Eu-Ne-AVb

Schneider, A.
   J. Gutenberg.   Am Fusse des Monumentes für Johann Gutenberg, bei
der Inauguration desselben in Stahl geschnitten.   Mainz, 14.
August 1837.
   Title from Mohr, Jubelfeste.   [2773]

Schneider, Friedrich, ed.
   Gedenkblätter zur Gutenbergfeier am 50. Jahrestage der Errichtung des Gutenbergdenkmals zu Mainz 14. Aug. 1837, herausgegeben von
den vereinigten Mainzer Buchdruckern und Buchhaendlern 1887.   [Mainz,
1887]   4to.   [2774]
   Eu-Ge-LB

Schreiber, Johann Heinrich.
Leistungen der Universität und Stadt Freiburg im Breisgau für
Bücher und Landkartendruck. Festrede gehalten bei der vierten
Säcularfeier der Typographie am 24. Juni 1840. Freiburg im Breis-
gau, Emmerling, 1840. 28p. 8vo.   [2775]
    Eu-De-LBb   Eu-Ge-LB

    Schriftproben der Hofbuchdruckerei von C. Macklot. Ausgegeben
24. Juni 1840. Carlsruhe, 1840. roy. 8vo.
    Title from Mohr, Jubelfeste.   [2776]

    Schriftproben der Schriftschneiderei, Schriftgiesserei, Stereo-
typengiesserei und der Buchdruckerei von Fr. B. Culemann & Sohn.
Junius 1840. Hannover, 1840.
    Title from Mohr, Jubelfeste.   [2777]

Schröder, W.
    Album des Gutenberg-Festes zu Hannover im Jahre 1840. Heraus-
gegeben von den Hofbuchdruckern Gebr. Jänecke. Hannover, Hahn,
1840. 6 prel. leaves, 108p. plates (1 col.) 21 cm.   [2778]
    NNGr   Eu-De-LBb   Eu-Ge-LSb

Schubert, F. L.
    Marsch zum Festzuge der vierten Säcularfeier der Erfindung der
Buchdruckerkunst. Für Pianoforte zu zwei und vier Händen. Leipzig,
Breitkopf & Härtel, 1840.
    Title from Mohr, Jubelfeste.   [2779]

Schuderoff, Jon.
    Vier Predigten von Gutenberg bis zum Amtsjubelfeste 1840. Neu-
stadt a.d.Orla, Wagner, 1841. x, 48p. 8vo.
    Title from Mohr, Jubelfeste.   [2780]

Schulz, Otto August, 1803-1860.
    Gutenberg, oder Geschichte der Buchdruckerkunst von ihrem Ursprung
bis zur Gegenwart. Eine Festgabe für jeden Gebildeten zur vierten
Saecularfeier des Typendrucks. Mit 8 Holzstichen. Leipzig, Schultz
und Thomas, 1840. iv, 123, [1]p. incl. plates. front. (port.)
3 fold. plates. 23 cm.   [2781]
    DLC   ICJ   ICN   MH   NNC   NNGr   Eu-De-BP   Eu-De-LBb
    Eu-Ge-LB   Eu-Ge-LSb

Schulze, Christian Ferdinand.
    Wechselwirkung zwischen der Buchdruckerkunst und der Fortbildung
der Menschheit. Eine Rede am Jubelfeste der Erfindung der Buchdruckerkunst den 24. Juni 1840 gehalten ... von Christian Ferdinand
Schulze ... Gotha, Engelhard-Reyhersch [1840] 18p. 22 cm.   [2782]
    NNC   Eu-De-LBb

Schumacher, A.
   Das Gutenbergs-Fest in Mainz.   Lustspiel in zwei Aufzügen.
Mannheim, 1837.   60p.   8vo.   [2783]
   Eu-De-LBb

Schuster, Anton.
   Die Erfindung der Buchdruckerkunst und deren Verbreitung in Bam-
berg.   Bamberg, 1890.   [2784]
   NNGr

Schwabe, Carl Ludwig, 1779-1851.
   Die Erfindung der Buchdruckerkunst und ihre Folgen.   Ein Vor-
breitungsschrift zur vierten Säkularfeier.   Von C. L. Schwabe,
Pastor in Kaditz bei Dresden.   Leipzig, George Wigand, 1840.
118p.   17.5 cm.   [2785]
   NN   NNC   Eu-De-LBb   Eu-Ge-LB   Eu-Ge-LSb

Schwarz, J. C. E.
   Predigt zum Gedächtniss der Erfindung der Buchdruckerkunst am
ersten Sonntage nach Trinitatis, in der Stadkirche zu Jena, gehalten
von Dr. J. C. E. Schwarz.   Jena, Friedrich Frommann, 1840.   23p.
22.5 cm.   [2786]
   NNC   Eu-De-LBb

Schwerdt, Heinrich.
   Festpredigt zur 400jährigen Jubelfeier der Buchdruckerkunst am
Johannistage 1840 über Luc I. 57-80 gehalten in Neukirchen bei
Eisenach.   Neukirchen, 1840.
   Title from Mohr, Jubelfeste.
   Reprinted in Sonntagsfeier (Darmstadt), no. 37, 1840.   [2787]

Schwetschke, Karl Gustav, 1804-1881.
   Vorakademische Buchdruckergeschichte der Stadt Halle.   Eine
Festschrift.   Mit einem Anhänge: I. Ehrenrettung des sächsischen
Merseburg, als des Druckorts "Marsipolis" und "Merssborg" vom 1473,
und mithin als der ältesten norddeutschen Druckstäte.   II. Supple-
mentarisches zu Hain, Ebert, Schaab und Wetter, und 2 Tafeln Abbildun-
gen.   Halle, Gebauersche Buchdruckerei, 1840.   viii, 126p.   [2788]
   DLC   ICJ   MB   Eu-De-LBb   Eu-Ge-LB

Seebode, Godofred.
   Michael Rellog spelis issintokoi phisikon phitimaton.   Quibus
nunc primum editis memoriam artis typographicae ante hoc quadringentos
annos feliciter inventae in ill. Gymnasio Gothano grate ac pie con-
celebrandem indicit etc.   Gotha, Litt. Engelhardo-Reyheriano, 1840.
8p.   4to.
   Title from Mohr, Jubelfeste.   [2789]

[Seyffarth, Gustav]
Unumstösslicher Beweis, dass im Jahre 3446 vor Christus am 7.
September die Sündfluth geendet habe und die Alphabete aller Völker
erfunden worden seien. Ein Beitrag zur Kirchengeschichte des alten
Testamentes und zur vierten Säcularfeier des Typendruckes. Leipzig,
Schulz & Thomas, 1840. 16p. 8vo.   [2790]
    Eu-De-LBb

Silbermann, Gustave, 1801-1876.
    Album typographique, publié à l'occasion de la quatrième fête
séculaire de l'invention de l'imprimerie, par G. Silbermann, imprimeur à Strasbourg.   Strasbourg, Impr. de G. Silbermann, 1840.
4 leaves.   36 plates (part col., incl. ports., coat of arms)
34.5x26 cm.
    Engraved throughout.
    One of the plates is accompanied by guard-sheet with descriptive
    letterpress.   [2791]
    DLC   MB   NjP   Eu-De-LBb   Eu-Ge-LB   Eu-Sz-BeG

----   Célébration de la fête séculaire de l'invention de l'imprimerie dans les siècles antérieures. Revue d'Alsace, 2d ser., vol.
1, 1835, p. 421-428.   [2792]

----   Quatrième fête séculaire de l'invention de l'imprimerie.
Revue d'Alsace, 2d ser., vol. 1, 1835, p. 187-190.   [2793]

----   Quatrième fête séculaire de l'invention de l'imprimerie
célébrée à Mayence. Revue d'Alsace, 2d ser., vol. 3, 1837. p. 344-
359.   [2794]

Sittenfeld, Julius, firm, printers.
    Beschreibung des vierten Säcularfestes der Erfindung der Buch-
druckerkunst, gefeiert in der Officin von Julius Sittenfeld, Berlin,
28. Juni 1840.   Berlin, 1840. 20p. 21 cm.   [2795]
    NNC   NNGr   Eu-De-LBb

Soldau, Gustav Theophile.
    Artis typographicae, a Joanne de Gutenberg inventae, sacra saecu-
laria facientibus statuamque aheneam, aere per tota, Europam collato,
inventori ponentibus, pie gratulantur.   Gissae, 1837. 4p. 4to.
    Title from Mohr, Jubelfeste.   [2796]

---- ----   [Metrical version by H. Hoffman]   (In Gedenkbuch an
die festlichen Tage ... Mainz, 1837)   [2797]
    NN   NNC

Soltwedel, Alex.
    Zum Gutenbergs-Jubiläum. Gutenberg an gewisse Literaten.   Parodie
von Schiller's Kapuzinerpredigt.   (In Funck, E. Buch deutscher Parodieen und Travestieen. Erlangen, 1840-1841. vol. 2, p. 308-312)   [2798]
    RPB

[Sommer, F. L.]
    Beschreibung des Jubelfestes... in der Officin in Potsdam am 25.
und 26. September 1840.   Mit Gutenbergs Portrait.   Potsdam, 1840.
24 leaves.   8vo.   [2799]
    Eu-De-LBb

Sommer, Ludwig.
    Chronologisch-historischer Wandkalender auf das Jahr 1700-2000
der christlichen Zeitrechnung.   Theoret.-prakt. Gedenkblatt zur
vierten Säcularfeier der Erfindung der Buchdruckerkunst.   Grosses
Tableau.   Berlin, 1840.   8p.   4to.
    Title from Mohr, Jubelfeste.   [2800]

    Special-Programm für die Jubelfeier der Erfindung der Buchdrucker-
kunst in St. Gallen.   Am Johannistage den 24. Juni 1840.   St. Gallen,
1840.   2p.   4to.
    Title from Mohr, Jubelfeste.   [2801]

Stadelmann, Johann Christian Friedrich.
    Festrede zur vierten Säcularfeier der Erfindung der Buchdrucker-
kunst, in dem Herzogl. Gymnasium zu Dessau am 29. Juni 1840 gehalten.
Dessau, Neubürger, 1840.   16p.   8vo.   [2802]
    Eu-De-LBb

----   Memoriam Joannis Gutenbergii artis typographicae inventoris
inter solemnia huius artis saecularia in Germania nunc quartum instaurata recolit eamque in ducali gymnasio Dessaviensi ... a. d. III.
Calendas Quintiles anni MDCCCXL celebrandum ... indicit.   Dessaviae,
1840.   Folio.   [2803]
    Eu-De-LBb

Stäger, Friedrich.
    Nacht und Morgenroth oder Guttenberg's gefeiert im vierten Jubel-
jahr der Buchdruckerkunst zu Halle an der Saale.   Halle a.d.S.,
1840.   28p.   8vo.   [2804]
    Eu-De-LBb

Stallbaum.
    De usu orationis ... mirifice aucto et amplificate.   Leipzig,
1840.   4to.
    Gymnas.-Programm zum Buchdrucker-Jubiläum.
    Title from Mohr, Jubelfeste.   [2805]

Starklof, L.
    Drei Tage in Mainz am Gutenbergfeste (14.,15. August 1837); eine
Skizze.   Mainz, 1837.   83p.   8vo.   [2806]

[Steffenhagen, Emil Julius Hugo] 1838-
    Zur Erinnerung an die Gutenberg-Ausstellung in Kiel.   Kiel, Druck
von Vollbehr & Riepen, 1900.   34p.   23 cm.   [2807]
    ICJ   MH

Steinhausen, Georg.
    Kulturgeschichtliche Bedeutung der Buchdruckerkunst.   Jugend,
part 1, no. 26, 1900, p. 430-433.   [2808]

    Stimmen alsatischer Sänger beim Gutenbergsfeste. (24., 25. und
26. Juni 1840)   [Strassburg, Ph. H. Dannbach, 1840]   35p.   21 cm. [2809]
    MB   NNC   Eu-De-LBb

Stöber, August.
    Die Erfindung der Buchdruckerkunst.   Ein Gespräch der elsässischen
Schuljugend gewidmet.   Strassburg, G. L. Schuler, 1840.   16p. 8vo. [2810]
    Eu-De-LBb   Eu-Ge-LSb

---- Gutenberg.   Toast.   Strassburg, G. L. Schuler, 1840.   1p.
4to.
    Title from Mohr, Jubelfeste.   [2811]

Stockmar & Wagner, firm, printers.
    Schatten und Licht.   Eine Festgabe zur vierten Säcularfeier der
Erfindung der Buchdruckerkunst am Johannistage 1840 zu Frankfurt a.M.
Dargebracht von Stockmar & Wagner, Buchdruckereibesitzer.   Frankfurt
am Main, Schmerder, 1840.   30p.   4to.   [2812]
    Eu-De-LBb   Eu-Sz-BeG

Stockmeyer, Immanuel, 1814-1895.
    Beiträge zur Baler Buchdruckergeschichte.   Von Immanuel Stock-
meyer und Balthasar Reber.   Zur Feier des Johannistages MDCCCXL.
Herausgegeben von der Historischen Gesellschaft zu Basel.   Basel,
Druck und Verlag der Schweighauserischen Buchhandlung, 1840.   viii p.,
1 leaf, 158p.   illus., fold. geneal. tab.   26 cm.
    Preface signed: Wilh. Wackernagel, Schreiber der Historischen
    Gesellschaft.
    "Neue Beiträge", by Dr. Streuber, appeared in the society's
    "Beiträge zur vaterländischen Geschichte", Basel, 1846, vol. 3,
    p. 65-124.   [2813]
    DLC   NN   NNGr   Eu-De-LBb   Eu-Ge-LB

Strassburg.
    Relation complète des fêtes de Gutenberg, célébrées à Strasbourg,
les 24, 25 et 26 juin 1840 ... Strasbourg, E. Simon, 1841.   2 prel.
leaves, 172p.   front., illus.   22 cm.
    p. 168-172: Publications relatives à la fête séculaire de l'in-
    vention de l'imprimerie célébrée en 1840.   [2814]
    DLC   MH   Eu-De-LBb   Eu-Ge-LSb

Strassburg.   Strassburger Industrie-Schule.
    Gutenberg, Erfinder der Buchdruckerkunst.   Eine historische
Skizze mit mehreren Zeichnungen und Facsimile autographisch ausge-
fuhrt von den Zoglingen der Strassburger Industrie-Schule.   1840.
26p.   22.5 cm.
    ICN   Eu-De-LBb   Eu-Ge-LSb   Eu-Ne-AVb   [2815]

Stückrad, Georg.
    Programm für das Gutenbergs-Jubiläum des 19. Jahrhunderts.
Offenbach, C. Washterschauser, 1837.   viii, 197p.   18.5 cm.   [2816]
    ICN   ICU   NNC   Eu-De-LBb   Eu-Ge-LSb

Sutter, Conrad, 1856-1927.
    Gutenberg-Feier Mainz 1900.   Orfizielle Darstellung des histori-
schen Festzuges nach den original Entwürfen von Conrad Sutter.   Verlag von L. Wilckens, Mainz [1900]   1 prel. leaf, [18] col. plates,
1 leaf.   20x29 cm.   [2817]
    ICN   MB   MH   NN   Eu-Ge-LB

    Tafel-Lied, gesungen zur vierten Säcularfeier ... auf dem Gröditz-
berge am St. Johannistage 1840.   Sorau, Rauert'sche Buchdruckerei,
1840.   4p.   8vo.
    Title from Mohr, Jubelfeste.   [2818]

    Tafellied.   Zur 400jährigen Jubelfeier der Buchdruckerkunst.
Elberfeld, Lucas, 1840.   4p.   8vo.
    Title from Mohr, Jubelfeste.   [2819]

    Tafellieder bei dem Festmahle zur vierten Säcularfeier der Erfin-
dung der Buchdruckerkunst am 25. September 1840.   Berlin, 1840.
16p.   8vo.
    Title from Mohr, Jubelfeste.   [2820]

    Tafellieder zur vierten Säcularfeier der Erfindung der Buchdrucker-
kunst in Mainz, geweiht dem Gastmahle im Hof zum Gutenberg (Casino)
am St. Johannistag den 24. Juni von N. M.   Mainz, Seifert'sche
Buchdruckerei, 1840.   8p.   8vo.
    Title from Mohr, Jubelfeste   [2821]

    Tafel-Lieder zur vierten Secularfeier der Erfindung der Buch-
druckerkunst.   24. Juni 1840.   [Rudolstadt, 1840]   8p.   8vo.
    Title from Mohr, Jubelfeste.   [2822]

Taubert, W.
    Gutenberg-Lieder, op. 51.   Berlin, 1840.   4to.   [2823]
    Eu-De-LBb

[Teubner, Richard]
    Deutsches Lied zur vierten Säcularfeier des Gutenberg-Festes.   In
Musik gesetzt von C. G. Reissinger.   Für eine Stimme und vierstimmig.
Leipzig, B. G. Teubner, 1840.   roy. 4to.
    Title from Mohr, Jubelfeste.   [2824]

    Text zum Finale der Jubel-Ouverture beim Gutenberg-Feste den 21.
Juni 1840.   Dresden, E. Blochmann, 1840.   4p.   8vo.
    Title from Mohr, Jubelfeste.   [2825]

Text zur Musik in der Kreuzkirche bei der vierten Säcularfeier
des Gutenberg-Festes am 21. Juni 1840. [Dresden, 1840] 7p. 8vo.
Te Deum laudamus by A. Romberg, translation by C. A. H. Clodius.
Title from Mohr, Jubelfeste.   [2826]

Texte zur Musikaufführung in der Thomaskirche bei Gelegenheit der
vierten Säcularfeier ... Leipzig, Breitkopf & Härtel, 1840. 7p. 8vo.
Title from Mohr, Jubelfeste.   [2827]

Theater der Stadt Leipzig. Am Vorabend der vierten Säcularfeier ...
23. Juni 1840. Leipzig, 1840. Folio.
Contents: Hans Sachs. Festoper mit Tanz in 3 Acten nach Dein-
hardstein's Drama bearteitet von Ph. Reger. Musik von A. Lort-
zing.
Title from Mohr, Jubelfeste.   [2828]

Theater in Leipzig. 26. Juni 1840. Theaterschau von Erfindung
der Buchdruckerkunst bis auf unsere Zeiten. Leipzig, 1840.
Contents: 1. Des turcken Vasnachtspiel von Hans Schnepperer
genannt Rosenplüt. 1450. 2. Dess Bawernknecht wil zwo Frawen
han. Ein Fassnachtspiel von Hans Sachs. 1551. 3. Absurda
Comoedia oder Herr Peter Squenz. Schimpfspiel von Andreas
Gryphius. 1640. 4. Sylvia. Ein Schäferspiel von Christ.
Fürchtegott Gellert. 1750. 5. Nathan der Weise. Dramat.
Gedicht von Lessing. 6. Egmont. Trauerspiel von Goethe.
7. Wilhelm Tell. Histor. Schauspiel von Schiller.
Title from Mohr, Jubelfeste.   [2829]

Thüringisch-Erfurter Gedenkbuch der vierten Säcular-Jubelfeier
der Erfindung der Buchdruckerkunst zu Erfurt am 26 und 27 Juli 1840.
Mit dem Portrait Gutenbergs ... Erfurt, In Commission bei L. Hilsen-
berg, 1840.   viii, 200p.   plates.   22 cm.   [2830]
    DLC   NN   NNGr   Eu-De-LBb   Eu-Ge-LP

Toropov, A. D., comp.
    Katalog predmetov, otnosiashchikhsia k chestvovaniiu 500-letiia
rozhdeniia Ioganna Gutenberga. Moskva, 1900. 13p.   [2831]
    Eu-Ru-MLe

[Tressen, Fr.]
    Jubelgesang bei der vierten Säcularfeier der Erfindung der Buch-
druckerkunst. Verden, im Juni 1840, druck von Tressen & Homkohl.
1p.   4to.
    Title from Mohr, Jubelfeste.   [2832]

Treunert, W.
    Gedichte und Lieder für Typographen und Schriftgiesser zur vierten
Säcularfeier der Buchdruckerkunst. Braunschweig, J. H. Meyer, 1840.
56p.   12mo.   [2833]
    Eu-De-LBb

Tsvetkov, I. V.
  Kratkii ocherk istorii knigopechataniia. K 500-letnemu ubileu
Gutenberga.   1400-1900.   St. Petersburg, I. V. Tsvetkova, 1900.
64p. illus.   [2834]
  Eu-Ru-MLe

  Ubilei Guttenberga.   Istoricheskii Vestnik, vol. 1, no. 31, 1900,
p. 303-304.   [2835]

  Uebersicht der merkwürdigsten und interessantesten Werke, Bilder
und Kupferstiche, welche am 24. Juni 1840 bei der vierten Jubelfeier der Erfindung der Buchdruckerkunst zur öffentlichen Beschauung
ausgestellt wurden.   Frankfurt a.M., 1840.   40p.   8vo.   [2836]
  Eu-De-LBb

Ullmann, Karl, 1796-1865.
  Rede bei dem vierten Säcularfeste der Erfindung der Buchdrucker-
kunst am 24sten Juni 1840 in der akademischen Aula zu Heidelberg
gehalten von Dr. C. Ullmann, derzeitigem Prorector.   Heidelberg,
Universitäts-Buchhandlung von Karl Winter, 1840.   36p.   21 cm.   [2837]
  MH   Eu-De-LBb   Eu-Ge-LSb

Umbreit, August Ernst.
  Die Ausstellung auf Typographie bezüglicher Gegenstände während
des vierten Säcularfeier der Buchdruckerkunst in Leipzig.   Börsenblatt für den Deutschen Buchhandel, vol. 7, 1840, col. 1949-1952,
1973-1977, 2005-2008.   [2838]

Ursin, Georg Frederik Krüger, 1797-1849.
  Bogtrykkerkunstens opfindelse og udvikling i 400 aar. En festgave
til dens fjerde jubilaeum. Af Georg Fr. Ursin.   Kjøbenhavn, Bianco
Luno, 1840.   96p.   front., illus.   20 cm.
  50 copies printed.
  NNC   Eu-De-LBb   Eu-Fr-PC   [2839]

Vater, J. K.
  Buchdrucker und Formenschneider.   Leipzig, 1840.   4to.
  Title from Mohr, Jubelfeste.   [2840]

Veit, Mor.
  Rede bei der Feier des vierten Säcularfestes der Erfindung der
Buchdruckerkunst in der Sittenfeld'schen Officin in Berlin am 28.
Juni.   Berlin, 1840.   7p.   8vo.
  Reprinted in Allgemeine Presszeitung, 1840, p. 505-510.   [2841]
  Eu-De-LBb

Volke, Wilhelm, 1854-
  Die Gutenbergfeier in Mainz.   Zentralblatt für Bibliothekswesen,
vol. 4, 1887, p. 463-465.
  Also reprint.   [2842]

Verzeichniss der ausgestellten Fahnen und Embleme, welche am 24ten
Juni 1840 bei der 4ten Jubelfeier der Erfindung der Buchdruckerkunst
vor den Abgeordneten einer jeden Innung getragen wurden.   Frankfurt
a.M., 1840.   18p.   8vo.   [2843]
    Eu-Ne-AVb

Verzeichniss der sämmtlichen Buchdruckereien mit ihrem Personal-
bestande und der Buchhandlungen in Mainz, niedergelegt in den Grund-
stein des Monumentes für Johannes Gutenberg am 8. Juli 1837. Mainz,
1837.   4p.   Folio.
    Title from Mohr, Jubelfeste.   [2844]

Die vierhundertjährige Jubelfeier der Erfindung der Buchdruckerkunst in Leipzig am 24., 25., 26. Juni. [Von G. K.]   Kamenz,
C. F. Krausche, 1840.   29p.   19 cm.   [2845]
    NNGr   Eu-De-LBb   Eu-Ge-LSb

Das vierte Jubiläum der Erfindung der Buchdruckerkunst am Johannistage 1840.   <u>Nationalkalender</u> (Switzerland), vol. 17, 1840.   [2846]

Vierte Säcularfeier der Erfindung der Buchdruckerkunst.   <u>Journal</u>
<u>für Buchdruckerkunst</u>, no. 11, 1840, p. 153-228; no. 1, 1841, p. 9-
15.   [2847]

Vierte Säcularfeier der Erfindung der Buchdruckerkunst am Johannistage den 24. Juni 1840.   <u>Wochen-Chronik</u> (Basel), June 26, 1840.
    Also reprint.   [2848]

Vierte Säcularfeier der Erfindung der Buchdruckerkunst durch
Johann Gutenberg in Mainz am 24. Juni 1840.   Festkantate.   Musik von
Ritter S. Neukomm.   Mainz, Kupferberg, 1840.   4p. 8vo.
    Latin text by M. G. Friedrich, followed by German translation.
    Title from Mohr, Jubelfeste.   [2849]

Das vierte Säcularfest der Erfindung der Buchdruckerkunst, begangen zu Stuttgart am 24. und 25. Juni 1840. Mit einer Ansicht des
Marktplatzes am Festtage und einer Abbildung des Festzuges. Stuttgart, Gedruckt bei J. Kreuzer, 1840.   91, [1]p.   front., facsim.,
fold. plate.   26 cm.   [2850]
    DLC   NNC   Eu-De-LBb   Eu-Ge-LSb   Eu-Sz-BeG

1440-1840.   Tafellied bei dem zur 400jährigen Jubelfeier der Erfindung der Buchdruckerkunst den 21. Juni 1840 stattfindenden Festmahle im Saale der Harmonie.   Gedichtet von einem jungen Zöglinge
des grossen Meisters. Dresden, B. G. Teubner [1840]   cover-title,
[2] leaves.   21 cm.
    Head and tail pieces.   [2851]
    NNGr

Vögelin, Sal.
Christoph Froschauer, erster berühmter Buchdrucker in Zürich, nach seinem Leben und Wirken, nebst Aufsätzen und Briefen von ihm und an ihm. Zur vierten Säcularfeier. Zürich, J. J. Ulrich, 1840. ii, 24p. roy 4to.   [2852]
    Eu-Ge-LB

Das Volksfest auf dem Marsfelde bei Leipzig am dritten Tage des 400jährigen Jubelfestes der Erfindung der Buchdruckerkunst den 26. Juni 1840. Poetisch dargestellt. Leipzig, Fischers Druckerei, 1840. 8p. 8vo.
    Title from Mohr, Jubelfeste.   [2853]

Vollmer, Hansjerg.
Das Buchdruckerfest zu Reutlingen beschrieben, am 24. Juni 1840. Reutlingen, J. J. Beck, 1840. 7p. 8vo.
    Poem in dialect.   [2854]
    Eu-De-LBb

Vom Gutenberg-Festzug im Mainz. Ueber Land und Meer, vol. 84, no. 42, 1900, p. 677.
    Signed: Fr. C.   [2855]

Vorholz, C.
Erinnerung an das Gutenbergsfest in Strassburg 1840. Indicateur de Strasbourg, no. 53, 1840.   [2856]

[----] Zur vierten Säcularfeier der Erfindung der Buchdruckerkunst am 24. Juni 1840. Gedicht. Carlsruhe, C. Macklot, 1840.
    Title from Mohr, Jubelfeste.   [2857]

Vortrag gehalten von dem Präsidium des erwählten engeren Comités zur Feier des Festes der Erfindung der Buchdruckerkunst am 24. Juni 1840 in der ersten Sitzung des erweiterten Comités. [Frankfurt a.M., 1840] Folio.
    Title from Mohr, Jubelfeste.   [2858]

Vorträge, gehalten bei der Jubelfeier der Erfindung der Buchdrucker-kunst in St. Gallen, den 24. Juni 1840. Als Anhang einige Tafelreden, gesprochen am Festmahle im Saale des Casino. St. Gallen, Scheitlin & Zollikofer, 1840. 35p. 8vo.   [2859]
    Eu-Ge-LSb

Wackerbarth, Graf.
Der Britten erste Heerfahrt nach China. Zum vierhundertjährigen Jubelfeste der Erfindung der Buchdruckerkunst mitgetheilt. Leip-zig, Druck von F. A. Brockhaus, 1840. 16p. 8vo.   [2860]
    Eu-De-LBb

Wackernagel, Wilhelm.
   Beiträge zur Basler Buchdruckergeschichte ... [Basel] 1840. 4to. [2861]
   Eu-Ge-LB

[————] Erster Trinkspruch am Buchdruckerfest zu Basel. 24. Juni
1840. Gedicht. [Basel, 1840] 4p. 4to.
   Title from Mohr, Jubelfeste.   [2862]

Wagner, Wilhelm.
   Die drei Tage der Enthüllungsfeier des Gutenbergs-Monuments am
14., 15. und 16. August 1837. Aufgefasst von einem Frankfurter Typographen. Mit Vorwort, vollständigen Festreden und Anhang. Zum Besten des Gutenberg Monuments hrsg. von Heller & Rohm, Buchdruckern
in Frankfort a.M.   Frankfort a.M. [1837?]   [2863]
   Eu-De-LBb   Eu-Ne-AVb

———— Gedicht. Das Frankfurter Journal an seine Leser am vierten
Säcularfeste der Erfindung der Buchdruckerkunst. Frankfurter
Journal, no. 176, June 24, 1840, p. 1.
   Also reprint.   [2864]

———— Gruss an Gutenberg bei der Enthüllung seines Monumentes am
14. August 1837. Frankfurt a.M., 1837. 4p. 8vo.
   Title from Mohr, Jubelfeste.
   Reprinted in Journal für Buchdruckerkunst, no. 6, 1837.   [2865]

———— Das Gutenberg-Fest in Mainz am 13-16 Aug. 1837. Journal für
Buchdruckerkunst, no. 9, 1837, col. 143-146.   [2866]

Walter, Friedrich.
   Bildung und Halbbildung. Ein Sendschreiben an die Gebildeten des
Preussischen Volks bei Gelegenheit der Thronbesteigung Friedrich Wilhelm IV. und des Gutenbergfestes in Berlin. Berlin, 1840. 31p.
8vo.   [2867]

Walther, Karl.
   Gedicht zum Festmahle des Jubiläums der Buchdruckerkunst in Göttingen, den 24. Juni 1840. Göttingen, Vandenhoeck & Ruprecht, 1840.
8p. 8vo.
   Title from Mohr, Jubelfeste.   [2868]

   Wann feiern wir das vierte Jubiläum der Erfindung der Buchdruckerkunst? Börsenblatt für den Deutschen Buchhandel, vol. 2, no. 45,
1835, p. 1259-1261.   [2869]

   Warum haben nur die Deutschen das Jubelfest der Buchdruckerkunst
gefeiert? Morgenblatt (Stuttgart), no. 183, 1840.   [2870]

Weber, Ferdinand.
Beschreibung des Gutenberg-Festes in Elberfeld. Am 25. Juli 1840.
Elberfeld, Schönian, 1840. 48p. 21 cm. [2871]
NNGr Eu-De-LBb

[Wegelin, Peter W.]
Beiträge zur Buchdrucker- und Literaturgeschichte St. Gallens.
Mit erläuternden und ergänzenden Anmerkungen. Eine Gelegenheits-
schrift zur Feier des bevorstehenden Buchdruckerjubiläums. St.
Gallen, 1835. 12mo. [2872]
Eu-De-LBb

------ Die Buchdruckereien der Schweiz. Mit erläuternden und ergänzenden Anmerkungen. Eine Gelegenheitsschrift zur Feier des vierten
Jubelfestes der Erfindung der Buchdruckerkunst. St. Gallen, Wartmann & Scheitlin, 1836. xviii, 180, 38p. 8vo. [2873]
Eu-De-LBb Eu-Sz-BeG

[------] Geschichte der Buchdruckereien im Kanton St. Gallen. Mit
einleitender Nachricht über die Erfindung der Buchdruckerkunst. Eine
Festgabe für die Theilnehmer an der Säkularfeier in St. Gallen am 24.
Juni 1840. St. Gallen, Zollikofer, 1840. viii, 108p. 8vo. [2874]
MH NNGr Eu-Ge-LBb

Wegweiser zu allen Sehenswürdigkeiten in Leipzig vom 22. bis 27.
Juni. Ein unermüdlicher Führer beim Gutenberg-Feste. Leipzig,
Rückmann, 1840. 36p. 32mo.
Title from Mohr, Jubelfeste. [2875]

Weimar's Album zur vierten Säcularfeier der Buchdruckerkunst am
24. Juni 1840. Weimar, gedruckt in der Albrecht'schen privil. Hofbuchdruckerei [In Kommission des Landes-Industrie-Comptoirs, 1840]
1 prel. leaf, iv, [12], 356p. 6 plates. 26 cm. [2876]
ICN IEN NNC NNGr NjP Eu-De-LBb Eu-Ge-LSb

Welcker, Philipp Heinrich.
Festgedicht bei der vierten Säcularfeier der Buchdruckerkunst
und beim Jubiläum des zweihundertjährigen Bestehens der Engelhard-
Reyherschen Buchdruckerei in Gotha ... Gotha, 1840. 24p. 8vo. [2877]
Eu-Ge-LSb

Wetter, Johann, 1795-1877.
Beantwortung der Frage: In welchem Jahre ist die Buchdruckerkunst
erfunden worden, und wann ist das Säcularfest der Erfindung zu feiern?
Mainz, 1837. 48p. 8vo. [2878]
Eu-De-LBb Eu-Ge-LB

Whibley, C.
The jubilee of the printing press. North American Review, vol.
171, 1900, p. 861-871. [2879]

Wigand.
Ausführliche Beschreibung der vierten Säcularfeier der Erfindung
der Buchdruckerkunst, wie sie am 24. 25. und 26. Juni 1840 zu Leip-
zig festlich begangen wurde, nebst einer historischen Einleitung.
Leipzig, 1840. 8vo. [2880]
Title from Bigmore & Wyman.

Willkommen und Gruss! Allen Theilnehmern an der bevorstehenden
vierten Säcularfeier ... gewidmet. [Leipzig, 1840] 1 leaf. Folio.
Title from Mohr, Jubelfeste. [2881]

Winterfeld, Carl von.
Dr. Martin Luther's deutsche geistliche Lieder, nebst den während
seines Lebens dazu gebräuchlichen Singweisen und einigen mehrstimmigen
Tonsätzen über dieselben von Meistern des XVI. Jahrhunderts. Heraus-
gegeben als Festschrift für die vierten Jubelfeier ... Mit eingedruck-
ten Holzschnitten nach Zeichnungen von A. Strähuber. Leipzig,
Breitkopf & Härtel, 1840. 1 leaf, 132p. 4to. [2882]
Eu-Ge-LB

Wolf, C. E.
Warum habe wir als evangelische Christen für die Erfindung der
Buchdruckerkunst Gott zu danken? Eine Predigt am 2. Sonntage nach
Trinit. den 28. Juni 1840 zum Gedächtniss des vierten Jubelfestes ...
gehalten. Saalfeld, Niese, 1840. 16p. 8vo. [2883]
Eu-De-LBb

Die wundersamen Sagen der Fauste: des Buchdruckers Faust, der
sich dem Teufel verschrieb und zur Hölle fuhr und des Dr. Faust,
des Schwarzkünstlers und Teufelbanners und seine Abenteuer in Auer-
bachs Keller zu Leipzig. Vorwort und Beitrag zur Jubelfeier des
Gutenberg-Festes in Leipzig. Mit zwei Lithogr. Leipzig, Cleve,
1840. 16p. 8vo. [2884]
Eu-De-LBb

Wurm.
Festrede zur Jubelfeier der Buchdruckerkunst in Hamburg am 24.
Juni 1840. Hamburg, 1840. 8vo.
Title from Mohr, Jubelfeste.
Reprinted in Börsenblatt für den Deutschen Buchhandel, no. 81-82,
1840. [2885]

Wüstemann, Ernst Friedrich, 1799-1856.
Oratio in quartis inventae artis Gutenbergianae solemnibus sacu-
laribus quae eadem secunda fuerunt officinae typographicae in urbe
Gotha conditae sacra saecularia in ill. Gymnasio gothano a. d. XXIV.
iun. MDCCCXL. habita ab Ernesto Frid. Wuestemanno ... Gothae, litteris
Engelhardo-Reyherianis [1840?] 22p. 21.5 cm. [2886]
DLC NN Eu-De-LBb

Zell, K.
-Festrede zur vierten Säcularfeier der Erfindung der Buchdruckerkunst am 24. Januar 1840, gehalten bei der Festversammlung im Rath-
haussaale.   Carlsruhe, Macklot, 1840.   12p.   roy. 8vo.
    Title from Bigmore & Wyman.   [2887]

Zobeltitz, Fedor von.
    Festschrift zum 500jährigen Geburtstage von Johann Gutenberg.
Allgemeines Literaturblatt, vol. 9, no. 50, 1900.   [2888]

----   Festschriften zur Gutenbergfeier.   Zeitschrift für Bücherfreunde, vol. 4, no. 7, Oct. 1900, p. 256-260; no. 8, Nov., p. 297-
299.   [2889]

----   Zu ehren Gutenbergs.   Der Türmer, vol. 2, part 2, no. 9,
June 1900, p. 226-235.   [2890]

    Zum Andenken an des 400jährige Jubiläum der Erfindung der Buch-
druckerkunst am 24. Juni 1840.   Gedicht.   Bremen, 1840.   Folio.
    Title from Mohr, Jubelfeste.   [2891]

    Zum Andenken an die Erfindung der Buchdruckerkunst und an die
vierten Säcularfeier derselben.   Königsberg, Degen'sche Buchdruckerei, 1840.   4p.   8vo.
    Title from Mohr, Jubelfeste.   [2892]

    Zum 5. December 1840.   Zwei Gedichte.   [Königsberg, 1840]
4p.   8vo.
    Title from Mohr, Jubelfeste.   [2893]

    Zum 50jährigen Jubiläum der Einweihung des Gutenberg Denkmals
in Mainz.   Mainzer Journal, vol. 40, no. 188, 1887.   [2894]

    Zum Gedächtniss der vierten Säcularfeier der Erfindung der Buch-
druckerkunst in Heidelberg am 24. Junius 1840 ... Heidelberg, Karl
Winter, 1840.   88p.   21 cm.   [2895]
    NNGr   Eu-De-LSb   Eu-Fr-PC   Eu-Go-LSb

    Zum Guttonbergs-Feste.   Den 5. December 1840.   Gedicht.   Königs-
berg, 1840.   1p.   8vo.
    Title from Mohr, Jubelfeste.   [2896]

    Zum 400jährigen Jubelfeste der Erfindung der Buchdruckerkunst.
Allgemeine Anzeiger und Nationalzeitung der Deutschen, no. 169,
June 24, 1840.   [2897]

    Zum vierten Jubelfeste Guttenbergs des Erfinders der Buchdrucker-
kunst, Zürich den 24ten Brachmonat 1836.   Zürich, Ulrichsche Offizin,
1836.   [2898]
    Eu-Sz-BoG

Zum vierten Säcularfeste der Erfindung der Buchdruckerkunst. Den Festtheilnehmern zur Erinnerung gewidmet. Ulm, Nübling, 1840.
Title from Mohr, Jubelfeste. [2899]

Zur Erinnerung an die Gutenbergs-Feier in Aachen am 25. Juli 1840. Aachen und Leipzig, 1840. 84p. 17 cm.
NNGr Eu-De-LBb [2900]

Zur Erinnerung an die vierten Säcularfeier der Erfindung der Buchdruckerkunst. Johannes Gutenberg oder Henne Gensfleisch zum Gutenberg. Flensburger Zeitung, no. 51, June 25, 1840. [2901]

Zur Erinnerung an Johann Gutenberg, den Erfinder der Buchdruckerkunst. Strassburg, F. G. Levrault, 1840.
Title from Mohr, Jubelfeste. [2902]

Zur Erinnerung der frohen Feier des Säcularfestes der Buchdruckerkunst zu Königsberg den 5. December 1840. Königsberg, Degen'sche Buchdruckerei, 1840. 4p. 8vo.
Title from Mohr, Jubelfeste. [2903]

Zur Feier der Erfindung der Buchdruckerkunst, am 24. Juni 1840. Lied. [St. Gallen, 1840] 1p. 4to.
Title from Mohr, Jubelfeste. [2904]

Zur Feier des vierten Säcular-Jubelfestes der Buchdruckerkunst, welche im Saale der hiesigen Ressource am 24. Juni 1840, vormittags 9 Uhr veranstaltet werden wird, ladet ergebenst ein die Oberlausitzische Gesellschaft der Wissenschaften ... Görlitz, 1840. 4to. [2905]
Eu-De-LBb

Zur Guttenbergs-Feier in Königsberg am 5. Dec. 1840. Drei Verse. Königsberg, 1840. 4to.
Title from Mohr, Jubelfeste. [2906]

Zur vierten Feier der Erfindung der Buchdruckerkunst. Deutsche Vierteljahresschrift, no. 2, 1840. [2907]

Zur vierten Jubelfeier der Erfindung der Buchdruckerkunst. Deutsche Vierteljahresschrift, no. 3, 1840, p. [133]-150. [2908]

Zur vierten Säcularfeier der Erfindung der Buchdruckerkunst. Dresden MDCCCXXXX. Druck von C. C. Meinhold & Söhne. 6p. Folio.
Title from Mohr, Jubelfeste. [2909]

Zur vierten Säcularfeier der Erfindung der Buchdruckerkunst. Indicateur de Strasbourg, no. 51, 1840.
Signed: B. [2910]

Zur vierten Saecularfeier der Erfindung der Buchdruckerkunst.
Indicateur de Strasbourg, no, 51, 1840.
  Signed: V.   [2911]

Zur vierten Säcularfeier der Erfindung der Buchdruckerkunst den 24.
Juni 1840, im Saale des Ballhofes. Rudolstadt, 1840. 4p. 8vo.
  Title from Mohr, Jubelfeste.   [2912]

Zur vierten Säcularfeier der Erfindung der Buchdruckerkunst durch
Johannes Gutenberg. Hamburg, Schuberth & Co., 1840. 4to.
  Title from Mohr, Jubelfeste.   [2913]

Zur vierten Säcularfeier der Erfindung der Buchdruckerkunst durch
Johannes Gutenberg, festlich begangen zu Königsberg am 5. December
1840, und Herrn Stadtrath George Friedrich Hartung, dem verehrten
Prinzipal der Hof- und Academischen Buchdruckerei der Hauptstadt
Preussens ehrerbietigst gewidmet von sämmtlichen Mitgliedern seiner
Offizin. Königsberg, 1840. 4p. Folio.   [2914]
  Eu-De-LBb

Zur vierten Säcularfeier der Erfindung der Buchdruckerkunst,
gefeiert zu Königsberg den 5. December 1840. Königsberg, Rosbach's
Druckerei, 1840. 8p. 8vo.
  Title from Mohr, Jubelfeste.   [2915]

Zürich. Museum-Gesellschaft.
  Denkschrift der Museumgesellschaft in Zürich. Zur Feier des 24.
Junius 1840. [Zürich] Zürcher & Furrer [1840] iv, 40p. facsims.
32 cm.   [2916]
  NNC   Eu-De-LBb   Eu-Ge-LSb

Zwanzig alte Lieder von den Nibelungen herausgegeben von Karl
Lachmann. Zur vierhundertjährigen Jubelfeier der Erfindung der Buch-
druckerkunst gedruckt bei Rud. Ludw. Decker. Berlin, 1840. Folio. [2917]
  Eu-De-LBb   Eu-Ge-LB

Zwei Festlieder. Lörrach, 1840.
  Title from Mohr, Jubelfeste.   [2918]

D.   20TH CENTURY

Aegerter, L.
  500 Jahre Buchdruck. Freie Rätier (Chur), Aug. 3, 1940.   [2919]

Alcock, J. J.
  John Guttenberg, the Lindbergh of typography. Tablet (Brooklyn),
Jan. 13, 1940, p. 13.   [2920]

American institute of graphic arts.
... Printing anniversary portfolio for schools, libraries and book
lovers.   New York, N. Y., The American institute of graphic arts
[1940]   13 pieces in portfolio.   53.5 cm.
    Anniversary emblem at head of title.
    Reproductions of examples of early printing, pamphlets on the
    history of printing, etc.   [2921]
    DLC

American institute of graphic arts. Printing anniversary committee.
... Manual of suggestions and methods for the American observance of
the five hundredth anniversary of the invention of printing from
movable type, compiled and issued by the Printing anniversary committee of the American institute of graphic arts.   New York, N. Y.
[1940]   cover-title, [16]p.   23 cm.
    Anniversary emblem at head of title.
    Bibliography: p. [11]-[13]   [2922]
    DLC   NNC

Anderson, Clarence.
    Printing is 500 years old! Duluth craftsmen hail Gutenberg's
gift to humanity.   Duluth News-Tribune (Duluth, Minn.), Nov. 3,
1940, cosmopolitan section, p. 12.   [2923]

Arnoldy, B.
    Celebration of the 500th anniversary of printing.   Share Your
Knowledge Review, vol. 21, no. 8, June 1940, p. 41.   [2924]

Bake.
    Johann Gutenberg's Halbjahrtausendfeier, 1940.   Zeitschrift für
Deutschlands Buchdrucker, vol. 46, 1934, p. 225-226.   [2925]

Bas, I.
    Velikos otkrytie; 500 let knigopechataniia.   Gosudarstvennoe
izdatel'stvo legkoii promyshlennosti, Moskva - 1940 - Leningrad.
36p.   illus.   22 cm.   [2926]
    McMurtrie

Becu, Teodoro, comp.
    Catalogo de la exposición del libro, que se celebra en la ciudad
de Buenos Aires bajo los auspicios del Ministerio de justicia e in-
strucción pública para conmemorar el quinto centenario de la invención de la imprenta, por Teodoro Becu.   Buenos Aires [G. Kraft ltda.]
1940.   4 prel. leaves, xi-xlvii, 273, [1]p.   front. (col. port.)
illus., facsims.   22 cm.
    "Bibliografia": p. 199-222.   [2927]
    DLC   MH   NN   NNGr

Beneš, Buchlovan B.
    Sonatina k pětistému výročí vynálezu umění knihtiskařského 1440-
1940 ... Praha, 1939.   15p.
    Title from Internationale Bibliographie des Buch und Bibliotheks-
wesen, 1939.   [2928]

Bergli-Hannes.
    500 Jahre Buchdruck.   Gedicht.   Volks-Zeitung (Spiess), no. 7,
July 5, 1940.   [2929]

Bingham, L. M.
    Printing industry; a review and recognition.   Connecticut Indus-
try, vol. 19, no. 1, Jan. 1941, p. 2-5.
    On the 500th anniversary celebration at Hartford, Conn.   [2930]

Björkbom, Carl, 1898-
    Johann Gutenberg.   Till 500 årsminnet av uppfinningen av boktryck-
arkonsten.   Stockholm, Skolan for Bokhantverk, 1940.   91p.
    Title from Zentralblatt für Bibliothekswesen, 1940.   [2931]

Bockwitz, Hans H.
    Welt des Buches und der graphischen Künste.   Schrifttum zum Guten-
bergjahr, 1940.   Archiv für Buchgewerbe und Gebrauchsgraphik, vol.
77, no. 7-8, 1940, p. 278-280.   [2932]

Börckel, Alfred, 1851-1928.
    Das Gutenbergmuseum in Mainz.   Klimsch's Jahrbuch, vol. 11, 1911,
p. 117-125.   [2933]

Boston. Public library.
    Five hundred years of printing; an exhibit of the work of famous
presses from Gutenberg to the present day, in the Treasure room of
the Boston public library, June-October, 1940.   Boston, Mass., The
Trustees of the Public library [1940]   cover-title, 27p. incl.
facsims.   27x20 cm.
    Signed: Zoltán Haraszti.   [2934]
    DLC   MB

Botkin, Betty.
    1940 brings milestones in printing of special interest to the new
world.   500th anniversary of Gutenberg's Bible and other important
dates in history of movable type to be given emphasis by exhibits in
Indiana schools and libraries.   Indianapolis Sunday Star, Mar. 3,
1940, part 6, p. 1.   [2935]

Cambridge. University. Fitzwilliam museum.
    Catalogue; an exhibition of printing at the Fitzwilliam museum,
6 May to 23 June 1940.   Cambridge [Eng.] The University press,
1940.   xi, 136p.   24 cm.   [2936]
    DLC   NN

Cary, Melbert Brinckerhoff, 1892-
   How the anniversary will be celebrated. Publishers' Weekly,
vol. 137, no. 1, Jan. 6, 1940, p. 64-65.   [2937]

   Celebrating the five hundredth anniversary of printing. Graphic
Arts Education, vol. 17, no. 1, 1939, p. 6.   [2938]

Chicago club of printing house craftsmen.
   Dinner to commemorate the five hundredth anniversary of the invention of printing, sponsored by the Chicago club of printing house
craftsmen, in cooperation with the Chicago graphic arts federation,
the unions in the printing trades, Chicago federated advertising
club, Old Time printers' association and 69 other organizations.
Stevens Hotel, Chicago, October 1, 1940.   [Chicago, 1940]   3p.
29 cm.   [2939]
   ICN   ICU

   The Chicago printing anniversary dinner; large and impressive
tribute to printing. Chicago Craftsman, vol. 12, no. 7, Oct. 1940,
p. 4-5.   [2940]

   Le 500me anniversaire de l'imprimerie. Le Sentier, Oct. 17,
1940.   [2941]

   Le 500me anniversaire de l'imprimerie au Musée Gutenberg suisse.
Patrie Suisse (Genève), July 13, 1940.   [2942]

Clemen, Otto Constantin, 1871-
   Gedichte zur zweiten Hundertjahrfeier zur Erinnerung an die Er-
findung der Buchdruckerkunst im Jahre 1640 in Leipzig. Gutenberg
Jahrbuch, vol. 15, 1940, p. 404-414.   [2943]

----- Luthers Lob der Buchdruckerkunst zur 500-Jahrfeier der Erfindung der Buchdruckerkunst, von D. Dr. Otto Clemen.   Zwickau (Sachsen), Verlag und druck von Johannes Heermann [1939]   2 prel. leaves,
5-25p.   facsim.   21.5 cm.   [2944]
   ICN

Cleveland. Public library.
   Printing exhibition: a guide and reading list for the exhibition
commemorating the 500th anniversary of the invention of printing.
Cleveland public library March 2-31, 1940.   [Cleveland, Ohio, 1940]
20p.   15.5 cm.   [2945]
   DLC   OCl

Collijn, Isak Gustaf Alfred, 1875-
   Nya forskningar till Gutenbergjubilecht, "Respice Domine", ett
ettbladstruck i den 36 radige Bibeltypen. Nordisk Boktryckarekonst,
vol. 41, no. 10, Oct. 1940, p. 351-353.   [2946]

- 360 -

Columbia university. Library.
... An exhibition commemorating the five hundredth anniversary of the
invention of printing, Low memorial library, January 15-April 15,
1940. [New York, 1940] 11p. 23 cm. [2947]
   DLC   NNC

Davis, Charles T.
   Etaoin-Shrdlu. Greater Pittsburgh, vol. 21, no. 8, Sept. 1940,
p. 10-11, 25.
   On Gutenberg's invention, printing in Pittsburgh, and paper-
making. [2948]

   Dem Andenken Gutenbergs, 500 Jahre Buchdruck. Alte und Neue
Welt (Einsiedeln), Dec. 1940. [2949]

Deutsch-Amerikanische Typographia. Typographia no. 7, New York.
   ... Five-hundred-year festival in memory of the invention of movable
type by Johann Gutenberg arranged on July 7, 1940 in the Brooklyn
labor lyceum by Typographica no. 7, branch of the International typographical union, veranstaltet diese Fünfhundert-Jahr-Feier zur Erinnerung an die Erfindung der beweglichen Buchstaben durch Johann Gutenberg, 7. Juli 1940, Brooklyn labor lyceum ... [New York city, Job printers, 1940] [24]p. illus. 23.5 cm.
   The dates 1440 and 1940 appear at head and foot of t.-p., respectively.
   "Program": p. [12] [2950]
   DLC   Eu-Sz-BeG

Dragulanescu, D.
   Le cinquième centenaire de l'imprimerie et la documentation
roumaine. Fédération International de Documentation. Communicationes, publication 174, vol. 7, pt. 4, 1941, p. 100-101. [2951]

Drugulin, W.
   Marksteine aus der Weltlitteratur in Originalschriften, hrsg. von
Johannes Baensch-Drugulin; Buchschmuck von L. Sütterlin. Zur Erin-
nerung an das fünfhundertjährige Geburtsfest des Altmeisters Johannes
Gutenberg. Leipzig, W. Drugulin, 1902. xiv, 116, 108, v, [1]p.
42 cm. [2952]
   DLC   ICJ   NjP   Eu-Ge-LB   Eu-Ge-LSb   Eu-Ne-AVb   Eu-Sz-BeG

Dwiggins, William Addison.
   The five hundred years. A time-problem, and its solution.
Print (New Haven, Conn.), vol. 1, no. 1, June 1940, p. 21-33.
   A hoax. [2953]

   Erinnerungsgabe der Stadt der Reichsparteitage Nürnberg zum
Gutenberg-Jahr 1940. Nürnberg, J. L. Schrag Verlag, 1940. 31p.
illus.

Contains on the left hand pages an address by Dr. Pfeiffer,
director of archives, on the part played by Nürnberg in the
development of German printing; on the right hand pages are
full-page illustrations of incunabula, etc.
Title from Douglas C. McMurtrie   [2954]

Eulenberg, Herbert, 1876-
   Huldigung an Gutenberg, eine Festdichtung zu seinem Angedenken,
von Herbert Eulenberg. [Hamburg, Genzsch & Heyse, 1928] 31,
[1]p.   20 cm. (Kleiner Druck der Gutenberg-Gesellschaft. Nr. 6) [2955]
   DLC ICN IU MH NjP Eu-De-MzG

Exposición del libro. Buenos Aires, 1940.
   Homenaje al V centenario de la imprenta. Catalogo general de la
Exposición del libro (portadas) en el Teatro del Pueblo Instituto
Argentino de artes gráficas. Federación gráfica bonaerense. Socie-
dad tipográfica bonaerense. [Buenos Aires] 1940. [38]p. 23 cm.[2956]
   DLC NN

---- Semana de homenaje conmemorando el 5⁰ centenario de la imprenta, 1440-1940, organizada por el Instituto Argentino de artes
gráficas, Sociedad tipográfica bonaerense, Federación gráfica bonaerense, y el Teatro del Pueblo, del 3 al 8 de Septiembre en el Teatro
del Pueblo. [Buenos Aires, 1940] cover-title, 7p. 23 cm.   [2957]
   DLC NN

   Exposición del libro. V centenario de la imprenta. Gutenberg
(Buenos Aires), vol. 40, no. 18, 1940, p. 54-55.
   On the book exhibit in the halls of the National commission on
fine arts, Buenos Aires, under the auspices of the Ministry of
justice and public instruction, in commemoration of the fifth
centenary of the invention of printing.   [2958]

Ferrigni, Mario.
   Gutenberg. Nel V centenario della invenzione della stampa 1440-
1940. 25 tavole fuori testo. Milano, Editore Ulrico Hoepli, 1940.
x, 200p. 8vo.   [2959]
   Eu-Sz-BeG

Fishenden, R. B.
   Printing and invention. Printing Review, vol. 9, no. 35 (commemorative issue), 1941, p. 59-67.   [2960]

   Five centuries of typography. World's Work, vol. 50, no. 6,
Oct. 1925, p. 581-582.   [2961]

   500 years of printing; history of art since its inception. Troy
Observer-Budget (Troy, N. Y.), May 19, 1940, section C, p. 5.   [2962]

500th anniversary of invention of printing being observed by world. Mainz, Strasbourg, where Gutenberg perfected movable type, imperiled by war along western front. Sunday Call (Newark, N. J.), May 5, 1940, p. 14. [2963]

Flebus, Francisco Amadeo.
    En el V centenario de la invención de la imprenta. El Obrero Grafico (Buenos Aires), 1940.
    Exact reference not available. [2964]

Forkert, Otto Maurice, 1901-
    Gutenberg and the Book of books and the lost art of the incunabula. Presenting in an illustrated lecture a subject of paramount interest today, since this year of 1940 is being celebrated throughout the world as the fifth centennial of the invention of printing. [Evanston, Ill., 1940] 4p. 29 cm. [2965]
    McMurtrie

──── The Gutenberg workshop at Chicago's Century of progress. American Printer, vol. 97, Aug. 1933, p. 24-26. [2966]

Frau, Manuel Ricra.
    1440-1940; V centenario de la imprenta. Gutenberg (Buenos Aires), vol. 40, no. 18, 1940, p. 53. [2967]

[Frazier, Julius L.]
    Five hundred years of printing. Inland Printer, vol. 105, no. 1, 1940, p. 35. [2968]

Freys, Ernst.
    Gutenberg-Festschriften. Historisches Jahrbuch der Görresgesellschaft, vol. 22, 1901, p. 374-397. [2969]

Flügner, O.
    Die Gutenberg-Reichsausstellung Leipzig, 1940. Messebuch der Deutschen Wirtschaft, 1939, p. 114-116. [2970]

Fuhrmann, Otto Walter.
    The 500th anniversary of the invention of printing [by] Otto W. Fuhrmann. New York, Phillip C. Duschnes, 1937. 34p., 1 leaf, incl. col. front. (port.) illus. (incl. facsims., 1 col.) 25 cm.
    "Six hundred copies ... have been printed on Archer paper." [2971]
    DLC   ICN   MB   NN

    500 Jahre Buchdruck. Schaffhauser Intelligenzblatt (Schaffhausen), July 13, 1940. [2972]

Garnett, Richard.
    The Festschrift of the Gutenberg anniversary. Printing Art Quarterly, vol. 3, Aug. 1904, p. 161-165. [2973]

Gehner, R. F.
    Printing quincentenary. Educational Forum, vol. 4, Nov. 1939,
p. 93-94.   [2974]

Giesecke, Albert.
    Gutenberg-Bildnisse. Die Zeugkiste, 1926, p. 94-98.
    Title from Bibliographie des Bibliotheks und Buchwesens, 1926.   [2975]

---- Wie sah Gutenberg aus? Monatsblätter für Bucheinbände und
Handbindekunst, vol. 2, no. 2, 1925-1926, p. 15-21.   [2976]

Graf, P. W.
    Die Tat.Gutenberg. Volk und Schrift, vol. 10, no. 2, 1939,
p. 37-39; no. 3, p. 20-26.   [2977]

Grollet, Pierre.
    Un anniversaria [l'arte della stampa]. Corriere del Ticino,
(Lugano), Oct. 31, 1940.   [2978]

[----] Un anniversaire [l'art de l'imprimerie]. Journal de
Genève, Sept. 27, 1940.   [2979]

Grolier Club, New York. Library.
    Portraits of Johannes Gutenberg, to be found in the library.
(In Grolier Club, New York. Officers, committees, etc.   1904.
p. 121-138)   [2980]
    ICN   NNGr

Grunau, Gustav.
    Über Gutenbergbildnisse. Gutenbergstube (Bern), vol. 3, no. 4,
1917, p. 89-92.   [2981]

Guppy, Henry, 1861-
    Evolution of the art of printing in commemoration of five hundredth
anniversary of the invention of the art of typography. Library
Bulletin, vol. 24, Oct. 1940, p. 198-233.   [2982]

    Gutemberg alla fiera. Gazetta Ticinese (Lugano), Oct. 4, 1940. [2983]

    Gutenberg and his invention; a bibliographical survey. Facts in
Review, vol. 3, 1941, p. 85-87.   [2984]

    The Gutenberg anniversary. Publishers' Weekly, vol. 130, no. 22,
Nov. 28, 1936, p. 2112.   [2985]

    A Gutenberg celebration in Mainz. British Printer, vol. 37, no.
218, 1924, p. 238.   [2986]

    Gutenberg, 500 Jahre Buchdruckerkunst. Luzerner Neuesten Nach-
richten, jubilee number, no. 290, 1940.   [2987]

Gutenberg Museum, Mainz. Publishers' Weekly, vol. 115, 1929,
p. 2367.   [2988]

Die Gutenberg-Reichsausstellung. Leipzig, 1940. Das Ergebnis
eines Wettbewerbes. Zentralblatt der Bauverwaltung, vol. 59, 1939,
p. 250-252.   [2989]

Gutenberg Reichsausstellung Leipzig, 1940, 15. Juni bis 20. Oktober ([zur] 500-Jahrfeier der Erfindung der Buchdruckerkunst). Mit
internationaler Beteiligung. Leipzig, Poeschel & Trepte, 1939.
10p.   2 plans (fold.) 4to.   [2990]
    Eu-Sz-BeG

Gutenberg to Morris. London Times, printing number, Sept. 10,
1912, p. 1-3.   [2991]

Gutenbergfeier der schweizerischen Buchdruckergewerkschaft Sektion
Olten. Morgen (Olten), Oct. 28, 1940.   [2992]

Die Gutenberg-Foiern in Leipzig und Mainz. Graphische Nachrichten,
vol. 19, no. 7, July 1940, p. 242-243.   [2993]

Gutenberg Fest in Mainz am 27., 28. und 29. Juni 1925. Zur Feier
des 25jährigen Jubiläums des Gutenbergmuseums und des 525 Geburtstages Gutenbergs.   [Frankfurt a.M., Gedruckt in der Bauerschen
Giesserei, 1925] [8]p.   25 cm.
    Caption titlo: Festfolge der Gutenbergfeier.   [2994]
    MiU

Gutenbergfest und Jahrtausendfeier. Zeitschrift für Deutschlands
Buchdrucker, vol. 37, no. 53, 1925.   [2995]

Gutenberg-Fest zu Mainz im Jahre 1900. Mainz, 1901. 4to.
Reprints of newspaper articles and notes on the festival.   [2996]
    Eu-Ge-LSb

Gutenberg-Fest zu Mainz im Jahre 1900. Zugleich Erinnerungs-Gabe
an die Eröffnung des Gutenberg-Museums am 23. Juni 1901. Mainz, In
Commission bei H. Quasthoff, 1901. 1 prel. leaf, 139p.   front.
24 cm.
    By Prof. Dr. Wilhelm Velke. Preface signed "Dr. Gassner, Ober-
    bürgermeister."   [2997]
    DLC ICJ ICN NN NNGr Eu-De-BP Eu-Ge-LB Eu-Ge-LSb
    Eu-Ne-GK

Gutenbergfestschrift, zur Feier des 25iaehrigen Bestehens des
Gutenbergmuseums in Mainz 1925. Hrsg. von A. Ruppel. Mainz, Verlag der Gutenberg-Gesellschaft [1925] 3 prel. leaves, ix-xvi, 448p.

illus., plates (part col.) facsims.   29 cm.   [2998]
    DLC   ICN   MB   MH   NN   NNC   NNGr   Eu-De-BP   Eu-Ge-LB
    Eu-Ne-AVb   Eu-Sz-BeG

    Gutenberg's discovery revolutionizes the art of book-making in the
15th century. Evanstonian, vol. 24, no. 3, Oct. 3, 1940, p. 6-7. [2999]

    Gutenberg's fame secure. Anniversary essay. Publishers' Weekly,
vol. 139, Jan. 1941, p. 71-72.   [3000]

    Gutenbergs neuesten Nachrichten, in geleimten Kleister, mit Ahlen-
spitzen garniert, als delikate Zeitung zur Johannisfeier 1937 des
Reichsbetriebsgemeinschaft Druck, Gau Sachsen.   Leipzig, 1937.
Folio.
    Title from Bibliographie des Bibliotheks und Buchwesens, 1937. [3001]

Hanson, Martin N.
    En sangers kald og nogle tanker i anledning af bogtrykkerkunstens
500-aar.   Odense, 1939.   24p.
    Title from Internationale Bibliographie des Bibliotheks und
Buchwesens, 1939.   [3002]

Hartford.   Committee for the celebration of the 500th anniversary
    of printing.
    500 years of printing, 1440-1940; an exhibition at the Connecticut
    state library in Hartford under the auspices of the Committee for the
    celebration of the 500th anniversary of printing, November 3-December
    5, 1940. Catalogue ... [Hartford, Printed by the Case, Lockwood &
    Brainard co., 1940]   65, [3]p.   24 cm.
    Illustration on t.-p.   [3003]
    DLC

Heidenheimer, Heinrich, 1856-
    Die Mainzer Presse und ihr Freundeskreis. Neue Mainzer Gutenberg-
bildnisse.   Mainzer Wochenschau, no. 25, June 22, 1930.   [3004]

---- Träumereien zur Gutenbergfeier.   Zeitschrift für Deutschlands
Buchdrucker, vol. 37, no. 46, 1925, p. 351-352.   [3005]

---- Zum Gutenberg-Tage.   Zeitschrift für Deutschlands Buchdrucker,
vol. 15, no. 25, 1903, p. 337-338.   [3006]

---- Zum Johannisfeste.   Zeitschrift für Deutschlands Buchdrucker,
vol. 13, no. 25, 1901, p. 288-290.   [3007]

---- Zum Johannistage.   Zeitschrift für Deutschlands Buchdrucker,
vol. 19, no. 25, 1907, p. 425-426.   [3008]

---- Zwei Gutenberg-Sinnbilder.   Mainzer Wochenschau, no. 28,
1928, p. 873-874.   [3009]

Heidenheimer, Heinrich, 1856-
Zwei Mainzer Dankbarkeitsfeiern, zum Gutenbergstage. Mainzer
Wochenschau, no. 25, June 22, 1930.   [3010]

Henry E. Huntington library and art gallery, San Marino, Calif.
Great books in great editions; an exhibition commemorating the
500th anniversary of the invention of printing. San Marino, Calif.,
The Huntington library, 1940. 47, [1]p. illus. (incl. facsims.)
24 cm.
"This exhibition was prepared by Roland Baughman and Robert
Schad."   [3011]
CSmH   DLC   MH   NNC

Herscher, Irenaeus.
1939 marks three centennials in the history of printing. Fran-
ciscan friars figure prominently in history of early printing press.
Printing celebrates three birthdays: 1439-1539-1639-1939. St. Bona-
venture Science Studies, vol. 8, no. 1, Nov. 1939, p. 21-24.   [3012]

----   The three-fold printing centennial. Proceedings of the Third
Convention of the Inter-American Bibliographical and Library Associa-
tion, Washington, D. C., February 23 and 24, 1940. (Inter-American
Bibliographical and Library Association publications, 2d ser., vol. 3)
New York, H. W. Wilson co., 1941. p. 21-60.
Also preprint.   [3013]

Hess, A.
Die Gutenberg-Reichsausstellung 1940. Börsenblatt für den
Deutschen Buchhandel, vol. 106, 1939.   [3014]

Himmelman, Leonard.
Books on printing [available at the Cincinnati public library].
A contribution of the printing high school, the School of graphic
arts, McMillan at Essex place, Cincinnati, Ohio, in celebration of
the 500th anniversary of the invention of typography. Compiled by
Leonard Himmelman, instructor. [Cincinnati, 1940] 12p. 18 cm. [3015]
DLC   OC

Holmström, C. T.
Gutenbergs Konst. Särtryck ur en artikel i Göteborgs Handels &
Sjofartstidning den 7 Febr. 1940 av C. T. Holmström. [Göteborg,
Oscar Isacsons Boktryckert A.-B., 1940] [1]p. 27 cm.   [3016]
McMurtrie

Hölscher, G.
Gutenberg als Drucker. Allgemeine Buchhändlerzeitung, no. 37,
1901.   [3017]

Horn, Gunnar.
   Gutenberg started something. Printing, the strongest influence
in course of western civilization. Scholastic Editor, vol. 19,
no. 6, Mar. 1940, p. 130, 135.   [3018]

Hugo, Victor Marie, comte, 1802-1885.
   Ceci tuera cela, par Victor Hugo. Mainz, Gutenberg-Gesellschaft,
1926. 40p. 24x19 cm. (Kleiner Druck der Gutenberg-Gesellschaft.
Nr. I)
      Added t.-p. in German: Hymnus auf die Druckkunst.
      Text in French and German on opposite pages.
      "'Ceci tuera cela' (Die Druckkunst wird die Baukunst töten) bildet
      das zweite Kapitel des fünften Buches in Victor Hugo's Roman 'Notre-
      Dame de Paris'. Herausgabe und Übersetzung besorgte Hanns Wilhelm
      Eppelsheimer. Textgestaltung auf Grund der 'Oeuvres complètes',
      Paris 1864 bei Alexandre Houssiaux." -- p. 40.   [3019]
   DLC   ICN   Eu-Fr-PN   Eu-Ge-LB

   Historic importance of the invention of printing reviewed. New
York Times, Feb. 18, 1940, section 6, p. 20.   [3020]

   Un hommage à Gutenberg par le Musée Gutenberg suisse. Revue
Suisse de l'Imprimerie, no. 210, Aug. 1940.   [3021]

   The invention of typography. A summary account of its place in
human history, now clarified by the events of its demi-millenial year.
Monotype Recorder (London), special number, Sept. 1940, p. 1-11.   [3022]

Jacot, L.
   Feicract zur Erinnerung an die Erfindung der Buchdruckerkunst, vor
500 Jahren, [von] L. Jacot [und] Karl J. Lüthi. Schweizerisches
Gutenbergmuseum, vol. 26, 1940, p. 69-80.   [3023]

Javitz, Romana.
   The library and this anniversary of printing. Publishers' Weekly,
vol. 137, no. 1, Jan. 6, 1940, p. 66-68.   [3024]

Jay, Leonard.
   1440:1940. Quincentenary of the invention of printing from movable
type. [Second title]: A tribute to the work of George W. Jones, master
printer, on the occasion of his eightieth birthday, by Leonard Jay ...
May, 1940. 12, [3]p. 30 cm.
      Bound as an insert into Printing Review, vol. 9, no. 35 (commemor-
      ative issue), 1941.   [3025]

   Johannes Gutenberg. 500 Jahre Buchdruck 1440-1940. Ausstellung
im Neuen Museum Olten. Das Volk (Olten), Oct. 19, 1940.   [3026]

Jones, George W.
    The inspirational moment of printing. Historical biography of
Fust and Gutenberg. Caxton Magazine, vol. 33, 1931, p. 86-90.   [3027]

    Jubeljahr der schwarzen Kunst. Deutsche Rundschau, vol. 263,
June 1940, p. 117-118.   [3028]

Kehrli, J. O.
    Neue Gutenberg Bildnisse. Schweizerisches Gutenbergmuseum,
vol. 16, no. 2, 1930, p. 71-72.   [3029]

Kleukens, Christian Heinrich, 1880-
    Gutenberg und der deutsche Geist. Die Westmark, 1934-1935,
p. 541-542.   [3030]

------ 1440 - 500 Jahre - 1940. St. Wiborada, vol. 4, 1937, p. 79-
83.   [3031]

Kretzman, Adalbert R.
    The leaden army conquers the world. Christmas Annual (Minnea-
polis, Augsburg publishing house), vol. 10, 1940, p. 37-42.   [3032]

Kunze, Horst.
    Gutenberg in der schönen Literatur. Archiv für Buchgewerbe und
Gebrauchsgraphik, vol. 74, 1937, p. 259-263.   [3033]

Lamartine, Alphonse Marie Louis de, 1790-1869.
    La imprenta, teloscopic del alma. Gutenberg (Buenos Aires),
vol. 40, no. 18, 1940, p. 34-37.
    From "El Conquistador" of Lamartine.   [3034]

Landolf, G.
    500 Jahre Buchdruckerkunst. Bemerkungen zum Jubiläum. Mit zwei
Abbildungen aus dem Schweizerischen Gutenbergmuseum. Der Bund,
Morgenblatt (Bern), Oct. 6, 1940.   [3035]

Lange, W.
    Gutenberg-Huldig. Hausbücher für Sachsen, vol. 11, 1922, p. 332-
336.   [3036]

    The lead soldiers of Gutenberg. British and Colonial Printer
and Stationer, July 4, 1940, p. 6-7.
    Account of a broadcast by the British broadcasting corporation
    entitled "The lead soldiers of Gutenberg," the script of which
    was written by Francis Meynell and Stephen Potter.   [3037]

Lenhart, John M.
    The quincentenary of the invention of printing. Pittsburgh
Catholic, May 11-June 15, 1939.   [3038]

Leumann, Carlos Alberto.
El invento de Gutenberg. Gutenberg (Buenos Aires), vol. 40,
no. 18, 1940, p. 23-25.   [3039]

Little, Evelyn Steel.
Twenty-six lead soldiers. Metallic types more powerful than guns.
This year, 1940, marks anninersary [sic] of one of the world's great
inventions. St. Bona Venture, Mar. 8, 1940, p. 13.   [3040]

Lorphèvre, G.
Histoire de l'imprimerie. Texte du film édité par la "Cinescopie."
Brussels, Cinescopie, 1938. 20p. illus.
Title from Bibliographie de Belgique, 1938.   [3041]

Lüthi-Tschanz, Karl Jakob, 1876-
Pour le demi-millónaire de l'art typographique. Le Gutenberg,
Organe de la Fédération Suisse des Typographes (Lausanne), no. 29,
July 19, 1940.   [3042]

---- Zur Erinnerung an die Erfindung der Buchdruckerkunst vor 500
Jahren. Ein Vortrag zum Feierakt im schweizerischen Gutenbergmuseum
in Bern, den 30. Juni 1940. Schweizerische Buchdrucker-Zeitung
(Zürich), no. 28, July 12, 1940.   [3043]

---- Zur Erinnerung an Johannes Gutenberg. Basler Nachrichten,
no. 305, Nov. 5, 1940.   [3044]

---- Zur Halbjahrtausend typographischer Kunst. Schweizer
Graphische Mitteilungen (St. Gallen), Oct. 1940. Same, Schweizer
Reklame (Zürich), Oct. 1940. Same, Fédération International de
Documentation. Communicationes, publication 174, vol. 7, pt. 4,
1941, p. 104-107.   [3045]

[McMurtrie, Douglas Crawford] 1888-
Advertising and publicity spotlighted by printing's 500th anni-
versary. Cincinnati, 1940. 6p. illus. (ports., facsims.)
30x23 cm.
Author's name from caption title.
"Reprinted from Markets of America."   [3046]
DLC

---- Algunos datos relativos a la invención de la imprenta, el
quinto centenario de la cual se celebra internacionalmente en 1940.
San Salvador, Ungo, 1940. viii, 35p. illus. 8vo.
Translation by Guillermo Ungo.
Also appeared in Anales Graficos (Buenos Aires), no. 1-6, 1941,
p. 11-20.   [3047]
CSmH MH NNC PU Eu-Sz-BoG

McMurtrie, Douglas Crawford, 1888-
    The birth of printing 500 years ago, by Douglas C. McMurtrie.
Chicago, Ill., Invention of printing anniversary committee, International association of printing house craftsmen, 1940. cover-
title, 1 prel. leaf, 24 numb. leaves. 27.5x21.5 cm.
    "Illustrated lecture for high school assemblies, Sunday schools,
Boy scout or Girl scout meetings, and other similar gatherings." [3048]
    DLC MH

---- The birth of the printing press. <u>Walther League Messenger</u>,
Aug.-Sept. 1940, p. 16-17, 48.   [3049]

---- Boxmakers join printers to commemorate 500th anniversary of
invention of printing. <u>Fibre Containers</u>, July 1940, p. 58-61.   [3050]

---- Brève histoire de l'imprimerie et des services qu'elle a
rendus à l'humanité. <u>La Patrie</u> (Montreal), May 12, 1940, magazine
section, p. 10-11, 17.   [3051]

---- Der Buchdruck; seine Erfindung und sein Nutzen der Menschheit.
<u>Sonntagsblatt der Täglichen Omaha Tribüne</u> (Omaha, Nebr.), Oct. 6,
1940, p. 4-5.   [3052]

---- Der Buchdruckerkunst; seine Erfindung und sein Nutzen der
Menschheit, von Douglas C. McMurtrie. Chicago, Ill., Invention of
printing anniversary committee, International association of printing
house craftsmen, 1940. cover-title, 14 numb. leaves. 27.5 cm. [3053]
    DLC ICU NN Eu-Sz-BcG

---- The Chicago dinner to commemorate the 500th anniversary of
the invention of printing. A talk over station WBBM, Chicago, Tuesday,
October 1, 1940, at 3 p.m. By Douglas C. McMurtrie, general chairman, "Chicago Printing Week". Chicago, Illinois, Chicago club of
printing house craftsmen, 1940. cover-title, 6 numb. leaves.
27.5 cm.   [3054]
    DLC IC ICU NN

---- Christians pay homage during 1940 to Bible printer Johann
Gutenberg. <u>Christian News</u>, Sept. 1940, p. 9-15.   [3055]

---- The commemoration in Dayton of the 500th anniversary of the
invention of printing; a radio interview with Douglas C. McMurtrie,
presented by station WING, Dayton, Ohio, October 18, 1940. Dayton,
Ohio, 1940. 11p. 15 cm.   [3056]
    DLC ICU NN

[----] The commemoration in Louisville of the 500th anniversary of
the invention of printing. An interview broadcast over station WAVE,
Louisville, Ky., October 20, 1940, 10:15 to 10:30 p.m. with Douglas

C. McMurtrie.   Louisville, Kentucky, Louisville club of printing
house craftsmen, 1940.   cover-title, 8 numb. leaves.   27.5 cm.   [3057]
   DLC   ICU   NN

McMurtrie, Douglas Crawford, 1888-
   Craftsmen active from coast to coast in celebration of 500th
anniversary of the invention of printing.   Share Your Knowledge
Review, vol. 21, no. 7, May 1940, p. 14-19.
   Also reprint.   [3058]

----   Five centuries of printing, by Douglas C. McMurtrie ...   [Chicago,
Ill.] International association of printing house craftsmen [1940?]
p. 14-19.   1 illus.   30.5 cm.
   Reprinted from New England Editor and Printer for November,
   1940.   [3059]
   DLC   ICU   NN

----   500 years of printing.   Kiwanis Magazine, vol. 25, Sept. 1940,
p. 520, 541-542.   [3060]

----   Five hundred years of printing.   Republican-Leader (Salem,
Ind.), July 11, 1940, p. 7; July 18, p. 7.   [3061]

----   500th anniversary of art of printing; credit for reproduction
of writing with movable type is given to Johann Gutenberg of Germany,
Reading Chronicle (Reading, Pa.), Sept. 13, 1940, p. 7.   Same,
Daily Item (Wakefield, Mass.), Aug. 27, 1940, p. 5.   [3062]

----   Five hundredth anniversary of printing being celebrated in
1940.   Milford Cabinet (Milford, N. H.), July 18, 1940.   [3063]

----   500th anniversary of printing observed in 1940.   Sanger
Herald (Sanger, Calif.), Aug. 2, 1940, p. 8.   [3064]

----   The 500th anniversary of the invention of printing.   East
Side Chamber News (New York City), vol. 13, no. 8, Aug. 1940, p. 6-7. [3065]

----   Five hundredth anniversary of the invention of printing.   An
address delivered before the sixth district conference of the International association of printing house craftsmen, on May 25, 1940,
Stevens hotel, Chicago, Ill.   Chicago, privately printed, 1940.
40p.   12.5 cm.
   Three hundred copies reprinted by students of the Chicago school
   of printing and lithography from the Proceedings of the sixth
   district conference of the International association of printing
   house craftsmen.   [3066]
   DLC   ICU   NN

----   500th birthday of printing.   Azusa Herald (Azusa, Calif.),
July 18, 1940, p. 2.   [3067]

McMurtrie, Douglas Crawford, 1888-
El invento de la impresion con tipos movibles.   Chicago,
1940.   4p.   31 cm.
   "Reproducido del numero de Abril, Mayo, Junio, 1940, de El Arte
Tipografico por estudiantes de Chicago school of printing."   [3068]
   DLC   ICU   NN

----   Gutenberg and the invention of printing.   Middletown Press
Saturday Magazine (Middletown, Conn.), June 8, 1940, p. 1, 3.   [3069]

----   Gutenberg is accredited with printing invention.   Greensboro
Daily News (Greensboro, N. C.), May 5, 1940, section 4, p. 1, 7.   [3070]

----   Gutenberg muere pobre.   El mundo celebra en 1940 el quinto
centenario de la invención de la imprenta.   Jamás dispuso el hombre
de palanca más poderosa para elevar su civilización.   Revista
Rotaria, May 1940, p. 14-16.   [3071]

----, ed.   Johann Gutenberg and his invention of printing.   A coast-
to-coast broadcast over the NBC blue network on August 4, 1940, in
tribute to the printing industry, sponsored by the International
association of printing house craftsmen, upon the opening of its
twenty-first annual convention ... Printed at Rochester, N. Y., in May,
1942, by the Publishing and printing department of the Rochester
Athenaeum and Mechanics institute for the Educational commission of
the International association of printing house craftsmen.   24p.
23 cm.   [3072]
   CU   DLC   IC   ICU   MH   NBuG   NN   Eu-Ge-LB

----   Looking back to Gutenberg.   Boston Business, vol. 3, no. 10,
Oct. 1940, p. 5, 56.   [3073]

----   1940 celebrated as 500th anniversary of Gutenberg's invention
of printing.   Illinois Journal of Commerce, vol. 22, no. 7, July
1940, p. 17-18, 33-36.   [3074]

[----]   Piecsetnia rocznica drukarstwa.   Wojna zaciemniła rocznicowe
obchody tam gdzie drukarstwo powstało.   Dziennik dla Wszystkich
(Buffalo, N. Y.), June 22, 1940, p. 6-7.   [3075]

----   A portfolio of informational articles on the invention of
printing and the beginnings of paper-making in the United States.
With suggested editorials and brief notes on these subjects prepared
by the International association of printing house craftsmen and distributed to newspapers with cooperation of the National editorial
association and Inland daily press association.   Chicago, Invention
of printing anniversary committee, International association of printing house craftsmen, 1940.   cover-title, [16] leaves.   27.5 cm.   [3076]
   DLC   ICU   NN

McMurtrie, Douglas Crawford, 1888-
  Printing: the story of its invention and its service to mankind. _Share_ _Your_ _Knowledge_ Review, vol. 21, no. 5, Mar. 1940,
p. 8-13.   [3077]

[————] Printing; the story of its invention and its service to
mankind. 500th anniversary of printing from movable types, 1440 ·
1940. Issued in the interest of a wider appreciation of the significance of printing to the community [by] Newark club of printing
house craftsmen, Advertising club of Newark. Newark, N. J. [Col-
yer printing company, 1940] cover-title, 15, [1]p. 23.5 cm.
  Author's name from caption title.   [3078]
  DLC NN NjN

[————] Printing; the story of its invention and its service to
mankind. Issued in the interest of a wider appreciation of the significance of printing to the community, on the occasion of the 500th
anniversary of the invention of printing, by the Chicago club of
printing house craftsmen. Chicago, 1940. 16p. 15.5 cm.
Buff wrappers.
  CtY DLC ICU MH NN
  The first specimen issue, distributed to clubs of printing house
  craftsmen throughout the country. About half a million copies
  were printed by the individual clubs in editions some of which
  are listed below:
  ———— ———— Issued ... by the Boston club of printing house craftsmen. Boston, 1940. Gray wrappers.
  ———— ———— Issued ... by the Cincinnati club of printing house
  craftsmen. Cincinnati, 1940. White wrappers.
  ———— ———— Issued ... by the Cleveland club of printing house
  craftsmen. Cleveland, 1940. Yellow wrappers.
  ———— ———— Issued ... by the Indianapolis club of printing house
  craftsmen. Indianapolis, 1940. White wrappers.
  ———— ———— Issued ... by the Minneapolis club of printing house
  craftsmen. Minneapolis, 1940. Brown wrappers.
  ———— ———— Issued ... by the Washington club of printing house
  craftsmen. Washington, D. C., 1940. Tan wrappers.   [3079]

[————] Printing; the story of its invention and of its service to
mankind. Issued in the interest of a wider appreciation of printing,
on the occasion of the five hundredth anniversary of the invention
of printing by the San Francisco club of printing house craftsmen.
[San Francisco] 1940. xvi p. 15.5 cm.
  Reset and in different format from the standardized editions. [3080]
  DLC NN

[————] Printing--the story of its invention and service to mankind. _Beckley_ Post-Herald (Beckley, W. Va.), allied printing
trades conference edition, Apr. 20, 1940, p. 4, 9.   [3081]

McMurtrie, Douglas Crawford, 1888-
    Printing's five hundred years of service, by Douglas C. Mc-
Murtrie. Chicago, Ill., Invention of printing anniversary committee,
International association of printing house craftsmen, 1940.   cover-
title, 1 prel. leaf, 17 numb. leaves.   27.5 cm.
    "Illustrated lecture for service clubs, Rotary, Kiwanis, Lions,
    etc." - 1st prel. leaf.   [3082]
    DLC   MH

----   The significance to religion of the invention of printing.
Being notes prepared for the information of Chicago clergymen in
preparing sermons or lectures relating to the 500th anniversary of
Gutenberg's invention. By Douglas C. McMurtrie, General chairman,
"Chicago Printing Week."   Chicago, Chicago club of printing house
craftsmen, 1940.   cover-title, 11 numb. leaves.   27.5 cm.   [3083]
    DLC   ICU   NN

----   They gave us paper. Paper Progress, vol. 4, no. 3, Oct.
1940, p. 20-22, 28-29.   [3084]

----   This year marks 500th anniversary of printing. Gutenberg
invention of 1440 made wide education possible. Star (Oneonta,
N. Y.), golden jubilee edition, 1940, p. 13B-14B.   [3085]

----   Two towns where printing was born 500 years ago are under pall
of war. Strasbourg and Mainz, where Johann Gutenberg developed the
movable type process, lie on opposite sides of the Siegfried-Maginot
lines. Historians now generally agree in recognizing the claims of
the unfortunate inventor. Kansas City Times, May 10, 1940, p. 22. [3086]

----   War blacks out celebrations in shrine cities of printing. Rest
of world celebrates 500th anniversary of Gutenberg's discovery. With
proofs of newspaper illustrations available in matrix form. Chicago,
Illinois, Invention of printing anniversary committee, International
association of printing house craftsmen, 1940.   cover-title, 3 numb.
leaves, [4] leaves of illustrations.   27.5 cm.   [3087]
    DLC   ICU   NN

----   Why we honor Gutenberg. Sweep away the cobwebs of 500 years
and he becomes a person -- erratic but likable. Born wealthy, he
died poor. Though sued often, he made and kept friends. By Douglas
C. McMurtrie.   Chicago [1940]   4p.   illus.   31 cm.
    Reprint from Rotarian, vol. 56, Feb. 1940, p. 36-38.
    Also appeared in Inland Printer, vol. 105, no. 1, Apr. 1940,
    p. 36-38.   [3088]
    DLC   ICU   NN

----   The world's greatest invention: printing. Graphic Arts
Monthly, vol. 12, no. 2, Feb. 1940, p. 10-12, 14, 16, 93.   [3089]

McMurtrie, Douglas Crawford, 1888-
  The world's greatest invention, printing, by Douglas C. Mc-
Murtrie ... Melbourne, The Hawthorn press, 1940.   2 prel. leaves,
13, [1]p.   illus. (facsims.)   21.5 cm.
  "Fifty copies of this book have been printed in honor of the
  five hundredth anniversary of the invention of printing."
  "Douglas C. McMurtrie, an appreciation," signed John Gartner:
  2d prel. leaf.   [3090]
  DLC

—— Worldwide commemoration in 1940 of the 500th anniversary of
the invention of printing.   Paterson Morning Call (Paterson, N. J.),
May 9, 1940, p. 2.   [3091]

[——] Worldwide commemoration of 500th anniversary of the invention of printing.   Brookline Chronicle, vol. 67, no. 22, May 30,
1940, p. 9, 23.   [3092]

—— The year 1940 celebrated as the 500th anniversary of the invention of printing, by Douglas C. McMurtrie.   Chicago, Ill., Invention of printing anniversary committee, International association of
printing house craftsmen, 1940.   cover-title, 9 numb. leaves.
27.5 cm.   [3093]
  DLC   MH

Manhattan college, New York. Library.
  The story of books since John Gutenberg.   An exhibition of books
held in the Cardinal Hayes library of Manhattan college, New York
city, in observance of the five-hundredth anniversary of the invention of printing from movable types.   January 15 - June 13, 1940.
[New York? 1940]   [12]p.   23 cm.   [3094]
  DLC   NN

Matthias, A.
  Gutenberg chez Les Typos.   Saynête typographique en trois tableaux.
La Chaux-de-Fonds, Imprimerie du National Suisse, 1907.   28p. 8vo.[3095]

Melchor, Frederic G.
  The anniversary year of 1940.   Publishers' Weekly, vol. 137,
no. 1, Jan. 6, 1940, p. 37.   [3096]

Meyer, Peter.
  500 Jahre Buchdruck.   Die Ostschweiz, Morgenblatt (St. Gallen),
Oct. 1, 1940.   [3097]

Meynell, Francis and Stephen Potter.
  The lead soldiers of Gutenberg.   Transmission: B.3.C. home service: Monday, June 24, 1940, 10.25-11.00 p.m.   [London? 1940]
18 leaves.   33 cm.

Broadcast commemorating the 500th anniversary of the invention
of printing with movable types.
Title from Douglas C. McMurtrie.   [3098]

Michigan. University. William L. Clements library of American
    history.
    Historic examples of American printing and typography; a guide to
an exhibition in the William L. Clements library at the University
of Michigan. 1. Five hundredth anniversary of the invention of
printing in Europe, 1440-1940. 2. Four hundredth anniversary of
the first printing in America, 1539-1939. 3. Three hundredth
anniversary of the first printing in what is now the United States,
1639-1939. [Ann Arbor, 1940] 66p. facsims. 23 cm. (Its
Bulletin XXXII)   [3099]
    DLC   MiU

Minneapolis, Minn. Citizens' committee on the commemoration of the
    500th anniversary of printing.
    Dinner commemorating anniversaries of international importance
to the graphic arts [program], Wednesday evening, March 13, 1940.
[Minneapolis, 1940] 20p. 21 cm.   [3100]
    MnU   NN

Noeb, Ernst.
    Zur Geschichte des Mainzer Gutenbergdenkmals. (In Gutenberg-
festschrift, zur Feier des 25iaehrigen Bestehens des Gutenbergmuseums
in Mainz 1925. Hrsg. von A. Ruppel. Mainz, Verlag der Gutenberg-
Gesellschaft [1925] p. 331-334)   [3101]
    DLC   ICN   MB   MH   NN   NNC   NNGr   Eu-De-BP   Eu-Ge-LB
    Eu-Ne-AVb   Eu-Sz-BeG

New York. Public library.
    .. An exhibition of printing from the 16th to the 20th century com-
memorating the five hundredth anniversary of printing from movable
types. [New York, Printed at the New York public library, 1940]
8p. 25.5 cm.
    At head of title: The New York public library, main exhibition
    room, January 15th to April 15th, 1940.   [3102]
    DLC   NN

----   Printing from the 16th to the 20th century. An exhibition
commemorating the five hundredth anniversary of the invention of
printing from movable types. A catalogue with an introduction by
Charles F. McCombs. New York, The New York public library, 1940.
24p. 2 facsims. (incl. front.) 25.5 cm.
    "Reprinted from the Bulletin of the New York public library of
    February 1940."
    Bibliographical footnotes.   [3103]
    DLC   NN

Newberry library, Chicago.
    500 years of printing; an exhibition in commemoration of the five-
hundredth anniversary of the European invention of printing from
movable type.   Chicago, The Newberry library [1940]   29, [1]p.
21.5 cm.
    "The exhibition was arranged and the catalog compiled by Ernst
    F. Detterer ... assisted by Gertrude Woodward ... March 1940."   [3104]
    CSmH   DLC   ICN   MH

    Nineteen-hundred and forty as the anniversary year of Gutenberg
Bible and other printing events discussed.   New York Times, Jan. 15,
1940, p. 13.   [3105]

Offenbach Monatsrundschau.
    Gutenberghoft der Offenbacher Monatsrundschau, herausgegeben im
Auftrage des Oberbürgermeisters der Stadt Offenbach a. Main.   1940.
112p.   illus.
    Contains, among other articles, the following: "Gutenberg, der
    Mann und das Work" (with facsimiles in color); Otto Hupp, "Die
    Anfänge des Buchdrucks" (on technical questions of letter forms);
    Heinrich Wallau, "Gutenberg, Erfinder, Techniker, Kunstler" (under-
    takes an analysis of letter forms; with illustrations).-   [3106]

Olmsted, Duncan H.
    The 500th anniversary of the invention of printing.   Petaluma
Argus-Courier (Petaluma, Calif.), Aug. 19, 1940, p. 6; Sept. 2,
p. 6.
    Third installment published two weeks later.   [3107]

Orcutt, William Dana.
    A keepsake printed in the year of the five hundredth anniversary
of the invention of printing and commemorating the thirty-fifth year
since the inauguration of the Society of printers, being the address
of William Dana Orcutt ... February 24, 1905.   Boston, Merrymount
press, 1940.
    Edition limited to 300 copies.   [3108]
    NN

Ormsbee, Arthur E.
    Wings of wisdom; delivered ... at the 500th anniversary of printing
celebration of the Typothetae of Philadelphia, at Franklin institute,
Philadelphia, Pennsylvania, May 16, 1940.   Share Your Knowledge
Review, vol. 22, no. 2, Dec. 1940, p. 18-23.   [3109]

Paoppi, Pablo.
    El libro y la imprenta.   Conferencia pronunciada por el Sr. Pablo
Paoppi, en el Teatro del Pueblo, en al acto de clausura de la "Semana
de Gutenberg."   Gutenberg (Buenos Aires), vol. 40, no. 18, 1940,
p. 85-88, 90-92.   [3110]

Pasadena, Calif. Public library.
Four thousand years of books; an exhibit honoring Gutenberg and his invention of printing in the year 1440. Exhibited by the Pasadena public library, January - 1940 - February. [Pasadena, Calif., Printed by the San Paszual press, 1940] 2 prel. leaves, 9p. 24.5 cm.
Catalogue compiled by Miss Bevis. cf. verso of t.-p.
On cover: To honor Gutenberg and bookmaking.
200 copies printed.   [3111]
CP   DLC

Petty, G. H.
The birth of civilization. <u>Share Your Knowledge Review</u>, vol. 22, no. 2, Dec. 1940, p. 24-25.   [3112]

Philadelphia. Free library.
The first printers and their books; a catalogue of an exhibition commemorating the five hundredth anniversary of the invention of printing, compiled by Elizabeth Morgan and Edwin Wolf, 2nd. [Philadelphia] The Free library of Philadelphia, 1940. 2 prel. leaves, 7-94p. illus. (facsims.) 26 cm.
"Authorities cited": p. 94.   [3113]
CSmH   CtY   DLC   PP   PU   ViU

Pierpont Morgan library, New York.
The fifteenth century book; an exhibition arranged for the 500th anniversary of the invention of printing; list of books exhibited with an introduction by Lawrence C. Wroth.   [New York] The Pierpont Morgan library, 1940. 30p.   23 cm.
"Printing and the rise of modern culture in the fifteenth century; an address delivered at the preview of the exhibition, January 16th, 1940, by Lawrence C. Wroth": p. 3-19.   [3114]
DLC   NN   NNP

Poeschel, Carl Ernst.
Deutscher Buchdruck gestern-heute-morgen. Vortrag gehalten vor der Gutenberg-Gesellschaft am 24. Juni 1925, zu Mainz ... Mainz, Gutenberg-Gesellschaft, 1927.   34p.   8vo.   (Beilage zur 25. Jahresbericht der Gutenberg-Gesellschaft)   [3115]
ICN   Eu-Ge-LB   Eu-Ne-AVb

Poulaille, Henri.
Le cinquième centenaire de l'imprimerie.   <u>Guilde du Livre</u> (Lausanne), no. 6-7, 1940.   [3116]

[Pratt, Anne S.]
Anniversary of the invention of printing.   <u>Yale University Library Gazette</u>, vol. 15, no. 1, July 1940, p. 9-16.   [3117]

Printing craft more than 500 years old. Gutenberg invention of
1440 made wide education possible. Milton Evening Standard (Milton,
Pa.), golden jubilee edition, May 10, 1941, section 2, p. 6.   [3118]

Printing's 500 anniversary. Process Engravers' Monthly, vol. 47,
Sept. 1940, p. 282.   [3119]

Proskurnin, N. P.
    500-letie izobreteniia knigopechataniia. Poligraficheskoe
Proizvodstvo, no. 6, 1940.   [3120]

    El quinto centenario de la invención de la imprenta. Anales
Graficos (Buenos Aires), Nov. 1940, p. 1-14.
    Articles by Leonidas Barleta and others.   [3121]

Ransom, Will.
    A brochure in honor of Gutenberg. [Stamford, Connecticut, Over-
brook press, 1940] [12]p. 26.5 cm.
    Keepsake no. 66 of American institute of graphic arts.
    Title from Douglas C. McMurtrie.   [3122]

---- Five hundred years of printing. Clement Comments, no. 150,
1940, p. 2-3. Same, Pacific Printer and Publisher, vol. 62, no. 6,
Dec. 1939, p. 20-21. Same, Publishers' Weekly, vol. 136, Aug. 5,
1939, p. 381-384. Same, Wilson Library Bulletin, vol. 14, 1939,
p. 312-313.   [3123]

---- Mother's birthday. Typothetae Bulletin, vol. 50, no. 5,
Dec. 1, 1939, p. 83-84.
    Title derived from the slogan of the United Typothetae of
America: "Printing--the Mother of Progress."   [3124]

---- Printing's 500th birthday. Trade Compositor, vol. 21, no. 2,
Feb. 1940, p. 7-9, 16.   [3125]

---- This anniversary year. Copco-Operator, Aug. 1940, p. 2-4.
    Cover-illustration: The first impression from movable type.
    Published by Central Ohio paper company, Columbus.   [3126]

Risley, Marius.
    Gutenberg's invention one of the world's greatest. German Fran-
ciscan honored on 500th anniversary of his gift to the printing industry. St. Bona Venture, vol. 14, no. 20, Mar. 1940, p. 1, 10.   [3127]

Rochat, Jules J.
    Cinquième centenaire. Les débuts de l'imprimerie. Journal du
Jura (Bienne), no. 193, Aug. 17, 1940.   [3128]

Rodenberg, Julius.
Die Gutenbergfeier in Mainz 27.-29. Juni 1925. Börsenblatt
für den Deutschen Buchhandel, vol. 92, no. 162, 1925, p. 11091.   [3129]

Rollins, Carl Purington.
The anniversary crop.   Saturday Review of Literature, vol. 23,
no. 11, Jan. 4, 1941, p. 11.   [3130]

---- Since Gutenberg. Notes commemorating three notable anniver-
saries. Part I: To 1800.   Print (New Haven, Conn.), vol. 1, no. 1,
June 1940, p. 1-20.   [3131]

Ruppel, Aloys Leonhard, 1882-
A mainzi Gutenberg-muzeum jubileums.   Magyar Bibliofil Szemle,
vol. 2, 1925, p. 43-45.   [3132]

---- A nyomdamuvesset vilagmuzeuma (Mainzban).   Magyar Konyvszemle,
n.s., vol. 36, 1929-1930, p. 184-189.   [3133]

---- A quelle date doit être commémoré le demimillénaire de l'art
de l'imprimerie?   Bibliofilia, vol. 38, 1936, p. 192-193.   [3134]

---- The anniversary of the Gutenberg museum.   Inland Printer,
vol. 75, 1925, p. 905-906.   [3135]

---- Die Bedeutung Gutenbergs für uns und unsere Verpflichtung ihm
gegenüber.   Graphische Nachrichten, vol. 16, 1937, p. 132-150.   [3136]

---- Boktryckkonstens världs-museum.   Nordisk Tidskrift för Bok
och Biblioteksväsen, vol. 17, 1930, p. 36-40.   [3137]

---- The coming world museum of the art of printing.   British
Printer, vol. 42, 1930, p. 226-228.   Same, Caxton Magazine, vol.
32, 1930, p. 152-156.   [3138]

---- Ehrenrettung Gutenbergs.   Germania, vol. 3, Apr. 1936.   [3139]

---- Die Errichtung des Mainzer Gutenberg-Denkmals, von Dr. Aloys
Ruppel ... Mainz, Verlag der Gutenberg-Gesellschaft, 1937.   48p.,
1 leaf.   plates.   21 cm.   (Kleiner Druck der Gutenberg-Gesellschaft.   Nr. 28)   [3140]
    DLC   ICN   Eu-Ne-AVb   Eu-Sz-BeG

---- Kleiner Führer durch das Gutenberg-Museum in Mainz, Abteilung
1: Haus zum römischen Kaiser; zusammengestellt von Dr. A. Ruppel und
Dr. A. Tronnier.   Mainz, Verlag der Gutenberg-Gesellschaft, 1934.
67p.   1 illus. (incl. plans)   21 cm.   (Kleiner Druck der Gutenberg-Gesellschaft.   Nr. 20)   [3141]
    DLC   ICN   Eu-Ne-AVb

Ruppel, Aloys Leonhard, 1882-
    Musée universel de l'imprimerie. Union Syndicale et Fédé-
ration des Syndicats des Maîtres Imprimeurs de France. Bulletin
Officiel, 1931, p. 345-346.   [3142]

----   Musée universel Gutenberg à Mayence.   Revue Rhenane, vol.
10, 1929-1930, p. 48.   [3143]

----   Il museo internationale dell' arte della stampa.   L'Archi-
ginnasio, vol. 25, 1930, p. 105-110.   [3144]

----   Svetoven muzej na pecatarsk. iskustvo.   Bulgarska Kniga,
vol. 2, 1930, p. 391-394.   [3145]

----   Wann soll das erste Halbjahrtausend der Buchdruckerkunst
gefeiert werden?   (In Gutenbergfestschrift zur Feier des 25iaehri-
gen Bestehens des Gutenbergmuseums in Mainz 1925. Hrsg. von A.
Ruppel.   Mainz, Verlag der Gutenberg-Gesellschaft [1925] p. 187-
192)   [3146]
    DLC ICN MB MH NN NNC NNGr Eu-De-BP Eu-Ge-LB
    Eu-Ne-AVb   Eu-Sz-BeG

----   Wann soll die 500-Jahrfeier der Druckkunst stattfinden?
Buchdrucker, vol. 3, 1936, p. 95-98. Same, Schweizerisches Gutenbergmuseum, vol. 22, no. 2, 1936, p. 83-86.   [3147]

----   Das werdende Weltmuseum der Druckkunst. Archiv für Bibliographie Buch und Bibliothekswesen, vol. 3, no. 2-3, 1930, p. 138-142.
Same, Graphische Jahrbücher, vol. 51, 1930, p. 116-118.   [3148]

----   Das werdende Weltmuseum der Druckkunst, von Dr. A. Ruppel ...
[Mainz, Gutenberg-Gesellschaft, 1930]   31, [1]p.   21 cm. (Kleiner
Druck der Gutenberg-Gesellschaft. Nr. 12)
    Caption title.
    Contains also translations into French, English, Italian, and
    Spanish, signed M. Audin, Victor Scholderer, Albano Sorbelli
    and Fernando Bruner y Prieto, respectively.   [3149]
    DLC ICU MB MH NNU-W Eu-De-BP Eu-Ge-LB Eu-Ne-AVb
    Eu-Sz-BeG

----   The world-museum of printing.   Penrose's Annual, vol. 33,
1931, p. 23-29.   [3150]

----   World-museum of the art of printing.   British and Colonial
Printer, vol. 106, no. 65, 1930, p. 84.   [3151]

----   World museum of typography at Mainz.   Book Collectors' Packet,
vol. 3, 1938, p. 8-9.   [3152]

Ruppel, Aloys Leonhard, 1882-
Zum Jubilaeum des Gutenberg-Museum in Mainz. Sammler, vol.
15, no. 7-8, 1925.   [3153]

Saurette, Joseph.
500 ans après Gutenberg. L'art de l'imprimerie, inventé par
Gutenberg, a provoqué des changements révolutionnaires dans le
monde. Recul de l'ignorance. La Patrie (Montreal), Mar. 10,
1940, magazine section, p. 12, 16.   [3154]

Scheewe, Ludwig.
Die Buchstadt Leipzig ehrt Gutenberg. 500-Jahrfeier der schwarzen
Kunst im Zeichen deutscher Waffensiege. Archiv für Buchgewerbe und
Gebrauchsgraphik, vol. 77, no. 7-8, 1940, p. 192-215.   [3155]

---- Leipziger Sonderausstellungen zur 500-Jahrfeier der Buchdruckerkunst. Archiv für Buchgewerbe und Gebrauchsgraphik, vol. 77, no. 7-8,
1940, p. 271-273.   [3156]

Schmidt, Alfred.
Die Gutenbergfeier in Mainz. Neue Wiesbadener Zeitung, July 1,
1925.   [3157]

Schneidereith & sons, Baltimore.
Wings for intelligence. Baltimore, Md., Press of Schneidereith
& sons, 1940. 23, [1]p. plates, 2 ports. (incl. front.) facsim.
21.5 cm.
"A keepsake, prepared in commemoration of the five hundredth anni-
versary of the invention of printing from movable types ... Written,
designed and printed for the ... friends of Schneidereith & sons,
Baltimore, Md."
"Seven hundred and fifty copies ... printed."   [3158]
DLC

Schoeller, Ludwig.
Gutenbergfeier in Wien. Archiv für Buchgewerbe und Gebrauchsgraphik, vol. 77, no. 7-8, 1940, p. 277.   [3159]

Sociedad tipografica bonaerense.
Reseña de los actos organizados por la Sociedad tipografica bonaerense, Instituto argentine de artes graficas, Federación grafica
bonaerense, en el Teatro del Pueblo. Gutenberg (Buenos Aires),
vol. 40, no. 18, 1940, p. 68, 82.
Review of the proceedings during "Gutenberg week" at Buenos
Aires, July 3-8, 1940.   [3160]

Steinberg, S. H.
Gutenberg's Germany. Its economic and cultural conditions.
Signature, no. 14, May 1940, p. 1-9.   [3161]

Stillwell, Margaret Bingham, 1887-
The Annmary Brown memorial, a booklovers' shrine [by] Margaret
Bingham Stillwell, curator.   Providence, R. I., Priv. print. [1940]
26p., 1 leaf. incl. front.   19.5 cm.
"A limited edition of six hundred copies ... has been printed in
observation of the 500th anniversary of the invention of printing,
for Eugene A. Clauss ... "   [3162]
CSmH   DLC   MH   NN   RPJCB

----   Fifteenth-century books in North American libraries; an
address delivered at the convocation held by Columbia university
and the American institute of graphic arts, in New York, January
19th, 1940, in commemoration of the five-hundredth anniversary of
the invention of printing.   [Portland, Maine, 1940]   14, 2, [1]p.
28 cm.   [3163]
DLC   NN   RPJCB

Struck.
Johann Gutenberg, der deutsche Meister.   Lübeck, H. G. Rathgens,
1940.   11p.
Title from Douglas C. McMurtrie.   [3164]

Sur quelques imprimeurs.   Union Syndicale et Fédération des
Syndicats des Maîtres Imprimeurs de France.   Bulletin Officiel, no.
12, Dec. 1929, p. 75, 90.   [3165]

Taylor, Joshua B.
Newspapers closely related with the past 500 years of printing.
Daily Journal (Wheaton, Ill.), Oct. 9, 1940.   [3166]

Troesch, Jean.
Le Musée Gutenberg suisse.   Journal de Genève, Dec. 29-30, 1940. [3167]

Tronnier, Adolph, 1875-
Gutenbergivisky muzej v Majnci.   Bibliologicni Visti, vol. 16,
1927, p. 64-74.   [3168]

----   Die Jahrhundertfeiern der Buchdruckerkunst, 1540-1940; Fest-
vortrag gehalten anlässlich der Festsitzung und Generalversammlung
der Gutenberg-Gesellschaft im Kurfürstl. Schlosse zu Mainz am 21.
Juni 1936, von Adolph Tronnier.   Mainz, Verlag der Gutenberg-Gesellschaft, 1937.   2 prel. leaves, 7-62p., 1 leaf.   (Kleiner Druck der
Gutenberg-Gesellschaft.   Nr. 29)   [3169]
DLC   NN   Eu-No-AVb

----   Mainz; die Gutenbergstadt 1440-1940.   Mainz, Zabern, 1940.
8p.   2 plates (fold.)   4to.   [3170]
Eu-Sz-BeG

Tronnier, Adolph, 1875-
   Vom Gutenberg-Museum zu Mainz am Rhein.   Rheinische Blätter,
vol. 5, 1928, p. 178-182.   [3171]

   250th anniversary of U. S. paper making. Paper makers join
printers for [500th] anniversary celebration. Lock Haven Express,
(Lock Haven, Pa.), Oct. 2, 1940, p. 3.   [3172]

Verndon, Eugène.
   Cinq siècles de typographie. Le Gutenberg, Organe de la Fédération Suisse des Typographes (Lausanne), no. 29, July 19, 1940. [3173]

   Viele Vorläufer und ein Genie. [Zum Jubilaeum der Buchdruckerkunst.] Vaterland (Luzern), Apr. 26, 1940.   [3174]

Wagner, Carl.
   Drei Hundertjahren in Leipzig zur Erinnerung an die Erfindung der
Buchdruckerkunst. 1640-1740-1840. Archiv für Buchgewerbe und
Gebrauchsgraphik, vol. 73, no. 4, 1936, insert p. i-iv, 5-36.
   Also reprint.   [3175]

Wagner, Wilhelm Jakob.
... Durch die Gassen um die Pressen; Besinnliches aus dem Reich der
schwarzen Kunst. [Mainz, Verlag der Gutenberg-Gesellschaft, 1939]
[29]p., 1 leaf. 25 cm. (Kleiner Druck der Gutenberg-Gesellschaft.
Nr. 33)   [3176]
   DLC   ICN

Walker art center, Minneapolis.
   Letters, words and books. An exhibition of 5000 years of the
graphic arts February 28 - April 25, 1940. Walker art center of the
Minnesota arts council. Minneapolis, 1940. 16p. 21.5 cm.
   Title from Douglas C. McMurtrie.   [3177]

Walter, J.
   Deux jubilés strasbourgeois demimillénaires en 1939 et 1940;
l'achèvement de la flèche de la cathédrale en 1439 et l'invention
de l'imprimerie en 1440. Strasbourg, 1939. 19p. 4to.
   Also appeared in La Vie en Alsace.
   Title from Bibliographie des Bibliotheks und Buchwesens, 1939. [3178]

Warde, Beatrice L.
   A master printer in a small town plans a reception to Gutenberg.
Caxton Magazine, vol. 42, no. 3, Mar. 1940, p. 33-34.   [3179]

Weiss, Karl.
   Zur Gutenbergfeier 1940. Ansprache an die Sektion St. Gallen-
Appenzell des Schweizerischen Buchdruckervereins am 23 November

1940 zu St. Gallen von Buchdrucker Karl Weiss und gedruckt in seiner
Officin. [St. Gallen, 1940] 16p. 22.5 cm.
   Title from Douglas C. McMurtrie. [3180]

Weldler, Norbert.
   Zum Gutenberg-Jubiläum. Das Bücherblatt (Zürich), no. 8, Sept.
1940. [3181]

Wentzcke, Paul and Gustav Mori.
   Strassburg und Frankfurt in den Anfängen der Buchdruckerkunst.
Beiträge zur Fünfhundertjahrfeier ihrer Erfindung. Frankfurt am
Main, Verlag Moritz Diesterweg, 1940. viii, 56p. 4to.
   Reprint from Elsass-Lothringisches Jahrbuch, vol. 19, 1940. [3182]
   Eu-Sz-BeG

Weyermann, J. J.
   Die 400jährige Gutenbergfeier in St. Gallen am 4. Juni 1840.
Schweizer Graphische Mitteilungen (St. Gallen), 1930, p. 159-160. [3183]

Wheelwright, William Bond.
   A red-letter year for printing and papermaking. Paper and Printing Digest, Sept. 1936, p. 3-5. [3184]

Windisch, Albert.
   Hymnus auf die Drucktype. (In Gutenbergfestschrift, zur Feier
des 25iaehrigen Bestehens des Gutenbergmuseums in Mainz 1925. Hrsg.
von A. Ruppel. Mainz, Verlag der Gutenberg-Gesellschaft [1925]
p. 5-8) [3185]
   DLC ICN MB MH NN NNC NNGr Eu-De-BP Eu-Ge-LB
   Eu-Ne-AVb Eu-Sz-BeG

Winship, George Parker, 1871-
   Five hundred years of printing. Christian Science Monitor,
weekly magazine section, May 4, 1940, p. 8-9. [3186]

   Worldwide commemoration in 1940 of 500th anniversary of the invention of printing from movable types. Townsman (Wellesley, Mass.),
Oct. 18, 1940. [3187]

Wyss, Arthur Franz Wilhelm, 1852-1900.
   Litteratur der Gutenberg-Feier. Historische Zeitschrift, vol.
87, 1901, p. 454-474. [3188]

Zedler, Gottfried, 1860-
   Per la celebrazione del quinto centenario dell' invenzione della
stampa. Bibliofilia, vol. 38, 1936, p. 446-459. [3189]

Zobeltitz, Fedor von.
   Mainzer Festtage. Berliner Lokal-Anzeiger, June 29, July 1,
1925. [3190]

Zum Gedächtniss an Johannes Gutenberg. Dem Toten zur Ehr', den Lebenden zur Lehr'. <u>Typographisches Mitteilungen</u>, vol. 15, 1918, p. 63-71. [3191]

Zum Gutenberg-Jubiläum. Feier veranstaltet durch die Sektion Solothurn der Schweizerischen Buchdruckergewerkschaft. <u>Solothurner Anzeiger</u>, Oct. 22, 1940. [3192]

Zum Gutenberg Jubiläum [über die Ausstellung im Schweizerischen Gutenbergmuseum]. <u>Oberländischen Volksblatt</u> (Interlaken), no. 142, Sept. 1940, p. 4. [3193]

Zur 500-Jahr-Feier der Erfindung der Buchdruckerkunst durch Johann Gutenberg. <u>Archiv für Buchgewerbe und Gebrauchsgraphik</u>, vol. 77, no. 7-8, 1940, p. 187-282.
    Also reprint. [3194]

Zur fünfzigjährigen Jubiläumsfeier der Typographia Interlaken. <u>Helvetische Typographia</u>, no. 44, 1932. [3195]

Bibliography [of Gutenberg printing]. <u>Norton's Literary Gazette</u>,
vol. 2, no. 2, 1852, p. 25; no. 3, p. 44; no. 4, p. 64; no. 5, p. 84;
no. 7, p. 128; no. 8, p. 148; no. 11, p. 213.
   Signed: S. A. A.   [3196]

Bigmore, Edward Clements, 1838?-1899.
   A bibliography of printing, with notes and illustrations. Comp.
by E. C. Bigmore and C. W. H. Wyman ... London, B. Quaritch, 1880-1886.
3 vols.   illus., plates, ports., facsims.   23 cm.
   Only 250 copies printed.
   Firt appeared in the Printing Times and Lithographer, n.s., vol.
   1-11, 1876-1886.
   Arranged alphabetically by authors, with some subject references
   and form headings -- e.g. "Parliamentary papers", "Periodical pub-
   lications".
   Biographical, historical and descriptive notes.   [3197]
   DLC   ICJ   MB   MH   MiD   NN   TxU   Eu-Fr-PN   Eu-Ge-LB

[Blades, William] 1824-1890.
   The invention of printing. A list of books published upon the
subject since 1868.   [n.p., 1887]   2 leaves.   24.5 cm.
   Printed on rectos only.   Headed "Lib. Assoc. 1887"   [3198]
   McMurtrie

Claudin, Anatole, 1833-1906.
... Les travaux sur l'histoire de l'imprimerie. Par M. A. Claudin ...
Paris, 1899.   cover-title, 22p.   24.5 cm.   (Congrès bibliogra-
phique international, tenu à Paris du 13 au 16 avril 1898, sous les
auspices de la Société bibliographique)
   "Extrait du Comte rendu des travaux."   [3199]
   DLC   Eu-Ge-LSb

Eckstein, Friedrich August.
   Schriften zur Secularfeier der Erfindung der Buchdruckerkunst.
<u>Allgemeine Literatur-Zeitung</u> (Halle), vol. 2, no. 111-114, 225-228,
and suppl. no. 105-107, 1840.   [3200]

   Festschriften zur vierten Säcularfeier der Erfindung der Buchdruckerkunst.   <u>Journal für Buchdruckerkunst</u>, no. 11, 1839, no. 2-4,
6, 9, 1840; no. 8-9, 1841.   [3201]

Gee, W. H.
   Works relating to bibliography, history of printing, bookbinding,
etc., catalogues of public and private libraries, sale and booksellers'
catalogues, on sale by W. H. Gee.   Oxford, 1880.   62p.   21 cm. [3202]
   Eu-Ge-LB   Eu-Ge-LE

Great Britain. Patent office.
A chronological list of works relating to the history and practise
of the art of printing [A. D. 1406-1855] ... being an appendix to the
abridgements of specifications of patents relating to printing.
London, 1861.   192p.   12mo.
    Proof sheets, by W. G. Atkinson, first librarian of the Patent
    office. The work was never completed.   [3203]
    Eu-Ge-LP

    Gutenberghiana.   Weber's Bibliopolisches Jahrbuch, 1841, p. 119-
138.   [3204]

Hoe, Richard March, 1812-1886.
    The literature of printing. A catalogue of the library illustra-
tive of the history and art of typography, chalcography and lithography, of Richard M. Hoe.   London, Privately printed at the Chiswick press, 1877.   2 prel. leaves, 149p., 1 leaf.   front. 18 cm.
    About 1500 titles arranged alphabetically by authors, with
    indexes of places and printers.
    The collection (with some additions) was sold in 1887.   [3205]
    DLC   ICJ   MiU-C   NN   NjP   Eu-Ge-LB

Hoe, Robert, 1839-1909.
... Catalogue of the library of Robert Hoe of New York [illuminated
manuscripts, incunabula, historical bindings, early English literature, rare Americana, French illustrated books, eighteenth century
English authors, autographs, manuscripts, etc.] ... to be sold by
auction ... by the Anderson auction company ... New York ... [New York,
D. Taylor & co., 1911-12]   8 vols. in 4.   fronts., plates, plan,
facsims,   23.5 cm.
    Part 1: Anderson catalogue no. 905-906.
    Each of the 4 parts issued in 2 vols.   [3206]
    DLC   ICJ   MB   MiU   NN   WaU

Hoffmann, Friedrich Lorenz, b. 1790.
    A bibliography of materials on the history of printing in Italy,
compiled in 1852 by Friedrich Lorenz Hoffmann ... Chicago, Ill., Committee on invention of printing, Chicago club of printing house
craftsmen, 1941.   3 prel. leaves, 2-29 numb. leaves.   27.5 cm.
(Contributions to the bibliography of printing, no. 7)
    "Published as a report on Work projects administration Official
    project no. OP65-1-54-273 (3) officially sponsored by the Chicago
    public library."
    Reprinted from the Bulletin du Bibliophile Belge, vol. 9, 1852,
    pages 1-21 and 97-113.   cf. leaf [1].   [3207]
    CSmH   DLC   IC   ICN   ICU   MH   NN   NNC

----   A bibliography of materials on the history of printing published in the Netherlands in the nineteenth century, as compiled in
1865-1867, by Friedrich Lorenz Hoffmann ... Chicago, Ill., Committee

on invention of printing, Chicago club of printing house craftsmen, 1940.   cover-title, 2-25 numb. leaves.   27.5 cm.   (Contributions to the bibliography of printing, no. 2)
   "Published as a report on Work projects administration Official project no. OP65-1-54-273 (3) officially sponsored by the Chicago public library."
   Reprinted from the Neuer Anzeiger für Bibliographie und Bibliothekwissenschaft, Jahrgang 1865, p. 273-289, and Jahrgang 1867, p. 317-322.   cf. leaf 2.   [3208]
   CSmH   DLC   IC   ICN   ICU   MH   NN   NNC

Hoffmann, Friedrich Lorenz, b. 1790.
   Chronological list of books and articles on the history of printing in Holland and Belgium, compiled 1856-1858, by Friedrich Lorenz Hoffmann ... Chicago, Ill., Committee on invention of printing, Chicago club of printing house craftsmen, 1941.   2 prel. leaves, 119 numb. leaves.   27.5 cm.   (Contributions to the bibliography of printing, no. 4)
   "Published as a report on Work projects administration Official ptoject no. OP65-1-54-273 (3) officially sponsored by the Chicago public library."
   "The present list was published serially in Le Bibliophile Belge, vol. 12 (2d ser., vol. 3), 1856, pages 1-12, 85-97, 180-188, 320-330, 380-389, and in vol. 13 (2d ser., vol. 4), 1857, pages 28-32, 159-175, 246-256, 273-285, and 337-349. Additions and corrections were published in vol. 14 (2d ser., vol. 5), 1858, pages 169-182, and 348-353." cf. leaf 1.   [3209]
   CSmH   DLC   IC   ICN   ICU   MH   NN   NNC

----   Essai d'une liste chronologique des ouvrages et dissertations concernant l'histoire de l'imprimerie en Hollande et en Belgique. Bulletin du Bibliophile Belge, vol. 12 (2d ser., vol. 4), 1856, p. 1-12, 85-97, 180-188, 320-330, 380-389; vol. 13 (2d ser., vol. 4), 1857, p. 28-32, 159-175, 246-256, 273-285, 337-349; vol. 14 (2d ser., vol. 5), 1858, p. 169-182, 348-353.   [3210]

----   Essai d'une liste des ouvrages concernant l'histoire de l'imprimerie en Italie.   Bruxelles, Heberle, 1852.   33p.   8vo.
   Reprint from Bulletin du Bibliophile Belge, vol. 9, 1852, p. 1-21, 95-113.   [3211]
   ICN   NN   Eu-Fr-PN

----   Verzeichniss und Beschreibung einiger von Niederlandern verfassten Werke und Aufsatze aus dem XIX. Jahrhundert, die Geschichte der Buchdruckerkunst betreffend.   Neuer Anzeiger für Bibliographie und Bibliothekwissenschaft, 1865, p. 273-289; 1867, p. 317-322.   [3212]

Josephson, Aksel Gustav Salomon, 1860-
The invention of printing as recorded in notes and colophons of fifteenth century books. A bibliographical essay. Bibliographical Society of America. Papers, vol. 11, 1917, p. 1-14. [3213]

Lepreux, Georges.
Les travaux sur l'histoire de l'imprimerie. Revue des Bibliothèques, vol. 22, 1912-1913, p. 499-501. [3214]

Linde, Antonius van der, 1833-1897.
Litteratur [on the invention of printing]. (In his Geschichte der Erfindung der Buchdruckkunst ... Berlin, A. Asher & Co., 1886. vol. 1, p. [i]-lvii) [3215]
DLC   ICJ   ICN   MB   MH   MdBP   NN   OCl   Eu-Ge-LB
Eu-Ge-LP   Eu-Ge-LSb   Eu-Ne-AVb   Eu-Ne-GK

A list of published materials in the Russian language on the invention of printing ... Chicago, Ill., Committee on invention of printing, Chicago club of printing house craftsmen, 1941. [i]-iv, 18 numb. leaves.   27.5 cm.   (Contributions to the bibliography of printing, no. 6)
"Published as a report on Work projects administration Official project no. OP65-1-54-273 (3) sponsored officially by the Chicago public library." [3216]
CSmH   DLC   IC   ICN   ICU   MH   NN   NNC

Literatur der Geschichte der Erfindung der Buchdruckerkunst. Neue Jahrbücher für Philologie und Padagogik, n.s., vol. 7, 1837, p. 337-339. [3217]

McMurtrie, Douglas Crawford, 1888-
Bibliographies [of materials on the invention of printing]. (In his The Book.   New York, 1937.   p. 608-618) [3218]
DLC   In   NN

Mohr, Louis, 1828-1886.
Die Jubelfeste der Buchdruckerkunst und ihre Literatur. Ein bibliographischer Versuch von Louis Mohr. Veröffentlicht bei Gelegenheit des vierhundertjährigen Jubiläums der Einführung der Buchdruckerkunst in Wien.   Wien, C. Graeser, 1886.   107p., 1 leaf.   21.5 cm.
Preface dated 1882.
"Aus der Oesterreichischen Buchdruckerzeitung abgedruckt und erweitert." [3219]
DLC   Eu-Ge-LB
1882 ed.:   ICN   Eu-Fr-PN   Eu-Ge-LSb

Ross, James.
Select bibliography of the art of printing to 1640. Librarian, vol. 10, 1920-1921, p. 28-31, 42-45, 78-83, 99-103, 119-126, 142-146, 165-168. [3220]

Schriften zum vierhundertjährigen Erinnerungsfeste der Erfindung
der Buchdruckerkunst.   Allgemeiner Anzeiger und National-Zeitung der
Deutschen, no. 169 et sqq., 1840.   [3221]

Stevens, Edward F.
    An outline of the history of printing.   Publishers' Weekly, vol.
118, Sept. 1930, p. 967-971.
    Also reprints.   [3222]

Umbreit, August Ernst.
    Ueber die Literatur der jüngsten Säcularfeier der Buchdrucker-
kunst.   Blätter für Literarische Unterhaltung, no. 15-17, 102-105,
1841.   [3223]

Winship, George Parker, 1871-
    The literature of printing.   Dolphin, vol. 3, 1938, p. 477-491.[3224]

ADDENDA

Beaudoin, Philippe.
    Gutenberg et l'imprimerie.   Montreal, Therien frères, 1940.
224p.   [3225]
    NN

Bockwitz, Hans H.
    Vorstufen der originalgraphischen Künste und der Buchdrucker-
kunst.   Archiv für Buchgewerbe und Gebrauchsgraphik, vol. 76,
no. 2, 1939, p. 71-84.   [3226]

Heyne, Hildegard.
    Der Holzschnitt.   Archiv für Buchgewerbe und Gebrauchsgraphik,
vol. 76, no. 2, 1939, p. 85-98.   [3227]

Reichel, Anton.
    Kupferstich und Radierung.   Archiv für Buchgewerbe und
Gebrauchsgraphik, vol. 76, no. 2, 1939, p. 99-124.   [3228]

ERRATA

Item 74, line 6   Add location symbol Eu-Ge-LSb

Item 259, line 8   For CLC, read DLC

Item 536, line 8   Add location symbols DLC   ICJ   Eu-Ge-LSb

Item 627, line 4   Add location symbol Eu-Ge-LSb

Item 993, line 1   For Nicolass, read Nicolaas

Item 1432   Cancel item number

Item 1455   Cancel item number

Item 1604, line 1   For Ettere, read Ettore

Item 2613, line 5   Add location symbol Eu-Ge-LB

Item 2806, line 4   Add location symbol Eu-De-LBb

Item 2867, line 6   Add location symbol Eu-De-LBb

Item 3095, line 4   Add location symbol Eu-Sz-BeG

INDEX TO AUTHORS

Item

Berlan, Francesco   1275, 1677
Berlin, IA. A.   1848
Berliner, A.   2287
Bernard, Auguste Joseph   147,
     316-320, 739, 864, 1592, 1700
Bernardi, Jacopo   1224-1226
Bernays, Heinrich   1678
Bernhart, Johann Baptist
                             1388,-1389
Bernhart, Mathias   1331
Berstett, August, freiherr von
                                   2288
Bertrand-Quinquet, Mme. Suzanne
     (Girieux)   225
Besold, Christoph   188
Bessmertny, Alexander   1390
Besso, Beniamino   321
Bettzeiche, Heinrich   2292
Beverswijk, J. M. van   866
Beyer, Fritz   1503
Beyssac, Gabriel M.   1530
Biedermann, F. F. von 2294, 2295
Biegelaar, A. J.   1209
Bigmore, Edward Clements   3197
Bignan, Anne   322
Bigot, Charles   740
Bilderdijk, Willem   868
Billig, J. C. G.   2296
Binger, H.   869, 870
Bingham, L. M.   2930
Binz, Gustav   596, 741
Birch-Pfeiffer, Charlotte   1849
Birkenfeld, Günther   1701, 1850
Björkbom, Carl   149, 1851, 2931
Björklund, F. C.   2297
Blades, William
                    323-326, 597, 3198
Blaizot, G.   598
Blaser, Fritz   2298, 2299
Blégier-Pierregrosse, le comte de
                                   1210
Bleyer, Hans   1852
Block, August   2301
Blum, André Salomon
                    82, 83, 599 - 601
Blumenfeld, J. C.   2302
Bocarmé, Albert Visart de   1252
Böck, Joseph   2303-2305

Item

Böckel, Ernst Gottfried Adolf
                                   2306
Bockenheimer, Karl Georg
                    1253, 1702, 1703
Bockenhoffer, Johann Philipp   189
Bockwitz, Hans H.
               1394, 1704, 2932, 3226
Bödeker, Hermann Wilhelm   2307
Boeclerus, Joannes Henricus   190
Boehm   327
Boeles, Willem Boele Sophius   873
Bogeng, Gustav Adolf Erich
                    602-604, 1679
Bohatta, Hanns   1531
Bohigas, Balaguer Pedro   605
Bohn, Henry George   330
Boisserand, M.   1593
Bolt, Hendrik   874
Boltz, Theodor   2057
Bömer, Alois   606, 1518, 1705
Bonné, D.   875
Boogaard, W.   876
Börckel, Alfred   331, 332, 1594
     1706-1709, 1853-1856, 2933
Bornet   607
Borovsky, F. A.   1483
Bösch, Hans   333
Bosscha, Hermann   877, 878
Botkin, Betty   2935
Bouchot, Henri François Xavier
     Marie   84, 85, 334-337, 742
Boudet, J. B.   338
Bowyer, William   879
Boxhorn, Marcus Zuerius   191-193
Boxman, A.   880, 881
Boysen, Karl   2308
Boze, C. G. de   1484
Bradbury, Henry Riley   339
Brage, H.   608
Brandes, Georg Morris Cohen   2309
Brechenmacher, Georg Friedrich
                                   2058
Brehm, C.   2020
Breitenbach, Edgar   1647
Breitkopf, Johann Gottlob Im-
     manuel   55, 227
Broadmann, G. A.   340
Broeckx, C.   1276

	Item		Item
Fritsch, Friedrich	407	Gessner, Christian Friedrich	
Frobenius, L.	1887		249, 2108
Froebel, Gunther	2433	Gethmann, E.	2455
Frölich, K.	2434	Ghesquière, Joseph Hippolyte	
Fromman, F. J.	2435		250, 251
Fruin, Robert	936-941, 1213	Ghinzoni, P.	1235
Fry, Francis	1296	Giesebrecht, Ludwig	2456, 2457
Frydlender, J.	768	Giesecke, Albert	2975, 2976
Fuchs, Johann Nicolas Heinrich		Giliberti, Francesco	411
	2099	Gilliodts-Van Severn, Louis	
Fuelleborn, Georg Gustav	2436		1256, 1257
Fugger, Jean George	246	Gillot, George	770
Fügner, O.	2970	Ginsburg, Percy	637
Fuhrmann, Otto Walter	19, 633,	Gleditzsch, Hermann	2458
634, 1407, 1684, 2971		Gleich, Ferdinand	2459
Fumagalli, Giuseppe	1232	Goebel, Theodor	1214, 2460
Funck, Johann Daniel	2100	Goetse, Christian Friedrich	
Funcke, Johann Michael	2101		2109, 2110
Fürstenau, Johann Hermann	247	Goetz, Walter	2461
Fürstenau, Philipp C. von	2024	Goldschmidt, Paul	2462
		Gollners, Johann	2111
		Gotthold, Friedrich August	
			1889, 2464
Gachet, Émile	1280, 1281	Gottner, G.	1890
Gage, Harry Lawrence	1297	Gottschalk, Paul	639
Gailer	2437	Gottsched, Johann Christoph	
Galeati, Paolo	408, 409		2112-2114
Gallotti, J.	20	Gottwald, Eduard	2466, 2467
Gema, Jean Pierre	769	Goudy, Frederic W.	640, 1739
Gando, François	248	Graberg, Fr.	2469, 2470
Garland, H.	1332	Graesse, J. G. T.	412
Garnett, Porter	1298	Graf, Andr. Christ.	2115
Garnett, Richard	2973	Graf, P. W.	1740, 2977
Garnier, Jacques Marie	58	Grant, George	413
Gasser, Johann Michael	2102	Graubel	2471
Gebhard, J. H.	943	Grellet, Pierre	2978, 2979
Gee, W. H.	3202	Gremps, P. Max	53
Geffcken, Johannes	153	Grey, Johanna	2472
Gehner, R. F.	2974	Grieben, Henry	2473
Geissler, P. C.	2448	Grieshaber	1891
Geldner, Ferdinand	1452	Groebe, Dirk	154
Geliger, P.	410	Grosch, Gottfried	2116, 2117
Gemeinhardt, Johann Casper	2104	Grosse, Ed.	2474
Gerlach, Benjamin Gottl.	2105	Grossman, Christian Gottlob	
Gerlings, Herman	945	Leberecht	2475
Gertner, Georg Michael	2106	Grotefend, Carl Ludwig	2476
Gertner, Johann Georg Christ.		Grotefend, George Friedrich	2477
	2107	Grover, Edwin Osgood	641, 642

	Item		Item
Grucker, M. T. G.	2478-2480	Hansen, Martin N.	3002
Grün, Karl	2481	Hanstein, Wolfram von	1908
Grunau, Gustav	2981	Hargrave, Catherine Perry	59
Grüneisen, Carl	2482	Hargreaves, C.	655
Grunert, Johann Friedrich	2119	Harless, Chr. Fr.	2527
Gubitz, F. W.	2483, 2484	Harris, John	254
Gueintz, Christian	2025	Hartenbach, J. Ritschel von	1608
Guibertus, Brother	643	Hartman, C. F.	2528-2532
Guicciardini, Lodovico	947-949	Hartshorne, Charles Henry	422
Guichard, Joseph Marie		Hartung, Johann Heinrich	2123
	155, 156, 1654	Harzen, Ernst	1655
Guillaume, B.	1741	Hase, Oscar von	2533
Guillot, Gaëtan	93, 94	Hasse, Friedrich Christian	
Gulberg, C. A.	2485	August	2534, 2535
Guppy, Henry	95, 96, 644, 645,	Hassler, Konrad Dieterich	
2982			2536, 2537
Gusman, Pierre	97, 98, 646,	Haton, Martial	2538
1299, 1558		Hauschild, J. G.	2539
Gutch, John Mathew	414	Hausrath, A.	2540
Gutner, Johann Gabriel	2026	Hauthal, Ferdinand	2541, 2542
Gutzkow, Karl	1907	Hawes, Stephen	423
		Haynes, Merritt Way	656
		Hazel, Oscar J.	773
Haapanen, Toivo	1538	Hazeu, Johann	953
Haarhaus, I. R.	1282	Hedenus, A. G.	2543
Haberland, L.	2521	Heffner, L.	424
Habermann, Carl Friedrich	2522	Heidenheimer, Heinrich 159, 774,	
Haebler, Konrad	157, 158,	1539, 1540, 1609, 1610, 1745,	
647-651, 1303, 1304, 1335,		2544-2546, 3004-3010	
1463, 1508		Hein, Gustav	2547
Hagelstange, Alfred	1607	Heinecken, Karl Heinrich von	
Hagen, Friedrich Heinrich von			99, 954
der	2523	Heinike, John C.	657
Hagenbach, Carl Rudolph		Heinlein, Heinrich	2548
	2318, 2524	Heinritz	2549
Hagenbusch, Johannes Theophius		Helbig, Henri Antoine	425-427,
	252	1453, 1454, 1541-1543, 1611,	
Hahn, R.	416	1667	
Hall, Charles Carter	417	Hell, Th.	2550
Hall, Charles W.	652	Heller	2551
Hallam, Henry	418	Heller, Johann Bernhard 2125, 2126	
Hallbauer, George Christian	253	Heller, Joseph	100
Haltaus, Karl Ferdinand	2526	Hellwald, Ferdinand von	428
Hamilton, Frederick William		Helmolt, H. F.	1909
	653, 654	Helquerra y Garcia, A. de la 1746	
Hänicker, Samuel	2121	Hendel, Johann Christian	2127
Hanov, Michael Christoph	2122	Henne	2552
Hansard, Thomas Curson	419-421	Henry, E.	658

	Item		Item
Melcher, Frederic G.	3096	Mone, Franz Joseph	1620
Mel'gunov, N. A.	2653	Monnoyer, Charles	115
Meller, Clara	1945	Moon, George Washington	1524
Melzer, C. Ph.	2654	Morelli, G.	1238
Memmel, Johann Casp.	2178	Mori, Gustav 802-805,	3182
Menapius, Gulielmus Insulanus	180	Morin, E.	1949
Mendelssohn-Bartholdy, Felix	2655	Morison, Stanley	690
Mentel, Jacques 1285-1287		Mornand, Pierre	691
Menz, Friedrich	2179	Morrison, Michael A.	2667
Merbach, P. A.	1946	Mortet, Paul Louis Charles	692
Mercier, Barthélemy	266	Mosche, C.	2668
Mercier, M. T.	2656	Moscherosch, Hans Michael	693
Merckenberger, Johann Wilhelm		Moser	1490
	2180	Moser, K.	2669
Merlin, Romain 66, 67		Motta, Emilio	1239
Méry, François Joseph Pierre		Müchler, Karl	2670
André	1064	Mueller, H.	494
Meschina, Carlo E.	487	Mueller, K.	1950
Metz, Friedrich	488	Müller, A.	2671
Metz, J. J.	1947	Müller, Bruno	1321
Metzner, Michael	2182	Müller, G. H.	1069
Meurling, Magn. G.	489	Müller, H.	2672
Meurs, Petrus van	1065	Müller, H. G.	1422
Meuschen, J. G.	2183	Müller, J. H.	2673
Meyer, Heinrich	2657	Müller, Joseph	1548
Meyer, L. E.	2658	Muller, Julius W. 1423,	1951
Meyer, Peter	3097	Müller, Nikolaus 2674-2680	
Meyer, Wilhelm	1547	Mullie, P. Jos.	30
Meyer-Köchlin, Val.	2659	Munch, Benedictus Guill.	267
Meynell, Francis	3098	Münden, Christian	2185
Mezger, G. C.	2660	Munsell, Joel	495
Micheletti, Giovanni Battista	801	Murr, Christoph Gottlieb von	1561
Middleton, Conyers	1066	Musper, Heinrich Theodor	
Middleton-Wake, Charles H.	490		1070-1072
Milchsack, Gustav	2661		
Minotto, A. S.	1237		
Mira, Giuseppe Maria	491	Nachod, O.	31
Misset, Eugène	1471	Nai, P.	1240
Mitkevich, V. F.	689	Natolinus, Joannis Baptistus	214
Modestov, A. P.	1948	Naudé, Gabriel	215
Mohnike, G.	2662	Naumann, C. J.	2683
Mohr, Louis 492,	3219	Naumann, Robert 1549,	1550
Mokelott, Alex 2663,	2664	Née de la Rochelle, Jean Fran-	
Moller, Daniel Wilhelm 212,	213	çois	2684
Möller, M. Johann Melchior	2184	Neeb, Ernst 1785, 1786,	3101
Møller, Peder Ludvig	493	Neff, P.	2685
Molsdorf, Wilhelm	1067	Nekrasova, I.	694
Mommnas, C.	1068	Nemeitz, Joachim Christoph	1658

	Item		Item
Thevet, André	1822, 1823	Vallet de Viriville, Auguste	
Thiboust, Claude Louis	286, 2238		559, 833, 834
Thiel, Rudolf	1825	Van Loon, Hendrik Willem	835
Thoma, Albrecht	828	Van Rensselaer, May King	75
Thorn	287	Varelen, J. E. van	1161
Thudichum, F.	829	Vater, J. K.	2840
Tiele, P. A.	1149, 1150	Vecchioni, Cesare	727
Timbs, John	551-553	Veit, Mor.	2841
Ting Wen Yuan	45	Velke, Wilhelm	1640, 2842
Tinker, C. B.	1441	Venturi, Lionello	139
Tiraboschi, Girolamo	288, 554	Verndon, Eugène	3173
Tissandier, Gaston	2001	Verreyt, Charles C. V.	1641
Toland, John	289, 290	Vester, Christian	223
Tollens, H. C.	1151	Vil'chinskii, O.	2007
Tomlinson, Charles	555	Villarroya, José	291
Tomlinson, Laurence Elliot	830	Villeneuve, J. de	292
Tonelli, Tommaso	556	Vinařický, Karel Alois	1828-1830
Toropov, A. D.	2831	Vinaritskii, K.	2008
Townsend, W. G. P.	138	Vincard, B.	560
Toze, Eobald	1152	Vincent, A.	1271
Tränckner, Christian	2002	Vitu, Auguste	561
Trautmann, Joan. Christoph	2239	Vogel, Emil Ferdinand	562
Trebusch	2003	Vögelin, Sal.	2852
Tressen, Fr.	2832	Volchanetskaia, E.	836
Treunert, W.	2833	Vollmer, Hansjerg	2854
Tribolet, H.	1777	Volpe, Riccardo	1250
Triqueti, H. de	831	Vorholz, C.	2856, 2857
Trocsanyi, Z.	1290	Vos, K.	1165
Troesch, Jean	3167	Vreese, Willem de	1166
Tronnier, Adolph [i.e. Heinrich		Vries, Abraham de	1167-1181
Ernst Adolph] 1153, 1492, 1514,			
1676, 1826, 1827, 3168-3171			
Tscherning, Andreas	2040	Wackerbarth, Graf	2860
Tsvetkov, I. V.	2834	Wackernagel, Wilhelm	2861, 2862
Tydeman, Hendrik Willem	1154	Wagner	2812
		Wagner, Carl	3175
		Wagner, Christian Ulrich	2243
		Wagner, Mag. Ph.	2244
Udal'tsov, A. D.	2005	Wagner, Wilhelm	2863-2866
Uhlendorf, Bernhard Alexander	726	Wagner, Wilhelm Jakob	3176
Ullmann, Karl	2837	Wal, F. van der	1183
Umbreit, August Ernst		Waley, Arthur	47
	558, 2838, 3224	Walker, E.	729
Ursin, Georg Frederik Krüger	2839	Wallau, Heinrich Wilhelm	
		1515, 1831, 1832, 3106
Valentine, U.	1444	Wallensis, Tho.	1516
Valkenburg, Cornelis van	1160	Wallmark, Peter Adam	1833